PAINT

A MANUAL OF PICTORIAL THOUGHT
AND PRACTICAL ADVICE

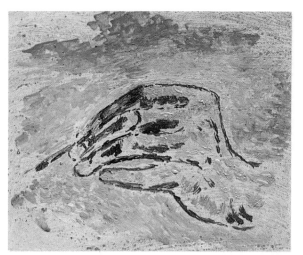

PAINT

A MANUAL OF PICTORIAL THOUGHT
AND PRACTICAL ADVICE

Jeffery Camp

DK

DORLING KINDERSLEY
LONDON · NEW YORK · STUTTGART · MOSCOW

To Dorothy and Alice

A DORLING KINDERSLEY BOOK

Art editor Sasha Kennedy
Project editor Neil Lockley

Senior editor Louise Candlish
Editor Timothy Hyman
Senior art editor Tracy
Hambleton-Miles

Senior managing editor Sean Moore
Deputy art director Tina Vaughan

Production controller Meryl Silbert
Picture research Lorna Ainger
Photography Andy Crawford

First published in Great Britain in 1996
by Dorling Kindersley Limited,
9 Henrietta Street, London WC2E 8PS

A CIP catalogue record for this book is
available from the British Library

ISBN O 7513 0211 2

Colour reproduction by Colourscan,
Singapore

Printed in Singapore by Toppan Printing
Co. (S) Pte Ltd

CONTENTS

JEFFERY CAMP

Born at Oulton Broad, Suffolk, England, in 1923, Jeffery Camp was taught at Lowestoft, then Ipswich School of Art before moving to Edinburgh College of Art in 1941. He was taught by William Gillies and John Maxwell and received Andrew Grant bursaries for study and travel. He has painted every kind of picture – trees in Constable's Suffolk, portraits, nudes, seascapes, skaters, bathers, fishermen, rocking and jiving dancers, and a large altarpiece for a Norwich church. For a short period he did abstract pictures. In 1961, he was elected a member of the London Group, to which in those days almost every good British artist belonged. Between 1963 and 1988, he taught at the Slade School of Fine Art, London University.

Jeffery Camp has exhibited widely. He has had one-man shows at the Gallerie de Seine, London (1958), Beaux Arts Gallery, London, run by Helen Lessore (1959, 1961, 1963), New Art Centre, London (1968), South London Art Gallery (Retrospective) (1973), Serpentine Gallery (1978), Bradford City Art Gallery (1979), Browse and Darby, London (1984), Nigel Greenwood, London (1986–87), and Browse and Darby, London (1993). He has also contributed to many Arts Council touring exhibitions, such as "Drawings of People", "Narrative Painting", "The British Art Show" (1979), and "The Proper Study: Contemporary Figurative Painting from Britain" (1984–85). The Royal Academy held a retrospective of his work in 1988, which then toured to the Royal Albert Memorial Museum, Exeter (1988), City Art Gallery, Manchester (1988), Laing Art Gallery, Newcastle-upon-Tyne (1989), School of Art Gallery, Norwich (1989), City Art Gallery, York (1989), and Usher Gallery, Lincoln (1989).

Jeffery Camp's work was shown at the Hayward Annual (1974), in the exhibition "British Painting 1952–1977" at the Royal Academy (1977), the Chantrey Bicentenary exhibition at the Tate Gallery, London (1981), "The Hard-Won Image", Tate Gallery (1984), "Proud and Prejudiced", Twining Gallery, New York (1985), "Salute to Turner", Agnew's, London (1989), and "Nine Contemporary Painters", Bristol Art Gallery, (1990). Jeffery Camp has won prizes at the John Moore's Liverpool exhibition, the Chichester National Art Exhibition, and the International Drawing Biennale, Middlesborough. His work is in the collections of the Nuffield Organization, the Department of the Environment, the Contemporary Arts Society, the British Council, the Royal Academy Chantrey Bequest, the Arts Council, and several public art galleries, including the Tate Gallery, as well as being in many educational departments and private collections. Jeffery Camp was elected a member of the Royal Academy in 1974.

FOREWORD

This book balances paint and words. William Blake's books do it at a high level, and when he watercolours Dante's *Inferno*, the power is on. It is said over and over, you cannot teach painting. Please take a brush and prove that painting is as natural as breathing; for I am tired of eye titivations with no paint, of Dada revivalist arch combinations of tricky materials with no paint. When Alice Neel, using an uncouth style, portrays Andy Warhol stark, in a corset, she enjoys journalism in paint. Warhol preserved in formaldehyde would attract more attention. In the fashion blaze of today it is difficult to make the tiny delicate touches of paint made by the young Lucian Freud or Michael Andrews, the gentle purity of a Euan Uglow pear, the rainbow beauty of a black complexion paint-rubbed by Craigie Aitchison, or long brush-drags on raw flax canvas by Francis Bacon seem exciting.

To paint the sea, I travel by train from London to Brighton, I enjoy staring at the passengers; usually I do not need to speak. Beyond them is the world we live in: slices of river, back gardens, factories, and a lot of very beautiful rural England. My fellow passengers do not mind or notice the grimy windows. They read newspapers and discuss problems; their eyes collect matter but they are not experiencing visually.

There are about 1,500 images in the following pages. If you are as shy as I am you will only succumb to a few of them, but you will enjoy having a full brush.

PREFACE
Copying, Practice, and Touch

WETTING THE WORLD WITH NEW PAINT will be glorious. They say you can teach drawing, but not painting. Most of us had one good teacher. Their teaching was verbal: school-books were informative, but sparsely illustrated. It is good that my publishers are specialists in combining words and pictures, and know how to make them flow. Soon all the world's children will be learning by word-images, as never before. Videos have also been excellent, but a book is read at a reader's pace, and can go with you anywhere: prison, beach, bathroom, train, or bed. Such a mass of words and images come together by the great skills of designers and editors. Probably, they secretly shudder at the inadequacy of my diagram-copies. But readers, more lenient, will concede that no reproduction will quite resemble a Titian. I hope they will rush to see the originals, and make their own fast, or long, copies.

> I actually go and draw from pictures to remind myself of
> what quality is, and what is actually demanded of paintings.
> Frank Auerbach

As a young artist, I thought copying was cheating. Children are "copycats", imitating each other's actions. It helps them to bully in the playground. Picasso bullied Velásquez by transform-copying his "Las Meninas" more than was necessary, and then said Goya and El Greco meant more to him. Copying is the way to find "the way".

> I think one's only hope of doing things that have a new
> presence, or at least a new accent, is to know what exists,
> and to work one's way through it, and to know that it is
> not necessary to do that thing.
> Frank Auerbach

Since I started writing this book, the "found object" no longer dominates the art scene. I believe paint is a good liquid for feeling, and there are enough young artists who know what paint can do, and will forgive my partial blindness to the metal objects, fats, kitsch, and assembled stuffs that some have found attractive. It was to some extent a "Dada Revival". Revivals are all around us: we fear "revival", and love "renaissance". But more than this, we seek the new. Take brushfuls of passion, and paint life as directly as the human voice is used in a Beatles song. Go in close, privately, intimately. If you paint a toenail, it can exist; be transcendental; ingrow; or become gangrenous. Whatever you know well can be a start, and you will surely paint new pictures. Be vulnerable, suffer, for paint has been spread for thousands of generations. It is one of the great languages of poetry.

Thames-side Chauvinism

London is a good city for painting in, and for finding out how to paint. Come to London. It is an enormous city. London is tight and varied, not as ornamental as Paris, not so built upward as New York. Not so archly – architect – dated as some cities. London is a hotch-potch. It is built so every building will deride its neighbour, and its inhabitants can love and insult one another at close range.

Anarchy thrives in this city, and what more lucid portrayal of the craze of London than Hyman's picture of the sprawl of London? The painter lives in a square on a hill about one mile north of the Thames. In this exhilarating, soaring picture he projects himself high, to see the sights of London in all directions. Such bird's-eye wandering is daring and rare. Kokoschka perched

high in great cities and brushed into the distance with bright colours – but Hyman is a free-flyer, and would not like to travel less in his pictures than Lorenzetti in his fresco at Siena.

Timothy Hyman is editing my text. We mostly agree, because we both subscribe to Odilon Redon's view of art, which puts "the logic of the visible at the service of the invisible".

A girl and a boy on a summer evening look towards the city as office lights reflect the Thames. At dusk the sensual, sexual anticipations take over from the stock market speculations of the day. Glass-filled girders strain with desire. London is glamorous. Its daffodil lights shimmer over the mud.

London Rainbows, 1989–90

The human projectile is prepared even to turn the British Museum on its pediment, and catch a yellow reflection in his spectacle lens. It is not easy to control so many energies, spaces, and weights of paint.

Timothy Hyman, *Myddelton Square, Springboard of London*, 1980s

The boardroom above the Thames. It is not bugged, but it has a computer. The staff have gone home.

"Paloma" (detail). Painted two days after Christmas, 1953. The child is playing with a toy; Picasso is playing with his paints.

After Picasso

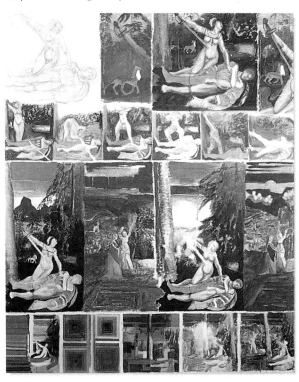

Adrian Berg, *Deutsch's Pyramus and Thisbe*, 1963

Ovid tells the story of Pyramus and Thisbe – how Thisbe, pursued by a lion, loses her veil; and when Pyramus finds it, covered in blood, he assumes her killed, and stabs himself. Thisbe, finding his body, also kills herself. Shakespeare makes use of the story in A Midsummer Night's Dream and, by parallel, in Romeo and Juliet. In the 1970s, Berg made his pictures burst with learning. He was educated in medicine, English, and art, and knew how to delve.

9

Practice and the Touching of Hands

P RACTICE IS A HURTFUL WORD for painters these days. You can be coached for sport, playing a musical instrument, and some examinations. Painting comes "naturally", some have thought. But then, nervously we consider – nothing else comes "naturally". Perhaps there are grounds for feeling insecure: as babies, we even had to learn to eat bananas. That is why we flung our custard at them! I will risk it. May I invite you to practise? Any young pianist's mother would do as much. Nobody would question her wisdom, so long as the child enjoyed hitting the keys. Practise! Practise, because painting is a skill. Practise, because every mark you make exposes you, as every word I write exposes me. It exposes, and can betray you, certainly. If you do not touch right, you lose your lover; if you do not brush right, your mark dies. If you will practise, I will offer you a helping hand, show-off that I am. All teachers are. I have painted for over 55 years, and taught for over 40 of them. I know a few ways for paintings to go wrong. I will give you a helping hand. I will give you a hand: it is your hand. All hands are good as models, because they are always available – "model" models. Now you have one hand for painting with, and one for posing. Use a mirror. Hands are mobile and difficult to paint; they are eloquent, and possess a language of movement. Hooligans bunch fists; Indians make their hands dance butterflies. Rembrandt painted three pairs of overlapping hands in "Jacob Blessing the Sons of Joseph". Hands tell of love in "The Prodigal Son" and "The Jewish Bride".

Make your own programme. Paint your "model-hand" with and without a mirror. Paint it roughly, dab by dab, day by day. You will gradually feel it getting easier. If you do it enough, you will become a "dab" hand! Paint someone else's hand; dab-copy a Picasso hand; then a Permeke hand. Practise till your brush wears out. The world-famous pianist, Benno Moiseiwitsch, wrestled – take care, your hands are special, keep them safe for practice.

If you paint a hand, you are launched. Enough! Your programme was rigorous. May I quote from Gide, quoting from Matisse? "Hands are the most difficult of all."

The dabs become hands

Paint these thin, serious, designed hands. No trace of caricature occurs; the arcs and design are too careful for that. Christian imagery is not for laughter.

After Rublev

The shape of the face is made squarish by adding the back of the hand, which is similar in shape to the light area of the face. The convex thumb and the convex cheek straighten as they push into each other. The drawing emphasizes straightness and pure arcs. Where one line is enough, one line is all that is used.

After Kitaj

Adam proclaims his death. Make tentative dabs for the frailty of an old arm, concave and disjointed, rather than plump and swinging.

After Piero della Francesca

*Practise in whatever way you wish.
Be wilful sometimes, careful at others.*

*Round and warm and elderly, one
hand finds comfort clasped in another.*

After Rembrandt

*Paint clasping hands.
Then other things will
clasp together, and
soon you will have a
composition. Here is a
body imitated by
clasping hands.*

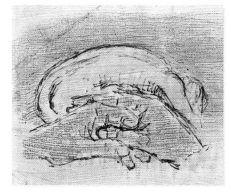

*"The Prodigal Son". Triangular and square. Richly
painted, the son is embraced by the father. The
generous use of earth pigment in a rich, oily sauce
is combined with compassionate hand gestures.*

After Rembrandt

*Rembrandt knew how to
overlay hands and clothes layer
upon layer to keep the terrors
of the world's harshness at bay.*

After Rembrandt

*Raw umber moves into the
pinkish ochres of the hands.*

After Corot

*The hand modifies the shape
of the face considerably.*

High on the Sistine Chapel ceiling, God releases Adam into the world.

After Michelangelo

The Language of Hands

BE HAPPY IF YOU HAVE ORIGINAL IDEAS, which bubble like pure spring water from the ground, or like new-forming clouds. We like paintings to be original in the West. In China, beautiful paintings are often made to closely resemble earlier versions. An eminent Chinese curator told me that most of the Chinese paintings in the British Museum were copies. To think of a painter in the West who resembles another is not so easy. Yet tradition is about some sort of resemblance; and, thinking in this way, a Manet is indeed slightly like a Goya.

Originality is innate. It is valuable. You will not lose it by returning to your ubiquitous model, your hand. The

explanatory hand is the most frequent illustration-diagram in craft-books. This practical hand will help to demonstrate sowing seeds, knitting, beating eggs, and carpentry. Imagine how various are the movements of a hand in a first-aid manual. Painting hands to order is very difficult. Practise some diagrams. Put your originality on hold. Allow your model hand to be in a "meaningless" pose, a "useless" position. (There is hardly any hand position, however unusual, which could not be used as part of a figure composition.) You need a lot of practice to do hands out of your head. For a real exercise in "How to do it", copy a ruthlessly cruel Japanese print.

After Degas

A singer using her hands to portray a poodle.

Aristocratically, he holds a glove. A glove can image a boneless hand, and on a hand be a second skin.

After Degas

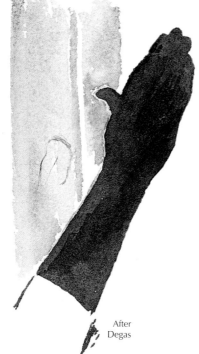

After Degas

The chanteuse gestures with a glove. The glove makes it possible to use a shape for a hand without the complication of separate fingers.

Describe the subtle differences.

After Manet

Practical hands: pointing to the bathroom, planting a seedling, and other things.

The hands grasp the sword in Hara-Kiri. A clear hand-mark in blood acts as a third hand. The hands are pulling the sword inwards for ritual disembowelling. The blood is made to be like a flower.

After Manet

Lucian Freud, *Girl with Roses*, 1947–48

The baby's hands with those of the mother　　　　After Renoir

The hands of the mother and child interweave. The edges are surprisingly red. He may have looked at Renoir.　After Picasso

Years ago in the art shop, there was no other customer than the young Freud, who was not getting the canvases he had ordered fast enough. He was pacing the floor: a panther about to leap. With energy, there can be hate, love, work, but best of all is painting. Freud channelled a tight sprung vitality into this hard-edged, Botticelli-brilliant, 'Baldung picture – unique for any time.

Lucian Freud, *Girl with Roses* (detail), 1947–48

Fingertips and Tradition

HOW WONDERFUL IS THE FINGERTIP touch in all great painting. How would a Watteau "Beau" give his girl the eye, except by the tender, tiny movements of the artist's fingertips, holding a small brush, tipping in details. The touch of a great artist is as sheer as an eyelash thrash. Large brushfuls of paint are also dependent on fingertip control. The plumpness of a massive Rubens thigh is also perfectly placed, and touch-steered. When your fingers have become watchmaker skilled you can become fast and fine. The diamond cutter cleaved the Kohinoor diamond with one blow.

Some are nervous, and eat their fingernails away. Some never look at them. Extravagantly, let fingernails be full fan-shaped views, miniature purple evening skies, with rising moons. The thumb moon is the grandest. More extravagantly, make them blood-red; black; false, or golden, for fashion; or razor-ended for horror movies; or long and quivering on Mozart's coloratura *Queen of the Night*. Nails are claws. Turner had a long one for watercolour-highlight scratching.

Fingernails and skies

Another attempt to make clear for myself where tradition lies. One pivot is always to be found in recent history; as with a scientist's balance, weighing Greek and Roman Art against what was to come. The main pivot is Poussin. After Poussin, all eyes were on Poussin and the past. Poussin's eyes were on the past, but also on Poussin when he did the celebrated self-portrait in the Louvre, Ingres copied the hand as part of "The Apotheosis of Homer", whereupon Seurat copied the Ingres with graphite. (There is a faint inscription which says, "There is genius.") Seurat in turn is also a pivot on which much present-day art balances. Go to the Louvre, and for an academic spree with a pencil, copy the pivotal wrists of Poussin, Ingres, and Seurat. Bonnard said modestly that he wished he had been taught by Moreau, as were Matisse and Rouault.

What would have been the effect on the great painter Edward Hopper of a hard traditional start, we will never know. I have copied Hopper hands to show a difference. His draughtsmanship is non-pivotal, neither traditional, nor even academic.

"The Embarrassing Proposition". On a surface stained with rose and Burnt sienna, barely touching the surface, brush in your thoughts, wet-in-damp, Flake white lies cool on the salmon-tinted surface.

After Watteau

Touch-dabs and fingerprints. The primed paper was brushed with Charcoal grey, ultramarine, and turpentine, then allowed to dry. White lead became hands. These were glazed when half-dry.

Clutching his portfolio; the ring is emphasized. Ingres was plainly not going to allow tradition, in the figure of Poussin, to escape him.

After Poussin

Poussin sitting in the corner of "The Apotheosis of Homer". Its secret is safe. Mark your formal discoveries in a notebook. Drawing focuses the attention.

After Ingres

"Creative Man". The fingernails on the podgy hand of a rich man. Mark the fingernails at many angles with a crayon.

After Orozco

Ingres' copy of Poussin's self-portrait hand, in "The Apotheosis of Homer". There are sharpeners for propelling pencils. I do not use them. A .03 lead keeps sharp if used at an angle. A point is useful for investigating the subtleties of great paintings.

After Seurat

"Creative Man". The fingernails come towards you.

After Orozco

A rising sun over waves is looking like a thumbnail. Dabs of watercolour work wonders.

In spite of being like magazine illustrations when compared with the grand tradition of drawing, drawing by shadows enabled Hopper to the great actuality of his pictures.

After Hopper

Brushes Make Shapes of all Kinds

Undulations

WARE OF MANET AND DAUMIER, both George Bellows and John Sloan made their American subjects grow as lively brush strokes. The children in Bellows' painting, "Forty two Kids" were called maggots by a critic. Maggots are brush stroke shaped.

On a white surface, paint a little blue dot. It is so small, it is almost colourless. A bee in the sky. Stroke a sequence: a blip, a blimp, a long wave, a longer wave. Scumble some fumbling marks. They move at different speeds. The top five lines are with a sable brush, the sixth with a hog-bristle brush, the seventh is done with a small sable brush, trying to make its marks look like a wide brush. Rarely believable!

The mark made by each kind of brush is full of character. The most common has a lozenge shape with pointed ends. If the brush is full of paint, it can make both round and oval marks. Howard Hodgkin uses round, dotting dabs. Bonnard uses similar splodges.

Renoir made his paintings of harmonizing ovals – as nudes, olive-trees, cats, babies, hats, and roses. The blimp shape is the most useful; it can have a tail, and will be like the thigh of a newt, or a leg running on a Greek vase.

Go at a fair pace. Undulate "riggers" or "writers" to make snakes, waves, and mountain ranges. Some brushes tend to make marks that resemble the sea, sky, grass, or hair – which is an embarrassment for painters aiming at abstract art, free from associations. They are often driven to using air-brushes, which present them with ghosts, or mists, or clean enamel surfaces that resemble walls, or doors. The pure abstract is as elusive as a temperature of absolute zero. The first in a jungle can cause the most visible clearance. They called Nature the jungle: Mondrian moved painting furthest from the jungle, but ended representing New York as "Broadway Boogie-woogie". His measures were his life, and beautifully simple, never minimal.

Brushes usually create fast movements if they move fast. But sometimes high-speed marks are painted slowly. Watch what the brush strokes do. Bonnard used a splayed brush to illustrate a famous book about a motor car.

Travelling strokes

16

*Dances on the Lowestoft pier usually ended with a fight.
Paint the swinging handbag. Use swing-speed gestures.*

Rainbow Pops, 1960

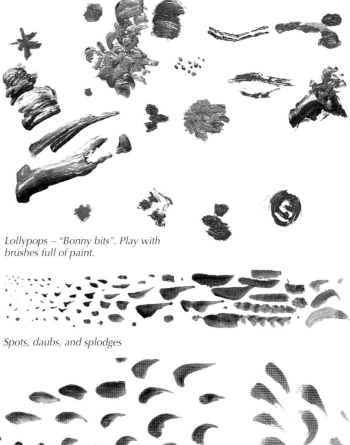

*Lollypops – "Bonny bits". Play with
brushes full of paint.*

Spots, daubs, and splodges

Slow splodges

The tails help the dollops to fall.

The tails help the dollops to rise.

Copy and Be Original

THE STYLES OF THE PAST were developed by copying. Paintings come from paintings. Think of a tree, then a Greek column. Greek temples led to Roman and Romanesque buildings. Giotto was an urgent stimulant for Masaccio, who in turn was painting's greatest all-time leaven. Piero and Uccello put columns in their pictures, then David, Ingres, and early Degas used more columns. Columns show a classical state of mind. Klee proposed the artist as a tree. Columns are not so frequent now, but painting continues to evolve. One last family tree: Giorgione knew Mantegna and Giovanni Bellini, and employed Titian, who knew Tintoretto, who was followed by El Greco, who was copied by Picasso – whom everyone has copied!

A unique originality is not possible, or desirable. An astronaut brought a little moon dust back to Earth, pounded it into paint, and made a picture of the moon. Truly a performance. The painting was usual. The story was a parable.

Pictures may take a long time to paint. In the past, shorter lives and shorter days used time more economically. Picasso did scores of copies of Velásquez' "Las Meninas", fast. Copy to expose secrets, while you stare in exploration. The results – like the diagrams in this book – may be wayward. But every mark you make is a contact with the original. Be inventive: scribble-copy, memory-copy, sample-copy, diagram-copy. Picasso gulp-copied. He was always racing.

After Courbet

A well palette-knifed nude by Courbet at Birmingham deserved to be copied. Courbet was a fat, strong painter, who looked at Rubens. Rubens was to be Cézanne's favourite painter. Courbet would have seen bodies tenderly painted by Rubens, and Rembrandt's superb "Bathshéba at the Bath" in the Louvre. Courbet inspired the thick, early Cézanne, and "Fauve" Matisse (Matisse owned a Courbet nude) and some of Balthus was first seen in Courbet.
I saw the bedclothes, curtains, and shadows had been arranged to make an area of nakedness that was at every point surprising – a body flat, full, and stylish.

Think of the glories of Poussin: of "Venus and Adonis" at Caen, of "Tancred and Ermina" at Leningrad, of "Cephalus and Aurora" in London. To copy an early, pastoral Poussin is to ramble with desire. To do a serious copy of "The Massacre of the Innocents" is the event of a lifetime. Uglow moulds the flesh without sweat, and as the paint goes on, with gentle application, the design tautens. The baby is built tight to bursting. Some blue areas of escape are allowed in this relentless picture. It is a small "machine".

Uglow was allowed to measure "The Massacre of the Innocents", at the Museé Condé at Chantilly. Overlappings make it more sculptural in the main action areas. Some areas are backdrops to the play – these resemble the simplifications of Burra. The bounding energy hoops male and female in a grand ellipse. The light areas of the body are rounded and simplified. An oval tongue cries within the stretching jowl, and the eyes are hard on the diagonal of the main square of light. No millimetre of a Poussin is left unconsidered – see how she scratches his back!

Euan Uglow, after Poussin,
The Massacre of the Innocents, 1979–81 (detail below)

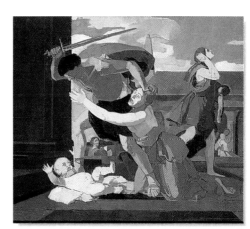

Piero's Baptism

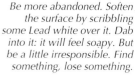

KENNETH CLARK TELLS US PIERO'S "BAPTISM" is divided into thirds horizontally, and into quarters vertically. It is all geometry and numbers if you feel like pursuing them. Or leave it to feeling and see what you find. Yes, relax, and see what you find.

Pure as freshly-squeezed oranges, or new-baked bread, great paintings are plainly good.

Piero della Francesca's "Baptism" is a beautiful picture – a great "copy", an alienation of a wonderful kind. The vision of God standing in a stream, imagined as in a dream. The figure in daylight, in clear air, alive. But made by way of a drawn design, a full-scale paper "cartoon" traced and transferred to the panel. Try not to mind my use of the word "copy". In this case, a unique authentic

After Piero della Francesca
A scribble

painting but done like an inspired copy, parallel to the cartoon, and painted never imitatively, but closely. The painting is transcendental. It moves in a mysterious way. It is the Holy Ghost.

Imagine-copy this "Baptism", painting it with the mind's eye, with an imagined brush. Move its tip, find the centre, mark the navel. Sable in the tiny trickle of water falling on the head. Scrub-copy the hill, partly hidden by a tree. Wetly rough in the "way of the cross". Alternatively, smooth in the delicate angel eyes, and tightly copy the falling measured folds, pure as Ionic columns. Choose whichever part of Piero's beneficent world you wish to dwell on.

A column-covered angel. The background detail is brushed in with comfortable dabs, and little editing.

An angels' head. Search, using fine pen, pencil, or crayon. Or paint marks to involve you intimately. Some baptisms are totally immersing.

A pastel pencil will decide how concentric the arcs are around the centre, and how the vertical gradation is controlled. Building a torso is like building a house, a tent, or Mount Fuji.

Be more abandoned. Soften the surface by scribbling some Lead white over it. Dab into it: it will feel soapy. But be a little irresponsible. Find something, lose something.

A line of hands and girdles. Join the distant landmarks to the near rhythms.

A brushed glance

Piero della Francesca, *The Baptism,* 1450s

Piero and Perfection

PIERO DELLA FRANCESCA'S "Baptism" is in the National Gallery, London, where a well-formed, uniformed girl stands guarding this perfect picture. She is talking to another guard about her pay and conditions. She cannot be mistaken for an angel, she is not built to the ordered measures of Ancient Greece, and she has no wings. On the left of the tree, from our view – therefore on the right-hand of Christ – are three angels who are as perfect as heaven. The tree is good, and Christ is good. Ellipsoid cirrus clouds float. Leaves pulsate as pads of green translucency. The whole picture fluctuates between perfection and human warmth. What could be better?

Paint a little perfection. Try copying a piece of pure angel. You will not use pimple mixture, or refer to the pictures by Lucian Freud. Piero della Francesca's divine measures are derived from Ancient Greece. No flesh sags. Forms are defined with true arcs and straightness, and surfaces are spread carefully.

Paint the man taking off his shirt, and some of the rough landscape above him, to feel the difference. Although the forms are clearly defined, the body is not idealized, and the bushes are made brusquely, even splodged.

The universe-symbols: circle, square, triangle.

After Piero della Francesca

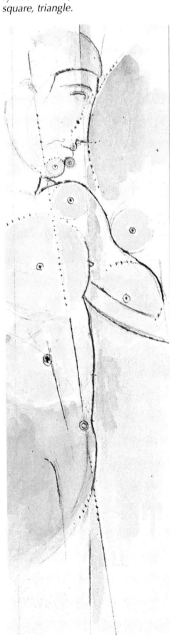

As in Ancient Greece, the forms are made of arcs and straight lines.

Watercolour, on top of a careful pencil drawing of the feet of an angel.

The body is not muscular, and the soft contours of the legs flow to toes that could almost peel a fruit.

After Piero della Francesca

Dabs are made over a blue underwash.

A free brushing with oil and turpentine

Use a soft bristle brush for the landscape background.

23

A Free Painting Extravaganza

IF YOU LEAVE THE DREAM, you paint dead paint. Around 40 years ago, painters decided to be free. They were not the only ones! Freedom was in the air. To watch Jackson Pollock on film dribbling paint, with hard, panting gasps at cigarettes, is to know that freedom has its arduous side. For Kandinsky and Klee, thinking in musical terms, freedom did not require muscles.

Come instead for a dab at real freedom. On a non-absorbent surface of shining white, dab with Cerulean blue. Imagine you are running – it is safer than jogging. Become entranced! The blue dab looks dark; add another mark close by, and it appears lighter. With freedom, we are allowed more colours. Now dab as if you were running by the river. Your deliberately planted feet are beginning to dance. The sight of the water has melted your touch: dabs are breaking into

flowers! Rainbows! Barges! And palm trees! The landscape is rhythmically passing you by. The brush marks are recognizably your own. As in a dream – on the edge of dreaming – painting....

Start, this time, by scrubbing a surface, making it an equal colour-tone all over. If the underpainting is buff, it is the padding that makes up 70 per cent of all painting, old and new. It is bread colour. In a painter like Titian, this padding is the support of glorious colours and the "the staff of life". But in the archive of the Slade school are stored Diploma "Life-studies". Most are bread colour; syrupy, and dead. Frightening, when you consider they were by young, lively people. It was required work at the beginning of this century. Dead paint can also be seen at the National Portrait Gallery, London; at animal art shops; and at communist and fascist historical galleries.

A snowman as a Christmas card. McLean is free to fashion enchanting colours

John McLean, *Snowman*, 1993

Freely brushed ideas about figures in the sky

Brushed blues over black bread colour

Where one mark leads to another. Extemporization is a large part of painting.

Blue and red dabs overlay each other, to make a painterly brushing, and to suggest the deep stress-space of a Polish astronomer.

Andrezej Jackowski, *The Tower of Copernicus*, 1983

Some of the rhythms of a restaurant still life. Half-baked is not baked at all.

After Picasso

An improvisation

Miró uses large fields of colour on which to place weightless, thin marks and symbols, and large, meticulously flat areas of paint. He is free. He maintains flatness, which with crayon I was unable to do. (No excuse really.)

After Miró

Wasps and passion-flowers, and a sunbathing girl, free and naked. Transparent scribbles are made on a surface the colour of honey sponge.

The Thames Open College of Painting

THE FURTHEST POINT FROM ENGLAND is near Fiji. It is beautiful. I shall never visit it, or even visit those great cultural centres which rival London for art stuff. London is homely, London is cosy; the right size for pictures, pedestrian easy, visually crazy, old, new, and useful. It has a lot of Turners.

I offer you a park bench. From it, you can teach yourself to paint. Take your art school with you, wherever is convenient. Mentally project wall-free art colleges for your delight, in Washington, Tokyo, Berlin, New York, Madrid, or Paris. A site in Central Park is fine, or a Tuileries bower; a Venetian gondola, a Berlin beer-cellar, or coffee and cakes in Vienna or Basel – chocky, creamy, and nice! Teach yourself well wherever you go. Treat yourself well wherever you go.

Enjoy a Thames Open College of Painting. Build it as André Malraux built his book, *The Museum Without Walls.* Build it at Trafalgar Square, where it can include the National Portrait Gallery for flattered faces, and the National Gallery for great paintings. You will tighten your mind for Mantegna, Poussin, and Bellini; expand it with Rubens, Picasso, and Titian, and make never-ending discoveries. The National Gallery is inexhaustible.

Thames riverboat

For your self-lectures use a bench in St. James' Park, near the pelicans. For practice, cogitation, self-examination, and the encouragement of squirrels, lie in a deckchair by the lake. No self-lecture bench is nearer to such a richness and variety of paintings to study. It is an easy walk to anywhere on the map tinted with yellow ochre.

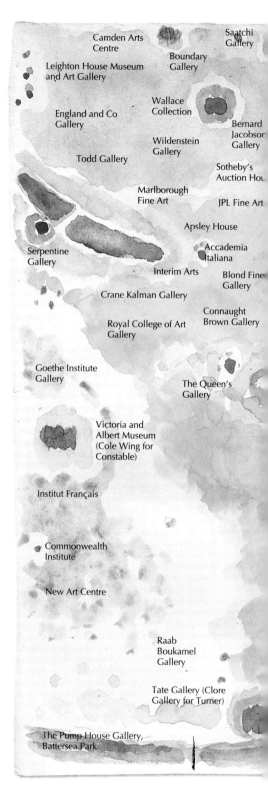

Camden Arts Centre
Saatchi Gallery
Leighton House Museum and Art Gallery
Boundary Gallery
Wallace Collection
England and Co Gallery
Bernard Jacobson Gallery
Wildenstein Gallery
Todd Gallery
Sotheby's Auction Hou
Marlborough Fine Art
JPL Fine Art
Apsley House
Serpentine Gallery
Accademia Italiana
Interim Arts
Blond Fine Gallery
Crane Kalman Gallery
Connaught Brown Gallery
Royal College of Art Gallery
Goethe Institute Gallery
The Queen's Gallery
Victoria and Albert Museum (Cole Wing for Constable)
Institut Français
Commonwealth Institute
New Art Centre
Raab Boukamel Gallery
Tate Gallery (Clore Gallery for Turner)
The Pump House Gallery, Battersea Park

Piero della Francesca's "Baptism" is repeated several times in this book: a sign of quality; it lives at the National Gallery, making all painters feel secure.

Nelson, pigeon-limed at Trafalgar Square. The pigeons are too numerous, and Nelson no longer suggests security. But the column helps in reading maps, and is high enough to climb and be newsworthy. It has yet to be part of a beautiful picture.

Second-hand bookstalls under Waterloo Bridge

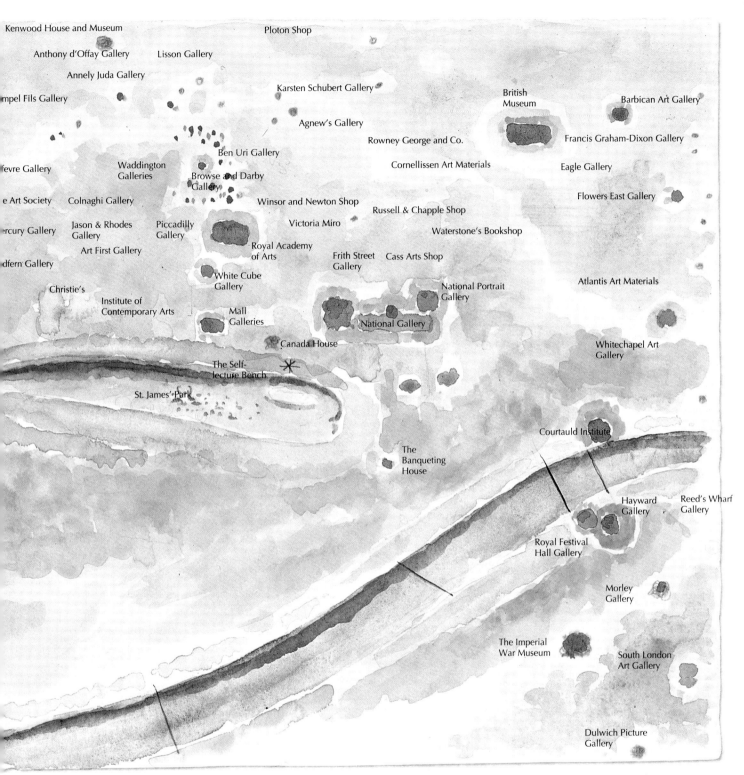

Kenwood House and Museum

Ploton Shop

Anthony d'Offay Gallery   Lisson Gallery

Annely Juda Gallery

Karsten Schubert Gallery

mpel Fils Gallery

British Museum

Barbican Art Gallery

Agnew's Gallery

Rowney George and Co.

Francis Graham-Dixon Gallery

Ben Uri Gallery

Cornellissen Art Materials

Eagle Gallery

fevre Gallery   Waddington Galleries

Browse and Darby Gallery

e Art Society   Colnaghi Gallery

Winsor and Newton Shop

Flowers East Gallery

Russell & Chapple Shop

rcury Gallery   Jason & Rhodes Gallery   Piccadilly Gallery

Victoria Miro

Waterstone's Bookshop

Art First Gallery

dfern Gallery

Royal Academy of Arts

Frith Street Gallery   Cass Arts Shop

Atlantis Art Materials

Christie's

White Cube Gallery

National Portrait Gallery

Institute of Contemporary Arts

Mall Galleries

National Gallery

Whitechapel Art Gallery

Canada House

The Self-lecture Bench

St. James' Park

The Banqueting House

Courtauld Institute

Hayward Gallery   Reed's Wharf Gallery

Royal Festival Hall Gallery

Morley Gallery

The Imperial War Museum

South London Art Gallery

Dulwich Picture Gallery

"The Thames Open College of Painting". New paintings come and go, as do dealers' galleries. For new art go northwards to Bond Street and Cork Street. The Institute of Contemporary Arts is in the park. For the Tate Gallery, go south. For the Arts Council's Serpentine Gallery go west, and for the Hayward Gallery go east. The many beautiful galleries for Old Masters are mapped in red and gold. Art colleges possess libraries. With the fees you are saving, make your own. Visit the stalls below Waterloo Bridge; walk up Charing Cross Road for bookshops of all kinds. The British Museum Library is world famous, and the National Art Library at the Victoria and Albert Museum calls itself a library of last resort! The green areas are practice areas: paint the lake, the Thames, ducks, swans, riverboats, sunbathers, and the enchanting multiracial picnics. Paint the bridges, buildings, flags, canoes, and litter.

Be inspired. Hold tight. Do not fall in. Mind the gap.

COLOURS
Studios, Children, and Skills

A STUDIO CHECKLIST: A WELL-EQUIPPED STUDIO, and some junk. Some painters can keep everything they need in a box no larger than a suitcase. My room almost buries me in the accumulations of years. To buy every item new would be expensive. Put everything you do not need in the attic – or convert the attic into a studio! Some of the items listed below are useful.

Here is more hand-practice. Your model hand is ready for you, and the exercise is suitably difficult. Let the palm face you and the tips of the fingers come towards you! Make dabs for the fingertips. Ugh! Stay with it, be encouraged. Look at the fingers of Piero della Francesca's "Madonna of the Annunciation". You are sailing: splay your fingers, pretend they are yacht-like and the dabbed fingers are flowing towards their tips, like the seams in a mainsail. After this, consider the palm of the hand as like a cushion – a square with convex sides, the thumb preventing symmetry. Paint the palm. It seems more vulnerable than the back. Here you encounter many of the problems of painting flesh. In strong daylight it is semi-transparent, and like a cuttlefish fluctuates gently between its blue-violet veins, vermilion lines, yellow-orange fat, and the pink complexion of rosy capillaries. Tickle it to know where the nerves are; scratch like a miser, and the flesh will be a warm pink.

For an extreme exercise, to be done only when in a good mood, make the palm hollow. Pour a little water into it. It is like a dew-pond. It has a visible meniscus. Paint it with a fine sable brush. The water trembles. Your touch must be as delicate as that of Vermeer. Refinement is limitless. I will exasperate you! With your sharpest sable, test your touch. Paint a robin's feather floating on a puddle. Touch it between held breaths. Lie low in a bath. Raise and lower your hand in the water. However thin the refraction makes the hand appear, it always seems real. A hand, seen at an extreme angle in the cinema, convinces. Draw the distorted view. Paint the lines of life, and the lines of fright, on the palm of a half-clasped hand.

Watercolour all the items you can think of, that a painter might need in a studio.
An easel. A good-tempered model. Neon lights. Blue daylight-simulation bulbs. A blind. A chaise-longue. A high stool with a hollowed seat. An invalid's adjustable bed-table. Coloured pencils. A brush-washer. Tubes and cans of paint. A mahlstick. A split-bamboo cane with a rubber band and charcoal. Watercolours. A claude-glass. Scissors. A magnifying glass. Binoculars (or a lightweight monocular) to take with you everywhere. A dipper. Brushes. Palette. Slide-viewer. Plan chest. Portfolio. Central heating. Pencils. Pin-board. Kneadable and stenographers' erasers. Pencil sharpeners. Fixative and varnish in aerosol cans. A table. Cutting knives. A projector. Spectacles. Armchair. Squeegee. Roller. Air-brush. Straightedge. Paint spray. Paint-stripper. Oil. Turpentine. Varnish. Wax. Clips. Clamps. Maps. Mirrors. Masking-tape. Fan. Radiant heater. Staple gun. Ladder. Carbon paper. Adhesive. Pastels. Sand. Sawdust. Sandpaper. Pigments. Protractor. Wedges. Sunhat. Acrylic medium. Stretchers. Canvas. Paper. Primer. Frames. Woodworking tools. Portcrayon. Tin and brass tacks. A sink. Greaseproof and tracing-paper. Drawing-board. Screen. Sponge. Blotting-paper. Plumb-line. Painting knives. Jars and tins. Rubbish-bin. Pens. Ink. Rag. Barrier cream. Gloves. A high window or skylight. A muller. Eggs. A T-square. Ruler. Drawing pins. Nails. Sodium benzoate. Canvas pliers. Magnifying glass. Blender badger. Masking tape.

A scribble-copy of the "Madonna" (from Frankfurt). She supports her breast with her hand. After van Eyck

Clasped hands

Two hands often say more than one.

Solomon takes the hand of the Queen of Sheba. The pricks of the pouncing are visible on the wall. After Piero della Francesca

"Madonna of the Annunciation" After Piero della Francesca

A half-closed hand

The lines as the hand closes

Palm of the hand

Large hands holding water After Rivera

A feather on a puddle

29

Painting Close to White

DEBUSSY ORCHESTRATED "LA MER" in the Grand Hotel at Eastbourne, whitened with many coats of paint since then. We think of a sheet of white paper as empty, of black surfaces as empty, and Turner probably felt his indigo sketchbook pages were empty. A sheet of white paper placed against a bright sky reflects only a tiny proportion of daylight. Eastbourne, because it is beside the sea and affluent, challenges the whiteness of white cliffs with white hotels. Retired ladies challenge the hotels with the whiteness of their hair, hats, and Crimplene. And all is bright until we see the foam! Eventually, we are obliged to close our eyes. Light is the whitest white.

When I was a student, Roberson made three consistencies of Lead white. It needed a Scottish "strengthy" effort to release the thickest white from its tube. This hard, pugged paint was different from the advertised paint of a buttery consistency, fashioned for amateur Impressionists. It was fine to spread with a palette-knife. Any colour could be moved into it; if you wiped the brush after each stroke, the marks were clear. Long ago, I got White lead from an ironmonger who knifed it out of a large drum. Wrapped in paper, it was heavy and gooey. Its long molecules allowed long, exact brushstrokes, the sort of flowing paint used by Rubens, Velásquez, Goya, and Manet. But Lead white is now less easy to obtain. I have found Roberson's Flake white is as heavy as lead.

Here are some whites the Old Masters did not have. The clearest, brightest white is Titanium white. But it is extremely opaque and in practice I find the more transparent whites have a greater versatility. Zinc white is a fine white. On its own, it keeps its whiteness better than other whites. Additions of Flake, Titanium, ▶

"Skulling" (detail)　　　　　　　　　　After Seurat

The yacht was too big. Seurat painted it when it was passing. He dabbed sparkling water across it, using blue, orange, Viridian, and ochreous white. It is not complete. But is a bright sketch. Painted on white, not the cigar-box mahogany he more often used.

Georges Seurat, *The Seine seen from the Island of La Grande Jatte*, 1888

Cherry blossom in spring. Twigs cast sharp, dark shadows on the tree-trunks and on the grass. The blossom bursts with whiteness. (Strangely, we end by painting most of the tree grey.)

Seurat was wonderfully sensitive, and with a perfect system he was able to paint with pale colours. So exactly are the gradations adjusted, our eyes are supported at every point.

▶ or Underpainting white prevent cracking. Underpainting white is a useful colour. It will cover opaquely, dries fast, does not crack, and its slight tooth makes it possible to paint thinly over it. It is made from titanium dioxide, ground in polymerised linseed oil. It contains a lead drier. Flake white and Silver white are Lead white with Zinc white added. Rutile titanium dioxide is the better crystalline form of Titanium white (also named Permanent white).

Obese over thin, fat over lean, oilier over less oily.

Winsor and Newton's oil painting primer is Titanium white in an oil-modified, synthetic thixotropic alkyd resin medium. Thixotropic means it brushes out well. The dictionary defines it as the property of certain gels, of liquifying when stirred or shaken, and returning to a gel state upon standing. Rowney's Gel, Wingel, Liquin, and Oleopasto are all gels that are thixotropic.

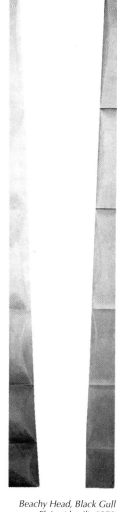

Beachy Head, Black Gull Flying, 1972

My picture is a tall picture. It usually has its middle at eye-level. It is a prospect of dazzling whiteness. The tone-range from lightest to darkest at the seaside is too great for the comfort of painters. Rembrandt did a drawing of himself by candle-light. How many candle-power for Beachy Head? It is partly due to the sea acting as a mirror, and clouds being white. I used tints in the painted border to suggest dawn and evening in the adjacent landscape. They helped the whiter parts to give off light. White cannot make light by itself. Robert Ryman's pictures have only the whiteness they were painted with, quiet enough for boardrooms and shiny new museums.

Beachy Head, Black Gull Flying (detail), 1972

Georges Seurat, *The Channel of Gravelines, Grand Fort-Phillipe,* 1890

The rose is fixed pencil. The sea is White lead laid on with a palette-knife. Done on skin (the thinnest) plywood. The grain is visible. Isolate with shellac if too absorbent.

White Rose (unfinished), 1970

Choose a Fine Lemon

THE BRIGHTEST PART OF A RAINBOW is greener than the lemon. But the fruit is bright yellow, and will freshen thought, just as it brightens food. Darken it carefully.

Take a small canvas. Scrub it with ultramarine, mixed with Burnt sienna or Burnt umber. With a pointed sable, or soft-haired bristle brush, filled with paint of the consistency of cream, make, touch by touch, little islands of Cremnitz white or Underpainting white, in lemon shapes. Continue with touches of Zinc yellow, ultramarine, and Charcoal grey. If you cannot make them sour enough, you might use a little viridian, or Cobalt green.

Braque's variations are on a black surface. Their priming contained sand-grit or sawdust, which prevented thin paint running down. It also took the paint off the brush.

After Braque

After Braque

Ben Nicholson used simple objects all his life, never human figures. A lemon is part of the brushwork design of this early painting. His art became as cool as Switzerland, when he grew older and lived there. He designed with great refinement.

After Nicholson

Lemons can be brushed in with yellow and brown on a white priming; or painted with Zinc yellow, mixed with black, on a black priming.

A cool black shows off the pale pinnacles of Tower Bridge, and makes the yellow fruit a bright juxtaposition with the naked visitor to London. The pale divisions of the lemon's flesh make a subtle, central star. The composition is made with star variations.

Tower Bridge Lemons, 1986

Dab yourself a free version of the famous witty "Fish hat".

After Picasso

After Manet

Lemons brushed with white

After Manet

Step-by-step dabs for constructing lemons. Sketch-paint with brown, mixed with yellow.

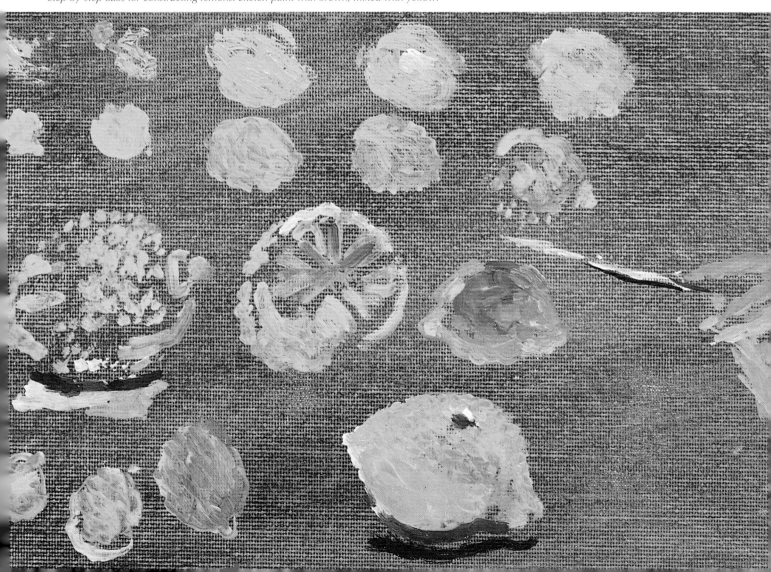

Greens

WHEN BUDS BREAK, the lyrical green mysteries of springtime burst and emerge. Winter is grey, brown, and blue. The fresh spring greens come early – tender and light. The late-summer greens are dark. The middle-summer leaves, as with human middle-years, are difficult to be excited by. Perhaps Paul Cézanne painted too slowly to do pictures of blossoming trees. But Cézanne did do some pale green landscapes, using tiny dabs.

The green colours are mysterious. Even the green gods from Frazer's *Golden Bough* would be daunted by the colourman's

chart. There seem to be more greens than there are other colours. Greens come and go. They are difficult – I mean, difficult to make simple visually, and certainly complex chemically. Camille Pissarro, who spent his life with leaves, and advised Lucien his son (in a letter) to mix primaries, might not have wanted to know that Prussian green is a blend of ferrous beta-napthol derivative and copper phthalocyanine. He would have approved of Chrome green, deep and light, being simple mixtures of Chrome yellow and Prussian blue. Cinnabar green is Raw sienna mixed with Chrome yellow and Prussian blue.

So far, Lucien Pissarro's parent would not have needed to worry. But the following greens are not blue-yellow mixtures. The lovely Cobalt greens (which Renoir used towards the end of his life, with Indian red, for bodies) and Cobalt turquoise, and Terre verte which was the underpainting for flesh in early Florentine and Sienese pictures. (Now it is sometimes tampered with by adding Viridian, which is a pity, because the character of the colour is changed.) Terre verte, if used in tempera, can be thick and dark. (See the trees in Sassetta.) The very opaque and beautiful Chromium oxide green (the transparent version has been lost) will not mix comfortably with weak colours. Try mixing it with Monastral blue, or its chemical relative, chromium sesquioxide (which is Viridian). We no longer have Emerald green (Veronese green) which was used by Cézanne. It is a great loss to painting. Cadmium emerald is a poor substitute.

Pissarro would not have wished to use Winsor emerald, and I do not know whether he used black. Black and lemon make a kind of green. There is excitement in mixing greens, especially when secondary colours are blended – violet and green, and orange and green – and when green is beaten into various kinds of submission by its complementary, red.

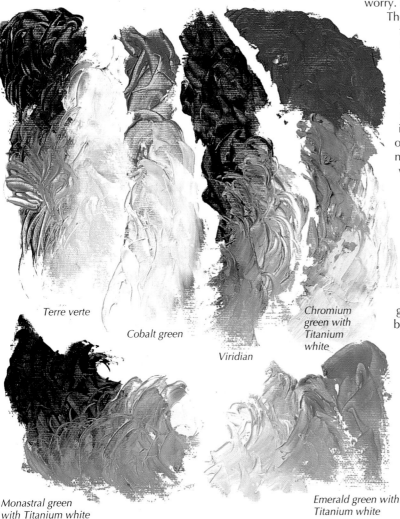

Terre verte

Cobalt green

Viridian

Chromium green with Titanium white

Monastral green with Titanium white

Emerald green with Titanium white

Nickel titanate with Ultramarine blue

Winsor yellow with Ultramarine blue

Yellow ochre with Ultramarine blue

| Viridian | Cobalt green | Chromium oxide green | Emerald green | Monastral green | Terre verte |

Cerulean blue with Nickel titanate

Cobalt blue with Nickel titanate

Cerulean blue with Winsor yellow

Cobalt blue with Winsor yellow

Ultramarine blue with Nickel titanate

Ultramarine blue with Winsor yellow

Davy's grey was mixed with oleopasto, so it would set quickly, and partly painted over with Viridian. The shawl was made with wonderfully orchestrated colours, probably by an old lady of genius. Certainly, I have never seen its equal. It was crocheted in short stripes, and wherever it was thrown down it looked beautiful. It seemed to make the painting very easy to do. The warmish Davy's grey is slightly yellowish and is activated by the greyed Ultramarine cloud shadows.

Hastings on the Pier, 1971

Cadmium red deep, Chromium oxide, and white

Chromium oxide green, white, and Cadmium red deep

Permanent rose, Viridian, and white

Viridian, Cadmium red deep, and white

35

Reds

SATURATED REDS HUM like mighty golden gongs. Matisse used the Cadmium reds. Vermilion is poisonous, and unless protected by glass or varnish, is affected by polluted air. Vermilion was the Old Masters' blood force for painting bodies. Little touches close to the contours made the White lead and ochres live. Used neat it is slightly warm, when diluted it gets warmer, when white is added it is considerably cooled. Craigie Aitchison uses saturated colour of fierce beauty. My free copies in oscillating colours show how pure Aitchison's colour is – like Stravinsky's orchestration, each instrument being made to sound new and profound.

Aitchison told me (rather as with alcohol in the days of Prohibition) where I could buy Vermilion scarlet. We are being deprived of our most important colours by our rulers. They think we must be protected from eating Emerald green, Naples yellow, White lead, Vermilion, Lemon yellow – and, alas, even more are threatened. Other colours, such as Lapis grey, never enter tubes for marketing reasons. Colours made from real pigments are granular, and move from the brush in special ways. They are as different as people. Dye colours cannot replace them. Nickel titanate is no replacement for the Lemon yellow used by Matisse.

Mary Potter was an inspired and sensitive painter of pale harmonies, by the sea. The light from the waves reflected on to the ceiling of her studio (formerly that of Benjamin Britten). She told the decorators to paint her room with brown, and then to give it a coat of pale scarlet – the sort of underpainting that Braque, from a family of decorators, might also have done. The great colourists woo their pigments into glow or subservience, with infinite pains.

A portrait of a girl named "Comfort" (detail). The colours approach those of flowers: pinks, orange-red, and poppy-red. After Aitchison

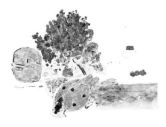

A ladybird beetle near a Henry Moore sculpture near the Tate Gallery, London.

Craigie Aitchison, *Dog in Red Painting* (detail), 1974–75

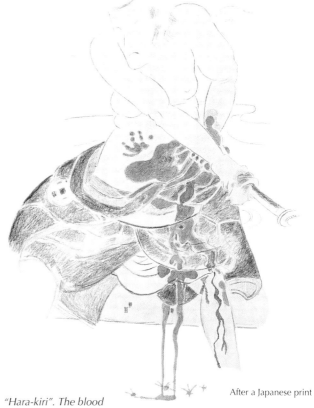

After a Japanese print

"Hara-kiri". The blood is designed like flowers, flowing like waterfalls, spattering like stars.

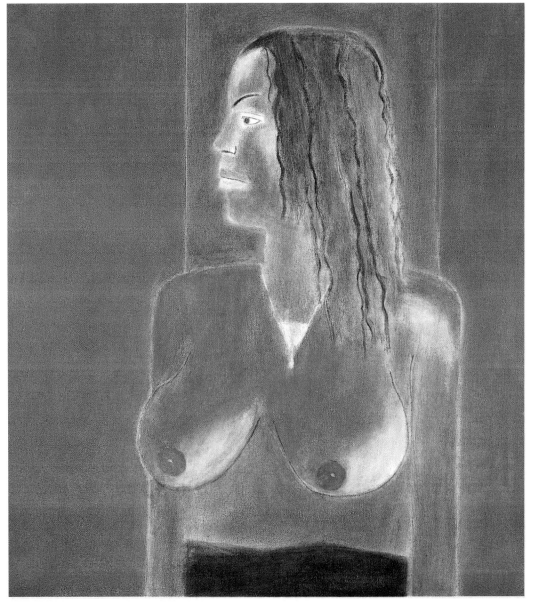

The skirt is painted like a dark Scottish island. The background is like a sunset of pink, howling at red. The girl is brown-black, and restful after a thorough brushing. The light is from below at the breasts, and from above at the forehead. Craigie's light is sometimes a little like a photograph's negative. This is really the inner light of a great imagination, and defies analysis. Practise rubbing colour on to canvas straight from the tube. Even the most opaque of colours such as Chromium oxide green can be scrubbed to a transparent lightness. Thicker colour can be kept in reserve to be added later.

Craigie Aitchison, *Portrait of Comfort* (detail), 1994

With experience, subtle differences are felt between Titanium white mixtures with Cadmium red deep and those with a Vermilion.

Cadmium red, diluted and mixed with Titanium white. Flesh colours tend to become heavy with these reds. For lighter weight mixtures, I might use Permanent rose with Zinc or Lemon yellow.

Vermilion, diluted and mixed with Titanium white. Cadmium scarlet will make wonderful glowing oranges with Cadmium lemon.

Cadmium scarlet, diluted and mixed with Titanium white. A pricked finger will smear in red and oxidize, darkening and leaving the flowery reds like the joyous reds of India to become Indian red, the densest opaque red.

"Pink Vase"   After Aitchison

Umbers

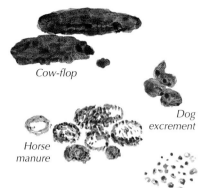

Cow-flop

Dog excrement

Horse manure

Rabbit droppings

BURNT AND RAW UMBERS are "earth" colours. They are mined, and consist of ferric oxide, silica, alumina, lime, and manganese oxides. They are intimate as dung. The brown of a cow-pat is the deep organ-note of a Braque. Horse manure is paler, and full of hay. Adding white to Raw umber reduces its strength of colour. Morandi used umbers weakened with white frequently. Perhaps the paint resembled pottery-clay, and since squarish pots in squarish formats were his habitual subjects, every nuance was clear enough. Umbers as liquids over white stain strongly. If you need them to be stronger when mixed with white, add a bright yellow: lemon yellow for Raw umber, Cadmium yellow for Burnt umber. Brown is a low-intensity yellow.

John Dodgson,
Small Nude, 1950s

On the right of this gentle picture, it is possible to make out a girl student holding a pencil at arm's length, sizing up the model. I do not know whether John Dodgson himself was a "measurer". He certainly considered every quantity with care, and as he painted, the composition would change. Here the knee became egg-shaped. The patches of brown paint (greyed sometimes with Cobalt blue) are divided exactly, and nothing is left to chance. (See the 15 millimetre-wide grey border – it was to have been covered by the frame!) Dodgson took as long as a picture required, and many of his paintings were lost in a studio fire. Dodgson possessed a fine painting by Bonnard. Bonnard would touch-up his own work, even when it was hanging in a museum.

Still life in Burnt umber   After Morandi

Raw umber with Lead white. Experiment with close-toned colours. They enhance one another, in a climate of pale brown. Pale discords make pleasurable buzzes.

Hang-gliders are made in beautiful colours. Here, a kite lies on the brown grass at Beachy Head. The fabrics reflect the sky.

Raw umber with Titanium white is much cooler than with Lead white.

John Dodgson would have liked the formal shaping of "La Poseuse", and Madeleine Knoblock, who was Seurat's girlfriend. There was a strong desire at the time to eliminate browns from the palette.

After Seurat

Burnt umber above, and below, Raw umber slightly diluted, showing the intensity when white is not added.

Burnt umber with Lead white, intensified on the right with yellow.

Burnt umber with Titanium white, intensified on the right with yellow.

Although some red is used, the umbers will do for most of the bodies and the beach.

Greys

A SIMPLE GREY IS A MIXTURE of black and white. (Lamp black and Lead white.) Battleship grey, perhaps. Winsor and Newton supply a mixture of Carbon black, Natural earth and Titanium dioxide, in five degrees of darkness. It is a heavy grey, but it can be wonderful as a support for other greys, or colours, as in Braque's studio pictures. A grey which made Battleship grey look clean, even enchanting, was called "sludge" by my father. He was keen on it, it was cheap – it was all the leftover colours mixed together, from a paint factory. It offended me, but it preserved ladders, tubs, tools, doors. He even dabbed it on his hat to make it waterproof. When you clean a palette, the resulting mixture can be dirty as sludge. With a restricted palette, the combination may be acceptable. Gillies said in an interview that he liked using the grey which accumulated in the corners of his watercolour box.

Usually, I try not to mix more than two colours. Burnt umber and ultramarine, for example, will make a useful grey. Davy's grey is made of slate. It can be sharpened by adding Monastral blue, or if you add ultramarine it approaches the beautiful Lapis

Norman Adams, *Study of the Sun – Evening, Staffin Bay, Skye,* 1965

grey, which is now no longer obtainable. (Lapis lazuli, and Ultramarine ash, were used in Piero della Francesca's greys.) A predominance of greys can make pure colours sing, and in a colourful picture the greys may become dominant.

Much Chinese painting is done with diluted black ink, and Thomas Girtin worked close to monochrome, as did many English watercolourists. In my diagram, the grey mixtures are, instead, very colourful. The beautiful greys that Klee obtained were by superimposing colour upon colour, and by juxtaposing broken colours. When painting with greys, think of them as colours.

My brushes are spoiled by my laziness. I have had some of them for more than 50 years. I was taught to clean brushes properly at the end of each painting day. You wiped them, and one at a time, rubbed them on soap, and then on your hand. (If you have allowed the brushes to become badly caked with dry paint, leave them in brush-cleaning fluid for a few days, then rub them against a scouring pad with washing-up liquid.) Sables do not keep their points well in oil. Sign-writers put Vaseline on them. (Remove it thoroughly before use.)

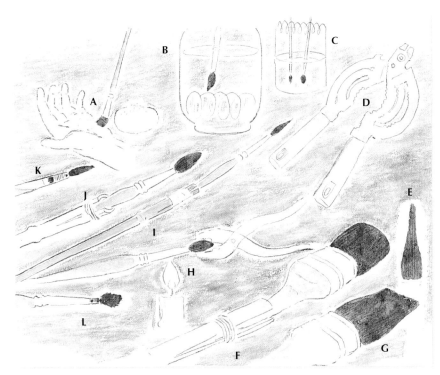

A Brushes soaped and rubbed in the hand

B A brush washer

C Watercolour brushes suspended in water by a spring

D A jar-opener is useful for undoing paint caps.

E Decorating brushes can have some of their outer hairs shortened.

F A decorating brush-handle can be cut to fit into a split bamboo stick, and bound.

G Decorating brushes hold too much paint for some purposes.

H Brushes whose hairs are worn short can be lengthened. Heat the ferrule, and pull – but not too hard or the ferrule can be cut round with a file.

I, J A watercolour brush set in split bamboo

K A sable in a quill can be set on a tapered stick, with a little adhesive.

L A brush that has been lengthened by heating is often fuzzy.

Black, and Transparent golden ochre, are used with Cremnitz white. Brighter colours are used for the cloud shadows.

Fishermen at Pakefield, 1963

1 *Chromium oxide green and Cobalt violet*

2 *Viridian and Cobalt violet*

3 *Viridian and Davy's grey*

4 *Viridian and Cadmium red deep*

5 *Cobalt blue and Davy's grey*

6 *Viridian and Permanent rose*

7 *Prussian blue and Burnt umber*

8 *Cerulean blue and Davy's Grey*

9 *Cerulean blue and black*

10 *Black with ultramarine*

11 *Black with ultramarine, but diluted*

12 *Burnt umber and ultramarine*

13 *Raw umber and ultramarine*

14 *Black*

15 *Black*

16 *Raw umber and Cobalt blue*

17 *Burnt umber and Cobalt blue*

18 *Cerulean blue and Burnt umber*

19 *Cerulean blue and Raw umber*

20 *Prussian blue and Davy's grey*

21 *Prussian blue and Light red*

22 *Cobalt blue and Light red*

Some of my hundreds of brushes. Do not throw brushes away. Often, they improve with wear, and are useful when fuzzy. Fan-shaped brushes are versatile.

Grey samples show how colourful and simple two-colour mixtures are, if placed side by side. Try as many permutations as you can. Some three or four colour mixtures may also be exciting. If you try mixing together all the colours of your normal palette, you will know what it looks like – you may wish to change the colours you use.

Braque had an enormous number of brushes. Some were in tins, ready for the fray. Miró, Braque, and Nolde would use frayed brushes to give a brushy mark. I knew a painter who rubbed his brushes on concrete.

Blacks

THE CLOCK BELONGED TO ZOLA. Cézanne painted the picture for Zola, in Zola's house, and Zola kept it all his life. If we understand that Miró, for example, depicts objects in oblique ways, and metaphors abound in art, we might dare to essay that Cézanne had painted his school days swimming companion, Zola, as a still life. Whatever its secret, "The Black Clock" is not just a dark setting for a teacup. This famous picture was done when Cézanne was 30. Its blacks are not as seductive as those in later works. As his pictures became more colourful, he would caress Peach black until he had coaxed it into being the most surprising colour in the picture. "The Black Clock" is a beautifully fashioned picture, using black generously. Cézanne built strongly on Spanish foundations and looked at Manet.

Blacks vary a lot. They are important colours, and, with whites, they are eloquent. El Greco, Velásquez, and Goya used semi-transparent whites and blacks throughout their pictures – black, sometimes like mantillas, flamenco-brilliant, over glimpses of flesh made with vermilion, ochre, white and black: a living abundance.

To experience the versatility of this great Spanish technique, make a canvas brownish. Then brush Cremnitz white where you wish. The lead helps it to set. An oily Bone black or Ivory black can then be brushed over it. White made oily will be cooled as it moves over black. Picasso did not use this way exactly, but he looked at Manet and brushed with black and white freely. He wanted to be the top branch of the great tree of Spanish painting, and copied "Las Meninas" over and over.

Try out every combination. With a brush, stir Cremnitz white, or some other Lead white, with Ivory black. Flake white is sometimes full of Lead white, you can tell by the weight. Do the same with Lamp black and Titanium white and compare them; the difference is enormous and will prove to you how necessary it is to examine the latent qualities in all colours.

Colours are from many sources. Some are from plants, some are minerals, others are synthetic. They are ground and put in tubes at the strength, hue, and darkness they become with oil added. Scarcely ever will they harmonize straight from the tube. ▶

The vest is pale black, and works paired with a darker green. The black face is blue.

The Jogger, 1983

Ivory black is warm.

Ivory black with Cremnitz white is warm.

Blue-black with Titanium white is cold.

Ivory black with Titanium white is cool.

Mars black with Cremnitz white. Mars black. Mars black with Titanium white is cool and dense.

Lamp black with Titanium white

Lamp black with Cremnitz white

Blue-black

Blue-black with Cremnitz white

Charcoal grey with Titanium white. Charcoal grey is transparent. Charcoal grey with Cremnitz white is warm.

Blue-black is Ivory black, mixed with ultramarine. If it is added to white, Blue-black does not make such warm greys at lower tones as Ivory black on its own. I add blues to Charcoal grey instead.

Davy's grey with Mars black added. When Davy's grey is used as if it were black, it makes a foundation for the last-minute application of Deep black.

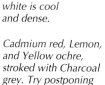

Cadmium red, Lemon, and Yellow ochre, stroked with Charcoal grey. Try postponing the use of black in a colourful picture until almost the end, then, supporting it on a grey or a colour, find how movingly it can sing. Uccello painted black over silver foil. Black over white can be sharp as a bell, precious as diamonds.

Leonard McComb, after Cézanne, *The Black Clock*, 1988

Leonard McComb, after Cézanne, *The Black Clock* (detail), 1988

▶ Mars black may be tinged red or not. It is the darkest of the iron oxides, and is thick and opaque. When mixed with Titanium white, it becomes a dense battleship grey that will cover anything. At the other extreme, Charcoal grey, which is really a black, will mix with Cremnitz white to be a warm, cloudy grey of a versatile transparency. Charcoal is often used in the preliminary drawing of paintings, and is allowed to mix in with subsequent daubings. Matisse and Picasso often painted in this way.

What courage he has to paint it full-size! McComb knows how to really look at paintings. His brush moves impetuously, almost ahead of sight; the brushing is like looking. If he'd had one of Rubens' apprentices to mix him a leady white, the paint facture might have been softer. The fold of the shell, which the writer Lawrence Gowing found so sensual, was straighter than the original. But this is an exuberant version of the mollusc. Zigzags generate energy. These undulations probably influenced Matisse's use of pattern. A zigzag done with a full brush is serpentine.

A free copy-dab of the shell. It has none of the weight of early Cézanne.

After Cézanne

Watercolours Can Enchant

STUART DAVIS INSISTED HIS PAINTINGS should be called drawings. Perhaps the difference between painting and drawing will become clear as we contemplate the forms dissolving in the splendours of British watercolour. As with ink landscape-drawing in China, British watercolour is regional and unique. It is rhythmical, of course, but not linear. Turner would scratch in movements, and Constable would flourish wetness. Turner used Rubens-like envelopes of spaciousness, without Florentine lines. He used body colour (gouache) on blue-grey paper, or highly worked watercolour on white paper, to move into miles of depth, to circle around the sun. It is strange that some of the widest, deepest expanses of landscape in art have been depicted on tiny sheets of paper.

Turner was the greatest European itinerant artist. Much would have been drawn in lead pencil and coloured in later. Back in England, the aristocrats, secure after the perils and delights of The Grand Tour, would recognize in Turner's paintings the high points of their visits. Do not stagger round Europe with a video camera built for boring. Be gentle with yourself: bring back delicate touches – the expressive movements of the brush, on distant mountains, as felt by you and no other.

Dab some blobs directly, to resemble a pomegranate.

A watercolour done in connection with a large painting. Cézanne would have used colours closer to simple primaries, but the hatching is similar.

Balthus, *Still Life with Leeks*, c. 1964

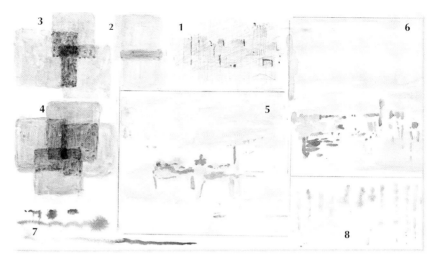

"Park Row". Davis liked speed, noise, energy, and visual slang. He wrote: "The city is man's greatest invention.... All my paintings affirm an urban continuity, a measurable juxtaposition." Gouache can be flatter than watercolour, and because of this the edges have to construe with each other more exactly. Davis said: "Drawing is the correct title for my work."

After Davis

John Sell Cotman was a great classical composer, the Poussin of watercolour. The most original painter in the Norwich School, he used a paper that had the appearance of dried porridge, and painted with the soft colours of burnt porridge.

1 *In Cotman pencil drawings, ticks for windows, birds, or cavities would be blacked-in hard: contours would be left for colour washes to define. Two applications for middle-tone. Four for the darks, gave five tones in all, enough for most purposes.*

2 *Two pale washes of colour give three tones*

3 *Three pale washes of colour give four tones*

4 *Four pale washes of colour give five tones*

5, 6 *Play with wet paper, and wet and dry marks, and pretend they depict San Giorgio Maggiore in Venice. This exercise is best done in a gondola on a calm day.*

7 *Ultramarine on wet, and on dry*

8 *Grey on wet paper*

Gillies lived in the village of Temple and painted the lowland hills of Scotland more beautifully than any other painter. He could draw fast. He did everything fast. Watercolour was natural for Gillies, his splodges each became part of the firmament. He made for innovations (although he trained in Paris). His compositions were very exact. He used only the simplest traditional materials – because that is all a genius ever needs.

William Gillies, Temple, Evening, 1940s

Gouache

WILLIAM GILLIES WAS NOT A VOLUBLE TEACHER. He said the minimum necessary, and always in the presence of the picture. He said in answer to a desperate enquiry: "It is the way you see it." Absolutely obvious, and sure to take years to accomplish! Look at the early works of any top artists to see how long it took for them to see their way. Henri Matisse was in his thirties before he did any original paintings, and many years older before he painted a Matisse that was all Matisse. Paul Gauguin was the slowest, he was in his forties before he could free himself from a slow Impressionism. (Carving, ceramics, and woodcuts were crafty activities that tempted him to greater freedom of invention.) It is what you bring to the thing seen that makes it possible to see, to paint.

Gillies watched the hills all the time. Cloud-shadow shape, cloud shape, field shape, cornstook shape. In this watercolour of "Border Fields, Longshaw", the hedged fields made lozenge-shapes, with pointed ends. Variations of lozenges (the old Basic Design "Family of Shapes") will hump up, to be clusters of foliage, or complete trees. He used pen and ink. He made thin pen lines for the horizon, and used a reed or bamboo pen, or a very flexible nib, or a piece of stick such as the wrong end of a paint brush to sweep in gestural, flowing, liquid lines of waterproof ink for the middle fields. Pen and gouache go well together. Gouache is a name for thick watercolour. Body colour. (Pigment, gum, and preservative.) Pen lines are so artificial, they will declare themselves even through rich applications of gouache. (Gouache is "designers' colour", watercolour with white added, to make it relatively opaque.) With his watercolour-whitewash, Gillies watered near and far: the underlying lines, like spines, would hold fields together, almost resembling a sequence of reclining bodies.

Pen lines over and pen lines under but not in this case, pen lines into wet gouache. John Maxwell and other Scottish painters enjoyed making their pen lines blur and run in the wetness. Two sheets of paper have been joined together, the join is barely visible.

Willam Gillies, *Border Fields, Longshaw* (detail), 1949

Terns on the Thames

Birch tree and a red bus at Clapham

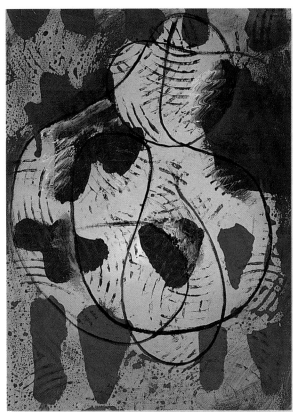

The Surrealists used rollers, resists, rubbings, combs, and anything that came to hand. Gouache would hold it all together.

Eileen Agar, *Untitled,* (no date)

William Gillies, *Border Fields, Longshaw,* 1949

Riverboat on the Thames

A Chestnut tree. Some painters rarely use strong contrasts, but dark colours can be dramatic. Fill a brush and be decisive.

Jewelled Water

SOME COLOURS ARE EXOTIC AS JEWELS. All colours are special. A pricked finger exudes a globule of ruby red, which dries to Indian red. Amethyst and sapphire, topaz and emerald, are like brushfuls of watercolour, and if the pigments are applied wetly, the jewel-quality remains. I am a glutton for colours. There is a Robert Rauschenberg painting that has, collaged across it, a colourman's chart of all available colours. I have all the colours depicted on these pages. I try not to use more than two or three at a time. Girtin used almost none. Klee makes it look as if there are more colours than exist in the world. Braque also is a master-chef. They change the priming, underpaint, and juxtapose colours to make optical mixtures.

Because I like having a lot of colours available, I enjoy using the box I made. You need a bundle of balsa wood (which is very strong and light) from a model-makers shop; a tube of balsa cement; a cutting knife; a long plastic hinge, or two short ones; some fine sandpaper; some white lacquer (spray it or brush it).

The cement dries quickly; you can make a box in a few minutes. The cement will secure the watercolour pans; a flanged edge will prevent the colours drying out. Tin boxes are rather unfriendly, but I also have a little metal box. It has a ring for the thumb, a built-in water container, and a tiny collapsible brush. It is good for making colour notes. It is difficult to decide which 12 colours to include. I settled on: Davy's grey, Viridian, Monastral blue, black, Burnt sienna, Ultramarine, Cerulean blue, Raw umber, Lemon yellow, Cadmium yellow, Cadmium red deep, and Permanent rose. Rice-water makes brushmarks happen; distilled water is advised by some. Oxgall, I am told, breaks surface tension.

Balsa wood; balsa cement; cutting knife; white lacquer; hinge; brush

Summer. Watercolour will combine well with pastel pencils to enhance a fixed, squared-up, pencil drawing from imagination.

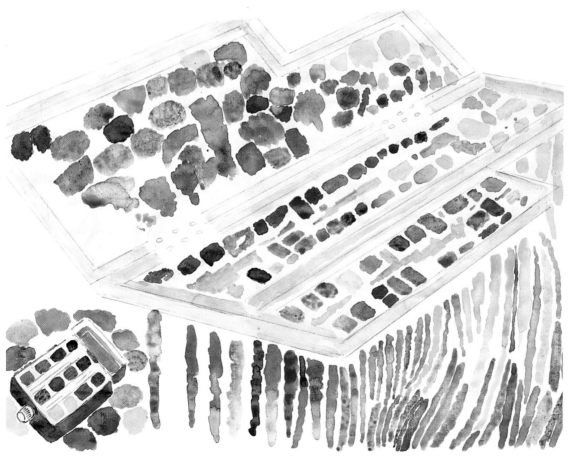

It is useful to group colours in families, they do not sully each other when wetted in the box as easily as contrasting colours, and their juxtapositions suggest fruitful harmonies. An example is Matisse's delight in the Cadmium yellows and reds. At a further extreme, van Gogh's economical earth palette (for potato eaters and weavers) was probably genuine

Naples yellow, Yellow ochre, Raw sienna, Raw umber, and black. The black family extends from the heavy opaque Mars black to the gentle transparent Charcoal black. (Some colourmen supply a transparent black.) The green family is very large, and beware of the colourmen counterfeiters whose muddled and mud making mixtures are given names to lure.

I often add watercolour to drawings when I get home. This is a view of Blackfriars Bridge.

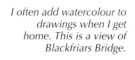

Laetitia and a blackbird at Kew. Bank paper makes watercolour hazardous because thin papers cockle.

Nicholas de Staël, after being abstract, painted his paints, jars, and brushes.

After de Staël

A set of Chinese materials, given to me by a grateful student. All I need now is to know the rituals.

Palettes

MY PALETTE WAS OLD AT AUCTION 50 years ago. A Stradivarius of palettes, it smelled of forbidden megilp. Its deep colour was sensible when primings were brown. You were supposed to rub the wood with oil when new. (If you normally paint on white, you can spray your palette with white car cellulose.) A good palette is balanced by being made thicker where it comes close to the body. It is useful to have a held palette, as the paint can be looked at against the subject, or with the picture as you work.

Artists have used a great variety of mixing apparatus. Bowls, foil pie-cases, cut-down bottles, jars. Bacon and Bonnard used plates. Picasso used wooden packing-cases, and the oil-absorbent boxes tubes are sold in. Rouault and Dunoyer de Segonzac used big tables. Early artists used fewer colours and their palettes were small. Cézanne's had to accommodate 15 colours. Tear-off paper palettes are unattractively floppy when nearly used-up.

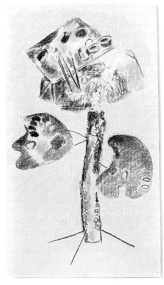

Braque made this palette support from a tree-trunk and wire.

My palette

Students, happily for teachers, continue to have palettes; for close to the palette may be found "The Work", almost always powerfully filled with Harrison's red, and dangerous to sensitive teachers. The survival method is to pick up the palette with alacrity, either for appraisal or attack. Discuss the setting of warm/cool, dark/light, opaque/transparent colours, in good order. Add some advice about removing old paint, and you are safe from "The Work" until the light dims. Harrison's red has its teeth drawn in poor light.

The glamour pages at the front of art books often show the encrusted palettes of the Masters. To remove old paint, blow hot air, or use a solvent, or hold face-down over a gas ring, as I was taught 56 years ago, and scrape with a three-cornered scraper. Sometimes, unused paint is scraped to the edges of the palette where it makes thick crusts. For Rouault, the rich accumulations of his enormous palette-table proved an inspiration.

Braque's plate-as-palette

After Gauguin

After Braque

After Corot

After El Greco

After Hogarth

After Avery

After David

After de Staël

After van Gogh

A brush washer. The spring suspends the brushes.

A base-board with greaseproof paper as a palette. The paper is kept taut by a spiked frame.

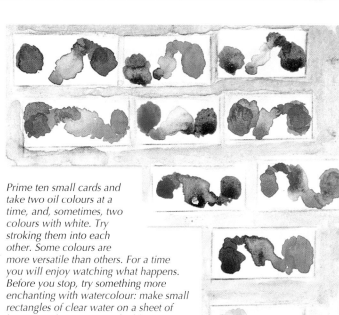

Prime ten small cards and take two oil colours at a time, and, sometimes, two colours with white. Try stroking them into each other. Some colours are more versatile than others. For a time you will enjoy watching what happens. Before you stop, try something more enchanting with watercolour: make small rectangles of clear water on a sheet of hot-pressed rag paper and add some strong colour at each end of the compartment, then add a drop of clear water. With a meniscus-leap, the colours will make towards each other, like trees in a "chemical garden".

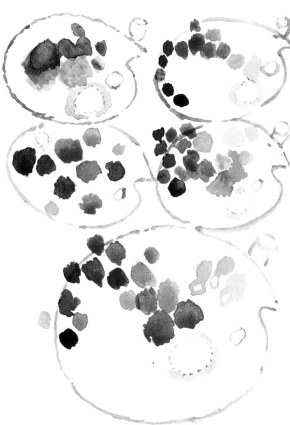

Play-paint some palettes with your chosen colours. One moves from light to dark, another is warm moving to cool. Another is haphazard, and another (a difficult choice) is for painting monochromes. Finally, decide what group of paints you really like to work with. Try two earths, two blues, crimson, two yellows, black, white, and red. This group moves opaquely outwards to transparency.

A colour circle

Making Paint

JOHN MAXWELL THOUGHT HIS RASH was caused by applying paint with his fingers. He said William Gillies also painted in this way. I think Gillies used brushes and painting-knives most of the time. But in Scotland, in Edinburgh, there seemed to be a great love of the look of paint. Maxwell and Gillies had studied in Paris, and would look at paint as thickly applied as that of Dunoyer de Segonzac. When they saw a beautiful picture, a "wee" cry of ecstasy would occur, a delight in its "bonny bits" be manifest. To paint thickly, you were urged to start with a large pile of white paint in the middle of your palette.

Palette-knifing began in England with Constable, and reached its greatest richness with Courbet. Rembrandt had painted thickly, and Soutine had understood the reason for this. Paint can be eloquent. Its special attraction, which is difficult to define, becomes clearer if you make your own paint. It can be very simple to do, for many pigments are finely divided and need only to be mixed with oil, using a spatula. For a start, you could mix cold-pressed linseed oil with Zinc white and two per cent beeswax. If you wore a mask, you could do the same mixture with White lead, which would really be like being an Old Master! This freshly mixed white is so responsive, one begins to sense how Rubens was able to paint a deer-hunt on a tiny panel. The pigment is in thin oil, flows well, and sets rapidly, ready to take thin glazes of colour, or a hound-whisker with a tiny brush.

The delights of paint are infinitely various. Peter Doig spatters in dollops galore: these make optical colours, and are substantial at a distance. Where the knife is used, these days, it has a congealed, constipated look. Eakins managed to combine knife and brush with hard edges. He lived close to the academic edge. A great painter.

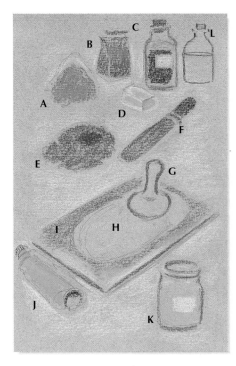

A *Pile of pigment*

B *Packet of pigment*

C *Bottle of pigment*

D *Beeswax*

E *Oil in a hollow made in the pigment*

F *Spatula*

G *Glass muller*

H *Paint being ground*

I *Ground-glass slab*

J *Empty tube*

K *Jar of paint*

L *Bottle of oil*

Somehow, the rough work, rough sea, and rough paint seemed to tell it the way it was. Although it is not long ago, it seems a remembrance of things past.

Nets, 1975

The straight lines of railway tracks turn into hand tracks, gestural knifings of paint – tracks that are not so different from the soft Scottish hills. Kossoff may have looked at Soutine, and Gillies would have looked at Munch. The thick paint makes doughty pictures: the raw, puggy stuff becomes real poetry, coming in big tins. These can be seen in John Lessore's painting of Kossoff's studio (see p.83).

Leon Kossoff, *View of Dalston Junction*, 1974

Painted with a brush, the Scottish Lowlands inspired it. A granular textured Cobalt green and Indian red would have been put on with a knife if the picture had been larger.

William Gillies, *Mount Lothian*, 1947

Colour Stores

USEUMS CONTROL THE AIR, and make a twilight for fear of fading. Cubists collaged newspapers, which have gone brown. Oils go yellow, wrinkle and crack. Pigments are changed for dye colours, which cost the manufacturers less. Preservatives, moisturizers, plasticizers, extenders, and driers are added to paint, for good, or profit. Lawrence Gowing gave hundreds of lectures on Cézanne. When I asked him what he mixed his colours with, he said he didn't know. There is so much we do not know. When I painted out-of-doors, insects would stick to my picture. I have never seen a midge leg on a Cézanne – do dealers pick them off?

It is probably not good to make complicated mixtures. Venice turpentine, copal varnish, megilp, and asphaltum may be better avoided, although most sticky mixtures will last a lifetime. This is not a recipe book. (Max Doerner and Ralph Meyer have written useful books on materials.) Art can be done with black, white, turpentine, and a little linseed oil. ("Guernica", for instance.) Bonnard used poppy oil; it is good for pale colours, because it is non-yellowing. If you want really thin paint, turpentine and cold-pressed linseed oil makes a basic medium. Use it with oil-paint that has been squeezed on to absorbent paper, and you will have paint as thin as ink.

My diagrams tell a little about the materials, but nothing is sure. Even Joseph Mallord William Turner's spit is not the same as spit today, nourished as we are on fast foods. (Spit contains enzymes, by the way, and is good for removing dirt from some kinds of oil painting.) Turpentine wets more than white spirit.

Daniel Miller, *Tubes of Paint*, 1994

They almost painted themselves.

Oil of spike (lavender oil) smells sweetly and dries slowly, although I have never used it. Eggs will make pigments adhere. Add equal parts of egg and oil to the same amount of water and shake. Add a little damar varnish, if you wish. Stand oil and turpentine in equal parts, added to the same amount of egg yolk with two parts of water, dries fast in both oil and tempera techniques.

Casein (which has been used by Balthus) makes a waterproof film that is strong on paper. Opal medium comes in tubes: it is beeswax, turpentine, and stand oil. It takes the shine out of paint.

Today, a visit to well-stocked artists' colour-store creates the same feelings I had as a child on Christmas mornings when I opened my presents. I was given a large watercolour box one year. Strangely, I fell in love with one colour which I remember to this day. It was a dull buff colour (which might have been a mixture of Chromium oxide green and white). Art shops are an inexhaustible lure. It is economical to remember that a million pound Cubist picture might be made of charcoal, yellowed newspaper, a dab or two, and some found objects. But Cubism was special and allowed many games with materials. Picasso, Braque, and Gris included granules of tobacco, beads, sand, sawdust, powdered cork, etc. And Dubuffet collaged with butterflies, dried leaves, flowers, and charred orange peel. Materials can be almost anything. Whole used paint tubes would be trowelled into John Maxwell's paintings. I had better stop before I include the vast array of collage materials used by Schwitters, Schnabel, Lanyon, Thubron, Rauschenberg, and Mellis, because that way lies sculpture.

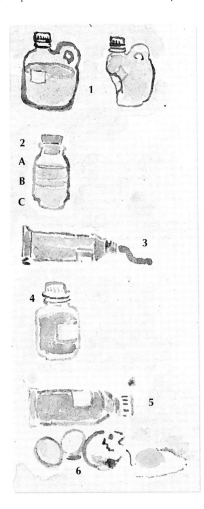

1 *Turpentine has an attractive smell. It is also toxic, so ventilate thoroughly. I found my paint was remaining sticky. I had tested the turpentine by putting a little on a piece of glass. It did not dry. Now I take care, and keep turpentine in the dark in a full container, and not for too long. If you squash the plastic container until the liquid is at the top, you can screw the cap on tight. Otherwise decant into full bottles.*

2 *The medium I like is probably too complicated to recommend. It is a combination of varnish, wax, turpentine and polymerized linseed oil.*

A *Stand oil. (Polymerized linseed oil.)*

B *Matt varnish. (Synthetic resin turpentine, and wax – not silicone.)*

C *Turpentine. Matisse is said to have had a little wax in his medium (which would have made it easier to remove the paint for his continual erasures).*

3 *The paint we buy in tubes is a mysterious mixture of constituents – to prevent settlement, or its failing to dry on the canvas, or going rancid in the tube. Nearly always the artist has to make intuitive adjustments. The substance is probably not worse than the impure paint of olden times. My earliest painting is now over 50 years old, and in good condition.*

4 *A tub of polymer emulsion paint*

5 *Acrylic emulsion paint, in a tube*

6 *Eggs*

My painting in oil – now over 50 years old.

They are painting the boat. Painters who paint pictures of painted boats, paint paint.

To show how impenetrable the description of materials has become, here is an example: "The equilibrium of dispersed particles is maintained using coalescing solvents. Disruption would cause the emulsion to 'break'. Antifreeze, water-softeners, preservatives and anti-foamers are required. And if the colours are to be in tubes, polyacrylate or cellulose thickeners are added." The guilds had their secrets. But now that scientists tell all, we must trust the colourmen. They charge a lot, and often cheat.

Rough pieces of cardboard would be used to make yacht paint look as precious as jewels.

After Wallis

Eye, Suffolk, 1945

55

Erasure

ANY OLD MASTERS were neat. Jan van Eyck "pencilled in" the details with a tiny brush on to a smooth surface. His mind was made up: why should he change it? Others in Italy would draw "cartoons", adjusting and pouncing and painting as they went.

The rough and repainted and "done-with-ease" look was (apart from Manet, Degas, and some Corot figure-paintings) a Matisse way. Matisse had visited, admired, and bought pictures by Renoir, who believed paintings should look handmade. To achieve the look of ease, Matisse worked hard. All difficulties must be washed out of sight. (For future scholars, he had each stage in the vast number of transformations recorded by photography.)

To make paint look inevitable and untramelled, however hard the journey, is an ambidextrous, athletic act. Actually, it needs three hands: in one, the absorbent, non-fluffy rag, in another, a brushful of solvent,

and in yet another, a brushful of new paint. Paint off! Paint on! Some painters are fast as fountains. Matisse's primings are of remarkable endurance. I looked at the surface of "The Rumanian Blouse" (which had suffered multiple erasures). The whites had a delicate watercoloured rainbow-paleness. Its survival may have been due to a small amount of gum arabic in the priming. (André Lhôte gives a recipe including gum.) Matisse had a little wax in his medium, which would have made the paint easier to dissolve and remove. Preliminary drawing on the canvas with charcoal, and its removal with rag and putty-rubber, would be part of this overall swingeing procedure. An awareness of these techniques by the spectators was taken for granted. Matisse was a great showman. He aimed at simplicity, without loss of meaning.

Emily (unfinished), 1989

The figure was drawn with charcoal directly from the girl, and later the Tower of London was added from the motif. Over the fixed charcoal, a turpentine wash of ultramarine is swept overall, and the board is laid flat. The blue goes into the interstices. Painting then proceeds, with simple mixtures.

The Houses of Parliament, veiled by drops of rain. The painting of the girl went wrong. Now the area has been given a coat of Underpainting white, with Viridian.

Eleven of the 22 states photographed by Matisse. The effect is of a sleepless body, at the mercy of Eros, but by 22 (at the end of October) the final nude has achieved repose. Starting in May, by June (at the tenth state) he is collaging and repainting fiercely. To paint as if he is making a collage, after erasure, is Matisses's middle-period style. Finally, paper is painted, cut, and stuck down for his last cut-out works.

After Matisse

After Matisse

A Nude at Dover (unfinished), 1993

You may prefer not to have to erase. If so, you may (if you do not think fast) adopt a cautious approach. I will give you the whole sequence. Some DIY stores supply hardboard ready-cut. Choose an attractive size and shape. It comes in $\frac{1}{8}$-inch thickness; or the $\frac{1}{4}$-inch which is very rigid. Coat it with adhesive, thinned for a first coat, then stronger for the second. (Acrylic medium is good.) Lay the dry fabric on the tacky surface, and smooth it from the middle outwards. When it is completely dry, give it a coat of acrylic gesso primer. (If you like a surface that has its pores filled, use a spatula, and scrape a mixture of White lead, oil, and gum arabic over it – or White lead and egg, or Underpainting white.) If you wish to paint a figure on the cliffs beside the sea, take the dry board and draw what you discover on your excursion. Then fix it. Paint samples of paint between the marks. This was at one time called "keeping the painting open". It makes for safety, and less erasure. But mind out that caution does not petrify.

Raindrops (unfinished), 1986

Partly unpainted, drawn on the spot, and partly erased. They were acrobats, and they must be free enough to move, so the surface is not to be lost. For very small, weightless pictures, primed plywood is ideal. You can obtain "skin plywood", $\frac{1}{16}$-inch thick.

Acrobats, 1991

Blue Against Yellow Does Not Make Green

THE UBIQUITY OF CHLOROPHYLL BLINDS us to green. Gauguin used the secondary colours, violet, orange, and green. They are more mysterious than the red, yellow, and blue that van Gogh liked. Green is the colour you obtain if you mix blue and yellow, but it is not the same if you put blue and yellow side by side. Weavers know this, and they also know how quantities change the resulting colours. Paul Klee taught textile composition at the Bauhaus, which involved weaving. Klee certainly knew what one coloured wool would do to another. Alternate blue and yellow threads are closer to the colour grey than the green obtained by mechanical mixing.

Colour surprises, and is practically impossible to measure even when on its own: when in pictures, it is totally, incommensurably weird. If you look at a spectrum analysis of ultramarine, you may be surprised at its complexity. Burn some salt, and by its light, see how a colourful picture turns monochrome (because the sodium spectrum is simple).

Matisse made tiny dots (almost as small as those in Seurat's "La Poudreuse"). Gradually, he made the dots larger   first pore-size, then pimple-size, finally boil-size. After this, he used the powerful reaction between colours, as when the green of a philodendron plant is placed against a red curtain. The undulating leaves make long edges for colours to meet and react with. For the rest of his life, large areas of colour would be made to meet each other. Seaweed, leaf, and heart shapes would brim with energy, or suffer in glory.

It is good to actually handle some large areas of colour. Cut straight lines into bright blue and yellow papers, and weave them together.

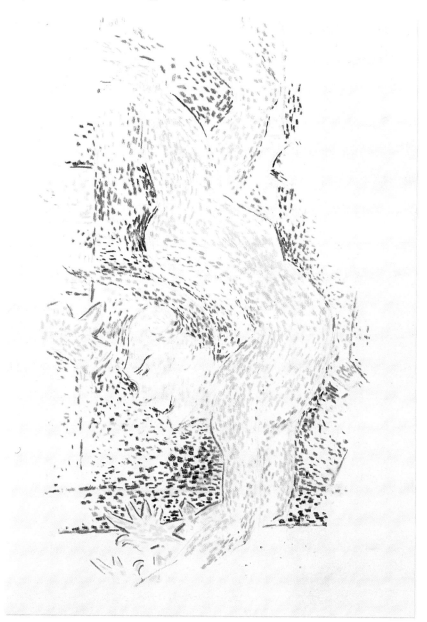

The sketch for "The Circus". The brushmarks are like a tailor's stitches (tacking), and French chalk markings.

After Seurat

"The Circus" was Seurat's last picture. He was 31. He had worked through the history of art, copying antique casts, Raphael, Ingres, and Delacroix. He painted at first a little like Corot, then somewhat as an Impressionist, then Pointillism, and finally, in a manner approaching Synthetic Cubism. Where would he have gone next? He had succumbed to the River and the Sea, and had done 170 cigar-box lids in front of "Nature". It looks as if he could have only gone one way. But there is a lust in the paint application that makes me believe he might have lived to be the great painter of bodies.

After Seurat

"Spinning and Weaving" can be hung any way up. It has patterns, and is the most complex picture painted in 1994. Cohen is a painter who thinks about music and mathematics and never loses his way in a rhythmic maze. The attachment to the surface (which weaving, or the tied surfaces of Cubism, achieves) would have had little interest for the heavy painters: Courbet, Rembrandt, or Rubens. Place a rough, white primed canvas supine. Make a solution of ultramarine, and swamp with it. Allow it to dry, the blue will settle in the hollows. Drag a brush filled with yellow of the consistency of cream across it. Some parts will be blue, some yellow, some greenish, and others an optical grey.

Bernard Cohen, *Spinning and Weaving,* 1994

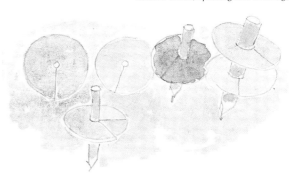

Little discs of cardboard will spin yellow and blue. If they were giving off pure coloured light, white would result. As it is, you obtain grey.

Coloured Squares

OFTEN A RECTANGLE will fill with squares. Squares appear more square if made wide. (Pure squares look narrow.) Squares are satisfying, and it often seems a shame to clutter them up. Rule-up some squares. (Use pale lines.) Believe you are going to fill the squares as enchantingly as did Paul Klee. He would use attractive surfaces of plastered burlap, or pasted paper or card. Klee was very experimental in his use of materials. Sometimes, the priming he used was absorbent. Sometimes, the pictures were called "magic squares", or some similar name. We can call our pictures fair names, but we cannot fill the squares as movingly as Paul Klee.

Watercoloured fillings for meadows

Fill some squares! Jeffrey Dennis' picture is made into compartments beautifully arranged and filled with foam-like circles. Fill squares with whatever attracts you most – wasps, larks, or even Boxer dogs. There is a sky by Magritte filled with raining men in bowler hats. My squares are rather sedate. Perhaps, if I were filling them in a studio in the Bauhaus and making the world's first pictures full of coloured squares, the sap would have risen. Noel Forster has an intimate feeling for the weave of canvas and paint. He makes flowing ways for rectangles to exist. Primary-coloured strokes have bound a rectangle into a larger rectangular canvas. Like a fault in a rock-face, he makes a slide in the harmony.

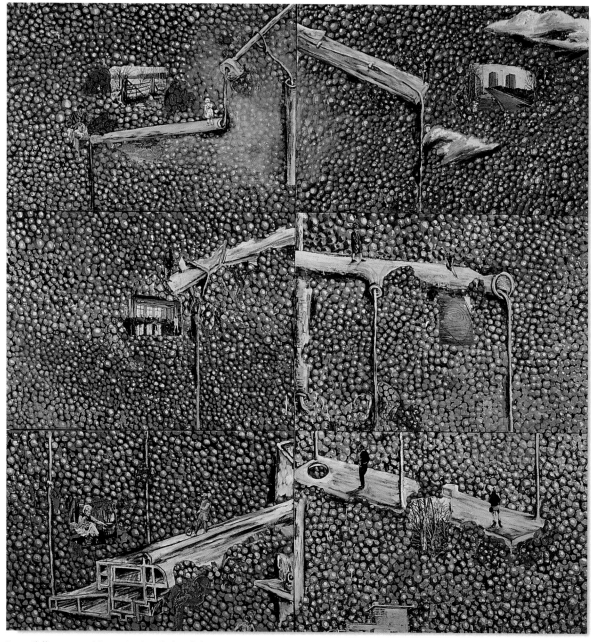

Beautifully arranged figurative interludes slide across rectangular compartments.

Jeffrey Dennis, *Heartwood*, 1989

Oil-painted fillings

Fill the squares, thinking of colours and squares. Then, if you feel mighty experimental, fill in the squares thinking of the night sky.

"Hardship by Drouth". Even here, there are rectangular ties. A line at an angle within a rectangle demands another at right-angles or parallel to it for resolution.

After Klee

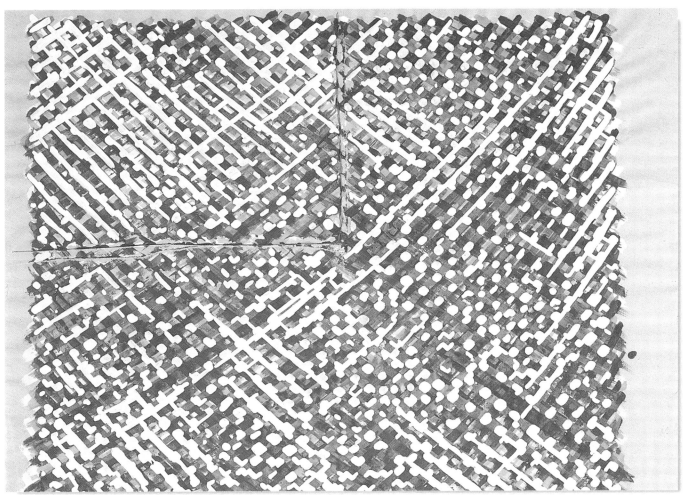

Bowed diagonally, criss-crossed, rectangled, dabbed until red, yellow, white, and blue shine silver-and-gold.

Noel Forster, *Untitled*, 1976

61

Primary Colours

Lowestoft is the most easterly seaside resort in Britain. Its coat-of-arms has the motto "Point du jour". Dawn comes early, but spring comes late. Each year the crashing daffodil colour of spring shocks me, and then a little later the laburnum trees demand that I paint them – and I always make them too yellow. Azo yellow is the kind of yellow advertisers know will – if used with black and white – be visible from Mars. The yellow of spring rivals Azo yellow. Bonnard would take laburnums and mimosa in his stride, claiming that pictures could not be too yellow. To find out something about the breakfast egg, consult Velásquez' painting "An Old Woman Frying Eggs". Then confront an egg itself.

One will do. Paint the white as a solid puddle-shape in bright white. We will call the white 100 per cent of light, and the yellow about 75 per cent of that. The yolk must glisten as the sun. Van Gogh used Yellow ochre, Chrome yellow, and white, striving to paint corn fields, lemons, sunflowers, buttercups, and even the sun, with the limited brightness of paint. "The Red Vineyard" was painted after an inspirational walk with Gauguin and it is a once-in-a-lifetime heartbreak. The artist desperately pitches at the sun, using the primary colours red, yellow, and blue. The effect is ravishing. A spiritual bonfire.

Red, yellow, and blue converge, hating each other. Hans Hoffman would have "push-pulled" them together.

Paul Klee played a violin. Noel Forster plays the piano. Forster likes entwining painted colours over woven surfaces. Klee taught weaving at the Bauhaus. Forster makes magical silvery webs out of red, blue, and yellow brush-rhythms. He rarely uses more complicated colours. They do not look Islamic, but are mesmeric and sublime – and his large paintings are almost mosque-complex.

Noel Forster, *Untitled*, 1992

The sun need not be round. It is seen so little, only in tiny flashes. This is probably a phoenix-feathered sun; or are they palm-leaves?

A Daffodil

The 15th-century floor of St. Mark's, Venice

The super-hued power-flower. Colours rotate, radiate, changing with their situation, frail yellow Flower Power compares with large areas of subdued, sharp, and edgy stone tones. Both seem to give out light.

"Peace" (detail)

After Picasso

The blue wooden bars swing around the red triangles. It is more representational than at first it seems. A self-portrayal as a small Greek island, bright and sunny in the blue Mediterranean. Red, yellow, and blue for happiness.

Joe Tilson, *Delian Apollo*, 1988

"Peace" After Picasso

An art deco lunette incorporating a rayed sun.

"Vision After the Sermon" After Gauguin

A fried egg. It seems like paint itself. The great float-splodge of egg white with its golden orb of yolk. Paint a target of creation.

"The Red Vineyard". The colours explode, jazzy as trumpets, briefly as primaries, when the sun leaves the fray, and drops towards the horizon. After van Gogh

"The Red Vineyard" After van Gogh

Suggestion

SOME EASY WAYS are saying it, placing it, or thinking it. Another way is by suggestion. Fast is not slick. Slick is incompetence, or the product of a horrible mind. Good painting is as fast as the painter can make it. Good painting can be slow, but most aware artists are in a hurry. An amusing game might be to guess each painter's dab-rate. Rubens, Goya, van Gogh, and Manet lost no time. Picasso's show-off speed we know from a film. White paint would fly off the brush on to thin paint fast as a laser, sure as a Japanese calligrapher. Suggestion in painting can be useful and wonderful. Goya, a Spaniard, had to be able to produce a bullfight crowd fast, and could suggest a coven of witches with a wave of his brush. Joseph Mallord William Turner RA was able, late in life, to suggest people in rooms, deer, trees, sunsets, and most things. Suggestion gained him enough time to go fishing. Petworth was full of suggestions.

Impressionism had to be fast enough to capture clouds. Pointillism was slower. The Ashcan artists had often been newspaper illustrators, with a daily deadline. American racers were Bellows, Sloan, and Whistler, but not Eakins. They certainly made the brush strokes move! I do not believe children can paint slowly, and I think Seurat would not paint fast. Suggestion is different from sketching – unless Constable, Turner, Toulouse-Lautrec or Boudin are doing the sketching.

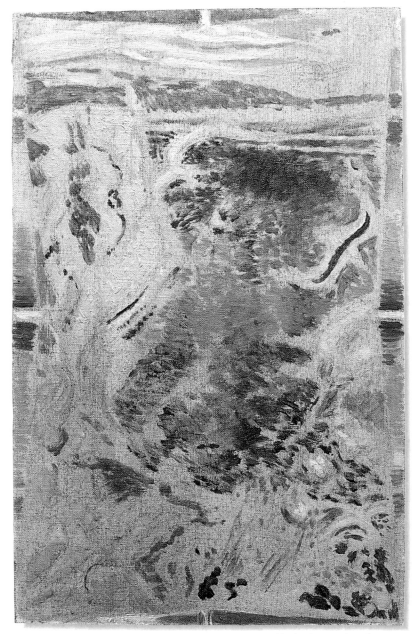

On the White Cliffs of Dover. Suggestion-dabs are instigated by birds, wavelets, flowers, sunbathers, and myself. The viewer enjoys deciphering these clues. A knowledge of the actual subject helps. Obviously, only tough, formal suggestion is worth having.

After Turner

After Turner

Donkeys touched in fast

A concourse at Petworth After Turner

The magnificent room with a round window that Lord Egremont put at the painter's disposal at Petworth House. After Turner

Choose quickly-moving subject matter to help make your painting faster – though William Gillies always painted at great speed, in the quiet landscape of lowland Scotland. Quick thinking does not require a fast subject. The influence of Dunoyer de Segonzac can be sensed. A delight in sumptuous resinous paint, but Segonzac is thicker.

William Gillies,
Lowland Landscape (detail), c. 1942

"Witches". Goya's late paintings are as haunted as the death of Duncan in Macbeth. Deafness may be lonely and quiet. Owl screeches and screams penetrate the silence. Forms loom out of the gloom.

After Goya

Daumier's drawings can resemble paintings. For an artist-caricaturist to be a painter's painter is surprising. When is drawing painting? He poses the question in a flurry of marks. Stuart Davis insisted his paintings were drawings. I think of drawings differently.

After
Daumier

65

Glazing

PRETEND YOU ARE PAINTING THE FIRST EVER – and painting particularly fast; slow up for a glaze. A glaze is a colour, thin and transparent enough to change the colour of underlying paint, and usually in a medium rich enough for it not to crack.

Stir the paint with a medium, to the consistency of double cream. With an almond-shaped brush (filbert brushes are too short) make a splodge; call it a brush stroke.

By a leap of imagination do a splodge, believe it to be a face – it is a face! Make a big splodge below – it is a body! You believe the marks you make are real? Good, you are secure. Splodge, splodge, splodge. Brushings are gifts; they will make you hands, arms, breasts, even mountains. Like the oriental story of the leap through the waterfall, a leap of imagination. Like St. John's "word" in the Bible, incarnate, the splodge lives, moves, and tunes in with the flux.

The flux was hot news for the newspaper illustrators of the Ashcan School. With splendid memories, they showed off at speed to meet daily deadlines. "Slick" is an abusive word. "Decorative" was derogatory, until Matisse made it plain that for him decorative was special. Slick is wonderful if it means the painter can get things done fast. Most great painters were in a hurry; fast, even slick, but never superficial. Manet, Hals, Tintoretto, Picasso, Dufy, Velásquez were fast. Chardin and Seurat may have been slow. Bellows was a wondrous, rapid brusher, equipped with the special flowing Maratta paint, as advised by Robert Henri. He dabbed swimmers' and boxers' muscles at speed. It is possible to increase the speed of painting, up to the speed of thought. If you go faster, the paintings become empty, like those done by chimpanzees. Make your own deadlines. Be a brave disciplinarian. Win some games. Be a good coach.

I scrub-splodged in poor, yellow light. However gloomy it is, once you begin dabbing, the colours usually behave.

Skiffle at Lowestoft, 1958

Stodgier, triangular daubs make hands "kippered" with rich glazes. Use White lead and think of pyramids.

Semi-transparent blue paint is supported on a strong, yellow base. A light touch is needed to keep the colours separate.

Hands. Fingertip touches touch in hands.

A Dabs very thinly glazed **B** A brown glaze
C Almost a glaze of pink **D** A palette-knife astray

*Oily dabs on paper. Picasso said: "I do not seek, I find."
Splodge and splodge until you find yourself living in paint.*

Bonnard's Diary

Bonnard said: "All art is composition. That's the key to it all." (This statement would be a cliché if stated by anyone other than Pierre Bonnard.)

Bonnard kept a two-day-per-page pocket diary. It served as a sketchbook. Whether the vivid sights that sparkle from its compartments were drawn close to the dates shown, I do not know. Each day he noted the weather, and most days that was "beau". He liked the informality of drawing across the printed divisions and dates, with a short soft pencil – the page almost as tiny as Constable's proper little sketchbooks. (They both had careful looks at the skies.) Bonnard was free to live and paint as he wished. Complete freedom is unnerving, and I sense his need was to tabulate his time and work: diary days, meal times, dog walks, Marthe's bath times. And the pieces of canvas were pinned to the wall, looking like various sizes of diary page. The studio-cum-landing was compartmented too, as views through windows, and postcards.

Bonnard like a prowling cat, always looking.

He said: "I like to work on an unframed canvas that is larger than the intended picture. This gives me room for alteration. I find this method very agreeable, especially for landscapes. For every landscape, you need a certain amount of sky and ground, water and verdure, and it is not always possible to establish their interrelation right from the start."

Just as the dachshund "Poucette" would move from smell to smell, so on his walks around the house and garden, the artist would scribble in the diary. He was fortunate and fulfilled, and rather lonely, painting his beautiful surroundings over and over.

John Maxwell, the Scottish artist, told his students to draw whatever they wanted to paint with a thick-leaded, blunt soft pencil on a little piece of paper – and then make the painting from it, with as little alteration as possible. The subjects you see close by, or on an excursion, are at the mercy of your fat black pencil. Perhaps you even possess an old (or new) diary. Even, perhaps, a dachshund, to help you follow your dream.

Bonnard saw a lot of different subjects on his walks. Diary pages.

After Bonnard

"Paysage du Cannet". McComb copied the central part. Bonnard was excited by the views around his newly-purchased house in the south of France.

After Bonnard

A scribble-drawing at Hastings Beach. (It would conform to John Maxwell's instructions, but was probably drawn with conté crayon.)

Overwhelmed by its beauty, McComb first said: "Bonnard had heaven in his head, and his work is starred in shimmering sunlight." Then: "Bonnard made gems of incomparable beauty." Then, when asked again: "Amongst the lemons, the greys, greens, dull oranges, wine-reds, a trace of glittering black across the space." Finally: "Across the waves of lemon-pinks, greys, azure blue-greens – finger-dabs of brown and black – glittering summer stars!" McComb did his copying three hours before the public ten o'clock opening time. And he went six days running.

Leonard McComb, Copy of a part of Bonnard's *Paysage du Cannet*, 1994

On the cliff, South Coast

"Terrace au Cannet". Painted with watercolour and gouache, soon after his wife died. Bonnard himself died about five years later. It has an unearthly icy summertime heat, a spiritual vision. Perhaps Marthe is the figure on the left. Some of the brush strokes look as if they were done with a bristle brush, which is often good for gouache, as it can keep the paint light and airy.

After Bonnard

A little drawing that resembles the view in McComb's copy.

After Bonnard

Detail

DETAILS AS SMALL AS A MOSQUITO'S FEELER, an eyelash, or a distant beak; details of bumble-bees, mice, midge-wings, and tiny grasses; all should live well under the brush. With good sight we see in detail. Indian miniatures try our seeing. Turner made drawings that dot ornaments and windows profusely. I lose patience drawing architecture. I find I am doing a window on the wrong building. Canaletto insists Mannerist wavelets and manikin figures combine with traced camera-obscura views, smooth and detailed, to become surfaces of resinous, sun-thick, oily gloss. Most paint has been smooth and glossy. A Vermeer is smooth as a lake on a windless day. Smooth, oily, resinous surfaces, when slightly wet, will gracefully receive tiny details of egg-tempera white (its water-wetness preventing it spreading). Cranach's "Adam and Eve" in the Courtauld Gallery, London,

shows how splendidly clearly lined grasses and pale details can lighten areas of dark paint, without mixing. Indian miniatures avoid "mechanical" mixture by overlaying patterns, colour over colour.

The most popular room at the Tate Gallery includes British Victorian and Pre-Raphaelite Brotherhood paintings. I really only enjoy Ford Madox Brown; he was not of the Brotherhood. The Pre-Raphaelites often made their details by painting sharp colours into tacky White lead surfaces. Some of the world's marvellous paintings are full of details; Jan van Eyck's "Madonna of Chancellor Rolin" in the Louvre is one.

Tackle a moth, brave a mouse, confront an oceanic insect: nothing is too small. They challenge the careful painter. You need a tiny brush. I wish you luck with the brush, and hope it points up well to delineate the mouse whiskers.

Mice

Moths

Bumble-bees and wasps hovering over borage

Van Gogh painted delicate subjects heavily. Discover what you can, daub, and discard. Two butterflies, a death's head moth, and a beetle.

Mice

Moths

A stag beetle: keep a sharp brush.   After Dürer

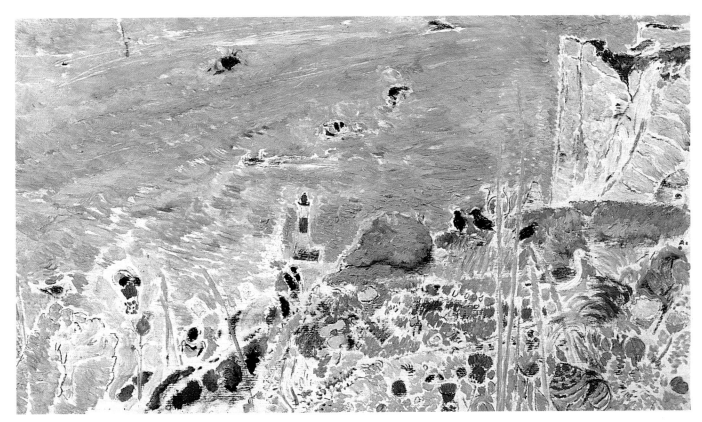

Bumble-bees at Beachy Head, 1990

Moth

Oceanic Insect, 1981

Verisimilitude

WITH GOOD EYESIGHT, what we see in a camera obscura does not surprise us. What we see is raw and accurate. High, near Edinburgh Castle, a lens projects a part of the city on to a white horizontal screen.

The material of sight surprises us if we find it in unusual places: a photorealist head nine feet high, or Central Park crushed into a book.

The manifest act of seeing is so wonderful that when we approach verisimilitude we must take care that we do not mean *like photography*. Photography is the world's light collected randomly, mechanically, by a lens.

It is what a temperament can do to the raw material of sight, that makes truth possible. It is when Velásquez brushes with a strange transforming passion close, but never too close, to eyesight. Then verisimilitude is truth. Vermeer was inspired by the pellucid charm of the camera obscura. But art need not approach physical sight so closely. Hokusai, Watteau, and Cézanne knew other ways to be truthful. Brueghel is universally believed even when Icarus falls out of the sky.

A backyard view in East London. Daniel Miller bought a house in Hackney, to be warm in winter. As he looked out of the

Stanley Spencer lying on a grave looks innocent and young. He is newly resurrected at Cookham churchyard.

window of his painting room, he saw back gardens. Each little walled plot eccentric in a particular way; small squabbles between man and nature. Lopped trees and grass patches; tiny stand-ins for the meadows and trees of grand estates, rendered bodged, burglar-alarmed, child-scribbled, dog-shaped, and twiggy.

Daniel painted it as a mass of present material to make intimate contact with his environment; then he would know his view. There must be no mannerism, just enough style to keep the twigs alive. A lot of patience, and a lot of looking.

Stanley Spencer worked in a similar way, painting Cookham as secure home views. Stanley was unique. I once saw him walking, and heard him talking. He was like an electric-sewing machine. No reworking was ever required. He was very fast. His was the gift that could make sense of the muddled English way of life. He could digest corrugated iron, chickens, pigs, mud, garden paths, old clothes and clothes-pegs, mangles, and Christ. Britain has thrown up other artists to deal with its dishevelled beauty. Bratby painted golden outdoor lavatories. Leon Kossoff jerk-dabbed junctions of rail. Burra watercoloured motorways and lorries in curious landscapes. John Nash painted rough and scrub and ponds.

"Montmartre"   After van Gogh

Overlooking Gillespie Park.

Daniel Miller, *Backlands*, 1990–91

Veiled by twigs, they rise naked and reluctant. One floor down, the cat food calls.

A first look at the new day: roses, bricks, and cats. From time to time, I notice what is happening in the house at the end of the garden. The figures struggling to get clothes on in time to go to work seem too large for the windows.

Paint some feline territorial prowls and squabbles on garden walls. Sketch in the waving paws before breakfast.

Arising with feet

After Vermeer

"A Street in Delft". This dry chalk diagram is to remind you of the famous "View of Delft". It is made with tiny drops of paint, into wet resinous paint. These effects are similar to the burrs made when the lens of a camera obscura is slightly out of focus. Vermeer chose subjects where sparkling dimpling liquid beauties could be presented.

Arising with violets. Bricks were stuck together with soft mortar, oozily it solidified. Brick-like rectangular dabs fill the rectangular pictures. Pectorals and window-panes, wardrobes and curtains meet cat tails and intimate tales.

Children's Art

MY FRIEND WILLIAM THOMSON taught at an Edinburgh Boy's Club. The older boys told the younger ones it was sissy to do art; sport was important. Unusually, he gave them paint in a range of soft colours. One of the resulting pictures is shown here. Could child art be more varied than we had thought?

Be generous. Children have the law on their side now: if you do not buy them lovely paints, they leave home immediately. When I was eight, I painted a mermaid with phosphorescent paint on my bedroom wall. If a child can spare you the time, she will teach you most of what you need to know. Late in life, Matisse said he wished to see like a child. One of Picasso's finest periods was soon after the Second World War, when his children were young. He loved to paint them with their toys.

Take a canvas and streak with a rich, deep, warm blue, made from ultramarine, Charcoal grey, and a little Permanent rose, thinned with turpentine. Share it with a child. Race to paint all the toys you can think of. He will give you tips, especially on new inventions. Take him to a children's museum, such as the Bethnal Green Museum in London, to see old toys. If there is any flagging of interest, treat Liquorice Allsorts as individual still lives.

The first childhood of a painter grows towards a second. Picasso said he never drew in a childlike way. I expect he was mistaken and forgot; or his special gift may have been to see brightly like a child all his life. Peter Pan's young friends were surnamed Darling. Children are not darlings. They are imitative: if parents fawn, they may fawn back. I was bored as a child. Little children demand repetition and are boring. Like Warhol soup, after he has advertized the advertisement, it is all the same – flour paste. Child vocabulary is small. Children pose questions continually, to get the attention of a parent, not for answers. Childhood is mysterious. The child makes rapid marks on paper, doing it as compulsively as it kicks.

Is there a survival mechanism preventing the infant from poking a finger in its baby sister's eye? A baby can distinguish at a glance between a card with 19 dots on it, and one with 18. I am unable to do this. Children are prodigies in music, mathematics, and sucking ice creams.

In Brueghel's "Children's Games", 84 games have been identified. Paint a game.

After Brueghel

Much child art surprises at first sight, then the pleasure wears off. But even after 50 years this seems a marvellous picnic poem. Mix gouache or other "body colour" *in several tones of, say, Burnt umber and other colours. The effect engendered can be as softly harmonious as Picasso's Pink period.*

"Yacht Girl"   After Picasso

A "pudding head", by Will

Various joke-shop items, sweets, and a bursting firework.

Watercoloured toys. Old toys are more simple and recognizable than new toys.

Liquorice Allsorts

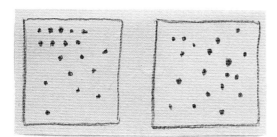

18 dots, or 19?

Toys in oil. Toys are often painted. Just play at painting.

The Stripes of Tutankhamun

KING TUTANKHAMUN was bandaged and embalmed, bound in stripes of fabric. His gold mask was striped with glass imitating lapis lazuli. Real lapis surrounded the eyes. Egyptian art is measured and layered throughout, from architecture to a small bead. Paul Klee was inspired by a visit to Egypt to paint profound layer upon profound layer; like striations of rock, like sandwiches of surprising colours. At Alum Bay on the Isle of Wight, they fill lighthouse-shaped vases with layers of coloured sand from the cliffs.

Straight lines are rare in the natural world, so it was possible for Wyndham Lewis, Léger, and Paul Nash to surprise in their day by ruling lines. Horizontal bands make us feel secure. Opposite the Albany is Savile Row, the home of the well-cut pinstriped suit. If we want to show how proper we are, we get well-striped-suited. Stripes bend, and camouflage zebras in forests. Stripes will make eloquent every departure from the strict and straight, however small; but also, wonderful wild variations, as in a Hockney swimming pool, surrounded with straight edges, where undulating water deforms the known straight race-track lines marked on the bottom.

Practise brushing lines: parallel, ruled, and free. The widest stripe is the rectangle of the picture. A small line is the warp of the canvas. Sign-writers know it is safer to make slightly fluctuating lines as straight lines than free-handed to attempt a perfect straightness. Max Bill of the Bauhaus made straight edges very straight. Only a laser would shake them. We live in a striped world. Stripe, then, and as you mark, consider whether you wish to stripe all your life. There seems to be a market for banded pictures. They fit well in frames, in rooms and offices where serious men in serious well-striped suits need calm environments. Stripe painters include: Scully, Stella, Barnett Newman, Noland, Klee, Riley, Jaray. The gold mask of Tut is a world image. Sam and Will Southward grasped it with conviction. The nose is much the same each time. The stripes are various and emphatic: yellow for gold, blue for the stripes. They made my copy look tame. A child's-eye view of Tut is our challenge. Two or three colours are enough to distress the Sphinx. A child's certainty is envied by me.

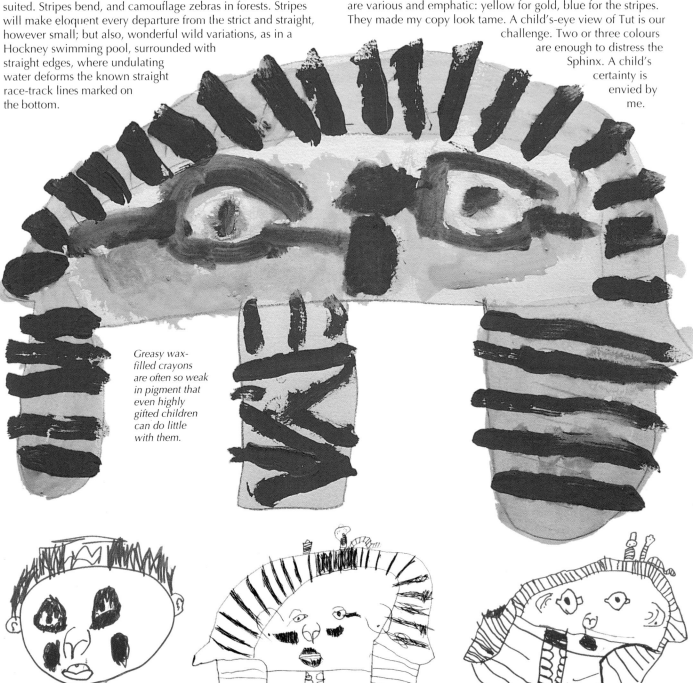

Greasy wax-filled crayons are often so weak in pigment that even highly gifted children can do little with them.

Drawings of Tut by Sam and Will

The striped head-dress of King Tutankhamun

This fractal has stripes curving like zebras. They are as active as African dancing.

Ruled lines almost blend with hand-drawn lines. But some people can draw straighter than I can. Obviously, the turquoise ones are hand-drawn.

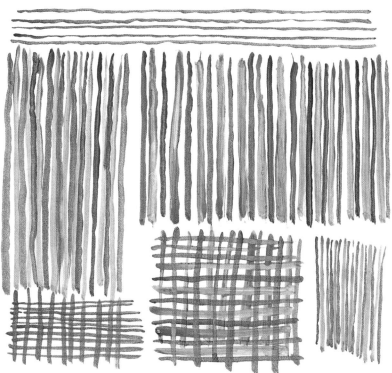

Practise striping. Mine are very wobbly. By the time I had done them, I was getting better. But stripes are always good unless you are unlucky. Practise striping with a brush; criss-cross, and you are close to tartan.

Rich Painting

I F YOU USE DARK HUES, be careful to keep them clear. Some colours are naturally dark: Ultramarine deep, Alizarin crimson, Monastral green, Prussian blue, and Mineral violet, for example. The support of a half-tone ground, or underpainting in colour, makes deep transparent colours look more secure when applied over them. Rich, dark colours over white must obey the "fat over lean" rule, or crazing, cracking, or bleeding will result. Underpainting white, a gel, a wax, even stand oil, fat oil, or

sun-thickened oil can be useful in preventing this. Try painting with colours straight from the tube. Without adding white, make the colours paler by scrubbing with a brush, scratching with the handle of the brush, scraping with a painting knife, or (if you like) using the teeth of a comb.

As the sun goes down, the red glass of Chartres Cathedral deepens like rubies before night takes over. The Daniele da Volterra "Descent from the Cross" mourns in blackened reds and pinks.

Matisse gave Smith sufficient confidence to paint near Cézanne's "Mont Sainte Victoire". He rarely added white to his rich colours.

Matthew Smith,
Provençal Landscape, 1935

Sutherland was isolated from Europe by the Second World War. Seeing Picasso's work freed him; looking at Blake and the young Palmer influenced him. Pembrokeshire inspired sumptuous gouache and crayon landscapes.

Graham Sutherland,
Landscape with Estuary, 1945

It is said Hitchens did trials on glass, then copied them on to canvas. I suspect even this would not be spontaneous enough for Hitchens' pantheistic bravura.

By using paint with a thick medium, with little mixing, and with close tones, twilight was made to glow.

Matthew Smith, *Winding Road – Cornish Landscape*, 1920

Ivon Hitchens
Tangled Pool, 1946

Lowland Scotland inspired Gillies most. He disliked the stridency of autumn colours, and (except on camping holidays to Iona or the Highlands) hardly needed mountains, or people. The west coast of Scotland is renowned for the saturation of its blue waters.

William Gillies, *Eildon*, 1949

The Working Drawing

PAINTERS VARY. I imagine Milton Avery, Modigliani, Matthew Smith, and Renoir splashed straight in and painted without a preliminary drawing. Some revise on the canvas. Some, like Edvard Munch, do different versions of the idea on new canvases. William Roberts did careful designs in full-colour, most perfectly squared-up for secure enlargement. (Sickert said that all drawings are improved by squaring-up.)

I am not neat. The making-up of my mind is desperate. I begin with thick, tough watercolour paper, and draw roughly the proportion of the picture. It is possible I will use all or some of the following: charcoal, knives, fixative, pencils, pastels, crayons, watercolour, putty (kneaded), rubbers, typewriter erasers, gouache, oil paint, collaged paper, spit, and tears. During this, and later, I consult drawings, done at various times, of the same

South Downland, 1992

subject. I do not mind how scuffed and rough the working drawing becomes, so long as all the shapes, and the subject matter, become exactly considered and disposed. It is like the plan of a circus: knowing where to put the cages, clowns, audience, and ring, and trying to pretend you are the ringmaster, and knowing all the time the "Big Top" may fall on you. But in the really good working drawing, if it is complete, the painter can move about in comfort as if in his own head.

The next stage I rather like. I transfer like a craftsman, watching each enlarged square, making arcs and straight lines, and thinking little about the subject depicted. Finally, primed ready for the explosive to go off, the picture can be painted as freely at arm's length, as Edvard Munch in the snow in his outdoor studio. After such a lot of preparation, the brush is keen to move, it still has a lot to do.

The weight of the various elements has to be measured intuitively. The main figures must not fall out of the sky.

South Downland (detail), 1992

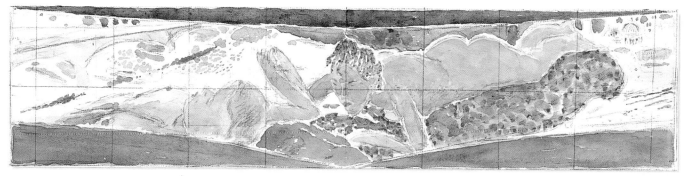

The Thames curves, and the painter can pretend it curves even more.

Extended Figures, 1992

Sickert said all drawings were improved by squaring-up.

William Roberts, *Folk Dance*, 1938

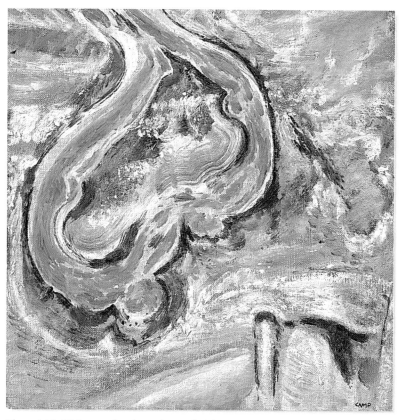

A working watercolour sketch for "South Coast". This was a preliminary drawing, but often what museums label "studies" are done when the picture is completely finished. Only the artist would know.

The paint is thick enough to keep them safe. Like mountainous contour maps. Repeated applications of paint make islands and the shapes stabilize the athletic rhythms of the subject.

Figures Somersaulting at Beachy Head, 1992

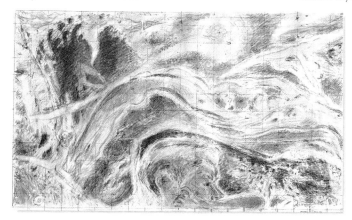

One of the working drawings for "South Downland". The self-portrait head was removed. The squares are visible. Watercolour and pastel pencils work well with each other.

A crayon moves the figures fast at Beachy Head. A self-portrait is making its exit. Bach sounds magnificent on various instruments. He did not always specify which ones. Rembrandt would use a variety of media to express his themes. A quill-pen drawing has a different effect from a heavy paint surface. He did a lot of schematic drawings that prepared the way.

Cloud Figures, Beachy Head, 1992

The Studio

THERE ARE FASHIONS IN ARTISTS' WORKPLACES. When Clement Greenberg passed away, a whole scene went with him. In the 1960s, David Sylvester, the famous perfect placer of pictures, who knew the needs of vast white museums, advised bright youth to paint big. To do this usually meant hiring a large space: in the United States a loft, or disused factory; in Britain, a big room, or a warehouse divided by screens. It slightly resembled an art college, or the corporate offices that, with the museums, were the main patrons for large pictures. Big pictures can be wonderful. Michelangelo's "Last Judgement" is large, but often the large pictures become inflated or decorative. In London's East End live countless painters of large canvases; many are poor; a large primed canvas costs as much as a bicycle. When in the days of the New York School, Jackson Pollock dribbled house paint, and massive rollings were harmonized by Rothko, excitement was in the air. Now that graffiti wet our cities, dribble and spray are everywhere.

Delacroix had a proper portrait-painter's studio with a waiting-room like a doctor. Monet had a waterlily-pond size studio. Alexander Lieberman's book, *The Artist in his Studio*, shows some of the great peacocks in their nests. Braque had a large area with several easels and palette supports, which he made himself out of tree branches with the bark left on. He mixed his paint in old paté or tomato-paste tins, one brush per tin. It looked very comfortable. I have usually worked in a room adjacent to my bedroom. It has nasty advantages. Gertrude Stein was sorry for painters because they could not get away from their pictures. She was right. The unfinished picture hangs on the bedroom wall, a horrible indictment. The artist desperately tries to make it better – starts touching it up when needing breakfast – or even takes it into the bathroom.

Any room will do to work in, if it fits you. L.S. Lowry looked comfortable; he had painted in his armchair in a Victorian parlour for many years. For a few weeks Nigel Greenwood lent me his beautiful gallery as a studio. It was blindingly light. It was the nearest I have been to having a "real studio" to work in. I had liked painting in the midst of landscape, in parks, on beaches, ice rinks, piers, bathing pools, dance-halls, or beside rivers. The weather could make things difficult. For years a Morris Traveller served as a tiny studio. It had good flat sliding windows. It went to the cliff edge at Pakefield, settling amongst the burdock, ragwort, nettles, and thistles. In winter, I put a paraffin heater in the rear, and an easel in the front, with a rug over my knees. I witnessed night and storms, mist, drizzle, buffeting winds, and at other times, the hot sun scorched. In a car you are often invisible; you can be very close to people's intimate gossip (usually about money, hospital, and television soaps). It was also luxurious painting watercolours in a rowing boat in the middle of the Waveney River, at Beccles in Suffolk. Monet and Daubigny had floating houseboat studios. William Gillies had a tent.

Although any part of a building will do for a studio (and I had a friend who painted secretly in the drawer of his government office), it is sometimes worth planning a studio. Make a sketch and a list of your needs. An easel can wind-up; the older ones can tip the canvas to an angle. A trolley and shelves will accommodate brushes, tubes of paint, a palette, brush washer, sketchbooks, straightedge, set square, clean rags, compass, watercolours, hi-fi, and art books.

For winter, have a lot of artificial light, and see that it resembles daylight and falls in the same direction. I suggest six 100-watt "daylight simulation" bulbs, and four eight-foot long "north light" or "colour matching" neon tubes. It is useful to pin drawings up. Bulldog clips are convenient. Paintings will hitch on to nails. If you get backache or a bent posture, hang up a trapeze.

Now that models are employed less, studios can be lonely rooms. Some of the greatest pictures are lonely pictures. Remember, your studio is your home to think in. If you need solitude, make it private.

After Monet

Timothy Hyman draws the monument built by Christopher Wren to commemorate the Fire of London.

Matisse would paint from his car. This is a poor copy of a beautiful picture, "The Windshield".

After Matisse

Lessore paints with gooey grey paint. The artist depicted is Leon Kossoff, who uses big tins. With so many grey days in England, it all looks very real.

John Lessore, *Artist And Model III*, 1988

Drawing a bonfire on the beach

Winslow Homer

Some days it can be comfortable drawing on the beach, but it is nearly always better in the shade of a boat or a windbreak.

After Goya

Goya at work with candle-holders around his hat.

Milton Avery painting out of doors, freely, with pure imagined colours.

OPEN AIR PAINTING
Wild and Urban Encounters

Windblown Lovers, Pakefield, 1960

The clay cliffs of Suffolk, where ragwort, bindweed, and thistles proliferate, are gale swept. The water is whipped into dark Ultramarine greys. It gobbles great chunks of the coast. Each girl has a boyfriend, except for the nearest, who appears ravished by the great North Sea itself.

Paint from the protection of a motorcar. The splodges will take over, until the rhythm becomes all-embracing.

Outside, the charging wind is holiday-brochure-bracing, blowing canvas against brush and stiffening necks. Lapis grey is no longer obtainable, but Davy's grey or black can be blued with ultramarine. "Blue-black" is a ready-mixed black. Blues are clear and poignant, but not necessarily as sad as country-singer "blues". The following are good, cold blues: Cyanine, Prussian, Monastral, and Manganese. Warmer blues (if blues can ever be thought of as warm) are Cobalt, Indigo, Cerulean, and Ultramarine, as well as Ultramarine ash. Paint on a blue ground for clean surprises.

*The stones in the wall are
fastidiously designed. Ravilious is
more descriptive than Seurat; but
it does feel like being on an island.*

Eric Ravilious, *Convoys Passing an Island*, c. 1940–1

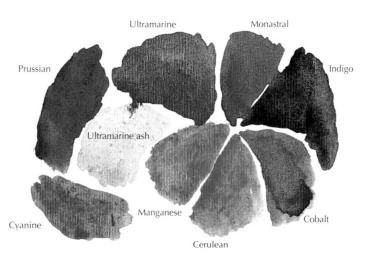

*Blues in watercolour are
naturally enchanting. To make
them equally beautiful in oil
needs more skill. Underpaint
and juxtapose.*

Ultramarine

Monastral

Prussian

Indigo

Ultramarine ash

Cyanine

Manganese

Cobalt

Cerulean

On a Clear Day You Can See France

DOVER PRIORY IS THE NAME OF THE RAILWAY STATION. From it, walk up high. The White Cliffs of Dover are known, but are seen mainly from the ferry. The terminal is noisy. The cliffs rise two-tiered, tinged off-white by soot. Further north, they are clean and bright. Small blue butterflies waver and flutter; deep in the grass, among knapweed, buttercups, and dandelions, lovers sweat. In the vastness, where cumulus clouds form and evaporate in blueness streaked with skeins of icy cirrus clouds, the flux is perfume-pathwayed, buzzed by bumble-bees, bees, flies, and wasps.

Give a canvas a scrub with a blue diluted with genuine turpentine, until it looks filled with desire. Make a little mark with blue-black. It is a jackdaw, I discover; the blip of white is turning into a yacht with its spinnaker filled. The undercut cliffs are set shimmering by a black flint beach.

The cliffs on either side of the Channel are marked by history. The choice is yours: Monet, Braque, Matisse, Turner, Seurat, Graham Bell, and many others dazzled their eyes here.

Do not fear past painting. With no food, you are anaemic. You cannot be in this world without ancestors. Do not fear to look at the English Channel. It has been looked at before. If you fear Impressionism, Cubism, or any of the past ways of painting, your art is weakened by fear. Past art is a protection from the dangers of academicism.

"The Cliff, Étretat"   After Braque

"Dieppe"   After Braque

The rock formation (rather like a flying buttress) allowed the water to be a larger part of the design.   After Monet

"Étretat"   After Matisse

Dover. On very thin plywood, small and light to carry

From eyehold to eyehold, grasp grass, chalk, thistle, flint, and wave, then, beyond the clouds looking back, see yourself looking towards France. Painting, like a magic carpet, will take you anywhere.

Dover, 1994

Dover above the ferry, with knapweed

A work-along drawing for "Dover" (see p.87). Push the components until you know the most eloquent arrangement.

Dover, 1994

Rain

RAIN IS SAD WITHOUT A RAINBOW. Liquids paint liquids. It has been said that Cotman, Constable, Crome, and other outdoor painters flourished in East Anglia because of the low rainfall. In autumn, the monster skies are splendid. We hardly see rain before it wets us. George Bellows painted approaching storms and rain-filled landscapes with a bravura use of dark transparent colours. Rain made Chinese minds glide like snails, and wring forth beautiful poems. Braque, Sickert, and van Gogh used short diagonal strokes on horizontal formats. Their surfaces were crusty: they did not want to imitate rain's liquidity.

Laetitia Yhap is the only painter who has made visual poetry from raindrops on window-panes. They are so exactly painted, the

surface tension of the water is visible. The golden toad's eye does not see the roundness of a headlight or consider the fast rain-marks, sharp as cat-scratches. The toad stays still as the stones. The picture is a liquid building of vapours condensing in a vast alembic-shaped vignette. Vignettes were used by Bewick, Whistler, and Turner in books and etchings. But used as it is here, it can imply a vastness, and make the falling rain important.

Thames, 1986

After Constable

After Constable

Constable was a miller's son, conscious of the weather. A windmill would turn according to the direction of the wind. He was excited by dew and rain, and made a physical engagement with the wetness, using big brushings of white and black over warm-coloured paper. (I expect he coated thick paper with White lead.) Constable's tiny sketches evoked large expanses of landscape and influenced Delacroix, and consequently French Impressionism.

After Rousseau

After Kandinsky

After Hiroshige

Hiroshige would make a hard poetry from rain traces, but here rain mysteriously obscures a hunting lodge called "The Temple", soft in the fall of leaves over the lake. Using paint as if it were mud, subdue a landscape, brush roughly thinking of a Turner storm.

Laetitia Yhap, *The Rain Storm*, 1967–69

After Braque   After Henri   After Seurat *Viewing Constable sketches*

Snow

I REMEMBER THE WHITE-ON-WHITE of snow on apple-blossom. Snow makes the White Cliffs of Dover appear chocolate-brown. It is soupy in London; slushy in Venice. But wherever snow goes, it is exciting.

When years ago I painted hard-blown snow, the streaks made it move fast, and straightness tied them to the picture plane. Brueghel painted dabs of snow liquidly, a little proud of the picture plane, slightly, lusciously law-breaking. But the flakes are small. When you copy a Brueghel picture you realize how perfect and painterly is his control. You find yourself dolloping too much, or snowballing a donkey. Much of the painting seems to be wet-in-wet.

Try some flaky dabs of paint on a dark surface: wet-on-dry, wet-on-wet, and in other ways. Brueghel's "Hunters in the Snow" is the greatest snow picture ever painted. The dogs' paws sink in the snow exactly the right amount. In "The Numbering of the People at Bethlehem", snowballing is done seriously. Brueghel's pictures work on every level.

A Hawksmoor church. St. George's in the east, with falling snow. The world is different for some. You may have a glowing log fire, but it is as likely you are protected from the snow-filled cold wind by the invisible warmth of central heating. The bent body is a dramatic subject against the dark dawn.

St. George's in the East, 1988

Snow flakes blown by severe winds at Pakefield. The long tails were painted from behind a large window.

Seaside Garden in Snow, 1960

Doig uses elaborate spotting – dark marks on light, and sometimes, really large light splodges, which jump forward to surprise, to create shocks of depth.

Peter Doig, *Hill Houses*, 1991

Various dots, splodges, and curlicues: liquid white on black; liquid white on wet black; black over white; spots with tails.

A Cat in the Snow

Snowballing. They wore many layers of clothing, and looked like walking haystacks. When I painted in the snow, I wore a flying suit and an overcoat.

After Brueghel

See if you can discover the luminous semi-transparent Brueghel way. Perhaps a golden ground will help.

After Brueghel

Snow crystals are circular.

Snow, 1960

Paint a snowball, or a ball of white wool. Like an old-time exercise.

Van Gogh and the Sun

THE CORN IS SOWN, GROWN, AND SCYTHED. Van Gogh, in the harness of his vocation, is held within his picture, like his weavers at their looms. The sower is a self-portrait of the artist, the tree is also one, and the whole picture, bisected by the horizon, is his cleft personality. Vincent is as harrowed as the field. Religion frightened him. As a parson's son, church law was on his back. He survived being a schoolmaster and an art dealer. He saw the degradation of poor miners. He wrote "Vincent" on the tree, loaded against a winter sky. It survives, a maimed but living cross with an amputated bough: the cut ear of the tree, a painful pink disc against the apple-green sky. (The apple-green of early Mondrian.) The picture is a symbolic prayer. An enormous sun palpitates against the head like a weighty halo. After the expulsion, toil punishes. The paint is worked hard with a Western force; the format is designed like the Japanese prints loved by the painter. If you think there was ever a comic face marked on the sun-disc, do not believe it: there is scarcely a trace of humour in the letters Vincent sent to Theo. Prussian blue was used for the figure and the tree. It can be a savage colour. Vincent wrote that time would tone down the Impressionists' unstable colours, and therefore not to be afraid of applying them too crudely. He asked to be sent Geranium lake. The tender pink clouds may have been a mixture of Geranium lake and white. Like his hope, this pink was destined to fade.

"The Sower". Hold a coin close and it obscures the sun. A coin-sized sun will not, however bright yellow, burn you a vision unless your painting is tiny. Looking at the sun fills your view with after images.

After van Gogh

"The Sower". A sun will become large as it approaches the horizon. Try painting a big area of Cadmium or Chrome yellow as a disc for the sun. What will the rest of your picture be like? Perhaps the sun will free you from a lax verisimilitude or habit.

After van Gogh

As if overcome by the heat, like a jerking raven trapped in the sun; Soutine-like, the Munch-mad heat-strokes of red paint are melting the Midi. These Bacons, when new, were shown at the Hanover Gallery in London and made it stink of drying paint.

Francis Bacon, *Studies for a Portrait of van Gogh*, 1957

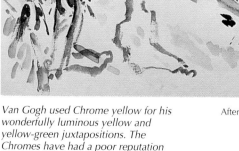

Van Gogh used Chrome yellow for his wonderfully luminous yellow and yellow-green juxtapositions. The Chromes have had a poor reputation for being blackened by polluted air. They are said to be improved, and should perhaps be used again. Chrome yellow is very intense.

After Bacon, after van Gogh

After van Gogh

After Millet

A smaller version of "The Sower". The simpler elements, the arc of the twig and the straighter furrow, may have been possible because it is smaller. It is rewarding to compare different versions. He did two copies, and several drawings, after Millet's "Sower". His figures swing into becoming images of power.

After
van Gogh

After van Gogh

After van Gogh

After van Gogh

"The Artist on his way to work". The "Sower" paintings were not actually done as self-portraits. The sowers spread hope as they stride across the fields. In this earlier painting, he depicted himself; trying to look blue as a peasant, and burdened with a painter's paraphernalia, he strides a little like a sower. But the time is August, and the shadow is from a hot sun.

This small picture inspired Francis Bacon's large, vividly coloured pictures. The painting-knives and large dripping brushes had never been used with such bravura before. The Bacons were very exciting, new, and melodramatic. But in the van Gogh, although the painter is weighed down, a bird may yet sing and the corn is bright.

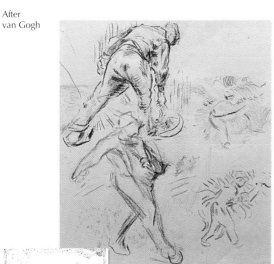

Small drawings were often in letters.

After van Gogh

After
van Gogh

After van Gogh

"A Weaver"

After
van Gogh

After van Gogh

"A Weaver". With a windmill outside the window, the picture is full of crosses. The weaver is imprisoned by overwork and poverty, and the loom resembles a torture-machine in its complicated woodwork: windlass, guillotine, rack. The painter knew the labyrinths of torment.

These early pictures of weavers were influenced by Rembrandt. The beautiful, heavy, grease-grey greens and hot browns are as moving as the bright colours of the later paintings.

After van Gogh

Leaves

Vine leaves, from being pale green, go paler and yellower and begin to flow with streams of wine-colour between the veins. The woodlands are soggy after rain. Over dark streams, the yellow chestnut-leaves float in the air, and lie in the mud. Make some Concorde-aeroplane shapes on Raw umber mud. The ginkgo leaves are exactly that shape. They are yellow. (The soft tawny, milky yellow that Vermeer floats into his pictures.) Ginkgo leaves look contented in the fall, but the horse chestnut leaves flame in Cadmium yellow rigor mortis, cracking with apparent agony, soused in the black mud.

Take a bag full of leaves. Paint them at home when it rains. Paint some simple green leaf shapes. Compare

Ginkgo leaves

them with the completely dead leaves, which can shrivel out of cognisance. Mud is difficult to recognize in small areas of a picture. It needs a whole woodland path to declare itself. There was a time, in the "Pop" era, when David Hockney might have labelled "mud" with a ticket (as they do paté, in delicatessens).

Adrian Berg has painted views of London's Regent's Park like musical firework displays – splendours of rockets, and Debussy or Ravel colour poems: like Roman fountains, concoctions of wonderful ruby leaves. Berg is a most inventive designer. Sometimes, he moves around his pictures, rotating the trees. Sometimes, they follow through the seasons: twiggy for winter, bud-bursting in spring.

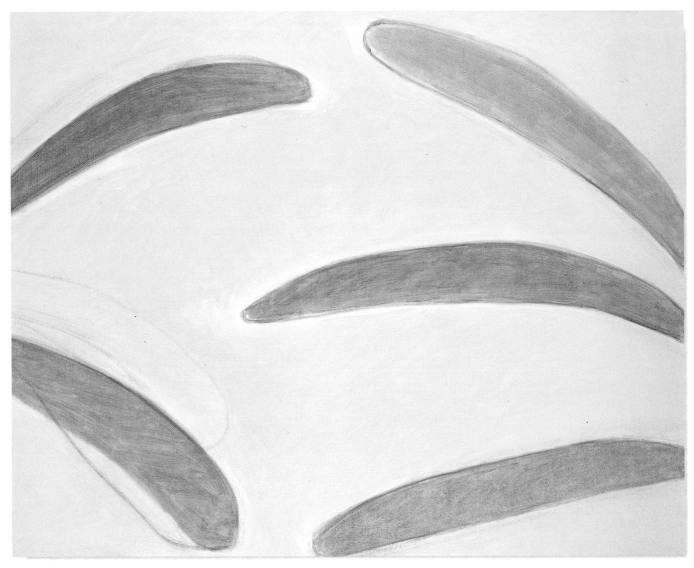

By doing a number of drawings, Kinley would gradually eliminate complications.

Peter Kinley, *Leaves*, 1977–78

Pinks sizzle and glow, discordant with orange (because in a rainbow, red would normally be darker than orange) but resolved here by being of equal darkness. Adrian lived beside Regent's Park.

Adrian Berg, *Gloucester Gate, Regent's Park, Night, Autumn*, 1981

Shrivelled leaves in pastel pencil

Vine leaves, with the curious wine-coloured streaks. Crimson capillary veins decorate the cheeks of drinkers. The leaves seem right to decorate Bacchus.

Horse chestnuts

Trial dabs on black

Try out green dabs for trees of scribble-foliage.

Leaves on mud

Chalk Landscape

BEACHY HEAD IS A "BEAUTY SPOT". What makes one vantage point right for beauty, rather than another, is useful to know. People visit Beachy Head to smoke, click a camera, cuddle a lover, pretend to push a parent over the edge, or throw a Coke tin. The danger is part of the fascination, with the possible dive to a death too far away for the gore to be seen. More than 20 jump every year.

A border of horizontals suggests a receding suggestion of skylines towards deep space, and the colours at the edges promote moods and times of day. (Violet for evening, lemon-green for morning.) When

the picture is square, or diamond-shaped and on its point, it has its angles at its edges. Stability is achieved by emphasizing horizontals and verticals: let the picture be active, and self-contained as a gyroscope.

Beachy Head is high. It makes the second-by-second dying of thoughts more intense – like gulls dropping from the cliffs, like leaps of consciousness, like quick film rushes towards death. The immense white chalk promontory can stand for whatever you want, and reflect any mood. Covered with snow, it is brown as chocolate. It changes colour week-by-week: blue, yellow, green, or dazzling white.

Beachy Head, Evening, 1975

The movements, dynamics, and depths are served by progressions. The compression of the stratified chalk is paralleled by the compressed design.

The lighthouse casts a long shadow, almost vertical; or it could be its reflection, on a special day. Cloud-shadows, and ripples, are damply rendered towards the edges.

This drawing almost maps a chunk of England. I enjoyed itemizing it, point-by-point, weed-by-weed: burdock, viper's bugloss, Carline thistle, sea poppy; chalky crack, black flint, jackdaw, and gull; and drawing the undulations of the downland as it reaches the sea a mile away. All is visible, vantage point to vantage point. Little has changed. Old postcards make contact with loved ones at the turn of the century: they show almost the same shape for the headland (and very proper messages). The perspective is controlled with a few "passages", and the weightlessness of a pencil point. Wild marjoram scents the air. The sea soothes.

Spatial ladders of flint and chalk shine. All the resources of Manganese and Cerulean blue, Cremnitz and Titanium white, charcoal and Charcoal grey, were involved.

Beachy Head, Black Gull Flying, 1972

I had watched the cliff-rescue team abseiling at night at Beachy Head. The spotlights made it dramatic. I had often imagined a figure falling from the high white cliffs, the lighthouse beams flashing. And, as if to show just how it would be, Andrews painted this self-portrait of his own narrow escape from death.

Michael Andrews, *Into the Tobasnich Burn: Glenartney. Saved by the Water*, 1991

"*Le Bec du Hoc*". Across the Channel, the coastal structures resemble Beachy Head. The diagram is of the picture in the Tate Gallery, London.

After Seurat

The shapes of the figures lying at Beachy Head, near the immense drop, resemble the silhouette of the downland against the sea.

Fishing

THE FISHING BEACH AT HASTINGS in East Sussex is at first sight picturesque. Its tall black huts, with caves and rocks in the background, are guidebook material. Only a few things change: the nets are no longer black, and satellites forecast the weather. But fish die in the nets when days are rough, and the shingle beach is swept to an angle by storms.

Laetitia Yhap paints the stuff of the past in the present, with new pictures, much as Benjamin Britten wrote music for the opera *Peter Grimes* (based on Crabbe's early 19th-century poem). She bravely analysed its ruthless, macho world, and was accepted by the fishermen. Perhaps they even realized the seriousness of her paintings as she kept warm with a hot-water bottle. She sees those on the beach straight and vulnerable, as they swear, lean, doze, or depart to collect the dole. The drawings are taken back to the studio, and memory does the rest.

A drawing of Laetitia Yhap, drawing on Hastings Beach

A very scribbly depiction of "Sou'westers". They were made of oilskin.

After Homer

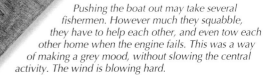

Pushing the boat out may take several fishermen. However much they squabble, they have to help each other, and even tow each other home when the engine fails. This was a way of making a grey mood, without slowing the central activity. The wind is blowing hard.

Launching the Boat, 1976

Laetitia Yhap,
The Jump, 1992

Often the first to leap ashore is the dog, barking with excitement, from the prow. The launching and beaching of the boat is dramatic. Catch the excitement with a pencil; dab in the first leap, and memorize all you cannot do fast enough.

A drawing of Laetitia Yhap, drawing on Hastings Beach

Laetitia Yhap, *The Steel Boat*
(Father and Son), 1988

*Most of the boats on
Hastings Beach are wooden,
and resemble boats throughout the
ages. Here, Laetitia Yhap made something
different. This steel boat looks hard, flat-plated, and
somewhat Cubist in design. The seagulls are so active, it is good to
have some plain central areas for the eyes to settle on: the peripheral
matter is held in place by the frame, which alludes in shape to a section through
a traditional rowing-boat. The construction is thorough, and the art is new.*

*Fishing can be gruelling. The
seagulls are desperate too. A foot
has left the picture. Compare the
compression of the boxed-in
design of "Exhaustion" with the
open space of "The Jump".*

Laetitia Yhap,
Exhaustion,
1992

*A smaller version of
"The Jump"*

Laetitia Yhap,
The Jump, 1992

*Bare or clothed, the body shape
is made to fit with the boat
shape. Rembrandt made the
thumb of a portrait come in front
of the frame. Here, thigh, waist,
and hands are coming forward.*

Laetitia Yhap,
Sun on his Back,
1991

In the Park

IT IS COLD AND "PARKY" some days, but there are shelters if it rains. Van Gogh painted four pictures of public parks. They were called "The Poet's Garden", and he did them to be hung in Gauguin's room, in the yellow house at Arles. The first was called "Public Garden with Weeping Tree" – it weeps citric lemon-yellow, brassy from the sky, and batters its way into the lush, green grass. Gauguin would certainly know he had arrived! "Entrance to the Public Garden" was another picture of a park. Parks are convenient. If you call a park "your outdoor studio", all sorts of benefits accrue. Trees and shrubs are often closer to human size, and flowers are large and special. Paths, benches, and fences are clear to see, and people are not upset if you stare at them. Usually, there are lavatories, and a café for drinks. It is possible to be remarkably private. Select a path that leads nowhere. If you are pretty, or magnetic in other ways, wear a Walkman radio (switched on or off) and you will be secure from interruption. A park is not like farm-land, or open country. Vincent would paint a park as a park.

A park in Arles. Using pastel pencils and watercolour, thrust colour with van Gogh impatience, person beyond person, up the park path.

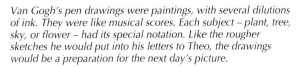

Van Gogh's pen drawings were paintings, with several dilutions of ink. They were like musical scores. Each subject – plant, tree, sky, or flower – had its special notation. Like the rougher sketches he would put into his letters to Theo, the drawings would be a preparation for the next day's picture.

A boat on the lake. The canvas was marouflayed to hardboard.   *Regent's Park, 1992*

Buckingham Palace. By including a large number of subjects, it becomes possible to choose those that mean most for future pictures. Fountains, geese, lake, and trees are easy of access, and the painter can practise his personal shorthand with a thick, soft-leaded clutch pencil. A soft Conté crayon makes painterly suggestions easy, sharpened charcoal is fast, and feels like paint; take a tin of fixative with you if the medium is likely to smudge.

Windblown chestnut tree flowers, with pigeons. Blank spaces become flower-candles.

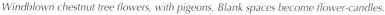

A juggler in the park. Juggle with a pencil and watercolour.   *A pen drawing in a park in Arles. Dense overlapping made clear as patterned paint marks.*

Learn to See

I VISITED A PATIENT IN A HOSPITAL in Florence and was surprised by the length and power of the staring on every side. Here in Britain, "An Englishman's home is his castle" – not only his home, but even his person may not be invaded by looking. Eye him and he may even ask you what you are staring at. I was shy when I first began painting, but I wanted to paint humans. "Know then thyself, presume not God to scan/The proper study of mankind is man." (Alexander Pope, *Essay on Man.*) I decided to be brave. I took a box of paints and a folding palette and sat in the middle of the action wherever I wanted to – roller-skating, dancing, swimming. I even painted a picture on the stage of a holiday camp while a knobbly-knees competition was in progress. The list of subjects is long. I had an insatiable appetite for looking. Museums, aquaria, public gardens and zoos, fishmongers, jazz clubs, trawlers, yachts, surfing, Rugby, promenading, parties, pubs.

Paint the world. Be committed. Paint as well as you can. The world is filled with half-felt pictures. The only paint we want is whole-hearted painting. It comes from intense, continuous looking at the life that surrounds us. You must be a voyeur, a professional snooping artist. You must cultivate the ability to be an observer everywhere. On hot randy beaches at Brighton, family beaches at Worthing, pretty adolescent beaches at Eastbourne. On tube trains. At parties. Indeed, wherever the rapacious, ravening, all-ingesting criminal eye will dare to go. Without this terrible visual appetite little can happen.

Just a "Peeping Tom", I stare towards the sea. I expect I am looking at a Japanese family on the beach. They are pale. They discover I am drawing them, their faces wreath with smiles. The creases on their faces are made especially for smiling. I am happy. They are difficult to draw. It is hot, humid, and windless. Boudin coped with wind and dazzle. Brighton is flashing and burning bright with sunlight. They enjoy being together. There is no tension or ill temper. The group is beautifully balanced. Though the clothes are vulgar, the wearers have poise. I find I cannot follow the form of "Mum's" tiger-striped bikini, linked as it is by lacings to a kind of side-apron. I decide with some relief to look instead at the simpler, nubile daughter. Her two-part garment is loud in yellow and black. Its abstract violence attacks her soft form at every point. I draw the boy. His elegance is sullied only by pink boxer shorts. His dental braces gleam in the sun.

The brilliance of the light after London is formidable. My eyes are tired at the end of the day – the perfect day, when the helter-skelter tower at the end of the pier shines, reflecting in the sea, and large jellyfish pump along in the green water.

Brighton Beach

Stylish hair on Clapham Common. Watercolour is added to a pencil drawing done on the common.

Afro Haircut, Clapham Common, 1983

Sunbathers and tankers at Worthing

Brighton Beach. An unfinished painting, drawn on the beach. Yachts and bathers. Make out what you can. I believe a helicopter is in the corner.

Boats and Bathers, 1992

Brighton from the Pier, 1993

Painted directly in the wind, at Lowestoft.

Parachute, 1954

Substance and Weight

Among the great sculptors, Donatello is the most like a painter. Clay is thick and waterbound like paint. Some pictures, which are hardly heavier than canvas, look as if they weigh a ton. "Beachy Head, Dawn" was about the accumulation of chalk over vast periods of time, together with the claustrophobic memory of reading Jules Verne's *Journey to the Centre of the Earth*. Weight in painting can be achieved in several ways. The obese Courbet knifed into dark earth colours (Raw sienna, Lead white, ochres, black, and umber), yet with great delicacy. The heavy opaque colours are the iron reds (Terra rosa, Veronese, Indian, and Light reds, and Caput mortuum) as well as vermilion, Mars black, and Chromium oxide green.

"E.O.W. Nude", 1953–4, by Frank Auerbach, painted when young, is the heaviest application of paint I know. A beautiful and determined painting, the image does not weigh much more optically than thin paintings by Matthew Smith, Renoir, or Rubens. A Rouault watercolour of a girl, using darkly flowing evocative lines, is as massive as a horse.

There is no reason why a cliff that weighs billions of tons should be painted with thicker paint than a Matthew Smith girl. But thick paint can add strength, help a canvas become an object, and establish a secure surface. Thick paint may be slow and hard work to do, it may not last well. It can be beautiful as tree-bark, or merely an oily excrement.

Watercolours are less heavy, usually. Nevertheless, Nolde, Rouault, and Burra make substantial pictures.

Clapham Common, 1980s

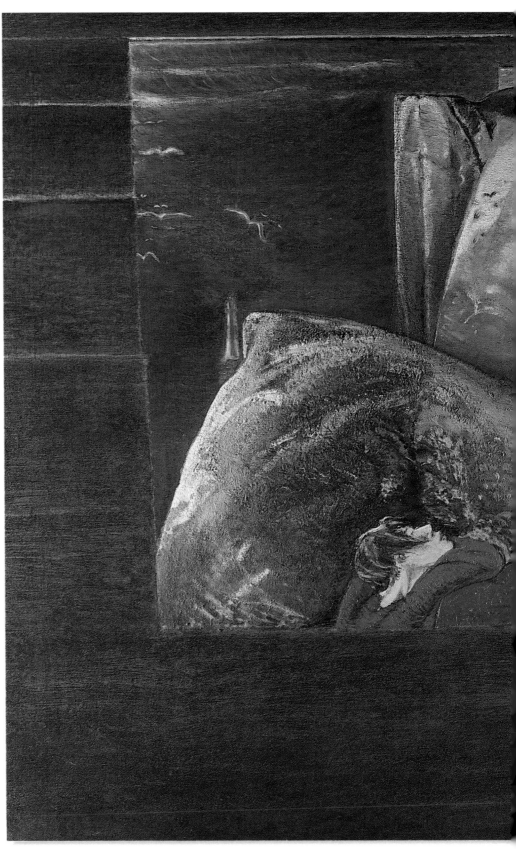

I often keep light colours low in my pictures. Here, the framework is made heavy at the base. A corpse feels heavy. Permeke painted large, earthy peasants with enormous hands. Masaccio was the first to paint "the human clay".

For Hodgkin, a frequent visitor to India, red probably means passion, rather than the pain of the West. The paint is heavy-laden. He scrubs and brushes red over green much as the painters of Indian miniatures overlay green patterns with red. He may have used "Liquin", a thixotropic medium.

Howard Hodgkin,
Foy Nissen's Bombay,
1975–77

Beachy Head, Dawn, 1975–84

Smith may have used Maroger's medium, which is still available. It pre-dates the gels that can be obtained now. The lavish brushing (using big dabs) – and the roundness – gives the fatness.

Matthew Smith,
Nude Girl, 1922–24

Death's Dark Tower

L EIGH IS ON THE NORTH SHORE OF THE THAMES ESTUARY. Anthony Farrell paints bravely the popular escape to Southend from "Town". He accepts the flux, the crowds, sea, and sky. John Constable looks stylish now but was considered a natural painter in his day. He changed the brown, ornamental tree into green foliage. He flicked in dew, snow, and light effects with a palette-knife. Hadleigh Castle is visible from Leigh, and caused a profound work by John Constable, whose noble style is style indeed, compared to the clear brave-faced Farrell confrontation of the Cockney invasion at Leigh-on-Sea. Although only a short distance from London, it is far enough for Farrell's freedom from fashion to be preserved. He neither uses conformist recipes for flatness, nor flirts with abstraction. From the long, long, Southend pier, watch him paint his son windsurfing, a balancing of wind, body, and water. He once copied "St. George and the Dragon" by Tintoretto. Anthony is a painter in mid-career. He makes painting seem like a bareback rider, balancing on tiptoe on a sweating horse at a gallop. The four little paintings are of winter, spring, summer, and autumn and were painted small for this book.

But the sea changes little with the seasons, compared to the tree-filled inland world of Constable. Constable did not depart wildly from the conventional design of the pictures of his time; and reading his lectures it seems he was unaware that pictures could be built as coloured architecture, as Seurat and Gris would design them later. Constable's style was like the fine handwriting of his time, or like the fine Georgian building style, ordered and serious in mode. Constable would apply paint with vigour and sketch fleeting effects. Gestural knifings of paint done directly from nature showed him to be a revolutionary painter. The last works such as "The Cenotaph" became nervous, colourless, and dryly monumental. (I remember the dismay of Scottish artists when Edinburgh's National Gallery acquired Constable's late painting, "Dedham Vale"; they thought it brown, very overworked, and dry.

Claude Lorraine was the envy of both Constable and Turner; like them, he studied out-of-doors. Constable copied a Claude, and Turner asked in his will for one of his pictures to be hung beside a Claude. This has been done in London.

Constable had an influence on Eugène Delacroix, but the French classical tradition was one of such firm drawing and design that some Constables look slack and billowy compared with a Chardin.

Constable was a great artist who was always threatened by perspective. His strong intuition enabled him to shape up the moisture of his leafy river pieces, yet his control of depth is not as lucid as Seurat's. Compare crayon drawings by Seurat with similar drawings by Constable. To paint "A Sunday Afternoon on the Island of La Grande Jatte", Seurat used the drawings imaginatively, making the figure groups smaller and higher on the picture, as they got further away. Anthony Farrell and Boudin do not do this.

Anthony Farrell, *Spring*, 1993

Leigh-on-Sea. The horizon is the other shore of the estuary.

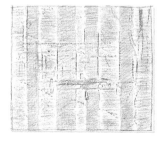

After Boudin

"Le Pont de Courbevoie". After
Mark the intervals on Seurat
tracing paper.

The drawing, "Le Pont de Courbevoie". Seurat said painting is the art of hollowing a surface.　　　After Seurat

Anthony Farrell, *Autumn*, 1993

Anthony Farrell, *Winter*, 1993

Anthony Farrell, *Summer*, 1993

A drawing for "A Sunday Afternoon on the Island of La Grande Jatte"

After Seurat

It takes no more than a few dots and a scribble to trigger a memory of Constable's "Haywain", Britain's best-known picture.

After Constable

"Hadleigh Castle"

After Constable

After Constable

After Constable

The pigeons flutter over the Thames near Somerset House. A large, awkward, foreshortened figure is held in place by the straight lines of the vertical railings.

Vastness

EYES CAN TRAVEL UP the tall silk of a Chinese painting, encountering mountain tops, trees, waterfalls, and sages. The intervals are for contemplation and rest – and recession. All the climbs towards the vastness are by the dilutions of ink.

Poets need little baggage. Anthony Eyton needed more, to brush bright figures at Western perspectival intervals on to the snow-slopes of a blue-grey mountain. But he travels light and constantly, without a razor, but with a few well-loved colours. Canvases are unwieldy, and take the wind like yachts. Traveller-painters are brave. Turner and Delacroix carried only little drawing-books, and when Turner was tied to a mast in a storm he took only his imagination.

An aside: how did Oskar Kokoschka, planting his feet high above the roofs of European cities, manage to have materials with him? Affluent when old, perhaps he bought them as he journeyed?

Beachy Head, Chasm, 1970s

Because there is a free choice of level when painting these cliffs, the disposition of figures is made easy.

The trees float as in a dream, blending close tones mysteriously. Fry is a much travelled artist and has crossed the desert.

A small figure is surrounded by wide, open space, created by expressive, intuitive brushing. Kondracki is the best Scottish painter-poet since Gillies. Hopper and Lowry use a central figure surrounded by large open spaces for moods of loneliness.

Henry Kondracki
On the Road Alone, 1989

Anthony Fry, *Mango and Rice Paddies, Thirunelli*, 1991

The contrasts of tone and colour are "open" (i.e. laid side by side, unmixed).

After Munch

He travels constantly, and – as was said of Sickert – his mixtures go with him. There are Eyton landscape subjects worldwide, from India to Brixton. As his brush thrusts, the spaces expand. With such constant practice over a long life, every gesture is decisive. He is one of the few remaining serious painters to work directly from the subject. Soutine, van Gogh, Bomberg, and Pissarro also did what Degas disgustedly called "standing about in fields".

Anthony Eyton, *Skiing*, 1990

When I was young, and lived on the East Anglian coast, the sea encroached considerably. Week by week, the cliffs receded. One day, a round tower stood on the beach as if by magic. It turned out to be a brick well. I seem drawn to the peninsular of chalk, the towering cliffs at Beachy Head. Here the risings are related to the various ages of humans.

Old and Young at Beachy Head, 1980s

109

A Marine Bullfight

PICASSO LIVED A LONG WHILE and made many new styles – his subjects were old. He painted simple, well-used themes, except for one spectacular subject, "The Bullfight", which is a complicated, difficult purge. It had been painted by Goya; Picasso felt the bull-drama in himself, and in art. The fisherman forks his fish with the same vehemence and deliberation as the matador plunges his sword into the bull. "Night Fishing at Antibes" was a sea-corrida against a balmy Beulah night, whose depths are charged with amethyst and black – all moves on. The girl groupies of the fishermen, dressed in the headscarf and snood of the time, are on tiptoe with excitement, the bosoms of the near biked "broad" ecstatic with pinkness spreading into the arms of her companion – although she has stayed cool, even inquisitive.

After Picasso

Diagram-copy small parts of this large picture, wherever you feel most involved. And if the main compositional ties (the schema) are seen to carry the meaning, pass over the details, and describe diagrammatically. Think in terms of a body, and the parts of a body. Picasso was always thinking in Picasso's-body terms. His own body, although small, was robust and good for use as a pattern.

Subjects are very important. They must make it possible for you to paint the shapes you need.

This is my favourite Picasso. I do not know what it contains. Sometimes, a scribble-think will make clear what is mysterious and determine the black, violet, and green areas of the night. The gradation from golden water to Viridian green below the boat revives memories of childhood dreams and strangeness below.

After Picasso

Electrically gleeful, the pink flapper licks a double-scooped ice, with a bluely lascivious tongue. Picasso often painted close to monochrome – the black-and-white of Spanish painting, of Ribera, Velásquez, and Goya. But in this picture, he went through every colour in the spectrum.

The light

The stars

A pen-scribble   After Picasso

"Night Fishing at Antibes"

The Polyphemus-eye-ruddy-moon-glowing light for attracting fish, in the centre, is like the peak of an erupting volcano. (In "Guernica", the electric light and oil lamp are at the summit of the design.) As advertisement designers know, the loudest attention-capturing colours are yellow with black. A little red increases the heat, and a little white takes it to white heat. Tear a black hoop around a square. Paint rays as black lines, add a yellow coil spiralling away to the right. The main red spiral is to show Picasso's passion is like a sun.

The reflection of the light After Picasso

A moon face After Picasso

A moon-pale face, grainily intent After Picasso

After Picasso

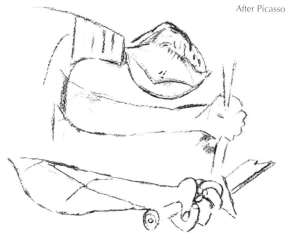

Thrusting arms. The lower arm, with a broken sword, is from "Guernica". After Picasso

Using a brush, and a brash will, crash through to beauty, shut your eyes to the particulars, and search out the massive, structural organ alembic and the toreador/sailor. After Picasso

Although Picasso copied figure-filled Poussins, this is almost the nearest he came to a figure landscape. After Picasso

Keys

Pablo Picasso was fond of the beach, and of a little beach hut. It is depicted in several of his lively paintings dating from the 1930s. An arm playful with desire, thrusts a key into the keyhole.

Léger, who had experimented with Cubism and abstraction, in order to prove to himself that almost any object could be used for art, took a ring of keys from his pocket, and painted it with a postcard of the "Mona Lisa" and a sardine-tin. Léger expanded the range of objects available to art. He painted roots, belts, corkscrews, ball-bearings, and spoons. He painted them as calmly as he could, with a control equal to that of a Japanese print. Léger hardly lifted his brush from its convoluted fluctuations. The bunch of keys makes a muddled image, but Léger sorts it out. Chance had presented him with more associations, perhaps, than he had expected.

Keys look stiff at first, then are found to be telling tales throughout past painting. St. Peter holds the keys of Heaven, Rodin's "The Burghers of Calais" give up keys – as happens also in Velásquez' "Surrender of Breda". In this large picture, the key becomes the focus, the interlocking point of the whole painting.

A key is usually rounded at the handle end, and squarer at the keyhole end; and these are connected by a shaft. The lock holds all the entrail-maze – mysteries of labyrinths, fractals, and uncrackable codes. Paint or draw some keys and other convoluted forms. Attempt a knot out of your head, it will quickly make clear your capabilities (some can imagine easily in three dimensions). Draw a granny knot, then a bowline, then a reef-knot. There are lots more. I rapidly became entangled. The elaborate margins of *The Book of Kells* were maze-like, and intended to keep the devil from reaching the sacred text.

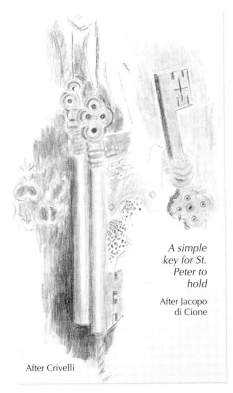

A simple key for St. Peter to hold

After Jacopo di Cione

After Crivelli

Crivelli's design is so tightly organized that these two long keys were able to be attached by cords, and stand in front of the tempera surface.

"The Keys of Heaven given to St. Peter by Christ". A bas-relief in the Victoria and Albert Museum, London.

After Léger   After Donatello

Playing at watercolouring locks, keys, and darknesses.

"The Surrender of Breda" (detail)   After Velásquez

"Key on Fire"
After Magritte

The symbol of his office, as Master of the Royal Horse.
After Velásquez

Keys and keyholes

"Fisherman's Huts"
After Braque

Various versions of Picasso's Beach hut
After Picasso

After Léger

"Mona Lisa with Keys"
After Léger

After Picasso

After Léger

Keys on a ring

After Léger

After Picasso

After Picasso

"The Surrender of Breda"   After Velásquez

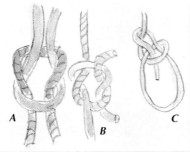

Knots: **A** *Reef* **B** *Granny* **C** *Bowline*

"Bather". A design wild with distortion, about a visit to a beach hut which was naughty with memories and some surrealism.

After Picasso

Art Holiday

A HOLIDAY WENT ON FOR YEARS, when like Matisse you lived in a hotel by the sea. Claude imagined a "golden age", and others yearned for Utopias of the future. Come then with me, as if it were in times gone by. You are in a little hotel almost by the sea. Jacques Tati as Monsieur Hulôt is enjoying the holiday. You think of Proust and Balbec; and settle, for your feet's sake, on low tide at Le Touquet. Your toes enjoy the wind-shivering glitter of the wavelets, and as Luchino Visconti directs the shutters to open, and a universal light floods in from the Lido at Venice, a pang of conscience assails you. You have lain on the hotel bed a full hour and have not unpacked your painting materials. You must be up before breakfast. The porter will carry an easel, croissants, a jug of coffee, and a dazzling white canvas. You will carry brushes and paints. The canvas will absorb the light and give it forth later, in Pimlico, London, where your sister will always enjoy it.

Enough of fancy. To work outside by the sea you have to be strong. The wind blows the palette, the brushes, the canvas, and your ears. Boudin must have been hardy. He was a starter for Monet, who also braved the weather. To work out-of-doors, it is useful to know a few versatile, fast ways. The St. Ives painters worked, if not outside, at least close to the beaches and the sea. Alfred Wallis was the most direct, and he worked from memory, with yacht enamel on pieces of cardboard, whose rough-cut shapes suggested his superb arrangements. Enamel had never before made such creamy waves. More artistically aware was Christopher Wood. (He had known Picasso and Cocteau in Paris.) Wood knew ways of coating white gesso with black, and scraping it, and painting – with the enchantment of glossy fresh enamel – many of the little beaches, boats, harbours, and churches of Cornwall. It seemed as if, because of the crinkled nature of the Cornish coast, the painter could be close to the subject. Add to this a concentration of Parisian Cubist space, and a new kind of condensed picture became possible.

The opposite thing, which Peter Lanyon did – since he wanted to paint open-space pictures – was to go gliding, climb over the rocks, and pick up evocative junk from the beaches. He made his own paint, by knifing up pigment with a glossy vehicle (such as stand oil and varnish) and thus took on some of the breadth of The New York School, where he won recognition before his youthful death.

"Fishing Boat at Sea". Take a piece of the sea-washed driftwood, or odd-shaped card, and to broaden your mind, paint in tune with its shape-surprises, as if you were building sandcastles.

After Wallis

Picasso and Matisse each painted large pictures on the theme of Joie de Vivre – *an idea of Arcadia.*

After Picasso

Gliding was Lanyon's sport. Its influence was apparent in the sweeping, cloud-like gestures of paint and open design.

Peter Lanyon,
Backing Wind, 1961

Wallis dabbed his way around his oddly cut shapes of cardboard (sometimes shoe-box card). In imagination it was as if he became the water washing against the rocks, jetties, inlets, and coves near St. Ives, Cornwall. He had begun painting at the age of 70, as he said, "for company".

Although technically Cornwall is a peninsular, after a whizz from its North Coast to its South Coast on a motorbike, or a flight in a glider, it seems like an island. Its artists, Nicholson, Wood, Lanyon, and Wallis, painted as if their surfaces were islands, and were to contain all the items they wished for. They distorted perspective, and played with their subjects as if they were toys. And everything was got in.

Alfred Wallis,
Penzance Harbour, (no date)

Christopher Wood, *Le Plage, Hotel Ty-Mad, Treboul*, 1930

Seaside Glare

JOHN WONNACOTT LIVES ON THE THAMES ESTUARY. Once it was an open sewer for London. When the tide is high, it is the sea coast; when low, it seems more like river mud. Wonnacott was taught by Frank Auerbach, as different from him as Gustave Moreau was from his pupil, Matisse. Not frightened of the glacial effect of white, Wonnacott explores, like Degas, the hinterlands of photographed effects – the terror-lands where so many have come to grief! Degas despised painting in the open air, but achieved some naturalistic race-course pictures. He scarcely painted the sea.

I found to my dismay that Gustave Courbet's small sea pictures were done from photographs. I had imagined his solid corpulence standing on the shoreline, like the older McTaggart in Scotland, with a rock hung from his easel, painting in the teeth of a gale. Wonnacott's beach has all the fright of a Pinter play about an English seaside holiday, with rain. He admires Lucian Freud's expanses of White lead flesh, and treats the dank shine of mud-banks with as much attention as Freud gives to the itchy veins, expansive buttocks, thighs, and hairy corners of post-natal bodies. They both try to tell it true, and believe that this is obtainable close to appearances – the "verisimilitude" Michael Andrews spoke of.

The pattern of the iron railings on Brighton Pier made watery whorls of light. The girl wore the shine like a flower. Chalk cliffs are in the distance.

Brighton, 1989

Whether this magnificent dark wave is painted over black, I do not know. These small pictures are often painted on dark grounds. When using a palette-knife, dip the paint into medium, then it will flow. Thick paint can have a nasty tightness if used straight out of the tube.

Gustave Courbet, *The Wave*, 1869

Ravilious was the clearest watercolourist ever. Water painting of water and light has always succeeded in Britain – land of the damp weather forecast. On humid days there is a chance of working wet-in-wet for longer. Ravilious knew the value of clear white paper. He scratches and uses masking fluid where useful.

Eric Ravilious, *Storm*, c. 1940–41

The Pre-Raphaelites painted their sharp colours into a White lead priming before it had dried.
Paul Gildea is a young painter who paints people (often actors) who take up extreme positions at his request in his compositions. They are brushed in fast on wet, white canvas. Gildea paints only while the subject is in front of him. Try painting into a stiff ground of wet Lead white with a soft long-haired bristle brush. Wipe the brush between brush strokes.

On beaches, the closer arcs are to straight lines, the bigger the expanse – especially if they curve outwards from the middle. The large number of notice-boards show fears of all kinds.

John Wonnacott, *Chalkwell Beach, Floodwater Overflow, Late Afternoon*, 1989–92

Rainbows

A RAINBOW WAS A PROMISE TO NOAH that there would be no more world floods. William Turner, John Constable, and Rubens painted fine rainbows. They are so exciting against dark skies that the tendency is to make them more colourful than they appear. If you place a prism in sunlight, you will see all the hues that are visible to the human eye. The bulk of the light is yellow-green. The hues are in harmony. Some are darker than others. If the natural overall tone is changed (as when a pale blue is placed against a deep orange) discords can occur. Colours of equal tone often enhance one another.

A rainbow in a fountain

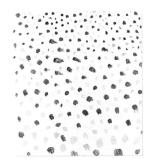

The further away the spots are from the eye, the greyer the effect. Close to the eye, the blue is blue and the yellow is yellow.

The human eye can distinguish an enormous number of tints. The stained glass at Chartres is wonderful. They probably used only a few colours, but it is lit from behind. Crayons can be more various. Here are about 78 hues of the 120 the manufacturers sell. (They include silver and gold.) This is only a tiny fraction of the thousands of tints used in Gobelin tapestries at the turn of the century.

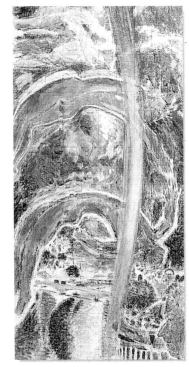

Rainbow, 1989–90

Crayon Spots

A double rainbow. This is puzzling – its colours are reversed, and it is shown against a light part of the sky. But as Constable was a master of sky painting, it must have happened.

After Constable

The fountains in Hyde Park in London did not make good rainbows, except when the wind shook them. They were red on the outside and violet on the inside. William Blake moved through the colours of the spectrum as he watercoloured his illustrations to Dante. Many great artists keep to a part of the spectrum-sequence of colours in building forms. Chagall used them particularly brightly, André Lhôte diagrammed the way Cézanne moved through the warm part of the spectrum to the cool blue (a blue that Cézanne said gave air to his pictures). Lhôte showed that you could move through the sequence orange-red-violet-blue (or by way of orange-yellow-green-turquoise-blue), which is more like moving around a colour circle than across a spectrum. But colour can build wonderfully.

Rain, Bowed, Thames, 1989–90

A nocturnal wake in rainbow colours. Aitchison used some of the darkest parts of the spectrum for the deep night, as his beloved Bedlington terrier ascended towards the golden ray from heaven. The waning moon illumines the yellow and green birds below the bright star. The tree yearns sadly from pink to blue. I have an irrational feeling night should have its rainbows.

Craigie Aitchison, *Wayney Going to Heaven*, 1986

Dive

ANCIENTLY, THE ELEMENTS ARE EARTH, AIR, FIRE, AND WATER. The setting sun, refracted in a polluted atmosphere, I thought of as "Fire". Thames mud could be "Earth". "Air" might choke an asthmatic. There is no swimming in the Thames: the "Water" would poison a bather. The Thames is too much encroached by government buildings and business greed. Wandering close to the water, I considered the concept of lowering the Thames Barrier, and gently allowing the water to rise; the cellars gradually submerging; Hansard and other records pulping, as a few more acres of water wash among the buildings….

A London aping Venice? No! Both cities are fine as they are. So I plunge in paint, in imagination; and in imagination, the waters are pure as thought in purest dreams. The down sun allows the electric lights to take over, and the yellow disc-eyes of Big Ben stare – witnessing the spirit's dive, from "Air" to "Water".

Fill a brush with semi-transparent paint, made liquid with turpentine; and on a pale grey ground, smother areas with thin, backward-moving paint of an advancing hue. (Warm colours come forward, cool colours recede, by their nature; so you have to work at it.) Load with cool paint the portions that you must make come forward. In the past, impasto was usual for light, advancing areas such as clouds. In these defiant days, the artist may be excited to do the unexpected. Over thick crumbles of Flake or Cremnitz white ("Lead white"), flick flecks of colour so that they will combine to equal the sodium-lighted, iridescent glamour of the roseate evening sky, and the clanging clock of Parliament, reflected in "Water".

Made in painted metal, the body enters an undulating wave.

Neil Jeffries, *Diver*, 1992

"The House in the Trees". Léger tried to do a different kind of Cubism from Picasso or Braque. It was not easy – to understand Cézanne, to be excited by the new, and not paint like Picasso. Cubist paintings by Braque and Picasso are similar; they signed their pictures on the back. Picasso acknowledged Léger, but said: "He is not really one of us."
    On primed canvas, with thin charcoal, mark straight lines. Where they do not meet other lines, they will lie on the surface. Arcs will evoke volumes; but they will also lie on the surface.
    Fix it. Then, with a soft brush, and a thin mixture of turpentine, black, and a little white, turn the surface pale grey. Then dab with red, blue, and green, until the surface is as substantial as you wish. This is an enjoyable exercise in the application of colours, and for watching them lie cleanly; and for considering how such an open style of painting was completely different from all of Léger's tightly closed manners after he returned from being a soldier.

After Léger

"The Divers". A little brush, with long Kolinsky sable hair, is called a "Writer" if pointed, and a "Rigger", or "Liner", if the hairs do not come to a point. Dip one in a sign-writer's consistency of paint, and try painting the kind of fluctuating contours Léger was to use for the rest of his life. Each movement is taken to a firm connection, or conclusion, usually making a closed shape. Each part resembles a factory-made component, to be assembled for the construction of a building.

After Léger

120

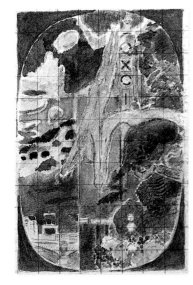

Diving Figures, the Thames, and a Bed of Roses

Undulate a Léger movement, slow as a slug, or bumptious as a Niki de Saint Phalle.

After Léger

Make a snake the Léger way, without lifting the brush, until the snake eats its tail. Now that the paint is flowing, move the liquid around a mask and watch it humanize.

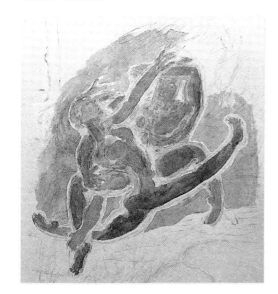

Falling Figures

Paint for yourself a pure spirit, close to the harsh House of Politics. Use your own means, and make it hurt!

A diver near Tower Bridge

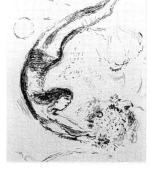

After Chagall

121

A Royal Pond

THE LAKE IN ST. JAMES' PARK lies between the Thames and Buckingham Palace. In the summer it supports a mass of wildfowl, which feed on soggy bread. Painters need not go voyaging. Cockneys or visitors can begin their pictures here. This little lake is at the centre of the world. It is the cosmopolitan pond. It sifts history like a pelican's beak. It is the essence of dust, bubbly green with fountain spray. There is more tame wildlife here than anywhere I know. Pigeons, black swans, ducks, sparrows, geese, and pelicans. It is a good place to take a little canvas. If you take it in a plastic bag, you will not be without models, since every bird and squirrel knows every rustle of every bag in the park. All around are old clubs. Members lie in quiet rooms, to the sound of geese and Pall Mall.

To the left of my picture, a cloud of pigeons. The fountain fails to move. The up-movement is opposed by the down-movement. I am driven to scratch. Beak-shapes are holding the design together. The crane is boring, the foliage is boring. Corot could use this "usual" green. Shall I blacken some yellow? If I had drawn the red beak of the black swan well enough, I could have painted it large…. On palest buff, try pencilling in, or marking with a tiny brush, every flicker and sparkle, goose eye, and feather, or part of a feather: rachis, barbule, barb, and vane. What I mean is, do not leave anything out which interests you. Be prepared to get in a muddle. Unless memory treats you badly, remember to remember the colour of every item.

Pen marks are fast, and pastel pencils suggest colour. Spray with odourless fixative if indoors.

A slightly more descriptive watercolour of the birds. Two of them had blue beaks. The dark shadow at the top moves them along. A hard, sharp pencil drawing on hot-pressed paper can be touched with colour from memory.

Water birds and ripples. Use a pencil and a small watercolour brush. Remember to memorize the colours and illuminate at leisure.

William Nicholson, *Two Black Swans On A Bank At Chartwell*, 1934

William Nicholson made pictures with a natural feeling for paint. He maintained a careful balance between subject and gesture. He painted brushy swans, and used the wrong end of a brush to scratch in twigs and necks. William was always painting different subjects, and they link his paintings, in my mind, with the poems of Thomas Hardy. Both Ben and his father achieved silvery harmonies.

Whites link the beak, fountain, and distant clouds. It is painted over grey.

Ben Nicholson liked to give his pictures an up-to-date appearance. The way at the time was to show off technique, and prove by a lot of scratching how wonderful a surface could be. Only occasionally was it necessary for him to depart from the simplest of subjects. Cornwall as a jug, or Switzerland as sanded hardboard! I decided a piece of a jug would become a swan's neck. Matisse talked frequently of the arabesque, the decorative beauty of swelling female throats and ogee rhythms.

Swans' necks are mysterious. Old depictions of sea-monsters had curvaceous necks. Pencil in the swoop. If you find the bird's neck sags a little, as if a taxidermist had failed to keep it smooth, take no notice. It is in his nature. Make it as smooth as the etching by Matisse. Later, when convenient, brush it as feathery as you wish, with black against black feathery wavelets on Cobalt green. White, lemon, and Cobalt green flow as foliage to the sky. A sky of Cobalt blue plumage: the sky, as a majestic blue bird whose neck enters the lake by way of the fountain.

Aim to be painting intuitively. Feel you are in there with the swans, and become each thing as you paint it. Undulate the paint as naturally as it comes. Think of a beak-like brush stroke extending as a swan's beak, the eye follows a neck, which is pursued by the body, which is trailed by wing tips, a tail, and a wake of foam.

Pigeons and Peacocks

S<small>T. MARK'S SQUARE IN VENICE</small> is full of fluttering pigeons. London's Trafalgar Square is grey with them – lusting, eating, grooming, sleeping. Many people enjoy filling the birds with bread. Cockney pigeons are grey as dusty roofs. Try and watercolour-sketch a pigeon. You must be fast. First, mark the white heart-shape above the beak – it is the only part you can be sure of. The rest is a flurry. At first, its body is small; then, if it is a male, it puffs its feathers to be large, then deflates instantly if it sees no chance of satisfaction. The patrolling is faster than it seems. Fanciers breed exotic birds. The wood-pigeon with its white collar and pale pink-over-grey is obviously beautiful, but then with feathery legs like ballerinas in fluffy trousers, comical and witty as close-clipped poodles, the dull taxi-dodging bird is common, and it is good to paint what is close to us. The pattern of feathers seems infinitely various. Try and get a feeling for the rhythm of the overlapping shapes, or you will never be believed. Even if your mind is full of the painted paradise-wings of the Italian Renaissance, an encounter with a peacock is always surprising.

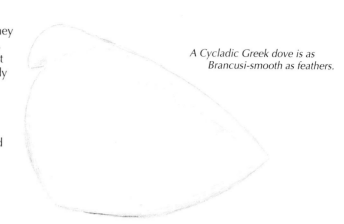

A Cycladic Greek dove is as Brancusi-smooth as feathers.

A pencil used on smooth paper is the swiftest way to secure information about birds.

The carmine-footed pigeons scatter water at the edge of the lake. Their feathers dishevelled, they are silhouetted against the clouds and a setting sun.

Daniel Miller, *Pigeon*, 1994

An elegant pigeon, in pencil and crayon

A feather. Draw it for a practice in refinement.

A watercoloured pigeon, with green-grey and pink-grey plumage

After Picasso

After Picasso

Pigeons resting, preening, and displaying

Some patterns make more convincing pigeons than others. The intuition must decide.

Pigeons and a cloud   After Léger

A girl, a boy, and a pigeon. Cover the pigeon with a thumb, and the figures almost cease to exist. A pigeon is often a lead-in for adjacent subject matter.

A pelican dozes among the pigeons at St. James' Park. Use crayon on rough paper until the only area of white paper left is a pelican.

Peacocks

Peacocks have such enormous tails, their heads look brainless. Once again a pencil is used, looking the bird in the eye, and watercolour is splashed in from memory. To do pure watercolour, you may rub out the pencil beginnings, or start with a little brush, and be a virtuoso.

City Splendours

Turner and the early Chinese painters steamed up the finest mists. Dickens wrote of the worst fogs, and of corpses floating in the Thames. T.S. Eliot made poetry out of "the yellow fog that rubs its back against the window panes". The Thames keeps mud moist, and reflects magnificent sunsets above Chelsea Reach. Whistler painted the nocturnal Thames softly absorbing fireworks. If you paint wet-into-wet with Lead white, with a light touch, it is not difficult to set off fireworks. To paint mist, squeeze the tones together as things get further away. Distance is achieved in the same way and is called "aerial perspective" (or "tone values"). Only sensitive artists are able to keep control. Seurat, because of the perfection of his design, could work close to white.

As the sun goes down over London's Primrose Hill, the fiery fairy lights glow;

Mud and mist near Vauxhall Bridge

historical, homely, and ghosted by so many admirable painters who would have walked up to the highest point, to see the domes and chimneys of the "great wen" emerging from the coal-fired fog with all the beauties of pollution. Turner, and later the Camden Town painters – among them Harold Gilman, Charles Ginner, Walter Sickert, and Spencer Gore – condensed the city to crimson and gold. The attachment Frank Auerbach may feel to Primrose Hill is for its centrality. London extends far in every direction. Lawrence Gowing said it felt as if every breath had already been breathed a hundred times.

Some deep-coloured paintings by Matthew Smith were done in Cornwall. Howard Hodgkin's brushings are as broad as those of Ivon Hitchens; his mergings intoxicate with voluptuous memories, and past epiphanies in Venice, India, and other faraway places.

The gold is made to shine in the rich blue of the sky. The ogee-arching rhythms counterchange through the picture.

Walter Sickert, *St. Mark's, Venice*, 1896–97

In the first of the trials that have become so effective in giving publicity to good and bad artists, Whistler received a farthing damages for not doing what Ruskin said he did.

After Whistler

Hodgkin's pictures depend to some extent on the close appreciation of the applied seductive caresses of paint. To reproduce them is an affront. To copy is an abuse of their bodies. It amused me to see what ravishing accident might occur on a wooden panel, with a Hodgkin in mind.

Slightly after Hodgkin

The streetlight gives out pure yellow, which knocks out all other colours. It gives a harsh atmosphere to the unloved suburbs, where the past is often no more to be seen.

*"London belongs to me",
went the popular music-
hall song of Sickert's
theatre world. Mauled,
scraped, daubed, knifed,
and smeared – a falling
empire of crimson
memories in the light of
the falling sun. Auerbach
always takes his paintings
to the edge. Here lies the
intimate oily argument of
painting today.*

Frank Auerbach,
*The Camden
Theatre*, 1976

*Leap through the
waterfall, brave the
rainbow shape. But
the golden silk takes
centuries to darken.*

After Wan-Wei

Paint the Thames

THE SUN OVER THE THAMES flashes reflections from its waters at every twist of its snaking way. If your art does not demand vastness, vistas, seas, or mountains, you can find in London views that resemble almost anywhere in the world. Those British who eat fine food in Italy sacrifice an "eel-and-pie" indigenous visual language. The robust smut of Hogarth's "Shrimp Girl" cannot survive too long away from its source.

Sometimes, the water is so low near the Tate Gallery, you can walk on the little islands of mud and junk close to the middle of the river. You can stand on the pasty clay of London's past, to draw the view through the spans of the bridges. After being a mud-lark, climb to the top of Tower Bridge and draw the river from the glass walkway, looking up or down river. Upriver, see the bridges, and many of the sights of London. Draw with that special sort of drawing found useful to painters: the chalky-charcoal-dusty-crayon-black-pencil-Titian-Bonnard-Sickerty kind of drawing, which confuses dashes and thumb marks. Add your personal abbreviated colour notes: "Raw umber and skim-milk" for the Thames, or "bath water after washing the dog". At home, coat the drawing with acrylic medium, or shellac, and dab it with some paint.

Each time you paint something from your memory, you will determine to memorize more thoroughly for the future. It is necessary to concentrate and to keep an open mind. Looking at the river, you missed seeing the geese fly by. Captivated by the tug, you did not care that the wasp on the glass was the same stinging yellow.

Big Ben at night. It is convenient to draw on the thinnest plywood and paint it the next day in oil.

The bridges looking up the river from Tower Bridge. Neatness is not required.

Hungerford Bridge

A youth, posed high, overlooking Somerset House from the Queen Elizabeth Hall. The roof was without shade and very hot.

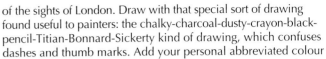

To explore the Thames between Vauxhall Bridge and Tower Bridge could take a lifetime. A pencil drawing is a quick, always available means of meeting a subject for the first time.

Hungerford Bridge

Hungerford Bridge

St. Paul's Cathedral from Hungerford Bridge

From London Bridge the view looking towards the Tower of London is complex as a lock. It is built around the unclad youth. In other directions are St. Paul's, Cannon Street Station, and Southwark Cathedral.

A squared-up drawing of the view from the glassed-in walkway of Tower Bridge. Across London Bridge, the office workers of the City run to catch their trains. Depict them any day after tea at a pose-run for you, umbrella and briefcase in hand.

St. Paul's with sleeper

Joggers on Westminster Bridge

Nocturnal Sparkles

TOWER BRIDGE CAN BE SEEN under Cannon Street railway bridge. The river glitters in glancing stripes. It is not far from "The Clink". Watercolour it, unless it is too dark to see. Often, if you paint in the dark, and you know where the colours are that you used in daylight, you will find only a little adjustment is needed next day. When it is too difficult to paint, mark circles for lights, and if you have a repertoire of signs for everything, and write in the colours, you will find it possible to paint the dreamy river with its staccato lights. Another way is to draw with conté crayon on rough-textured paper, as Seurat did.

When painting a dark picture, underpaint with a paler than half-tone warm grey (not too fat) and paint on it with brushfuls of darker medium-rich colour. The Matthew Smith way of painting, with jammy, dark, transparent colours, with no white. Alla prima, was a success for him, but is liable to bleeding and cracking. (Fortunately, Smith did not need to repaint.)

From Bermondsey. I kept the big contrasts to the edges of forms. The tiny silver glitter seemed – along with the heat of the sky – to express the flagrant urgency of the city.

The Sights of London, 1985

From within the Royal Festival Hall. Long, vertical windows are crossed by the river and Embankment. The pier moves at an angle. Using a pencil is the most convenient way to assemble the complicated flickers of the river at dusk. While the fading light allows a lot to be seen. Lights are continually being switched. The middle dusk is the colourful time.

Three bridges. London Bridge is in the middle. (Munch liked painting reflections of the sun or moon as golden columns in the water.) When a boat goes by, the vertical tranquillity will shatter into a diagonal wildness.

If the main forms are drawn at dusk, the positions of the brighter lights can be recorded when they are switched on later. The arches of Waterloo Bridge have their own illumination. This causes a surprise lightening at the centre of the picture.

Victor Willis, *Waterloo Bridge, 1995*

Hungerford Bridge at Charing Cross. Circles and points show where the lights are. While darkness can be evolved by overlapping layers of transparent paint, it is useful to keep in mind some opaque mixtures for elimination. Mars black with Titanium white, for example, will obliterate most things. Some other combinations for density are: Cobalt blue with Caput mortuum, Chromium oxide green, and Mars black.

The horizontals of the buildings, the Embankment, the ripples, and the vertical reflections make a calm setting for the naked figure, who looks towards Somerset House. Close tones make a twilight. I tried to make a pale nocturne.

Moonrise Over Somerset House, 1987

"Courbevoie Factories by Moonlight".   After Seurat
The paper gives you the sparkle. Conté crayon (soft grade, then fix) with Michallet paper or Ingres paper, which also has ribs.

A girl sleeps, and the trawler passes in the blackness. This painting is close to the limit of darkness, for a design to work. There have been darker pictures, even pure black pictures. Ad Reinhardt has painted blues against blacks, which are so dark it is difficult to distinguish them. To sleep is to die a little. The night, full of strangeness goes on without us. Ships pass in the night. It is often rewarding to paint night pictures, it is easy to hide areas of little interest in gloom and (thinking of Rembrandt) to bring up important parts as impasto.

PARTS OF THE BODY

Births and Stories

PICTURES ARE LIKE CHOSEN FRIENDS. Wherever you are in the world, you are in known company. Although it is good to see pictures in the countries where they were painted, it is also wonderful to see Brueghel in Vienna. Scribble a copy of

Rembrandt's "A Woman Bathing" (now in London). It is of Hendrickje Stoffels; she bore him a daughter in 1654, the year this picture was painted. A Rembrandt looks at home in London. A Matisse painting sends the viewer seeking Mediterranean warmth.

I wonder how much Degas thought about Rembrandt. Here, he enjoyed the brandish and "déshabillé". See the brave thrust for the nose, and the marks on the arm, like staples to join it to the background.

Edgar Degas,
A Woman Combing Her Hair, 1904–05

My own self-portrait and a chalk copy of Sickert's late self-portrait "The Servant Of Abraham", which was such an inspiration to the painters at the Beaux Arts Gallery – before Helen Lessore was obliged to sell it to the Tate Gallery.

After Sickert

A hesitant pose. The crayons make the plumpnesses by means of hollowing marks. Rembrandt models with impasto.

After Bonnard

Rembrandt, *A Woman Bathing*, 1654

132

Kossoff lives in the paint until it is all his own picture – hollowing, realizing, impasting – with passion, because he admires Rembrandt so much.

The Rembrandt was cleaned until the wood showed, using solvents. I feel that with microchip control there will, in the future, be dry ways of removing dirt, and only dirt, from pictures, and that liquids penetrate too deeply.

Leon Kossoff, *A Woman Bathing*
(*Study after Rembrandt*), 1982

Body Cuts and Paul Klee

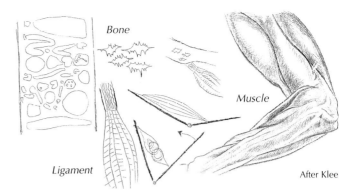

Bone

Muscle

Ligament

After Klee

PAUL KLEE, AT 23, WAS A PARAGON STUDENT. He wrote in his diary that he would continue to study anatomy with medical students – "More as a means than an end". He dissected cadavers from 8.30 a.m. till 10.30 a.m. and attended a life class at night. Klee's anatomy studies involved taking the body to pieces. In composing a picture he often seems to be putting it together again piece by piece. Klee's youthful anatomy drawing is hatched in the same direction as those of left-handed Leonardo da Vinci. Some lines follow the muscle fibres. In Edinburgh College of Art, the muscles were drawn on a living model with charcoal. I had learned the bones and the origins and insertions of the muscles at Lowestoft Art School from a skeleton and a book. More recently, I became interested in books of photographs of dissections, but found them too difficult to draw from. The Greek sculptor Praxiteles would have thought little of Arnold Schwarzenegger, the hero of the film "Pumping Iron", who proudly believed he was building his body harmoniously, muscle by muscle. His face did not fit his thighs.

Pablo Picasso said: "I want to say the nude, I don't want to do a nude as a nude. I want only to say breast, say foot, say hand or belly. I don't want to paint the nude from head to foot…to find the way to say it, that's enough."

The little diagram above is the body in pieces. Sculptors since Rodin seem to be able to accept dismembered bodies, legless, headless, armless, never breastless. Mediaeval reliquaries were sometimes in the form of arms and hands.

Muscled figure

After Klee

After Picasso

After Klee

"Outburst of Fear"

Dissecting the right knee

After Eakins

Claude Rogers, *Nude*, 1960s

Paint a canvas thinly with flesh colour, a mixture of Permanent rose, lemon, and Raw umber over white – do not use artificial limb paint or Flesh pink. Flesh pink is the nastiest colour ever invented. Dab in without lines all the parts of the body as you think of them. Dab with childlike thrusts, not artistically but to make a piece of body. Sometimes strange things happen, a nipple becomes a rose, a pelvis becomes a lobster. The whole canvas surface changes to a body or a face, then the belly and navel are an apple – Chagall and Gorky could be extravagant. Continue to dab-report all the sags and plumpnesses and unnamed pieces, even dimples, freckles, scars, and pores – leave nothing out a painter's imagination can encompass.

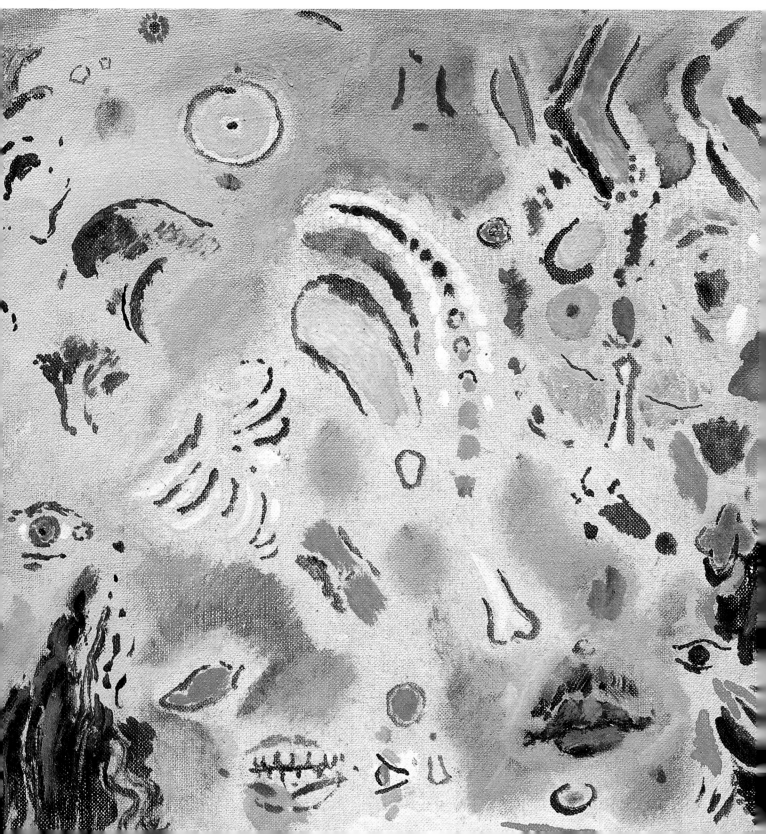

Life

MY EDITOR, TIMOTHY HYMAN, who is younger than I am, kindly tries to protect me from being labelled a fogey whenever I write positively about life rooms, but I battle on because this is the first period for hundreds of years that has tried to manage without them. There were private schools of drawing, and academies, in Italy by the 16th century. Giambattista Tiepolo did a drawing of one (which might have been Lazzarini's Academy). The students were depicted sitting around a nude model. There is also a Rembrandt drawing of a similar arrangement. I suspect that great masters, even as early as Giotto, might have seen to it that their apprentices drew from each other.

In Hyman's time, the Slade school had an Indian summer of "Life": Coldstream's measuring "Life", Auerbach's luscious, thick "Life", Michael Andrews' making-up-your-mind "Life", Claude Rogers' secure "Life", my "Life", and even other "Life". Because students came to believe that their futures depended on their producing personal pictures for fame, self-fulfilment, the market, and their final graduation

exhibition, some of the life rooms became empty. The rich, old, and famous Matisse could send round to his local film studios for six beautiful girls to model for him. For others less fortunate, there is the life room, where a human being will lie still for you, for as long as you wish, while you endeavour to find a wondrous shape that will do justice to a unique mouth and allow you to move a brushing of golden watercolour towards a round belly. Such rooms were – once upon a time, and only occasionally – quiet retreats for strong contemplation. Matisse spoke of the almost religious feeling he had when painting from the model.

What are the alternatives? Mouths are everywhere. Those of relatives and friends are available, but sometimes they refuse to be still. You have to give them drinks and nuts, and they have appointments. Very few will stand naked with arms strung to the ceiling for you.

You can hang a plumb-line in a life room, but you do not have to use it. The models link students with the common existence in the world outside. Many were memorable. Miss Deladier's big toe; graceful old Mancini, of a famous family of Italian

After Clemente

Mouths, eyes, nostrils, and ears show little heads looking out. Whatever use Clemente might once have had for life rooms, he is unlikely to use one now.

Watercoloured lips

After Léger

After Léger

Lips that hardly needed a life class

A model resting. Often the best poses are in the breaks.

This was painted in a life class at Chelsea School of Art. Two models are posing, and one student seems to have little on.

Andrew, a friend, posing, warmed by wine.

Bonnat's studio in the Ecole des Beaux Arts. There are between 30 and 40 students visible. These Parisian life classes were for the acquisition of skills, not for gentle inspiration. If you were a long way from the model, you were not very advanced in the art world.

▶ Italian models (he would have hairy sweets in his dressing-gown for the students); the beautiful Renoir-shaped girl who had a back street abortion, and died. Actors "resting", jugglers resting, black, undulant pregnant girls. A young mother looking after her baby. A very fat girl with opalescent thighs. Girls so beautiful no boys could deserve them. And they all had mouths.

Gleyre said to Monet, "Here you have a dumpy little man with big feet, so you have given him big feet! It's very ugly, that sort of thing! Instead, you should always have the Antique in mind!" Well, Gleyre is obviously one teacher we would not listen to today. But to be fair, if a student at Julian's did not wish to be corrected, he was allowed to turn his canvas to face the wall.

Eakins' Academy

MATISSE, EAKINS, BALTHUS, AND DEGAS could paint from the model wonderfully well. Thomas Eakins studied at the Pennsylvania Academy of Fine Art in Philadelphia, and then at the Ecole des Beaux-Arts in Paris, where he was taught by Jean Léon Gérôme. He then returned to Pennsylvania. Eakins was a brilliant teacher. He visited twice weekly for short periods, as Gérôme had done. He thought young men better at drawing than young women, but that women should be given an equal chance, and taught as seriously as those studying medicine. Eakins was against drawing antique plaster casts, which he considered was imitating imitations. Instead, the students were encouraged to work from life using a brush, which Eakins thought more powerful than a point or stump. Painting was to be done from the middle of forms, working outwards. Modelling in clay or wax helped to make figures substantial. Athletes, trapeze artists, cows, and horses were engaged as models. He had little

interest in art history or aesthetics, but was keen on perspective, and the reflecting or refracting qualities of water. He constructed pictures seriously, slowly, and exactly. No painter knew more about how a rower's arm muscles moved, when sculling on wavelets (done strictly in perspective). Firm as a fortress, Eakins' brownish brushmarks

The ladies' clay modelling class at Pennsylvania Academy of Fine Arts. They are sculpting a cow. The cow did not have to wear a mask.

helped to build the best of the French tradition in America. Eakins' ideas were carried on by Anschutz, and I think Matisse would have agreed with the teaching; but not with the cloths and masks that the models were required to wear. Hypothetically, if the over-tasteful Clement Greenberg had been less powerful, if Edward Hopper had been better trained, then on the shoulders of Thomas Eakins, on the back of Degas, on the broad back of the biggest painting tradition ever, American painters would have shattered the world with greatness.

But be content. Nobody knows what might have been. When painters are killed in war, die young, are ill or poor, it affects the course of art more than such chances in other vocations. The spiritual starvation that has killed painting in past periods is close to us. If the painter lives in the wrong place and knows only the wrong people, there is little chance of learning this profound and sensitive language. There is one painter who suffered no such privations. Balthus' parents were artists, and knew Bonnard. Rilke helped him to see pictures, and Rodin's sculptures, and to love reading. He lived in Paris, travelled, and copied the art he liked and aspired to emulate. With his passionate temperament and long life, the scions of tradition could send out tendrils rare enough in our days. Sometimes, the life of art seems to hang by a thread.

After Eakins

An early life drawing, and a drawing from the antique

After Matisse

This charcoal drawing is of a very frequent position, which does not involve the complications of the face, and is as far removed from the syrupy salon decorum pose as Degas could get.

Edgar Degas, *Woman Drying Herself,* c. 1903

A masked model shows
the prudery of the time.
Eakins' teaching of
human anatomy caused
his dismissal.

After
Eakins

The 21-year-old
Thomas Eakins
painting when
naked. Eakins
may have been
painting Fussell
at the same time.

After
Fussell

The satisfaction to be obtained
watching sports is about muscles
moving well. Here combined with art,
the arms are muscled strongly like oars.

After
Eakins

After
Masaccio

A copy by Balthus
of Masaccio

After
Balthus

After Eakins

Robert Henri in the dissection room
at the Pennsylvania Academy.

The model poses against a painting of a woodland scene.

Balthus, La Toilette, 1958

139

Folds of Life

What cosmic jest or anarch blunder
The human integral clove asunder
And shied the fractions through life's gate?

Herman Melville

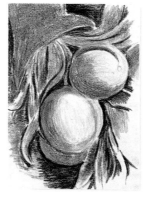

After Mantegna

*The cleavage folds
of peaches*

SUMO WRESTLERS LOOK LIKE massive cells dividing. Through microscopes we can watch cells divide, and sense a resemblance in this unfolding to the shapes of larger forms. There is a kind of cleavage visible – in peaches, pectorals, buttocks, breasts, and in art. When it is good and simple, it may approach the divided spherical form.

The roundness of cells has been closely approached by the sculptors Arp, Barbara Hepworth, Henry Moore, Constantin Brancusi, Naum Gabo, and several Cornish pebbled coves. In Plato's *Symposium* a figure is described, as a perfect combination of male and female – the state to which men and women desire to return. To realize how words are less concrete than paint, try to paint such a combination. It has two spines; knee and knee; thigh and thigh; stomach and stomach; breast and chest; and kissing lips.

To paint the living figure, a feel for symmetry, cleavage, and balance is fundamental. Brush with subtlety, nuance by nuance, with eyes travelling down the body, and find temple balancing temple, cheek/cheek, eyebrow/eyebrow, eye/eye and so on. The central line of the body makes delicate balances visible – dimple by dimple, hairy patch by hairy patch. Even when canvases are abstract, a vertical division will not fail to suggest a man's erect spine. Mondrian, whose recreation was dancing, knew the level of his hips and the direction of his pumps.

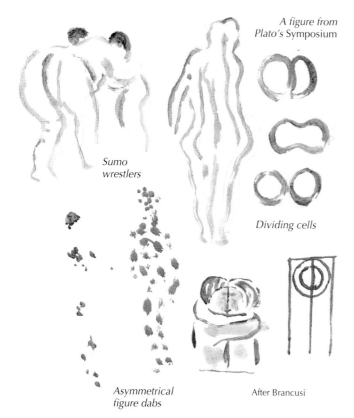

*A figure from
Plato's Symposium*

*Sumo
wrestlers*

Dividing cells

*Asymmetrical
figure dabs*

After Brancusi

*A row of sleepers in an
air-raid shelter.*

*It has two breasts, but
otherwise seems bisexual,
and asymmetrical enough to
be the figure suggested by
Plato's Symposium.*

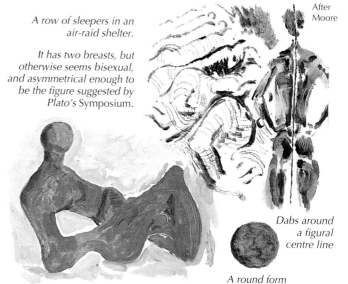

After Moore

After Moore

*Dabs around
a figural
centre line*

A round form

*One face looking in
two directions*   After Donatello

*Cleavage and
equal wings*   After Mantegna

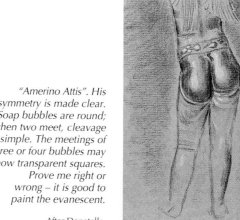

*"Amerino Attis". His
symmetry is made clear.
Soap bubbles are round;
when two meet, cleavage
is simple. The meetings of
three or four bubbles may
show transparent squares.
Prove me right or
wrong – it is good to
paint the evanescent.*

After Donatello

140

A figure with legs apart at Beachy Head. A three-quarter view of an almost symmetrical pose. An unfinished picture severely cut. Horizontally.

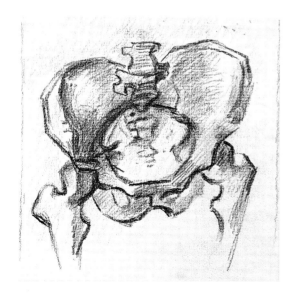

A drawing from a sketchbook. The vertical symmetry is plain in the pelvis. Only in the soft parts of the body (brain and abdomen) does the figure become substantially asymmetrical.

After van Gogh

By following a monograph on Mondrian, see how the complicated colours and shapes of landscape gave way to simpler balancings. For example, a pier made as a vertical was surrounded by crosses for waves. Later, as here, simpler elements were balanced obliquely.

After Mondrian

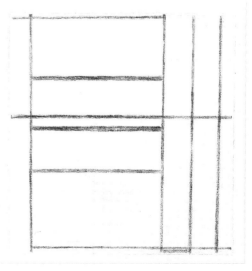

Profiles

THE PROFILE OF BATTISTA SFORZA cuts across the blue infinity of the sky like ivory. It links to points and measures innumerable. Try and see what moving a ruler around uncovers. Her husband, Federigo da Montefeltro, lost his eye and damaged his nose in a tournament. Piero, knowing that all parts of the Duke were valuable to God, carefully measured the moles and acne, and delicately touched them in. It seems as if there was good feeling and humour when they posed so exactly opposite each other, with these such disparate noses. Portraits in the 15th century were often in profile. Pisanello and Alberti made medals of profiles: they are formal, and require less information than three-quarter views. The piece above the lip and the piece between the eyebrows are hollows, so are invisible from the side. Profiles have to be invented.

After Piero della Francesca

Profile tracings of Battista Sforza. Sforza looks towards the Duke.

Rosie and Juliet, her mother, seem alike and closer in age than I expected. When Rosie laughed, the transformation was incredible; the resemblance to her mother instantaneously included the sparkle of her father. The media continually remind us of the DNA double-helix. We sense a necklace of genes making a family likeness. We feel it is important, like "begat" in the Bible. Ask some close relatives to pose for you, nose beside nose. William Coldstream painted both W.H. Auden and his mother as separate portraits. Auden's big, boy-like English face was to collapse, becoming drink-wrinkled. His mother certainly looked like him, in the form of an overused tent.

The temple is where the early photographers would ask their sitters to put a hand, so as to prevent movement. The angular furrow at the temple expresses the sort of thinking Rodin's "Thinker" does.

With two mirrors, do a sequence of self-portrait sketches: turning, watching the nose disappearing behind the cheek. Do the same, drawing someone else.

A three-quarter view. Full faces show more than profiles, but less than three-quarter views.

Laetitia in profile in an aeroplane

Juliet in profile looks towards Rosie

Dorothy and Alice

A profile tracing of Battista Sforza, with an added thickness to the contour where the forms are more substantial. After Piero della Francesca

The temple of Gorgeous Macaulay. A square hairline, but the temple possesses a diagonal darkness. After Aitchison

Nose-to-nose

WHEN LOVERS ARE NOSE-TO-NOSE, eye-to-eye, eyelids, like bridges, span the world. The undulations of the body initiate sensual expressions. Some portions are simple, obvious, and have simple names; the eye can weep or wink. The piece between the eye and eyebrow is involved when the very expressive eyebrow is raised in question, or lowered to frown. The nameless areas are important for painters. For a child, the face is a nose, a mouth, and two eyes. But painters can self-educate, until the body is seen totally, as a realm of visual sensation.

Outside the ivory tower of art, murder, work, sleep, touch, smell, and taste – indeed, all our experiences modify or intensify visual responses. Play a little: as an opening gambit, list some specialists for particular parts of the body. Gentileschi and Géricault were good for severed heads; Renoir for rounding plumpness; Castagno and Botticelli for bright clear eyes. Giovanni Bellini for veins, Grünewald for scabs, and Mantegna for open, singing, or howling mouths. Every mortal item, named or

After Picasso
"Marguerite"

not, will express your body-minded will. Play some more: mark some strange places. What do you feel about the valleys between the fingers? Is the crease above the navel agreeing with a new double chin? Have you considered the corner of the mouth?

Look at nostrils, even at nose-hairs. The orifices of the body engage us, as do caves. It is a physical shock to see a cow put its tongue up its nose. The frontal portrait is structurally difficult, unless you have a way with nostrils. Children, babies, the snub-nosed, and pigs show two holes. Hockney, van Gogh, and Picasso could do these with single dabs. People with cream fed, well-found noses must have harmonious nostrils, swept sideways, and increased to counteract perspective. The vertical nose and horizontal nostrils give the portrait stillness and dignity.

Take a notebook, and walk through a gallery rich in Botticelli noses, sketch-copying with a blunt, black pencil. The more you concentrate, the more significant the shapes become, however small. The nostril as a world of wonder?

Skeletal nasal holes

After Ensor

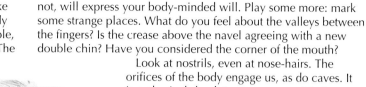

Even the baby is coughing in the chill blasts of flu-filled air.

After Daumier

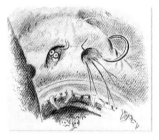

After Brueghel

Above the maw of Hell, an owl roosts in one nostril, and from the other, twigs grow downwards. With a dotting sable, explore the nooks and crannies of this strange world. Most of Brueghel's inventions are based on what he has seen in the life around him.

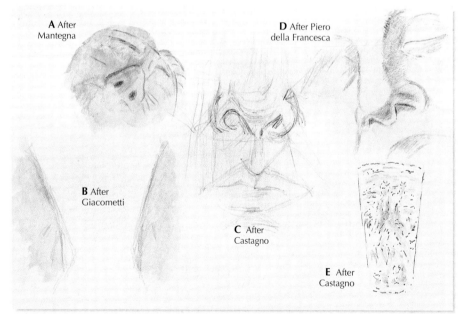

A After Mantegna

D After Piero della Francesca

B After Giacometti

C After Castagno

E After Castagno

After Gauguin

After Titian

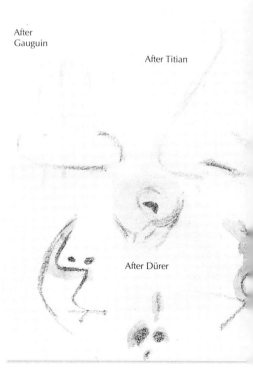

After Dürer

A *The nostril position declares the angle of the head.*

B *All our seeing is done between blurred noses. I can see a small part of my nose if I look askance. If I saw all of it, it would be the height of a man at three metres, or as high as a distant mountain. The right eye sees the right side of the viewing nose, and the left eye sees the left side. This leaves an attractive shape, rather like the shield of Castagno's "David".*

C *One round nostril, and one angular*

D *"The Sleeping Soldier" – possibly a self-portrait – whose nose is again foreshortened*

E *The shield-shaped "David"*

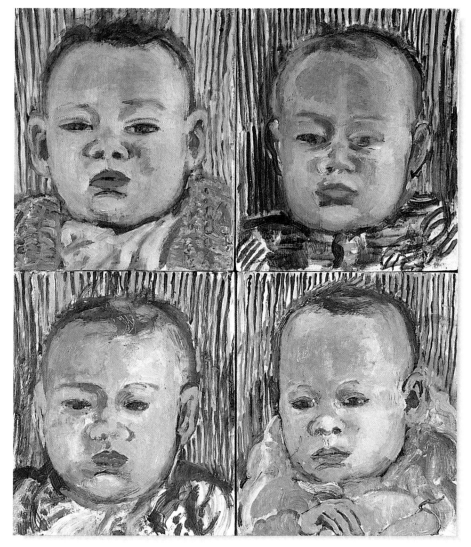

The committed parent-painter will never stop doing it. Never stop brushing in babies. Your baby is crying, brush the baby's nose. Baby has a cold – paint the streaming sore. Baby is at a party, nose in pink jelly with cream. Paint a baby each day until the little darling believes it to be normal for adults to play in this way.

Daniel Miller,
Joe Four Times, 1988

Cartilages, cavities, sinuses, and snot. The nasal connection to the lungs and air passages – imperfectly, epiglottally separated from the food gullet – is not a very good arrangement.

Start several little paintings, and fidget after fidget, dab after dab, gradually, around the nostrils, plump, baby faces will accrue.

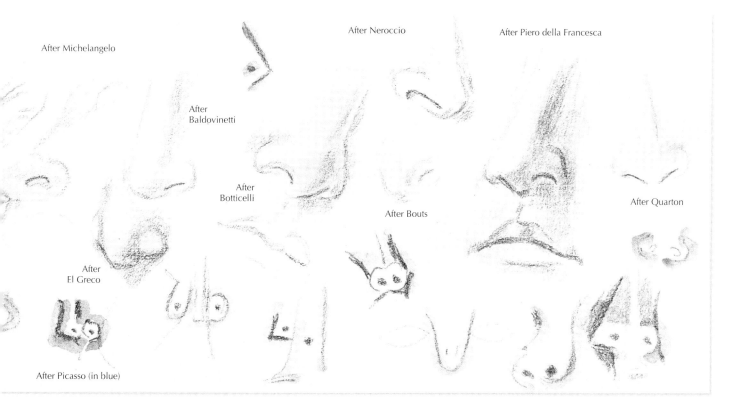

After Michelangelo

After Neroccio

After Piero della Francesca

After
Baldovinetti

After
Botticelli

After Bouts

After Quarton

After
El Greco

After Picasso (in blue)

The Philtrum

Agutter-shaped runnel is not often an attractive feature. It is difficult for some people to know whether to grow a moustache. The moustache we do not dare to paint was worn by the mad Hitler: a nasty little black carpet, it was the focus of massive adulation. How could a countenance appear if we beheld it newly, as when Miranda saw Ferdinand for the first time in Shakespeare's *Tempest*? We have minds full of faces. An empty mind would be equally surprised by ogres, unknown animals, and humans.

The philtrum is the least familiar part of a face. It is often surprising. When I had a copy-look at Donatello's "St. George", I found he had swept the forms up to the nostrils, with very little runnel. His "Judith" is wide-guttered, with

After Picasso

almost no pause at the lips. I had expected a dimple below the nose, a finger-touch in the clay. But great art continually surprises. Much of the great Italian painting that follows benefits from Donatello's controlled depths. He practised sculpture in-the-round, and also at all the levels of relief, short of painting. Mantegna was able to paint pictures that resembled bas-relief sculptures. Try doing some diagram-copies of several overlips from Mantegna's "Camera degli Sposi".

The ageing process is apparent; but although young lips can jut almost as far forward as a nose-tip, and in old folk the philtrum-angle can relax, there is less of a law about it than I had expected. Using a slab of clay, try incising or modelling in shallow relief.

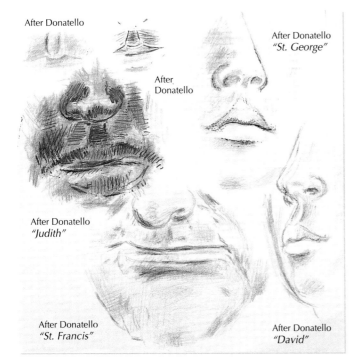

After Donatello

After Donatello

After Donatello "St. George"

After Donatello "Judith"

After Donatello "St. Francis"

After Donatello "David"

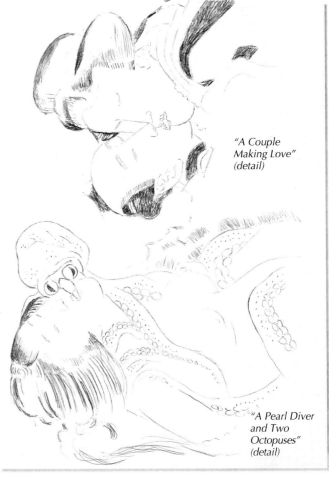

"A Couple Making Love" (detail)

"A Pearl Diver and Two Octopuses" (detail)

After Hokusai

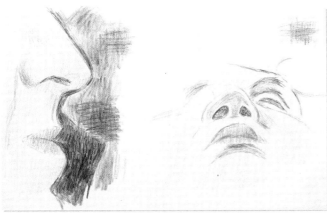

Look at the family in Mantegna's "Camera degli Sposi". Theoretically, philtrum-angles can monitor the ageing process. Touch in some philtra next time you have a family or friends at your mercy.

The philtrum, as reflected by Gonzagas.

Towards a kiss

Coldstream called the undernose part of the face "The Rower". It is sometimes useful to think in oblique terms when confronted by demanding sitters avid for likeness.

After Picasso

After
Picasso

After
Picasso

A moustache which has taken charge of the picture.

After Léger

Kissing, while frequent in the world and in films, is rare in painting. Picasso is the only artist to enter the fray, even painting the insides of mouths and thrashing of tongues.

After
Mantegna

After
Mantegna

The sensual lips of Francesco Gonzaga

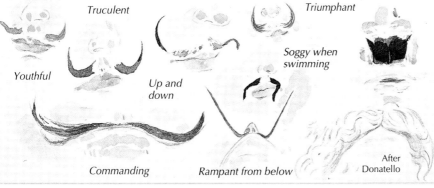

Truculent

Triumphant

Youthful

Soggy when swimming

Up and down

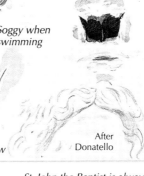

Commanding

Rampant from below

After
Donatello

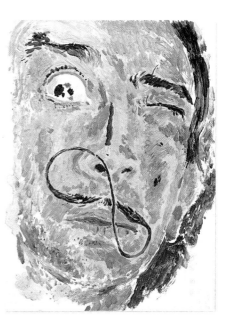

A moustache can be grotesque, yet cherished by the wearer. Dali's waxed horns were very long. The Dali "Gigolo" moustache could be variously expressive.

St. John the Baptist is always hirsute. Patriarchal whiskers fill up the philtrum.

Dali as a window-dresser and Surrealist so aggravated Picasso by his commercial exploits he nicknamed him "Avida Dollers".

Round Heads

CIRCLES, AND CIRCLES THAT LOOK BACK at you, and circles who know you. Klee, Matisse, and Léger all, for a short time, painted featureless circles to stand for heads. This was new. Although recognizable forms accompanied them, these circles were abstract. Much of the material in older pictures was abstract – Italian Renaissance figures were surrounded by patterned surfaces, marbling would often be juxtaposed with gold (and most gold is non-figurative). Using the word "abstract" loosely, it could be said that the head on the right of Matisse's monumental "Bathers by a River", and a nimbus in a 15th-century Italian painting, are both almost abstract.

When Goya put crowd-fillings into his little pictures of bullfighting, he used suggestion-dabs. They were confidence tricks, helped by memory. The people were made with oval dabs and scribble; only occasionally were features indicated. Try some crowd-like calligraphy, using brushfuls of gooey cream paint over a brown-toned ground. If you do it small, your bluff will not be called. A Goya bull-ring format is dramatic, as bent on drama as a theatre's proscenium stage. The crowd Goya portrays is contained by the fenced ring, and is entirely believable.

I ask too much! Here is an exercise, which is about a subtle incarnation: touch softly! For this eclipse of intelligence, make ovoids of pale paint. One can be as round as a halo, or a billiard ball; another can be as exact as a Brancusi egg; let another be a rough bonce, an oval dab like a face in a Goya crowd; another can be as real as a very special aunt.

All kinds of circle, knob, or oval may stand in for a head. Matisse, or a child, will paint a head as a simple oval. (Matisse knew that added features would sway the attention away from other parts of his picture.) Picasso, Schlemmer, Brancusi, Gris, and Klee designed heads close to abstraction, which meant close to the simplicity of a circle. But the less formal painters of the time, such as Miró and Dali, painted heads as curvy as in dreams – bendy knobs and soft fungus crania. And curiously, and frequently, Italian artists employed a dressmaker's dummy: these and other figments were used to disconcert by Carra, de Chirico, Morandi (to begin with) and others. An oval for a head can be an equivalent, an evasion, or an unsettling symbol. Ultimately, an android is not a lovable human being.

Ovals and scribble make a crowd in an etching.　　After Goya

Ellipse-shaped hats and little flicks of White lead make up the suggested crowd, keen to see the horn killing the toreador. A bullfight is massively complicated, simplifying heads allows the main theme of courage and death to be shown carefully.　　After Goya

Early bubble-heads after Morandi. He was really yearning for the pot-shapes which would occupy him for the rest of his life.

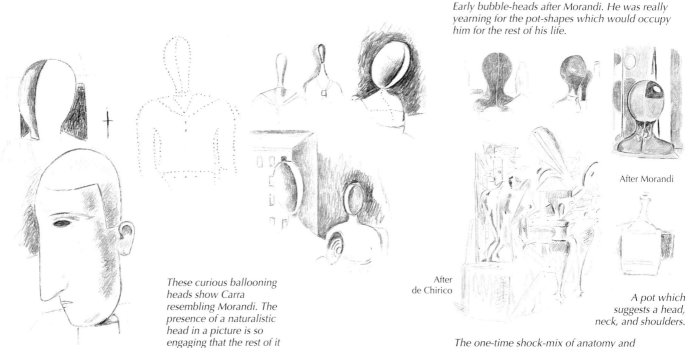

These curious ballooning heads show Carra resembling Morandi. The presence of a naturalistic head in a picture is so engaging that the rest of it may lose in importance.　　After Carra

After de Chirico

The one-time shock-mix of anatomy and geometrical instruments.

After Morandi

A pot which suggests a head, neck, and shoulders.

The simple use of circles for heads allows Léger a corresponding freedom with colour.

After Léger

Simplified heads

After Avery

After Picasso

After
Matisse

Simple heads

*Bubble-heads   After
and a funnel   de Chirico*

*A featureless face   After
Avery*

*A simplified head.   After
Brush lines to become   Léger
rectangles and rectangles
to be plump as faces.*

After Miró

Circles transforming from abstract to faces.

Feet

MARK TWAIN'S *INNOCENTS ABROAD* found the museums of Italy more than their feet could endure, and containing numberless "Madonna with Child" depictions, which were all the same. A tourist of stamina has always been able to do three galleries in the time I need for looking at a single Watteau. They do not see how various are Madonnas. It was an excuse to paint a girl and a baby – often a local girl who wanted her pride and joy to be on show for ever in her church. This was the ultimate baby show. The formal religious placing was in the middle of the picture, as it should be. But look at the dandling: the positions, and the feet are so various, even Mark Twain would be persuaded! For there are no gold haloes at the toes. They are the feet of God made man. These wonderful pudgy, unruly babies are the way in: like the free dreamy predellas, these feet are the rewards for those who linger. (There is a ravishing book called *The Predella*. The painter Craigie Aitchison once said, "No-one should be without it".)

Diamond-shaped pictures often have fewer inactive parts than rectangular pictures. They will include more items. This picture is in relief and still surprises me. It is a painting of feet and alludes to buttercups, dandelions, a plate, a table, a chair, thighs, clouds and the wide ocean, dark grass, and the colours of passion.

Dandelions, 1970

Your own feet will model for you, separating areas of pebbly beach, and sparkle. On the whole, if your feet are warm they make better models than hands.

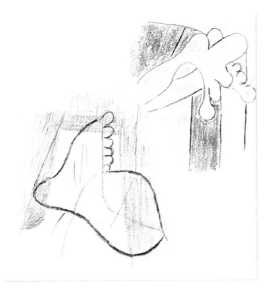

Make-believe feet, feet that nobody can believe in – but Pablo's feet are always neat and clean, and good to look at.

After Picasso

Patricia holds her new baby. Try drawing the feet with a pencil. The mother's hands enfold the baby, whose hands enfold its own head. The feet are contained in the triangle of the elbow. All fits together so lucidly it would be a shame to alter it much. All babies should be drawn continually. They grow up fast. Patricia will paint continuously and know her baby's feet better than her own.

Study the toes of babies in the laps of Madonnas.

After Cranach

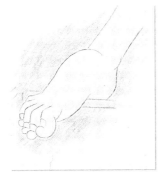

This foot pushes against the edge of a boat as the sword enters the stomach. Copy to see how wonderfully designed are the toes in this Japanese print.

After a Japanese print

Copy with a sharp point (or a 0.3mm Pentel propelling pencil) the perfectly composed feet of Christ in the late "Piéta" by Botticelli. There is no place for uneven toenails here, and the wounds are clean as well-cut marble. Your disciplined style cannot fail to approach a "foils-man" precision for really hard, sharp definition. Thinly prime hot-pressed watercolour paper with a Zinc white watercolour (sometimes called "Chinese white"), then with a sharp 6H pencil, incise it true.

After Botticelli

151

Cherubs

CHERUBS ARE NOT MUCH LIKE BABIES, but let us pretend. Be rejuvenated. Flattery gets results. Today, you will paint. Your child is a wonder! Unique in the world! This certainly is true. On the assumption of parental love and proximity, and however beautiful, plain, or hideous your offspring has turned out to be, she is still bound to be of overwhelming interest to you – and therefore, the subject you should paint. Judging by the enormous population of cherubs, putti, and Madonna-lapped babies in world art, you are not the only painter to be holding the baby. The new race of parent-painters mix the paint, tell children stories, change nappies one-handed, as never before. Rubens, the great master of the picture-filling cherub, would have had a wet-nurse. Babies, unless they are asleep, move a lot, but usually have only a few set positions. Start

Will, attempting to look cherubic

several sketches. One or more will be lucky. In any case, you know your way around your paragon. Rubens found that gessoed boards, streaked brown, and not too absorbent, would take creamy White lead paint from his tiny brushes most accurately, and as fast as he was thinking. To see how he did it, find the little panels, scattered in many museums around the world. (I have a book that reproduces 140 of them.) Whatever your ultimate way, the Rubens touch is redoubtable. Considering the ease with which the Old Masters expressed adult desires using cherubs (I'm thinking of Mantegna, Titian, Rubens, Poussin, and others), it is strange how rarely cherubs are to be found in paintings today. But with such encouragement you will paint your best beloved. He can be a pictorial device for space control, or a darling portrayal to please a grandparent.

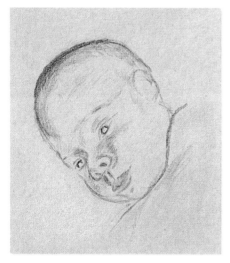

The pupils of the eyes are usually dark. This baby's irises are dark, and the middles are bright reflections.

A fairly placid baby, swept in intuitively, leaves the rectangle in turmoil.

Daniel Miller, *Dora*, 1994

The mask-like area of the face is where the artist has concentrated most. The hands are oval swirls. With your baby on your knee and one arm free, brush in cherry lips, peach cheeks, blackcurrant eyes, fast, before a new aroma causes a change.

After Modersohn-Becker

With a pen and slightly diluted non-waterproof black ink, sketch around some cherubs in Mantegna's "Camera degli Sposi". Poussin's cherubs, or those by Titian are well worth copying. From William Blake's A Cradle Song:

After Mantegna

Sweet babe, in thy face
Soft desires I can trace
Secret joys and secret smiles,
Little pretty infant wiles.

Almost as though kissed or
pressed against a window-pane,
Dora is lively and only a little way
towards being a cherub.

Daniel Miller, *Dora*, 1994

A sleeping child will keep still until a dream comes along. Draw her in graphite pencil. Additions with a pastel pencil will suggest the colour.

She was the top painter of real babies and I suppose shows up cherubs to be pictorial, rather than of this world.

After Modersohn-Becker

First Steps

SOME ANIMALS HATCH AND LEAVE the egg ready for life. Not humans. Trauma follows trauma. In 1943, Picasso painted "First Steps": a child learning to walk. It is a self-portrait. It has Picasso eyes staring into the future, tottering forward, anxious. Wartime increased angst.

Goal follows goal. The learning can often be embarrassing. Learning multiplication tables can take too long; or caresses fail. Mothers guide. Picasso painted pictures of most of the stages of life. Even a child holding its mother's hand becomes a little monument, and, scribble-pen at the ready, drawing a peeing baby becomes a spree. When he was old he painted "Nude Man and Woman 1971". It resembles the great "First Steps". The man, who is Picasso again, of a great age and with no goals left, totters forwards. He is as nervous as ever.

I expect Paddy's other hand is being held. He is closer to the water than grown-ups. The duck is big enough to swamp a yacht. It is a water-filled picture, with near boats and far boats. His knees are the shape of the water.

Henry Kondracki, *Paddy*, 1992

"First Steps" (in chalk)   After Picasso

"Paloma Asleep". All the parts of the body are presented clearly.   After Picasso

"Dandling a Baby". Pen and ink can be fast. These sketches call to mind the fast quill drawings of Rembrandt. Great painters build on the common life around them. The protecting mother. The Madonna and Child. The enfolding, caring, even smothering, loving relationships are important themes for painting.

After
Picasso

"First Steps"   After Picasso

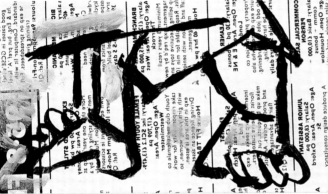

(Picasso tried doing the feet first on newspaper.) Picasso did criss-crossed soles for the feet in "First Steps". As I looked at late Picasso paintings with the undersides of feet in mind, I realized how continuously Cubist he remained even to the end. Explaining each part of the body in an innocent way: top of foot, side of foot, sole of foot. Although Degas was not childlike in the same way, he also did drawings of nudes and ballet dancers from the back, front, and side. It is an instinctive way, aiming at complete realization, without making sculpture. Picasso does not usually repeat soles or other features. His economy allows a frontal eye, and a profile eye.

"The Child's Face". The drooping eyes of the mother are two waning moons on their backs. She will worry at his every step. The wartime pictures were done in blacks and greys and were profound, anxious, angular, and fearful.

After Picasso

Rough sketches of "Nude Man and Woman"

A little girl holding her mother's hand   After Picasso

After Picasso

After Picasso

Knees

SHRINKS WRITE ABOUT "THE GOOD BREAST" but never refer to the back of the knee. All joints complicate – and we do not have knees in mind so much as other parts of the body. This may be why painters avoid knee-backs. Also, knees break the long rhythm joining leg and thigh. It is interesting to note how cunningly the passionate artist smooths the tender back of the female knee. Pierre Bonnard noticed how, when bodies are young, the knee-joint is flexible, almost double-jointed. The gastrocnemius muscle tendon (as a pad with fat, covering the meeting of the femur and tibia bones) is forced backward between the "hamstring" muscles. (They join the thigh to the leg.) This is most pronounced when the girl wears high-heeled shoes. (Chinese foot binding and the fashion for high heels show a dissatisfaction with the natural shape of the female leg.) To me, most legs are visually bountiful. But Bonnard made girls on high court shoes, stalked like flowers, into beautiful paintings, and the near-dislocation makes all the difference.

Ingres smoothed the knee-back of his "Bather of Valpinçon", whereas Oedipus, looking at the Sphinx, has muscular knees. Skateboarders and scrubbers wear knee-pads, rarely used in pictures.

After Ingres

Knees tilted by high-heeled shoes

After Bonnard

Natural knees. Paint some knees simply. Knees, elbows, and knuckles can look odd on humans. Where are the knees of dogs, kittens, and sparrows? Draw from armour (at the Wallace Collection, London) space-suits, puppets, or lay figures for knee variations.

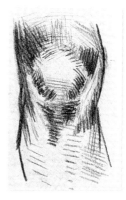

"Mars and Venus". Mars is with Venus, and Venus shows willing by covering the back of Mars' knee with her paler leg.

After Veronese

"Knees" from a sketchbook. Van Gogh was a great self-teacher, focusing problem after problem. Look to see ways to worry – draw knees. He suffered over knees, brave as a footballer. Rembrandt etched knees, and made them dumplings, dimpled and real.

After van Gogh

"Women in an Interior" (detail). Formalized knees. Later on, Léger dispensed with patellas altogether.

After Léger

The knee is as high as a mountain. The sharp points and edges are wayward as Nature. Compare the gradations with those of Léger. Stahl's pictures are often large. He breaks a lot of old-time rules about tone and recession. Here, it is as if, climbing an enormous leg, his brush is slipping in little, meaningful items, unrelated compositionally to the immense background of sea. Late Poussin included giants, and surprising scale-jumps, but everything remained formal. Stahl's awkward poetry concerns an oceanic, eerie feeling about distant travels.

Andrew Stahl, China Beach, 1992

Armpits and Violet

THE HAIR OF THE HEAD, chest, armpits, and beard join shadow-darks to help make areas of flesh live luminously. There is a Matisse of a girl with her arms above the head. He liked poses where the rhythms could be dolphin-smooth and dolphin-long. The tufts of hair are exultantly brushed in, above breast level: the contrasts are bright as starlings on stone. The armpit is a complicated structure. Muscles from the back, front, and side leave a hollow for hair, sweat, and shadow. Brush it in cleverly with dark paint, and you have a shoulder.

We are naturally drawn to certain artists: others, just as good or better, we pass by, sometimes for years, and then we want to look at them. I cannot look at Memlinc for long and am only now beginning to be able to look at Tiepolo. (His son, Domenico, was never a problem.) Zurburán remains for me a mystery. David is difficult for many – there is a leathery, guillotine dullness that does not beckon.

But early or late, move into David's corpse-pallor and curious satisfactions take over. With the arm down, David has drawn a shoulder, with classical restraint, a formal rigor. Do you think him a killjoy? Extinguish for a little the peacock colours of today, and engage with this hard, arched arm. It is squared-up for enlargement with white chalk, and pounce holes.

Consider figs and armpits. Fig-leaves never succeeded in quenching desire.

A green stalk increases the violet of its hairs, until it reaches a violet flower.

Lilac is First in the Year, Violet is the End of the Rainbow

The end of the spectrum, the end of the day. Funereal when with black, violet colours the end of the year with Michaelmas-daisies, buddleia, and asters.

If you use the many available transparent dye colours, support them on greys or whites. Alizarin crimson is very dark. Permanent rose and Permanent magenta are strong and can be mixed with Cobalt, Ultramarine, and Cerulean blues. Various violet dyes can be as fierce as endorsing ink. The pale Cobalt violet that Bonnard used is expensive but good. Other darker violets are Cobalt violet dark, and Mineral violet. Strange pigment colours are the sticky Ultramarine red, and the weak but permanent Potters' pink. Rose madder is durable and dear: it will mix gently and transparently with Ultramarine blue. Crimson lake has been made durable, and is comparatively cheap. Mauve is made in red and blue shades, and, like Winsor violet, is a dye colour.

Black seems to have been added to the red and to the contrasting green of the fig. It is really a still life about a sailor's love life, and the sea.

Edward Burra,
The Green Fig, 1933

Fig-leaves

After David   *Watercolour flows erotically and triangularly.*   After Clemente

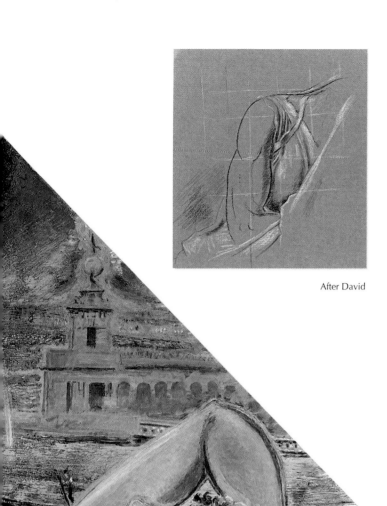

After Matisse

Rainbow in Venice,
1985

The colour of a ripe fig is between violet
and green. Some colours will only mix
cleanly if the mixing is done optically.
Cobalt violet, dabbed lightly against
Cobalt green, makes violet-green.
Viridian will increase the darkness. Stab
into the indigo-velvet-fruit. The interior
flesh is crimson and gold, in a covering
of apple-green as pale as pastry.

The Massive Eye Lock

GUIDES AND LECTURERS in front of pictures sometimes say: "See how the eyes follow you around the room." We feel we move our eyes, directing them at will, much as we point an electric torch. Scientists say that eyes flit about all over the place rather as flies fly. We direct our attention without being aware of this. The limitation of the activity of the eye may account for the relaxation of looking through binoculars.

Since we are not taught to look at pictures, do we naturally "go for a walk with a line" as with Paul Klee, or comprehend immediately. Snakes and ladders? Perhaps we take the physical looking at pictures too much for granted. Oriental reading of pictures is different. The movements of people's eyes when looking at famous pictures have been charted as dots, clustering around certain attractive areas. Great painters know how to direct the attention of the viewer.

No painter, however astute, can move the eyes of a dog lover away from a trace of dog. Bonnard's slightest dabs about his dachshund are sufficient to engage the attention of a dog lover. Bonnard is very good at controlling the spectator's attention over his surfaces.

Ninety years of staring in and out. The poignant expression is fearful of death's imminence.

Piero and the great painters are always painting encounters between humans. Piero paints eyes with vitality, the whites of the eyes bright as in Japanese prints and vividly directed. It is difficult to know how much the painter relies on spectator knowledge of the direction of a glance for the drama within his picture. Even if we cover the eyes, we remember the direction somewhat, and even upside-down (as with Baselitz), some of the effect survives.

The design with eye is strong when storytelling, and such linkages could not be made in a purer design. Figurative art is seen to be strong when Piero della Francesca, using tiny triangles and circles for eyes, links them to a massive design telling stories of love, war, annunciation, revelation, and monumental calm.

"The eyes follow you around the room." The guide is aware that something mysterious is going on. It would be truer to say eyes move your eyes through the picture. But he might be close, for we confront eyes with eyes. All figurative pictures have at least a ghost mirror to them. Francis Bacon, the great croupier, insisted on glass and frames, and these would part reflect the punter.

After Picasso

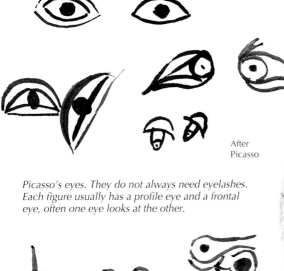

After Picasso

Picasso's eyes. They do not always need eyelashes. Each figure usually has a profile eye and a frontal eye, often one eye looks at the other.

One of the most dramatic eye-to-eye encounters is when Judas betrays Christ in the fresco in Padua by Giotto.

After Giotto

160

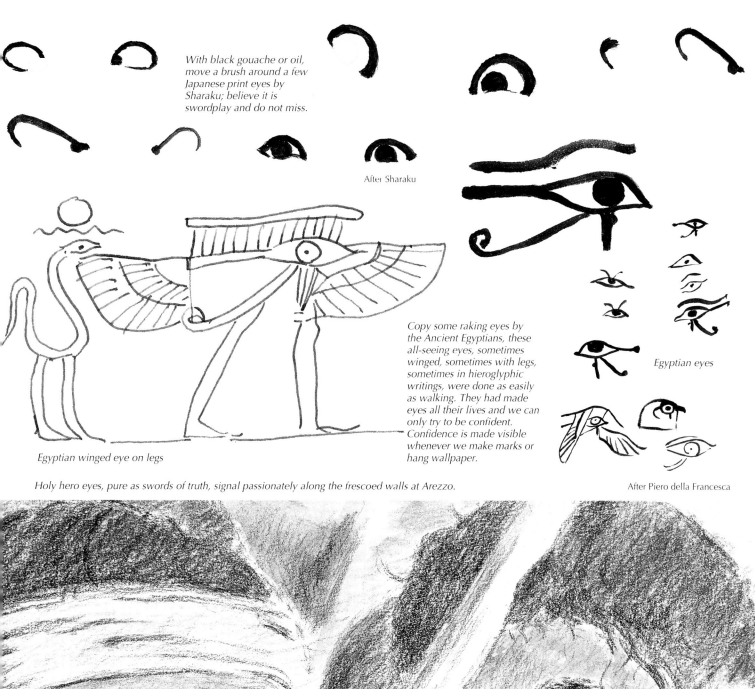

With black gouache or oil, move a brush around a few Japanese print eyes by Sharaku; believe it is swordplay and do not miss.

After Sharaku

Copy some raking eyes by the Ancient Egyptians, these all-seeing eyes, sometimes winged, sometimes with legs, sometimes in hieroglyphic writings, were done as easily as walking. They had made eyes all their lives and we can only try to be confident. Confidence is made visible whenever we make marks or hang wallpaper.

Egyptian eyes

Egyptian winged eye on legs

Holy hero eyes, pure as swords of truth, signal passionately along the frescoed walls at Arezzo.

After Piero della Francesca

Modigliani

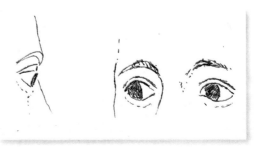

WE HAVE BECOME ACCUSTOMED to the blank eyes of ancient sculptures. Once they were filled with precious stones. Modigliani was a sculptor, a painter, and a Cubist. He could get a good likeness. He would fill the eye-shapes with a simple colour or even criss-crosses. The eyes of Neil Jeffries are central and over life-size to confront the onlooker dramatically.

Brush self-portrait eyes, or stare into the eyes of the beloved. Make little marks and dabs for wink-eyes, sultry eyes, and wide eyes, and then double mirrored, or as requested of your partner, side-long glancing eyes – these are the flashing, healthy, heaven-sent eyes of Piero.

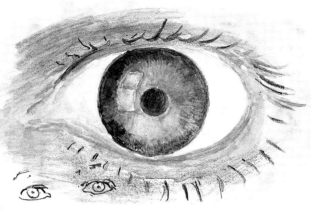

Piero exaggerated eye irises in "The Death of Adam" at Arezzo. A profile iris is actually painted in front of an eyelid and often the circular irises are very large and dramatic.

After Piero della Francesca

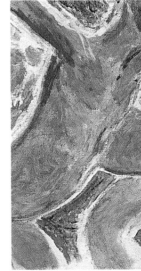

A profile turned until the eye is no longer visible. It is difficult to do but Piero knew how to do it. Adam's eye in profile is clear and high on the wall as he looks for the last time. "The Death of Adam" is at Arezzo.

After Piero della Francesca

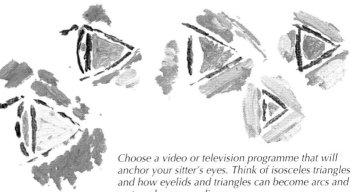

Choose a video or television programme that will anchor your sitter's eyes. Think of isosceles triangles and how eyelids and triangles can become arcs and watercolour some diagrams.

The tiniest marks against the white of the eye will make a directional glance.

Modigliani eyes, like ancient statues stare mysteriously ahead.

After Modiglia

These are the eyes of the young sculptor Neil Jeffries near the Thames at Chelsea.

Chelsea (detail), 1988

My eyes move towards the viewer and away from a panoramic view over the sea (not seen here).

South Coast (detail), 1990

Crayon the whites of the eyes at night, small against the mysterious dark rocks and caves of Rock-a-Nore.

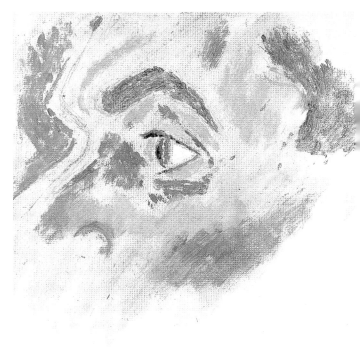

Once again I wanted to make a clear triangle of the profile eye. It rhymes with the angular background.

Spectacles

SPECTACLES DISTORT AND CHANGE the dimensions of everything. Hollywood stars would pretend to be ugly ducklings and turn into glamorous swans when their spectacles were removed. Spectacles are the frames of eyes, and change people's appearance as much as picture frames alter pictures. In portraiture, spectacles can take over. Picasso's portrait of "Jaime Sabartes" is mainly glasses. Sickert made Hugh Walpole around a circular lens. William Coldstream's painting of Lord Thomson was a bespectacled barrier, and a barrage of measurement marks. The camouflage and partial disguise that spectacles provide, makes life easier for the sitter. Hockney lives his life behind enormous lenses. Vuillard's mother wore little ovals. Some people appear so naked, if they remove their glasses you expect them to blush.

Choosing spectacle frames is the nearest many people come to abstract art, and the choice is very serious: for a politician in the public eye, a millimetre mistake might change his election chances.

Dark glasses were fashionable when abstract artists taught at the Slade. They even wore them in winter, as protection against "Jungle Art"!

Try variations of a circle in a square. Try hoop against hoop. Spectacle lenses can be thick and convex. A goldfish bowl is thicker. Fishes are eye-shaped; eyes are spherical. Paint eyes through a goldfish bowl. Paul Klee in "The Thinking Eye" placed a simple fish-shape in a rectangle, as a representation of a fish tank. If we call the rectangular tank a spectacle frame, the fish becomes an eye; and if the eye is a fish, then it is a symbol for the Resurrection.

Often improprieties reflect from Anthony Green's spectacles. In his self-portrait surrounded by fireworks, he probably remembered a little mirror in a favourite picture, "The Arnolfini Marriage" portrait by Jan van Eyck in London's National Gallery – a most proper arrangement.

The mind's eye version of an eye is a sphere, shuttered by arc-shaped eyelids. Looked at carefully, an eye is more complicated. The eyelids are not pure arcs, and the orb eye has a projecting cornea; and when you try painting the turned eye, the elastic eyelid surprises. If the eye also wears a contact lens, the forms are even less predictable.

Doodle some rounded forms within some rectangular formats.

Anthony Green, *Cannes/The Lover*, 1977

Anthony Green posesses the visual gluttony of Carpaccio, Stanley Spencer, and the old German masters.

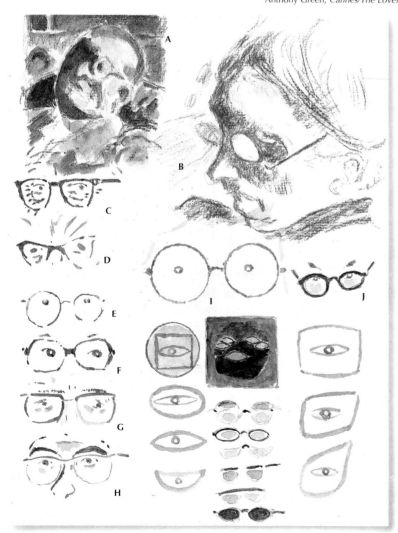

A	Hugh Walpole, after Sickert
B	Mrs Vuillard, after Vuillard
C	Coldstream
D	Gowing
E	Eurich
F	Mary Potter
G	Michael Andrews
H	Anthony Green
I	Hockney
J	Le Corbusier

Anthony Green, *Cannes/ The Lover* (detail), 1977

Anthony Green uses hardboard with a white acrylic priming. It is more difficult to manoeuvre small details in oil than in oily tempera, or even when using fine grain canvas, but he works bravely brusquely and the images shine forth with surprising force.

The spectacles of various famous people

Eyes within ovals and rectangles. Pupils, irises, and lenses are somewhat eccentric.

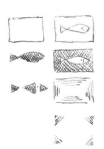

After Klee

An oblique view makes an even more complicated self-portrait.

Spectacle still lives

Brush-doodle some doodles.

"Self-portrait". Baseball, or other sporting eyeshades might be useful. A straw hat is comfortable. Chardin is so swathed, bespectacled, and shaded it is easy to realize that he was professional, and warm and as great as they come.

After Chardin

165

Staring Skull Heads

THE CLOSEST PART WE HAVE to the mind is the skull. The best teachers have known the importance of learning the bones. Eakins, Anschutz, and McComb are examples. McComb would place a skull at the same height beside his portrait model. It made for a serious atmosphere. Late Picasso self-portraits relate to skulls. Picasso painted numerous absinthe glasses, but even more skulls. Cézanne had several skulls on his shelves. Skulls vary, and I think we do not see certain heavy European skulls; most are from India. The finest drawn skulls are by Leonardo da Vinci. Hans Baldung painted an "Allegory of Vanity". Death drips some flesh, but is skeletal. He waves an hourglass over a beautiful girl, who holds a hand-mirror.

Skulls are head-shaped, but are made up of small, concave surfaces that are home to muscles – together with fat, these create the plumpnesses. Make studies of skulls if you can. Blur your way into the hollows. New skulls and skeletons are pale. Bratby painted them with pale ochres. These are cheaper than most colours; thick painters often use them.

Edvard Munch's predicament was horrible. Rooms with choking and dying loved-ones filled his mind and drove him crazy and drunken. We are able to endure agony if an end to it is in sight. The idea of a terminal ache appals.

A painted metal sculpture

After
Neil Jeffries

After
Redon

A swamp flower, which is a sickly visage. Skulls have a greater ferocity.

Self-portraits in old age, with various frightened, ghostly, and ghastly heads

After Munch

"Anais Faure on her Death Bed". It contrasts with the Expressionism of Munch.

After Seurat

In old age, Munch shows himself as if embracing Death, but also gently pushing him away. "Half in Love with Easeful Death."

After Munch

"Self-portrait at 2.15 a.m." and "Self-portrait: The Night-Wanderer"

After Munch

Study for "Death in the Sick-room"

After Munch

As if measuring Munch for a coffin, the clock will continue into the future. They both have faces and hands. The clock has an escapement, but for the painter there is no escape.

After Munch

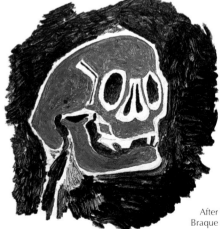

After Braque

"A Death's Head". Violet and black are the colours for memento mori. (Latin for "remember you must die".)

Flying Figures

HOWEVER HARD YOU WAVE YOUR ARMS, you will not rise an inch. There is a lot of great art that depicts figures in the air. Certainly, if there is no more than clouds to support them, it must be imagination they depend on to keep them in the sky.

An enormous rain-cloud over a flat expanse. Draw with a soft pencil on rough paper. Fix and watercolour it from memory.

Eastern England is flat. The skies are enormous. In the autumn, they build like sheep and lambs to the zenith; when low-lighted at evening, they appear solid enough to sit on. To make lowland figures steady, a long, horizontal shadow can be attached to the feet; to settle them compositionally, the heads can be attached to the horizon. Koninck, Cuyp, and Boudin knew how to manage low horizons.

Leaving the low cliffs of East Anglia, for the high chalk promontories of the South Downs, I could see the figures in the sky, hang-gliding in bright colours. Bodies can be put anywhere, on any level, or in the sky. It took me a long while to feel free to put figures anywhere, and to soar adolescents over Venice. I could not give Nancy, Daniel, and Francis wings. I had to be fearful, and spare them an Icarus fate.

Paint the sky. Here are a few gerbil-shaped cumulus clouds seducing a desirable angora-rabbit-shaped cloud. It is all about stroking! With turpentine and medium, swish a canvas with pale Cobalt violet, then stroke it with pale Cobalt green until it is as blue as it will go. Into this damp surface, using a pointed sable brush, mark out a few cloud shapes with ultramarine: into the middles, brush in a whitish-blackish grey, or a whitish-violetish grey mixture.

Various flying figures from the Dante illustrations Blake was employed on at his death. Inverted figures will fall or fly.

After Blake

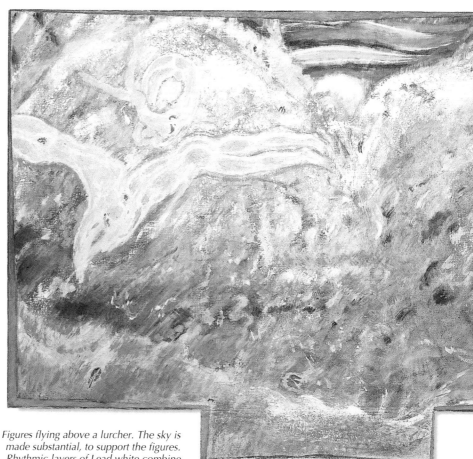

Figures flying above a lurcher. The sky is made substantial, to support the figures. Rhythmic layers of Lead white combine with liquids to hurry movements along with brush and stripe at greyhound speeds. Pop artists incorporated a greater variety of formal devices than I do and could change speeds more easily.

Isle of Wight, 1991

"The Dance". Diving and acrobatics were nearly flying. Léger painted everything – even comet tails.

After Léger

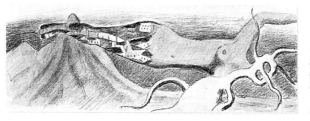

"Great Journeys". A tree and a village-figure float over a mountain. Invention approaches imagination.

After Magritte

A self-portrait, Tower Bridge, and
two grappling figures

Nash painted various flowers in the sky. Here,
the sunflower seems to rotate. He often used
a painting knife (a small trowel) and did not
dilute the buttery paint.

Paul Nash,
Eclipse of the Sunflower, 1945

After Tiepolo

After Tiepolo

"Allegory with Venus and Time". Her breasts
are even further apart than the
floating hemispheres by Léger.
Tiepolo used clouds
creatively.

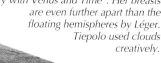

The paper-dart shape of the hang-glider
fits well in the diamond shape. A long format was
intended to suggest the vast spaces at Beachy Head.
Concave frameworks might have been more expansive.

Red Kite Lift-off, 1978

Yourself in Fur

ETER PAUL RUBENS PAINTED A GRAND SOUVENIR – a world-famous painting of his wife, Helena Fourment, posing as Aphrodite. It was called "Little Fur" in his will. If we are enjoying a happy time, we are almost immediately disturbed at the anticipation of its passing. The great performances of music are sometimes preserved on disc. In the past, they remained only as a memory. Mortal, we clutch at souvenirs: tapes, videos, photographs, perfumes, letters, even locks of hair. Rubens was schooled in the grand tradition of Italy, by copying and practising. Imagine, extravagantly, that you are the Prince of Painters, with all his powers at your command. Helena has just left a hot bath, and stands in her fur wrap enjoying the cool night air, anticipating the warming-panned bed. Your dream allows that you are indeed Rubens, and are contentedly watching Helena from the soapy warmth of the bath. Suddenly, you become aware, and everything falls into place: a hide-and-seek of texture. Tomorrow, one of the wonders of the world will be achieved. The result hangs in Vienna, and for around 350 years, has embodied a wonderful moment for the artist.

Rubens had previously copied "The Lady in a Fur Cloak" by Titian, which is also in Vienna. (The Rubens copy is owned privately.) He learned by copying. Be daring! Be cautious! I know the dangers of copying paintings as old as this. But art can also be a source of real and sustaining power.

Stay with Helena. She is no ordinary woman. Rubens had known her as a child of 5 – 1 of 11 children. He chose and married her when he was 53, and she 16. Do not expect your copy to come alive. Only the brimming confidence of Peter Paul could achieve this Pygmalion miracle. But stay with Helena. She changes all the time. Make dabs for what you discover.

All the features are at their fullest. The hard little animal nose flares its nostril within the invented shadow, which belies the illumination from the shoulder below – which is made to reflect on to the chin and eyebrow. The plumpness is controlled by a sharp, contrasting pearl earring, and a highlight in the far eye. More enigmatic than the "Mona Lisa". There is no naturalism in this wonder concoction. Copy her vitality and wit. Does she whisper a naughty joke? Mark where the cherry cherub lips come together. See how, at the wild limits of possibility, the eyes are enormous, and will bounce meanings across the room.

Be up to date. Anoint your body with moisturising cream. Be your own model. Helena as Aphrodite is a sumptuous spectacle because of the textural contrasting of fur and flesh. As you leave the shower, there is no fur – but an enormous fluffy towel will be more colourful. Drape it carefully around you. Its long rhythms will camouflage a boasting abdomen. (For ruined feet, wear socks.) If you continue to fret, arrange a ravishing accompaniment of flowers and fruit, even attract your cat with a sardine. Paint a self-portrait as lurid as cosmetics.

In large mirrors, the students of Chelsea Art School are painting self-portraits. The girls know what they look like, and what they want to look like. They invent their appearances considerably. Take the girl rattling in a tube train. She makes a large brushing of "blusher", with an almost unbelievable skill. Aided by a tiny mirror (and with the train rattling hard as a road drill) a sure hand sweeps in a narrow line round the eyes, raising the corners minutely. Then, as the train lurches from a stop, mascara is added. Ever since Ancient Egypt and before, girls have changed their appearance. Gwen John would have done her self-portrait "plain", with no-nonsense mouse-brown eyelashes.

A line-up for a portrayal of self

A sketch of the whole picture

After Rubens

After Rubens' copy of Titian

After Rubens

The newly married Rubens in his garden   After Rubens

Use a rich medium, and paint over a streaky underpainting.

After Rubens

After Rubens

An oily scribble over black

After Rubens

A fluffy towel will enhance your smoothest attractions and can leave the exact shape of flesh you need for your painting.

On the underground railway, a girl applies lipstick. In Ancient Greece and Egypt, mirrors were only as bright as you could polish copper. Hand-mirrors were a frequent accompaniment to the figure.

A scribble-copy of Helena

After Rubens

Peter Paul Rubens, *Helena Fourment with Fur Cloak*, 1638–40

Self-portrait

JOHN DONNE ENDED A POEM, "Death, thou shalt die." For Bacon, Death was the end. Francis Bacon gambled, and drank champagne, and there must have been many times when he looked at himself in the big, circular, paint-spattered mirror in his studio, sore with a hangover, pursued by The Furies (Bacon read Aeschylus); and other times, elated by a gambling win, when his reflection in the mirror, beyond the paint-spots, was pleasurable, like Narcissus reflected in a pool. Francis Bacon did a lot of self-portraits. Accidents in paint were cherished, but his "accidents" were really more like violent gestures done with a lifetime's experience – a fly-fisherman casting. He did not miss. Willem de Kooning and Jackson Pollock would also set the paint flying at this time.

Most bodies resemble each other, in the main. One way to have a body-compendium at your disposal is to prop up three mirrors and be between them. You will surprise yourself, and unsettle your nearest and dearest. Palliate by inviting them to join you; you then have two models, and an enormous number of reflections. Draw-paint everything; act out useful performances because painting depends as much on acting as does grand opera.

Then do some paintings of your own face (before plastic surgeons make face-transplants general). Move a long-haired brush around as if you know you will be lucky. Curiously, only a little repainting will be needed; intuition, as usual, is in command. Try again, this time beside a large mirror, and use a small make-up mirror. Closely explore your features one at a time, brushing diagrams as you go. Dab at your nostrils, dilate them attractively. Open your mouth, paint an arch of flashing teeth. Tint your lips with cosmetic flair. Do not miss any part of the visage-compendium. It looks different every time.

Put the mirror aside. Imagine you are Narcissus. The pool is as round as Bacon's mirror, the water is rippled, obscured as the looking-glass, blotchy with paint. But however disturbed the water, you know you are substantial, and when it calms, you will be "present". "Presence" was a term much used, at one time – for example, Rembrandt surrounded his subjects with darkness, and achieved "presence". Bacon often used three gold-framed, glass-covered canvases, and would paint the figure in each, at about the size of a reflected onlooker. The floor was painted as if continuous with the carpet of the gallery. They achieved a "presence". My mother, who had been a nurse, said it is a great pity we cannot turn our bodies inside-out. Bacon, who liked a book called *Positioning for Radiography* and another, more colourful book on wounds, would probably have agreed.

After Picasso

The frontal top is combined with a profile.

Skulls in hats

After Ensor

Francis Bacon, *Head VI*, 1949

Oil on a black ground, a free variation on a self-portrait

After Bacon

A free brush drawing of myself

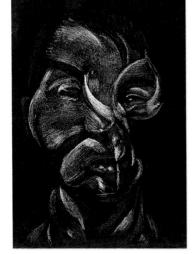

Crayon variation-copies of a Bacon self-portrait. They were often done in threes.

An intuitive, freely-brushed painting

Daniel Miller, *Self-Portrait*, 1977

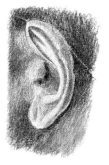

After Mantegna

After Mantegna

Self-portrait, ear

A hand-mirror will search out features. Non-protuding ears, and fundamental regions will require two mirrors.

After Seurat

Self-portrait, nose

Stories

ASKED WHETHER HE BELIEVED in God, Matisse said: "Yes, when I am working." Paint only what you believe in: once you start painting, you will find yourself more of a believer – or more gullible, or more inventive – than you expected.

For about 30 years, Paula Rego has painted the fright and fortune of European folk-tales. Animals are made to act out cruelties and inhibitions. Sometimes, a friend will pose as a toad, and sometimes the stories are Rego's own, impregnable and special. Acrylic is dabbed on paper (later supported on canvas). She begins on the floor, almost as a child might play, but completes the picture vertically. As a child she was safe in her playroom, but the dark corners of the house were grim with terrors: blind mice had their tails cut off with a carving-knife, and far, far worse. Paula Rego says: "When the pictures are going well you just can't wait for the next morning to come. And that's very good. A very good feeling. Painting is practical, but it's magical as well. Being in this studio is like being inside my own theatre."

Today, stories can be told vividly. Although Rembrandt's "Belshazzar's Feast" is a wonderful illustration, it strains our period vision – but not as much as Rubens' "Samson and Delilah". William Blake's Dante watercolours are icicle-crisp and sharp as flames, and some of them are time-free. Stories were left out of painting for nearly a century, but now we do what we like, and we are "narrative" if we like to be. Ken Kiff has led me into many strange grottoes and dells to confront the beasts he imagines. For his "Echo and Narcissus", Kiff used acrylic on paper. Ovid told stories that often fitted the ideas of artists more easily than the big biblical themes. (For instance, it was difficult to accommodate 13 at a long table for "The Last Supper", although Stanley Spencer made it into an exciting picture of feet – or hundreds of toes!) The itinerant story-teller is no longer awaited in the village, yet Coleridge's *Ancient Mariner* continues to hold us spellbound in a book, or when read aloud – and David Jones' illustrations of Coleridge, and other subjects, are superb story drawings.

Take up your brush. Do not fear. Believe everything you tell yourself. You will paint your favourite story: the one that makes you shiver, the one living in the fastnesses of your being and tearing you from the practical.

Family life is made up of stories, themes, and surprises. There is no need for any other subject. Remove their clothes, make everybody superb in long, charcoal swathes: the rhythms will not date. Then paint them in strong colours: challenge the stained-glass of the Sainte Chapelle in Paris. As Norbert Lynton wrote of Eileen Cooper: "Paint the family and you end up a 'history painter'. History painting used to be the most highly valued category of art, because it demanded such directorial talents..."

Green is telling the story of his childhood, as remembered in the London flat where he lived for many years. The grandest doll's-houses come apart. Green's flat is no doll's-house, it is furnished detail by detail to be present. The viewer is caught impaled, as on Royal occasions, in a time warp.

Eileen Cooper, *Woman Surprised by a Young Boy*, 1991

After Cooper

Ken Kiff, *Echo and Narcissus (Number 81 of the sequence)*, 1977

Anthony Green, *Victory in Europe: The Greens*, 1945

The woman is playing with the dog, possibly even telling it a story. The picture's story is of buff, pink, and grey, and it is a little frightening.

Paula Rego, *Snare*, 1987

175

Gwen John

Augustus John learned a kind of sweeping line drawing from Tonks. It was swishy and not very useful. It was less slick than Tonks, but compared with Sickert's workmanlike drawings, or the gentle poetry of his sister, Gwen, it was too polished to be good for anything, except its august boast. But Augustus was fond of his sister, and by his example showed exactly what she did not need. She went and found a greater ego in Rodin (an even faster draughtsman, and a great sculptor). She met Picasso, whose enormous ego had a brilliant pencil to go with it. Plainly, surrounded by so much macho puff and virtuosity, she was left only a little space for spiritual retreat: a tiny room, a chair, a softly filtering light falling on a table and a book, a stillness punctuated only by the silent paw-falls of her cats. Her technique for painting was frugal and sufficient and no different from the one she had learned at the Slade. Flax canvas tacked to a stretcher was sized with warm rabbit skin glue, then coated with a half-chalk ground, left rather absorbent. She used only a few primary colours – the main one bright, the others less bright. They were mixed with half-and-half turpentine and oil with more oil added as the painting proceeded. She had been taught to paint tonally, sight-size. But what they could not teach was Gwen's feather-light touch, the delicate crumbles, the pale colours, or the power of her spirit. (Have you ever tried to break a feather with a straight pull?) Gwen posed for Auguste Rodin. It is difficult to imagine him posing in Gwen's cane chair!

Probably "Sweet" again

A soft-coloured watercolour.

Gwen John,
Faded Dahlias, 1925

Gwen's beloved cat (called both "Sweet" and "Edgar Quinet"). She would search all night, by moonlight, when the cat went missing.

After
Gwen John

After
Gwen John

The quiet room with its simple contents – a book, a table, a chair, and a view through a window.

After Gwen John

She used dove-soft greys and almost no line, still as a pudding, with simplest composition. The near cheek and a cat's eye are on the middle division, and her invisible breasts half-way up (detail below).

Gwen John, *Girl with Cat*, 1920 (detail below)

Gwen John, *Flowers in a Vase*, 1925

Good Humour at Court

MANTEGNA IS AN ARTIST of serious moods. He painted the family of the Duke of Mantua, in the Ducal Palace. A visit to it can change a painter's life. Swathes of fruit and foliage decorate the castle. The "Camera degli Sposi" is full of painted people. Mantegna must have intensified the lives of the Duke, his family, dogs, horses, dwarf, and servants – whose portraits are uniquely recorded on the walls. Art historians try to discover the identities of those depicted – whether, for example, a small profile portrait in Naples is Francesco Gonzaga, pretending to be four years older so as to be Cardinal Deacon, and shown in Mantua full-face, and grown-up. The wonderful

surprise of the "Camera" comes when you look up at a circle of painted blue sky (the oculus) and find Mantegna, the serious painter, in relaxed mood, depicting smiling faces looking down, and playful babies. A gentle comedy of this kind does not fade.

Make a diagram of the ceiling. Its lovely design is unfathomable, but rule up what diagrammatic links you can. Clues may be buried in the cloud. The cloud is concentric, as are many of the forms. Paint with gouache, or oil, some of the Putti against the blue-eye-paradise-firmament. Their butterfly-wings would not keep them aloft without Mantegna's art.

After Mantegna

Using wax crayon pencils. 		*After Mantegna*

"Francesca Gonzaga".
Copy from Mantegna
to engage with the
structural power of
painting. The force
that raised
Renaissance domes.

After Mantegna

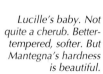

Lucille's baby. Not
quite a cherub. Better-
tempered, softer. But
Mantegna's hardness
is beautiful.

Is she a good friend, a servant, a relative? Some 		*After Mantegna*
light reverberates around the face – it is almost
Impressionism. Perhaps she is the children's nurse.

Andrea Mantegna, *Oculus, from
"The Painted Room" (Camera Picta),
in the Gonzaga Palace, Mantua,
1465–74*

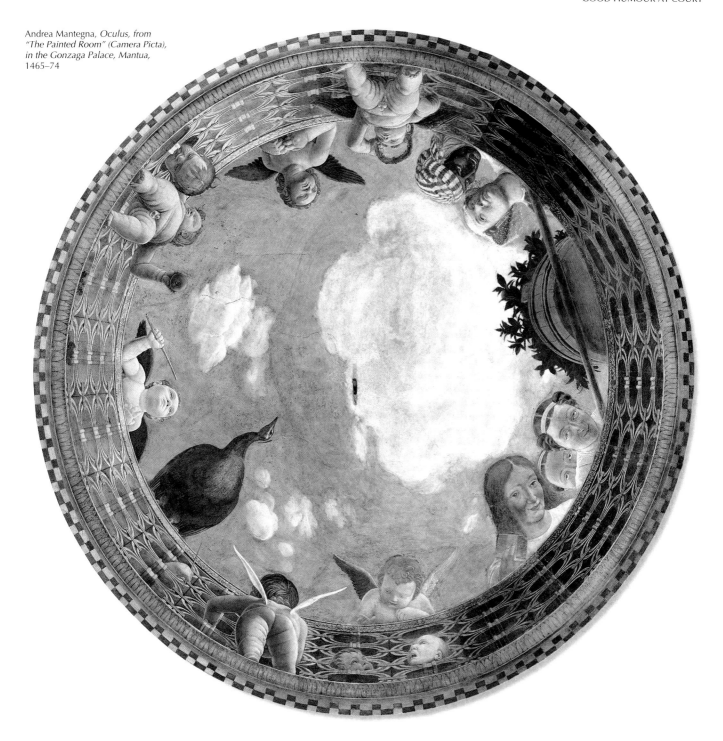

Cherubs playing
(using pastel pencils)   After Mantegna

A tracing, to suggest a few
of the links you may find.
Mantegna fitted everything
together with watchmaker
precision, and the
counterpoint of Bach – and
"three pounds of walnut oil".

Using pastel-pencils on grey paper. It is
possible to buy very soft pastel-pencils.
If you use these they require a special
sharpener – I used a medium hardness.

After Mantegna

179

Birth

After Modersohn-Becker

PAULA MODERSOHN-BECKER WROTE: "I know I shall not live very long. But why is that so sad? My sensuous perceptions grow sharper, as if I were supposed to take in everything within the few years that will be offered to me…."

History hurts. We would like to change it, and bring back the gifted who died young – Masaccio, Raphael, Gaudier-Brzeska, Harold Gilman, Eric Ravilious, Christopher Wood – and to know what would happen to their art. Old Master lives were short, compared with present expectations. Centuries are fixed by men, but 1900 seemed like a new beginning. Painters launched on a time of great innovatory painting. The Barnes Collection Matisse, "Joie de Vivre", was a large new painting of 1906. If Picasso had died before he painted "Les Demoiselles d'Avignon" in 1907, would we guess the years of Cubism? Braque would have soothed us. A far worse historical hurt was the death from heart attack in 1907, 19 days after giving birth to her baby girl, of Paula Modersohn-Becker aged 31. For now we do not know how a great woman artist would have painted through the years.

Paula Modersohn-Becker was unique. Women artists of the past (Artemisia Gentileschi, for example) were excellent but thought like men. Paula painted and thought as a woman. She painted a woman's subjects, and what is a surprise, did it with a tough strength. (Mothers have always said girls are healthier and easier to raise than boys; and women generally outlive men by several years.)

She knew exactly what she wanted and needed, and went for it. An extract from Marie Bashkirtseff's diary shows the difficulty of the time: "I know I could be somebody, but with petticoats what do you expect one to do? Marriage is the only career for women. Men have 36 chances, women have only one." But at 21, Paula wrote: "In art one is usually totally alone with oneself. My whole week has consisted of nothing but work and inspiration. I work with such passion that it shuts out everything else."

She had gone to an art school in London when 16, and the Berlin School of Art for Women at 20; lived in an art-village, Worpswede, at 21; attended the Academie Cola Rossi in Paris at 27, and later, the Beaux-Arts anatomy class.

The almost closed eyes show contentment.   After Modersohn-Becker

Breast-feeding a baby

A rough diagram   After Gauguin

A beautiful black girl awaits her baby. A monumental verticality meets a taut hemisphere.

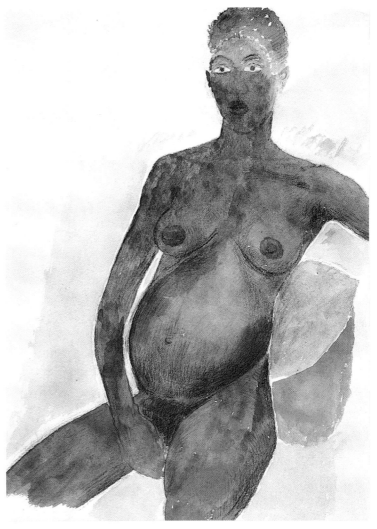

After Modersohn-Becker

A pregnant black girl firm as a gourd or fig makes one think of an aubergine.

The diagrammatic way Modersohn-Becker copied was rough, even wayward, but it aided memory and understanding. Try marking as a diagram a Gauguin painting with ten chalky dabs.

After Modersohn-Becker

The suckling baby is blended into the shadows of Tahiti. Paula was influenced by Gauguin's once-for-ever way of painting.

After Gauguin

Mother and Child

Paula loved Clara Westhoff, who married Rilke. When in Paris, where she went on long visits, she looked at art and found what she needed from the past: the rough, coarse-grained texture in Rembrandt, as well as the many individual qualities of Maillol, Munch, Vuillard, Bonnard, Michelangelo, van Gogh, Millet, Goya, and Gauguin. In the Louvre, she studied sculpture. Her copies were slight mementos – like tracings done with an elbow. But she knew that her open sketches would leave spaces for the swathes of paint she could move with such power.

When she was not visiting Paris, she lived in an artists' colony at Worpswede with her husband Otto Modersohn. They often painted the same subjects. She thought of birches as female, and pine trees as strong men, painted the people in the poorhouse, and peasant mothers nursing babies and children over and over, and self-portraits over and over.

A prehistoric mother goddess

"Through drawing I wanted to feel how a body has grown." (Rilke writing about Rodin: "There was no part of the human body that was unimportant to him.")

"All along", Paula Modersohn-Becker wrote, "I have striven to give the heads, drawn or painted, the simplicity of nature. Now I felt deeply how I can learn from antique heads, how they are seen in the large, and with such simplicity! Forehead, eyes, mouth, nose, cheeks, chin, that is all."

About a favourable criticism Paula said: "The criticism gave me satisfaction rather than pleasure. The real pleasures, the overwhelmingly beautiful hours are experienced through art, without being noticed by others. The same applies to the sad ones." In 1937, the Nazis seized 70 Becker pictures as "degenerate" art. She left some four hundred paintings and about one thousand drawings, and I would like to see all of them.

Rilke (who was Rodin's secretary for a time). The simplification resembles the pre-Cubist Picasso, when he was looking at African sculptures, and painted Gertrude Stein. Paula looked at Greco-Roman encaustic coffin-lid portraits – in order to make the "human clay" weigh as heavy as the world.

After Modersohn-Becker

"An Old Woman". The rough chalk drawings resemble those of van Gogh using "mountain chalk".

After Modersohn-Becker

After Modersohn-Becker

"Mother and Child"

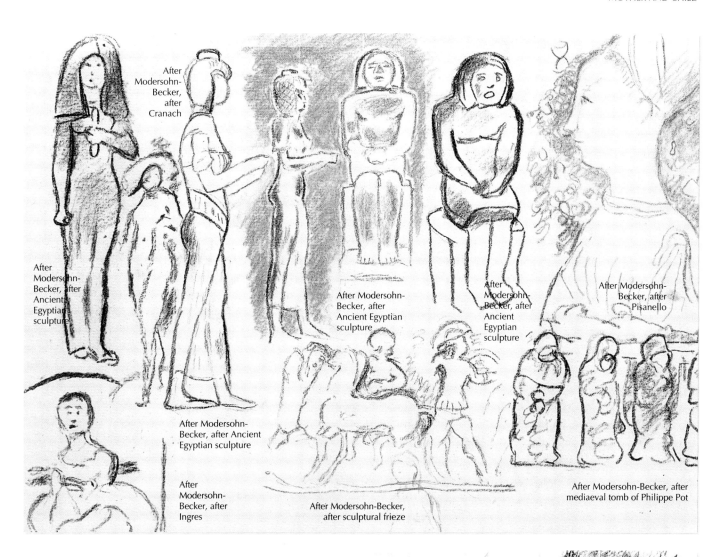

After Modersohn-Becker, after Cranach

After Modersohn-Becker, after Ancient Egyptian sculpture

After Modersohn-Becker, after Ancient Egyptian sculpture

After Modersohn-Becker, after Ancient Egyptian sculpture

After Modersohn-Becker, after Pisanello

After Modersohn-Becker, after Ancient Egyptian sculpture

After Modersohn-Becker, after Ingres

After Modersohn-Becker, after sculptural frieze

After Modersohn-Becker, after mediaeval tomb of Philippe Pot

Gauguin and Paula Modersohn-Becker looked at Ancient Egyptian and Etruscan art, which helped them to make heavy figures without fat.
Gauguin's Tahitian figures, although monumental, were tightly nubile.

After Modersohn-Becker

After Rembrandt

Rembrandt's "Bathshéba" has a rounded, noble body, and a beautiful profile face. Paula copied her to be a young girl with a perky body and a three-quarter viewed peasant head.

"Mother and Child"   After Modersohn-Becker

Lively Death and Deep Despair

WHEN TOLD HE HAD got the positions of his fighters wrong, George Bellows said: "It is of two men trying to kill each other." The great painter Gerard David painted a flaying, which I can hardly bear to look at. Titian painted "The Flaying of Marsyas" – which is one of the summits of art. Negro spirituals wail with pain. Initiation ceremonies involve pain. Max Beckmann knew about sufferings in hospital in wartime. Agonies abound, great painters digest them. Carpaccio made a picture of one thousand martyrdoms.

Great art can be cathartic. Poor art makes agony sordid. Michelangelo's "Last Judgement" shows a muscular youth being bitten. There are three to weigh him down. His knees are squeezing, he is in the closed foetal position, protecting his centre. The lowest devil has baby horns, the middle one a nasty tongue and eagle's claws. (A Mannerist mask is roughed-

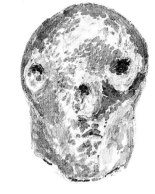

After Picasso
"Skull" (bronze)

up and made alive.) The warm adolescent is thrust hard-edged against a cold blue sky, doom laden with leaden grey clouds. He has nothing to hope for. He is the ultimate, obvious image of despair, and has haunted me always. My copy misses the suffering, but I discovered some technical ingredients: the chopped-out sculptural coming-and-going of the drawing, which supports the paint; then the strangeness of the fingers. (Rodin's "Thinker" is a distant free-copy.) When images possess such power, the arts seem to come together – and this one would illustrate Hamlet's soliloquy, or breathe with a late Beethoven quartet.

Mahler made death symphonic. Life tilts at death. Munch made a lot of it; his dying relatives drove him alcoholic. Rembrandt's mother, wrinkled as a corpse, would have allowed him to forget death's imminence. Painters keep death in place. Crows came for van Gogh, magpies for Brueghel, a shrike for Bosch, a corset for Matisse.

"Dempsey through the Ropes"　　　After Bellows

"Stag at Sharkeys"　　　After Bellows

A howl from Hell　　　After Michelangelo

McFadyen knows the hard end of the city. Paint the next nasty thing you see, purge your system. In the north of England they compete at making ugly grimaces. The toothless win. For the adolescent, despair confronts acne, sores, and boils. Francis Bacon painted a moving picture from a Muybridge photograph of a spastic child. Painters shout, and never weep.

Jock McFadyen, Even Dwarves..., 1987

Icarus flew too near the sun and melted his wings. Rubens' freshly mixed lead pigment melted flesh into the painted sky.　　　After Rubens

"Death and the Maiden"　　　After Baldung

"Envy"　　　After Munch

A woman with a
dead child

After Picasso

"Self-portrait
and Monsters"

After Michelangelo

After Michelangelo

After Picasso

*A young man, damned, and falling to Hell – on the end wall of the Sistine Chapel. He
had more than acne to worry him. Meet terror with a brush. Paint horror intimately.*

Max Beckmann, *Birds' Hell*, 1938

Creamy White Players

RECREATIONS CAN LEAD to a large inventory of forms. Join me to watch cricket on Clapham Common in south London. You need not follow the score! Ruskin started his Italian journeys with sketchbooks, a carriage, and horses, not far from here. We will turn him in his grave. Here, the freezer-bag keeps the cucumber sandwiches cool, the jar of water is at hand, the watercolour box and a sheet of rag paper – "hot-pressed", "NOT", or "rough" surfaced. We will choose "rough". The fine and springy sable brushes are at our command. It only remains to wet the brush, and start the "game".

Be relaxed. Turnover to "automatic". Mess with the paint. Do not fear Ruskin. His detailed investigations were honourable and interesting. But Dürer also watercoloured a hare with every hair in place, an owl feathered neatly, and a lovely clump of lush grasses. Never mind. We will allow ourselves to make a mess, and let the runny colour flow. The white flannels absorb most green at the legs. The parching, orange common turns the shirts pale blue. Perhaps the blue in the sky was a mistake: the blue of the shirts is so pale, it survives no rivalling blue…. Think in terms of rounded splurges of Terre verte and black – then all will become leafy, leafy shadows, and balls of tousled hair. I was caught out when I added blue to the sky. I could remove the blue! I could leave the blue! Feel free to accept, from the vast complications of nature, more than you can control.

Allow the mind to expand, and from the unfinished or empty pieces and from stabs, marks, and blobs attempting the depiction of nature, controlled pictures may one day grow. On this occasion I mean by Nature, all that is visible, sitting on the grass in the middle of this common. An area for the common people, and for a painter, a common source. But commons are not meadows. Humanly grubby commons absorb trash, orange peel, dog poop, Coke cans, cigarette packets, and sun cream. Picasso advised painters of the need to dirty their hands. Rodin arranged for a different prospect: several naked models would move around in his studio, and he would draw them when interested. Janacek would collect street conversation for use in his operas. Seek a richness from which to select and adapt. Common sources give life to all the arts.

When you have nothing more you feel strongly about; when it comes on to rain; when the joggers have run home. When a red bus would unsettle your greens; when pollen has filled your eyes – STOP. Do not fill in. Leave unfinished. If there is a calamity, remove the offending piece with a typist's eraser. Hard watercolour paper will accept erasure using a razor blade or cutting knife, or obscure mistakes using acrylic Titanium white delicately.

Clapham Common, 1984

The child on the left has become displaced. Never mind. If I had not drawn him there I would not have recorded him at all. The girl below him is smoking a cigarette. Some people quickly moved away, leaving me with little more than a nose, or a hooded eye. Some artists are always finalists, but most need to pry around in preparation for their important works.

A pencil drawing becomes full of activity when a background of brown-green watercolour is brushed in. A dog leaps for a stick. A jogger jogs. Discover what forms motivate painters you admire. Look at their history. See how Leon Kossoff, for instance, concentrates on people walking in the streets or underground stations. Then makes surprising swimming pools full of people and copies early Cézannes. See how, in this way, he carries his life's work forward.

A pencil drawing is watercoloured with black. It is almost monochrome.
Tiny additions of green and orange make it full of colour.

Flowers and Nudes

FLOWERS OFTEN COME WRAPPED IN PAPER. An unwrapped body is almost as full of character as a countenance. When flowers are unwrapped, some are more like nudes than others. Roses, lilies, and tulips are smooth: they do not embarrass. The unclothed body is vulnerable and meaningful. The mind touches it at every point. It can be eloquent as paint. No cloth, gaiter, or shoe rivals it as subject matter. A bath of nude is flower-like, fubsy, or rude. Try painting a body against a tulip. Fix it so the parts most similar are adjacent; make the colours equal, and the tones and textures equal. Allow your mind to slip. Paint a tulip as a figure, and a figure as a tulip.

Flowers can be enormous. Georgia O'Keeffe painted very large pictures, sometimes of the middles of flowers. The "Two Calla Lilies" could be seen as made of very pale nudes. A very large tulip could be with a tiny naked body.

"Woman-Flower" resembles one of Picasso's flat ceramics from Vallauris.

After Picasso

Lily and nude

The green-blanketed girl resembles a bursting bud.

A flower-like abstraction

Georgia O'Keeffe loved the dry blankness of the hot, red desert, and painting enormous flowers. (A black hollyhock was one metre across.) This picture called "Two Calla Lilies on Pink" is erogenous – like a Mae West invitation to her pink boudoir, without the girl.

After O'Keeffe

Smooth paper and waxy crayon pencils are sleek enough for tulip textures. Hot-pressed watercolour paper is nearly like the China clay-filled process papers that are smooth as nudes.

Beyond the body is a rose bush, and the sea. The bedclothes are like petals surrounding the nude, cream around pink.

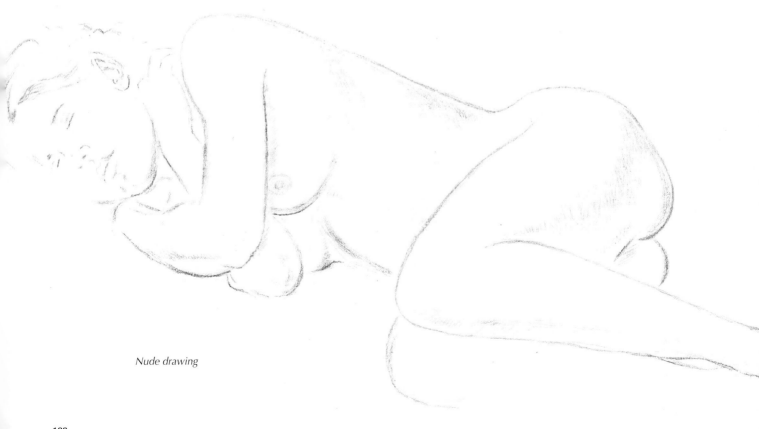

Nude drawing

*Smooth, rhythmic
curves make
bodies flower-like.
Brancusi-smooth
and flower-like as
the youthful
Madonnas of
Botticelli.*

After Modigliani

*Apple-blossoms
bloom so fast, you
have to try and
draw at Giacometti
speed.*

*The flower has reduced
the bottle to being weightless.
The stalk has become
important: the effect is stiff.*

Euan Uglow,
*Orange-flower
in Bottle,* 1983

"The Campers". The flower-shapes comment on the girl-shapes.

After Léger

STILL AND FAST LIFE
Animals, Objects, and Flowers

THE RISING BIRDS OF LIGHT pass the falling birds of darkness. Birds inspire artists, and cause mortals to flap in dreams. Painters have filled their pictures with angels' wings: without genius, the wings of Icarus (waxed on) will not adhere. The wings of the heavy bodies of painted angels are a problem anatomically: for instance, in Annunciations one set of shoulder blades has to serve both for pointing and for flying! Design some wings. Odilon Redon was good at it. Braque painted hundreds of birds – some were boomerang-shaped, some like paper aeroplanes. Wings can be used to express all moods, from the evil harpies by William Blake, to the sacred pinions of Poussin's "Pegasus". The recording angel in Blake's *Illustrations to Dante* has pale wings; and a devil in hell (Canto 28) has dark, transparent wings, batlike, angular, "draculant".

A wing of a blue roller on vellum. I did not make it hard, sharp, delicate, and soft – or detail the tiny feathers sufficiently. I missed the airy secret – the radiating sequences whose exactness enables air to be thick enough for flight. Dürer was even drawing the spines of feathers.

After Dürer

The Dove from "The Baptism"

After Piero della Francesca

Magpies

Braque's birds fly with eloquence.   After Braque

A harpy   After Blake

Dabs become birds

Seagull   After Avery   *Magpies*

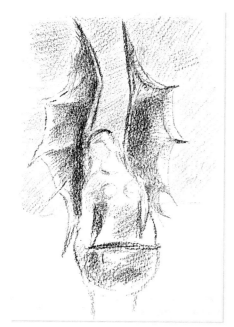

"Les Tenebres". Dark Wings   After Redon   *Magpies*   After Brueghel   *Songbirds in snow*

Cats and Pets

Horses have us as pets. Picasso petted and painted a goat, cats, dogs, an owl, and pigeons – but our real pets are cats and dogs. You can have pet rats and alligators, but it is not the same. We have adapted to dogs and cats; they even sleep in their owners' beds. Goats, stoats, and hedgehogs are never allowed under the duvet. Cats are fastidious (except for the tom's rancid perfume), and we think we understand them. Cats, if you warm them, will pose well. Black cats, like those of Manet, are easier than white. Carefully manipulate a blob of black, and it will become a cat. Use Burnt umber and ultramarine or other colours for spectral blacks. Cats are tabby, striped, Siamese, slinky, tail-less, dappled, and hairless.

After Bonnard

Try pencilling around the sphinx-like, eagle-like, mysterious presence of an Ancient Egyptian feline sculpture – more monumental and sacred than any other cats. (They mummified cats!)

We owe a lot of great art to the waving tails of cats. How much "Fritz" (Paul Klee's cat) physically did in applying colour, I do not know; but I believe he was the inspiration for many of Klee's paintings. Balthus did a self-portrait of "H.M. The King of Cats". His cats have massive heads, and are important in many of his paintings of young girls. Paint pets! Unlike some infants, they do not mind, and there is much to enjoy. They are not as testing as a torso, but keep the brush moving! Encourage a child to play with a cat and a balloon. When the balloon bursts, you can continue from memory.

After Auberjonois

"A Cat and a Girl"   *After Balthus*

A screaming cat   After Auberjonois   *Scribbles of several Bonnard cats*   After Bonnard

Klee's cat "Fritz"

"Pets"

After Klee *Playing with a cat*

After Balthus

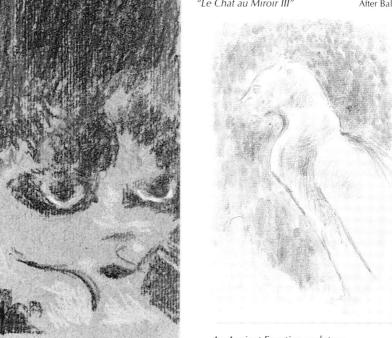

After Ensor

As Ensor became older in Ostend, he became eccentric. Perhaps he looked at Hieronymus Bosch.

After Bonnard

An early, almost Art Nouveau design

"Le Chat au Miroir III" After Balthus

An Ancient Egyptian sculpture

Horses

ONCE THERE WERE HORSES EVERYWHERE…. It was the horses' day off at the stables, except for one. She would pose for me. A bay. I wondered if a naked man on a horse would seem special. It was: they brought a potent symbolism with them. David sat without a saddle; the thighs encircling the horse's back were tense. The horse looked at me in a boss-eyed, disconcerting way. The willow leaves pointed all ways, and met the nettles, willow-herb, mullein, and blackberries; beyond were the boletus-toadstool-shaped, deer-nibbled oaks of Richmond Park. Picasso did gouaches of youths and horses (probably from drawings of circus people). Horses are difficult. Degas, Géricault,

"Diary sketch"
After Bonnard

Delacroix, Seurat, and Stubbs kept quite close to their appearance, but Chinese horses can vary a lot; and one of Bonnard's last works would have surprised Stubbs.

George Stubbs made a book of horse anatomy after cutting horses up in layers. The smell must have ensured privacy. The famous vine at Hampton Court was planted with a dead horse to feed on. For a bay-coloured horse, use Burnt sienna, an earth colour, a low-tone orange of great versatility.

Try scrubbing from thick to thin; but be careful when adding white – unless you want lifeless, doughy, flesh mixtures.

In Bonnard's diary are scribbled memory-aids for his penultimate painting, "The Circus Horse". Laugh at my messy diagram-copies, and discuss with me. Has he painted his last self-portrait as a Pagliacci-clown-weeping-horse, whose skull-eyes are confronting the artist when he was young, brush in hand? Bid farewell to Bonnard, acting in a sweet nightmare, with a winged dream horse; an image which haunts and dwells in the mind. Try copying this vision – an accretion of tentative scrubs of paint – and good luck be with you.

In the gloom as I left the bath, a tiny mirror caught a crinkly, wrinkly old horse's eye. My reflection.

"The Circus Horse"

After Bonnard

After Seurat

Youth on a polo pony

When you have tried all that the colour can do on its own, try adding yellow or red to Burnt sienna, the results are astonishing.

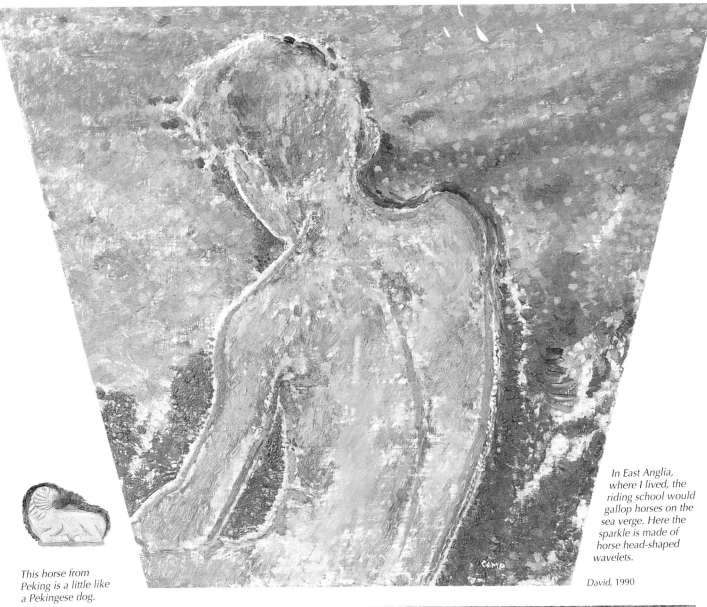

In East Anglia, where I lived, the riding school would gallop horses on the sea verge. Here the sparkle is made of horse head-shaped wavelets.

David, 1990

This horse from Peking is a little like a Pekingese dog.

David on a horse

A Horse near the Serpentine, 1992

Race Horses

CARS ARE ADJUSTED, wetted, and polished, and horses are wetted and groomed. Their smell does us no harm. Despite the robots of the Twenties and Léger's "Art Méchanique", advertisers are unable to make cars love back. Horses have long eyelashes, and floor teenage girls with their soulful frantic eyes. The whites of the eyes are surprisingly far back. Horses are difficult to draw, but easier to paint. Colour in the centres of forms first, as these change less than the edges of the silhouette. Look at a book of Géricault's horses, George Stubbs' *Anatomy of the Horse*, and Muybridge's *Animals in Motion*.

I went to Sandown Park race-course to see the horses. Not such open country as Newmarket, but there were wide views from the stadium. I felt the racing life was

After an Egyptian brush drawing

in some ways a version of all human activity. Binoculars covered much of it: the place where the winner was greeted; the toffs; the owners; the trainers; the punters; and the jockeys in pretty silks – some young, some shrunken.

Scribble-sketch the cars, the picnics, champagne, beer tins, fish and chips, and the bookies. The gamblers standing indoors surrounded by television screens and thick smoke are depressing to behold, as they yearn only for money. I had a vision of the "Night Mare" whinnying through an art world of collectors and dealers. It was time to go and stand close to the lush grass of the track. The "field" galloped by me in one-hundredth of a second. I remember the blundery hooves, whips, and tails. Stubbs and Degas would have known what to make of it.

After Ryder

Albert Pinkham Ryder used all kinds of makeshift techniques, resulting in cracking and yellowing. His "The Race Track" or "Death on a Pale Horse" compares the sharp curve of Death's scythe with the roundness of the course. The time-track of life where all are ultimately coursed and scythed.

After Ryder

After Rousseau

Scythes, skeletons, and emaciated horses excruciate in tumbrils of horror in Brueghel's "Triumph of Death".

After Brueghel

"War. It passes, terrifying, leaving despair, tears and ruin everywhere." Henri Rousseau painted a curious Russian story involving a chestnut horse dyed black; inspired at the same time by "The Apocalypse", where the fire and sulphurous smoke issuing from the horses mouths, and a like power in their serpent-tails, kills a third of mankind. Ravens with bloody beaks obey the loud angel who tells all the birds to eat the flesh.

Painters of a certain temper have seemed to enjoy painting Hell, and knew what went on there. Medieval art is rich in "Dooms"; here, birds are shown enthusiastically biting the impious.

After the Angers Apocalypse tapestries

Degas uses the pointed end of the brush for bursting energy. Eakins and Degas were among the first to know (by photography) how horses really moved their legs at speed. Muybridge used banks of cameras with trip-wires, but scratchy paint is faster than photographs.

Edgar Degas, *Jockeys*, c. 1890

A long neck speeds up a gallop.

After Auberjonois

Draw with hurtful Indian ink lines from photographs.

Pegasus and the 'Oss

After being a student at Edinburgh, I painted the lush, undisturbed Suffolk countryside. My paints, rag, palette, brushes, and even the painting – all of which I carried in a basket – were warm in the sun, and I felt part of the hedge and the high grasses, the air thick with pollen. While I sat deep in umbellifera and nettles painting, a man invited me to see his collection of pictures. They were hung frame to frame, every picture was of a horse – he said he "knew an 'oss". I expect his aesthetic appreciation was slight, so it is fortunate he did not see my painting of "the noble creature". I felt rural: dug a celery trench, rushed from tree to tree, dabbing fast as the buds burst into flower. I followed a horse as it moved around a field. In those days, my sheets of paper became filled with detached hooves, manes, fetlocks, and other pieces of horse.

Happy the horse! Adored by girls, the noble horse, with whom no boyfriend can compare. Paint with watercolour the loved, lovely eyes, which make the jodhpured swoon.

Roger and Angelica, and a fine, winged horse

After Redon

Thinking of Bonnard's diary sketches, and his advice about moving a pencil with ease, do sketch-drawings at a good pace, while looking at a large book of horse photographs. Keep up a flow, using a dryish brush, if

you like, or a pen. Look at Eadweard Muybridge's Animals in Motion – too small, but seeing a sequence of movements can help in arriving at an image. Degas and Eakins found these sequential photographs useful.

This winged horse, Pegasus, looks somewhat Chinese.   After Redon

Pegasus. The stables breed for speed, while the artists design sunken eyes.   After Redon

After Redon

A nocturnal being, of the White Goddess/Night Mare family, perhaps?   After Redon

After Gauguin

The powdery, pastel pencil surface has a decorative, slow-motion, tapestry-like security. It is in the shade of hot sunlight. In the original, small strokes of colour are painted on a canvas almost as rough as sackcloth, but not so hairy. (When canvas is too hairy, stretch it, and pass a flame across it fast, and do not set it on fire!) Because there is little gesture, Gauguin and Bonnard depend on the colours buzzing on the spot.

The paint marks are too active for this rough daub to look like Gauguin. Many paintings work by moving rhythms vigorously through and across the picture. Animals invite a galloping application. Munch and Manet have made horses gallop towards the spectator. There is a Courbet in Munich of a riderless horse which crosses the canvas dramatically.

After Gauguin

The soulful eye of the horse

That house filled with horse paintings had none more important than by "Sartorius". This rough is about "Hambletonian", a famous racehorse of the time, by the great artist Stubbs.

After Stubbs

Lurchers, Pigdogs, and Mastiffs

WERE THE CHINESE able to enter the lives of their subjects? Well, they concentrated on the lives of snails in ways pop-artists never did. David Hockney's dachshunds care nothing for dogs on television. Some of us pursue sights as urgently as dogs smell trails. London transforms yard by yard, glance by glance; as Cézanne said, "Only turn the head and there are many subjects". The city is a smell-paradise for dogs. Do they care for the smells we smell? Coffee, croissants, fried bacon? Perfumes and Thames mud? The triggers of emotion are mysterious. William Blake wrote: "How do you know but ev'ry bird that cuts the airy way, is an immense world of delight, closed by your senses five?"

Jock McFadyen owns a fine poodle, George. He is McFadyen's watchdog, and keeps his dog forms right. Two dogs smell. They symbolize degradation but are themselves actually overjoyed by the odour trail. Litter is offensive to the upper classes, but McFadyen's pictures are bought by nobs for safe slumming. The gemlike cars and houses are remote enough to be charming.

Jock McFadyen, *Copperfield Road*, 1990 (detail below)

D'Arcy hunts a thrown ball so fast he almost disappears, then returns triumphant. At other times he is still as a lizard, instantly entranced. Paint with animal urgency.

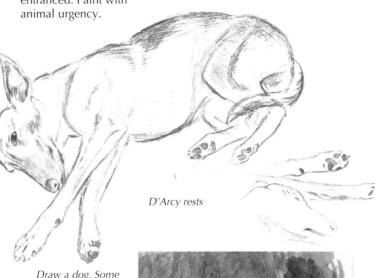

D'Arcy rests

Draw a dog. Some dogs can be asked to keep still. The entranced state D'Arcy drops into seems to be like the painting state. Trances can be entered fast or slow; films show Matisse drawing quickly. The lizard may be still but its tongue is fast. Be aware: the lurcher of the imagination is a greyhound. Except for the nose, a dachshund is not like a wolf; and except for the peeing, a wolf is not like a pekingese.

After Mantegna

Susan and D'Arcy enjoying the night air.

Dogs, bone-formal, in the "Camera degli Sposi" in Mantua.

D'Arcy at night. London and St. Paul's in the distance. The side panels declare that he is indoors, the haloed edges of the dog allow the sky dabs to fall back from the animal who is in a monumental pose.

D'Arcy in Islington, 1992

D'Arcy running at full-speed. His owner, daffodils, clouds, ocean, even the dog itself, are demolished in the energetic clifftop rush.

D'Arcy Running, 1992

Owls

GOYA'S OWLS accompanied witches, and when Shakespeare wrote of mysterious foul deeds, he shook nature with storms, while owls screeched. Owls are symbols of wisdom, are quiet as a falling feather and possess tiny brains. Picasso had a pet owl. It meant that any pair of circles could be brushed into being an owl, whenever he did not want them to become a skull, or one of his popping-eyed late self-portraits.

The top part of a decoy. (The tethered owl is on a long pole, carried by a boy.)

After Goya

A conjuration of owls and witches

After Goya

Pen-copy a pet owl

After Picasso

A wise owl. In humans an owl-look does not denote wisdom. Standing with a deep grey streaky ground, paint an equal dabbing of grey of the same darkness for the body. Flick in the breast feathers and eye with creamy white. Then paint with darks until the bird looks ready to hoot.

After Bosch

Paint a tantric sexual oval, topping it with two circles for eyes. Make a flying bird-shape become a flesh-tearing beak. Let the brush take charge: like a decoy owl on its string, it will go in for the kill. Hardly more than a doodled pair of circles with an oval, and you have an owl to play with.

After
Picasso

After Bosch

Dab into wet white:
skulls become owls,
sometimes.

After Picasso

After Bosch

Penned and crayoned skulls

After Picasso

An African mask, with circles
for supernatural eyes.

Cats sometimes resemble owls
and accompany witches.

Fish and Crustaceans

AT BIRTH WE CRIED AT THE DRY AIR. Fish out of water gasp. Water attracts us. To see fish alive, visit the Brighton Aquarium, gloomy after the brilliance of seaside light. Its old tanks are conducive to drawing a strange eel, or a Nursing Shark. Light may come from below, which is eerie, and the eye of a spectator seen through a tank is like an extra small fish in a shoal. Michael Andrews braved aquaria kitsch to paint schools of tropical fish. On television, fish perform so well the "box" seems to fill with water. Fish are strange. (Even stranger when brought up from deep water.) Klee, Redon, Picasso, and Matisse painted fish in all their strangeness, as wildly as in nature. The fish of Hieronymus Bosch fly people through the sky. Soutines's herrings are about poverty. Choose from the often magnificent still-life arrangements on the fishmonger's slab. Most kinds of fish – lobsters, prawns, oysters, and crabs – have been painted superbly by Chardin, Ensor, Goya, Picasso, and Braque – but never Cézanne. I expect fish did not stay fresh long enough for him to complete his slow pictures. Goldfish in bowls circulated continuously for Matisse.

After Picasso

After Picasso

After Picasso

After Picasso

The surprise of their tiny circle eyes combines with their ravenous mouths for Picasso comedy.

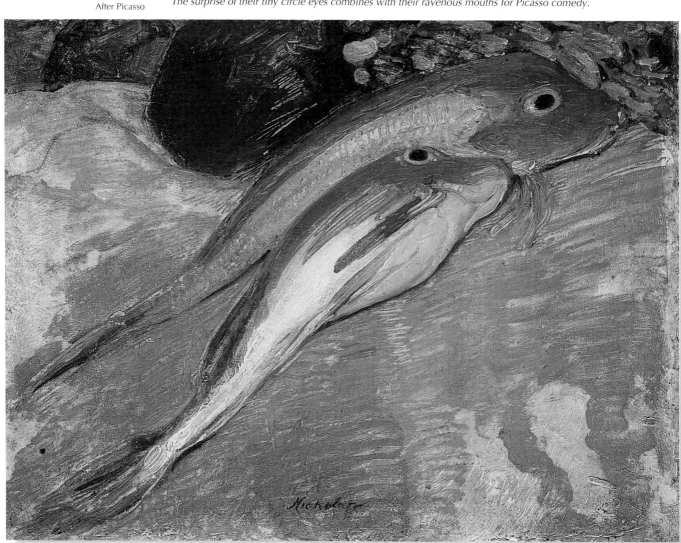

Painted with a succulent affection, and few colours. The touch has followed the spiny sliminess, and climaxed at the large dark eyes.

William Nicholson, *Gurnards*, 1931

Fish carrying people. So exact is the Bosch world we believe his dreams. Copy and do not make them comical.

After Bosch

The catch spread on the beach. By an obliging fisherman perhaps.

After Matisse

Marouflay (stick) canvas to wood. The flatness of the surfaces are emphasized. The small head begins a sequence of overlappings within the picture.

Mackerel, 1971

The fish are deliberately made ornamental.

After Carra

Fish are comical. The large lips and round eyes are funny. Sharpen greasy crayons and try a Trumpet fish.

After Ensor

Herrings symbolize poverty.

After de Chirico

The Nursing Shark

The eel resembles an aunt who is an "old trout".

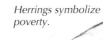

Sunflowers

THE SIGNS FOR PUBLIC HOUSES named "The Sun" have human features and flame-like rays. Van Gogh gave up preaching, and spent his last ten years tuning in to the brightness and life-giving force of the sun. Do not look at the sun: it blinds. Through blackened glass it is boring. But feel its warmth waken your bones.

Make diagram-drawings and scribble paintings of van Gogh's sun-marks; the beautiful daubed rounds of close yellows, creamy oranges, and apple-greens. He was endlessly inventive, no one can copy the sun and see.

In a picture, the sunflower is a symbolic face as powerful, and as paint-shattering as the sun. Van Gogh gave Gauguin two pictures of sunflower heads in exchange for his picture of Martinique, then relentlessly filled the rooms in the Yellow House (where Gauguin was to sleep) with six sunflower masterpieces.

Aspire to beat the sun in your picture, let colours batter each other until they glow like beaten gold. The van Gogh sunflowers, as we remember them, are bright yellow; but in actuality, they are mainly ochres. Matisse painted the sun black. A yellow house need not be round to be the sun.

After Blake

Sunflowers have been subjects for John Bratby, Georges Braque, Norman Adams, Paula Modersohn-Becker, Piet Mondrian, Emil Nolde, and William Blake. But when Blake came to the end of his wonderful series of illustrations for Dante's vision, his feelings rebelled; the mystical white rose of chastity, which supports the Queen of Heaven in glory, became a sunflower, sepalled and dishy as a flying saucer. It is well worthwhile to copy. Examining William Blake's Dante designs, copy-follow the body-forming rhythms of Blake's imagination that urgently contruct Earth, Heaven, Purgatory, and Hell. Like most of us, Blake was more puzzled by Heaven; the highest points are less lusty. Pencil-scribble lines; strengthen, swell, and sharpen, using a tiny brush. Follow the vision, which gradually takes charge. Like the plots of William Shakespeare, these night-gowns, from Gothic sources, and Michelangelo engraving-derived bodies are second-hand. But Blake is world-shaking.

Picasso said: "It's the sun in the belly with a million rays. The rest is nothing. It's only for that reason that Matisse is Matisse – it's because he carries the sun in his belly."

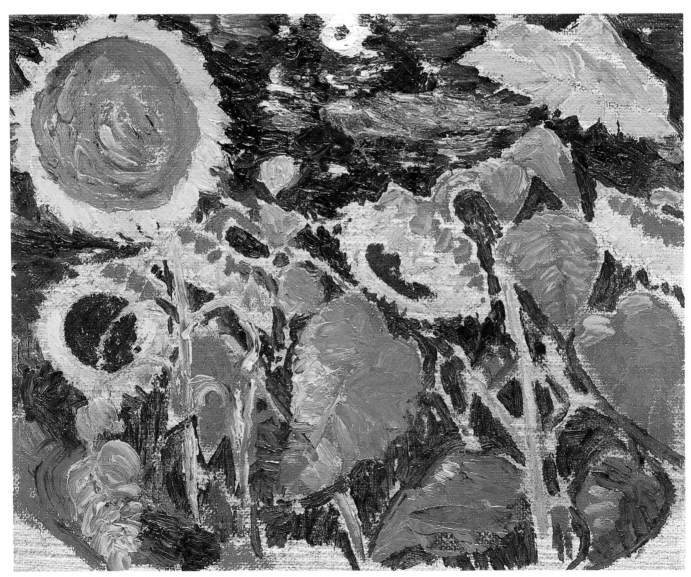

The rough shapes on the right are shown to be sunflowers by the circular flowers on the left, sunflowers at night are mysterious: as are eclipses.

Sunflowers, 1993

A whirling sunflower becoming a flaming sun.

After
Paul Nash

Graham Sutherland found swelling forms and ogees in Blake, which he could use.

After
Sutherland

The sun descends, jackdaws fly roughly, like fragments of burnt paper in the wind. The feather flutters, random in the up-draught. Use light, broken marks, for a subject that is little heavier than clouds. Clouds are a pretend steam bath for the reddening sun.

Beachy Head, Sun,
and Feather, 1989

Late, eccentric suns by Giorgio de Chirico. The dark, distant sun is connected to a lighter, closer sun on the easel.

Other suns

After de Chirico

Sunflower heads

The Queen of Heaven in Glory (Paradiso Canto 31)

After Blake

Diagrams of over 30 corn circles. Whoever did them, they suggest sun-engendered forms.

Sun-diagrams that move and rotate

Daisy

ISTANCING BY OVERLAPPING is especially hazardous when subjects are not easily recognizable. Unwittingly trendy, throwing pollen to the wind, the child wore a daisy-chain. I wanted to paint daisies and clover. Both are small. Nurserymen have bred daisies to be large, and in many colours, but I like the common daisy. This year daisies throve. No painter has painted clover; with eyes baby-high I overlapped flower over flower; recession on the level. It did not work! The clover looked like chrysanthemums.

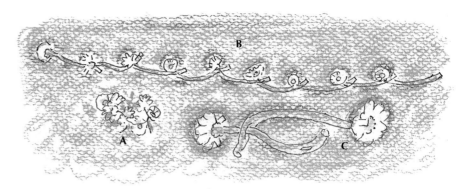

"Chrysanthemum"   After Hokusai

In most landscape paintings where the eye-level is low, some overlapping is involved.

Plain and muddled daisy-chains:

A *Seen end-on, no-one would know it was a daisy-chain.*

B *Daisies in chains.*

C *Wounded daisies await enchainment.*

"The Resurrection, Cookham". The revived girl in Cookham churchyard buries her face in a small sunflower, or big yellow daisy. Most flowers can be thought of as having faces.

After Spencer

The clover's size is made clear by a mouse.

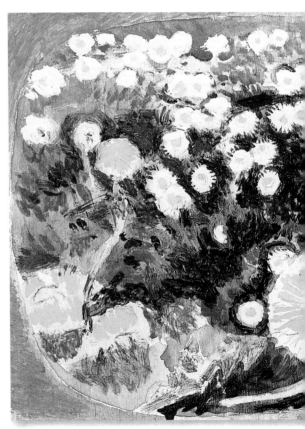

Daisies look their natural size, because dandelions have not been bred large. Clouds of daisies like starry meadows mirror the Milky Way.

Although Gainsborough planted water-ducks so he could put them in foregrounds, close-ups are still rare in painting, although frequent in photographs. Corot played safe, treating the middle distance as the foreground.

Battersea Power Station, 1993

Daisies, 1993

To make the clover appear its proper size, I introduced a blackbird. A cockney blackbird's "manor", grub-rich daisy and clover embellished – a bird paradise. Paint him black enough and he might sing.

Roses

WHEN ANDY WARHOL silk-screened Marilyn Monroe, the erotic lips were squeezed on to canvas, over and over. There were red rosebud lips for all. Fashion designers are much kissed: after clothes shows their cheeks are lipsticky and high with perfume. Renoir and Balthus painted roses as if they were the

Rose buds, sharp edged with watercolour

girls of their dreams. Picasso had a rose period but rarely painted roses. Corot painted a rose as sumptuously as Chardin painted raspberries.

Inhale the rose heavy air, and paint a rich, deep, red rose, with Cremnitz or Underpainting white, over a copper-coloured priming. Matthew Smith might have used "Maroger's Medium", we could use a thixotropic gel. When the rose shape is set, sweep in the luscious transparent plum and mulberry colours. Permanent rose is cleaner than Alizarin crimson, but not as dark. For the depths of the flower, use Cobalt violet, Manganese violet, or Mineral violet.

Permanent rose and Permanent magenta are light-fast. Even when pale, Genuine rose, Madder, and Rose madder deep have stood the test of time. Rose doré is a paler, slightly scarlet form. The Madder plant is getting rarer. Use it only for enchantment.

Historians divide time into periods, "Ages" of Stone, Iron, Bronze, and then came times for Glass, Plastics, and the Media. Warhol lived in the Media Age. Andy was a personality of massive media dissemination. Like Dali, he had been a window-dresser, and used every media-means to make himself known: the press, film, radio, books, magazines, television, and the reproduction and repetition of photographs. Images were printed in paint: Marilyn Monroe was dabbed and squeezed through a silk-screen. Having Marilyn repeated a lot of times on a traditional, primed canvas from the Warhol Factory was good for selling to museums, and to the rich. The pictures were tasteful. Silk-screening flattens automatically, and flattening has been one of the easy ways of making art look advanced. The repetition makes a pattern. A Warhol is easy to recognize and looks decorative. Shocking pink, acid greens; cows, giant flowers, and for the serious viewer, motor accidents and electric chairs. Wow! That was the Media Age. Now for ours. An electronic era? A rose is a rose is a rose – a Gertrude Stein reminder.

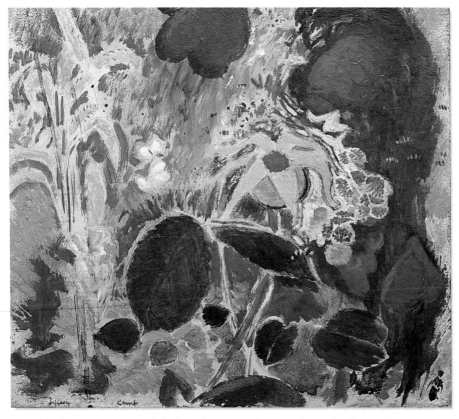

A rosehip. In autumn, roses are full of surprises, wasps, hips, earwigs, and falling petals.

Rosebuds opening, soft pinks against orange chalks

A soft, old ash-pink rose

A wild rose by the sea. Rub and scrub until all the shapes edge up to each other, and clouds allude to knees, and breasts allude to petals, and the softness of summer haze is flower-like in the circular format.

The old rose is angular and concave.

After Balthus

Lips

The rose is not having an easy time; although not sick, it is being soaked by rain. Drops are forming necklaces on its petals and a flying worm is approaching (only partly visible).

After Corot

Roses can be eloquent, petal-sweet or maliciously thorny.

After Warhol

A frightening, repulsive flatness occurs if lips are pressed against glass.

Grasses and Moths

GRASS CAN BE SCRUBBED in casually, or be an assemblage of grass-blade-shaped brush marks. If you care as much about the wonder of it as van Gogh, it becomes a tragic meditation. (His letters tell of the pain of red and green, and he painted poppies severely red against the grasses.) But grass is complex and can be treated like portraiture. Stanley Spencer and Albrecht Dürer knew the way to do this, and would paint each grass as a separate subject, of graceful filaments. Sometimes, van Gogh would almost fill his picture with grass, looking down on it. I have made grass less heavy. It is possible, on cliffs or hills, to see grass from below. It is dry and light as froth, and softens the margins of rivers. Try some light gouache over grey, or fill the interstices with water or sky colour. For filaments and flecks, you might use masking fluid (a rubber solution that peels off). The pale shapes left can be modified afterwards. Edward Bawden, Paul Nash, Eric Ravilious, and others scratched in dry and wet watercolour and used wax crayons as resists.

Sit in the long, blowing grass on the cliffs near the sea, and touch in the tiny seeds and distant yachts. Do not disturb the dozing moth. Moths are mysterious – silent and camouflaged by day, and at night, harmlessly disturbing. They are furry, like tiny mice, with crawly legs and feelers. They flutter in the grass. Some are fast and small enough to enter a nostril or water an eye. Odilon Redon was inspired by real moths to invent imaginatively.

Scented herbage of my breast
Leaves from you I yield, I write, to be perused best afterwards,
Tomb-leaves, body-leaves growing up above me, above death,
Perennial roots, tall leaves – O the winter shall not freeze your delicate leaves,
Every year shall you bloom again – out from where you retired you shall emerge again.

Walt Whitman, *Leaves of Grass*

Whitman was thinking of those slain in the American Civil War, pushing up the grass.

Foreground grasses, and a moth. The grasses increase the vibrancy of the blue.

Moth and
Grasses, 1993

These complex overlappings in the views above and below must be done clearly, each item presented somewhat obviously, in its characterful shape: jackdawy; appley; grassy; yachty; lighthousey; skyey; seay; finally, painterly.

Cut an apple in half and pencil in the many tiny items around it: jackdaws; grasses; yachts; the lighthouse; a knife; another painter; a seagull...then fill in around them with small brushfuls of background colour until it looks real.

Beachy Head, Grass, and Apples, 1993

Real artists follow their desires. Inveigled even to play with subjects as light as thistledown. Daniel Miller has not feared to follow this dead moth's camouflage – a merge of pink and brown, almost disappearing into twilight greys.

Daniel Miller, *Moth*, 1993

Grasses over the lighthouse, Beachy Head. The cliff, like an immense convexity, subtends the hollow space.

Beachy Head,
Jackdaws, 1993

On a wood panel – all is done by suggestion. At the top right are the leaves of a horse chestnut tree. The picture could be continued.

The moth hovers, made frantic by the oil lamp. It is almost weightless, painted with a pale dragging brush. Balthus painted on rough surfaces. His slow rhythms make for quiet moods.

After Balthus

Redon would wander from form to form. After looking at living moths, the mysteries would thicken. Browns joined pinks or reds on umber nights.

After Redon

Shine

LEONARD MCCOMB is aware of tradition, and enjoys working within it. He has made the rarely painted aubergine exist as a "Still Life". McComb works within the easel-painting categories of the last 200 years: Still Life, Portrait, Landscape, and Nude. He does not get his categories mixed, as I do. Usually, McComb places the main subject close to the centre of the picture. The categories have a long history. Remove the storyline and altarpiece framework, extract the arrows, and St. Sebastian becomes a Nude. Remove the figures from Giovanni Bellini's "Agony in the Garden", and you can call it a *Landscape*. Steal the blue cloak from the Madonna, and a cushion from Christ, and you have a *Portrait*. Remove everything else from a Signorelli reredos, and a Still Life full of fruit remains.

The aubergine shape resembles many other subjects – slugs, leeches, beetles, and hedgehogs.

Sacred sculptures are oiled and stroked smooth by hands. Constantin Brancusi rubbed and smoothed his sculptures to a keen finesse. Gloss is attractive. In the old days, enamelling was called "coach-painting". It involved doing a lot of rubbing, and using sun-thickened linseed oil, or stand oil with varnish, and the longer it took to dry, the better. Lead, cobalt, and manganese driers might weaken the paint film.

Slick gloss is unpleasant, but armour by Giorgione shines beautifully. With your discriminating eyes, paint an aubergine, dark and glossy. And perhaps, if a beetle scuttles by, paint it large and scarlet. Or if a shiny lacquered "Beetle" car comes by, paint it any size you like. The traditional categories are all-embracing. Use a gel, or the oil-vehicles of the past – and may your subjects shine!

A thick, rich palette-knifing of aubergine-coloured paint. On the fruiterer's counter, it shone with wine-black brightness. Painting with knives is painting with shines. (But, with beeswax added, Mary Potter made pictures that did not shine.)

Leonard McComb,
Aubergine, 1994–95

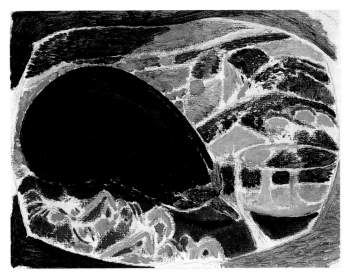

My aubergine is accompanied by two affectionate heads, a glass of stout, puddles on the cliffs, and the sea. It is done using the very poisonous Emerald green, which Cézanne liked to use.

An Eggplant

After Matisse

Hen's eggs decorated with figures. Painter friends who were given boiled eggs for tea by Patrick Symons, were encouraged to decorate an egg for Easter. With a small brush, see if you can ornament a simple, perfect, natural egg. Passionately. If you cannot incorporate the whole Easter story, paint a celandine, king cup, or buttercup. The unprimed eggshell surface is enticing, the surface-area of an egg is surprisingly large. Try painting with a brushful of golden Cadmium yellow, as if it were the yolk.

Every time we take the top off an egg there is a surprise: delicate as a flower. Real eggs are much deeper surprises than Fabergé eggs.

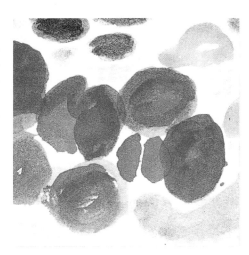

Blobs beginning to look like ladybird beetles. They swell to suggest plumpness. If shines had been added they would have blown up like balloons.

Puddles on the cliffs are egg-shaped, but flat ovals naturally tend to become plump. Puddles must be kept flat.

Manet's Last Apple

I T MIGHT HAVE BEEN THOUGHT A "STUDY" if the painter had been young. But it is one of Manet's final statements. Pencil copying is fast, copying with paint is technically demanding. Do it elaborately only to help in penetrating the thought of a painter you particularly admire. On a simply primed surface, think with brush in hand, aiming at discovery.

A little before Manet's grisly end in 1883, he painted an apple on a plate. I hoped, as I copied a little piece, that I would find its quick, bright, oily secret. I felt the ease of Goya and Velásquez. I made it almost as swollen as a fruit by Edward Burra; a cross between an apple, a grapefruit, and a melon. It made me thirsty. After a lifetime making grand figure compositions, Manet painted violets, asparagus, clematis, an apple, and a lemon, each on its own. Courbet may have been the first to do a pear alone. Somehow it seems, by doing these subjects in isolation, a new awareness in painting was born.

An apple seems a modest subject, but it will test you. Pose the apple simply. Mine is against the sea, a near-circle in a near-square. Paint your apple robustly. It will not look like mine, or like any other painted apple. Think of all the pippins painted by famous artists. Scribble-copy from Milton Avery, Paula Modersohn-Becker, Giacometti, Picasso, Manet, de Chirico, Matisse, Balthus, Magritte, Cézanne, Klee, Renoir. They all look like apples. The essence of apple is secret. Artists may think they know the right conditions for its distillation. But good pictures of apples are rare.

A sculptor's drawings. Follow with a small brush and thin grey paint.

After Giacometti

After Manet

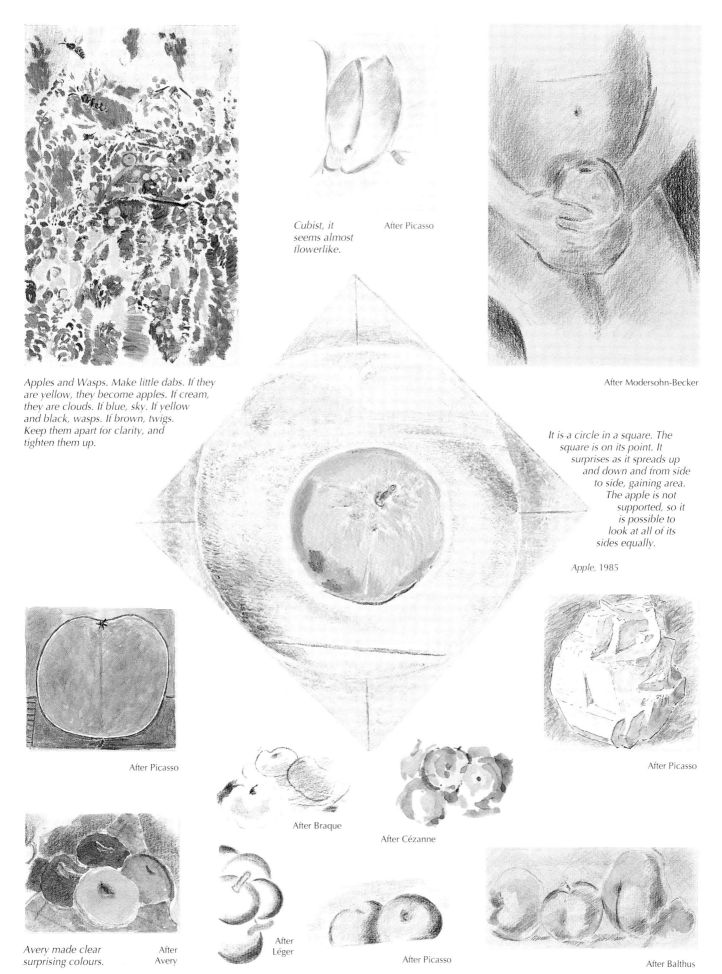

Cubist, it seems almost flowerlike.

After Picasso

After Modersohn-Becker

Apples and Wasps. Make little dabs. If they are yellow, they become apples. If cream, they are clouds. If blue, sky. If yellow and black, wasps. If brown, twigs. Keep them apart for clarity, and tighten them up.

It is a circle in a square. The square is on its point. It surprises as it spreads up and down and from side to side, gaining area. The apple is not supported, so it is possible to look at all of its sides equally.

Apple, 1985

After Picasso

After Picasso

After Braque

After Cézanne

Avery made clear surprising colours.

After Avery

After Léger

After Picasso

After Balthus

217

Apple

Patrick George said in 1994 that although his measuring way of thinking had not changed, he did not now make arm's-length measurements so often. Vermeer used a camera obscura. William Coldstream and Patrick George did not. They looked carefully, and believed what their eyes showed them. (The resulting pictures were scarcely as soft as Graham Bell, or designed as hard as Seurat.) George thinks two-eyed, measures one-eyed, and paints a solution. When an apple is close, the eyes see around it a little. I wonder what would be the effect of a prolonged viewing, wearing widely-spaced prismatic lenses? Would we see extra-stereoscopically? A distant view, seen upside-down with your head between your legs, is surprisingly spatial. Patrick George marks out an apple with feeling, to be non-scrumptious, no show-apple, and naturally green as seen. And he paints in quick perspective.

Here is a tract, a credo: an inoculation against obscurity, the ubiquity of puffed, fixed, developed photographs: those shiny seducers, which Degas, Sickert, and Hockney squeezed life into, at personal hazard. Photographs contain a lot of information you do not need, and little which is useful, while a good paint-drawing contains all that is needed and little else. Polaroids attract and engender sloth.

Painting directly from a subject is demanding. I have worked longer than was comfortable in windy, cold, or excessively hot places. It is good to look a long while at something special. The subject fixes itself in your mind like a nest full of eggs which may hatch soon or late. Making art is rarely comfortable. Even in the studio something will ache, or be difficult to see. Out-of-doors, aiming for verisimilitude or precision in the teeth of a howling gale can be agonizing.

Paint fragments of a bitten apple

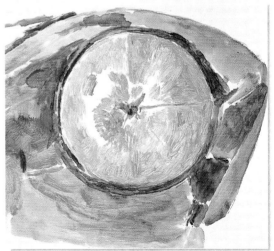

Apples oily on black

Make fat, tart, lemon-green dabs radiate, like a star in a faceted circle, within a raw, umber oblong, framed within a rectangle.

Paint glowingly, close-tonally, on a dark ground without white.

Patrick George's apple. The voluptuous fruit offers itself to the artist, who gives it a careful viewing, and with long practice in looking, brushes it in drily; and dismisses it, with as much juice as it had before, and curiously present on the cardboard.

Patrick George,
Apple I, 1994

Apple and Hang-glider, 1991

Hang-gliders, high on Beachy Head. The wind whistles through the fingers, harness, and rigging. By the sea, when waves become large enough to be spectacular, conditions are brutal. At Beachy Head, for hang-gliders to soar, the wind must be strongly from the South-east. (The bigger you are, the bigger the kite must be.)

Patrick George, *Apple II,* 1994   *Seaside apples*

It has been said of Cézanne that his paintings were done with the tip of the brush. Certainly, his touch was sensitive. He may have used the responsive "mongoose" hair brushes (mottled grey and fairly springy). Meaningful touches are only possible if the paint is of just the right consistency. A carefully prepared canvas helps the paint to leave the brush consistently.

Lemon

IMAGINE, IF YOU WILL, a solid lemon, flat. Paint some lemons. They hang on black twigs in Italy in winter. On a small, rectangular canvas, previously brushed with Lead white, with some brush strokes of Zinc yellow, white, and transparent Golden ochre, caress and form a lemon shape. Dab it with little strokes, thinking in terms of circles of various sizes, each trying to escape. Then do something similar to the background, dabbing in circles as if each were trying to nudge the fruit. Make arcs at the corners of the canvas, thus preventing the background slipping from the level of the lemon. (It is as if you were tucking the lemon up in bed, and making it secure in its picture.) Concentrate. Paint carefully, and all will happen intuitively, even beautifully. Paint at your natural pace.

Matisse used Lemon yellow at its brightest. Lemon can be modified subtly towards pink, with Permanent rose, or towards green with Light cobalt green. Think of the rose-tinted glasses on the lights of St. Mark's Square in Venice – golden posies against the sharp mystery of the lagoon.

Paint a lemon as flat as you can. It is ovoidal, with cones pointing away from a central sphere. Examine possible colours. Lemons are dimpled, and move through the spectrum, from Monastral green towards Burnt umbery-lemony-orange. I have described a lemon: solid, ripe, and sculptural. But you desire

Little Renoir-like dabs

flatness, because flatness allows the colour to shine bright and clear. Imagine a garden roller has squashed the lemon flat to become bigger in area, and pictorially closer in size to that of a real fruit.

Next, place a lemon on a surface. Perhaps you can describe the shape of the shadow – a long half-moon, with added half-moon additions at each end, and a straighter variation beneath. You will see, after this description, that painting is not easy to describe in words. If you are dismayed by the shadow, hang the lemon up by a thread, or arrange it, free from shadow, on glass. For another lemon exercise, cut the lemon in half. Its segments form a radiant rose-window of juice, like solid juice hanging in space. Braque painted lemons with thin, transparent paint; this was supported on a dark ground containing particles of powdered cork, sand, or sawdust (this prevents the paint running down). You do not have to paint a shadow. (Gauguin said shadows were "optional".) Dream a lemon. A lemon dream is less an exercise, more an inspiration – which is learning's goal.

Renoir caressed lemons with small strokes of a brush and Matisse found cursive, casual ways of drawing on canvas with charcoal so that this, the brightest yellow fruit, could be used for areas of explosive colour. Cézanne and van Gogh enjoyed using Chrome yellow and Chrome orange.

Expanding and contracting marks

Semi-transparent paint over black

Reflections, and a yellow lemon gleams in the night.

Tower Bridge Lemons, 1986

Charcoal energizes even pale yellows.

After Matisse

Painting lemons by painting backgrounds

Various brown-yellow mixtures

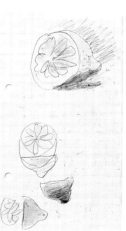

Exploratory scribble-diagrams in the manner of Claes Oldenburg

Opposite: the cut surface of a lemon – almost trompe l'oeil.

Pear

T HE TWO WARS SPOILED MY PARENTS' LIVES. Claude Rogers said his life had been blighted. Harold Gilman escaped the enormous slaughter of the First World War, only to die of the great influenza epidemic that followed. In the boredom and blight of war and its aura, fear stalks sensitive artists. William Coldstream, reacting against the specious dealer-led Parisian arty painting of between the wars, invented and developed an unprecedented way of painting. Using arm's length measuring with thumb and pencil, closing one eye,

he made cautious, continually adjusted touch-diagrams, which gradually became sensuous pictures. He accepted certain limits of colour, gesture, and design. The measuring marks, cutting the cone of vision, might be vermilion. He painted some very fine portraits during the 1940s, very slowly. All measurements of Time are disturbing and frightening: watches, clocks, pendulums, and the hourglass "Sands of Time". The measurement marks invented by William Coldstream are the marks of his decisions in time, the spore of his fear.

Euan Uglow, *Oval Pear*, 1974

I have looked at Euan Uglow's painting of a pear for 30 years. Its measures continue to move me. He has always painted pears: they are the cornerstones of his art. He makes strong pears, marking them as a sculptor points stone, establishing safe eye-holds and nodal points. He uses the same process

for a nude, a duck, a loaf, and the things chosen are mostly rounded and are placed against flat backgrounds. Seurat wrote: "They see poetry in what I do, but I just apply my method."

The shadow cast by a blue steel rod is plotted meticulously. The rod implies a central stalk, a visible spine. The whole is like a strong girl with a healthy complexion.

Euan Uglow, *Pear*, 1982

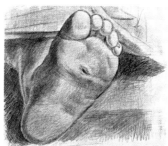

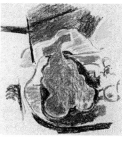

The dead Christ's big toe is pear-shaped. It is from imagination.

After Mantegna

A flat pear, which, except for its context, could be a toad or the back of a woman.

After Braque

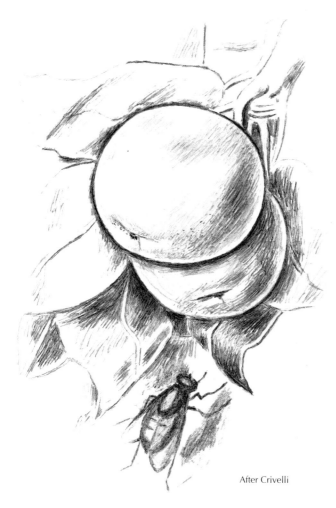

After Crivelli

An apple, imagined with a lively roundness, and a fly for life's transience. Flattening is achieved by making strong-contrast outlines as hoops.

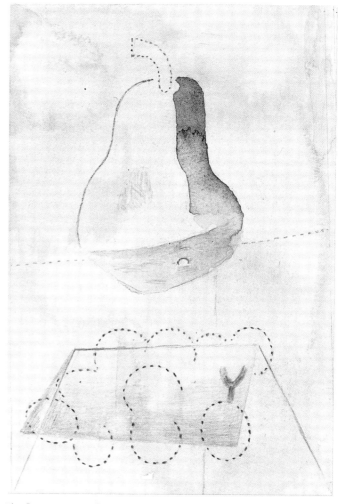

A poor diagram to suggest some edges by Uglow. Apples, pears, stomachs, thighs, and loaves made flat, and with arcs of fixed extent pressing against background areas. Although under firm control, geometric, and tested by eye, the subjects are most sensuous, and he knows pears are less still than apples.

After Uglow

The flattest pears are by Stuart Davis. Flat is simpler than bas-relief. Bas-relief is simpler than free-standing sculpture. To be flat, simple, and good, you must be very good!

After Davis

After Pissarro

After Pissarro

After Gris

After Gris, copying Cézanne

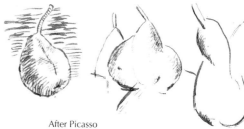

After Picasso

Sandwich

WE ARE HUNGRY AND NEED a snack. We are open to suggestion. Here is a sandwich shop, its window full. The sandwiches look like mouths full of lettuce, cheese, and mayonnaise ready to greet you, and tongues of ham ready to lick you. Where a rogue is selling sandwiches in the park, the filling is a smarm of lard and it is called a Pork Sausage Sandwich. In The City, sandwiches are meals, and customers give exact orders. But the mouth-shape is a confidence-trick: the stuff is in the middle and nowhere else, then it is sliced so that the stuff is more visible.

Bonnard knew how to compare paint with food. Here is tomato ketchup out of a tube, a knife full of Naples yellow as butter, and a brushful of brown ochre depicting bread.

Paint some sandwiches out of your head. From the filling side they are ogee-shaped. Put into them your favourite foods. You can be inventive, or you can look at the menu-board. It is mostly a new subject matter, for sandwiches are rarer in art than guitars. The texture and colour of brown bread will enhance many colours. Think of beef, horseradish, and wholemeal bread. Or go for it: mix avocado, gorgonzola and anchovy in a bap. Some Scandanavians enjoy open sandwiches, which really are still lives.

Before the age of spread bread, Bonnard lived in a world of tarts, oysters, strawberries, and wondrous sweetmeats. Each had its special basket or dish, and a gardener, servant, or cook was pleased that Bonnard would eat or paint it.

A portrait of Bonnard. The nose is a long arc. Redon has lessened the spectacles. After Redon

If it helps, think of it as a still life. With pastel pencils, draw two brown sandwiches with tomato slices. Almost a face: with a prawn nose, it almost grins.

A pen-drawn sandwich with crayoned filling is a fast food sketch.

No longer a sandwich-shape: a torpedo of French bread, bursting with ham, onions, tomatoes, and mayonnaise.

The side-on ogee sandwich.

Scribble the bread texture. The white and green bulb of spring onion entices.

A pizza slice. Pen in the olives, anchovies, and pepperoni.

A samosa. The pastry purses are nicely triangular, but secretive till bitten.

Two sandwiches in a plastic carton. Record the various textures, shiny to rough. The more elaborately you do it, the more hungry you will become.

A pile of sandwiches in a shop window. A tower of deceit?

End-on sandwich-mouths with hammy lips, or pink with seafood relish.

Pierre Bonnard's table of visual and edible delights. Bonnard did not need elaborate materials to make his pictures. A bowl of cherries; peaches; an orange and a lemon. A little rectangular palette (the kind which fits in a painting box); a set of watercolours; a can of oil; five or six brushes (square, not round as I had expected); and plenty of newspaper and rags. The fruit bowl and the smeared palette resembled each other in 1937 to the short-sighted Bonnard. Without his glasses, all was a mingle of colours.

"Strawberries". Paint them till the juice oozes soft and strong.   After Bonnard

With watery marks, see what is on the large tablecloth. Two blues move between shadows and objects, making straight linkages. The blues oppose the creams, oranges, and yellows; obviously begun on a day when Bonnard's diary entry was "Beau".

After Bonnard

The cats have seen the oysters. Take a pen and some slightly diluted (use distilled water if possible) Indian, non-waterproof ink, and scratch around some Bonnard foods. They are so delicious you will want to eat the paint. Watch the marks you make. Each medium can enchant, and be as mouth-watering as a Bonnard raspberry cream. Remove rotten pieces fast, or the rot will spread. (By "rotten pieces", I mean your mistakes.)

Bicycle

Train-spotters, car thieves, and Tour de France cyclists are all in thrall to machines. Hell's Angels embrace their bikes. When young, I was not more attached to my bicycle than to my knees or my roller-skates – they were all a part of me. I felt closest to Jeffrey Dennis' "Brink of Dissolution" when I remembered flying over the handlebars after braking on a steep hill. He has tubed and conduited his way through his pictures. Now, in "A Journey Postponed", he paints the tubes of a bicycle and says: "At a certain point, the circular elements were giving me an uneasy sensation of instability, as if the painting were about to whizz off the studio wall; and it seemed necessary to slow the whole thing down, by letting the components drift apart and embed themselves in the field of bubbles. (The sustaining and defining 'atmospheric pressure' for the other elements.)" He pondered the truth of Flann O'Brien's long discourse on bicycles in *The Third Policeman*: "On how, with excessive use, bicycle, rider, and ground start to interchange their qualities."

When Braque and Léger were young (and girls were wearing bloomers) bicycles meant freedom and emancipation – The Open Road! Years later, Braque painted the machine nostalgically, slightly decoratively, and in one picture, including in large letters "MON VELO" (my bike). Bicycles are popular and pollution-free, as Amsterdam, Cambridge, and all wise places know. Bikes can be bright-coloured, riders can take up wonderful poses. You can recline on bicycles. Paint them as lively diagrams of happiness.

A rather tentative assembly of the components. See how confidently he eliminates and even truculently deals with the spokes in "The Big Julie".   After Léger

"The Big Julie". Obviously cloudily, touchily fond of his machine in 1929. Ten years later, harder pristine bicycles accompanied family outings jauntily.   After Léger

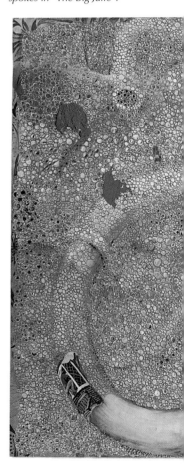

The bike would take Braque, when young, from Paris to the Normandy coast. In this mess-copy, apple blossoms are suggested – casually depicted, as if the spectator would know all about it anyway.   After Braque

Bicyclists, intent on entering The City of London, via the heavily engineered Tower Bridge. Use tiny sable brushes to suggest these complexities.

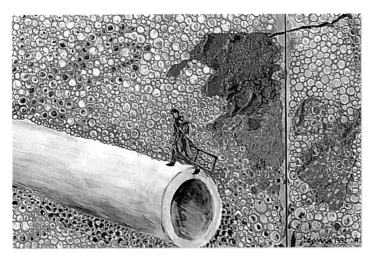

Jeffrey Dennis, *A Journey Postponed* (detail), 1992

Dennis says: "I like the idea that a painting may only reach its resolution when the entire structure is on the brink of dissolution." The artist, struggling to erect his deckchair in time for the end of the universe, is seen more than once.

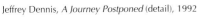

Bicycles are triangles, lines, circles, and, unlike the fast-forward tilt of a runner, the rider is looped. Choose swinging lines to make him race. Or paint the velocipede of olden times leaning quietly.

Jeffrey Dennis, *A Journey Postponed*, 1992

After Braque

After Braque

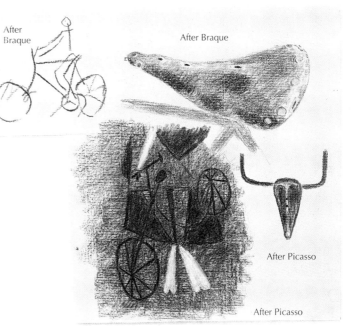

After Picasso

After Picasso

The girl's bicycle in "Night Fishing at Antibes".

Still and Fast Life

IN GRIS' PAINTINGS, MOUNTAINS come indoors through the window, transforming to become all sorts of things. Cubism demands transformation. Windows are also important exits. The three top Cubists were Braque, Picasso, and Gris; but almost all good artists since have been Cubist to some extent. The changes in painting this century have often been about still life on a table. Familiar, even humdrum objects were chosen, challenging the painter to make a new kind of beauty. Cubism was the biggest change in depictive ways, and Gris, before he died, had pursued the picture more thoughtfully and thoroughly than any other painter. It would have been exciting to see what came next.

After Picasso

The last Gris are concise objects, in "enamel", "house", or "coach" type paint. (De Chirico had a similar surface, and Picasso had bought a good commercial paint called "Ripolin".) Into this "enamel" Gris would sometimes melt a thicker, knifed paint.

Chardin was the grand artist of still life. He would prepare wonderful, rich surfaces as carefully as cheese makers ripen Camembert. Graham Crowley prepares his paint surfaces so that, at a latter stage, they can receive colour glazes. His "Kitchen Life II" was an onslaught of the nasty utensils.

Test out with watercolour your own reactions to kitchen stuff: knives; graters; choppers; forks. Kitchens can be nervy.

"The View Across the Bay" is one of several late pictures by Gris where the outdoors comes indoors. A cloud, or a mountain, turns into a napkin, or a compôte, and tables or windows serve as false frames. Once the main areas are filled in, lines are made parallel to the ripples on the bay: the guitar strings, the staves on the music-paper and the wood grain of the table. The yacht and the flag also act as triangular patches of sunlight.

Victor Willis, after Gris, *The View Across the Bay*, 1995

Hard sparks and ectoplasm, the terrors of the kitchen – not easy to compare them with Gris' gentle float through the window.

Graham Crowley, *Kitchen life II*, 1982

A scrub-in copy of a kitchen group.

After Chardin

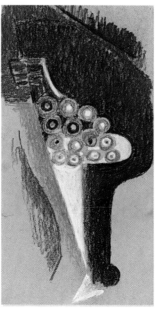

After Gris

After Picasso

The mountains join a violin, and resemble the tablecloth. The top of the carafe is joined to the near mountain.

After Gris

Scribble around some late Gris. His designs became increasingly elided.

After Gris

Watercolour blurs are energized by the Celtic rhythm-lines of the great Welsh poet of In Parenthesis *and* The Anathemata. *Indoor rhythms join outdoor rhythms through the window.*

David Jones,
Curtained Outlook, 1932

IMAGINATION

Symbols, Theories, and Artists

WE SEE THINGS ALL THE TIME our eyes are open. Walking through a wood, we may see no toadstools; then, finding them tasty, we see them everywhere. What we see is what we decide to see. Inevitably, painters and less specialist viewers see things differently. Perhaps the separation is greater today than in the past, because so much of our looking is channelled through photography, film, video, and television. This brightly-lit media version of the world may make it less easy to enter a painted world. And photos can also be made shapely.

"Young and Old at Beachy Head", is without any trace of photographic vision. I will try and describe its shapes. It is about people of various ages. A false frame is a little like a

crystalline four-pointed star. Its straightnesses suggest wide-open spaces: rhythmic brush strokes rush at the sheer cliff. At Beachy Head, the verticals stabilize, as do the horizontal lines in the frame that make linear equivalents for multiple horizons and distance and the layers of chalk. High-up are the birds and bird-shaped pieces of sky. At the left, a feather sinks, as magpies whizz by. In the centre, a black-backed gull is active (when seen as a gull), but seen as a vertical mark, it is stabilizing. The humans are mostly depicted in pairs. A black girl is given a pickaback by a ginger boy. To the right, a boy puts on a pullover close to a jackdaw and two old people. Above a lighthouse, lovers kiss, and my eyebrow resembles a looping-the-loop seagull.

A realization of Goya's "Drunken Mason". In Goya's other, similar picture, "The Wounded Mason", the friends are very serious.

Laetitia Yhap,
Drunk, 1990s

A sketch-copy of "The Wounded Mason"

After Goya

The flats have dated, but this beautifully arranged painting will continue to slide eerily into our consciousness.

Michael Andrews, *Flats*, 1959

230

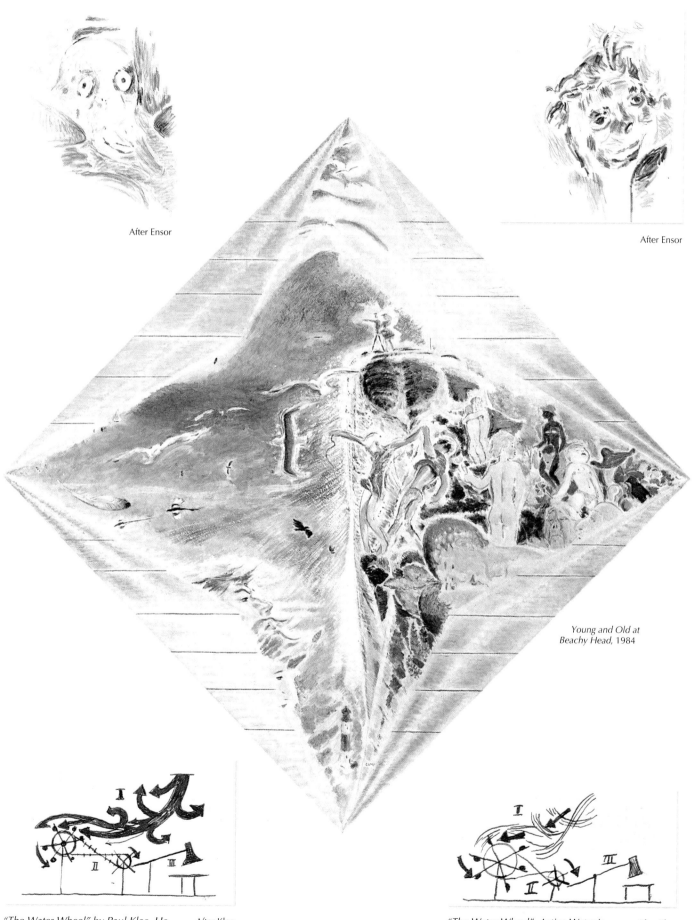

After Ensor

After Ensor

Young and Old at Beachy Head, 1984

"The Water Wheel" by Paul Klee. He is being theoretical. A pedagogical confidence trick – but fruitful.

After Klee

"The Water Wheel". Active Water is arrowed (I). The wheels are median (II). The hammer is passive (III).

After Klee

Teaching and Learning

YOU CAN LEARN MORE by teaching than by being taught. For a young student, art is glamorous. I had not heard of Cézanne before attending Ipswich Art School. My ignorance was sniffed at by the teacher of painting there, a Mr Fortin. This made me find things out. I read Gerstle Mack's book on Cézanne. Cézanne was glamorous. Doing painting was intoxicating. If you are fortunate, and if the art you admire is poor, a good teacher or cultured friend will sniff in a superior way. Tradition is secured by sniffing. When the "way" is healthy, a sneer is not needed. I learned a lot from being smiled at in a lukewarm way. Teaching is done by coaxing, cajoling, nodding, sneering, and by demonstration.

Teachers have a tiny number of star pupils, and they always believe there are more. To teach well is to lie convincingly, to encourage in the most discouraging circumstances, even when the student's work is failing. Failures are inevitable in the beginning. If the student is gifted, he will find his way. There have been avenues of teaching which have been good for the teachers. Max Bill, Kandinsky, Klee, Moholy-Nagy, Oscar Schlemmer and others had the resources of the Bauhaus at their disposal. Figurative painters teaching at the Slade school before the 1960s also enjoyed facilities of a different kind, and some worked from the 16 models who posed in various rooms throughout the building. A prolonged looking at the figure can generate compelling images in paint. Correction in the past could be scathing: Henry Tonks was a disciplinarian and made girl students weep. I taught at the Slade after 1960. It made me nervous. We were so polite, it was slow getting through doors. Most of the staff spoke with the "thrown" university voice of Sir William Coldstream and wore suits. During the next ten years, those in suits became aware that Pablo Picasso and Jackson Pollock did not wear suits.

Students in those days did not have shows of pictures, but were expected to produce studies and acquire skills. The work was placed in a room and assessed. Most were given a diploma. The students fought month after month to rid themselves of examination requirements. Meanwhile, the art scene made other demands. Star teachers showed the use of masking tape, photographs, spraying, and how fashionably to cover the white walls of new museums throughout the world. Things were being done in art that had never been done before, and 20 years later they are being done again. But such dramatic furores as those at the first performance of Stravinsky's *Rite of Spring* cannot happen again. The big changes in art have been made, yet some continue to yearn for an "avant-garde". The big mistake the art schools made was to believe it possible to learn to be a painter by doing art. Previously, students had done exercises. They did them cleverly, tastefully, usefully, and it bored them. It did not leave much time for original painting.

A brush drawing of two models

Corporeity

In 1907, John Fothergill (one of the first Slade students to be taught by Tonks) wrote *The Teaching of Drawing at the Slade*:

> Art comprises colour, form and the spiritual element. (The spiritual element is dictated by the artist's character and is not susceptible to teaching.) Drawing being colourless, the pursuit of drawing is to represent form. A good drawing is the simplest statement in light and shade of the artist's comprehension of forms.

It was, he wrote, research into (and not judgement on) the forms in nature which enabled the draughtsman to represent forms, and which gave rise to emotion. But style occurs only when research ceases. True style is not manner, but the expression of a clear understanding of the raw material.

> Colour, silhouette, pattern of the form, light and shade together give us the idea of an object's corporeity. But not from the eyes alone. For this corporeity is learnt from infancy by touch and our ability to move.

In the light of this testimony, it is interesting to consider the fixed point of view and measurements practised by Coldstream, Uglow, and Patrick George. The mystery of establishing corporeity by drawing was – in the light of the philosophy of Bishop ▶

A figure lying down in a life room transformed to become part of an imagined, rainbowed, stormclouded night.

Summer Storm, 1976

▶ Berkeley – fascinating to David Bomberg and other artists. In simple terms, Berkeley stated material objects have no independent being, but exist only as concepts of a human (or divine) mind. "The spirit in the mass" aimed at by Bomberg's Borough Group – which included Auerbach and Kossoff – was a response to this belief.

To teach in an important art school is to confront ignorance, erudition, strongly-held views, no technique, and some skill. This mix is energy-absorbing and most good artists teach less if their paintings are in demand. (Matisse gave up teaching in his own art school after one year. He found he was giving the same advice over and over.) Here is Thomas Eakins after a visit to the Prado, Madrid, where he particularly liked Ribera and Velásquez. He said: "Rubens is the nastiest, most vulgar, noisy painter that ever lived. His men are twisted to pieces. His modelling is always crooked and dropsical and no marking is ever in its right place."

He would not mind if all Rubens' paintings were burned up! But Rubens was Cézanne's favourite painter, "the prince of painters". Good art schools thrive on controversy and excess.

A Spanish model, with a seascape background.

Youth posing

A girl posing, with an added sea background.

An Edge is Not a Line

HEALTH AND EFFICIENCY WAS A NUDIST magazine which expunged all pubic hair from its photography.

In 1939, two spinsters ran Lowestoft Art School. I would draw an old naked man. My lines were cautious. I believed if I drew the model often I would improve. I drew in Lowestoft, Ipswich, and in Edinburgh, where nudes were warmed electrically most days, and even at night. I continued to draw, and as "The Athens of the North" had more contact with Paris than London, some art crept in. I thought it dreadful to draw by using shadows. It never occurred to me that when Seurat used shadows in his drawings they were special.

Miss Musson, the principal of my first art school, had received The King's Prize for a stumped drawing from life, blended using a "Tortillon Stump" of coiled paper and black chalk (sauce). Highlights were removed using kneaded bread. Even such shade drawings could have finesse when done by Picasso, Seurat, Degas, or Matisse (for they were all taught in this way).

When is a drawing a painting? Stuart Davis said his paintings were drawings; Philip Guston said: "It is an old ambition to make drawing and painting one."

Seurat was able to make scribble-darkened drawings of great beauty and subtlety. Drawing by edge-emphasis, and without much line, Seurat knew when drawing could seem like painting.

Eakins' colleague and successor at the Pennsylvania Academy of the Fine Arts in Philadelphia was Thomas Anschutz. Anschutz advised: "Don't copy shades on your paper so as to make round things round. Every line and every shade on a drawing should mean something. The shade on one part of the body must be studied with relation not only to the shades next to it but all over the body." Eakins' robust paintings were not achieved by copying shadows but by modelling with shading. The Pennsylvania Academy also taught clay modelling. Together with dissection and measurement, it was a thorough training for painting mass; and for this the students at Penn. were expected to be manly, healthy, and efficient.

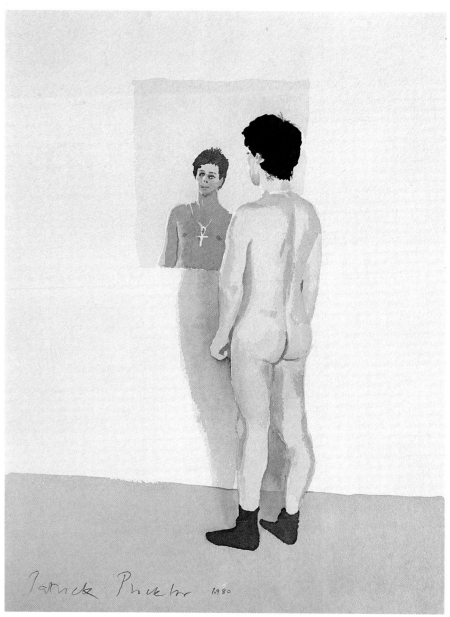

Use conté crayon on Ingres paper.   After Seurat

Polygonals on Michallet paper   After Seurat

The mirror shows the face.... The shadow suggests the front of the body. The blacks are daring. The touch is sensuous. Procktor called him "Narcissus"; the watercolour flowed delicately. The shadow is important and central.

Patrick Procktor, *Nude Boy, 1980*

Shadows and openings are used for melancholy. Pencil-hatch shadows and sunlight is prepared.   After Hopper

A transparent hat

Cloud shadows

De Chirico used shadows dramatically, for strangeness and loneliness.

After de Chirico

Seurat copied Angelica in oil and also in crayon with no lines. Copy Seurat's crayon study after Ingres' "Angelica Chained to a Rock". It is plain that even if Seurat might save her, Ingres would be more likely to add another chain. As you pencil or chalk-paint her, you will notice the cunning freeing and loosing of the edge by making "passages" between the form and the background. Seurat copied Angelica in oil with maximum contrasts and an acceptance of vigorous distortion. In the drawing, a goitrous throat was of considerable interest to Matisse, who found ways of using it. As you move along the far contours, trying to avoid making lines, you will sense Ingres' influence on Degas and other later artists. Ingres had incorporated The Simple State – a balance of quantities, using arcs and a straightness that he found in Poussin, David, Raphael, and Greek sculpture.

After Seurat, after Ingres

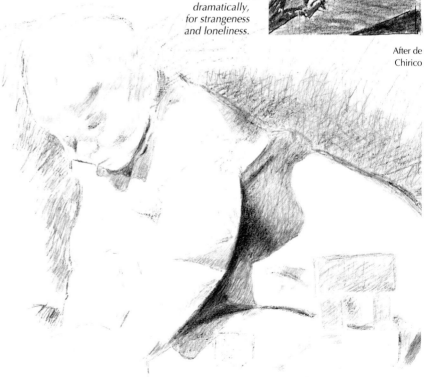

A solidly constructed baby, modelled by shading, is cut across by battlements of hard shadows, as if the painter were trying to demolish the infant. The tones bind the solid to the background. The background is of leaves suggested by palette-knife strokes, reminiscent of Courbet.

After Hopper

235

Extreme and Simple Painting

L ESS IS MORE, but sometimes less is less. It is good to know about all kinds of painting; Albers made an expensive book of silk-screened diagrams. Art colleges bought it for teaching colour. An orange would be seen to buzz on a pink of equal darkness. Matisse worked towards simplicity, but was certain that the young should not take a shorter cut than he had. "The Open Window, Collioure" is dark; I have wondered whether it was always dark (you can still see the railings underneath the black). Compared with Ad Reinhardt's paintings, it is complex. Minimal painters worked close to emptiness and sometimes achieved it.

If an aged curator ever mounts an exhibition of the almost plain rectangles by Newman, Turnbull, Marden, Palermo, Kelly, Ryman, Charlton, Plumb, Graubner, Yves Klein, Joseph etc., perhaps the view will be clear. Yves Klein, an expert at judo and self-promotion, piled galleries with ultramarine powder, rollered-blue canvases, and filled sponges with blue pigment. He induced

After Matisse

When reproduced in a book, the cut-outs were printed as opaque. But in the original the paper had been transparently brushed, and the streaking gave lightness and energy.

beautiful, blued, nude girls to squirm against large canvases. He lectured on Vermeer blue and Zen blue and I hope he had seen the blue zenith by Giotto at Padua. The simple, rolled rectangles by Rothko remain resonant. They are never blue, but sometimes are soft as sunsets. He became rich, and greys took over; he became depressed. Perhaps he should have heeded Delacroix' warning: "A taste for simplicity cannot last long." Cézanne thought Delacroix a great colourist. Here is a list of Delacroix' colours:

White; Naples yellow (the original pigment); Zinc yellow; Yellow ochre; Brown ochre; Vermilion; Venetian red; Cobalt blue; Emerald green (poisonous, so no longer available); Burnt lake; Raw sienna; Burnt sienna; Vandyke brown (different now); Peach black; Raw umber; Prussian blue; Mummy; Florentine brown; Roman lake; Citron yellow; the original Indian yellow.

With a palette of this complexity, it is clear simplicity was not Delacroix' intention. The bright colours of today are simpler.

If enough Cobalt blue is used, charcoal lines left visible will appear golden-black. The campanile acts as a foil.

Venice, 1976

Examine with watercolour the cut-outs of late Matisse. They are extreme, but complex.

After Matisse

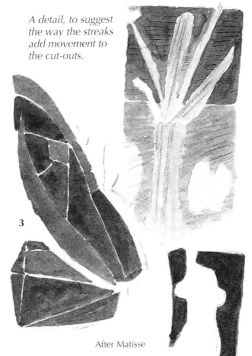

A detail, to suggest the way the streaks add movement to the cut-outs.

3

Simple heads, without features. (**1**) is brushed in, and (**2**) had its head made by wiping off background paint using a rag. Bonnard said: "A brush in one hand, a rag in the other." The thigh of (**3**) is made of a complex collaging of blue paper. The seams are evident, making his thought visible. As blue as the Mediterranean.

After Matisse

After Matisse

Cobalt green and Cobalt violet

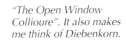

Green and lilac mix optically.

"The Open Window Collioure". It also makes me think of Diebenkorn.

After Matisse

The spectrum of Ultramarine blue is unexpected: it contains red, blue, and green. Try brushing warm blues over cold blues, and cold blues over warm blues. ▶

◀ Cobalt Violet

Ultramarine blue over Manganese blue ▶

◀ Cobalt violet over Cobalt green. With careful manipulation, Viridian and Cobalt violet (in oil) will make a blue-grey. Here is a lilac-grey.

Manganese blue over ultramarine ▶

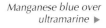

◀ Cobalt violet over Viridian

A landscape of verticals and horizontals

After Seurat

Ultramarine over Turquoise blue ▶

Read and Write

WILLIAM BLAKE LEARNED ITALIAN late in life so he could read Dante. In *The Divine Comedy*, a serpent, with six feet, fastens itself upon Agnello the thief. With its middle feet it clasped his belly, with those in front it seized his arms, then fixed its fangs in both his cheeks. The hind feet it spread along his thighs. Eventually, this hideous monster and thief were entwined, and, as if they had been molten wax, they stuck together and mingled their colours until they were "neither two nor one" (Canto 25). For William Blake it was good to put painting and words together. His transparent watercolours were right for the *Inferno*. Watch and copy his flame-shapes turning into fingers and curls. The stuff of his pictures was assembled strangely. Muscles from Michelangelo, gowns from Gothic art, words from Dante, rainbowed miracles from English watercolour. They came together just once in history at the point of a brush. Graham Sutherland looked at Blake to his advantage – but Blake is rarely understood. John Maxwell thought he was one of the world's ten draughtsmen. Blake probably did not see naked figures often enough, but imagination crackled from the brushed water, and the superbly drawn Botticelli Dante drawings are not more exciting.

Some painters are good writers. Michelangelo wrote famous sonnets. Turner's poems were poor. Klee wrote letters, a journal, and two influential notebooks, *The Thinking Eye* and *The Nature of Nature*. I recommend the letters of Cézanne, Degas, Pissarro, and Gauguin (who also wrote *Noa-Noa* and an *Intimate Journal*). Read Delacroix' *Journal*, and above all van Gogh's letters, which change everyone's life. If you have a mammoth monograph open as you read, you can follow his life visually day by day. He was a superb writer. Matisse wrote usefully. Redon wrote well. Picasso aphorized with genius. Stanley Spencer could not stop writing. I enjoyed the early books by Kenneth Clark (his *Rembrandt and the Italian Renaissance* makes clear the breadth of Rembrandt's sources) and Sickert's *A Free House*. I can only list a few books, but books have meant a lot to me. (Sickert's wife said whenever she visited his studio, he was reading.)

Here are a few more:

Gris by Kahnweiler; *Matisse* by Pierre Schneider; *Interviews with Francis Bacon* by David Sylvester; *Constable* by C.R. Leslie; *Blake* by Gilchrist; *In Parenthesis* by David Jones; and *David Hockney* by David Hockney. Other recent painter-writers to explore could be Josef Herman, Paul Nash, R.B. Kitaj, Lawrence Gowing, Wyndham Lewis, Gilbert and George, Andrew Forge, Timothy Hyman, Frank Auerbach, Kandinsky, Mondrian, Dali, William Feaver, Seurat, Redon, and Herbert Read.

Demon-wings can be bat-like, Dracula-like.

After Blake

After Blake

A rough copy of Agnelli the thief being absorbed. All arts meet as poetry. The sculptor Michelangelo's sonnet set by Benjamin Britten becomes a song.

Sickert painting the nude with his writing arm (when not found reading by his wife).

Walter Sickert, *Studio Painting of a Nude*, 1911–12

After Gauguin

Copy-diagrams, after some idols painted by Gauguin in Tahiti.

Cylinders and Joints

CÉZANNE, THE FATHER-FIGURE FOR CUBISTS, recommended seeing nature as cone, cylinder, and sphere. It was a critic who muddled things by bringing in cubes. Cubic joints are awkward even in David Lynch's science fiction film *Dune*. A crystalline body is a shock. Léger's early pictures were "open", and made of cylinders. For Matisse, favouring cones, the path was simpler. (In billiards, a game Mozart was fond of, the traces of the moving balls are cylinders, jointing as they strike the cushions. Sometimes, we see only the balls.) A cigarette is a cylinder. Its stubs, and smoke, are present-day subjects. A whole gamut of facial contortions are built around smoking. Van Gogh, Beckmann, and Edvard Munch used cigarettes, pipes, and clouds of smoke in pictures. Philip Guston was a most rampant cigarette-smoking painter, devoting an enormous canvas to an ashtray of "dog-ends". Internationally famous for sweet, abstract paintings, he spent his last years caricaturing his smoking and drinking problems, and painting monster shoes, and parts of his face. Sometimes a wrinkle, an eyeball, a cigarette-butt, and a cloud of smoke were sufficient.

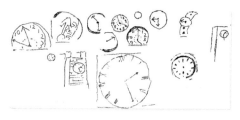

After Guston

Clocks from Guston's pictures. He said he measured his life in "Camel" cigarette butts.

After Guston

1 *John Cage*　　　**2** *Self-paintings with cigarettes*　　　**3** *Richard Nixon*

After Léger

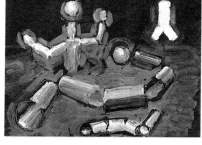

Daub in a tubular way from imagination. Or cut a postal-tube almost through. (This was done on black-painted paper.) Although it suited Cézanne and Léger, seeing in terms of cylinders or planes has never seemed very useful to me. Too many complications arise.

"Cabal". Guston used very few colours – red, blue, black, and white – when abstract or figurative. There are single colour (monochrome) pictures by Dufy, who found vermilion a versatile pigment.　After Guston

After Léger

Léger's Cubism was rather impure, open – even decorative. Paint using simple elements, as did Léger, until your personal style takes over.　After Léger

Measuring

MEASURING DISTORTS THE IMAGE. Patrick George measures the strangely foreshortened view of Susan. Most portraits in the past were posed like Madonnas; head frontal, dead centre, and higher than the middle. This portrait is close to the middle horizontally, but lower than expected. Thus he breaks the mould, and thus a sensitive eccentric artist flouts tradition. Giovanni Bellini felt arms imaged best when roughly two heads long and half a head thick. Patrick George softly brushes in arms no longer than a nose. Fed by the abstract practice of his time, this play of marks, arrived at by eye, comes to resemble one of Mondrian's analytical compositions – a pyramidal staircase of dabs. (Cézanne liked triangular structures, but would not have measured.) Degas did several little-known landscapes involving sharply receding perspective (which may have been demonstrations for Boudin's

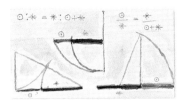

To get the "golden cut" for a given line.

pupil Braquaval). Stylistically, Patrick George's overlapping tree-lines slightly resemble those by Degas: their pictures would not show the viewer around the whole estate, as Rubens' paintings did.

"Dynamic symmetry" was thought valuable: find out by way of Piero, Klee, Seurat, the Bauhaus, Le Modulor, Ad Quadratum, and Basic Design. But one of the effects of using dynamic symmetry in landscape was that if the edge of a tree-trunk was placed on the golden section, it tended to disrupt the flat surface – emphasizing the rift between tree and distance excessively. And if, alternatively, the centre of the tree-trunk was placed on the golden section, the effect might be a bit sedate, like Georgian architecture. Yet any formal devices (and there are thousands: numberings, measurings, surveys, and geometrics) which make painting feel a serious activity are valuable. For a start, it is good to know where the centre of your canvas is.

Various measures are visibly marked around the edge of the panel.

Taking a Photograph, 1954

Edgar Degas, Landscape with Rocks, 1892

Victor Pasmore, *Suburban Garden*, 1947

THE·PILGRIM'S·PROGRESS
FROM·THIS·WORLD·TO
THAT·WHICH·IS·TO·COME
BY·JOHN·BUNYAN

ILLUSTRATED·BY·W·STRANG

LONDON·JOHN·C·NIMMO
MDCCCXCV

THE
PILGRIM'S PROGRESS

FROM THIS WORLD TO THAT
WHICH IS TO COME

DELIVERED UNDER THE SIMILITUDE OF A DREAM; WHEREIN IS
DISCOVERED THE MANNER OF HIS SETTING OUT; HIS
DANGEROUS JOURNEY; AND SAFE ARRIVAL
AT THE DESIRED COUNTREY

"*I have used Similitudes.*"—Hos. xii. 10

BY

JOHN BUNYAN

WITH FOURTEEN ETCHINGS BY WILLIAM STRANG

THE BANNER OF TRUTH TRUST

THE BANNER OF TRUTH TRUST
3 Murrayfield Road, Edinburgh EH12 6EL
PO Box 621, Carlisle, Pennsylvania 17013, USA

*

Reprinted from the edition of 1895
published by John C Nimmo Ltd

*

First Banner of Truth Trust Edition 1977
Reprinted 1979
Reprinted 1990
ISBN 0 85151 259 3

*

Printed and bound in Great Britain at
The Camelot Press Ltd. Southampton

LIST OF ETCHINGS

DESIGNED AND ETCHED BY

WILLIAM STRANG

The AUTHOR's Apology for his Book.

WHEN at the first I took my Pen in hand,
 Thus for to write; I did not understand
That I at all should make a little Book
In such a mode: Nay, I had undertook
To make another; which, when almost done,
Before I was aware, I this begun.

 And thus it was: I writing of the Way
And Race of Saints in this our Gospel-day,
Fell suddenly into an Allegory
About their Journey, and the Way to Glory,
In more than twenty things, which I set down;
This done, I twenty more had in my crown,
And they again began to multiply,
Like sparks that from the coals of fire do fly.
Nay then, thought I, if that you breed so fast,
I'll put you by yourselves, lest you at last
Should prove ad infinitum, *and eat out*
The Book that I already am about.

 Well, so I did; but yet I did not think
To show to all the World my Pen and Ink
In such a mode; I only thought to make
I knew not what: nor did I undertake

Thereby to please my Neighbour ; no not I,
I did it mine ownself to gratifie.

  Neither did I but vacant seasons spend
In this my scribble ; nor did I intend
But to divert my self in doing this,
From worser thoughts, which make me do amiss.

  Thus I set Pen to Paper with delight,
And quickly had my thoughts in black and white.
For having now my Method by the end,
Still as I pull'd, it came ; and so I penn'd
It down ; until it came at last to be
For length and breadth, the bigness which you see.

  Well, when I had thus put mine ends together,
I shew'd them others, that I might see whether
They would condemn them, or them justify :
And some said, let them live ; some, let them die ;
Some said, John, print it ; others said, Not so.
Some said, It might do good, others said, No.

  Now was I in a straight, and did not see
Which was the best thing to be done by me :
At last I thought, Since ye are thus divided,
I print it will ; and so the case decided.

  For, thought I, Some, I see, would have it done,
Though others in that Channel do not run :
To prove then who advised for the best,
Thus I thought fit to put it to the test.

  I further thought, if now I did deny
Those that would have it thus, to gratifie ;
I did not know but hinder them I might
Of that which would to them be great delight.
For those that were not for its coming forth,
I said to them, Offend you, I am loth ;

Yet since your Brethren pleased with it be,
Forbear to judge, till you do further see.

 If that thou wilt not read, let it alone;
Some love the meat, some love to pick the bone:
Yea, that I might them better palliate,
I did too with them thus *Expostulate:*

 May I not write in such a stile as this?
In such a method too, and yet not miss
Mine end, thy good? why may it not be done?
Dark Clouds bring Waters, when the bright bring none.
Yea, dark or bright, if they their Silver drops
Cause to descend; the Earth, by yielding Crops,
Gives praise to both, and carpeth not at either,
But treasures up the Fruit they yield together;
Yea, so commixes both, that in her Fruit
None can distinguish this from that; they suit
Her well, when hungry: but if she be full,
She spues out both, and makes their blessings null.

 You see the ways the Fisher-man doth take
To catch the Fish; what Engines doth he make?
Behold how he engageth all his Wits;
Also his Snares, Lines, Angles, Hooks, and Nets:
Yet Fish there be, that neither Hook, nor Line,
Nor Snare, nor Net, nor Engine can make thine;
They must be grop't for, and be tickled too,
Or they will not be catch't, what e're you do.

 How doth the Fowler seek to catch his Game
By divers means, all which one cannot name?
His Gun, his Nets, his Lime-twigs, light and bell:
He creeps, he goes, he stands; yea, who can tell
Of all his postures, Yet there's none of these
Will make him master of what Fowls he please.

Yea, he must Pipe and Whistle, to catch this,
Yet if he does so, that Bird he will miss.
If that a Pearl may in a Toad's head dwell,
And may be found too in an Oyster-shell;
If things that promise nothing, do contain
What better is than Gold; who will disdain,
(That have an Inkling of it,) there to look,
That they may find it?   Now my little Book,
(Though void of all those paintings that may make
It with this or the other Man to take)
Is not without those things that do excel
What do in brave, but empty, notions dwell.

Well, yet I am not fully satisfied,
That this your Book will stand when soundly try'd.
Why, what's the matter! it is dark, what tho'!
But it is feigned: What of that I tro?
Some men by feigning words, as dark as mine,
Make truth to spangle, and its rayes to shine.
But they want solidness: Speak man thy mind:
They drownd the weak; Metaphors make us blind.

Solidity, indeed, becomes the Pen
Of him that writeth things Divine to men:
But must I needs want solidness, because
By Metaphors I speak; Was not God's Laws,
His Gospel-Laws, in older time held forth
By Types, Shadows and Metaphors?   Yet loth
Will any sober man be to find fault
With them, lest he be found for to assault
The highest Wisdom: No, he rather stoops,
And seeks to find out what by pins and loops,
By Calves; and Sheep; by Heifers, and by Rams,
By Birds, and Herbs, and by the blood of Lambs.

God speaketh to him : And happy is he
That finds the light, and grace that in them be,
 Be not too forward therefore to conclude
That I want solidness ; that I am rude :
All things solid in shew, not solid be ;
All things in parables despise not we,
Lest things most hurtful lightly we receive ;
And things that good are, of our souls bereave.
 My dark and cloudy words they do but hold
The Truth, as Cabinets inclose the Gold.
 The Prophets used much by Metaphors
To set forth Truth; Yea, whoso considers
Christ, his Apostles too, shall plainly see,
That Truths to this day in such Mantles be.
 Am I afraid to say that holy Writ
Which for its Style and Phrase puts down all Wit,
Is every where so full of all these things,
(Dark Figures, Allegories) yet there springs
From that same Book, that lustre, and those rays
Of light, that turn our darkest nights to days.
 Come, let my Carper, to his Life now look,
And find There darker lines than in my Book
He findeth any : Yea, and let him know,
That in his best things there are worse lines too.
 May we but stand before impartial men,
To his poor One, I durst adventure Ten,
That they will take my meaning in these lines
Far better than his Lies in Silver Shrines.
Come, Truth, altho' in Swaddling-clouts, I find
Informs the Judgment, rectifies the mind ;
Pleases the Understanding, makes the Will
Submit ; the Memory too it doth fill

With what doth our Imagination please ;
Likewise it tends our troubles to appease.

Sound words I know, Timothy *is to use,*
And old Wives Fables he is to refuse ;
But yet grave Paul, *him no where doth forbid*
The use of Parables ; in which lay hid
That Gold, those Pearls, and precious stones that were
Worth digging for ; and that with greatest care.

Let me add one word more.   O man of God !
Art thou offended ? dost thou wish I had
Put forth my matter in another dress,
Or that I had in things been more express ?
Three things let me propound, then I submit
To those that are my betters, (as is fit).

1. *I find not that I am denied the use*
Of this my method, so I no abuse
Put on the Words, Things, Readers, or be rude
In handling Figure, or Similitude,
In application ; but, all that I may,
Seek the advance of Truth, this or that way :
Deny'd, did I say ? Nay, I have leave,
(Example too, and that from them that have
God better pleased by their words or ways,
Than any man that breatheth now a-days)
Thus to express my mind, thus to declare
Things unto thee, that excellentest are.

2. *I find that men (as high as Trees) will write*
Dialogue-wise ; yet no man doth them slight,
For writing so : Indeed if they abuse
Truth, cursed be they, and the craft they use
To that intent ; But yet let Truth be free
To make her salleys upon Thee, and Me.

Which way it pleases God : For who knows how,
Better than he that taught us first to Plough,
To guide our Mind and Pens for his Design ?
And he makes base things usher in Divine.

   3. *I find that holy Writ in many places*
Hath semblance with this method, where the cases
Do call for one thing, to set forth another ;
Use it I may then, and yet nothing smother
Truth's golden Beams ; Nay, by this method may
Make it cast forth its rays as light as day.

   And now, before I do put up my Pen,
I'll shew the profit of my Book, and then
Commit both thee and it unto that hand
That pulls the strong down, and makes weak ones stand.

   This Book it chalketh out before thine eyes
The man that seeks the everlasting Prize ;
It shews you whence he comes, whither he goes,
What he leaves undone ; also what he does :
It also shews you how he runs, and runs
Till he unto the Gate of Glory comes.

   It shows too, who set out for life amain,
As if the lasting Crown they would attain :
Here also you may see the reason why
They lose their labour, and like Fools do die.

   This book will make a Traveller of thee,
If by its Counsel thou wilt ruled be ;
It will direct thee to the Holy Land,
If thou wilt its Directions understand :
Yea, it will make the slothful, active be ;
The Blind also delightful things to see.

   Art thou for something rare, and profitable ?
Wouldest thou see a Truth within a Fable ?

*Art thou forgetful? wouldest thou remember
From* New-year's-day *to the last of* December *?
Then read my fancies, they will stick like Burs,
And may be to the Helpless, Comforters.*

   *This Book is writ in such a Dialect,
As may the minds of listless men affect :
It seems a Novelty, and yet contains
Nothing but sound and honest Gospel-strains.*

   *Would'st thou divert thyself from Melancholy ?
Would'st thou be pleasant, yet be far from folly ?
Would'st thou read Riddles, and their Explanation ?
Or else be drownded in thy Contemplation ?
Dost thou love picking meat ?   Or wouldst thou see
A man i' th' Clouds, and hear him speak to thee ?
Would'st thou be in a Dream, and yet not sleep ?
Or, wouldest thou in a moment laugh, and weep ?
Wouldest thou lose thyself, and catch no harm ?
And find thyself again without a charm ?
Would'st read thyself, and read thou know'st not* **what***,
And yet know, whether thou art blest or not,
By reading the same lines ?   O then come hither,
And lay my Book, thy Head, and Heart together.*

                        JOHN BUNYAN.

THE

PILGRIMS PROGRESS:

IN THE SIMILITUDE OF A DREAM.

A S I walked through the wilderness of this world, I lighted on a certain place, where was a Den, and I laid me down in *that* place to *The Jail.* sleep: And as I slept, I dreamed a Dream. I dreamed, and behold *I saw a Man cloathed with* Isa. 64. 6. *rags, standing in a certain place, with his face* Luke 14. 33. *from his own house, a Book in his hand, and a* Hab. 2. 2. *great Burden upon his back.* I looked, and saw 30. him open the Book, and read therein; and as he read, he wept and trembled; and not being able longer to contain, he brake out with a lamentable cry, saying, *What shall I do?* *His Outcry.*

Acts 2. 37.

In this plight therefore he went home, and refrained himself as long as he could, that his wife and children should not perceive his distress; but he could not be silent long, because that his trouble increased: Wherefore at length he brake his mind to his wife and children; and thus he began to talk to them: *O my dear Wife,* said he, *and you the*

Children of my bowels, I your dear friend am in myself undone, by reason of a Burden that lieth hard upon me: moreover, I am for certain informed, that *This World.* *this our City will be burned with fire from Heaven; in which fearful overthrow, both myself, with thee my wife, and you my sweet babes, shall miserably* *He knew no Way of Escape as yet.* *come to ruin, except* (*the which yet I see not*) *some Way of escape may be found, whereby we may be delivered.* At this his relations were sore amazed; not for that they believed that what he had said to them was true, but because they thought that some frenzy distemper had got into his head; therefore it drawing towards night, and they hoping that sleep might settle his brains, with all haste they got him to bed: But the night was as troublesome to him as the day; wherefore, instead of sleeping, he spent it in sighs and tears. So when the morning was come, they would know how he did; he told them *worse* and *worse;* he also set to talking to them again, but they began to be hard- *Carnal Physick for a sick Soul.* ened; they also thought to drive away his distemper by harsh and surly carriages to him: Sometimes they would deride, sometimes they would chide, and sometimes they would quite neglect him: Wherefore he began to retire himself to his Chamber, to pray for and pity them; and also to condole his own misery: He would also walk solitarily in the fields, sometimes reading and sometimes praying; and thus for some days he spent his time.

Now I saw, upon a time, when he was walking in the fields, that he was (as he was wont) reading in his Book, and greatly distressed in his mind;

CHRISTIAN IS TROUBLED

and as he read, he burst out, as he had done before, crying, *What shall I do to be saved?*

Acts 16. 30, 31.

I saw also that he looked this way, and that way, as if he would run; yet he stood still, because (as I perceived) he could not tell which way to go. I looked then, and saw a Man named *Evangelist* coming to him, and asked, *Wherefore dost thou cry?*

He answered, Sir, I perceive by the Book in my hand, that I am condemned to die, and after that to come to Judgment; and I find that I am not willing to do the first, nor able to do the second.

Heb. 9. 27. Job 16. 21, 22. Ezek. 22. 14.

Then said *Evangelist*, Why not willing to die, since this life is attended with so many evils? The man answered, Because, I fear that this Burden that is upon my back, will sink me lower than the grave; and I shall fall into *Tophet*. And, Sir, if I be not fit to go to Prison, I am not fit to go to Judgment, and from thence to Execution; and the thoughts of these things make me cry.

Isa. 30. 33.

Then said *Evangelist*, If this be thy condition, Why standest thou still? He answered, Because I know not whither to go. Then he gave him a *Parchment Roll*, and there was written within, *Fly from the Wrath to come.*

Conviction of the Necessity of flying. Mat. 3. 7.

The Man therefore read it, and looking upon *Evangelist* very carefully, said, Whither must I fly? Then said *Evangelist*, pointing with his finger over

---

Christian *no sooner leaves the World but meets* Evangelist, *who lovingly him greets With Tidings of another: And doth shew Him how to mount to that from this below.*

a very wide field, Do you see yonder *Wicket Gate?* The man said, No: Then said the other, Do you see yonder Shining Light? He said, I think I do. Then said *Evangelist,* Keep that Light in your eye, and go up directly thereto, so shalt thou see the Gate; at which, when thou knockest, it shall be told thee what thou shalt do. So I saw in my dream that the Man began to run: Now he had not run far from his own door, but his Wife and Children perceiving it, began to cry after him to return; but the Man put his fingers in his ears, and ran on crying, *Life! Life! Eternal Life!* So he looked not behind him, but fled towards the middle of the Plain.

The Neighbours also came out to see him run, and as he ran some mocked, others threatened, and some cried after him to return; Now among those that did so, there were two that were resolv'd to fetch him back by force. The name of the one was *Obstinate*, and the name of the other *Pliable*. Now by this time the Man was got a good distance from them; but however, they were resolved to pursue him, which they did, and in a little time they overtook him. Then said the Man, Neighbours, *Wherefore are you come?* They said, To persuade you to go back with us; but he said, That can by no means be: You dwell (said he) in the City of *Destruction*, (the place also where I was born) I see it to be so: And dying there, sooner or later, you will sink lower than the grave, into a place that burns with Fire and Brimstone: Be content, good neighbours, and go along with me.

What, said *Obstinate*, and leave our Friends and our Comforts behind us!

Yes, said *Christian*, (for that was his name) because that all *which you shall forsake*, is not worthy to be compared with a little of that, that I am seeking to enjoy; and if you will go along with me, and hold it, you shall fare as I myself; for there where I go, is enough and to spare; come away and prove my words.

2 Cor. 4. 18.
Rom. 8. 18.

Luke 15. 17.

Obst. What are the things you seek, since you leave all the World to find them?

Chr. I seek an *Inheritance incorruptible, undefiled, and that fadeth not away:* And it is laid up in Heaven, and safe there, to be bestowed, at the time appointed, on them that diligently seek it. Read it so, if you will, in my Book.

1 Pet. 1. 4.

Heb. 11. 16.

Obst. Tush, said *Obstinate*, away with your Book; will you go back with us, or no?

Chr. No, not I, said the other; because I have laid my hand to the Plough.

Luke 9. 62.

Obst. Come then, neighbour *Pliable*, let us turn again, and go home without him; There is a Company of these craz'd-headed coxcombs, that when they take a fancy by the end, are wiser in their own eyes than seven men that can render a Reason.

Pli. Then said *Pliable*, Don't revile; if what the good *Christian* says, is true, the things he looks after are better than ours; my heart inclines to go with my Neighbour.

Obst. What! more Fools still? Be ruled by me, and go back; who knows whither such a brain-sick fellow will lead you? Go back, go back and be wise.

Chr. Nay, but do thou come with me, neighbour *Pliable;* there are such things to be had which I spoke of, and many more Glories be-

Christian *and* Obstinate *pull for* Pliable's *Soul.*

sides; if you believe not me, read here in this Book, and for the truth of what is express'd therein, behold all is confirmed by the Blood of him that made it.

Heb. 9. 17, 18, 19, 20, 21.

Pli. Well, neighbour *Obstinate*, (said *Pliable*) I begin to come to a point, I intend to go along with this good man, and to cast in my Lot with him; but, my good companion, do you know the way to this desired place?

Pliable *contented to go with* Christian.

Chr. I am directed by a man whose name is *Evangelist*, to speed me to a little Gate that is before us, where we shall receive instructions about the Way.

Pli. Come then, good neighbour, let us be going. Then they went both together.

Obstinate *goes railing back.*

Obst. And I will go back to my place, said *Obstinate*: I will be no companion of such misled fantastical fellows.

Talk between Christian *and* Pliable.

Now I saw in my dream, that when *Obstinate* was gone back, *Christian* and *Pliable* went talking over the plain; and thus they began their discourse.

Chr. Come, neighbour *Pliable*, how do you do? I am glad you are persuaded to go along with me; and had even *Obstinate* himself but felt what I have felt of the Powers and Terrors of what is yet unseen, he would not thus lightly have given us the back.

Pli. Come, neighbour *Christian*, since there are none but us two here, tell me now further, what the things are? and how to be enjoyed, whither we are going?

Chr. I can better conceive of them with my Mind,

THE SLOUGH OF DESPOND

than speak of them with my Tongue : But yet since *God's things unspeakable.* you are desirous to know, I will read of them in my Book.

Pli. And do you think that the words of your Book are certainly true?

Chr. Yes verily, for it was made by him that cannot lye.   Tit. 1. 2.

 Pli. Well said, what things are they?

Chr. There is an endless Kingdom to be inha-   Isa. 45. 17. bited, and everlasting Life to be given us, that we   John 10. 27, 28, 29. may inhabit that Kingdom for ever.

Pli. Well said; and what else?

Chr. There are Crowns of Glory to be given us ;   2 Tim. 4. 8. and Garments that will make us shine like the Sun   Rev. 22. 5. Mat. 13. 43. in the firmament of Heaven.

Pli. This is very pleasant; and what else?

Chr. There shall be no more crying, nor sorrow ;   Isa. 15. 8. for he that is Owner of the place will wipe all tears   Rev. 7. 16, 17. ch. 21. from our eyes.   4.

Pli. And what company shall we have there?

Chr. There we shall be with Seraphims, and   Isa. 6. 2. Cherubims, Creatures that will dazzle your eyes   1 Thes. 4. 16, 17. Rev. 5 to look on them : There also you shall meet with   11. thousands, and ten thousands that have gone before us to that place ; none of them are hurtful, but loving and holy, every one walking in the sight of God, and standing in his presence with acceptance for ever : In a word, there we shall see the Elders with their golden Crowns : There we shall see the Holy Virgins with their golden Harps : There we   Rev. 4. 4. shall see men, that by the World were cut in pieces,   Rev. 14. 1, burnt in flames, eaten of beasts, drowned in the   2, 3, 4, 5. John 12. 25. Seas, for the Love that they bare to the Lord of

2 Cor. 5. 2,
3, 5.

the place; all well, and cloathed with Immortality, as with a garment.

Pli. The Hearing of this is enough to ravish one's heart; but are these things to be enjoyed? How shall we get to be Sharers thereof?

Isa. 55. 12.
John 7. 37.
John 6. 37.
Rev. 21. 6.
Rev. 22. 17.

Chr. The Lord the Governor of the country, hath recorded *that* in this Book, the substance of which is, if we be truly willing to have it, he will bestow it upon us freely.

Pli. Well, my good companion, glad am I to hear of these things; come on, let us mend our pace.

Chr. I cannot go so fast as I would, by reason of this Burden that is on my back.

The Slough of Despond.

Now I saw in my dream, that just as they had ended this talk, they drew nigh to a very *miry Slough* that was in the midst of the plain, and they being heedless, did both fall suddenly into the bog. The name of the Slough was *Despond.* Here therefore they wallowed for a time, being grievously bedaubed with the dirt; and *Christian,* because of the Burden that was on his back, began to sink in the mire.

Pli. Then said *Pliable,* Ah! neighbour *Christian,* where are you now?

Chr. Truly, said *Christian,* I do not know.

Pli. At that *Pliable* began to be offended, and angrily said to his fellow, Is this the happiness you have told me all this while of? If we have such ill

It is not enough to be Pliable.

speed at our first setting out, what may we expect 'twixt this and our Journey's end? May I get out again with my Life, you shall possess the brave Country alone for me. And with that he gave a desperate Struggle or two, and got out of the mire on that side of the Slough which was next to his own house; so away he went, and *Christian* saw him no more.

Wherefore *Christian* was left to tumble in the Slough of *Despond* alone; but still he endeavoured to struggle to that side of the Slough that was still further from his own house, and next to the Wicket Gate; the which he did, but could not get out because of the Burden that was upon his back: But I beheld in my dream, that a man came to him, whose name was *Help*, and asked him, *What he did there?* Christian in Trouble seeks still to get further from his own house.

Chr. Sir, said *Christian*, I was directed this way, by a man called *Evangelist*, who directed me also to yonder Gate, that I might escape the Wrath to come. And as I was going thither, I fell in here.

Help. But why did you not look for the Steps? *The Promises.*

Chr. *Fear* followed me so hard, that I fled the next way, and fell in.

Help. Then, said he, *Give me thy hand;* so he gave him his hand, and he drew him out, and set him upon sound Ground, and bid him go on his way. Help lifts him out. Psa. 40. 2.

Then I stepped to him that plucked him out, and said, Sir, wherefore, (since over this place is the way from the City of *Destruction* to yonder Gate,) is it, that this plat is not mended, that poor Travellers might go thither with more security? And he said unto me, This *miry Slough* is such a place as cannot be mended: It is the descent whither the scum and filth that attends Conviction for Sin doth continually run, and therefore it is called the Slough of *Despond;* for still as the Sinner is awakened about his lost condition, there ariseth in his Soul many fears and doubts, and discouraging apprehensions, which all of What makes the Slough of Despond.

them get together, and settle in this place : And this
is the reason of the badness of this ground.

Isa. 35. 3, 4. It is not the pleasure of the King that this place
should remain so bad ; his labourers also have, by
the directions of his Majesties Surveyors, been for
above this sixteen hundred years employ'd about
this patch of ground, if perhaps it might have been
mended : Yea, and to my knowledge, said he, *here*
hath been swallowed up at least twenty thousand cart
loads ; yea, Millions of wholsome Instructions, that
have at all seasons been brought from all places of
the King's dominions (and they that can tell, say,
They are the best materials to make good ground of
the place) if so be it might have been mended ; but
it is the Slough of *Despond* still ; and so will be when
they have done what they can.

True, there are, by the direction of the Lawgiver,

*The Promises
of Forgiveness
and Accept-
ance to Life
by Faith in
Christ.*
certain good and substantial Steps, placed even
through the very Midst of this Slough ; but at such
time as this place doth much spue out its filth, as
it doth against change of weather, these steps are
hardly seen, or if they be, men, through the dizziness
of their heads, step besides ; and *then* they are
bemired to purpose, notwithstanding the steps be

1 Sam. 12.
23.
there ; but the ground is good when they are once
got in at the Gate.

*Pliable is got
home, and is
visited by his
Neighbours.
His Enter-
tainment by
them at his
return.*
Now I saw in my dream, that by this time *Pliable*
was got home to his house again. So his Neighbours
came to visit him ; and some of them called him
wise man for coming back ; and some called him
Fool for hazarding himself with *Christian ;* others
again did mock at his *Cowardliness ;* saying, ' Surely
since you began to venture, I would not have been

so base to have given out for a few Difficulties.' So *Pliable* sat sneaking among them. But at last he got more Confidence, and then they all turned their tales, and began to deride poor *Christian* behind his back. And thus much concerning *Pliable*.

Now as *Christian* was walking solitary by himself, he espied one afar off, come crossing over the field to meet him, and their hap was to meet *just as they were crossing the way of each other*. The gentleman's name that met him, was Mr. *Worldly Wiseman*, he dwelt in the town of *Carnal Policy*, a very great town, and also hard by from whence *Christian* came. This Man then, meeting with *Christian*, and having some inckling of him (for *Christian's* setting forth from the City of *Destruction*, was much noised abroad, not only in the town where he dwelt, but also it began to be the *Town-talk* in some other places) Master *Worldly Wiseman* therefore having some guess of him, by beholding his laborious going, by observing his sighs and groans, and the like; began thus to enter into some Talk with *Christian*. *Mr.* Worldly Wiseman *meets with* Christian.

World. How now, good fellow, whither away after this burdened manner? *Talk between Mr.* Worldly Wiseman *and* Christian.

Chr. A burdened manner indeed, as ever, I think, poor creature had! And whereas you ask me, *Whither away?* I tell you, Sir, I am going to yonder Wicket Gate before me; for there, as I am informed, I shall be put into a Way to be rid of my heavy Burden.

World. Hast thou a Wife and Children?

Chr. Yes; but I am so laden with this Burden, that I cannot take that Pleasure in them as formerly: methinks, I am as if I had none. 1 Cor. 7. 29.

World. Wilt thou hearken to me if I give thee counsel?

Chr. If it be good, I will; for I stand in need of good counsel.

Mr. Worldly Wiseman's *Counsel to* Christian. *World.* I would advise thee then, that thou with all speed get thyself rid of thy Burden; for thou wilt never be settled in thy mind till then: Nor canst thou enjoy the Benefits of the Blessings which God hath bestowed upon thee, till then.

Chr. That is that which I seek for, even to be rid of this heavy Burden; but get it off myself, I cannot: Nor is there a Man in our country, that can take it off my shoulders; therefore am I going this Way, as I told you, that I may be rid of my Burden.

World. Who bid thee go this Way to be rid of thy Burden?

Chr. A Man that appeared to me to be a very great and honourable person; his name, as I remember, is *Evangelist.*

Mr. Worldly Wiseman *condemns* Evangelist's *Counsel.* *World.* Beshrew him for his counsel, there is not a more dangerous and troublesome way in the world, than is that unto which he hath directed thee; and that thou shalt find, if thou wilt be ruled by his counsel. Thou hast met with something (as I perceive) already; for I see the dirt of the Slough of *Despond* is upon thee; but that Slough is the Beginning of the sorrows that do attend those that go on in that Way: Hear me, I am older than thou; thou art like to meet with, in the way which thou goest, Wearisomeness, Painfulness, Hunger, Perils, Nakedness, Sword, Lions, Dragons, Darkness, and in a word, Death, and what not? These things are certainly true, having been confirmed by many Testimonies. And why should a man so carelessly cast away himself, by giving heed to a Stranger?

Chr. Why, Sir, this Burden upon my back is more terrible to me, than are all these things which you have mentioned: Nay, methinks I care not what I meet with in the way, if so be I can also meet with Deliverance from my Burden. *The Frame of the Heart of a young Christian.*

World. How camest thou by thy burden at first?

Chr. By reading this Book in my hand.

World. I thought so; and it is happened unto thee as to other weak men, who, meddling with things too high for them, do suddenly fall into thy distractions; which distractions do not only unman men (as thine I perceive have done thee) but they run them upon desperate ventures, to obtain they know not what. *Mr.* Worldly Wiseman *does not like that* Men should be serious in read-*ing the* Bible.

Chr. I know what I would obtain; it is Ease for my heavy Burden.

World. But why wilt thou seek for ease this way, seeing so many Dangers attend it? especially, since (hadst thou but patience to hear me) I could direct thee to the obtaining of what thou desirest, without the dangers that thou in this way wilt run thyself into: Yea, and the Remedy is at hand. Besides, I will add, that instead of these dangers, thou shalt meet with much Safety, Friendship, and Content.

Chr. Pray, Sir, open this secret to me.

World. Why in yonder Village (the village is named *Morality*) there dwells a gentleman, whose name is *Legality*, a very judicious man (and a man of a very good name) that has skill to help men off *Mr.* Worldly *prefers* Mo-rality *before the Strait Gate.*

with such Burdens as thine is, from their shoulders; yea, to my knowledge, he hath done a great deal of good this way: Ay, and besides, he hath skill to cure those that are somewhat crazed in their wits with their Burdens. To him, as I said, thou may'st go, and be help'd presently. His house is not quite a mile from this place; and if he should not be at home himself, he hath a pretty young man to his Son, whose name is *Civility*, that can do it (to speak on) as well as the old Gentleman himself: There, I say, thou may'st be eased of thy Burden, and if thou art not minded to go back to thy former habitation, as indeed I would not wish thee; thou may'st send for thy Wife and Children to thee to this Village, where there are houses now stand empty, one of which thou mayest have at reasonable rates: Provision is there also cheap and good, and that which will make thy Life the more happy is, to be sure there thou shalt live by honest neighbours, in Credit and good Fashion.

Christian *snared by Mr.* Worldly Wiseman's *Words.* Now was *Christian* somewhat at a stand; but presently he concluded, If this be true which this gentleman hath said, my wisest course is to take his advice; and with that he thus further spoke.

Chr. Sir, which is my way to this honest man's house?

Mount Sinai. *World.* Do you see yonder high Hill?

Chr. Yes, very well.

World. By that Hill you must go, and the first house you come at is his.

So *Christian* turned out of his way, to go to Mr. *Legality's* house for help: But behold, when he was got now hard by the Hill, it seemed so high, and also that side of it that was next the Wayside, did hang so much over, that *Christian* was afraid to venture further, lest the Hill should fall on his head; wherefore there he stood still, and he wot not what to do. Also his Burden now seemed heavier to him than while he was in his Way. There came also flashes of fire out of the Hill, that made *Christian* afraid that he should be burned : Here therefore he sweat and did quake for Fear. And now he began to be sorry that he had taken Mr. *Worldly Wiseman's* counsel; and with that he saw *Evangelist* coming to meet him; at the sight also of whom he began to blush for Shame. So *Evangelist* drew nearer and nearer; and coming up to him, he looked upon him with a severe and dreadful countenance, and thus began to reason with *Christian*.

Christian afraid that Mount Sinai would fall on his Head. Exod. 19. 18. Ver. 16. Heb. 12. 21.

Evangelist findeth Christian under Mount Sinai, and looketh severely upon him.

Evan. What doest thou here, *Christian ?* said he : At which words, *Christian* knew not what to answer; wherefore at present he stood speechless before him Then said *Evangelist* farther, Art not thou the Man that I found crying without the walls of the City of *Destruction ?*

Evangelist reasons afresh with Christian.

Chr. Yes, dear Sir, I am the Man.

Evan. Did not I direct thee the Way to the little Wicket Gate ?

Chr. Yes, dear Sir, said *Christian*.

Evan. How is it then that thou art so quickly turned aside ? for thou art now out of the way.

Chr. I met with a gentleman so soon as I had got over the Slough of *Despond*, who persuaded me, that I might, in the village before me, find a man that could take off my Burden.

Evan. What was he ?

Ch. He looked like a gentleman, and talked much to me, and got me at last to yield ; so I came hither : But when I beheld this Hill, and how it hangs over the way, I suddenly made a stand, lest it should fall on my head.

Evan. What said that gentleman to you ?

Ch. Why, he asked me whither I was going ? And I told him.

Evan. And what said he then ?

Ch. He asked me if I had a family ? And I told him : But, said I, I am so loaden with the Burden that is on my back, that I cannot take pleasure in them as formerly.

Evan. And what said he then ?

Ch. He bid me with speed get rid of my burden ; and I told him 't was Ease that I sought : And, said I, I am therefore going to yonder Gate, to receive farther direction how I may get to the place of deliverance. So he said that he would shew me a better way, and short, not so attended with Difficulties, as the Way, Sir, that you set me in ; which way, said he, will direct you to a gentleman's house that hath skill to take off these Burdens : So I believed him, and turned out of *that* Way into *this*, if haply I might be soon eased of my Burden. But when I came to this place, and beheld things as they are, I stopped for fear (as I said) of danger : But I now know not what to do.

Evan. Then (said *Evangelist*) stand still a little, that I may shew thee the words of God. So he stood trembling. Then said *Evangelist*, See that ye refuse not him that speaketh ; for if they escaped not, who refused him that spake on Earth, much

Heb. 12. 25.
Evangelist
convinces
Christian *of*

more shall not we escape, if we turn away from him *his Error.*
that speaketh from Heaven. He said, moreover,
Now the just shall live by faith; but if any man Heb. 10. 38.
draws back, my soul shall have no pleasure in him.
He also did thus apply them, *Thou art the man*
that art running into this misery: Thou hast begun
to reject the counsel of the Most High, and to draw
back thy foot from the Way of Peace, even almost
to the hazarding of thy Perdition.

Then *Christian* fell down at his foot as dead,
crying, *Wo is me, for I am undone!* At the sight
of which, *Evangelist* caught him by the right hand,
saying, *All manner of Sin and Blasphemies shall be* Mat. 12.
forgiven unto men; be not faithless, but believing: Mark 3.
Then did *Christian* again a little revive, and stood
up trembling, as at first, before *Evangelist.*

Then *Evangelist* proceeded, saying, Give more
earnest Heed to the things that I shall tell thee of.
I will now shew thee who it was that deluded thee,
and who it was also to whom he sent thee. The
man that met thee, is one *Worldly Wiseman,* and Mr. Worldly
rightly is he so called; partly, because he savoureth Wiseman *de-scribed by*
only the doctrine of this world; (therefore he always Evangelist.
1 John 4. 5.
goes to the town of *Morality* to church) and partly,
because he loveth that doctrine best; for it saveth Gal. 6. 12.
him from the Cross; and because he is of this carnal
temper, therefore he seeketh to pervert my ways,

When Christians unto Carnal Men give ear,
Out of their Way they go, and pay for't dear.
For Master Worldly Wiseman *can but shew*
A Saint the way to Bondage and to Wo.

Evangelist *discovers the deceit of Mr. Worldly Wiseman.* though right. Now there are three things in this man's counsel that thou must utterly abhor.

1. His turning thee out of the Way.

2. His labouring to render the Cross odious to thee.

3. And his setting thy feet in that way that leadeth unto the administration of Death.

First, Thou must abhor his turning thee out of the Way; yea, and thine own Consenting thereto; because this is to reject the counsel of God for the sake of the counsel of a *Worldly Wiseman.* The Lord says, *Strive to enter in at the Strait Gate,* the Luke 13. 24. gate to which I sent thee; *for strait is the Gate* Mat. 7. 13, 14. *that leadeth unto Life, and few there be that find it.* From this little *Wicket Gate,* and from the Way thereto, hath this wicked man turned thee, to the bringing of thee almost to destruction: hate, therefore, his turning thee out of the Way, and abhor thyself for hearkening to him.

Secondly, Thou must abhor his labouring to render Heb. 11. 25, 26. the Cross odious unto thee; for thou art to *prefer it before the treasures in Egypt:* Besides, the King of Mark 8. 35. Glory hath told thee, *That he that will save his life* John 12. 25. Mat. 10. 39. Luke 14. 26. *shall lose it:* And, *he that comes after him, and hates not his Father, and Mother, and Wife, and Children, and Brethren, and Sisters, yea and his own Life also, he cannot be my Disciple.* I say therefore, for a man to labour to persuade thee that That shall be thy Death, without which, the Truth hath said, thou canst not have Eternal Life: This doctrine thou must abhor.

Thirdly, Thou must hate his setting of thy feet in the way that leadeth to the ministration of Death. And for this thou must consider to whom he sent thee, and also how unable that Person was to deliver thee from thy Burden.

He to whom thou wast sent for Ease, being by name *Legality*, is the son of the Bondwoman which now is, and is in bondage with her children, and is in a mystery this Mount *Sinai*, which thou hast feared will fall on thy head. Now if she with her children are in Bondage, how canst thou expect by them to be made free? This *Legality*, therefore, is not able to set thee free from thy Burden. No man was as yet ever rid of his Burden by him; no, nor ever is like to be: Ye cannot be justified by the Works of the Law; for by the deeds of the law no man living can be rid of his burden: Therefore Mr. *Worldly Wiseman* is an alien, and Mr. *Legality* a cheat: And for his son *Civility*, notwithstanding his simpering looks, he is but a hypocrite, and cannot help thee. Believe me, there is nothing in all this noise that thou hast heard of this sottish man, but a design to beguile thee of thy Salvation, by turning thee from the Way in which I had set thee. After this, *Evangelist* called aloud to the Heavens for confirmation of what he had said; and with that there came Words and Fire out of the Mountain under which poor *Christian* stood, that made the hair of his flesh stand up: The words were thus pronounced, *As many as are of the Works of the Law, are under the Curse; for it is written, Cursed is every one that continueth not in all things which are written in the Book of the Law, to do them.*

Now *Christian* looked for nothing but Death, and began to cry out lamentably; even cursing the time in which he met with Mr. *Worldly Wiseman;* still

Gal. 4. 21, 22, 23, 24, 25, 26, 27. The Bondwoman.

Gal. 3. 10.

calling himself a thousand fools for hearkening to his counsel : He also was greatly ashamed to think that this gentleman's arguments, flowing only from the Flesh, should have that prevalency with him as to cause him to forsake the right Way.   This done, he applied himself again to *Evangelist* in words and sense as follows :

Chr. Sir, what think you ?   Is there Hopes ? may I now go back, and go up to the *Wicket Gate ?* Shall I not be abandoned for this, and sent back from thence ashamed ? I am sorry I have hearkened to this man's counsel ; but may my Sin be forgiven ?

Evan. Then said *Evangelist* to him, Thy Sin is very great, for by it thou hast committed two evils ; thou hast forsaken the Way that is good, to tread in forbidden paths ; yet will the man at the Gate receive thee, for he has *good will* for men ; only, said he, take heed that thou turn not aside again, lest thou perish from the Way, when his wrath is kindled but a little.   Then did *Christian* address himself to go back ; and *Evangelist*, after he had kissed him, gave him one smile, and bid him God speed ; So he went on with haste, neither spake he to any man by the way ; nor if any asked him, would he vouchsafe them an answer.   He went like one that was all the while treading on forbidden ground, and could by no means think himself safe, till again he was got into the Way which he left to follow Mr. *Worldly Wiseman's* counsel : So in process of time *Christian* got up to the Gate.   Now over the Gate there was written, *Knock, and it shall be opened unto you.*   He knocked therefore more than once or twice, saying,

Christian *enquires if he may yet be happy.*

Evangelist *comforts him.*

Psalm 2. *last Verse.*

Mat. 7. 8.

May I now enter here? Will he within
Open to sorry Me, though I have bin
An undeserving Rebel? Then shall I
Not fail to sing his lasting Praise on high.

At last there came a grave person to the Gate, named *Goodwill*, who asked, Who was there? and whence he came, and what he would have?

Chr. Here is a poor burdened Sinner. I come from the City of *Destruction*, but am going to Mount *Zion*, that I may be delivered from the Wrath to come; I would therefore, Sir, since I am informed that by this Gate is the Way thither, know if you are willing to let me in?

Goodwill. I am willing with all my heart, said he; and with that he opened the Gate. *The Gate will be opened to broken-hearted sinners.*

So when *Christian* was stepping in, the other gave him a pull: Then said *Christian*, what means that? The other told him, A little distance from this Gate, there is erected a strong castle, of which *Beelzebub* is the captain; from thence both he, and them that are with him, shoot arrows at those that come up to this Gate, if haply they may die before they can enter in. Then said *Christian*, I rejoice and tremble. So when he was got in, the man of the Gate asked him who directed him thither. *Satan envies those that enter the Strait Gate. Christian entered the Gate with joy and trembling. Talk between Goodwill and Christian.*

Chr. Evangelist bid me come hither and knock, (as I did) and he said, that you, Sir, would tell me what I must do.

He that will enter in must first without
Stand knocking at the Gate, nor need he doubt,
That is a knocker, but to enter in,
For God can love him, and forgive his sin.

Goodw. An open Door is set before thee, and no man can shut it.

Chr. Now I begin to reap the Benefits of my hazards.

Goodw. But how is it that you came alone?

Chr. Because none of my neighbours saw their danger, as I saw mine.

Goodw. Did any of them know of your coming?

Chr. Yes, my Wife and Children saw me at the first, and called after me to turn again: Also some of my neighbours stood crying and calling after me to return; but I put my fingers in my ears, and so came on my way.

Goodw. But did none of them follow you to persuade you to go back?

Chr. Yes, both *Obstinate* and *Pliable*: But when they saw that they could not prevail, *Obstinate* went railing back; but *Pliable* came with me a little way.

Goodw. But why did he not come through?

Chr. We indeed came both together, until we came at the Slough of *Despond*, into the which we also suddenly fell, and then was my neighbour *Pliable* discouraged, and would not adventure further. Wherefore, getting out again on that side next to his own house, he told me, I should possess the brave country alone for him: So he went *his* way, and I came *mine.* He after *Obstinate*, and I to this Gate.

A man may have company when he sets out for Heaven, and yet go thither alone.

Goodw. Then said *Goodwill*, Alas, poor man, is the Cœlestial Glory of so small esteem with him, that he counteth it not worth running the hazard of a few difficulties to obtain it?

Chr. Truly, said *Christian*, I have said the truth

of *Pliable*, and if I should also say all the truth of
myself, it will appear there is no betterment 'twixt Christian *ac-cuseth himself*
him and myself. 'Tis true, he went back to his own *before the*
house, but I also turned aside to go in the way *Man at the Gate.*
of Death, being persuaded thereto by the carnal
arguments of one Mr. *Worldly Wiseman.*

Goodw. Oh! did he light upon you? What, he
would have had you have sought for ease at the
hands of Mr. *Legality;* they are both of them a
very cheat; but did you take his counsel?

Chr. Yes, as far as I durst; I went to find out
Mr. *Legality*, until I thought that the Mountain that
stands by his house would have fallen upon my head;
wherefore there I was forced to stop.

Goodw. That mountain has been the death of
many, and will be the death of many more: 'Tis
well you escaped being by it dashed in pieces.

Chr. Why truly I do not know what had become
of me there, had not *Evangelist* happily met me
again as I was musing in the midst of my *dumps:*
But it was God's Mercy, that he came to me again,
for else I had never come hither. But now I am
come, such a one as I am, more fit indeed for death
by that mountain, than thus to stand talking with
my Lord: But O! what a Favour is this to me, that
yet I am admitted entrance here?

Goodw. We make no objections against any, not- Christian *com-forted again.*
withstanding all that they have done before they
come hither. They in no wise are cast out; and John 6. 37.
therefore, good *Christian*, come a little way with me,
and I will teach thee about the way thou must go. Christian *di-*
Look before thee; dost thou see this narrow way? *rected yet on his Way.*
THAT is the way thou must go. It was cast up by

the Patriarchs, Prophets, Christ and his Apostles, and it is as strait as a *Rule* can make it: This is the Way thou must go.

Christian
afraid of los-
ing his Way. *Chr.* But, said *Christian*, are there no turnings nor windings, by which a Stranger may lose his way?

Goodw. Yes, there are many ways *butt* down upon this; and they are crooked and wide: But *thus* thou mayst distinguish the right from the wrong, Mat. 7. 14. the Right only being strait and narrow.

Christian
weary of his
Burden. Then I saw in my dream, That *Christian* asked him further, If he could not help him off with his Burden that was upon his back? For as yet he had not got rid thereof, nor could he by any means get it off without help.

*There is no
deliverance
from the guilt
and burden of
Sin, but by
the death and
blood of
Christ.* He told him, As to thy Burden, be content to bear it, until thou comest to the place of *Deliverance;* for there it will fall from thy back of itself.

Then *Christian* began to gird up his loins, and to address himself to his Journey. So the other told him, That by that he was gone some distance from the Gate, he would come at the house of the *Interpreter*, at whose door he should knock, and he would shew him excellent things. Then *Christian* took his leave of his Friend, and he again bid him God speed.

Christian
comes to the
House of the
Interpreter. Then he went on till he came at the house of the *Interpreter*, where he *knocked* over and over; at last one came to the door, and asked, Who was there?

Chr. Sir, here is a Traveller, who was bid by an acquaintance of the Good Man of this house, to call here for my profit; I would therefore speak with the Master of the house: So he called for the Master of the house; who after a little time came to *Christian,* and asked him what he would have?

Chr. Sir, said *Christian,* I am a man that am come from the City of *Destruction,* and am going to the Mount *Zion;* and I was told by the Man that stands at the Gate, at the head of this way, that if I called here, you would shew me excellent things, such as would be a help to me in my Journey.

Inter. Then said the *Interpreter,* Come in; I *He is enter-* will shew thee that which will be profitable to thee. *tain'd.* So he commanded his man to light the Candle, and *Illumination.* bid *Christian* follow him: So he had him into a private room, and bid his man open a door; the which when he had done, *Christian* saw the picture *Christian sees* of a very grave Person hang up against the wall; *a brave pic-ture.* and this was the fashion of it, It had eyes lifted up *The fashion of the picture.* to Heaven, the best of Books in his hand, the Law of Truth was written upon his lips, the World was behind his back; it stood as if it pleaded with men, and a Crown of Gold did hang over its head.

Chr. Then said *Christian,* What means this?

Inter. The man whose picture this is, is one of a thousand; he can beget children, travel in birth with *1 Cor. 4. 15.* children, and nurse them himself when they are *Gal. 4. 19.* born. And whereas thou seest him with eyes lift up to Heaven, the best of Books in his hand, and the Law of Truth writ on his lips; it is to shew thee, that his work is to know and unfold dark things to *The meaning* Sinners; even as also thou seest him stand as if *of the pic-ture.* he pleaded with men; and whereas thou seest the World as cast behind him, and that a Crown hangs over his head; that is to shew thee, that slighting and despising the things that are present, for the love that he hath to his Master's service, he is sure in the World that comes next, to have Glory for his reward. Now, said the *Interpreter*, I have shewed thee this picture first, because the man whose picture this is, is the only man whom the Lord of the place whither thou art going, hath authorized to be thy Guide in all difficult places thou may'st meet with in the Way: Wherefore take good heed to what I have shewed thee, and bear well in thy mind what thou hast seen; lest in thy Journey thou meet with some that pretend to lead thee right, but their way goes down to death.

Why he shew-ed him the pic-ture first.

Then he took him by the hand, and led him into a very large parlour that was full of dust, because never swept; the which after he had reviewed a little while, the *Interpreter* called for a man to sweep. Now when he began to sweep, the dust began so abundantly to fly about, that *Christian* had almost therewith been choaked. Then said the *Interpreter* to a *Damsel* that stood by, bring hither Water, and sprinkle the room; the which when she had done, it was swept and cleansed with pleasure.

Chr. Then said *Christian*, What means this?

Inter. The *Interpreter* answered, This *parlour* is the heart of a man that was never sanctified by the sweet Grace of the Gospel: The *dust* is his Original Sin, and inward Corruptions that have defiled the whole man. He that began to sweep at first, is the *Law;* but she that brought Water, and did sprinkle it, is the *Gospel.* Now, whereas thou sawest that so soon as the first began to sweep, the dust did so fly about, that the room by him could not be cleansed, but that thou wast almost choaked therewith; this is to shew thee, that the Law, instead of cleansing the heart (by its working) from Sin, doth revive, put strength into, and increase it in the soul, even as it doth discover and forbid it, for it doth not give Power to subdue. _{Rom. 7. 6.}

Rom. 7. 6.
1 Cor. 15. 56.
Rom. 5. 20.

Again, as thou sawest the *Damsel* sprinkle the room with Water, upon which it was cleansed with pleasure; this is to shew thee, that when the Gospel comes in, the sweet and precious influences thereof to the heart, then, I say, even as thou sawest the *Damsel* lay the dust by sprinkling the floor with Water, so is Sin vanquished and subdued, and the soul made clean, through the Faith of it, and conse-quently fit for the King of Glory to inhabit.

John 15. 3.
Ephes. 5. 26.
Acts 15. 9.

I saw, moreover, in my dream, That the *Inter-preter* took him by the hand, and had him into a little room, where sat two little children, each one in his chair. The name of the eldest was *Passion*, of the other *Patience*. *Passion* seemed to be much discon-tent, but *Patience* was very quiet. Then *Christian* asked, What is the reason of the discontent of *Passion ?* The *Interpreter* answered, the Governor of them would have him stay for his best things, 'till the beginning of the next year; but he will have all now: But *Patience* is willing to wait.

Rom. 16. 25, 26. 1 John 5. 13.

He shewed him Passion and Patience.

Passion will have it now.

Patience is for waiting.

Then I saw that one came to *Passion*, and brought him a bag of Treasure, and poured it down at his feet; the which he took up and rejoiced therein, and withall laughed *Patience* to scorn: But I beheld but a while, and he had lavished all away, and had nothing left him but rags.

Passion hath his desire.

And quickly lavishes all away.

Chr. Then said *Christian* to the *Interpreter*, Ex-pound this matter more fully to me.

The matter expounded.

Inter. So he said, These two lads are Figures; *Passion* of the men of *this* World, and *Patience* of the men of That which is to come : For as here thou seest, *Passion* will have all now, this year; that is to say, in this world; so are the men of this world : They must have all their good things now, they cannot stay till next year, that is, until the next World, for their portion of good.   That proverb, *The Worldly man for a bird in the hand.* *A Bird in the Hand is worth two in the Bush,* is of more authority with them, than are all the Divine testimonies of the Good of the World to come. But as thou sawest, that he had quickly lavished all away, and had presently left him nothing but rags; so will it be with all such men at the End of this world.

Chr. Then said *Christian,* Now I see that *Patience* *Patience had the best Wisdom.* has the best Wisdom, and that upon many accounts. 1. Because he stays for the *best* things.   2. And also because he will have the Glory of his, when the other has nothing but rags.

Inter. Nay, you may add another, to wit, the Glory of the next World will never wear out; but these are suddenly gone.   Therefore *Passion* had *Things that are First must give place, but things that are Last are lasting.* not so much reason to laugh at *Patience,* because he had his good things first, as *Patience* will have to laugh at *Passion,* because he had his best things last; for *first* must give place to *last,* because *last* must have its time to come; but last gives place to nothing; for there is not another to succeed : He therefore that hath his portion *first,* must needs have a Time to spend it; but he that has his portion *last,* must have it lastingly : Therefore it is said of Dives, *In thy* *Luke 16.* *Lifetime thou receivedst thy good things, and likewise*

Lazarus *evil things; but now he is comforted, and thou* Dives *had his good things first.*
art tormented.

Chr. Then I perceive it is not best to covet things
that *are* now, but to wait for things to come.

Inter. You say truth : *For the things that are seen
are* Temporal; *but the things that are not seen are* 2 Cor. 4. 18.
Eternal: But though this be so, yet since things *The first things are but*
present, and our fleshly appetite are such near *Temporal.*
neighbours one to another ; and again, because things
to come, and carnal Sense, are such Strangers one to
another: Therefore it is, that the first of these so
suddenly fall into *Amity*, and that *Distance* is so
continued between the second.

Then I saw in my dream, that the *Interpreter* took
Christian by the hand, and led him into a place
where was a Fire burning against a wall, and one
standing by it, always casting much water upon it, to
quench it; yet did the Fire burn higher and hotter.

Then said *Christian*, What means this ?

The *Interpreter* answered ; This Fire is the Work
of Grace that is wrought in the heart; he that casts
water upon it, to extinguish and put it out, is the
Devil: But in that thou seest the Fire notwithstanding burn higher and hotter, thou shalt also see the
reason of that. So he had him about to the back
side of the wall, where he saw a Man with a Vessel
of Oil in his hand, of which he did also continually
cast (but secretly) into the Fire.

Then said *Christian*, What means this ?

The *Interpreter* answered, This is *Christ*, who
continually with the Oil of his Grace maintains the
work already begun in the heart: By the means of
which, notwithstanding what the Devil can do, the

2 Cor. 12. 9. souls of his people prove gracious still. And in that thou sawest, that the Man stood behind the wall to maintain the Fire; this is to teach thee, That it is hard for the Tempted to see how this Work of Grace is maintained in the soul.

I saw also, that the *Interpreter* took him again by the hand, and led him into a pleasant place, where was builded a stately Palace, beautiful to behold; at the sight of which, *Christian* was greatly delighted; he saw also upon the top thereof certain persons walking, who were cloathed all in Gold.

Then said *Christian*, May we go in thither?

Then the *Interpreter* took him and led him up toward the Door of the Palace; and behold, at the Door stood a great Company of men, as desirous to go in, but durst not. There also sat a man at a little distance from the door, at a table side, with a book, and his inkhorn before him, to take the name of him that should enter therein: He saw also, that in the doorway stood many men in armour to keep it, being resolved to do to the men that would enter, what hurt and mischief they could. Now was *Christian* somewhat in a maze: At last, when every man started back for fear of the armed men, *Christian* saw a man of a very stout countenance, come up to the man that sat there to write, saying, *Set down my*

The Valiant Man. *name, Sir;* the which when he had done, he saw the man draw his Sword, and put an Helmet upon his head, and rush toward the Door upon the armed men, who laid upon him with deadly force: But the man, not at all discouraged, fell to cutting and hacking most fiercely. So after he had received and given many wounds to those that attempted to keep him out, he cut his way through them all, and pressed forward into the Palace; at which there was a pleasant voice heard from those that were within, even of those that walked upon the top of the Palace, saying,

Come in, Come in;
Eternal Glory thou shalt win.

So he went in, and was cloathed with such garments as they. Then *Christian* smiled, and said, I think verily I know the meaning of this.

Now, said *Christian*, let me go hence. Nay, stay (said the *Interpreter*) till I have shewed thee a little more, and after that thou shalt go on thy way. So he took him by the hand again, and led him into a very dark room, where there sate a man in an Iron Cage. *Despair like an Iron Cage.*

Now the man, to look on, seemed very sad: he sat with his eyes looking down to the ground, his hands folded together, and he sighed as if he would break his heart. Then said *Christian*, What means this? At which the *Interpreter* bid him talk with the man.

Then said *Christian* to the man, What art thou? The man answered, I am what I was not once.

Chr. What wast thou once?

Man. The man said, I was once a fair and flourishing Professor, both in mine own eyes, and also in the eyes of others: I once was, as I thought, fair for the Cœlestial City, and had then even Joy at the thoughts that I should get thither. *Luke 8. 13.*

Chr. Well, but what art thou now?

Man. I am now a man of *Despair*, and am shut

up in it, as in this Iron Cage. I cannot get out;
O, *Now* I cannot.

Chr. But how camest thou in this condition?

Man. I left off to watch, and be sober; I laid the
reins upon the neck of my lusts; I sinned against
the Light of the Word, and the Goodness of God:
I have grieved the Spirit, and he is gone; I tempted
the Devil, and he is come to me; I have provoked
God to Anger, and he has left me; I have so hardened my heart that I *cannot* repent.

Then said *Christian* to the *Interpreter*, But is
there no Hopes for such a man as this? Ask him,
said the *Interpreter*.

Chr. Then said *Christian*, Is there no Hope, but
you must be kept in the Iron Cage of Despair?

Man. No, none at all.

Chr. Why? The Son of the Blessed is very pitiful.

Heb. 6. 6.   *Man.* I have crucified him to myself afresh; I have
Luke 19. 14. despised his Person, I have despised his Righteousness, I have counted his Blood an unholy thing, I
Heb. 10, 28, have done despite to the Spirit of Grace: There-
29.   fore I have shut myself out of all the Promises, and
there now remains to me nothing but Threatnings,
dreadful Threatnings, fearful Threatnings of certain
Judgment and fiery Indignation, which shall devour
me as an Adversary.

Chr. For what did you bring yourself into this
condition?

Man. For the Lusts, Pleasures, and Profits of
this World; in the enjoyment of which, I did then
promise myself much delight: But now every one
of those things also bite me, and gnaw me, like a
burning Worm.

Chr. But canst thou not now repent and turn?

Man. God hath denied me Repentance. His Word gives me no encouragement to believe; yea, himself hath shut me up in this Iron Cage: Nor can all the men in the world let me out. O Eternity! Eternity! How shall I grapple with the Misery that I must meet with in Eternity!

Inter. Then said the *Interpreter* to *Christian,* Let this man's Misery be remembred by thee, and be an everlasting Caution to thee.

Chr. Well, said *Christian,* this is Fearful; God help me to watch and be sober, and to pray that I may shun the Cause of this man's misery. Sir, is it not time for me to go on my way now?

Inter. Tarry till I shall show thee one thing more, and thou shalt go on thy way.

So he took *Christian* by the hand again, and led him into a chamber, where there was one rising out of bed; and as he put on his raiment, he shook and trembled. Then said *Christian,* Why doth this man thus tremble? The *Interpreter* then bid him tell to *Christian* the reason of his so doing: So he began and said, This night as I was in my sleep, I dreamed, and behold the Heavens grew exceeding black; Also it thundred and lightned in most fearful wise, that it put me into an agony. So I looked up in my dream, and saw the clouds rack at an unusual rate; upon which I heard a great sound of a Trumpet, and saw also a Man sit upon a Cloud, attended with the Thousands of Heaven: They were all in flaming ɪ Cor. 15. 52. fire, also the Heavens were in a burning flame, I ɪ Thess. 4. heard then a Voice, saying, Arise ye Dead, and Jude 15.

John 5. 28.
2 Thess. 1. 8.
Rev. 20. 11,
12, 13, 14.
Isa. 26. 21.
Mich. 7. 16,
17.
Psalm 5. 1, 2,
3.
Dan. 10. 7.
come to Judgment; and with that the Rocks rent, the Graves opened, and the Dead, that were therein, came forth; some of them were exceeding glad, and looked upward; and some sought to hide themselves under the mountains: Then I saw the Man that sat upon the Cloud, open the Book, and bid the World draw near. Yet there was, by reason of a fierce Flame which issued out and came before him a convenient distance betwixt him and them, as

Mal. 3. 2, 3.
Dan. 7. 9, 10.
Mat. 3. 12.
Chap. 13. 30.
Mal. 4. 1.
betwixt the Judge and the Prisoners at the bar. I heard it also proclaimed to them that attended on the Man that sat on the Cloud, *Gather together the Tares, the Chaff and Stubble, and cast them into the burning Lake;* and with that the bottomless Pit opened, just whereabout I stood; out of the mouth of which there came, in an abundant manner, smoak, and coals of fire, with hideous noises. It was also

Luke 3. 17.
said to the same Persons, *Gather my Wheat into the Garner.* And with that I saw many catch'd up and

1 Thess. 4.
16, 17.
carried away into the clouds, but I was left behind. I also sought to hide myself, but I could not, for the Man that sat upon the Cloud still kept his Eye upon

Rom. 2. 14,
15.
me: My Sins also came into my mind; and my Conscience did accuse me on every side. Upon this I awaked from my sleep.

Chr. But what was it that made you so afraid of this sight?

Man. Why, I thought that the Day of Judgment was come, and that I was not ready for it: But this frighted me most, that the Angels gathered up several, and left me behind; also the Pit of Hell opened her mouth just where I stood. My Conscience too afflicted me; and, as I thought, the Judge had always his Eye upon me, shewing Indignation in his countenance.

Then said the *Interpreter* to *Christian*, Hast thou considered all these things?

Chr. Yes, and they put me in *Hope* and *Fear.*

Int. Well, keep all things so in thy mind, that they may be as a *goad* in thy sides, to prick thee forward in the Way thou must go. Then *Christian* began to gird up his loins, and to address himself to his Journey. Then said the *Interpreter*, The *Comforter* be always with thee, good *Christian;* to guide thee in the Way that leads to the City. So *Christian* went on his Way, saying,

Here I have seen Things rare and profitable,
Things pleasant, dreadful, Things to make me stable
In what I have begun to take in hand;
Then let me think on them, and understand
Wherefore they shewed me were, and let me be
Thankful, O good Interpreter, *to thee.*

Now I saw in my dream, That the highway up which *Christian* was to go, was fenced on either side with a wall, and that wall was called *Salvation.* Isa. 26. 1. Up this way therefore did burdened *Christian* run, but not without great difficulty, because of the Load on his back.

He ran thus till he came at a place somewhat ascending, and upon that place stood a *Cross*, and a little below, in the bottom, a Sepulchre. So I saw in my dream, That just as *Christian* came up with the *Cross*, his Burden loosed from off his shoulders, and fell from off his back, and began to tumble, and so continued to do, till it came to the mouth of the Sepulchre, where it fell in, and I saw it no more.

When God releases us of our Guilt and Burden, we are as those that leap for Joy.

Then was *Christian* glad and lightsome, and said with a merry heart, *He hath given me Rest by his Sorrow, and Life by his Death.* Then he stood still a while to look and wonder; for it was very surprizing to him, that the sight of the Cross should thus ease him of his Burden. He looked therefore, and looked again, even till the springs that were in his

Zech. 12. 10.

head sent the waters down his cheeks. Now, as he stood looking and weeping, behold three Shining

Mar. 2. 5.

Ones came to him and saluted him, with *Peace be to thee;* so the first said to him, *Thy Sins be forgiven;* the second stript him of his rags, and cloathed him

Zech. 3. 4.

with Change of Raiment; the third also set a Mark

Eph. 1. 13.

on his forehead, and gave him a Roll, with a Seal upon it, which he bid him look on as he ran, and that he should give it in at the Cœlestial Gate; so they went their way. Then *Christian* gave three leaps for Joy, and went on singing:

A Christian can sing, tho' alone, when God doth give him the Joy of his Heart.

Thus far did I come laden with my Sin;
Nor could ought ease the grief that I was in,
Till I came hither: What a place is this!
Must here be the beginning of my bliss?
Must here the Burden fall from off my back?
Must here the strings that bound it to me crack?
Blest Cross! blest Sepulchre! blest rather be
The Man that there was put to Shame for me!

I saw then in my dream, that he went on thus, even until he came at the bottom, where he saw, a little out of the way, three men fast asleep, with Fetters upon their heels. The name of the one was *Simple*, another *Sloth*, and the third *Presumption*.

Simple, Sloth and Presumption.

Christian then seeing them lie in this case, went to them, if peradventure he might awake them ; and cried, You are like them that sleep on the top of a mast, for the Dead Sea is under you, a Gulph that hath no bottom : Awake, therefore, and come away ; be willing also, and I will help you off with your Irons. He also told them, If he that goeth about like *a roaring Lion*, comes by, you will certainly become a Prey to his teeth. With that they looked upon him, and began to reply in this sort : *Simple* said, *I see no Danger :* *Sloth* said, *Yet a little more Sleep :* And *Presumption* said, *Every Tub must stand upon his own bottom.* And so they lay down to sleep again, and *Christian* went on his Way.

Prov. 23. 34.

1 Pet. 5. 8.

There is no Persuasion will do if GOD *openeth not the eyes.*

Yet was he troubled to think, that men in that danger should so little esteem the kindness of him that so freely offered to help them, both by the awakening of them, counselling of them, and proffering to help them off with their Irons. And as he was troubled thereabout, he espied two men come tumbling over the wall, on the Left Hand of the narrow Way ; and they made up apace to him. The name of the one was *Formalist*, and the name of the other *Hypocrisy*. So, as I said, they drew up unto him, who thus entered with them into discourse.

Chr. Gentlemen, Whence came you, and whither do you go ?

Christian talked with them.

Formalist and *Hypocrisy.* We were born in the land of *Vain-Glory*, and are going for Praise to Mount *Sion.*

Chr. Why came you not in at the Gate which standeth at the beginning of the Way ? Know you

John 10. 1. not that it is written, That *he that cometh not in by the Door, but climbeth up some other way, the same is a Thief and a Robber ?*

Form. and *Hyp.* They said, That to go to the Gate for entrance, was by all their countrymen

They that come into the Way, but not by the Door, think that they can say something in Vindication of their own Practice. counted too far about ; and that therefore their usual way was to make a short cut of it, and to climb over the wall, as they had done.

Chr. But will it not be counted a trespass against the Lord of the City, whither we are bound, thus to violate his revealed Will ?

Form. and *Hyp.* They told him, That as for that, he needed not to trouble his head thereabout ; for what they did, they had *Custom* for, and could produce, if need were, Testimony that would witness it, for more than a thousand years.

Chr. But, said *Christian*, will your Practice stand a Trial at Law ?

Form. and *Hyp.* They told him that *Custom*, it being of so long standing as above a thousand years, would doubtless now be admitted as a thing legal by an impartial Judge : And besides, said they, if we get into the Way, what's matter which way we get in ? If we are in, we are in : Thou art but in the Way, who, as we perceive, came in at the Gate ; and we are also in the Way, that came tumbling

---

Who's this ? The Pilgrim. *How ! 'Tis very true.*
Old things are pass'd away ; all's become New.
Strange ! He's another Man, upon my word ;
They be fine Feathers, that make a fine Bird.

CHRISTIAN LOSES HIS BURDEN

over the wall : Wherein now is thy condition better than ours ?

Chr. I walk by the Rule of my Master, you walk by the rude working of your fancies. You are counted Thieves already by the Lord of the Way, therefore I doubt you will not be found true men at the End of the Way. You come in by yourselves without his Direction ; and shall go out by yourselves, without his Mercy.

To this they made him but little answer ; only they bid him look to himself. Then I saw that they went on every man in his way, without much Conference one with another ; save that these two men told *Christian*, That as to *Laws* and *Ordinances*, they doubted not but they should as conscientiously do them as he. Therefore, said they, we see not wherein thou differest from us, but by the *Coat* that is on thy back, which was, as we trow, given thee by some of thy neighbours to hide the shame of thy nakedness.

Chr. By Laws and Ordinances you will not be saved, since you came not in by the Door. And as for this *Coat* that is on my back, it was given me by the Lord of the Place whither I go ; and that, as you say, to cover my nakedness with. And I take it as a token of his kindness to me ; for I had nothing but Rags before ; and besides, thus I comfort myself as I go : Surely, think I, when I come to the Gate of the City, the Lord thereof will know me for good, since I have his *Coat* on my back! a *Coat* that he gave me freely in the day that he stript me of my Rags. I have moreover a Mark in my forehead, of which perhaps you have taken no notice, which one

Gal. 2. 16.

Christian *has got his Lord's Coat on his back, and is comforted therewith: He is comforted also with his Mark and his Roll.*

of my Lord's most intimate Associates fixed there
in the day that my Burden fell off my shoulders.   I
will tell you, moreover, that I had then given me
a Roll sealed, to comfort me by reading, as I go on
the Way ; I was also bid to give it in at the Cœlestial Gate, in token of my certain going in after it ;
all which things I doubt you want, and want them,
because you came not in at the Gate.

To these things they gave him no answer, only
they looked upon each other, and *laughed.*   Then I
saw that they went on all, save that *Christian* kept

Christian has talk with him-self. before, who had no more talk but with himself, and
that sometimes sighingly, and sometimes comfort-
ably : Also he would be often reading in the Roll,
that one of the Shining Ones gave him, by which he
was refreshed.

I beheld then, that they all went on till they came

He comes to the hill Diffi-culty. to the foot of the hill *Difficulty*, at the bottom of which
was a Spring.   There were also in the same place
two other ways besides that which came strait from
the Gate ; one turned to the left hand, and the other
to the right, at the bottom of the hill : but the narrow
Way lay right up the hill, and the name of the going
up the side of the hill is called *Difficulty*.   *Christian*

Isa. 49. 10. now went to the Spring, and drank thereof to refresh
himself, and then began to go up the Hill, saying :

This Hill, though high, I covet to ascend,
The Difficulty will not me offend.
For I perceive the Way to Life lies here :
Come pluck up Heart, let's neither faint nor fear ;
Better, though difficult, *the Right Way to go,*
Than Wrong, though easy, *where the End is Wo.*

The other two also came to the foot of the hill; but when they saw that the hill was steep and high; and that there were two other ways to go; and supposing also that these two ways might meet again with that up which *Christian* went, on the other side of the hill: Therefore they were resolved to go in those ways. Now the name of one of those ways was *Danger*, and the name of the other *Destruction*. So the one took the way which is called *Danger*, which led him into a great Wood, and the other took directly up the way to *Destruction*, which led him into a wide field, full of dark Mountains, where he stumbled and fell, and rose no more. *The danger of turning out of the Way.*

I looked then after *Christian*, to see him go up the hill, where I perceived he fell from running to going, and from going to clambering upon his hands and his knees, because of the steepness of the place. Now about the midway to the top of the hill, was a pleasant *Arbour*, made by the Lord of the Hill, for the refreshment of weary Travellers; thither therefore *Christian* got, where also he sat down to rest him : Then he pulled his Roll out of his bosom, and read therein to his Comfort; he also now began afresh to take a review of the Coat or Garment that was given him as he stood by the Cross. Thus pleasing himself a while, he at last fell into a Slumber, and thence into a fast Sleep, which detained him in that place until it was almost night: and in his Sleep his Roll fell out of his hand. Now as he was sleeping, there came one to him, and awaked him, saying, *Go to the ant, thou Sluggard; consider her ways, and be wise:* And with that *Christian* suddenly started *A Word of Grace.* *He that sleeps is a Loser.* Prov. 6. 6.

up, and sped him on his Way, and went apace till he came to the top of the hill.

Now when he was got to the top of the hill, there came two men running against him amain ; the name of the one was *Timorous*, and of the other *Mistrust* : To whom *Christian* said, Sirs, What's the matter you run the wrong way ? *Timorous* answered, That they were going to the City of *Zion*, and had got up that difficult place : But, said he, the farther we go, the more Danger we meet with ; wherefore we turned, and are going back again.

Christian meets with Mistrust and Timorous.

Yes, said *Mistrust*, for just before us lies a couple of Lions in the Way ; (whether sleeping or waking we know not) and we could not think, if we came within reach, but they would presently pull us in pieces.

Chr. Then said *Christian*, You make me afraid : But whither shall I fly to be safe ? If I go back to mine own country, that is prepared for Fire and Brimstone, and I shall certainly perish there : If I can get to the Cœlestial City, I am sure to be in safety there : I must venture ; to go back, is nothing but death ; to go forward, is Fear of death, and Life everlasting beyond it : I will yet go forward. So *Mistrust* and *Timorous* ran down the hill, and *Christian* went on his Way. But thinking again of what he had heard from the men, he felt in his bosom for his Roll, that he might read therein, and be com-

Christian shakes off Fear.

Shall they who Wrong begin yet Rightly end ?
Shall they at all have Safety for their friend ?
No, no, in head-strong manner they set out,
And head-long will they fall at last no doubt.

forted; but he felt, and found it not. Then was Christian *missed his Roll wherein he used to take Comfort.*
Christian in great distress, and knew not what to
do; for he wanted that which used to relieve him;
and that which should have been his Pass into the
Cœlestial City. Here therefore he began to be much
perplexed, and knew not what to do; at last he be- *He is perplexed for his Roll.*
thought himself that he had slept in the Arbour that
is on the side of the hill; and falling down upon his
knees, he asked God Forgiveness for that his foolish
act, and then went back to look for his Roll. But
all the Way he went back, who can sufficiently set
forth the sorrow of *Christian's* heart? Sometimes
he sighed, sometimes he wept, and oftentimes he chid
himself for being so foolish to fall asleep in that place
which was erected only for a little refreshment from
his weariness. Thus therefore he went back, carefully looking on this side and on that, all the way as
he went, if happily he might find the Roll that had
been his comfort so many times in his Journey. He
went thus till he came again in sight of the Arbour Christian *bewails his foolish Sleeping.*
where he sat and slept; but that sight renewed his
sorrow the more, by bringing again even afresh, his
evil of sleeping into his mind. Thus therefore he
now went on bewailing his sinful sleep, saying, *O* Rev. 2. 1 Thess. 5. 7, 8.
wretched Man that I am! that I should sleep in the
Day-time! that I should sleep in the midst of Difficulty! that I should so indulge the Flesh, as to use
that rest, for ease to my flesh, which the LORD of the
Hill hath erected only for the relief of the Spirits
of Pilgrims! How many steps have I took in vain!
(Thus it happen'd to *Israel*, for their Sin they were
sent back again by the way of the Red Sea) and I
am made to tread those steps with Sorrow, which I

might have trod with Delight, had it not been for
this sinful Sleep. How far might I have been on
my Way by this time! I am made to tread those
steps thrice over, which I needed not to have trod
but once: Yea, now also I am like to be benighted,
for the Day is almost spent: O that I had not slept!
Now by this time he was come to the *Arbour* again,
where for a while he sat down and wept; but at last
(as *Christian* would have it) looking sorrowfully
down under the settle, there he espied his Roll; the
which he with trembling and haste catched up and
put into his bosom. But who can tell how joyful
this man was, when he had gotten his Roll again?
For this Roll was the Assurance of his Life, and
Acceptance at the desired Haven. Therefore he
laid it up in his bosom, gave Thanks to GOD for
directing his eye to the place where it lay, and with
Joy and Tears betook himself again to his Journey.
But, O how nimbly now did he go up the rest of the
Hill! Yet, before he got up, the Sun went down
upon *Christian;* and this made him again recall the
vanity of his sleeping to his remembrance; and thus
he again began to condole with himself: O thou
sinful Sleep! how for thy sake am I like to be
benighted in my Journey: I must walk without the
Sun, darkness must cover the path of my feet, and I
must hear the noise of doleful creatures, because of
my sinful Sleep! Now also he remembered the story
that *Mistrust* and *Timorous* told him of, how they
were frighted with the sight of the Lions. Then
said *Christian* to himself again, These Beasts range
in the Night for their prey, and if they should meet
with me in the dark, how should I shift them? How

*Christian find-
eth his Roll
where he lost
it.*

should I escape being by them torn in pieces? Thus he went on his Way; but while he was thus bewailing his unhappy miscarriage, he lift up his eyes, and behold there was a very stately palace before him, the name of which was *Beautiful,* and it stood just by the Highway side.

So I saw in my dream, that he made haste and went forward, that if possible he might get Lodging there. Now before he had gone far, he entered into a very narrow Passage, which was about a furlong off the Porter's lodge, and looking very narrowly before him as he went, he espied two Lions in the way. Now, thought he, I see the dangers that *Mistrust* and *Timorous* were driven back by. (The Lions were chained, but he saw not the chains.) Then he was afraid, and thought also himself to go back after them, for he thought nothing but death was before him: But the Porter at the Lodge, whose name is *Watchful,* perceiving that *Christian* made a Halt, as if he would go back, cried unto him, saying, Is thy Strength so small? Fear not the Lions, for Mark 13. 14 they are chain'd, and are placed there for Trial of Faith, where it is, and for Discovery of those that have none: Keep in the *midst* of the Path, and no hurt shall come unto thee.

Then I saw that he went on trembling for fear of the Lions; but taking good heed to the directions of the Porter, he heard them roar, but they did him no harm. Then he clapt his hands, and went on till he came and stood before the Gate where the Porter was. Then said *Christian* to the Porter, Sir, What house is this? and, May I lodge here to-night? The Porter answered, This house was built by the

Lord of the Hill, and he built it for the relief and security of Pilgrims. The Porter also asked whence he was, and whither he was going?

Chr. I am come from the City of *Destruction*, and am going to Mount *Zion;* but because the Sun is now set, I desire, if I may, to lodge here to-night

Porter. What is your Name?

Chr. My name is now *Christian*, but my name at the first was *Graceless:* I came of the race of
Gen. 9. 27. *Japheth*, whom God will persuade to dwell in the Tents of *Shem*.

Port. But how doth it happen that you come so late? The Sun is set.

Chr. I had been here sooner, but that, wretched man that I am, I slept in the *Arbour* that stands on the Hill-side! Nay, I had, notwithstanding that, been here much sooner, but that in my Sleep I lost my Evidence, and came without it to the brow of the Hill, and then feeling for it, and finding it not, I was forced, with Sorrow of Heart, to go back to the place where I slept my Sleep, where I found it, and now I am come.

Port. Well, I will call out one of the Virgins of this place, who will, (if she likes your Talk) bring you in to the rest of the Family, according to the rules of the house. So *Watchful* the Porter rang a bell, at the sound of which came out of the door

---

Difficulty is behind, Fear is before,
Though he's got on the Hill, the Lions roar.
A Christian man is never long at Ease:
When one fright's gone, another doth him seize.

of the house a grave and beautiful damsel, named *Discretion*, and asked why she was called?

The Porter answered, This man is in a Journey from the City of *Destruction* to Mount *Zion*, but being weary and benighted, he asked me if he might lodge here to-night: So I told him I would call for thee, who, after Discourse had with him, mayest do as seemeth thee good, even according to the Law of the house.

Then she asked him, whence he was, and whither he was going? And he told her. She asked him also, how he got into the Way? and he told her. Then she asked him, what he had seen and met with in the Way? and he told her. And at last she asked his Name? So he said, It is *Christian;* and I have so much the more a desire to lodge here to-night, because by what I perceive, this Place was built by the Lord of the Hill, for the relief and security of Pilgrims: So she smiled, but the water stood in her eyes: And after a little pause, she said, I will call forth two or three more of the Family. So she ran to the door and called out *Prudence, Piety,* and *Charity;* who after a little more discourse with him, had him into the Family; and many of them meeting him at the Threshold of the House, said, Come in, thou blessed of the Lord; this House was built by the Lord of the Hill, on purpose to entertain such Pilgrims in. Then he bowed his head, and followed them into the House: So when he was come in, and set down, they gave him something to drink, and consented together that until Supper was ready, some of them should have some particular discourse with *Christian*, for the best

Improvement of Time, and they appointed *Piety*, and *Prudence*, and *Charity*, to discourse with him; and thus they began:

Piety *discourses him.*

Piety. Come, good *Christian*, since we have been so loving to you, to receive you into our House this night, let us, if perhaps we may better ourselves thereby, talk with you of all things that have happened to you in your Pilgrimage.

Chr. With a very good will, and I am glad that you are so well disposed.

Piety. What moved you at first to betake yourself to a Pilgrim's Life?

How Christian *was driven out of his own Country.*

Chr. I was driven out of my Native Country by a dreadful sound that was in mine ears; to wit, That unavoidable destruction did attend me, if I abode in that place where I was.

Piety. But how did it happen that you came out of your Country this Way?

Chr. It was as God would have it; for when I was under the fears of destruction, I did not know whither to go; but by chance there came a Man, even to me, (as I was trembling and weeping,)

How he got into the Way to Zion.

whose name is *Evangelist*, and he directed me to the Wicket Gate, which else I should never have found, and so set me into the Way that hath led me directly to this House.

Piety. But did you not come by the House of the *Interpreter?*

A Rehearsal of what he saw in the Way.

Chr. Yes, and did see such things there, the remembrance of which will stick by me as long as I live: Especially three things, to wit, How Christ, in despite of *Satan*, maintains his Work of Grace in the heart; how the Man had sinned himself quite out of hopes of God's Mercy; and also the dream of him that thought in his sleep the Day of Judgment was come.

Piety. Why, Did you hear him tell his dream?

Chr. Yes, and a dreadful one it was, I thought; it made my heart ache as he was telling of it; but yet I am glad I heard it.

Piety. Was that all that you saw at the House of the *Interpreter?*

Chr. No, he took me and had me where he showed me a stately Palace, and how the people were clad in Gold that were in it; and how there came a venturous man, and cut his Way through the armed men that stood in the Door to keep him out; and how he was bid to come in, and win Eternal Glory: Methought those things did ravish my heart! I could have staid at that good man's house a twelve-month, but that I knew I had further to go.

Piety. And what saw you else in the Way?

Chr. Saw! Why, I went but a little further, and I saw one, as I thought in my mind, hang bleeding upon a Tree; and the very Sight of him made my Burden fall off my back, (for I groaned under a weary Burden) but then it fell down from off me. 'Twas a strange thing to me, for I never saw such a thing before: Yea, and while I stood looking up, (for then I could not forbear looking) Three Shining Ones came to me: One of them testified that my Sins were forgiven me; another stript me of my Rags, and gave me this 'broidered Coat which you see; and the third set the Mark which you see in my forehead, and gave me this sealed Roll; (and with that he plucked it out of his Bosom.)

Piety. But you saw more than this, did you not?

Chr. The things that I have told you, were the best; yet some other small matters I saw, as namely I saw three men, *Simple, Sloth,* and *Presumption,* lie asleep a little out of the Way as I came, with Irons upon their heels; but do you think I could awake them! I also saw *Formality* and *Hypocrisy* come tumbling over the wall, to go (as they pretended) to *Zion,* but they were quickly lost; even as I myself did tell them, but they would not believe: But, above all, I found it *hard work* to get up this Hill, and as hard to come by the Lions mouths: and truly if it had not been for the good man, the Porter that stands at the Gate, I do not know, but that, after all, I might have gone back again; but now I thank God I am here, and I thank you for receiving of me.

Then *Prudence* thought good to ask him a few questions, and desired his answer to them.

Prudence *discourses him.*

Prudence. Do you not think sometimes of the Country from whence you came?

Christian's *thoughts of his Native Country.*

Heb. 11. 15, 16.

Chr. Yea, but with much *Shame* and *Detestation:* Truly, if I had been mindful of that Country from whence I came out, I might have had opportunity to have returned; but now I desire a better Country; this is, a Heavenly.

Prud. Do you not yet bear away with you some of the things that then you were conversant withal?

Christian *distasted with Carnal Cogitations.*

Chr. Yes, but greatly against my will; especially my inward and carnal Cogitations, with which all my countrymen, as well as myself, were delighted; but now all those things are my Grief; and might I but choose mine own things, I would choose never to

think of those things more; but when I would be   Christian's
doing of that which is best, that which is worst is   *Choice.* Rom. 7.
with me.

Prud. Do you not find sometimes, as if those
things were vanquished, which at other times are
your Perplexity?

Chr. Yes, but that is but seldom; but they are
to me Golden Hours, in which such things happen   Christian's
to me.   *Golden Hours*

Prud. Can you remember by what Means you
find your annoyances at times, as if they were vanquished?

Chr. Yes, when I think what I saw at the Cross,   *How* Christian
that will do it; and when I look upon my 'broidered   *gets Power*
Coat, that will do it; also when I look into the Roll   *against his*
that I carry in my bosom, that will do it; and when   *Corruptions.*
my thoughts wax warm about whither I am going,
that will do it.

Prud. And what is it that makes you so desirous
to go to Mount *Zion?*

Chr. Why, there I hope to see him *alive* that did   *Why* Chris-
hang *dead* on the Cross; and there I hope to be rid   *tian would be*
of all those things, that to this day are in me an An-   *at Mount Zion.*
noyance to me: There they say there is no Death,   Isa. 25. 8.
and there I shall dwell with such Company as I like   Rev. 21. 4.
best. For, to tell you truth, I love him, because I
was by him eased of my Burden; and I am weary
of my inward Sickness: I would fain be where I
shall die no more, and with the Company that shall
continually cry, *Holy, Holy, Holy.*

Then said *Charity* to *Christian,* Have you a Fa-   Charity *dis-*
mily? Are you a married man?   *courses him.*

Chr. I have a Wife and four small Children.

Charity. And why did you not bring them along with you?

Christian's
*Love to his
Wife and
Children.*
Chr. Then *Christian* wept and said, Oh! how willingly would I have done it! but they were all of them utterly averse to my going on Pilgrimage.

Cha. But you should have talked to them, and have endeavoured to have shown them the Danger of being behind.

Chr. So I did; and told them also what God had shewed to me of the destruction of our City; but I seemed to them as one that mocked, and they believed me not.

Cha. And did you pray to God that he would bless your Counsel to them?

Chr. Yes, and that with much Affection; for you must think that my Wife and poor Children were very dear unto me.

Cha. But did you tell them of your own Sorrow, and Fear of Destruction? For I suppose that destruction was visible enough to you?

Chr. Yes, over, and over, and over. They might
Christian's
*Fears of per-
ishing might be
read in his
very Counte-
nance.*
also see my Fears in my Countenance, in my Tears, and also in my trembling under the apprehension of the Judgment that did hang over our heads; but all was not sufficient to prevail with them to come with me.

Cha. But what could they say for themselves why they came not?

*The Cause
why his Wife
and Children
did not go with
him.*
Chr. Why, my Wife was afraid of losing this World; and my Children were given to the foolish Delights of Youth: So what by one thing and what by another, they left me to wander in this manner alone.

Cha. But did you not with your vain Life damp all that you by Words used by way of persuasion to bring them away with you?

Chr. Indeed I cannot commend my Life, for I am conscious to myself of many failings therein: I know also, that a man by his Conversation may soon overthrow what by Argument or Persuasion he doth labour to fasten upon others for their good. Yet, this I can say, I was very wary of giving them occasion, by any unseemly action, to make them averse to going on Pilgrimage. Yea, for this very thing, they would tell me I was too precise, and that I denied myself of things (for their sakes) in which they saw no evil. Nay, I think I may say, that, if what they saw in me did hinder them, it was my great Tenderness in sinning against God, or of doing any Wrong to my Neighbour. *Christian's good Conversation before his Wife and Children.*

Cha. Indeed *Cain* hated his brother, because his own works were Evil, and his brother's Righteous; and if thy Wife and Children have been offended with thee for this, they thereby shew themselves to be implacable to good; and thou hast delivered thy soul from their Blood. *1 John 3. 12. Christian clear of their Blood if they perish. Ezek. 3. 19.*

Now I saw in my dream, That thus they sat talking together until Supper was ready. So when they had made ready, they sat down to meat: Now the Table was furnished with fat Things, and with Wine that was well refined; and all their talk at the Table was about the LORD of the Hill; as, namely, about what HE had done, and wherefore HE did what HE did, and why HE had built that House; and by what they said, I perceived that HE had been a *great Warrior*, and had fought with, and slain him that *What Christian had to his Supper. Their Talk at Supper-Time.*

Heb. 2. 14,
15.
had the Power of Death, but not without great Danger to himself, which made me love him the more.

For, as they said, and as I believe, (said *Christian*) he did it with the Loss of much Blood; but that which put Glory of Grace into all he did, was, that he did it of pure Love to his Country. And besides, there were some of them of the Houshold that said, they had seen and spoke with him since he did die on the Cross; and they have attested, that they had it from his own lips, that he is such a Lover of poor Pilgrims, that the like is not to be found from the East to the West.

They moreover gave an Instance of what they affirmed, and that was, He had stript himself of his Glory, that he might do this for the Poor; and that they heard him say and affirm, *That he would not dwell in the Mountain of* Zion *alone.* They said

Christ makes Princes of Beggars.
1 Sam. 2. 8.
Ps. 113. 7.
moreover, That he had made many Pilgrims princes, though by nature they were beggars born, and their original had been the dunghill.

Thus they discoursed together till late at night; and after they had committed themselves to their Lord for Protection, they betook themselves to rest:

Christian's Bed-chamber.
The Pilgrim they laid in a large upper chamber, whose window opened towards the Sun-rising: The name of the chamber was *Peace*, where he slept till break of Day, and then he awoke and sang,

Where am I now! Is this the Love and Care
Of Jesus; *for the men that Pilgrims are,*
Thus to provide! That I should be forgiven,
And dwell already the next door to Heaven!

So, in the morning, they all got up; and, after some more discourse, they told him that he should not depart till they had shewed him the *Rarities* of that place. And first they had him into the Study, where they shewed him Records of the greatest antiquity; in which, as I remember my dream, they shewed him first the *Pedigree* of the Lord of the Hill, that he was the Son of the Ancient of Days, and came by an Eternal Generation: Here also was more fully recorded the Acts that he had done, and the Names of many hundreds that he had taken into his service; and how he had placed them in such Habitations, that he could neither by Length of Days, nor Decays of Nature, be dissolved.

Christian had into the Study and what he saw there.

Then they read to him some of the worthy Acts that some of his Servants had done: As how they had subdued Kingdoms, wrought Righteousness, obtained Promises, stopped the Mouths of Lions, quenched the Violence of Fire, escaped the Edge of the Sword, out of Weakness were made strong, waxed valiant in Fight, and turned to Flight the Armies of the *Aliens.*

Heb. 11. 33, 34.

Then they read again in another part of the Records of the House, where it was shewed how willing their Lord was to receive into his Favour, any, even any, though they in time past had offered great Affronts to his Person and Proceedings. Here also were several other histories of many other famous things, of all which *Christian* had a view: As of things both Ancient and Modern; together with Prophecies and Predictions of things that have their certain accomplishment, both to the dread and amazement of Enemies, and the comfort and solace of Pilgrims.

Christian *had into the Armory.*

The next day they took him, and had him into the Armory, where they shewed him all manner of Furniture, which their Lord had provided for Pilgrims, as Sword, Shield, Helmet, Breast-plate, *All-Prayer*, and Shoes that would not wear out. And there was here enough of this to harness out as many men, for the service of their Lord, as there be Stars in the Heaven for multitude.

They also shewed him some of the Engines with which some of his Servants had done wonderful

Christian *made to see Ancient things.*

things. They shewed him *Moses'* Rod, the Hammer and Nail with which *Jael* slew *Sisera*, the Pitchers, Trumpets, and Lamps too, with which *Gideon* put to Flight the Armies of *Midian.* Then they shewed him the Ox's Goad, wherewith *Shamgar* slew Six Hundred men. They shewed him also the Jaw-Bone with which *Samson* did such mighty Feats: They shewed him moreover the Sling and Stone with which *David* slew *Goliah* of *Gath;* and the Sword also with which their Lord will kill the Man of Sin, in the Day that he shall rise up to the Prey. They shewed him besides many excellent things, with which *Christian* was much delighted. This done, they went to their Rest again.

Then I saw in my dream, That on the morrow he got up to go forwards, but they desired him to stay till the next day also; and then said they, we

Christian *shewed the Delectable Mountains.*

will (if the day be clear) show you the Delectable Mountains; which, they said, would yet farther add to his Comfort, because they were nearer the desired Haven than the place where at present he was; so he consented and staid. When the morning was up, they had him to the top of the House, and bid

him look South : So he did ; and behold, at a great ^{Isa. 33. 16,}
Distance, he saw a most pleasant mountainous Coun- ^{17.}
try, beautified with Woods, Vineyards, Fruits of all
sorts, Flowers also, with Springs and Fountains,
very delectable to behold. Then he asked the
name of the Country. They said, It was *Emanuel's
Land;* and it is as common, said they, as this *Hill*
is to and for all the Pilgrims. And when thou
comest there, from thence thou mayest see to the
Gate of the Cœlestial City, as the Shepherds that
live there will make appear.

Now he bethought himself of setting forward, and Christian *sets*
they were willing he should. But first, said they, *forward.*
let us go again into the Armory : So they did ; and
when he came there, they harnessed him from head Christian *sent*
to foot, with what was of Proof, lest perhaps he *away armed.*
should meet with Assaults in the Way. He being
therefore thus accoutred, walketh out with his
Friends to the Gate, and there he asked the Porter,
If he saw any Pilgrim pass by ? Then the Porter
answered, Yes.

Chr. Pray, did you know him ? said he.

Port. I asked his name, and he told me it was
Faithful.

Chr. O, said *Christian,* I know him ; he is my
Townsman, my near neighbour, he comes from the
place where I was born : How far do you think he
may be before ?

Port. He is got by this time below the Hill.

Chr. Well, said *Christian,* good *Porter,* the Lord *How* Christian
be with thee, and add to all thy blessings much *and the* Porter
increase for the kindness that thou hast shewed to *greet at part-*
me. *ing.*

Then he began to go forward; but *Discretion, Piety, Charity,* and *Prudence,* would accompany him down to the foot of the Hill. So they went on together, reiterating their former discourses, till they came to go down the Hill. Then said *Christian,* As it was *difficult* coming up, so, (so far as I can see,) it is *dangerous* going down. Yes, said *Prudence,* so it is; for it is a hard matter for a man to go *The Valley of* down into the Valley of *Humiliation,* as thou art *Humiliation.* now, and to catch no slip by the Way; therefore, said they, are we come out to accompany thee down the Hill. So he began to go down, but very warily; yet he caught a slip or two.

Then I saw in my dream, That these good Companions (when *Christian* was got down to the bottom of the Hill) gave him a loaf of bread, a bottle of wine, and a cluster of raisins; and then he went his Way.

But now in this Valley of *Humiliation,* poor *Christian* was hard put to it; for he had gone but a little Way, before he espied a foul *Fiend* coming over the field to meet him: His name is *Apollyon.* Then did *Christian* begin to be afraid, and to cast in his mind whether to go back or to stand his ground. But he considered again, that he had no Armour for *Christian has* his back, and therefore thought that to turn the back *no Armour for* to him might give him greater advantage, with ease *his back.* to pierce him with his Darts; therefore he resolved

---

Whilst Christian *is among his godly friends,*
Their golden mouths make him sufficient 'mends
For all his griefs; and when they let him go,
He's clad with northern steel from top to toe.

to venture, and stand his ground: For, thought he, Christian's *Resolution on the approach of* Apollyon. had I no more in mine Eye than the saving of my life, 'twould be the best way to stand.

So he went on, and *Apollyon* met him: Now the Monster was hideous to behold: He was cloathed with scales like a fish; (and they are his Pride) he had wings like a dragon, feet like a bear, and out of his belly came fire and smoke, and his mouth was as the mouth of a lion. When he was come up to *Christian*, he beheld him with a disdainful countenance, and thus began to question with him.

Apollyon. Whence come you? and whither are *Discourse betwixt* Christian *and* Apollyon. you bound?

Chr. I am come from the City of *Destruction*, which is the Place of all Evil, and am going to the City of *Zion*.

Apol. By this I perceive thou art one of my subjects; for all that country is mine, and I am the Prince and God of it. How is it then that thou hast run away from thy King? Were it not that I hope thou mayest do me more service, I would strike thee now at one blow to the ground.

Chr. I was born indeed in your Dominions, but your Service was hard, and your wages such as a man could not live on; *for the Wages of Sin is Death;* Rom. 6. 23. therefore, when I was come to years, I did as other considerate persons do, look out, if perhaps I might mend myself.

Apol. There is no prince that will thus lightly lose his subjects, neither will I as yet lose thee; but since thou complainest of thy service and wages, be content to go back; what our Country will afford, I do here Apollyon's *Flattery.* promise to give thee.

Chr. But I have let myself to another, even to the King of princes, and how can I, with fairness, go back with thee ?

Apol. Thou hast done in this according to the Proverb, changed *a Bad for a Worse:* But it is ordinary for those that have professed themselves his Servants, after a while to give him the slip, and return again to me : Do thou so to, and all shall be well.

Apollyon *un-*
dervalues
Christ's Ser-
vice.

Chr. I have given him my Faith, and sworn my Allegiance to him, How then can I go back from this, and not be hanged as a Traitor ?

[Apollyon
pretends to be
merciful.
1st Edit. 1678
only.]

Apol. Thou didst the same to me, and yet I am willing to pass by all, if now thou wilt turn again and go back.

Chr. What I promised thee was in my non-age ; and besides, I count that the Prince under whose Banner now I stand, is able to absolve me ; yea, and to pardon also what I did as to my Compliance with thee : And besides, (O thou destroying *Apollyon*) to speak Truth, I like his Service, his Wages, his Servants, his Government, his Company, and Country, better than thine ; and therefore leave off to persuade me further, I am his servant, and I will follow him.

Apollyon
pleads the
grievous Ends
of Christians,
to dissuade
Christian *from*
persisting in
his Way.

Apol. Consider again, when thou art in cool blood, what thou art like to meet with in the Way that thou goest. Thou knowest, that for the most part, his Servants come to an ill End, because they are transgressors against me and my Ways. How many of them have been put to shameful deaths ! And besides, thou countest his service better than mine, whereas he never came yet from the Place where he is, to deliver any that served him out of our hands: But as for me, how many times, as all the World very well knows, have I delivered, either by Power or Fraud, those that have faithfully served me, from him and his, though taken by them? And so I will deliver thee.

Chr. His forbearing at present to deliver them, is on purpose to try their Love, whether they will cleave to him to the End: And as for the ill end thou sayest they come to, that is most glorious in their account: But, for present Deliverance, they do not much expect it; for they stay for their Glory, and then they shall have it, when their Prince comes in his, and the Glory of the Angels.

Apol. Thou hast already been unfaithful in thy service to him; and how dost thou think to receive Wages of him?

Chr. Wherein, O *Apollyon!* have I been unfaithful to him?

Apol. Thou didst faint at first setting out, when thou wast almost choaked in the Gulph of *Despond*; thou didst attempt wrong ways to be rid of thy Burden, whereas thou shouldest have stayed till thy Prince had taken it off. Thou didst sinfully sleep, and lose thy choice Things. Thou wast also almost persuaded to go back at the sight of the Lions: And when thou talkest of thy Journey, and of what thou hast heard and seen, thou art inwardly desirous of Vain-glory in all that thou sayest or dost.

Apollyon pleads Christian's Infirmities against him.

Chr. All this is true, and much more, which thou hast left out; but the Prince whom I serve and honour, is merciful and ready to forgive: But besides, these Infirmities possessed me in thy Country; for there I sucked them in, and I have groaned under them, been sorry for them, and have obtained Pardon of my Prince.

Apollyon in a Rage falls upon Christian.

Apol. Then *Apollyon* broke out into a grievous Rage, saying, I am an Enemy to this Prince; I hate his Person, his Laws, and People: I am come out on purpose to withstand thee.

Chr. Apollyon, beware what you do; for I am in the King's highway, the Way of Holiness; therefore take heed to yourself.

Apol. Then *Apollyon* straddled quite over the whole breadth of the Way, and said, I am void of Fear in this matter; prepare thyself to die; for I swear by my infernal Den, That thou shalt go no further: Here will I spill thy Soul!

And with that he threw a flaming Dart at his breast; but *Christian* had a Shield in his hand, with which he caught it, and so prevented the danger of that.

Then did *Christian* draw; for he saw it was time to bestir him; and *Apollyon* as fast made at him, throwing Darts as thick as hail; by the which, notwithstanding all that *Christian* could do to avoid it,

Christian wounded in his Understanding, Faith, and Conversation.

Apollyon wounded him in his *head*, his *hand*, and *foot*. This made *Christian* give a little back: *Apollyon*, therefore, followed his Work amain, and *Christian* again took Courage, and resisted as manfully as he could. This sore Combat lasted for above half a day, even till *Christian* was almost quite spent. For you must know that *Christian*, by reason of his Wounds, must needs grow weaker and weaker.

Then *Apollyon* espying his opportunity, began to

gather up close to *Christian*, and wrestling with him, gave him a dreadful Fall; and with that *Christian's* Sword flew out of his hand.   Then said *Apollyon, I am sure of thee now:* And with that he had almost pressed him to Death; so that *Christian* began to despair of Life.   But, as God would have it, while *Apollyon* was fetching of his last blow, thereby to make a full end of this good man, *Christian* nimbly reached out his hand for his Sword, and caught it, saying, *Rejoyce not against me, O mine Enemy! when I fall I shall arise;* and with that gave him a deadly thrust, which made him give back, as one that had received his mortal wound.   *Christian* perceiving that, made at him again; saying, *Nay, in all these things we are more than Conquerors, through him that loved us.*   And with that *Apollyon* spread forth his Dragon's wings, and sped him away, that *Christian* saw him no more.

In this Combat no man can imagine, unless he had seen and heard as I did, what yelling and hideous roaring *Apollyon* made all the time of the fight: He spake like a Dragon: And on the other side, what sighs and groans burst from *Christian's* heart. I never saw him all the while give so much as one pleasant look, till he perceived he had wounded *Apollyon* with his two-edged Sword; then, indeed, he did smile, and look upward: But it was the dreadfullest Fight that ever I saw.

Apollyon cast-eth Christian down to the Ground.

Christian's Victory over Apollyon.
Mic. 7. 8.

Rom. 8. 37.
Jam. 4. 7.

A brief Relation of the Combat, by the spectator.

A more unequal Match can hardly be:
Christian *must fight an Angel; but you see*
The Valiant Man, by handling Sword and Shield,
Doth make him, tho' a Dragon, quit the field.

Christian
*gives God
Thanks for
Deliverance.*
So when the Battle was over, *Christian* said, I will here give Thanks to him that hath delivered me out of the mouth of the *Lion,* to him that did help me against *Apollyon.* And so he did; saying,

Great Beelzebub, *the Captain of this Fiend,*
Design'd my Ruin; therefore to this end
He sent him harness'd out; and he with rage,
That hellish was, did fiercely me engage:
But blessed Michael *helped me, and I,*
By dint of Sword, did quickly make him fly:
Therefore to him let me give lasting Praise,
And Thank, and bless his holy Name always.

Then there came to him a Hand with some of the leaves of the Tree of Life, the which *Christian* took and applied to the wounds that he had received in the battle, and was healed immediately. He also sat down in that place to eat bread, and to drink of the bottle that was given him a little before; so being refreshed, he addressed himself to his Journey, with *Christian goes
on his Journey
with his Sword
drawn in his
hand.* his Sword drawn in his hand; for he said, I know not but some other Enemy may be at hand. But he met with no other affront from *Apollyon* quite through this Valley.

Now at the end of this Valley was another, called, *The Valley of
the* Shadow of
Death. *The Valley of the Shadow of Death,* and *Christian* must needs go through it, because the Way to the Cœlestial City lay through the midst of it: Now this Valley is a very solitary place. The prophet *Jere-* Jer. 2. 6. *miah* thus describes it: A wilderness, a land of desarts, and of pits; a land of drought, and of the shadow of death, a land that no man (but a Christian) passeth through, and where no man dwelt.

CHRISTIAN FIGHTS APOLLYON

Now here *Christian* was worse put to it than in his fight with *Apollyon;* as by the sequel you shall see.

I saw then in my dream, That when *Christian* was got to the borders of the *Shadow of Death,* there met him two men, children of them that brought up *The Children of the Spies go back.* an evil report of the good land, making haste to go back; to whom *Christian* spake as follows: Numb. 13.

Chr. Whither are you going?

Men. They said, Back! Back! And we would have you to do so too, if either Life or Peace is prized by you.

Chr. Why! What's the matter? said *Christian.*

Men. Matter! said they, we were going that Way as you are going, and went as far as we durst; and indeed we were almost past coming back; for had we gone a little farther, we had not been here to bring the news to thee.

Chr. But what have you met with? said *Christian.*

Men. Why we were almost in the Valley of the Psal. 44. 19. Shadow of Death, but that by good hap we looked Psal. 107. 10. before us, and saw the danger before we came to it.

Chr. But what have you seen? said *Christian.*

Men. Seen! Why the Valley itself, which is as dark as pitch: We also saw there the Hobgoblins, Satyrs, and Dragons of the Pit: We heard also in that Valley a continual howling and yelling, as of a people under unutterable misery, who there sat bound in affliction and irons; and over that Valley Job 3. 5. hangs the discouraging clouds of Confusion: Death ch. 10. 22. also doth always spread his wings over it. In a word, it is every whit dreadful, being utterly without Order.

Jer. 2. 5.

Chr. Then said *Christian*, I perceive not yet, by what you have said, but that this is my Way to the desired Haven.

Men. Be it thy Way, we will not choose it for ours.

So they parted, and *Christian* went on his Way, but still with his Sword drawn in his hand, for fear lest he should be assaulted.

I saw then in my dream, so far as this Valley reached, there was on the right hand a very deep Psal. 69. 14. Ditch: That Ditch is it, into which the blind have led the blind in all ages, and have both there miserably perished. Again, behold, on the left hand, there was a very dangerous Quag, into which, if even a good man falls, he finds no bottom for his foot to stand on: Into that Quag King *David* once did fall, and had, no doubt, therein been smothered, had not he that is able plucked him out.

The pathway was here also exceeding narrow, and therefore good *Christian* was the more put to it; for when he sought, in the Dark, to shun the Ditch on the one hand, he was ready to tip over into the Mire on the other: Also when he sought to escape the Mire, without great carefulness he would be ready to fall into the Ditch. Thus he went on,

---

*Poor man! where art thou now? Thy Day is
    Night:
Good man, be not cast down, thou yet art right.
Thy Way to Heav'n lies by the Gates of Hell:
Chear up, hold out, with thee it shall go well.*

and I heard him here sigh bitterly : For besides the dangers mentioned above, the pathway was here so dark, that oftimes, when he lift up his foot to set forward, he knew not where, or upon what, he should set it next.

About the midst of this Valley, I perceived the mouth of Hell to be, and it stood also hard by the Wayside : Now, thought *Christian*, what shall I do ? And ever and anon the flame and smoke would come out in such abundance, with sparks and hideous noises, (things that cared not for *Christian's* Sword, as did *Apollyon* before) that he was forced to put up his Sword, and betake himself to another Weapon, called *All Prayer :* So he cried, in my hearing, *O* Eph. 6. 18. *Lord, I beseech thee, deliver my Soul.* Thus he went Psal. 116. 4. on a great while, yet still the flames would be reaching towards him : Also he heard doleful voices, and rushings to and fro, so that sometimes he thought he should be torn in pieces, or trodden down like mire in the streets. This frightful sight was seen, and these dreadful noises were heard by him for several miles together : And coming to a place, where he thought he heard a Company of *Fiends* coming forward to meet him, he stopt, and began to muse what Christian *put* he had best to do : Sometimes he had half a thought *to a stand, but* to go back ; then again he thought he might be half-*for a while.* way through the Valley : He remembred also, how he had already vanquished many a danger ; and that the danger of going back might be much more than for to go forward ; so he resolved to go on : Yet the *Fiends* seemed to come nearer and nearer : But when they were come even almost at him, he cried out with a most vehement voice, *I will walk in the*

Strength of the Lord God: So they gave back, and came no further.

One thing I would not let slip: I took notice that now poor *Christian* was so confounded, that he did not know his own voice: And thus I perceived it: Just when he was come over-against the mouth of the burning Pit, one of the Wicked Ones got behind him, and stept up softly to him, and whisperingly suggested many grievous Blasphemies to him, which he verily thought had proceeded from his own mind. This put *Christian* more to it than any thing that he met with before, even to think that he should now blaspheme him that he loved so much before; yet, if he could have helped it, he would not have done it: But he had not the discretion either to stop his ears, or to know from whence those Blasphemies came.

Christian made believe that he spake Blasphemies when 'twas Satan that suggested them into his mind.

When *Christian* had travelled in this disconsolate condition some considerable time, he thought he heard the voice of a man, as going before him, saying, *Though I walk through the Valley of the Shadow of Death, I will fear none Ill, for thou art with me.*

Psal. 23. 4.

Then was he glad; and that for these reasons:

First, Because he gathered from thence, that some who feared God were in this Valley as well as himself.

Job 9 10.

Secondly, For that he perceived God was with them, though in that dark and dismal state: And why not, thought he, with me? Though by reason of the impediment that attends this place, I cannot perceive it.

Thirdly, For that he hoped (could he overtake them) to have Company by-and-by.

So he went on, and called to him that was before; but he knew not what to answer: For that he also thought himself to be alone. And by and by the Day broke: Then said *Christian, He hath turned the Shadow of Death into the Morning.* Amos 5. 8.

Now Morning being come, he looked back, not out of desire to return, but to see, by the Light of the Day, what Hazards he had gone through in the Dark: So he saw more perfectly the Ditch that was Christian *glad at Break of* Day. on the one hand, and the Quag that was on the other; also how narrow the Way was which led betwixt them both; also how he saw the Hobgoblins, and Satyrs, and Dragons of the Pit, but all afar off: For after break of Day they came not nigh, yet they were discovered to him, according to that which is written, *He discovereth deep things out of Darkness, and bringeth out to Light the shadow of death.* Job 12. 22.

Now was *Christian* much affected with his deliverance from all the dangers of his solitary Way; which dangers, though he feared them more before, yet he saw them more clearly now, because the light of the day made them conspicuous to him; and about this time the Sun was rising, and this was another Mercy to *Christian:* For you must note, that though the first part of the Valley of the Shadow of Death was dangerous, yet this second part, which *The second part of this Valley very dangerous.* he was yet to go, was, if possible, far more dangerous: For, from the place where he now stood, even to the end of the Valley, the Way was all along set so full of snares, traps, gins, and nets here, and so full of pits, pitfalls, deep holes, and shelvings down there, that had it now been dark, as it was when he came the first part of the Way, had he had a thousand Souls, they had in reason been cast away ; but, as I said, just now the Sun was rising. Then said he, *His Candle shineth on my head, and by his Light I go through Darkness.*

Job 29. 3.

In this Light therefore he came to the end of the Valley. Now I saw in my dream, that at the end of this Valley lay blood, bones, ashes, and mangled bodies of men, even of Pilgrims that had gone this Way formerly : And while I was musing what should be the reason, I espied a little before me a Cave, where two giants, *Pope* and *Pagan*, dwelt in old Time ; by whose power and tyranny the men, whose bones, blood, ashes, *&c.* lay there, were cruelly put to death. But by this place *Christian* went without much danger, whereat I somewhat wondered : But I have learnt since, that *Pagan* has been dead many a day ; and as for the other, though he be yet alive, he is, by reason of age, and also of the many shrewd brushes that he met with in his younger days, grown so crazy and stiff in his joints, that he can now do little more than sit in his Cave's mouth, grinning at Pilgrims as they go by, and biting his nails, because he cannot come at them.

So I saw that *Christian* went on his Way ; yet, at the sight of the *Old Man*, that sat in the mouth of the Cave, he could not tell what to think, 'specially because he spake to him, though he could not go after him ; saying, *You will never mend, till more of you be burnt.* But he held his peace, and set a good face on't, and so went by, and catched no hurt. Then sang *Christian :*

O World of Wonders! (I can say no less)
That I should be preserv'd in that Distress
That I have met with here! O blessed be
That Hand that from it hath deliver'd me!
Dangers in darkness, Devils, Hell, and Sin,
Did compass me, while I this Vale was in:
Yea Snares, and Pits, and Traps, and Nets did lie
My Path about, that worthless, silly I
Might have been catch'd, entangled, and cast down:
But since I live, let JESUS *wear the Crown.*

Now, as *Christian* went on his Way, he came to a little ascent, which was cast up on purpose, that Pilgrims might see before them: Up there, therefore, *Christian* went; and looking forward, he saw *Faithful* before him upon his Journey: Then said *Christian* aloud, *Ho, ho: So, ho: Stay, and I will be your Companion.* At that *Faithful* looked behind him; to whom *Christian* cried again, *Stay, stay, till I come up to you.* But *Faithful* answer'd, *No, I am upon my Life, and the Avenger of Blood is behind me.*

At this *Christian* was somewhat moved, and putting to all his strength, he quickly got up with *Faithful,* and did also overrun him; so the *last* was first. Then did *Christian* vain-gloriously smile, because he had gotten the start of his Brother: But not taking good heed to his feet, he suddenly stumbled and fell, and could not rise again, until *Faithful* came up to help him. *Christian over-takes Faithful.*

Then I saw in my dream, they went very lovingly on together, and had sweet discourse of all things that had happened to them in their Pilgrimage; and thus *Christian* began. *Christian's Fall makes Faithful and he go lovingly together.*

Chr. My honoured and well beloved Brother *Faithful*, I am glad that I have overtaken you; and that God has so tempered our Spirits, that we can walk as Companions in this so pleasant a path.

Faith. I had thought, dear Friend, to have had your Company quite from our town, but you did get the start of me: Wherefore I was forced to come thus much of the Way alone.

Chr. How long did you stay in the City of *Destruction*, before you set out after me on your Pilgrimage?

Their talk about the Country from whence they came.

Faith. Till I could stay no longer; for there was great talk presently after you were gone out, that our City would, in a short time, with Fire from Heaven, be burned down to the ground.

Chr. What, did your Neighbours talk so?

Faith. Yes, 'twas for a while in everybody's mouth.

Chr. What and did no more of them but you come out to escape the danger?

Faith. Though there was, as I said, a great Talk thereabout, yet I do not think they did firmly believe it. For in the heat of the discourse, I heard some of them deridingly speak of you and of your desperate Journey (for so they called this your Pilgrimage:) But I did believe, and do still, that the end of our City will be with fire and brimstone from Above: And therefore I have made my escape.

Chr. Did you hear no talk of neighbour *Pliable*?

Faith. Yes, *Christian*, I heard that he followed you till he came at the Slough of *Despond*; where, as some said, he fell in: But he would not be known to have so done; but I am sure he was soundly bedaubed with that kind of dirt.

Chr. And what said the neighbours to him?

Faith. He hath, since his going back, been had *How* Pliable *was accounted* greatly in derision, and that among all sorts of *of, when he* people; some do mock and despise him, and scarce *got home.* will any set him on work. He is now seven times worse than if he had never gone out of the City.

Chr. But why should they be so set against him, since they also despise the Way that he forsook?

Faith. O, they say, Hang him; he is a turncoat! he was not true to his Profession! I think God has stirred up even his enemies to hiss at him, and make Jer. 29. 18. him a proverb, because he hath forsaken the Way. 19.

Chr. Had you no talk with him before you came out?

Faith. I met him once in the streets, but he leered away on the other side, as one ashamed of what he had done: So I spake not to him.

Chr. Well, at my first setting out, I had hopes of that man; but now I fear he will perish in the over-throw of the City. For it has happened to him 2 Pet. 2. 22. according to the true proverb, *The dog is turned to his vomit again; and the sow that was washed, to her* The Dog and *wallowing in the mire.* the Sow.

Faith. They are my fears of him too, but who can hinder that which will be?

Chr. Well, neighbour *Faithful* (said *Christian*) let us leave him, and talk of things that more imme-diately concern ourselves. Tell me now what you have met with in the Way as you came: For I know you have met with some things, or else it may be writ for a Wonder.

Faith. I escaped the *Slough* that I perceive you fell into, and got up to the Gate without that danger; only I met with one whose name was *Wanton*, that had like to have done me a mischief.

Faithful *assaulted by* Wanton.

Chr. 'Twas well you escaped her Net: *Joseph* was hard put to it by her, and he escaped her as you did; but it had like to have cost him his Life. But what did she do to you?

Gen. 39. 11, 12, 13.

Faith. You cannot think (but that you know something) what a flattering tongue she had; she lay at me hard to turn aside with her, promising me all manner of Content.

Chr. Nay, she did not promise you the Content of a good Conscience.

Faith. You know what I mean; all carnal and fleshly content.

Prov. 22. 14.

Chr. Thank God you have escaped her: The abhorred of the Lord shall fall into her ditch.

Faith. Nay, I know not whether I did wholly escape her, or no.

Chr. Why, I trow, you did not consent to her desires?

Faith. No not to defile myself; for I remembered an old Writing that I had seen, which said, *Her*

Prov. 5. 5. Job 31. 1.

steps take hold of Hell. So I shut mine eyes, because I would not be bewitched with her looks: Then she railed on me, and I went my way.

Chr. Did you meet with no other assault as you came?

Faith. When I came to the foot of the Hill called *Difficulty*, I met with a very aged Man, who asked

He was assaulted by Adam the First.

me what I was? and whither bound? I told him, that I was a Pilgrim, going to the Cœlestial City.

Then said the old man, Thou lookest like an honest fellow; wilt thou be content to dwell with me, for the Wages that I shall give thee? Then I asked him his name, and where he dwelt? He said his name was *Adam the first,* and I dwell in the town of *Deceit.* I asked him then, What was his Work? Eph. 4. 22. and what the Wages that he would give? He told me, that his *Work* was *many delights;* and his *Wages,* that I should be his Heir at last. I further asked him, what House he kept, and what other Servants he had? So he told me, that his House was maintained with all the dainties in the world; and that his *servants* were those of his own begetting. Then I asked, how many children he had? He said, that he had but three daughters, *The Lust of the Flesh,* 1 John 2. 16. *The Lust of the Eyes,* and *The Pride of Life;* and that I should marry them all, if I would. Then I asked, how long Time he would have me live with him? And he told me, As long as he lived himself.

Chr. Well, and what conclusion came the old man and you to at last?

Faith. Why, at first I found myself somewhat inclinable to go with the man, for I thought he spake very fair; but looking in his forehead, as I talked with him, I saw there written, *Put off the Old Man with his Deeds.*

Chr. And how then?

Faith. Then it came burning hot into my mind, whatever he said, and however he flattered, when he got me home to his house, he would sell me for a Slave. So I bid him forbear to talk, for I would not come near the door of his house. Then he reviled me, and told me, that he would send such a one after me, that should make my Way bitter to my Soul. So I turned to go away from him; but just as I turned myself to go thence, I felt him take hold of my Flesh, and give me such a deadly twitch back, that I thought he had pulled part of me after himself: This made me cry, *O wretched Man!* So I went on my Way up the Hill.

Rom. 7. 24.

Now when I had got above half way up, I looked behind me, and saw one coming after me, swift as the wind; so he overtook me just about the place where the Settle stands.

Chr. Just there, said *Christian*, did I sit down to rest me; but being overcome with Sleep, I there lost this Roll out of my bosom.

Faith. But, good brother, hear me out: So soon as the man overtook me, he was but a word and a blow; for down he knocked me, and laid me for dead. But when I was a little come to myself again, I asked him, Wherefore he served me so? He said, Because of my secret inclining to *Adam the First:* And with that he struck me another deadly blow on the breast, and beat me down backward; so I lay at his foot as dead as before. So when I came to myself again, I cried him mercy: But he said, I know not how to show mercy; and with that knocked me down again. He had doubtless made an end of me, but that one came by, and bid him forbear.

Chr. Who was that, that bid him forbear?

Faith. I did not know him at first; but as he went by, I perceived the holes in his hands and in his side: Then I concluded that he was our Lord. So I went up the Hill.

Chr. That Man that overtook you, was *Moses.* He spareth none, neither knoweth he how to shew mercy to those that transgress his Law.

Faith. I know it very well; it was not the first time that he has met with me. 'Twas he that came to me when I dwelt securely at home, and that told me he would burn my house over my head, if I staid there.

Chr. But did you not see the House that stood there on the top of that Hill, on the side of which *Moses* met you?

Faith. Yes, and the Lions too, before I came at it; but for the Lions, I think they were asleep; for it was about Noon : And because I had so much of the Day before me, I passed by the Porter, and came down the Hill.

Chr. He told me indeed, That he saw you go by ; but I wish you had called at the House ; for they would have shewed you so many rarities, that you would scarce have forgot them to the day of your death. But pray tell me, Did you meet nobody in the Valley of *Humility?*

Faith. Yes, I met with one *Discontent*, who would willingly have persuaded me to go back again with him : His reason was, For that the Valley was al-together without *Honour*. He told me moreover, That there to go, was the way to disobey all my Friends, as *Pride, Arrogancy, Self-Conceit, Worldly-Glory*, with others, who, he knew, as he said, would be very much offended, if I made such a Fool of myself as to wade through this Valley.

Chr. Well, and how did you answer him ?

Faith. I told him, That although all these that he

Faithful's *an-swer to* Dis-content. named, might claim kindred of me, and that rightly, (for indeed they *were* my relations, *according to the Flesh*) yet since I became a Pilgrim, they have disowned me, as I also have rejected them; and therefore they were to me now, no more than if they had never been of my lineage : I told him moreover, That as to this Valley, he had quite misrepresented the thing; for before *Honour* is *Humility*, and a *Haughty Spirit* before a *Fall.* Therefore, said I, I had rather go through this Valley to the honour that was so accounted by the Wisest, than choose that which he esteemed most worthy our affections.

Chr. Met you with nothing else in that Valley ?

He is assaulted with Shame.

Faith. Yes I met with *Shame;* but of all the men that I met with in my Pilgrimage, he, I think, bears the wrong name. The other would be said Nay, after a little argumentation, (and somewhat else): But this bold-faced *Shame* would never have done.

Chr. Why, what did he say to you ?

Faith. What! why he objected against *Religion* itself; he said, 'Twas a pitiful, low, sneaking business for a man to mind *Religion;* he said that a tender Conscience was an unmanly thing; and that for a man to watch over his Words and Ways, so as to tie up himself from that hectoring liberty that the brave *Spirits of the Times* accustomed themselves unto, would make him the ridicule of the Times. He objected also, That but *few* of the *Mighty, Rich,* or *Wise*, were ever of my opinion; nor any of *them* 1 Cor. 1. 26. neither, before they were persuaded to be fools, and ch. 3. 18. Phil. 3. 7. 8. to be of a voluntary fondness to venture the Loss John 7. 48. of all, for nobody else knows what. He moreover objected the base and low estate and condition of those that were chiefly the Pilgrims of the times in which they lived; also their Ignorance, and want of understanding in all Natural Science. Yea, he did hold me to it at that rate also, about a great many more things than here I relate; as that it was a shame to sit whining and mourning under a sermon, and a shame to come sighing and groaning home: That it was a shame to ask my neighbour Forgiveness for petty faults, or to make Restitution where I have taken from any. He said also, That Religion made a man grow strange to the Great, because of a few Vices, (which he called by finer names) and made him own and respect the Base, because of the same Religious Fraternity: And is not this, said he, a Shame?

Chr. And what did you say to him?

Faith. Say! I could not tell what to say at first. Yea, he put me so to it, that my blood came up in my face; even this *Shame* fetched it up, and had almost beat me quite off. But at last I began to consider, That that which is highly esteemed among Luke 16. 15. Men, is had in abomination with God. And I thought again, this *Shame* tells me what *men* are; but it tells me nothing what *God* or the *Word of God* is. And I thought moreover, That at the Day of Doom we shall not be doomed to Death or Life, according to the hectoring spirits of the world, but according to the Wisdom and Law of the Highest. Therefore, thought I, what God says, is best, though all the men in the world are against it: Seeing then that God prefers his Religion; seeing God prefers a tender Conscience; seeing they that make themselves fools for the Kingdom of Heaven, are wisest; and that the poor man that loveth Christ, is richer than the greatest man in the world that hates him; *Shame*, depart, thou art an Enemy to my Salvation; shall I entertain thee against my Sovereign Lord? How then shall I look him in the Face at his Coming? Should I now be *ashamed* of his Ways and Servants, how can I expect the blessing? But indeed this *Shame* was a bold villain: I could scarce shake him out of my company: Yea, he would be haunting of me, and continually whispering me in the ear, with some one or other of the Infirmities that attend Religion; but at last I told him, it was but in vain to attempt further in this business; for those things that he disdained, in those did I see most Glory: And so at last I got past this importunate one. And when I had shaken him off, then I began to sing:

Mar. 8. 38.

> *The Tryals that those men do meet withal,*
> *That are obedient to the Heavenly Call,*
> *Are manifold and suited to the Flesh,*
> *And come, and come, and come again afresh;*
> *That now, or some time else, we by them may*
> *Be taken, overcome, and cast away.*
> *O let the Pilgrims, let the Pilgrims then*
> *Be vigilant, and quit themselves like Men.*

Chr. I am glad, my Brother, that thou didst withstand this villain so bravely; for of all, as thou sayest, I think he has the wrong name; for he is so bold as to follow us in the streets, and to attempt to put us to shame before all men, that is, to make us ashamed of that which is Good; but if he was not himself audacious, he would never attempt to do as he does; but let us still resist him; for notwithstanding all his bravado's, he promoteth the Fool, and none else. The Wise shall inherit Glory, said *Solo-* Prov. 3. 35. *mon;* but Shame shall be the promotion of Fools.

Faith. I think we must cry to Him for help against *Shame*, that would have us be valiant for Truth upon the earth.

Chr. You say true: But did you meet nobody else in that Valley?

Faith. No not I; for I had Sun-shine all the rest of the Way through that, and also through the Valley of the Shadow of Death.

Chr. It was well for you; I am sure, it fared far otherwise with me; I had for a long season, as soon almost as I entered into that Valley, a dreadful Combat with that foul Fiend *Apollyon;* yea, I thought verily he would have killed me, especially when he got me down, and crushed me under him, as if he would have crushed me to pieces. For as he threw me, my Sword flew out of my hand; nay, he told me, he was *sure of me:* but I cried to God, and he heard me, and delivered me out of all my troubles. Then I entered into the Valley of the *Shadow of Death*, and had no Light for almost half the Way through it. I thought I should have been killed there over and over; but at last Day brake, and the Sun rose, and I went through that which was behind with far more ease and quiet.

Moreover I saw in my dream, that as they went on, *Faithful,* as he chanced to look on one side, saw a man whose name was *Talkative,* walking at a dis-

tance besides them (for in this place there was room
enough for them all to walk.) He was a tall man,
and something more comely at a distance, than at
hand : To this man *Faithful* addressed himself in
this manner.

Faith. Friend, Whither away ? are you going to
the Heavenly Country ?

Talk. I *am* going to that same Place.

Faith. That is well ; then I hope we may have
your good company ?

Talk. With a very good will will I be your Companion.

Faith. Come on then, and let us go together, and
let us spend our time in discoursing of things that
are profitable.

Talk. To talk of things that are good, to me is
very acceptable, with you, or with any other ; and I
am glad that I have met with those that incline to so
good a work : For to speak the truth, there are but
few that care thus to spend their time (as they are in
their Travels) but choose much rather to be speaking
of things to no profit ; and this hath been a Trouble
to me.

Faith. That is indeed a thing to be lamented ;
for what thing so worthy of the use of the tongue
and mouth of men on Earth, as are the things of
the God of Heaven ?

Talk. I like you wonderful well ; for your sayings
are full of conviction ; and I will add, What thing is
so pleasant, and what so profitable, as to talk of the
Things of God ?

What things so pleasant ? (that is, if a man hath
any delight in things that are wonderful) for instance :

If a man doth delight to talk of the History, or the Mystery of things; or if a man doth love to talk of Miracles, Wonders, or Signs, where shall he find things recorded so delightful, and so sweetly penned, as in the Holy Scripture?

Faith. That's true; but to be profited by such things in our talk, should be that which we design.

Talk. That is it that I said; for to talk of such things is most profitable; for by so doing, a man may get Knowledge of many things; as of the vanity of Earthly things, and the benefit of things Above: (Thus in general) but more particularly; by this a man may learn the necessity of the New Birth; the insufficiency of our Works; the need of Christ's righteousness, *&c.* Besides, by this a man may learn what it is to repent, to believe, to pray, to suffer, or the like: By this also, a Man may learn what are the great Promises and consolations of the Gospel, to his own comfort. Farther, by this a Man may learn to refute false opinions, to vindicate the Truth, and also to instruct the Ignorant.

Faith. All this is true, and glad am I to hear these things from you.

Talk. Alas! the want of this is the cause that so few understand the need of Faith, and the necessity of a work of Grace in their soul, in order to Eternal Life; but ignorantly live in the works of the Law, by which a man can by no means obtain the Kingdom of Heaven.

Faith. But, by your leave, Heavenly knowledge of these is the Gift of God; no man attaineth to them by human industry, or only by the talk of them.

Talkative's fine discourse.

O brave Talkative.

Talk. All this I know very well. For a man can receive nothing, except it be given him from Heaven; all is of Grace, not of works: I could give you an hundred Scriptures for the confirmation of this.

Faith. Well then, said *Faithful,* what is that one thing that we shall at this time found our discourse upon?

O brave Talkative.

Talk. What you will: I will talk of things Heavenly, or things Earthly; things Moral, or things Evangelical; things Sacred, or things Prophane; things past, or things to come; things foreign, or things at home; things more essential, or things circumstantial; provided that all be done to our Profit.

Faithful *beguiled by* Talkative.

Faith. Now did *Faithful* begin to wonder; and stepping to *Christian,* (for he walked all this while by himself) he said to him, (but softly,) What a brave Companion have we got? Surely this man will make a very excellent Pilgrim.

Christian *makes a discovery of* Talkative, *telling* Faithful *who he was.*

Chr. At this *Christian* modestly smiled, and said, This man, with whom you are so taken, will beguile, with this Tongue of his, twenty of them that know him not.

Faith. Do you know him then?

Chr. Know him! Yes, better than he knows himself.

Faith. Pray what is he?

Chr. His name is *Talkative;* he dwelleth in our town; I wonder that you should be a stranger to him, only I consider that our Town is large.

Faith. Whose son is he? And whereabout doth he dwell?

Chr. He is the son of one *Say-well*, he dwelt in *Prating-Row;* and he is known of all that are acquainted with him, by the name of *Talkative* in *Prating-Row;* and notwithstanding his fine tongue, he is but a sorry fellow.

Faith. Well, he seems to be a very pretty man.

Chr. That is, to them that have not a thorough acquaintance with him; for he is best abroad, near home he is ugly enough: Your saying that he is a *pretty man*, brings to my mind what I have observed in the work of the Painter, whose pictures shew best at a distance; but very near, more unpleasing.

Faith. But I am ready to think you do but *jest*, because you *smiled*.

Chr. God forbid that I should *jest*, (though I smiled) in this matter, or that I should accuse any falsely; I will give you a further discovery of him: This man is for any company, and for any *talk;* as he *talketh now* with you, so will he talk when he is on the *ale-bench:* And the more Drink he hath in his crown, the more of these things he hath in his mouth: Religion hath no place in his heart, or house, or conversation; all he hath lieth in his *tongue*, and his religion is to make a noise therewith.

Faith. Say you so! then am I in this man greatly deceived.

Chr. Deceived! you may be sure of it: Remember the proverb, *They say, and do not; but the* Mat. 23. *Kingdom of God is not in word, but in power.* He ¹ Cor. 4. 20. talketh of Prayer, of Repentance, of Faith, and of Talkative the New Birth; but he knows but only to *talk* of *talks, but does not.*

them.   I have been in his Family, and have observed him both at home and abroad; and I know

His House is empty of Religion.

what I say of him is the truth.   His house is as empty of religion, as the white of an egg is of savour.   There is there neither Prayer, nor sign of Repentance for Sin: Yea, the brute in his kind,

He is a Stain to Religion. Rom. 2. 24. 25.

serves God far better than he.   He is the very stain, reproach, and shame of Religion to all that know him; it can hardly have a good word in all that end of the Town where he dwells, through him. Thus, say the common people that know him, *A*

The Proverb that goes of him.

Saint abroad, and a Devil at home.   His poor family finds it so, he is such a churl; such a railer at, and so unreasonable with his servants, that they neither know how to do for, or speak to him.   Men that

Men shun to deal with him.

have any dealings with him, say, 'Tis better to deal with a *Turk* than with him, for fairer dealing they shall have at their hands.   This *Talkative* (if it be possible) will go beyond them, defraud, beguile, and over-reach them.   Besides, he brings up his sons to follow his steps; and if he findeth in any of them *a foolish Timourousness,* (for so he calls the first appearance of a tender conscience) he calls them Fools and blockheads; and by no means will employ them in much, or speak to their commendations before others.   For my part, I am of opinion, that he has, by his wicked Life, caused many to stumble and fall; and will be, if God prevent not, the ruin of many more.

Faith. Well, my brother, I am bound to believe you; not only because you say you know him, but also because, like a Christian, you make your reports of men.   For I cannot think that you speak these things of Ill-will, but because it is even so as you say.

Chr. Had I known him no more than you, I might perhaps have thought of him as at the first you did : Yea, had he received this report at their hands only that are enemies to Religion, I should have thought it had been a slander. (A lot that often falls from bad mens mouths, upon good mens names and professions :) But all these things, yea, and a great many more as bad, of my own knowledge, I can prove him guilty of. Besides, good men are ashamed of him ; they can neither call him *brother* nor *friend;* The very naming of him among them, makes them blush, if they know him.

Faith. Well, I see that *saying* and *doing* are two things, and hereafter I shall better observe this distinction.

Chr. They are two things indeed, and are as diverse, as are the Soul and the Body; for as the *The carcass of Religion.* Body without the Soul is but a dead carcass, so *saying*, if it be alone, is but a dead carcass also. The Soul of Religion is the Practick part : *Pure Religion* *Jam* 1. 27. *and undefiled, before God and the Father, is this, To* *See ver. 23, 24, 25, 26.* *visit the fatherless and widows in their affliction, and to keep himself unspotted from the World.* This *Talkative* is not aware of; he thinks that *hearing* and *saying* will make a good Christian ; and thus he deceiveth his own soul. Hearing is but as the sowing of the seed : Talking is not sufficient to prove that fruit is indeed in the Heart and Life; and let us assure ourselves, that at the day of Doom, men *See Matt.* 13. shall be judged according to their Fruit: It will not *and* ch. 25. be said then, *Did you believe?* But were you *Doers*' or *Talkers* only? And accordingly shall they be judged. The end of the world is compared to our harvest; and you know men at harvest regard nothing but fruit. Not that any thing can be accepted, that is not of Faith; but I speak this to shew you how insignificant the profession of *Talkative* will be at that Day.

Faith. This brings to my mind that of *Moses*, by which he described the beast that is clean. He is such an one that parteth the hoof, and cheweth the cud; not that parteth the *hoof* only, or that cheweth the *cud* only. The hare cheweth the cud, but yet is unclean; because he parteth not the hoof. And this truly resembleth *Talkative;* he cheweth the cud, he seeketh Knowledge, he cheweth upon the Word; but he divideth not the hoof, he parteth not with the Way of Sinners; but as the hare, he retaineth the foot of a dog or bear, and therefore is unclean.

Chr. You have spoken, for ought I know, the true Gospel sense of those texts. And I will add another thing: *Paul* calleth some men, yea, and those great *Talkers* too, *Sounding Brass*, and *Tink-ling Cymbals;* that is, as he expounds them in another place, *Things without life, giving sound.* Things without life, that is, without the true Faith and Grace of the Gospel; and consequently, things that shall never be placed in the Kingdom of Heaven among those that are the Children of Life: Though their *sound* by their *talk*, be as it were the tongue or voice of an Angel.

Faith. Well, I was not so fond of his company at first, but I am as sick of it now. What shall we do to be rid of him?

Marginal notes:

Lev. 11. Deut. 14.
Faithful *convinced of the badness of* Talkative.

1 Cor. 13. 1, 2, 3. ch. 14. 7.
Talkative *like to things that sound without Life.*

Chr. Take my advice, and do as I bid you, and you shall find that he will soon be sick of your company too, except God shall touch his heart and turn it.

Faith. What would you have me to do?

Chr. Why, go to him, and enter into some serious discourse about the *Power of Religion;* and ask him plainly, (when he has approved of it, for that he will) whether this thing be set up in his Heart, House, or Conversation.

Faith. Then *Faithful* stept forward again, and said to *Talkative, Come, what chear? How is it now?*

Talk. Thank you, well; I thought we should have had a great deal of talk by this time.

Faith. Well, if you will, we will fall to it now; and since you left it with me to state the question, let it be this: How doth the Saving Grace of God discover itself, when it is in the Heart of Man?

Talk. I perceive then that our talk must be about the *Power of Things:* Well, 'tis a very good question, and I shall be willing to answer you. And take my answer in brief, thus: *First,* Where the Grace of God is in the heart, it causeth there a great Outcry against Sin. *Secondly,* *Talkative's false discovery of a Work of Grace.*

Faith. Nay, hold, let us consider of one at once: I think you should rather say, It shews itself by inclining the soul to abhor its Sin.

Talk. Why, what difference is there between crying out against, and abhorring of Sin?

Faith. Oh! a great deal: A man may cry out against Sin, of Policy, but he cannot abhor it but by virtue of a godly antipathy against it: I have heard *The Crying out against Sin, no sign of Grace.*

many cry out against Sin in the Pulpit, who yet can abide it well enough in the Heart, House, and Con-

Gen. 39. 15. versation. *Joseph's* Mistress cried out with a loud voice, as if she had been very holy; but she would willingly, notwithstanding that, have committed uncleanness with him. Some cry out against Sin, even as the mother cries out against her child in her lap, when she calleth it slut and naughty girl, and then falls to hugging and kissing it.

Talk. You lie at the Catch, I perceive.

Faith. No, not I, I am only for setting things right. But what is the second thing whereby you would prove a discovery of a Work of Grace in the heart?

Talk. Great Knowledge of *Gospel-Mysteries.*

Faith. This sign should have been first; but first

Great Knowledge no sign of Grace.
1 Cor. 13. or last, it is also false; for Knowledge, great knowledge may be obtained in the mysteries of the Gospel, and yet no Work of Grace in the Soul. Yea, if a man have all Knowledge, he may yet be nothing; and so consequently be no child of God. When Christ said, *Do you know all these things?* And the disciples had answered, Yes: He added, *Blessed are ye, if ye do them.* He doth not lay the blessing in the *knowing* of them, but in the *doing* of them. For there is a knowledge that is not attended with doing: *He that knoweth his Master's will, and doth it not.* A man may know like an Angel, and yet be no Christian; therefore your sign is not true. Indeed, to *know*, is a thing that pleaseth Talkers and Boasters; but to *do*, is that which pleaseth God. Not that the heart can be good without knowledge; for without that, the heart is naught. There is there-

fore knowledge and knowledge; knowledge that *Knowledge and know-ledge.* resteth in the bare speculation of things, and know-ledge that is accompanied with the grace of Faith and Love; which puts a man upon doing even the Will of God from the Heart: The first of these will serve the *Talker;* but without the other, the true Christian is not content. *Give me Understanding,* *True Knowledge attended with Endeavours.* *and I shall keep thy Law; yea, I shall observe it with my whole Heart.* Psal. cxix. 34.

Talk. You lie at the Catch again; this is not for edification.

Faith. Well, if you please, propound another sign how this work of Grace discovereth itself where it is.

Talk. Not I, for I see we shall not agree.

Faith. Well, if you will not, will you give me leave to do it?

Talk. You may use your liberty.

Faith. A Work of Grace in the Soul discovereth *One good sign of Grace.* itself, either to him that hath it, or to standers by. John 16. 8.

To him that hath it, *thus;* It gives him Conviction Rom. 7. 24. John 16. 9. of Sin, especially the defilement of his Nature, and Mark 6. 16. Ps. 38. 18. the Sin of Unbelief, (for the sake of which he is sure Jer. 31. 19. to be damned, if he findeth not Mercy at God's hand, Gal. 2. 16. Acts 4. 12. by faith in Jesus Christ.) This fight and sense of Matt. 5. 6. Rev. 21. 6. things worketh in him sorrow and shame for Sin: He findeth, moreover, revealed in him the Saviour of the World, and the absolute necessity of closing with him for Life, at the which he findeth hungrings and thirstings after him; to which hungrings, *&c.* the Promise is made. Now according to the strength or weakness of his faith in his Saviour, so is his Joy and Peace, so is his love to Holiness, so are his desires to know him more, and also to

serve him in this World. But though, I say, it discovereth itself thus unto him, yet it is but seldom
that he is able to conclude, that this is a Work of
Grace, because his Corruptions now, and his abused
Reason, make his mind to misjudge in this matter;
therefore in him that hath this Work, there is required a very sound judgment, before he can with
steadiness conclude that this is a Work of Grace.
To others it is thus discovered:

Rom. 10. 10.
Phil. 1. 27.
Matt. 5. 9.
John 14. 15.
Ps. 50. 23.
Job 42. 5, 6.
Ezek. 20. 43.

1. By an *experimental confession* of his *Faith in
Christ.* 2. By a Life answerable to that confession,
to wit, *a life of Holiness:* heart-holiness, family-holi-
ness, (if he hath a family,) and by conversation-holi-
ness in the world; which in the general teacheth him
inwardly to abhor his Sin, and himself for that, in
secret; to suppress it in his family, and to promote
holiness in the world; not by *talk* only, as an hypocrite or talkative person may do, but by a practical
subjection in Faith and Love to the Power of the
Word: And now, Sir, as to this brief description of
the Work of Grace, and also the discovery of it, if
you have ought to object, object; if not, then give
me leave to propound to you a second question.

Talk. Nay, my part is not now to object, but to
hear: Let me therefore have your second question.

Faith. It is this: Do you experience the first

*Another good
sign of Grace.*

part of the description of it? And doth your Life
and Conversation testify the same? Or standeth your
Religion in *Word* or *Tongue,* and not in *Deed* and
Truth? Pray, if you incline to answer me in this,
say no more than you know the God above will say
Amen to; and also nothing but what your Conscience
can justify you in: *For not he that commendeth him-*

self, is approved, but whom the Lord commendeth.
Besides, to say, I am thus, and thus, when my conversation, and all my neighbours, tell me I lie, is
great wickedness.

Talk. Then *Talkative* at first began to blush ; but *Talkative not pleased with Faithful's Question.*
recovering himself, thus he replied : You come now
to Experience, to Conscience, and God ; and to appeal
to him for justification of what is spoken : This kind
of discourse I did not expect : nor am I disposed to
give an answer to such questions, because I count
not myself bound thereto, unless you take upon
you to be a *Catechizer;* and though you should
so do, yet I may refuse to make you my Judge :
But I pray will you tell me why you ask me such
questions ?

Faith. Because I saw you forward to talk, and *The reason why Faithful put him to that question.*
because I knew not that you had ought else but
Notion. Besides, to tell you all the truth, I have
heard of you, that you are a man whose Religion
lies in Talk, and that your Conversation gives this
your mouth-profession the lie. They say you are *Faithful's plain dealing to Talkative.*
a Spot among Christians ; and that Religion fareth
the worse for your ungodly conversation ; that some
already have stumbled at your wicked ways, and that
more are in danger of being destroyed thereby ; your
Religion, and an ale-house, and covetousness, and
uncleanness, and swearing, and lying, and vain com-
pany-keeping, *&c.* will stand together. The proverb
is true of you, which is said of a whore, to wit, *That
she is a Shame to all Women,* so you are a shame to
all professors.

Talk. Since you are ready to take up Reports, *Talkative flings away from Faithful.*
and to judge so rashly as you do, I cannot but con-

clude you are some peevish or melancholy man, not fit to be discoursed with, and so Adieu. *Farewall*

Chr. Then came up *Christian,* and said to his brother, I told you how it would happen; your Words and his Lusts could not agree: He had rather leave your Company, than reform his Life; but he is gone, as I said, let him go, the Loss is no man's but his own; he has saved us the trouble of going from him; for he continuing (as I suppose he will do) as he is, he would have been but a Blot in our Company: Besides, the Apostle says, *From such withdraw thyself.*

A good rid-dance.

Faith. But I am glad we had this little discourse with him; it may happen that he will think of it again; however, I have dealt plainly with him, and so am clear of his blood, if he perisheth.

Chr. You did well to talk so plainly to him as you did; there is but little of this faithful dealing with men now a days, and that makes Religion so stink in the nostrils of many as it doth; for they are these talkative fools, whose Religion is only in word, and are debauched and vain in their conversation, that (being so much admitted into the fellowship of the godly) do puzzle the world, blemish Christianity, and grieve the sincere. I wish that all men would deal with such, as you have done; then should they either be made more conformable to Religion, or the company of Saints would be too hot for them. Then did *Faithful* say,

> *How* Talkative *at first lifts up his plumes!*
> *How bravely doth he speak! How he presumes*

To drive down all before him! But so soon
As Faithful *talks of* Heart-work, *like the Moon*
That's past the Full, into the Wane he goes;
And so will all, but he that Heart-work *knows.*

Thus they went on talking of what they had seen by the Way, and so made that Way easy, which would otherwise, no doubt, have been tedious to them; For now they went through a Wilderness.

Now when they were got almost quite out of this Wilderness, *Faithful* chanced to cast his eye back, and espied one coming after them, and he knew him. Oh! said *Faithful* to his brother, who comes yonder? Then *Christian* looked, and said, It is my good friend *Evangelist;* Ay, and my good friend too, said *Faithful,* for 'twas he that set me the Way to the Gate. Now was *Evangelist* come up unto them, and thus saluted them : *Evangelist overtakes them again.*

Evangelist. Peace be with you, dearly beloved ; and, Peace be to your helpers.

Chr. Welcome, welcome, my good *Evangelist;* the sight of thy countenance brings to my remembrance thy ancient kindness and unwearied labouring for my Eternal Good. *They are glad at the sight of him.*

Faith. And a thousand times Welcome, said good *Faithful;* thy company, O sweet *Evangelist,* how desirable is it to us poor Pilgrims!

Evan. Then, said *Evangelist,* How hath it fared with you, my Friends, since the time of our last parting? What have you met with, and how have you behaved yourselves?

Then *Christian* and *Faithful* told him of all things that had happened to them in the Way; and how, and with what difficulty, they had arrived to that place.

His Exhortation to them.

Evan. Right glad am I, said *Evangelist*, not that you met with Trials, but that you have been Victors, and for that you have (notwithstanding many weaknesses) continued in the way to this very day.

I say, right glad am I of this thing, and that for mine own sake and yours; I have sowed, and you have reaped; and the Day is coming, when both he that soweth, and they that reaped, shall rejoice together; that is, if you hold out; for in due time ye shall reap, if you faint not. The Crown is before you, and it is an uncorruptible one; so run, that you may obtain it. Some there be that set out for this Crown, and after they have gone far for it, another comes in and takes it from them: Hold fast therefore that you have, let no man take your Crown: You are not yet out of the gunshot of the Devil: You have not resisted unto Blood, striving against Sin: Let the Kingdom be always before you, and believe stedfastly concerning things that are invisible: Let nothing that is on this side the other World get within you: And above all, look well to your own Hearts and to the Lusts thereof, for they are deceitful above all things, and desperately wicked; set your faces like a flint; you have all power in Heaven and Earth on your side.

John 4. 36.
Gal. 6. 9.
1. Cor. 9. 24, 25, 26, 27.

Rev. 3. 11.

They do thank him for his Exhortation.

Chr. Then *Christian* thanked him for his exhortation; but told him withal, that they would have him speak farther to them for their help the rest of the Way; and the rather, for that they well knew that he was a Prophet, and could tell them of things that might happen unto them, and also how they might resist and overcome them. To which request *Faithful* also consented. So *Evangelist* began as followeth :

Evan. My Sons, you have heard in the words of the truth of the Gospel, that you must through many Tribulations enter into the Kingdom of Heaven. And again, That in every City, Bonds and Afflictions abide in you ; and therefore you cannot expect that you should go long on your Pilgrimage without them, in some sort or other : You have found some thing of the truth of these Testimonies upon you already, and more will immediately follow ; for now, as you see, you are almost out of this Wilderness, and therefore you will soon come into a Town that you will by and by see before you; and in that Town you will be hardly beset with enemies, who will strain hard but they will kill you ; and be you sure that one or both of you must seal the testimony which you hold, with Blood ; but be you faithful unto Death, and the King will give you a Crown of Life. He that shall die there, although his death will be unnatural, and his pains perhaps great, he will yet have the better of his fellow ; not only because he will be arrived at the Cœlestial City soonest, but because he will escape many miseries that the other will meet with in the rest of his Journey. But when you are come to the Town, and shall find fulfilled what I have here related, then remember your Friend, and quit yourselves like men, and commit the keeping of your souls to your God (in well-doing), as unto a Faithful Creator.

Then I saw in my dream, that when they were got out of the Wilderness, they presently saw a Town before them, and the name of that Town is

He predicteth what troubles they shall meet with in Vanity Fair, and encourageth them to Steadfastness.

He whose lot it will be there to suffer, will have the better of his brother.

Vanity, and at the Town there is a Fair kept, called *Vanity-Fair:* It is kept all the year long; it beareth the name of *Vanity-Fair*, because the Town where it is kept, *is lighter than Vanity;* and also, because all that is there sold, or that cometh thither, is *Vanity.* As is the saying of the Wise, *All that cometh is Vanity.*

Isa. 40. 17.
Eccles. 1.
ch. 2. 11, 17.

This Fair is no new erected business, but a thing of ancient standing : I will shew you the original of it.

*The Antiquity
of this Fair.*
Almost five thousand years agone, there were Pilgrims walking to the Cœlestial City, as these two honest persons are; and *Beelzebub, Apollyon*, and *Legion*, with their companions, perceiving by the path that the Pilgrims made, that their Way to the City lay through this Town of *Vanity*, they contrived here to set up a Fair; a Fair, wherein should be sold *all Sorts of Vanity*, and that it should last all

*The merchan-
dize of this
Fair.*
the year long; therefore, at this Fair, are all such merchandizes sold, as houses, lands, trades, places, honours, preferments, titles, countries, kingdoms, lusts, pleasures ; and delights of all sorts, as whores, bawds, wives, husbands, children, masters, servants, lives, blood, bodies, souls, silver, gold, pearls, precious stones, and what not ?

And moreover, At this Fair there is at all times to be seen jugglings, cheats, games, plays, fools, apes, knaves, and rogues, and that of every kind.

Here are to be seen too, and that for nothing,

Behold Vanity-Fair! *the Pilgrims there
Are chain'd, and ston'd beside :
Even so it was our* LORD *pass'd here,
And on Mount* Calvary *dy'd.*

thefts, murders, adulteries, false-swearers, and that of a blood-red colour.

And as in other fairs of less moment, there are the several rows and streets under their proper names, where such and such wares are vended: So here likewise, you have the proper places, rows, streets, (*viz.* Countries and Kingdoms) where the wares of this Fair are soonest to be found: Here is the *Britain* row, the *French* row, the *Italian* row, the *Spanish* row, the *German* row, where several sorts of vanities are to be sold. But as in other fairs, some one commodity is as the chief of all the fair, so the ware of *Rome* and her merchandize is greatly promoted in this Fair: Only our *English* nation, with some others, have taken a dislike thereat. *The Streets of this Fair.*

Now, as I said, the Way to the Cœlestial City lies just through this Town, where this lusty Fair is kept; and he that will go to the City, and yet not go through this Town, must needs go out of the World. The Prince of Princes himself, when here, went through this Town to his own Country, and that upon a *Fair-day* too: Yea, and as I think, it was *Beelzebub*, the Chief Lord of this Fair, that invited him to buy of his Vanities; yea, would have made him Lord of the Fair, would he but have done him reverence as he went through the Town. Yea, because he was such a Person of Honour, *Beelzebub* had him from street to street, and shewed him all the Kingdoms of the World in a little time, that he might, (if possible) allure that Blessed One, to cheapen and buy some of his Vanities; but he had no mind to the merchandize, and therefore left the Town, without laying out so much as one farthing 1 Cor. 5. 10. *Christ went through this Fair.* Mat. 4. 8. Luke 4. 5, 6, 7. *Christ bought nothing in this Fair.*

upon these Vanities. This Fair, therefore, is an ancient thing, of long standing, and a very great Fair.

The Pilgrims enter the Fair. Now these Pilgrims, as I said, must needs go through this Fair. Well, so they did; but behold,

The Fair in a hubbub about them. even as they entered into the Fair, all the people in the Fair were moved, and the Town itself, as it were, in a hubbub about them; and that for several reasons: For,

The First cause of the hubbub. First, The Pilgrims were cloathed with such kind of Raiment as was diverse from the Raiment of any that traded in that Fair. The people, therefore, of the Fair made a great Gazing upon them:

1 Cor. 2. 7. 8. Some said they were fools; some they were bedlams; and some they were outlandish men.

The second cause of the hubbub. Secondly, And as they wondered at their apparel, so they did likewise at their speech; for few could understand what they said; they naturally spoke the language of *Canaan;* but they that kept the Fair were the men of this World: So that from one end of the Fair to the other, they seemed barbarians each to the other.

Third cause of the hubbub. Thirdly, But that which did not a little amuse the merchandizers, was, that these Pilgrims set very light by all their wares; they cared not so much as to look upon them; and if they called upon them to buy, they would put their fingers in their ears, and cry, *Turn away mine eyes from beholding Vanity;* and look upwards, signifying, That their trade and traffick was in Heaven.

Fourth cause of the hubbub. One chanced mockingly, beholding the carriages of the men, to say unto them, *What will ye buy?*

Prov. 23. 23. But they looking gravely upon him, said, *We buy the*

Truth. At that, there was an occasion taken to despise the men the more; some mocking, some *They are mocked.* taunting, some speaking reproachfully, and some calling upon others to smite them. At last things *The Fair in a hubbub.* came to an hubbub, and great stir in the Fair, insomuch that all order was confounded. Now was word presently brought to the Great One of the Fair, who quickly came down and deputed some of his most trusty Friends to take these men into examination, about whom the Fair was almost overturned. *They are examined.* So the men were brought to examination; and they that sat upon them, asked them, Whence they came, whither they went, and what they did there in such an unusual Garb? The men told them, That they were Pilgrims and Strangers in the World, and that *They tell who they are, and whence they came.* they were going to their own country, which was the Heavenly *Jerusalem;* and that they had given none *Heb.* 11. 13, occasion to the men of the Town, nor yet to the 14, 15, 16. merchandizers, thus to abuse them, and to let them in their Journey: Except it was for that, when one asked them what they would buy, they said, they would *buy the Truth.* But they that were appointed to examine them, did not believe them to be any *They are taken for Madmen.* other than Bedlams and Mad, or else such as came to put all things into a confusion in the Fair. There- *[They are not believed.* 1st fore they took them and beat them, and besmeared Edit.] them with dirt, and then put them into the Cage, *They are put in the Cage.* that they might be made a Spectacle to all the men of the Fair. There therefore they lay for some time, and were made the objects of any man's Sport, or Malice, or Revenge; the Great One of the Fair laughing still at all that befell them: But, the men *Their behaviour in the Cage.* being patient, and not rendring railing for railing, but contrariwise blessing, and giving good words for bad, and kindness for injuries done; some men in the Fair that were more observing, and less prejudiced than the rest, began to check and blame the baser sort for their continual abuses done by them to the men : They therefore in angry manner let fly at them again, counting them as bad as the men in the Cage, and telling them that they seemed Con federates, and should be made partakers of their misfortunes. The other replied, that for ought they could see, the men were quiet and sober, and intended nobody any harm : And that there were many that traded in their Fair, that were more worthy to be put into the Cage, yea, and Pillory too, than were the men that they had abused. Thus, after divers words had passed on both sides, (the men behaving themselves all the while very wisely and soberly before them) they fell to some blows among themselves, and did harm one to another. Then were these two poor men brought before their examiners again, and there charged as being guilty of the late hubbub that had been in the Fair. So they beat them pitifully, and hanged irons upon them, and led them in chains up and down the Fair, for an example and a terror to others, lest any should further speak in their behalf, or join themselves unto them. But *Christian* and *Faithful* behaved themselves yet more wisely, and received the ignominy and shame that was cast upon them, with so much meekness and patience, that it won to their side (though but few in comparison of the rest) several of the men in the Fair. This put the other Party yet into a greater rage, insomuch that they concluded the

The men of the Fair do fall out among themselves about these two men.

They are made the Authors of this disturbance.

They are led up and down the Fair in chains, for a terror to others.

Some men of the Fair won over to them.

death of these two men. Wherefore they threatned, *Their adver-*
that neither Cage nor irons should serve their turn, *saries resolve to kill them.*
but that they should die for the abuse they had
done, and for deluding the men of the Fair.

Then were they remanded to the Cage again, *They are*
until further order should be taken with them. So *again put into the Cage, and*
they put them in, and made their feet fast in the *after brought to Tryal.*
stocks.

Here also they called again to mind what they had
heard from their faithful friend *Evangelist*, and were
the more confirmed in their ways and sufferings, by
what he told them would happen to them. They
also now comforted each other, that whose Lot it
was to suffer, even he should have the best on't;
therefore each man secretly wished that he might
have that preferment: But committing themselves
to the All-wise dispose of Him that ruleth all things,
with much content they abode in the condition in
which they were, until they should be otherwise
disposed of.

Then a convenient time being appointed, they
brought them forth to their Tryal, in order to their
condemnation. When the time was come, they
were brought before their enemies, and arraigned.
The Judge's name was Lord *Hate-Good:* Their
indictment was one and the same in substance,
though somewhat varying in form; the contents
whereof was this:

That they were Enemies to, and Disturbers of their *Their Indict-*
Trade: That they had made Commotions and Divi- *ment.*
sions in the Town, and had won a Party to their own
most dangerous Opinions, in contempt of the Law of
their Prince.

Faithful's an-
swer for him-
self.
Then *Faithful* began to answer, That he had
only set himself against that, which had set itself
against Him that is higher than the Highest. And,
said he, as for Disturbance, I make none, being
myself a man of Peace; the parties that were won
to us, were won by beholding our Truth and Innocence, and they are only turned from the worse to
the better. And as to the King you talk of, since
he is *Beelzebub*, the Enemy of our Lord, I defy him
and all his angels.

Then proclamation was made, That they that had
ought to say for their Lord the King against the
Prisoner at the Bar, should forthwith appear, and
give in their evidence. So there came in three
witnesses, to wit, *Envy, Superstition*, and *Pickthank:*
They were then asked, if they knew the Prisoner at
the Bar; and what they had to say for their Lord
the King against him.

Envy *begins.*
Then stood forth *Envy*, and said to this effect:
My Lord, I have known this man a long time, and
will attest upon my oath before this honourable
Bench, that he is——

Judge. Hold—Give him his Oath.

So they sware him: Then he said, My Lord, this
man, notwithstanding his plausible name, is one of
the vilest men in our Country; he neither regardeth
Prince nor People, Law nor Custom: but doth all
that he can to possess all men with certain of his
disloyal notions, which he in the general calls *Principles of Faith and Holiness*. And in particular, I
heard him once myself affirm, *That Christianity and
the Customs of our town of Vanity, were diametrically
opposite, and could not be reconciled.* By which saying,

my Lord, he doth, at once, not only condemn all our laudable doings, but *us* in the doing of them.

Judge. Then did the Judge say to him, Hast thou any more to say?

Envy. My Lord, I could say much more, only I would not be tedious to the Court. Yet if need be, when the other gentlemen have given in their evidence, rather than any thing shall be wanting that will dispatch him, I will enlarge my testimony against him. So he was bid stand by.

Then they called *Superstition*, and bid him look upon the Prisoner: They also asked, what he could say for their Lord the King against him? Then they sware him; so he began:

Super. My Lord, I have no great acquaintance Superstition with this man, nor do I desire to have further know- *follows.* ledge of him; however, this I know, That he is a very pestilent fellow, from some discourse that the other day I had with him in this Town; for then talking with him, I heard him say, That our Religion was naught, and such by which a man could by no means please God. Which saying of his, my Lord, your Lordship very well knows what necessarily thence will follow, to wit, *that we still do worship in vain, are yet in our Sins, and finally shall be damned:* And this is that which I have to say.

Then was *Pickthank* sworn, and bid say what he knew in the behalf of their Lord the King, against the Prisoner at the Bar.

Pick. My Lord and you gentlemen all; this fellow Pickthank's I have known of a long time, and have heard him *testimony.* speak things that ought not to be spoke; for he hath railed on our noble Prince *Beelzebub*, and hath spoke

contemptibly of his honourable Friends, whose
names are, the Lord *Old-Man*, the Lord *Carnal-
Delight*, the Lord *Luxurious*, the Lord *Desire of
Vain-Glory*, my old Lord *Leachery*, Sir *Having
Greedy*, with all the rest of our nobility; and he hath
said moreover, That if all men were of his mind, if
possible, there is not one of these noblemen should
have any longer a being in this Town. Besides, he
hath not been afraid to rail on you, my Lord, who
are now appointed to be his Judge, calling you an
ungodly Villain, with many other such-like vilifying
terms, with which he hath bespattered most of the
gentry of our Town.

When this *Pickthank* had told his tale, the Judge
directed his speech to the Prisoner at the Bar, say-

ing, Thou 'Renegade,' Heretick, and Traitor, hast
thou heard what these honest gentlemen have
witnessed against thee?

Faith. May I speak a few words in my own
defence?

Judge. Sirrah, sirrah, thou deservest to live no
longer, but to be slain immediately upon the place;
yet that all men may see our Gentleness towards
thee, let us see what thou hast to say.

Faith. 1. I say then, in answer to what Mr. *Envy*
hath spoken, I never said ought but this, That what
rule, or laws, or custom, or people, were flat against
the Word of God, are diametrically opposite to

Now, Faithful, *play the Man, speak for thy God;
Fear not the Wicked's malice, nor their rod:
Speak boldly, man, the Truth is on thy side;
Die for it, and to Life in triumph ride.*

Christianity. If I have said amiss in this, convince me of my error, and I am ready here before you to make my recantation.

2. As to the second, to wit, Mr. *Superstition*, and his charge against me, I said only this, That in the worship of God there is required a Divine Faith: but there can be no Divine Faith without a Divine Revelation of the Will of God. Therefore, whatever is thrust into the worship of God, that is not agreeable to Divine Revelation, cannot be done but by an human Faith, which Faith will not profit to eternal Life.

3. As to what Mr. *Pick-Thank* hath said, I say (avoiding terms, as that I am said to rail, and the like) that the Prince of this Town, with all the rablement, his attendants, by this gentleman named, are more fit for being in Hell, than in this Town and Country; *and so the Lord have Mercy upon me.*

Then the Judge called to the Jury (who all this *The Judge's* while stood by to hear and observe) Gentlemen of *speech to the Jury.* the Jury, you see this man about whom so great an uproar hath been made in this Town: You have also heard what these worthy gentlemen have witnessed against him: Also you have heard his Reply and Confession: It lieth now in your breasts to hang him, or save his life; but yet I think meet to instruct you into our Law.

There was an act made in the days of *Pharaoh* Exod. 1. the Great, servant to our Prince, that lest those of a contrary Religion should multiply, and grow too strong for him, their males should be thrown into the river. There was also an act made in the days Dan. 3. of *Nebuchadnezzar* the Great, another of his servants, that whoever would not fall down and worship his Golden Image, should be thrown into a Fiery Furnace. There was also an act made in the days of *Darius*, That whoso for some time called upon any God but him, should be cast into the Lions Den. Now the substance of these Laws this Rebel has broken, not only in thought (which is not to be borne) but also in word and deed; which must therefore needs be intolerable.

Dan. 6.

For that of *Pharaoh*, his Law was made upon a supposition, to prevent mischief, no Crime being yet apparent; but here is a Crime apparent. For the second and third, you see he disputeth against our Religion; and for the Treason he hath confessed, he deserveth to die the Death.

The Jury and their names.

Then went the Jury out, whose names were Mr. *Blind-man*, Mr. *No-good*, Mr. *Malice*, Mr. *Love-lust*, Mr. *Live-loose*, Mr. *Heady*, Mr. *High-mind*, Mr. *Enmity*, Mr. *Lyer*, Mr. *Cruelty*, Mr. *Hate-light*, and Mr. *Implacable;* who every one gave in his private verdict against him among themselves, and afterwards unanimously concluded to bring him in Guilty, before the Judge. And first among themselves, Mr. *Blindman* the fore-man said, I see clearly that this man is an Heretick. Then said Mr. *No-good*, Away with such a fellow from the earth. Ay, said Mr. *Malice*, for I hate the very looks of him. Then said Mr. *Love-lust*, I could never endure him. Nor

Every one's private Verdict.

Brave Faithful *! Bravely done in word and deed !*
Judge, witnesses, and jury have, instead
Of overcoming thee, but shewn their rage,
When they are Dead, thou'lt Live, from age to age.

I, said Mr. *Live-loose,* for he would always be condemning my Way. Hang him, hang him, said Mr. *Heady.* A sorry Scrub, said Mr. *High-mind.* My heart riseth against him, said Mr. *Enmity.* He is a Rogue, said Mr. *Lyer.* Hanging is too good for him, said Mr. *Cruelty.* Let's dispatch him out of the way, said Mr. *Hate-light.* Then said Mr. *Implacable,* Might I have all the World given me, I could not be reconciled to him, therefore let us forthwith bring him in Guilty of Death. And so they *They conclude to bring him in Guilty of Death.* did; therefore he was presently condemned to be had from the place where he was, to the place from whence he came, and there to be put to the most cruel Death that could be invented.

They therefore brought him out, to do with him *The cruel death of Faithful.* according to their Law; and first they scourged him, then they buffeted him, then they lanced his flesh with knives: after that they stoned him with stones, then pricked him with their swords; and last of all, they burnt him to ashes at the Stake. Thus came *Faithful* to his end.

Now I saw, that there stood behind the multitude *Chariot and horses take away Faithful.* a Chariot and a couple of horses waiting for *Faithful,* who (so soon as his adversaries had dispatched him) was taken up into it, and straitway was carried up through the clouds with Sound of Trumpet, the nearest way to the Cœlestial Gate. But as for *Christian,* he had some respite, and was remanded back *Christian still a Prisoner. [early edits. 'is still alive.']* to prison; so he there remained for a space: But he that over-rules all things, having the Power of their rage in his own Hand, so wrought it about, that *Christian* for that time escaped them, and went his way. And as he went he sang, saying;

The Song that Christian *made of* Faithful *after his death.*

Well, Faithful, *thou hast faithfully profest*
Unto thy Lord, *with Him thou shalt be blest;*
When faithless ones, with all their vain delights,
Are crying out under their hellish plights:
Sing, Faithful, *sing, and let thy Name survive;*
For tho' they kill'd thee, thou art yet alive.

Now I saw in my dream, that *Christian* went not forth alone ; for there was one whose name was *Hopeful,* (being made so by the beholding of *Christian* and *Faithful* in their words and behaviour, in their sufferings at the Fair) who joined himself unto him, and entring into a brotherly covenant, told him, that he would be his companion.   Thus one died to make testimony to the Truth, and another rises out of his ashes to be a companion with *Christian* in his Pilgrimage.   This *Hopeful* also told *Christian,* that there were many more of the men in the Fair that would take their time, and follow after.

Christian *has* another companion.

There are more of the men of the Fair *will follow.*

So I saw, that quickly after they were got out of the Fair, they overtook one that was going before them, whose name was *By-ends ;* so they said to him, What countryman, Sir ? and how far go you this Way ?   He told them, that he came from the town of *Fair-speech,* and he was going to the Cœlestial City, (but told them not his name.)

They overtake By-ends.

Prov. 26. 25.

From *Fair-speech,* said *Christian?* is there any good that lives there ?

By-ends. Yes, (said *By-ends,*) I hope.

Chr. Pray, Sir, what may I call you ?

By-ends. I am a Stranger to you, and you to me : If you be going this Way, I shall be glad of your company : If not, I must be content.

By-ends *loth to tell his* name.

Chr. This town of *Fair-speech* (said *Christian*,) I have heard of it, and, as I remember, they say it's a wealthy place.

By-ends. Yes, I will assure you that it is, and I have very many Rich Kindred there.

Chr. Pray, who are your kindred there, if a man may be so bold?

By-ends. Almost the whole Town: And in particular my Lord *Turn-about*, my Lord *Time-server*, my Lord *Fair-speech*, (from whose ancestors that town first took its name:) Also Mr. *Smooth-man*, Mr. *Facing-both-ways*, Mr. *Any-thing*, and the parson of our parish, Mr. *Two-tongues*, was my mother's own brother by father's side: And, to tell you the truth, I am become a Gentleman of good quality, yet my great grandfather was but a waterman, looking one way and rowing another, and I got most of my estate by the same occupation.

Chr. Are you a married man?

By-ends. Yes, and my wife is a very vertuous woman, the daughter of a vertuous woman; she was my Lady *Feigning's* daughter, therefore she came of a very honourable family, and is arrived to such a pitch of breeding, that she knows how to carry it to all, even to prince and peasant. 'Tis true, we somewhat differ in Religion from those of the stricter sort, yet but in two small points: First, We never strive against Wind and Tide. Secondly, We are always most zealous when Religion goes in his Silver Slippers; we love much to walk with him in the street, if the Sun shines and the People applaud him.

The wife and kindred of By-ends.

Where By-ends differs from others in Religion.

Then *Christian* stept a little aside to his fellow *Hopeful*, saying, It runs in my mind that this is one

By-ends of *Fair-speech;* and, if it be he, we have as
very a Knave in our company as dwelleth in all
these parts.   Then said *Hopeful,* Ask him, methinks he should not be ashamed of his Name.   So
Christian came up with him again, and said, Sir,
You talk as if you knew something more, than all
the world doth; and, if I take not my mark amiss,
I deem I have half a guess of you : Is not your name
Mr. *By-ends* of *Fair-speech?*

By-ends. That is not my name, but indeed it is a
nick-name that is given me by some that cannot
abide me, and I must be content to bear it as a
Reproach, as other good men have borne theirs
before me.

Chr. But did you never give an occasion to men
to call you by this name?

By-ends. Never! never! The worst that ever I
did to give them an occasion to give me this name
was, that I had always the Luck to jump in my
judgment with the present Way of the Times, whatever it was, and my Chance was to get thereby; but
if things are thus cast upon me, let me count them
a blessing; but let not the malicious load me therefore with reproach.

Chr. I thought indeed that you were the man
that I had heard of; and, to tell you what I think,
I fear this name belongs to you more properly than
you are willing we should think it doth.

By-ends. Well, if you will thus imagine, I cannot
help it : You shall find me a fair company-keeper, if
you will still admit me your associate.

Chr. If you will go with us, you must go against
Wind and Tide; the which, I perceive, is against

How By-ends
got his name.

*He desires to
keep company
with* Chris-
tian.

THE SCOURGING OF *FAITHFUL*

your opinion : You must also own Religion in his Rags as well as when in his Silver Slippers ; and stand by him too when bound in Irons, as well as when he walketh the streets with Applause.

By-ends. You must not impose, nor lord it over my faith ; leave me to my Liberty, and let me go with you.

Chr. Not a Step further, unless you will do in what I propound, as we.

Then said *By-ends,* I shall never desert my old Principles, since they are harmless and profitable. If I may not go with you, I must do as I did before you overtook me, even go by myself, until some overtake me that will be glad of my company. By-ends *and* Christian *part.*

Now I saw in my dream, that *Christian* and *Hopeful* forsook him, and kept their distance before him ; but one of them looking back, saw three men following Mr. *By-ends,* and behold, as they came up with him, he made them a very low congee ; and they also gave him a compliment. The mens names were Mr. *Hold-the-World,* Mr. *Money-love,* and Mr. *Save-all;* men that Mr. *By-ends* had formerly been acquainted with ; for in their minority they were school-fellows, and taught by one Mr. *Gripe-man,* a school-master in *Love-gain,* which is a market-town in the county of *Coveting,* in the north. This School-master taught them the Art of Getting, either by violence, cozenage, flattery, lying, or by putting on a guise of Religion ; and these four gentlemen had attained much of the Art of their Master, so that they could each of them have kept such a school themselves. *He has new companions.*

Well, when they had, as I said, thus saluted each

other, Mr. *Money-love* said to Mr. *By-ends*, Who are they upon the road before us? For *Christian* and *Hopeful* were yet within view.

By-ends's character of the Pilgrims. *By-ends.* They are a couple of far country-men, that *after their mode* are going on Pilgrimage.

Money-love. Alas! why did they not stay, that we might have had their good company; for they, and we, and you, Sir, I hope, are all going on Pilgrimage?

By-ends. We are so, indeed; but the men before us are so rigid, and love so much their own notions, and do also so lightly esteem the opinions of others, that let a man be never so godly, yet if he jumps not with them in all things, they thrust him quite out of their company.

Mr. *Save-all.* That's bad; but we read of some that are *righteous over-much*, and such mens Rigidness prevails with them to judge and condemn all but themselves; but I pray *what*, and *how many* were the things wherein you differed?

By-ends. Why they, after their head-strong manner, conclude that it is their Duty to rush on their journey all weathers, and I am for waiting for Wind and Tide. They are for hazarding all for God at a clap, and I am for taking all advantages to secure my Life and Estate. They are for holding their notions, though all other men be against them; but I am for Religion, in what, and so far as the Times and my safety will bear it. They are for Religion when in Rags and Contempt, but I am for him when he walks in his Golden Slippers in the sunshine, and with Applause.

Mr. *Hold-the-World.* Ay, and hold you there still,

good Mr. *By-ends;* for, for my part, I can count him but a Fool, that having the Liberty to keep what he has, shall be so unwise as to lose it. Let us be wise *as Serpents;* it's best to make hay when the Sun shines; you see how the Bee lieth still all winter, and bestirs her only when she can have Profit with Pleasure. God sends sometimes rain, and sometimes sun-shine: If they be such fools to go through the first, yet let us be content to take fair weather along with us. For my part, I like that Religion best, that will stand with the security of God's good blessings unto us: For who can imagine, that is ruled by his Reason, since God has bestowed upon us the good things of this Life, but that he would have us keep them for his Sake. *Abraham* and *Solomon* grew rich in Religion. And *Job* says, That a good man *shall lay up Gold as Dust.* But he must not be such as the men before us, if they be as you have described them.

Mr. *Save-all.* I think that we are all agreed in this matter, and therefore there needs no more words about it.

Mr. *Money-love.* No, there needs no more words about this matter indeed; for he that believes neither Scripture nor Reason, (and you see we have both on our side) neither knows his own Liberty, nor seeks his own Safety.

Mr. *By-ends.* My brethren, we are, as you see, going all on Pilgrimage, and for our better diversion from things that are bad, give me leave to propound unto you this question:

Suppose a man, a Minister, or a Tradesman, *&c.* should have an advantage lie before him, to get the good blessings of this life, yet so as that he can by no means come by them, except, in appearance at least, he becomes extraordinary zealous in some points of Religion that he meddled not with before; may he not use this Means to attain his End, and yet be a right honest man?

Mr. *Money-love.* I see the bottom of your question; and, with these gentlemen's good leave, I will endeavour to shape you an answer: And first, to speak to your question as it concerns a *Minister* himself. Suppose a Minister a worthy man, possess'd but of a very small benefice, and has in his eye a greater, more fat and plump by far; he has also now an opportunity of getting of it, yet so as by being more studious, by preaching more frequently and zealously, and, because the temper of the people requires it, by altering of some of his Principles; for my part, I see no reason but a man may do this; (provided he has a Call) ay, and more a great deal besides, and yet be an honest man. For why?

1. His desire of a greater benefice is lawful, (this cannot be contradicted) since 'tis set before him by Providence; so then he may get it if he can, making no question for Conscience sake.

2. Besides, his desire after that benefice makes him more studious, a more zealous Preacher, *&c.* and so makes him a better man, yea, makes him better improve his parts, which is according to the Mind of God.

3. Now as for his complying with the temper of his people, by dissenting, to serve them, some of his Principles, this argueth, 1. That he is of a Self-denying temper. 2. Of a sweet and winning deport-

ment. 3. And so more fit for the ministerial function.

4. I conclude then, that a minister that changes a *small* for a *great*, should not, for so doing, be judged as covetous; but rather, since he is improved in his parts and industry hereby, be counted as one that pursues his Call, and the opportunity put into his hand to do Good.

And now to the second part of the question, which concerns the *Tradesman* you mentioned: Suppose such a one to have but a poor employ in the world, but, by becoming Religious, he may mend his market, perhaps get a rich wife, or more and far better customers to his shop. For my part, I see no reason but this may be lawfully done. For why?

1. To become *Religious* is a Vertue, by what Means soever a man becomes so.

2. Nor is it unlawful to get a rich wife, or more custom to my shop.

3. Besides, the man that gets these by becoming religious, gets that which is good of them that are good, by becoming good himself; so then here is a good Wife, and good Customers, and good Gain, and all these by becoming Religious, which is good: Therefore, to become religious to get all these, is a good and profitable Design.

This answer thus made by this Mr. *Money-love* to Mr. *By-ends's* question, was highly applauded by them all; wherefore they concluded upon the whole, that it was most wholsome and advantageous. And because, as they thought, no man was able to contradict it, and because *Christian* and *Hopeful* were yet within call, they jointly agreed to assault them with the question as soon as they overtook them; and the rather, because they had opposed Mr. *By-ends* before. So they called after them, and they stopt and stood still till they came up to them; but they concluded, as they went that not Mr. *By-ends*, but old Mr. *Hold-the-World* should propound the question to them, because, as they supposed, their answer to him would be without the remainder of that heat that was kindled betwixt Mr. *By-ends* and them, at their parting a little before.

So they came up to each other, and after a short salutation, Mr. *Hold-the-World* propounded the question to *Christian* and his fellow, and bid them to answer it if they could.

Chr. Then said *Christian*, Even a babe in Religion may answer ten thousand such questions. For, if it be unlawful to follow Christ for loaves, as it is *John* 6. how much more abominable is it to make of him and Religion a Stalking-horse to get and enjoy the World? Nor do we find any other than Heathens, Hypocrites, Devils, and Witches, that are of this opinion.

1. *Heathens;* for when *Hamor* and *Sechem* had a mind to the daughters and cattle of *Jacob*, and saw that there was no ways for them to come at them, but by becoming circumcised; they said to their companions, If every male of us be circumcised, as they are circumcised, shall not their cattle, and their substance, and every beast of theirs be ours? Their Daughters and their Cattle were that which they sought to obtain, and their Religion the stalking-horse they made use of to come at them. Read the whole story, *Gen.* 34. 20, 21, 22, 23.

2. The Hypocritical *Pharisees* were also of this Religion : Long Prayers were their Pretence ; but to get widows houses was their Intent, and greater damnation was from God their Judgment, *Luke* 20. 46, 47.

3. *Judas* the Devil was also of this Religion ; he was religious for the Bag, that he might be possessed of what was therein ; but he was lost, cast away, and the very Son of Perdition.

4. *Simon* the Witch was of this Religion too ; for he would have had the Holy Ghost, that he might have got Money therewith, and his sentence from *Peter's* mouth was according, *Acts* 8. 19, 20, 21, 22.

5. Neither will it out of my mind, but that that man that takes up Religion for the world, will throw away Religion for the World ; for so surely as *Judas* designed the world in becoming religious, so surely did he also sell religion and his Master for the same. To answer the question therefore affirmatively, as I perceive you have done ; and to accept of, as authentick, such answer, is both Heathenish, Hypocritical, and Devilish ; and your Reward will be according to your Works. Then they stood staring one upon another, but had not wherewith to answer *Christian. Hopeful* also approved of the soundness of *Christian's* answer, so there was a great Silence among them. Mr. *By-ends* and his company also staggered and kept behind, that *Christian* and *Hopeful* might out-go them. Then said *Christian* to his fellow, If these men cannot stand before the sentence of men, what will they do with the sentence of God ? And if they are mute when dealt with by

vessels of Clay, what will they do when they shall be rebuked by the flames of a devouring Fire?

The Ease that Pilgrims have, is but little in this life.

Then *Christian* and *Hopeful* out-went them again, and went till they came at a delicate plain, called *Ease*, where they went with much content; but that plain was but *narrow*, so they were quickly got over it. Now at the further side of that plain was a

Lucre hill a dangerous hill.

little hill called *Lucre*, and in that hill a *Silver-Mine*, which some of them that had formerly gone that way, because of the rarity of it, had turned aside to see; but going too near the brink of the pit, the ground, being deceitful under them, broke, and they were slain: Some also had been maimed there, and could not, to their Dying-day, be their own men again.

Then I saw in my dream, that a little off the

Demas at the hill Lucre.

road, over against the *Silver-Mine*, stood *Demas* (gentleman-like) to call to passengers to come and

He calls to Christian *and* Hopeful *to come to him.*

see; who said to *Christian* and his fellow, Ho! turn aside hither, and I will shew you a thing.

Chr. What thing so deserving, as to turn us out of the Way?

Demas. Here is a *Silver-Mine*, and some digging in it for Treasure; if you will come, with a little pains, you may richly provide for yourselves.

Hopeful *tempted to go, but* Christian *holds him back.*

Hope. Then said *Hopeful*, Let us go see.

Chr. Not I, said *Christian*, I have heard of this place before now, and how many have there been slain; and besides, that treasure is a Snare to those that seek it; for it hindreth them in their Pilgrimage.

Then *Christian* called to *Demas*, saying, Is not

the place dangerous ? Hath it not hindred many Hos. 4. 18.
in their Pilgrimage ?

Demas. Not very dangerous, except to those that
are careless ; but withal, he *blushed* as he spake.

Chr. Then said *Christian* to *Hopeful*, Let us not
stir a Step ; but still keep on our Way.

Hope. I will warrant you, when *By-ends* comes
up, if he hath the same Invitation as we, he will
turn in thither to see.

Chr. No doubt thereof, for his principles lead him
that way, and a hundred to one but he dies there.

Demas. Then *Demas* called again, saying, But
will you not come over and see ?

Chr. Then *Christian* roundly answered, saying, Christian
Demas, Thou art an Enemy to the right ways of *roundeth up* Demas.
the Lord of this Way, and hast been already con- 2 Tim. 4. 10.
demned for thine own turning aside, by one of his
Majesties Judges : And why seekest thou to bring
us into the like condemnation ? Besides, if we at
all turn aside ; our Lord the King will certainly hear
thereof, and will there put us to shame, where we
would stand with boldness before him.

Demas cried again, That he also was one of their
Fraternity ; and that if they would tarry a little, he
also himself would walk with them.

Chr. Then said *Christian*, What is thy name ?
Is it not the same by the which I have called thee ?

Demas. Yes, my name is *Demas*, I am the son of
Abraham.

Chr. I know you ; *Gehazi* was your great grand- 2 Kings 5. 20.
father, and *Judas* your father, and you have trod Matt. 26. 14, 15.
their steps ; it is but a devilish prank that thou Ch. 27. 1, 2,
usest : Thy father was hang'd for a Traitor, and 3, 5, 6.

thou deservest no better reward. Assure thyself, that when we come to the King, we will do him word of this thy behaviour. Thus they went their Way.

By this time *By-ends* and his companions were

By-ends *goes over to* Demas. come again within sight, and they at the first beck went over to *Demas.* Now, whether they fell into the pit by looking over the brink thereof, or whether they went down to dig, or whether they were smothered in the bottom by the damps that commonly arise, of these things I am not certain; but this I observed, that they never were seen again in the Way. Then sang *Christian:*

By-ends *and* Silver Demas *both agree;*
One calls, the other runs, that he may be
A Sharer in his Lucre, so these two
Take up in this World, and no further go.

They see a strange Monument. Now I saw, that just on the other side of this plain, the Pilgrims came to a place where stood an old *Monument*, hard-by the highway side, at the sight of which they were both concerned, because of the strangeness of the form thereof, for it seemed to them as if it had been a *Woman* transformed into the shape of a Pillar; here therefore they stood looking and looking upon it, but could not for a time tell what they should make thereof: At last *Hopeful* espied written above upon the head thereof, a writing in an unusual hand; but he being no scholar, called to *Christian* (for he was learned) to see if he could pick out the meaning; so he came, and after a little laying of letters together, he found the same to be this,

Remember Lot's Wife. So he read it to his fellow; after which they both concluded that that was the Pillar of Salt into which *Lot's* wife was turned, for Gen. 19. 26. her looking back with a *covetous heart*, while she was going from *Sodom* for safety. Which sudden and amazing sight, gave them occasion of this discourse.

Chr. Ah, my brother! this is a seasonable sight; it came opportunely to us after the invitation which *Demas* gave us to come over to view the hill *Lucre;* and had we gone over, as he desired us, and as thou wast inclined to do, (my brother), we had, for ought I know, been made ourselves, like this Woman, a spectacle for those that shall come after, to behold.

Hope. I am sorry that I was so foolish, and am made to wonder that I am not now as *Lot's* wife; for wherein was the difference betwixt her Sin and mine? She only looked back, and I had a desire to go see; let Grace be adored, and let me be ashamed, that ever such a thing should be in mine heart.

Chr. Let us take notice of what we see here, for our help for time to come : *This* woman escaped one Judgment, for she fell not by the destruction of *Sodom;* yet she was destroyed by another; as we see, she is turned into a Pillar of Salt.

Hope. True, and she may be to us both *Caution*, and *Example; caution*, that we should shun her sin; or a sign of what Judgment will overtake such as shall not be prevented by this caution : So *Korah, Dathan*, and *Abiram*, with the two hundred and fifty men that perished in their sin, did also become a sign Numb. 26. 9; or *example* to beware. But above all, I muse at one 10. thing, to wit, how *Demas* and his fellows can stand so confidently yonder to look for that treasure, which this woman, but for looking behind her after, (for we read not that she stept one foot out of the Way) was turned into a Pillar of Salt; especially since the Judgment which overtook her did make her an example, within sight of where they are : For they cannot choose but see her, did they but lift up their eyes.

Chr. It is a thing to be wondred at, and it argueth that their heart is grown desperate in the case; and I cannot tell who to compare them to so fitly, as to them that pick pockets in the presence of the Judge, or that will cut purses under the Gallows. It

Gen. 13. 13.

is said of the men of *Sodom, that they were sinners exceedingly,* because they were sinners *before the Lord,* that is, in his Eyesight, and notwithstanding the Kindnesses that he had shewed them; for the land

Ver. 10.

of *Sodom* was now like the *Garden of Eden heretofore.* This therefore provoked him the more to Jealousy, and made their plague as hot as the fire of the Lord out of Heaven could make it. And it is most rationally to be concluded, That such, even such as these are, that shall sin in the Sight, yea, and that too in Despite of such examples, that are set continually before them to caution them to the contrary, must be partakers of severest Judgments.

Hope. Doubtless thou hast said the truth; but what a Mercy is it, that neither thou, but especially I, am not made myself this example? This ministreth occasion to us to thank God, to fear before him, and always to remember *Lot's* wife.

I saw then, that they went on their way to a

A River.
Psal. 65. 9.

pleasant river; which *David* the King called *the river of God;* but *John, the river of the Water of*

Life. Now their Way lay just upon the bank of this River: Here therefore *Christian* and his companion walked with great delight; they drank also of the water of the River, which was pleasant and enlivening to their weary spirits. Besides, on the banks of this River, on either side, were *green Trees,* that bore all manner of fruit; and the leaves of the trees were good for Medicine; with the fruit of these trees they were also much delighted; and the leaves they eat to prevent Surfeits, and other diseases that are incident to those that heat their blood by Travels. On either side of the River was also a meadow, curiously beautified with lillies; and it was green all the year long. In this meadow they lay down and slept; for here they might *lie down safely.* When they awoke, they gathered again of the fruit of the trees, and drank again of the water of the River, and then lay down again to sleep. Thus they did several days and nights. Then they sang:

Rev. 22.
Ezek. 47.

Trees by the River.
The fruit and leaves of the trees.

A Meadow in which they lie down to sleep.
Psal. 23. 2.
Isa. 14. 30.

Behold ye, how these Crystal Streams do glide
(To comfort Pilgrims) by the Highway side.
The Meadows green, besides their fragrant smell,
Yield dainties for them: And he that can tell
What pleasant Fruit, yea, Leaves, these Trees do
yield,
Will soon sell all, that he may buy this Field.

So when they were disposed to go on, (for they were not as yet at their Journey's end), they eat and drank, and departed.

Now I beheld in my dream, that they had not journied far, but the River and the Way for a time parted, at which they were not a little sorry, yet they durst not go out of the *Way*. Now the way from the River was rough, and their feet tender by Numb. 21. 4. reason of their travels. *So the Soul of the Pilgrims were much discouraged, because of the way.* Wherefore still as they went on, they wished for better Way. Now a little before them, there was on the *By-Path-* Left Hand of the road a *Meadow*, and a Stile to go *Meadow.* *One Tempta-* over into it, and that meadow is called *By-Path-* *tion makes way Meadow.* Then said *Christian* to his fellow, If this *for another.* meadow lieth along by our Wayside, let us go over into it. Then he went to the Stile to see, and behold a Path lay along by the Way on the other side of the fence. 'Tis according to my wish, said *Christian*, here is the easiest going ; come, good *Hopeful*, and let us go over.

Strong Chris- *Hope.* But how if this Path should lead us out of *tians may lead* *weak ones out* the Way ? *the way.*

Chr. That's not likely, said the other ; look, doth it not go along by the Wayside ? So *Hopeful*, being persuaded by his fellow, went after him over the Stile. When they were gone over, and were got into the Path, they found it very easy for their feet ; and withal, they looking before them, espied a man walking as they did, (and his name was *Vain Confidence*), so they called after him, and asked him, whither that Way led ? He said, to the Cœlestial *See what it is* Gate : Look, said *Christian*, did not I tell you so ? *too suddenly to* *fall in with* By this you may see we are right ; so they followed, *Strangers.* and he went before them. But behold, the Night came on, and it grew very dark ; so that they that were behind lost the sight of him that went before.

He therefore that went before (*Vain-Confidence* Isa. 9. 16.
by name), not seeing the way before him, fell into a *A Pit to catch the Vain-glo-*
deep Pit, which was on purpose there made by the *rious in.*
Prince of those grounds, to catch *vain-glorious* fools
withal, and was dashed in pieces with his fall.

Now *Christian* and his fellow heard him fall. So
they called to know the matter, but there was none *Reasoning be-*
to answer, only they heard a groaning. Then said *tween Chris-*
Hopeful, Where are we now? Then was his fellow *tian and Hopeful.*
silent, as mistrusting that he had led him out of the
Way; and now it began to rain, and thunder and
lighten in a very dreadful manner; and the water
rose amain.

Then *Hopeful* groaned in himself, saying, *Oh
that I had kept on my Way!*

Chr. Who could have thought that this Path
should have led us out of the Way?

Hope. I was afraid on't at the very first, and
therefore gave you that gentle caution. I would
have spoke plainer, but that you are older than I.

Chr. Good brother, be not offended, I am sorry *Christian's*
I have brought thee out of the way, and that I have *Repentance for leading his*
put thee into such imminent Danger; pray, my *brother out of the Way.*
brother, forgive me; I did not do it of an Evil
Intent.

Hope. Be comforted, my brother, for I forgive
thee; and believe too, that this shall be for our
good.

Chr. I am glad I have with me a merciful
brother: But we must not stand thus; let's try to
go back again.

Hope. But, good brother, let me go before.

Chr. No, if you please, let me go first; that if

there be any danger, I may be first therein, because by my means we are both gone out of the way.

Hope. No, said *Hopeful,* you shall not go first; for your mind being troubled, may lead you out of the Way again.   Then for their Encouragement,

Jer. 31. 21. they heard the Voice of one, saying, *Let thine Heart be towards the Highway; even the Way that*

They are in danger of drowning as they go back. *thou wentest, turn again.*   But by this time the Waters were greatly risen, by reason of which, the Way of going back was very dangerous. (Then I thought that it is easier going out of the way when we are in, than going in when we are out.)   Yet they adventured to go back, but it was so dark, and the Flood was so high, that in their going back, they had like to have been drowned nine or ten times.

Neither could they, with all the skill they had, get again to the Stile that night.   Wherefore at last, lighting under a little shelter, they sat down there 'till the Day brake; but being weary, they fell asleep.   Now there was, not far from the place

They sleep in the grounds of Giant De- spair. where they lay, a castle, called *Doubting-Castle,* the owner whereof was *Giant Despair,* and it was in his grounds they now were sleeping; wherefore he getting up in the morning early, and walking up

He finds them in his ground, and carries them to Doubting- Castle. and down in his fields, caught *Christian* and *Hope- ful* asleep in his grounds: Then with a *grim* and *surly* voice, he bid them awake, and asked them

---

The Pilgrims now, to gratify the Flesh,
Will seek its Ease; *but, oh! how they afresh*
Do thereby plunge themselves new Griefs into!
Who seek to please the Flesh, themselves undo.

whence they were, and what they did in his grounds. They told him they were Pilgrims, and that they had lost their Way. Then said the *Giant*, You have this night trespassed on me, by trampling in and lying on my grounds, and therefore you must go along with me. So they were forced to go, because he was stronger than they. They also had but little to say, for they knew themselves in a Fault. The *Giant* therefore drove them before him, and put them into his castle, in a very dark Dungeon, nasty and stinking to the spirit of these two men: Here then they lay from *Wednesday* morning till *Saturday* night, without one bit of bread, or drop of drink, or Light, or any to ask how they did: They were therefore here in evil case, and were far from Friends and Acquaintance. Now in this place *Christian* had double sorrow, because 'twas through his unadvised haste that they were brought into this distress.

The Grievousness of their Imprisonment.

Psal. 88.

Now Giant *Despair* had a wife, and her name was *Diffidence :* So when he was gone to bed, he told his wife what he had done, to wit, That he had taken a couple of Prisoners, and cast them into his *Dungeon*, for trespassing on his grounds. Then he asked her also, what he had best to do further to them. So she asked him what they were, whence they came, and whither they were bound? and he told her. Then she counselled him, that when he arose in the morning, he should beat them without any mercy: So when he arose, he getteth him a grievous crab-tree cudgel, and goes down into the *Dungeon* to them, and there first falls to rating of them as if they were dogs, although they gave him

On Thursday
Giant Despair
*beats his Pri-
soners.*

never a word of distaste : Then he falls upon them, and beats them fearfully, in such sort, that they were not able to help themselves, or to turn them upon the floor. This done, he withdraws, and leaves them there to condole their misery, and to mourn under their distress : So all that day they spent the time in nothing but sighs and bitter Lamentations. The next night she talking with her husband about them further, and understanding that they were yet alive, did advise him to counsel them to make away themselves : So when morning was come, he goes to them in a surly manner, as before, and perceiving them to be very sore with the stripes that he had given them the day before, he told them, That since they were never like to come out of that place, their only way

On Friday
Giant Despair
*counsels them
to kill them-
selves.*

would be forthwith to make an end of themselves, either with Knife, Halter, or Poison : For why, said he, should you choose Life, seeing it is attended with so much Bitterness ? But they desired him to let them go ; with that he looked ugly upon them, and rushing to them had doubtless made an end of them himself, but that he fell into one of his fits (for

*The Giant
sometimes has
Fits.*

he sometimes in Sun-shine weather fell into fits) and lost, for a time, the use of his hand : Wherefore he withdrew, and left them as before, to consider what to do. Then did the Prisoners consult between themselves, whether 'twas best to take his counsel or no ; and thus they began to discourse :

Christian *be-
gins to despair.*

Chr. Brother, said *Christian,* what shall we do ? The life that we now live is miserable ! For my part, I know not whether 'tis best to live thus, or to

Job 7. 15.

die out of hand. *My Soul chooseth Strangling rather than Life,* and the Grave is more easy for me than this Dungeon! Shall we be ruled by the Giant?

Hope. Indeed our present condition is dreadful, and death would be far more welcome to me, than *thus* for ever to abide: But yet let us consider, the Lord of the Country to which we are going, hath said, Thou shalt do no Murder, no not to another man's person; much more then are we forbidden to take his counsel, to kill ourselves. Besides, he that kills another, can but commit murther upon his body: But for one to kill *himself,* is to kill Body and Soul at once. And moreover, my brother, thou talkest of ease in the grave, but hast thou forgotten the Hell, whither for certain the Murderers go? For no Murderer hath Eternal Life, &c. And let us consider again, that all the Law is not in the hand of *Giant Despair;* others, so far as I can understand, have been taken by him, as well as we; and yet have escaped out of his hands. Who knows, but that God, who made the world, may cause that *Giant Despair* may die, or that, at some time or other, he may forget to lock us in; or but he may in short time have another of his fits before us, and may lose the use of his limbs? And if ever that should come to pass again, for my part I am resolved to pluck up the heart of a Man, and to try my utmost to get from under his hand. I was a fool that I did not try to do it before; but however, my brother, let's be patient, and endure a while, the time may come that may give us a happy release: But let us not be our own murderers. With these words *Hopeful* at present did moderate the mind of his brother; so they continued together

Hopeful com-forts him.

(in the Dark) that day in their sad and doleful
condition.

Well, towards evening the *Giant* goes down into
the Dungeon again, to see if his prisoners had taken
his counsel; but when he came there, he found
them alive; and truly alive was all; for now, what
for want of bread and water, and by reason of the
Wounds they received when he beat them, they
could do little but breathe. But I say, he found
them alive; at which he fell into a grievous rage,
and told them, that seeing they had disobeyed his
counsel, it should be worse with them than if they
had never been born.

At this they trembled greatly, and I think that
Christian fell into a Swoon; but coming a little to
himself again, they renewed their discourse about
the *Giant's* counsel, and whether yet they had best

Christian still dejected.

take it or no. Now *Christian* again seemed to be
for doing it, but *Hopeful* made his second reply as
followeth.

Hopeful comforts him again, by calling former things to remembrance.

Hope. My Brother, said he, remembrest thou not,
how valiant thou hast been heretofore? *Apollyon*
could not crush thee, nor could all that thou didst
hear, or see, or feel, in the valley of the Shadow
of Death; what hardship, terror, and amazement
hast thou already gone through, and art thou now
nothing but Fear? Thou seest that I am in the
Dungeon with thee, a far weaker man by nature
than thou art; also this *Giant* has wounded me as
well as thee, and hath also cut off the bread and
water from my mouth, and with thee I mourn
without the Light. But let's exercise a little more
patience; remember how thou playedst the Man

W.S.

CHRISTIAN AND HOPEFUL IN THE DUNGEON

at *Vanity Fair*, and was neither afraid of the chain nor cage, nor yet of bloody Death; wherefore let us (at least to avoid the Shame that becomes not a Christian to be found in) bear up with patience as well as we can.

Now night being come again, and the *Giant* and his wife being in bed, she asked him concerning the prisoners, and if they had taken his counsel: To which he replyed; They are sturdy rogues, they choose rather to bear all hardships, than to make away themselves. Then said she; Take them into the castle-yard to-morrow, and shew them the *Bones* and *Skulls* of those that thou hast already dispatch'd, and make them believe e're a week comes to an end, thou also wilt tear them in pieces, as thou hast done their fellows before them.

So when the morning was come, the *Giant* goes to them again, and takes them into the castle-yard, and shews them as his wife had bidden him: These, said he, were Pilgrims as you are, once, and they trespassed in my grounds, as you have done; and when I thought fit, I tore them in pieces, and so within ten days I will do you; go, get you down to your Den again; and with that he beat them all the way thither. They lay therefore all day on *Satur-day* in a lamentable case, as before. Now, when night was come, and when Mrs. *Diffidence* and her husband the *Giant* were got to bed, they began to renew their discourse of their prisoners; and withal, the old *Giant* wondered that he could neither by his Blows nor Counsel bring them to an end. And with that his wife replied; I fear, said she, that they live in hope that some will come to relieve them, or

On Saturday the Giant threatned, that shortly he would pull them in pieces.

that they have picklocks about them, by the means
of which they hope to escape.   And say'st thou so,
my dear, said the *Giant;* I will therefore search
them in the morning.

Well, on *Saturday* about midnight they began to
pray, and continued in Prayer till almost break of
day.

Now, a little before it was Day, good *Christian,*
as one half amazed, brake out in this passionate
speech ; What a Fool, quoth he, am I, thus to lie in
a stinking dungeon, when I may as well walk at

A Key in
Christian's
bosom called
Promise, *opens*
any lock in
Doubting-
Castle.

liberty ? I have a key in my bosom, called *Promise,*
that will I am persuaded open any lock in *Doubting-
Castle.*   Then said *Hopeful,* That's good news, good
brother, pluck it out of thy bosom and try.

Then *Christian* pulled it out of his bosom, and
began to try at the dungeon door, whose bolt (as he
turned the Key) gave back, and the door flew open
with ease, and *Christian* and *Hopeful* both came out.
Then he went to the outward door that leads into
the *castle-yard,* and with his key opened that door
also.   After he went to the Iron Gate, for that must
be opened too, but that lock went very hard, yet the
Key did open it.   Then they thrust open the gate
to make their escape with speed ; but that gate as it
opened made such a creaking, that it waked *Giant
Despair,* who hastily rising to pursue his prisoners,
felt his limbs to fail, for his fits took him again, so
that he could by no means go after them.   Then they
went on, and came to the King's Highway again,
and so were safe, because they were out of his
jurisdiction.

Now, when they were gone over the Stile, they

began to contrive with themselves what they should do at that Stile, to prevent those that should come after from falling into the hands of *Giant Despair*. So they consented to erect there a pillar, and to en- *A Pillar erected by Christian and his fellow.* grave upon the side thereof this sentence; ' Over 'this Stile is the way to *Doubting-Castle*, which is 'kept by *Giant Despair*, who despiseth the King of 'the Cœlestial Country, and seeks to destroy his 'holy Pilgrims.' Many therefore that followed after, read what was written, and escaped the danger. This done, they sang as follows:

Out of the Way we went, and then we found
What 'twas to tread upon forbidden ground.
And let them that come after have a care,
Lest heedlessness makes them as we to fare,
Lest they for trespassing, his Pris'ners are,
Whose Castle's Doubting, and whose name's Despair.

They went then till they came to the *Delectable* *The Delectable Mountains.* *Mountains;* which mountains belong to the Lord of that Hill, of which we have spoken before; so they *They are refreshed in the mountains.* went up to the mountains, to behold the Gardens and Orchards, the Vineyards, and Fountains of water; where also they drank and washed themselves, and did freely eat of the vineyards. Now there was on the tops of those mountains, Shepherds feeding their Flocks, and they stood by the Highway side.

Mountains delectable they now ascend,
Where Shepherds be, which to them do commend
Alluring things, and things that Cautions are,
Pilgrims are steady kept, by Faith and Fear.

The Pilgrims therefore went to them, and leaning upon their staves, (as is common with weary Pilgrims, when they stand to talk with any by the way) they *Talk with the Shepherds.* asked, *Whose Delectable Mountains are these? And whose be the Sheep that feed upon them?*

John 10. 11.   *Shepherd.* These mountains are *Emmanuel's Land*, and they are within sight of his City; and the Sheep also are his, and he laid down his Life for them.

Chr. Is this the Way to the Cœlestial City?

Shep. You are just in your Way.

Chr. How far is it thither?

Shep. Too far for any, but those that shall get thither indeed.

Chr. Is the Way safe or dangerous?

Shep. Safe for those for whom it is to be safe, *but* *Hos.* 14. 9. *Transgressors shall fall therein.*

Chr. Is there in this place any Relief, for Pilgrims that are weary, and faint in the Way?

Shep. The Lord of these mountains hath given us *Heb.* 13. 1, 2. a Charge *not to be forgetful to entertain strangers,* therefore the Good of the place is even before you.

I saw also in my dream, That when the *Shepherds* perceived they were Way-fairing men, they also put questions to them, (to which they made answer as in other places) as, Whence came you? And how got you into the Way? And by what Means have you so persevered therein? For, but few of them that begin to come hither, do shew their face on these mountains. But when the Shepherds heard their answers, being pleased therewith, they looked *The Shepherds welcome them.* very lovingly upon them, and said, *Welcome to the Delectable Mountains.*

The Shepherds, I say, whose names were *Know-* *The names of the Shepherds.* *ledge, Experience, Watchful,* and *Sincere,* took them by the hand, and had them to their tents, and made them partake of that which was ready at present. They said, moreover, We would that you should stay here a while, to be acquainted with us, and yet more to solace yourselves with the good of these Delectable Mountains. They then told them, That they were content to stay; so they went to their Rest that night, because it was very late.

Then I saw in my dream, That in the morning the Shepherds called up *Christian* and *Hopeful* to walk with them upon the Mountains: So they went forth with them, and walked a while, having a pleasant prospect on every side. Then said the Shepherds one to another, Shall we shew these Pilgrims some Wonders? So when they had concluded to do it, they had *They are* them first to the Top of an Hill, called *Error,* which *shewn wonders.* was very steep on the furthest side, and bid them *The Mountain of Error.* look down to the bottom. So *Christian* and *Hopeful* looked down, and saw at the bottom several men dashed all to pieces by a Fall that they had from the top. Then said *Christian,* What meaneth this? The Shepherds answered, Have you not heard of them that were made to err, by hearkning to *Hymeneus* 2 Tim. 2. 17, and *Philetus,* as concerning the Faith of the Resur- 18. rection of the body? They answered, Yes. Then said the Shepherds, Those that you see lie dashed in pieces at the bottom of this mountain are they; and they have continued to this day unburied, (as you see) for an Example for others to take heed how they clamber too high, or how they come too near to the brink of this Mountain.

Then I saw that they had them to the top of
Mount Cau-
tion.
another mountain, and the name of that is *Caution*,
and bid them look afar off: Which when they
did, they perceived, as they thought, several men
walking up and down among the Tombs that were
there: And they perceived that the men were
blind, because they stumbled sometimes upon the
Tombs, and because they could not get out from
among them. Then said *Christian, What means
this?*

The Shepherds then answered, Did you not see
a little below these mountains a Stile that led into
a Meadow, on the left hand of this Way? They
answered, Yes. Then said the Shepherds, From
that Stile there goes a path that leads directly to
Doubting-Castle, which is kept by Giant *Despair*,
and these men (pointing to them among the Tombs)
came once on Pilgrimage, as you do now, even till
they came to that same Stile. And because the
right Way was rough in that place, they chose to go
out of it into that Meadow, and there were taken by
Giant *Despair*, and cast into *Doubting-Castle;* where,
after they had a while been kept in the Dungeon, he
at last did put out their Eyes, and led them among
those Tombs, where he has left them to wander to
this very day, that the saying of the Wise Man
Prov. 21. 16.
might be fulfilled, *He that wandereth out of the Way
of Understanding, shall remain in the Congregation
of the Dead.* Then *Christian* and *Hopeful* looked
one upon another, with tears gushing out, but yet
said nothing to the Shepherds.

Then I saw in my dream, That the Shepherds
had them to another place in a bottom, where was

a door in the side of an Hill, and they opened the door, and bid them look in : They looked in therefore, and saw that within it was very dark and smoky ; they also thought that they heard there a rumbling noise, as of fire, and a Cry of some tormented, and that they smelt the scent of brimstone. Then said *Christian, What means this ?* The Shepherds told them, This is a by-way to Hell, a way that Hypocrites go in at ; namely, such as sell their Birth-right with *Esau ;* such as sell their Master, with *Judas ;* such as blaspheme the Gospel, with *Alexander ;* and that Lie and dissemble, with *Ananias* and *Sapphira* his wife.

A By-way to Hell.

Then said *Hopeful* to the Shepherds, I perceive that these had on them, even every one, a shew of Pilgrimage, as we have now, had they not ?

Shep. Yes, and held it a long time too.

Hope. How far might they go on Pilgrimage in their day, since they notwithstanding were thus miserably cast away.

Shep. Some further, and some not so far as these Mountains.

Then said the Pilgrims one to another, *We had need cry to the* Strong *for strength.*

Shep. Ay, and you will have need to use it, when you have it, too.

By this time the Pilgrims had a desire to go forwards, and the Shepherds a desire they should ; so they walked together towards the end of the mountains. Then said the Shepherds one to another, Let us here shew to the Pilgrims the Gates of the Cœlestial City, if they have skill to look through our *Perspective-Glass.* The Pilgrims then lovingly

The Shepherds Perspective-Glass.

accepted the motion : So they had them to the top of an high hill, called *Clear*, and gave them the Glass to look.

The hill Clear.

Then they essayed to look, but the Remembrance of that last thing that the Shepherds had shewed them, made their hands shake ; by means of which impediment, they could not look steadily through the Glass ; yet they thought they saw something like the Gate, and also some of the Glory of the place. Then they went away and sang this song :

The fruits of Servile Fear.

> *Thus by the Shepherds Secrets are reveal'd,*
> *Which from all other men are kept conceal'd :*
> *Come to the Shepherds then, if you would see*
> *Things deep, Things hid, and that Mysterious be.*

When they were about to depart, one of the Shepherds gave them a *Note of the Way*. Another of them bid them *Beware of the Flatterer*. The third bid them *Take Heed that they sleep not upon the Inchanted Ground*. And the fourth bid them *God Speed*. So I awoke from my Dream.

A two-fold Caution.

And I slept, and dreamed again, and saw the same two Pilgrims going down the mountains along the highway towards the City. Now a little below these mountains on the Left Hand, lieth the country of *Conceit ;* from which country there comes into the Way in which the Pilgrims walked, a little crooked lane. Here therefore, they met with a very brisk lad, that came out of that country ; and his name was *Ignorance*. So *Christian* asked him *From what Parts he came, and whither he was going*.

The country of Conceit, *out of which came Ignorance.*

Ignor. Sir, I was born in the country that lieth off Christian *and* there, a little on the left hand, and am going to the Ignorance *have some talk* Cœlestial City. *together.*

Chr. But how do you think to get in at the Gate? for you may find some difficulty there.

Ignor. As other good people do, said he.

Chr. But what have you to shew at that Gate, that the Gate should be opened to you?

Ignor. I know my Lord's Will, and have been a *The Grounds* good liver; I pay every man his own; I Pray, Fast, *of Ignorance's Hope.* pay Tithes, and give Alms, and have left my country, for whither I am going.

Chr. But thou camest not in at the Wicket-Gate that is at the Head of this Way; thou camest in hither through that same crooked lane, and therefore I fear, however thou mayest think of thyself, when the reckoning-day shall come, thou wilt have laid to thy charge, that thou art a Thief and a Robber, instead of getting admittance into the City.

Ignor. Gentlemen, ye be utter Strangers to me, I *He telleth* know you not; be content to follow the Religion of *every one he is but a Fool.* your country, and I will follow the Religion of mine. I hope all will be well; and as for the Gate that you talk of, all the world knows that that is a great way off our Country; I cannot think that any men in all our parts, do so much as know the way to it; nor need they matter whether they do or no, since we have, as you see, a fine pleasant green lane, that comes down from our country the next way into it.

When *Christian* saw that the man was wise in his own conceit, he said to *Hopeful* whisperingly, *There* Prov. 26. 12. *is more hopes of a Fool than of him.* And said moreover, *When he that is a Fool walketh by the* Eccles. 10. 3.

How to carry it to a Fool.

Way, his wisdom faileth him, and he saith to every one, that he is a Fool. What, shall we talk further with him, or out-go him at present, and so leave him to think of what he hath heard already; and then stop again for him afterwards, and see if by Degrees we can do any good of him? Then said *Hopeful,*

Let Ignorance *a little while now muse*
On what is said, and let him not refuse
Good Counsel to embrace, lest he remain
Still ignorant of what's the chiefest Gain.
God saith, Those that no Understanding have,
(*Altho' he made them*) *them he will not save.*

Hope. He further added, It is not good, I think, to say all to him at once; let us pass him by, if you will, and talk to him anon, *even as he is able to bear it.*

So they both went on, and *Ignorance* he came

Matt. 12. 45.
Prov. 5. 22.

after. Now when they had passed him a little way, they entered into a very dark lane, where they met a man whom seven devils had bound with seven strong cords, and were carrying of him back to the door that they saw on the side of the Hill: Now good *Christian* began to tremble, and so did *Hopeful* his companion: Yet, as the devils led away the man, *Christian* looked to see if he knew

The Destruction of one Turn-away.

him; and he thought it might be one *Turn-away* that dwelt in the town of *Apostasy.* But he did not perfectly see his face; for he did hang his head like a thief that is found. But being gone past, *Hopeful* looked after him, and espied on his back a paper, with this inscription, *Wanton Professor, and dam-nable Apostate.* Then said *Christian* to his fellow, Now I call to remembrance that which was told me, of a thing that happened to a good man hereabout. The name of the man was *Little-Faith*, but a good man, and he dwelt in the town of *Sincere.* The thing was this: At the entering in of this passage, there comes down from *Broad-way-gate*, a lane called *Dead-man's-lane;* so called, because of the Murders that are commonly done there: And this *Little-Faith* going on Pilgrimage, as we do now, chanced to sit down there and slept: Now there happened at that time to come down that *Lane* from *Broad-way-gate*, three sturdy Rogues, and their names were *Faint-heart, Mistrust, and Guilt,* (three brothers) and they espying *Little-Faith* where he was, came galloping up with speed: Now the good man was just awakened from his sleep, and was getting up to go on his Journey. So they came up all to him, and with threatning language bid him *stand.* At this *Little-Faith* looked as white as a clout, and had neither power to fight nor fly. Then said *Faint-Heart*, Deliver thy purse; but he making no haste to do it, (for he was loth to lose his Money) *Mistrust* ran up to him, and thrusting his hand into his pocket, pull'd out thence a bag of silver. Then he cried out, Thieves, thieves. With that *Guilt*, with a great club that was in his hand, struck *Little-Faith* on the head, and with that blow fell'd him flat to the ground; where he lay bleeding as one that would bleed to death. All this while, the Thieves stood by: But at last, they hearing that some were upon the road, and fearing lest it should

Christian telleth his companion a story of Little-Faith. *Broad-way-Gate. Dead-man's lane.* *Little-Faith robbed by Faint-Heart, Mistrust, and Guilt.* *They got away his Silver and knocked him down.*

be one *Great Grace*, that dwells in the city of *Good-Confidence*, they betook themselves to their heels, and left this good man to shift for himself. Now after a while, *Little-Faith* came to himself, and getting up, made shift to scrabble on his Way. This was the story.

Hope. But did they take from him all that ever he had?

Little-Faith *lost not his best things.*

Chr. No: The place where his Jewels were, they never ransack'd; so those he kept still: But, as I was told, the good man was much afflicted for his loss; for the thieves got most of his spending-money.

1 Pet. 4. 18.

That which they got not, (as I said) were Jewels; also he had a little odd money left, but scarce enough to bring him to his Journey's end; nay, (if I was not mis-informed,) he was forced to beg as he went, to keep himself alive; for his Jewels he might not sell: But beg and do what he could, *he went* (as we say) *with many a hungry belly*, the most part of the rest of the Way.

Little-Faith *forced to beg to his Journey's end.*

Hope. But is it not a wonder they got not from him his Certificate, by which he was to receive his admittance at the Cœlestial Gate?

[*'No' only in* 1st. edit.] *He kept not his best things by his own Cunning.* 2 Tim. 1. 14. 2 Pet. 2. 9.

Chr. 'No,' ('tis a wonder) but they got not that; though they missed it not through any good cunning of his: for he being dismay'd with their coming upon him, had neither power nor skill to hide any thing, so 'twas more by good Providence than by his Endeavour, that they miss'd of that good thing.

Hope. But it must needs be a Comfort to him, that they got not this Jewel from him.

Chr. It might have been great comfort to him, had he used it as he should: But they that told me

the story, said, that he made but little use of it all
the rest of the Way; and that because of the Dismay
that he had in their taking away of his money:
Indeed he forgot it a great part of the rest of his
Journey; and besides when, at any time it came into
his mind, and he began to be comforted therewith,
then would fresh thoughts of his Loss come again
upon him, and those thoughts would swallow up all.

Hope. Alas, poor man! This could not but be a *He is pitied by both.*
great grief unto him!

Chr. Grief! Ay, a grief indeed. Would it not
have been so to any of us, had we been used as he,
to be robbed and wounded too, and that in a strange
place, as he was? 'Tis a wonder he did not die
with grief, poor heart; I was told that he scattered
almost all the rest of the Way with nothing but
doleful and bitter complaints: Telling also to all
that overtook him, or that he overtook in the Way
as he went, where he was robbed, and how; who
they were that did it, and what he lost; how he
was wounded, and that he hardly escaped with his
life.

Hope. But 'tis a wonder that his Necessities did
not put him upon *selling* or *pawning* some of his
Jewels, that he might have wherewith to relieve
himself in his Journey.

Chr. Thou talkest like one upon whose head is *Christian*
the Shell to this very day: For What should he *snubs his fellow for unadvised speaking.*
Pawn them? or to whom should he sell them? In
all that country where he was robbed, his Jewels
were not accounted of; nor did he want that Relief
which could from thence be administered to him;
besides, had his Jewels been missing at the Gate of

the *Cœlestial City*, he had (and that he knew well enough) been excluded from an Inheritance there, and that would have been worse to him than the appearance and villany of ten thousand thieves.

Hope. Why art thou so tart, my brother; *Esau* sold his birth-right, and that for a mess of pottage, and that birth-right was his greatest Jewel; and if he, why might not *Little-Faith* do so too?

Heb. 12. 16.

A discourse about Esau *and* Little-Faith.

Chr. Esau did sell his birth-right indeed, and so do many besides, and by so doing exclude themselves from the chief blessing, as also that caitiff did; but you must put a difference betwixt *Esau* and *Little-Faith*, and also betwixt their estates. *Esau's* birth-right was Typical, but *Little-Faith's* Jewels were not so. *Esau's* belly was his God, but *Little-Faith's* belly was not so. *Esau's* Want lay in his fleshly appetite, *Little-Faith's* did not so: Besides, *Esau* could see no further than to the fulfilling of his Lusts; *For I am at the point to die*, said he, *and what good will this birth-right do me?* But *Little-Faith*, though it was his lot to have but a *little faith*, was by his little faith kept from such extravagancies, and made to see and prize his Jewels more, than to sell them as *Esau* did his birth-right. You read not any where that *Esau* had Faith, no, not so much as a little; therefore no marvel if where the Flesh only bears sway, (as it will in that man where *no* faith is to resist) if he sells his birth-right, and his Soul and all, and that to the Devil of Hell; for it is with such, as it is with the ass, *who in her occasions cannot be turned away.* When their minds are set upon their lusts, they will have them, whatever they cost; but

Esau *was ruled by his* Lusts. Gen. 25. 32.

Esau *never had Faith.*

Jer. 2. 24.

Little-Faith was of another temper, his mind was on things Divine; his livelihood was upon things that were Spiritual and from above; therefore, to what end should he that is of such a temper, sell his Jewels, (had there been any that would have bought them) to fill his mind with empty things? Will a man give a penny to fill his belly with Hay? or can you persuade the *turtle-dove* to live upon carrion like the *crow?* Though *faithless* ones can for carnal lusts, pawn, or mortgage, or sell what they have, and themselves outright to boot; yet they that have Faith, *Saving faith*, though but a little of it, cannot do so. Here therefore, my brother, is thy mistake. *Little-Faith could not live upon Esau's pottage.* *A comparison between the turtle-dove and the crow.*

Hope. I acknowledge it; but yet your severe Reflexion had almost made me angry.

Chr. Why, I did but compare thee to some of the birds that are of the brisker sort, who will run to and fro in trodden paths with the shell upon their heads: But pass by that, and consider the matter under debate, and all shall be well betwixt thee and me.

Hope. But, *Christian*, these three fellows, I am persuaded in my heart, are but a company of Cowards: Would they have run else, think you, as they did, at the noise of one that was coming on the road? Why did not *Little-Faith* pluck up a greater heart? He might, methinks, have stood one brush with them, and have yielded when there had been no Remedy. *Hopeful swaggers.*

Chr. That they are Cowards, many have said, but few have found it so in the time of Trial. As for a great heart, *Little-Faith* had none; and *No great heart for God where there is but little Faith.*

I perceive by thee, my brother, hadst thou been the man concerned, thou art but for a brush, and then to yield.   And verily, since this is the height

We have more Courage when out, than when we are in.

of thy stomach, now they are at a distance from us, should they appear to thee, as they did to him, they might put thee to second thoughts.

But consider again, they are but journey-men thieves, they serve under the King of the bottomless

Psal. 5. 8.
[Prov. 28.
15?]
Christian *tells his own Experience in this case.*

Pit; who, if need be, will come in to their aid himself, and his voice is *as the Roaring of a Lion.*   I myself have been engaged as this *Little-Faith* was, and I found it a terrible thing.   These three villains set upon me, and I beginning like a *Christian* to resist, they gave but a call, and in came their Master; I would, (as the saying is) have given my life for a penny; but that, as God would have it, I was cloathed with Armour of Proof.   Ay, and yet, though I was so harnessed, I found it hard work to quit myself like a Man; no man can tell what in that combat attends us, but he that hath been in the Battle himself.

Hope. Well, but they ran, you see, when they did but suppose that one *Great-Grace* was in the way.

Chr. True, they have often fled, both they and their Master, when *Great-Grace* hath but appeared; and no marvel, for he is the *King's Champion:* But I tro, you will put some difference between *Little-*

The King's Champion.

Faith and the *King's Champion.*   All the King's subjects are not his Champions, nor can they, when tried, do such feats of War as he.   Is it meet to think, that a little child should handle *Goliah* as *David* did ?   Or, that there should be the strength of an *ox* in a *wren?* Some are strong, some are weak; some have great Faith, some have little; this man was one of the weak, and therefore he went to the walls.

Hope. I would it had been *Great-Grace* for their sakes.

Chr. If it had been he, he might have had his hands full : For I must tell you, that though *Great-Grace* is excellent good at his weapons, and has and can, so long as he keeps them at sword's point, do well enough with them; yet, if they get within him, even *Faint-heart, Mistrust,* or the other, it shall go hard, but they will throw up his heels. And when a man is down, you know, what can he do?

Whoso looks well upon *Great-Grace's* face, shall see those scars and cuts there, that shall easily give demonstration of what I say. Yea, once I heard he should say, (and that when he was in the combat) *We despaired even of Life.* How did these sturdy rogues and their fellows make *David* groan, mourn, and roar? Yea, *Heman* and *Hezekiah* too, though Champions in their day, were forced to bestir them, when by these assaulted; and yet notwithstanding they had their Coats soundly brushed by them. *Peter,* upon a time, would go try what he could do; but though some do say of him, that he is the Prince of the Apostles, they handled him so, that they made him at last afraid of a sorry Girl.

Besides, their King is at their whistle; he is never out of hearing; and if at any time they be put to the worst, he, if possible, comes in to help them : And of him it is said, *The Sword of him that layeth at him cannot hold; the Spear, the Dart, nor* Job 41. 26. Leviathan's sturdiness.

the Habergeon; he esteemeth Iron as Straw, and Brass as rotten Wood. The Arrow cannot make him fly; Sling-stones are turned, with him, into stubble; Darts are counted as stubble; he laugheth at the shaking of a Spear. What can a man do in this case? 'Tis true, if a man could at every turn have Job's horse, and had Skill and Courage to ride him, he might do notable things. For his neck is clothed with Thunder; he will not be afraid as the grasshopper; the Glory of his nostrils is terrible; he paweth in the Valley, rejoyceth in his Strength, and goeth out to meet the Armed Men. He mocketh at Fear, and is not affrighted, neither turneth back from the Sword. The Quiver rattleth against him, the glittering Spear, and the Shield. He swalloweth the ground with fierceness and rage, neither believeth he that it is the sound of the Trumpet. He saith among the Trumpets, Ha, ha; and he smelleth the Battle afar off, the Thundering of the captains and the Shoutings.

But for such footmen as thee and I are, let us never desire to meet with an Enemy, nor vaunt as if we could do better, when we hear of others that they have been foiled, nor be tickled at the thoughts of our own Manhood, for such commonly come by the worst when tried. Witness *Peter*, of whom I made mention before; he would swagger, ay, he would; he would, as his vain mind prompted him to say, do better, and stand more for his Master than all men; but, who so foiled and run down by these villains as he?

When therefore we hear that such Robberies are done on the King's Highway, two things become us

Job 39. 19.
The excellent mettle that is in Job's *horse.*

to do: First, to go out harnessed, and to be sure to take a Shield with us; for it was for want of that, that he that laid so lustily at *Leviathan* could not make him yield; for indeed, if that be wanting, he fears us not at all. Therefore, he that had Skill, hath said, *Above all, take the Shield of Faith, wherewith* Eph. 6. 16. *ye shall be able to quench all the fiery Darts of the Wicked.*

'Tis good also that we desire of the King a *Con-* 'Tis good to *voy*, yea that he will go with us himself. This made have a Convoy. *David* rejoyce when in the valley of the Shadow of Death; and *Moses* was rather for dying where he Exod. 33. 15. stood, than to go one Step without his God. O, my brother, if he will but go along with us, what Psal. 3. 5, 6, need we be afraid of ten thousands that shall set 7, 8. & 27. 1. 2, 3. themselves against us? but without him, *the proud Helpers fall under the Slain.* Isa. 10. 4.

I, for my part, have been in the fray before now; and though (through the Goodness of him that is best) I am, as you see, alive, yet I cannot boast of my manhood. Glad shall I be, if I meet with no more such brunts; though I fear we are not got beyond all danger. However, since the Lion and the Bear have not as yet devoured me, I hope God will also deliver us from the next uncircumcised *Philistine.* Then sang *Christian:*

> *Poor* Little-Faith! *Hast been among the Thieves?*
> *Wast robb'd? Remember this; Whoso believes,*
> *And gets more Faith, shall then a Victor be*
> *Over ten thousand; else scarce over three.*

So they went on, and *Ignorance* followed. They went then till they came at a place where they saw

A way and a Way. a way put itself into *their Way*, and seemed withal to lie as strait as the Way which they should go; and here they knew not which of the two to take, for both seemed strait before them; therefore here they stood still to consider. And as they were thinking *The Flatterer finds them.* about the Way, behold a man black of Flesh, but covered with a very light Robe, came to them, and asked them why they stood there? They answered, They were going to the Cœlestial City, but knew not which of these Ways to take. Follow me, said the man, it is thither that I am going. So they followed him in the Way that but now came into the *Christian and his fellow deluded.* road, which by Degrees turned, and turned them *so* from the City, that they desired to go to, that in a little time their faces were turned away from it; yet they followed him. But, by and by, before they were *They are taken in a Net.* aware, he led them both within the compass of a Net, in which they were both so entangled, that they knew not what to do; and with that, the *White robe fell off the black man's back:* Then they saw where they were. Wherefore there they lay crying some time, for they could not get themselves out.

They bewail their condition. *Chr.* Then said *Christian* to his fellow, Now do I see myself in an Error. Did not the Shepherds bid us beware of the Flatterers? As is the saying of the Wise Man, so we have found it this day: *A Prov. 29. 5. man that flattereth his neighbour, spreadeth a Net for his feet.*

Hope. They also gave us a Note of Directions about the Way, for our more sure finding thereof; but therein we have also forgotten to read, and have not kept ourselves from the paths of the Destroyer. Here *David* was wiser than we; for, saith he, *Con-*

cerning the works of men, by the Word of thy Lips, Psal. 17. 4.
I have kept me from the paths of the Destroyer.
Thus they lay bewailing themselves in the Net.
At last they espied a Shining One coming toward A Shining
them with a Whip of small cord in his hand. When *One comes to them with a*
he was come to the place where they were, he asked *Whip in his hand.*
them whence they came, and what they did there.
They told him, that they were poor Pilgrims going
to *Zion,* but were led out of their Way by a black
man, cloathed in white, who bid us, said they, follow
him, for he was going thither too. Then said he
with the Whip, It is *Flatterer,* a false Apostle, that
hath transformed himself into an Angel of Light. Prov. 29. 5.
So he rent the Net, and let the men out. Then Dan. 11. 32. 2 Cor. 11. 13,
said he to them, Follow me, that I may set you in 14
your Way again; so he led them back to the Way
which they had left to follow the *Flatterer.* Then *They are exa-*
he asked them, saying, Where did you lie the last *mined, and convicted of*
night? They said, With the Shepherds, upon the *Forgetfulness.*
Delectable Mountains. He asked them then, If they
had not of those Shepherds a *note of direction* for
the Way? They answered, Yes. But, did you,
said he, when you were at a stand, pluck out and
read your Note? They answered, No. He asked *Deceivers fine*
them, Why? They said, They forgot. He asked *spoken.* Rom. 6. 18.
moreover, If the Shepherds did not bid them beware Deut. 25. 2.
of the *Flatterer?* They answered, Yes. But we 2 Chron. 6. 26, 27.
did not imagine, said they, *that this fine-spoken man* Rev. 3. 19,
had been he.

Then I saw in my dream, That he commanded
them to *lie down;* which when they did, he chas- *They are*
tized them sore, to teach them the good Way *whipt and sent on their Way.*
wherein they should walk: And as he chastized

them, he said, *As many as I love, I rebuke and chasten; be zealous, therefore, and repent.* This done, he bids them go on their Way, and take good heed to the other directions of the Shepherds. So they thanked him for all his Kindness, and went softly along the right Way, singing;

> *Come hither, you that walk along the Way,*
> *See how the Pilgrims fare, that go astray:*
> *They catched are in an intangling Net,*
> *'Cause they good Counsel lightly did forget:*
> *'Tis true, they rescu'd were, but yet you see*
> *They're scourg'd to boot: Let this your Caution be.*

Now, after a while, they perceived afar off, one coming softly, and alone, all along the highway to meet them. Then said *Christian* to his fellow, Yonder is a man with his back toward *Zion*, and he is coming to meet us.

Hope. I see him, let us take heed to ourselves now, lest he should prove a *Flatterer* also. So he

The Atheist *meets them.*

drew nearer and nearer, and at last came up unto them. His name was *Atheist*, and he asked them whither they were going.

Chr. We are going to the Mount *Zion.*

He laughs at them.

Then *Atheist* fell into a very great Laughter.

Chr. What is the meaning of your laughter?

Atheist. I laugh to see what ignorant persons you are, to take upon you so tedious a journey, and yet are like to have nothing but your Travel for your pains.

They reason together.

Chr. Why, man? Do you think we shall not be received?

Atheist. Received! There is no such place as you dream of in all this World.

Chr. But there is in the World to come.

Atheist. When I was at home in mine own country, I heard as you now affirm, and from that hearing went out to see, and have been seeking this City these twenty years, but find no more of it than I did the first day I set out. Jer. 22. 13. Eccl. 10. 15.

Chr. We have both heard, and believe that there is such a place to be found.

Atheist. Had not I, when at home, believed, I had not come thus far to seek: but finding none, (and yet I should, had there been such a place to be found, for I have gone to seek it further than you) I am going back again, and will seek to refresh myself with the things that I then cast away, for hopes of that which I now see is not. *The Atheist takes up his content in this World.*

Chr. Then said *Christian* to *Hopeful,* his fellow, *Is it true which this man hath said?* *Christian proveth his brother.*

Hope. Take heed, he is one of the *Flatterers;* remember what it hath cost us once already for our hearkening to such kind of fellows. What! No Mount *Zion?* Did we not see from the *Delectable* mountains, the Gate of the City? Also, are we not now to walk by Faith? Let us go on, said *Hopeful,* lest the man with the Whip overtake us again. *Hopeful's gracious Answer. 2 Cor. 5. 7. Remembrance of former Chastisements, is a Help against present Temptations.*

You should have taught *me* that Lesson, which I will round you in the ears withal: *Cease, my Son, to hear the Instruction that causeth to err from the Words of Knowledge:* I say, my brother, cease to hear him, and let us Believe to the saving of the soul. *Prov. 19. 27. Heb. 10. 39.*

Chr. My brother, I did not put the question to

thee, for that I doubted of the Truth of our belief myself, but to prove thee, and to fetch from thee a

The Fruit of an honest heart.
1 John 2. 11, 21.

Fruit of the honesty of thy heart. As for this man, I know that he is blinded by the God of this world. Let thee and I go on, knowing that we have belief of the Truth, and no Lie is of the truth.

Hope. Now do I rejoice in hope of the Glory of God : So they turned away from the man ; and he laughing at them, went his way.

They are come to the Enchanted ground.
Hopeful begins to be drowzy.

I saw then in my dream, that they went till they came into a certain Country, whose air naturally tended to make one drowzy, if he came a Stranger into it. And here *Hopeful* began to be very dull and heavy of sleep ; wherefore he said unto *Christian*, I do now begin to grow so drowzy, that I can scarcely hold up mine eyes : Let us lie down here, and take one nap.

Christian keeps him awake.

Chr. By no means, (said the other) lest sleeping we never awake more.

Hope. Why, my brother ? Sleep is sweet to the labouring man ; we may be refreshed if we take a nap.

Chr. Do you not remember, that one of the Shepherds bid us beware of the Enchanted ground ? He meant by that, that we should beware of Sleep-

1 Thes. 5, 6.

ing ; wherefore let us not sleep as do others ; but let us watch and be sober.

He is thankful.

Hope. I acknowledge myself in fault ; and had I been here alone, I had by sleeping run the danger of Death. I see it is true, that the Wise Man saith,

Eccl. 4. 9.

Two are better than one. Hitherto hath thy company been my mercy ; *And thou shalt have a good reward for thy labour.*

Chr. Now then, *said Christian,* to prevent drow- *To prevent*
ziness in this place, let us fall into good discourse. *Drowziness*
Hope. With all my heart, said the other. *they fall to*
Chr. Where shall we begin ? *good discourse.*
Hope. Where God began with us, but do you *Good discourse*
begin if you please. *preventeth*
Chr. I will sing you first this song. *drowziness.*

When Saints do sleepy grow, let them come hither, *The dreamer's*
And hear how these two Pilgrims talk together, *note.*
Yea, let them learn of them in any wise
Thus to keep ope' their drowzy slumb'ring eyes ;
Saints Fellowship if it be manag'd well,
Keeps them awake, and that in spite of Hell.

Chr. Then *Christian* began, and said, I will ask *They begin at*
you a question. How came you to think at first of *the beginning*
doing as you do now ? *of their Con-*
Hope. Do you mean, how came I at first to look *version.*
after the Good of my Soul ?
Chr. Yes, that is my meaning.
Hope. I continued a great while in the delight of
those things which were seen and sold at our Fair;
things which I believe now would have (had I continued in them still) drowned me in perdition and
destruction.
Chr. What things were they ?
Hope. All the treasures and riches of the World.
Also I delighted much in rioting, revelling, drink- *Hopeful's* life
ing, swearing, lying, uncleanness, sabbath-breaking, *before Con-*
and what not, that tended to destroy the Soul. *version.*
But I found at last, by hearing and considering of
things that are Divine, which indeed I heard of you,

as also of beloved *Faithful*, that was put to death for his faith and good living in *Vanity-Fair*, *That the end of these things is Death.* And that for these things sake, the wrath of God cometh upon the children of disobedience.

Rom. 6. 21, 22, 23. Eph. 5. 6.

Chr. And did you presently fall under the power of this conviction ?

Hope. No, I was not willing presently to know the Evil of Sin, nor the Damnation that follows upon the commission of it ; but endeavoured, when my mind at first began to be shaken with the Word, to shut mine eyes against the light thereof.

Hopeful at first shuts his eyes against the Light.

Chr. But what was the Cause of your carrying of it thus to the first workings of God's blessed Spirit upon you ?

Reasons of his resisting the Light.

Hope. The causes were, 1. I was ignorant that this was the work of God upon me. I never thought that by awakenings for Sin, God at first begins the Conversion of a Sinner. 2. Sin was yet very sweet to my Flesh, and I was loth to leave it. 3. I could not tell how to part with mine old Companions, their presence and actions were so desirable unto me. 4. The hours in which Convictions were upon me, were such troublesome and such Heart-affrighting hours, that I could not bear, no not so much as the Remembrance of them upon my heart.

Chr. Then, as it seems, sometimes you got rid of your Trouble.

Hope. Yes, verily, but it would come into my mind again, and then I should be as bad, nay worse than I was before.

Chr. Why, what was it that brought your Sins to mind again ?

Hope. Many things ; as,

1. If I did but meet a Good man in the streets ;
or,

2. If I have heard any read in the Bible ; or,

3. If mine head did begin to ache ; or,

4. If I were told that some of my neighbours were sick ; or,

5. If I heard the bell toll for some that were dead ; or,

6. If I thought of Dying myself ; or,

7. If I heard that sudden Death happened to others.

8. But especially when I thought of myself, that I must quickly come to Judgment.

Chr. And could you at any time, with ease, get off the Guilt of Sin, when by any of these ways it came upon you ?

Hope. No, not latterly ; for then they got faster hold of my Conscience ; and then, if I did but think of going back to Sin, (though my mind was turned against it) it would be double Torment to me

Chr. And how did you do then ?

Hope. I thought I must endeavour to mend my Life ; for else, thought I, I am sure to be damned.

Chr. And did you endeavour to mend ?

Hope. Yes ; and fled from, not only my Sins, but sinful company too, and betook me to religious duties ; as Praying, Reading, weeping for Sin, speaking Truth to my neighbours, *&c.* These things I did, with many others, too much here to relate.

Chr. And did you think yourself well then ?

Hope. Yes, for a while ; but at the last my Trouble

When he had lost his Sense of Sin, what brought it again.

When he could no longer shake off his Guilt by sinful courses, then he endeavours to mend.

Then he thought himself well.

came tumbling upon me again, and that over the neck of all my reformations.

Chr. How came that about, since you were now reformed ?

Reformation at last could not help, and why.
Isa. 64. 6.
Gal. 2. 16.
Luke 17. 10.

Hope. There were several things brought it upon me, especially such sayings as these : *All our Righteousnesses are as filthy rags.   By the Works of the Law, no man shall be justified.   When ye have done all things, say, We are unprofitable:* With many more such like.   From whence I began to reason with myself thus : If all my Righteousnesses are filthy rags ; if by the Deeds of the Law no man can be justified ; and if when we have done *all* we are yet unprofitable, then 'tis but a folly to think of Heaven by the Law.   I further thought thus : If a man runs a hundred pounds into the shop-keeper's Debt, and after that shall pay for all that he shall fetch ; yet his old Debt stands still in the Book uncross'd, for the which the shop-keeper may sue him, and cast him into Prison, till he shall pay the debt.

His being a Debtor by the Law troubled him.

Chr. Well, and how did you apply this to yourself ?

Hope. Why, I thought thus with myself; I have by my Sins run a great way into GOD's Book, and that my now Reforming will not pay off that score ; therefore I should think still, under all my present amendments, But how shall I be freed from that Damnation that I have brought myself in danger of by my former Transgressions ?

Chr. A very good application ; but pray go on.

Hope. Another thing that hath troubled me even since my late amendments is, that if I look narrowly into the best of what I do now, I still see Sin, new

Sin, mixing itself with the best of that I do; so that *His espying* now I am forced to conclude, that notwithstanding *bad things in* my former fond Conceits of myself and duties, I have *his best Du-* committed Sin enough in one duty to send me to *ties troubled* Hell, tho' my former life had been faultless. *him.*

Chr. And what did you do then?

Hope. Do! I could not tell what to do, till I *This made* brake my mind to *Faithful*, for he and I were well *him break his* acquainted. And he told me, that unless I could *ful, who told* obtain the Righteousness of a man that never had *him the way* sinned; neither mine own, nor all the Righteous-*to be saved.* ness of the World could save me.

Chr. And did you think he spake true?

Hope. Had he told me so when I was pleased and satisfied with mine own amendments, I had called him Fool for his pains; but now, since I see mine own Infirmity, and the Sin that cleaves to my best performance, I have been forced to be of his opinion.

Chr. But did you think, when at first he suggested it to you, that there was such a man to be found, of whom it might justly be said, That he never committed Sin?

Hope. I must confess the words at first sounded *At which he* strangely, but after a little more talk and company *started at pre-* with him, I had full conviction about it. *sent.*

Chr. And did you ask him, What man this was, and how you must be justified by him?

Hope. Yes, and he told me it was the Lord Jesus, *Heb.* 10. that dwelleth on the right hand of the Most High: *Rom.* 4. And thus, said he, you must be justified by him, *Col.* 1. even by trusting to what he hath done by himself *1. Pet.* 1. in the days of his flesh, and suffered when he did *A more par-* *ticular Dis-* *covery of the*

Way to be saved. hang on the Tree. I asked him further, how *that* Man's righteousness could be of that efficacy, as to justify another before GOD? And he told me, He was the Mighty GOD, and did what he did, and died the Death also, not for himself, but for me; to whom His doings, and the worthiness of them, should be imputed, if I believed on him.

Chr. And what did you do then?

He doubts of Acceptation. *Hope.* I made my objections against my believing, for that I thought he was not willing to save me.

Chr. And what said *Faithful* to you then?

Mat. 11. 28.
He is better instructed. *Hope.* He bid me go to him and see; then I said it was Presumption; he said No, for I was Invited to come. Then he gave me a Book of Jesus his inditing, to encourage me the more freely to come; and he said concerning that Book, That every jot Mat. 24. 35.
Psal. 95. 6.
Dan. 6. 10.
Jer. 29. 12, 13. and tittle thereof stood firmer than Heaven and earth. Then I asked him what I must do when I came: And he told me, I must entreat upon my knees, with all my heart and soul, the Father to reveal him to me. Then I ask'd him further, how I Ex. 25. 22.
Lev. 16. 2.
Num. 7. 8, 9,
Heb. 4. 16. must make my supplication to him? And he said, Go, and thou shalt find him upon a Mercy-Seat, where he sits all the year long, to give Pardon and Forgiveness to them that come. I told him, that I knew not what to say when I came. And he bid *He is bid to Pray.* me say to this effect:

God be merciful to me a Sinner, and make me to know and believe in Jesus Christ; for I see, that if his Righteousness had not been, or I have not Faith in that Righteousness, I am utterly cast away. Lord, I have heard that thou art a merciful God, and hast ordained that thy Son Jesus Christ should be the Saviour of the World; and moreover, that thou art willing to bestow upon such a poor sinner as I am, (and I am a sinner indeed) Lord, take therefore this opportunity, and magnify thy Grace in the Salvation of my soul, through thy Son Jesus Christ. Amen.

Chr. And did you do as you were bidden?

Hope. Yes; over and over, and over.   *He prays.*

Chr. And did the Father reveal his Son to you?

Hope. Not at the first, nor second, nor third, nor fourth, nor fifth; no, nor at the sixth time neither.

Chr. What did you do then?

Hope. What! why I could not tell what to do.

Chr. Had you not thoughts of leaving off Praying?

Hope. Yes; an hundred times twice told.   *He thought to leave off praying.*

Chr. And what was the reason you did not?

Hope. I believed that that was true, which had *Durst not leave off praying, and why.* been told me, *to wit,* That without the Righteousness of this Christ, all the World could not save me; and therefore thought I with myself, if I leave off, I die, and I can but die at the Throne of Grace. And withal this came into my mind, *If it tarry, wait for it, because it will surely come, and will not tarry.* So *Habb.* 2. 3. I continued Praying, until the Father shewed me his Son.

Chr. And how was he revealed unto you?

Hope. I did *not* see him with my bodily eyes, but *Eph.* 1. 18, with the eyes of mine Understanding; and thus it *19.* was. One day I was very sad, I think sadder than *Christ is re-* at any one time of my Life; and this sadness was *vealed to him, and how.* through a fresh sight of the greatness and vileness of my Sins.   And as I was then looking for nothing but *Hell*, and the everlasting Damnation of my Soul, suddenly, as I thought, I saw the Lord Jesus looking down from Heaven upon me, and saying, *Believe on the Lord Jesus Christ, and thou shalt be saved.*

Acts 16. 30, 31.

But I replied, Lord I am a great, a very great Sinner: And he answered, *My Grace is sufficient for thee.*   Then I said, but Lord, what is Believing? And then I saw from that saying, [*He that cometh to me shall never hunger, and he that believeth on me shall never thirst*] that Believing and Coming was all one; and that he that came, that is, ran out in his heart and affections after Salvation by Christ, he indeed believed in Christ.   Then the water stood in mine eyes, and I asked further, But Lord, may such a great Sinner as I am, be indeed accepted of thee, and be saved by thee?   And I heard him say, *and him that cometh to me, I will in no wise cast out.*   Then I said, But how, Lord, must I consider of thee in my coming to thee, that my Faith may be placed aright upon thee?   Then he said, *Christ Jesus came into the World to save Sinners.   He is the end of the Law for Righteousness to every one that believes.   He dyed for our Sins, and rose again for our Justification: He loved us, and washed us from our Sins in his own blood: He is Mediator between God and us: He ever liveth to make Intercession for us.*   From all which I gathered, that I must look for Righteousness in his Person, and for Satisfaction for my Sins by his Blood; that what he did in Obedience to his Father's Law, and in submitting to the Penalty thereof, was not for himself, but for him that will accept it for his Salvation, and be

2 Cor. 12. 9.

John 6. 35.

John 6. 37.

1 Tim. 1. 15.
Rom. 10. 4.
Chap. 4.

Heb. 7. 24, 25.

thankful. And now was my heart full of joy, mine eyes full of tears, and mine affections running over with love to the Name, People, and Ways of Jesus Christ.

Chr. This was a Revelation of Christ to your soul indeed; But tell me particularly what effect this had upon your spirit?

Hope. It made me see that all the World, notwithstanding all the righteousness thereof, is in a state of Condemnation. It made me see that God the Father, though he be just, can justly justify the coming Sinner: It made me greatly ashamed of the Vileness of my former life, and confounded me with the sense of mine own Ignorance; for there never came thought into my heart before now, that showed me so the beauty of Jesus Christ: It made me love a Holy Life, and long to do something for the honour and glory of the name of the Lord Jesus; Yea, I thought that had I now a thousand gallons of blood in my body, I could spill it all for the sake of the Lord Jesus.

I then saw in my dream, that *Hopeful* looked back and saw *Ignorance*, whom they had left behind, coming after. Look, said he to *Christian*, how far yonder youngster loitereth behind?

Chr. Ay, ay, I see him; he careth not for our company.

Hope. But I trow it would not have hurt him, had he kept pace with us hitherto.

Chr. That's true, but I warrant you he thinketh otherwise.

Hope. That I think he doth; but however, let us tarry for him. So they did.

Young Igno-
rance *comes
up again.
Their talk.* Then *Christian* said to him, Come away man,
why do you stay so behind?

Ignorance. I take my pleasure in walking alone,
even more a great deal than in company, unless I
like it the better.

Then said *Christian* to *Hopeful*, (but softly) Did
I not tell you he cared not for our company: But
however, said he, come up, and let us talk away
the time in this solitary place. Then directing
his speech to *Ignorance*, he said, Come how do
you? How stands it between God and your Soul
now?

Ignorance's
Hope, and the
Ground of it. *Ignor.* I hope well, for I am always full of good
motions, that come into my mind, to comfort me
as I walk.

Chr. What good motions? Pray tell us.

Ignor. Why, I think of GOD and Heaven.

Chr. So do the Devils and damned souls.

Ignor. But I think of them, and desire them.

Chr. So do many that are never like to come
Prov. 13. 4. there. The soul of the Sluggard desires, and hath
nothing.

Ignor. But I think of them, and leave all for
them.

Chr. That I doubt; for leaving of all is a hard
matter; yea, a harder matter than many are aware
of. But why or by what, art thou persuaded that
thou hast left all for GOD and Heaven?

Ignor. My Heart tells me so.

Prov. 28. 26. *Chr.* The Wise Man says, *He that trusts his own*
heart, is a fool.

Ignor. This is spoken of an evil heart, but mine
is a good one.

Chr. But how dost thou prove that?

Ignor. It comforts me in hopes of heaven.

Chr. That may be through its *Deceitfulness;* for a man's Heart may minister comfort to him in the Hopes of that thing for which he yet has no Ground to hope.

Ignor. But my Heart and Life agree together, and therefore my Hope is well grounded.

Chr. Who told thee that thy Heart and Life agree together?

Ignor. My Heart tells me so.

Chr. Ask my Fellow, if I be a Thief? Thy Heart tells thee so! Except the Word of God beareth witness in this matter, other testimony is of no value.

Ignor. But is it not a good Heart that has good Thoughts? And is not that a good Life, that is according to God's Commandments?

Chr. Yes, that is a good Heart that hath good Thoughts; and that is a good Life that is according to God's Commandments: But it is one thing indeed to have these, and another thing only to think so.

Ignor. Pray what count you good thoughts, and a life according to God's commandments?

Chr. There are good thoughts of divers kinds; some respecting ourselves, some God, some Christ, and some other things.

Ignor. What be good thoughts respecting ourselves?

Chr. Such as agree with the Word of God. *What are good thoughts.*

Ignor. When do our thoughts of ourselves agree with the Word of God?

Chr. When we pass the same Judgment upon ourselves which the Word passes. To explain myself: The Word of God saith of persons in a Natural Condition, *There is none Righteous, there is none that doth good;* it saith also, *That every imagination of the heart of a man is only Evil, and that continually;* and again, *The imagination of man's heart is Evil from his youth.* Now then, when we think thus of ourselves, having *Sense* thereof, then are our thoughts good ones, because according to the Word of God.

Rom. 3.
Gen. 6. 5.

Ignor. I will never believe that my heart is thus bad.

Chr. Therefore thou never hadst one good thought concerning thyself in thy life. But let me go on. As the Word passeth a judgment upon our *Heart,* so it passeth a judgment upon our *Ways,* and when our thoughts of our *Hearts* and *Ways* agree with the judgment which the Word giveth of both, then are both good, because agreeing thereto.

Ignor. Make out your meaning.

Psal. 125. 5.
Prov. 2. 15.
Rom. 3.

Chr. Why, the Word of God saith, That man's ways are crooked ways, not good, but perverse: It saith, They are naturally out of the good Way, that they have not known it. Now when a man thus thinketh of his ways, I say, when he doth sensibly, and with Heart-humiliation thus think, then hath he good thoughts of his own ways, because his thoughts now agree with the judgment of the Word of God.

Ignor. What are good thoughts concerning God?

Chr. Even (as I have said concerning ourselves) when our thoughts of God do agree with what the

Word saith of him ; and that is, when we think of his Being and Attributes as the Word hath taught ; of which I cannot now discourse at large : But to speak of him with reference to us, then we have right thoughts of God, when we think that he knows us better than we know ourselves, and can see Sin in us when and where we can see none in ourselves : When we think He knows our inmost thoughts, and that our heart, with all its depths, is always open unto his eyes : Also when we think that all our Righteousness stinks in his nostrils, and that therefore he cannot abide to see us stand before him in any Confidence, even of all our best performances.

Ignor. Do you think that I am such a Fool as to think God can see no further than I ? Or, that I would come to God in the best of my Performances ?

Chr. Why, how dost thou think in this matter ?

Ignor. Why, to be short, I think I must believe in Christ for Justification.

Chr. How! Think thou must believe in Christ, when thou seest not thy need of him! Thou neither seest thy original nor actual Infirmities, but hast such an opinion of thyself, and of what thou dost, as plainly renders thee to be one that did never see a necessity of Christ's personal Righteousness to justify thee before God. How then dost thou say, I believe in Christ ?

Ignor. I believe well enough for all that.

Chr. How dost thou believe ?

Ignor. I believe that Christ died for sinners, and *The Faith of* that I shall be justified before God from the Curse, Ignorance. through his gracious acceptance of my obedience to his law. *Or thus*, Christ makes my Duties, that are religious, acceptable to his Father by virtue of his Merits, and so shall I be justified.

Chr. Let me give an answer to this confession of thy Faith.

1. Thou believest with a *fantastical* Faith ; for this faith is no where described in the Word.

2. Thou believest with a *false* Faith, because it taketh Justification from the Personal Righteousness of Christ, and applies it to thy own.

3. This Faith maketh not Christ a justifier of thy person, but of thy actions ; and of thy person, for thy actions sake, which is false.

4. Therefore this Faith is deceitful, even such as will leave thee under Wrath in the day of God Almighty ; For true *Justifying Faith* puts the soul (as sensible of its lost condition by the Law) upon flying for refuge unto Christ's Righteousness : (which righteousness of *his* is not an act of Grace, by which he maketh, (for Justification,) *thy* Obedience accepted with God ; but *his* Personal Obedience to the Law, in doing and suffering for us what that requireth at our hands.   This righteousness, I say, true Faith accepteth ;) under the skirt of which, the soul being shrouded, and by it presented as spotless before God, it is accepted, and acquit from Condemnation.

Ignor. What! would you have us trust to what Christ in his own Person has done without us ? This conceit would loosen the reins of our Lust, and tolerate us to live as we list : For, what matter how we live, if we may be justify'd by Christ's Personal Righteousness, from all, when we believe it.

Chr. Ignorance is thy Name ; and as thy name is,

so art thou; even this thy answer demonstrateth what I say. *Ignorant* thou art of what *Justifying Righteousness* is, and as ignorant how to secure thy Soul through the Faith of it from the heavy Wrath of GOD. Yea, thou also art ignorant of the true effects of Saving Faith in this righteousness of Christ, which is to bow and win over the heart to God in Christ, to love his Name, his Word, Ways, and People, and not as thou ignorantly imaginest.

Hope. Ask him if ever he had Christ revealed to him from Heaven?

Ignor. What! You are a man for Revelations! I believe that what both you and all the rest of you say about that matter, is but the fruit of distracted brains. *Ignorance jangles with them.*

Hope. Why man! Christ is so hid in God from the natural apprehensions of all Flesh, that he cannot by any man be savingly known, unless God the Father reveals him to them.

Ignor. That is your Faith, but not mine; yet mine, I doubt not, is as good as yours, though I have not in my head so many Whimsies as you. *He speaks reproachfully of what he knows not.*

Chr. Give me leave to put in a word: You ought not so slightly to speak of this matter; For this I will boldly affirm, (even as my good companion hath done) that no man can know Jesus Christ but by the revelation of the Father; yea, and Faith too, by which the soul layeth hold upon Christ, (if it be right) must be wrought by the exceeding greatness of his mighty Power; the working of which Faith, I perceive, poor *Ignorance!* thou art ignorant of. Be awakened then, see thine own wretchedness, and fly to the Lord Jesus; and by his righteousness. *Matt. 11. 27.* *1 Cor. 12. 3.* *Eph. 1. 18, 19.*

which is the righteousness of GOD, (for he himself is GOD) thou shalt be delivered from Condemnation.

*The Talk
broke up.*

Ignor. You go so fast, I cannot keep pace with you : Do you go on before; I must stay a while behind. Then they said,

> *Well*, Ignorance, *wilt thou yet foolish be*
> *To slight good Counsel, ten times given thee?*
> *And if thou yet refuse it, thou shalt know,*
> *E're long, the Evil of thy doing so.*
> *Remember, man, in time ; stoop, do not fear ;*
> *Good Counsel taken well saves ; therefore hear.*
> *But if thou yet shalt slight it, thou wilt be*
> *The Loser*, Ignorance, *I'll warrant thee.*

Then *Christian* addressed himself thus to his fellow :

Chr. Well, come my good *Hopeful*, I perceive that thou and I must walk by ourselves again.

So I saw in my dream, that they went on apace before, and *Ignorance* he came hobbling after. Then said *Christian* to his companion, It pities me much for this poor man; it will certainly go ill with him at last.

Hope. Alas! there are abundance in our town in his condition, whole families, yea, whole streets, (and that of Pilgrims too;) and if there be so many in our parts, how many, think you, must there be in the place where he was born?

Chr. Indeed the Word saith, *He hath blinded their eyes, lest they should see,* &c.

But now we are by ourselves, What do you think of such men? Have they at no time, think you,

Convictions of Sin, so consequently fears that their state is dangerous?

Hope. Nay, do you answer that question yourself, for you are the elder man.

Chr. Then I say, sometimes (as I think) they may; but they being naturally ignorant, understand not that such convictions tend to their Good; and therefore they do desperately seek to stifle them, and presumptuously continue to flatter themselves in the way of their own hearts.

Hope. I do believe, as you say, that Fear tends much to men's good, and to make them right at their beginning to go on Pilgrimage. *The good Use of Fear.*

Chr. Without all doubt it doth, if it be right; for so says the Word, *The Fear of the Lord is the beginning of Wisdom.* Job 28. 28. Psal. 111. 10. Prov. 1. 7. ch. 9. 10.

Hope. How will you describe right fear?

Chr. True or right fear is discovered by three things: *Right Fear.*

1. By its rise, It is caused by saving Convictions for Sin.

2. It driveth the soul to lay fast hold of Christ for Salvation.

3. It begetteth and continueth in the soul a great Reverence of God, his Word and Ways, keeping it tender, and making it afraid to turn from them, to the right hand or to the left, to any thing that may dishonour God, break its peace, grieve the Spirit, or cause the enemy to speak reproachfully.

Hope. Well said; I believe you have said the truth. Are we now almost got past the Enchanted ground?

Chr. Why, art thou weary of this discourse?

Hope. No, verily, but that I would know where we are.

Chr. We have not now above two miles further to go thereon. But let us return to our matter. *Why ignorant persons do stifle Convictions.* Now the Ignorant know not that such convictions *1. In general.* that tend to put them in Fear, are for their Good, and therefore they seek to stifle them.

Hope. How do they seek to stifle them?

2. In particular. *Chr.* 1. They think that those fears are wrought by the Devil; (tho' indeed they are wrought of God;) and thinking so, they resist them, as things that directly tend to their overthrow. 2. They also think that these fears tend to the spoiling of their Faith, (when, alas! for them, poor men that they are, they have none at all!) and therefore they harden their hearts against them. 3. They presume they ought not to fear, and therefore in despite of them wax presumptuously confident. 4. They see that those fears tend to take away from them their pitiful old Self-holiness, and therefore they resist them with all their might.

Hope. I know something of this myself; before I knew myself, it was so with me.

Talk about one Temporary. *Chr.* Well, we will leave, at this time, our neighbour *Ignorance* by himself, and fall upon another profitable question.

Hope. With all my heart, but you shall still begin.

Chr. Well then, did you not know, about ten years ago, one *Temporary* in your parts, who was a forward man in religion then?

Where he dwelt. *Hope.* Know him! yes, he dwelt in *Graceless*, a town about two miles off of *Honesty*, and he dwelt next door to one *Turnback*.

Chr. Right, he dwelt under the same roof with him. Well, that man was much awakened once; I believe that then he had some sight of his Sins, and of the Wages that were due thereto. *He was to-wardly once.*

Hope. I am of your mind, for (my house not being above three miles from him) he would oft times come to me, and that with many tears. Truly I pitied the man, and was not altogether without Hope of him: But one may see, it is not every one that cries, *Lord, Lord,*———

Chr. He told me once, That he was resolved to go on Pilgrimage, as we do now; but all of a sudden he grew acquainted with one *Saveself*, and then he became a stranger to me.

Hope. Now, since we are talking about him, let us a little enquire into the Reason of the sudden back-sliding of him and such others.

Chr. It may be very profitable, but do you begin.

Hope. Well then, there are, in my judgment, four reasons for it.

1. Though the Consciences of such men are awakened, yet their Minds are not changed: There-fore, when the power of Guilt weareth away, that which provoked them to be religious ceaseth: Wherefore they naturally turn to their own course again; even as we see the dog that is sick of what he hath eaten, so long as his sickness prevails, he vomits and casts up all: Not that he doth this of a free mind (if we may say a dog has a mind) but because it troubleth his stomach; but now, when his sickness is over, and so his stomach eased, his desires being not at all alienated from his vomit, he turns him about and licks up all; and so it is true *Reasons why towardly ones go back.*

2 Pet. 2. 22. which is written, *The dog is turned to his own vomit* *again.*   This I say ; being hot for Heaven by virtue only of the sense and fear of the torments of Hell ; as their sense of hell and the fears of damnation chills and cools, so their desires for Heaven and Salvation cool also : So then it comes to pass, that when their Guilt and Fear is gone, their desires for Heaven and happiness die, and they return to their course again.

2. Another reason is, they have slavish fears that do over-master them ; I speak now of the fears that Prov. 29. 25. they have of men : *For the fear of men bringeth a* *Snare.*   So then though they seem to be hot for Heaven so long as the flames of Hell are about their ears, yet when that terror is a little over, they betake themselves to second thoughts, namely, that 'tis good to be wise, and not to run (for they know not what) the hazard of losing all, or at least of bringing themselves into unavoidable and unnecessary Troubles, and so they fall in with the World again.

3. The Shame that attends Religion lies also as a block in their way ; they are proud and haughty, and Religion in their eye is low and contemptible : Therefore when they have lost their sense of Hell, and Wrath to come, they return again to their former course.

4. Guilt, and to meditate Terror, are grievous to them ; they like not to see their misery before they come into it, though perhaps the Sight of it first, if they loved that sight, might make them fly whither the righteous fly and are safe ; but because they do, as I hinted before, even shun the thoughts of guilt and terror, therefore when once they are rid of their

awakenings about the terrors and wrath of God, they harden their hearts gladly, and chuse such ways as will harden them more and more.

Chr. You are pretty near the business, for the bottom of all is, for want of a change in their Mind and Will. And therefore they are but like the felon that standeth before the Judge; he quakes and trembles, and seems to repent most heartily; but the bottom of all is, the fear of the halter; not that he hath any detestation of the offence, as it is evident, because, let but this man have his liberty, and he will be a thief, and so a rogue still; whereas, if his mind was changed, he would be otherwise.

Hope. Now I have shewed you the Reasons of their going back, do you shew me the Manner thereof.

Chr. So I will willingly.

How the Apostate goes back.

1. They draw off their thoughts, all that they may, from the remembrance of God, Death, and Judgment to come.

2. Then they cast off by *degrees* private duties, as Closet-Prayer, Curbing their Lusts, Watching, Sorrow for Sin, and the like.

3. Then they shun the company of lively and warm Christians.

4. After that they grow cold to publick duty, as Hearing, Reading, Godly Conference, and the like.

5. Then they begin to pick holes, as we say, in the coats of some of the Godly, and that devilishly, that they may have a seeming colour to throw Religion (for the sake of some infirmity they have spied in them) behind their backs.

6. Then they begin to adhere to, and associate themselves with carnal, loose, and wanton men.

7. Then they give way to carnal and wanton discourses in secret; and glad are they if they can see such things in any that are counted honest, that they may the more boldly do it through their Example.

8. After this, they begin to play with little Sins openly.

9. And then being hardened, they shew themselves as they are. Thus being launched again into the gulph of misery, unless a Miracle of Grace prevent it, they everlastingly perish in their own deceivings.

Now I saw in my dream, that by this time the Pilgrims were got over the Enchanted ground, and entering into the Country of *Beulah*, whose air was very sweet and pleasant, the Way lying directly through it, they solaced themselves there for a season. Yea, here they heard continually the singing of birds, and saw every day the flowers appear in the earth, and heard the voice of the turtle in the land. In this country the Sun shineth night and day; wherefore this was beyond the valley of the *Shadow of Death*, and also out of the reach of Giant *Despair*, neither could they from this place so much as see *Doubting-Castle*. Here they were within sight of the City they were going to; also here met them some of the inhabitants thereof: For in this land the *Shining Ones* commonly walked, because it was upon the borders of Heaven. In this land also the contract between the Bride and the Bridegroom was renewed: Yea, here, *as the Bride-*

Isa. 62. 4.
Cant. 2. 10, 11, 12.

Angels.

Isa. 62. 5.

groom rejoyceth over the Bride, so did their God re-
joyce over them. Here they had no want of corn Ver. 8.
and wine; for in this place they met with abundance of what they had sought in all their Pilgrimage. Here they heard voices from out of the
City, loud voices, saying, *Say ye to the Daughter of* Ver. 11.
Zion, Behold thy Salvation cometh! Behold his Re-
ward is with him! Here all the inhabitants of the
Country called them, *The holy People, the Redeemed* Ver. 12.
of the Lord, Sought out, &c.

Now, as they walked in this land, they had more
Rejoycing than in parts more remote from the
Kingdom to which they were bound; and drawing near to the City, they had yet a more perfect
View thereof: It was builded of Pearls and precious Stones; also the streets thereof were paved
with Gold, so that by reason of the natural glory
of the City, and the reflection of the Sun-beams
upon it, *Christian* with desire fell sick; *Hopeful*
also had a fit or two of the same disease: Wherefore here they lay by it a while, crying out because
of their pangs; *If you see my Beloved, tell him that*
I am sick of Love.

But being a little strengthned, and better able
to bear their sickness, they walked on their Way,
and came yet nearer and nearer, where were orchards, vineyards and gardens, and their gates
opened into the High-way. Now as they came up
to these places, behold the gardener stood in the
Way, to whom the Pilgrims said, Whose goodly
vineyards and gardens are these? He answered, Deut. 23. 24.
They are the KING'S, and are planted here for his
own delight, and also for the solace of Pilgrims: So

the gardener had them into the vineyards, and bid them refresh themselves with dainties; He also shewed them: *there* the King's walks and the arbours, where he delighted to be: And here they tarried and slept.

Now I beheld in my dream, that they talked more in their sleep at this time, than ever they did in all their Journey; and being in a muse thereabout, the gardener said even to me, Wherefore musest thou at the matter? It is the nature of the fruit of the grapes of these vineyards to go down so sweetly, as to cause the lips of them that are asleep to speak.

So I saw that when they awoke, they addressed themselves to go up to the City. But as I said, the reflection of the Sun upon the City (for the City was pure gold) was so extremely glorious, that they could not as yet with open face behold it; but through an *instrument* made for that purpose. So I saw that as they went on, there met them two Men in raiment that shone like gold, also their faces shone as the light.

Rev. 21. 18.
2 Cor. 3. 18.

These men asked the Pilgrims whence they came? and they told them. They also asked them where they had lodged, what difficulties and dangers, what comforts and pleasures they had met with in the Way? And they told them. Then said the men that met them, You have but two Difficulties more to meet with, and then you are in the City.

Christian then and his Companion asked the men to go along with them, so they told them they would: But, said they, you must obtain it by your own

Faith. So I saw in my dream that they went on together till they came within Sight of the Gate.

Now I further saw, that betwixt them and the Gate was a River, but there was no bridge to go over, and the river was very deep. At the sight therefore of this River, the Pilgrims were much astounded, but the men that went with them, said, You must go through, or you cannot come at the Gate.

The Pilgrims then began to enquire if there was *Death is not* no other Way to the Gate; to which they answered, *welcome to Nature,* Yes, but there hath not any, save two, to wit, *Enoch* *though by it we pass out of* and *Elijah*, been permitted to tread that path, since *this world* the foundation of the World, nor shall until the last *into Glory.* *1 Cor. 15. 51,* Trumpet shall sound. The Pilgrims then (especi- *52.* ally *Christian*) began to despond in his mind, and looked this way and that, but no way could be found by them, by which they might escape the River. Then they asked the Men if the Waters were all of a depth? They said, No; yet they could not help *Angels help us* them in that case; *For*, said they, *you shall find it* *not comforta- bly through* *deeper or shallower, as you believe in the King of* *Death.* *the Place.*

They then addressed themselves to the Water, and entring, *Christian* began to sink, and crying out to his good friend *Hopeful*, he said, I sink in deep Waters; the Billows go over my head, all the Waves go over me. *Selah.*

Then said the other, Be of good cheer, my Bro- *Christian's* ther, I feel the bottom, and it is good. Then said *Conflict at the hour of Death.* *Christian*, Ah! my friend, the sorrows of Death have compassed me about, I shall not see the Land that flows with milk and honey. And with that a

great darkness and horror fell upon *Christian,* so
that he could not see before him.   Also here he in
a great measure lost his senses, so that he could
neither remember nor orderly talk of any of those
sweet refreshments that he had met with in the
Way of his Pilgrimage.   But all the words that he
spake still tended to discover, that he had Horror
of Mind, and Heart-Fears that he should die in that
River, and never obtain Entrance in at the Gate.
Here also, as they that stood by perceived, he was
much in the troublesome thoughts of the Sins that
he had committed, both since and before he began
to be a Pilgrim.   'Twas also observed, that he was
troubled with apparitions of Hobgoblins and evil
Spirits; for ever and anon he would intimate so
much by words.   *Hopeful* therefore here had much
ado to keep his brother's head above water, yea
sometimes he would be quite gone down, and then
e're a while he would rise up again half dead.   *Hopeful* also would endeavour to comfort him, saying,
Brother, I see the Gate, and Men standing by to
receive us; but *Christian* would answer, 'Tis you,
'tis you they wait for; you have been *Hopeful* ever
since I knew you.   And so have you, said he to
Christian.   Ah, brother! said *he,* surely if I was
right, he would now rise to help me, but for my Sins
he hath brought me into the snare, and hath left me.
Then said *Hopeful,* My Brother, you have quite
forgot the text, where it is said of the Wicked,
Psal. 73. 4, 5. *There is no Bands in their Death, but their Strength
is firm, they are not troubled as other men, neither
are they plagued like other men.*   These troubles and
distresses that you go through in these Waters, are

no sign that God hath forsaken you, but are sent to try you, whether you will call to mind that which heretofore you have received of his Goodness, and live upon him in your Distresses.

Then I saw in my dream, That *Christian* was as in a muse a while. To whom also *Hopeful* added these words, *Be of good cheer, Jesus Christ maketh thee whole:* And with that *Christian* brake out with a loud voice, Oh, I see him again! and he tells me, When thou passest through the Waters, I will be with thee; and through the Rivers, they shall not overflow thee. Then they both took courage, and the Enemy was after that as still as a stone, until they were gone over. *Christian* therefore presently found Ground to stand upon, and so it followed, that the rest of the River was but shallow: Thus they got over. Now upon the bank of the River on the other side, they saw the two shining men again, who there waited for them: Wherefore being come up out of the River, they saluted them, saying, *We are Ministring Spirits sent forth to minister to those that shall be Heirs of Salvation;* Thus they went along toward the Gate. Now you must note, that the City stood upon a mighty Hill, but the Pilgrims went up that Hill with ease, because they had these two men to lead them up by the arms; also they had left their *mortal Garments* behind them in the River; for though they went in with them, they came out without them. They therefore went up here with much agility and speed, though the Foundation upon which the City was framed was higher than the Clouds; They therefore went up through the

Christian delivered from his Fears in Death.

Isa. 43. 2.

The Angels do wait for them so soon as they are passed out of this World.

They have put off Mortality.

region of the air, sweetly talking as they went, being comforted, because they safely got over the River, and had such glorious Companions to attend them.

The talk that they had with the Shining Ones was about the Glory of the place, who told them, that the Beauty and Glory of it was inexpressible. There, said they, is *Mount Sion, the Heavenly Jerusalem, the innumerable Company of Angels, and the Spirits of just men made Perfect.* You are going now, said they, to the Paradise of GOD, wherein you shall see the *Tree of Life,* and eat of the neverfading Fruits thereof; and when you come there you shall have white Robes given you, and your walk and talk shall be every day with the KING, even all the days of Eternity. There you shall not see again such things as you saw when you were in the lower region upon the earth, to wit, Sorrow, Sickness, Affliction, and Death, *for the former things are passed away.* You are going now to *Abraham, Isaac,* and *Jacob,* and to the Prophets, men that God hath taken away from the Evil to come, and that are now resting upon their beds, each one walking in his Righteousness. The men then asked, What must we do in the Holy Place? To whom it was answered, You must there receive the Comfort of all your Toil, and have Joy for all your Sorrow; you must reap what you have sown, even the fruit of all your Prayers and Tears, and Sufferings for the King by the Way. In that place you must wear Crowns of Gold, and enjoy the perpetual sight and vision of the *Holy One, for there you shall see him as he is.* There also you shall serve him

Heb. 12. 22, 23, 24.

Rev. 2. 7.

& 3. 4.

Rev. 22. 7.

Isa. 57. 1, 2. & 65. 16, 17.

Gal. 6. 7.

1 John 3. 2.

continually with Praise, with Shouting, and Thanks-
giving, whom you desired to serve in the World,
though with much difficulty because of the Infirmity
of your Flesh. There your eyes shall be delighted
with seeing, and your ears with hearing the pleasant
Voice of the *Mighty One.* There you shall enjoy
your Friends again, that are gone thither before
you; and there you shall with joy receive even
every one that follows into the Holy Place after
you. There also you shall be cloathed with Glory
and Majesty, and put into an equipage fit to ride out
with the *King of Glory.* When he shall come with
Sound of Trumpet in the Clouds, as upon the wings
of the Wind, you shall come with him; and when 1 Thes. 4.
he shall sit upon the Throne of Judgment, you Jude 14.
shall sit by him; yea, and when he shall pass Sen- Dan. 7. 9, 10.
tence upon all the workers of Iniquity, let them be 1 Cor. 6. 2, 3.
Angels or men; you also shall have a voice in that
Judgment, because they were his and your Enemies.
Also when he shall again return to the City, you
shall go too with sound of Trumpet, and be ever
with him.

Now while they were thus drawing towards the
Gate, behold a company of the Heavenly Host came
out to meet them; to whom it was said by the other
two Shining Ones, These are the men that have
loved our Lord, when they were in the World, and
that have left all for his Holy Name, and he hath
sent us to fetch them, and we have brought them
thus far on their desired Journey, that they may go
in and look their Redeemer in the face with Joy.
Then the Heavenly Host gave a great shout, say-
ing, *Blessed are they that are called to the Marriage* Rev. 19. 9.

Supper of the Lamb. There came out also at this time, to meet them, several of the King's Trumpeters, cloathed in white and shining raiment, who with melodious noises and loud, made even the Heavens to echo with their sound. These Trumpeters saluted *Christian* and his fellow with ten thousand Welcomes from the world; and this they did with shouting and Sound of Trumpet.

This done, they compassed them round on every side; some went before, some behind, and some on the right-hand, some on the left, (as 'twere to guard them through the upper regions) continually sounding as they went with melodious noise, in notes on high; so that the very sight was to them that could behold it, as if Heaven itself was come down to meet them. Thus therefore they walked on together; and as they walked ever and anon these Trumpeters, even with joyful sound, would, by mixing their musick with looks and gestures, still signify to *Christian* and his brother how welcome they were into their company, and with what gladness they came to meet them: And now were these two men, as 'twere, in Heaven before they came at it; being swallowed up with the sight of Angels, and with hearing their melodious notes. Here also they had the City itself in view, and they thought they heard all the bells therein to ring, to welcome them thereto; but above all, the warm and joyful

Now, now look how the holy Pilgrims ride,
Clouds are their Chariots, Angels are their Guide;
Who would not here for him all Hazards run?
That thus provides for His, *when this world's done.*

thoughts that they had about their own dwelling there with such Company, and that for ever and ever; Oh! by what tongue or pen can their glorious Joy be expressed! Thus they came up to the Gate.

Now, when they were come up to the Gate, there was written over it in letters of Gold, *Blessed are* Rev. 22. 14. *they that do his Commandments, that they may have right to the Tree of Life, and may enter in through the Gates into the City.*

Then I saw in my dream, that the shining men bid them call at the Gate, the which when they did, some from above looked over the Gate; to wit, *Enoch, Moses,* and *Elijah, &c.* to whom it was said, These Pilgrims are come from the City of *Destruction,* for the Love that they bear to the King of this place; and then the Pilgrims gave in unto them each man his Certificate, which they had received in the beginning; those therefore were carried in to the King, who when he had read them, said, Where are the men? to whom it was answered, They are standing without the Gate. The King then commanded to open the Gate, *that the Righteous Nation,* said he, *that* Isa. 26. 2. *keepeth Truth, may enter in.*

Now I saw in my dream, that these two men went in at the Gate; and lo, as they entered, they were transfigured: and they had raiment put on that shone like Gold. There was also that met them, with Harps and Crowns, and gave them to them, the harps to praise withal, and the crowns in token of honour. Then I heard in my dream, that all the bells in the City rang again for joy; and that it was said unto them, *Enter ye into the Joy of our Lord.*

I also heard the men themselves say, that they sang
with a loud voice, saying, *Blessing, Honour, Glory,
and Power, be to Him that sitteth upon the Throne,
and to the Lamb, for ever and ever.*

Rev. 5. 13,
14.

Now, just as the Gates were opened to let in the
men, I looked in after them; and behold the City
shone like the Sun, the streets also were paved with
Gold, and in them walked many men with Crowns
on their heads, Palms in their hands, and Golden
Harps to sing praises withal.

There were also of them that had wings, and they
answered one another without intermission, saying,
Holy, Holy, Holy is the Lord: and after that, they
shut up the Gates : which when I had seen, I wished
myself among them.

Now, while I was gazing upon all these things,
I turned my head to look back, and saw *Ignorance*
coming up to the River-side; but he soon got over,
and that without half the Difficulty which the
other two men met with. For it happened that
there was then in that place one *Vain-Hope,* a ferry-
man, that with his boat helped him over : so he, as
the other, I saw did ascend the Hill, to come
up to the Gate, only he came alone; neither did
any man meet him with the least encouragement.
When he was come up to the Gate, he looked up
to the Writing that was above, and then began to
knock, supposing that Entrance should have been
quickly administred to him : But he was asked by
the men that looked over the top of the Gate,
Whence come you ? And what would you have ?
He answered, I have eat and drank in the Presence of the King, and he has taught in our streets.

*Ignorance
comes up to the
River, and
Vain-Hope
ferrys him
over.*

Then they asked him for his Certificate, that they might go in and shew it to the King; so he fumbled in his bosom for one, and found none. Then, said they, Have you none? but the man answered never a word. So they told the King, but he would not come down to see him, but commanded the two shining Ones that conducted *Christian* and *Hopeful* to the City, to go out and take *Ignorance* and bind him hand and foot, and have him away. Then they took him up, and carried him through the air to the door that I saw in the side of the Hill, and put him in there. *Then I saw that there was a* Way to Hell, *even from the* Gates of Heaven, *as well as from the* City of *Destruction.* So I awoke, and behold it was a Dream.

The Conclusion.

NOW, Reader, I have told my Dream to thee,
See if thou canst Interpret it to me,
Or to Thyself, or Neighbour; but take heed
Of mis-interpreting; for that, instead
Of doing Good, will but thyself abuse:
By misinterpreting, Evil ensues.

Take heed also that thou be not extreme
In playing with the out-side *of my dream:*
Nor let my Figure or similitude
Put thee into a Laughter, or a Feud;
Leave this for Boys and Fools; but as for thee,
Do thou the Substance *of my matter see.*

Put by the curtains, look within my vail,
Turn up my metaphors, and do not fail;
There, if thou seekest them, such things thou'lt find
As will be helpful to an honest mind.

What of my dross *thou findest here, be bold*
To throw away, but yet preserve the Gold.
What if my Gold be wrapped up in ore?
None throws away the Apple for the Core.
But if thou shalt cast all away as vain,
I know not but 'twill make me dream again.

The End of the First Part.

THE PILGRIM'S PROGRESS

FROM THIS WORLD TO THAT
WHICH IS TO COME

The Second Part

DELIVERED UNDER THE SIMILITUDE OF A DREAM
WHEREIN IS SET FORTH THE MANNER OF THE
SETTING OUT OF CHRISTIAN'S WIFE AND CHILDREN
THEIR DANGEROUS JOURNEY, AND SAFE ARRIVAL
AT THE DESIRED COUNTREY

" I have used Similitudes."—Hos. xii. 10

BY

JOHN BUNYAN

The AUTHOR'S Way of sending forth his

Second Part of the Pilgrim.

G O now, my little Book, to every place,
    Where my first Pilgrim has but shewn his Face:
Call at their door: If any say, Who's there?
Then answer thou, Christiana is here.
If they bid thee Come in, then enter thou,
With all thy boys: And then as thou know'st how;
Tell who they are, also from whence they came;
Perhaps they'l know them by their looks or name:
But if they should not, ask them yet again,
If formerly they did not entertain
One Christian a Pilgrim? If they say,
They did, and were delighted in his Way,
Then let them know, that those related were
Unto him: Yea, his Wife and Children are.
    Tell them that they have left their House and Home:
Are turned Pilgrims, seek a World to come:
That they have met with Hardships in the Way,
That they do meet with Troubles night and day:
That they have trod on Serpents, fought with Devils,
Have also overcome a many evils.
Yea, tell them also of the next, who have
Of Love to Pilgrimage, been stout and brave
Defenders of that Way, and how they still
Refuse this World, to do their Father's will.

Go tell them also of those dainty things,
That Pilgrimage *unto the* Pilgrim *brings :*
Let them acquainted be too, how they are
Beloved of their King, under his Care ;
What goodly Mansions for them he provides,
Tho' they meet with rough Winds and swelling Tides,
How brave a Calm they will enjoy at last,
Who to their Lord, and by his Ways hold fast.
  Perhaps with heart and hand they will embrace
Thee, as they did my firstling, and will grace
Thee, and thy fellows, with such cheer and fare,
As shew will, they of Pilgrims *Lovers are.*

1. OBJECTION.

But how, if they will not believe of me
That I am truly thine ; 'cause some there be
That counterfeit the Pilgrim and his Name,
Seek, by Disguise, to seem the very same,
And by that means have brought themselves into
The hands and houses of I know not who.

ANSWER.

  'Tis true, some have of late to counterfeit
My Pilgrim, to their own, my Title set ;
Yea, others half my Name and Title too
Have stitched to their Book, to make them do ;
But yet they by their Features do declare
Themselves not mine to be, whose e'er they are.
  If such thou meet'st with, then thine only way
Before them all, is, to Say out thy Say,
In thine own native Language, which no man
Now useth, nor with ease dissemble can.
If, after all, they still of you shall doubt,
Thinking that you, like Gipsies, *go about*
In naughty wise, the Country to defile,
Or that you seek good people to beguile

With things unwarrantable, send for me,
And I will testify you Pilgrims *be ;*
Yea, I will testify that only you
My Pilgrims *are ; and that alone will do.*

2. OBJECT.

But yet, perhaps, I may enquire for him,
Of those that wish him damned life and limb.
What shall I do, when I at such a door
For *Pilgrims* ask, and they shall rage the more ?

ANSWER.

Fright not thyself, my Book, for such bugbears
Are nothing else but Ground for groundless fears,
My Pilgrim's *Book has travell'd Sea and Land,*
Yet could I never come to understand
That it was slighted or turn'd out of door
By any Kingdom, were they Rich or Poor.
  In France *and* Flanders, *where men kill each other,*
My Pilgrim *is esteem'd a Friend, a Brother.*
  In Holland *too, 'tis said, as I am told,*
My Pilgrim *is with some worth more than Gold.*
  Highlanders *and* Wild Irish *can agree,*
My Pilgrim *should familiar with them be.*
'Tis in New England *under such advance,*
Receives there so much loving countenance,
As to be trim'd, new-cloath'd, and deck'd with gems
That it may shew its features and its limbs,
Yet more, so comely doth my Pilgrim *walk,*
That of him Thousands daily sing and talk.
  If you draw nearer Home, it will appear,
My Pilgrim *knows no ground of shame or fear ;*
City and Country will him entertain
With, Welcome, Pilgrim, *yea, they can't refrain,*
From smiling, if my Pilgrim *be but by,*
Or shews his head in any Company.

Brave Gallants do my Pilgrim *hug and love,*
Esteem it much, yea, value it above
Things of a greater bulk; yea, with delight,
Say, my Lark's *leg is better than a* Kite.

Young Ladies, and young Gentlewomen too,
Do no small kindness to my Pilgrim *shew;*
Their cabinets, their bosoms, and their hearts,
My Pilgrim *has, 'cause he to them imparts*
His pretty riddles, in such wholsome strains,
As yields them Profit double to their Pains
Of reading; yea, I think I may be bold
To say, some prize him far above their Gold.

The very Children that do walk the street,
If they do but my Holy Pilgrim *meet,*
Salute him will, will wish him well, and say,
He is the only stripling of the day.

They that have never seen him, yet admire
What they have heard of him, and much desire
To have his Company, and hear him tell
Those Pilgrim *stories, which he knows so well.*

Yea, some who did not love him at the first,
But call'd him Fool *and* Noddy, *say they must,*
Now they have seen and heard him, him commend;
And to those whom they love, they do him send.

Wherefore, my Second Part, *thou need'st not be*
Afraid to shew thy head; none can hurt thee,
That wish but well to him that went before,
'Cause thou com'st after with a second store,
Of things as good, as rich, as profitable,
For Young, for Old, for Stagg'ring, and for Stable.

3. OBJECT.

But some there be that say, *He laughs too loud;*
And some do say, *His Head is in a Cloud.*
Some say, *His Words and Stories are so dark,*
They know not how by them to find his mark.

ANSWER.

One may (I think) say, Both his laughs and cries
May well be guess'd at by his wat'ry eyes.
Some things are of that nature, as to make
One's Fancy checkle, while his Heart doth ake;
When Jacob *saw his* Rachel *with the sheep,*
He did at the same time both kiss and weep.

Whereas some say, A Cloud is in his Head,
That doth but shew how Wisdom's covered
With its own mantles, and to stir the mind
To a search after what it fain would find.
Things that seem to be hid in words obscure,
Do but the Godly mind the more allure,
To study what those sayings should contain,
That speak to us in such a cloudy strain.

I also know a dark Similitude
Will on the Fancy more itself intrude,
And will stick faster in the Heart and Head,
Than things from Similies not borrowed.

Wherefore, my Book, let no discouragement
Hinder thy travels: Behold, thou art sent
To Friends, not foes, to Friends that will give place
To thee, thy Pilgrims, and thy Words embrace.

Besides, what my first Pilgrim left conceal'd,
Thou, my brave Second Pilgrim *hast reveal'd;*
What Christian *left lock'd up, and went his Way,*
Sweet Christiana *opens with her Key.*

4. OBJECT.

But some love not the method of your first;
Romance they count it, throw't away as dust.
If I should meet with such, What should I say?
Must I slight them as they slight me, or nay?

ANSWER.

My Christiana, *if with such thou meet,*
By all means in all Loving wise them greet;

Render them not reviling for revile;
But if they frown, I prithee on them smile:
Perhaps 'tis Nature, or some ill report,
Has made them thus despise, or thus retort.

 Some love no cheese, some love no fish, and some
Love not their Friends, nor their own house or Home.
Some start at pig, slight chicken, love not fowl,
More than they love a cuckow, or an owl.
Leave such, my Christiana, *to their Choice,*
And seek those, who to find thee will rejoice;
By no means strive, but in all humble wise,
Present thee to them in thy Pilgrim's guise.

 Go then, my little Book, and shew to all
That entertain, and bid thee Welcome shall,
What thou shalt keep close, shut up from the rest,
And wish what thou shalt shew them, may be blest
To them for good, may make them chuse to be
Pilgrims better by far, than thee or me.

 Go then, I say, tell all men who thou art,
Say, I am Christiana, *and my part*
Is now with my four Sons to tell you what
It is for men to take a Pilgrim's *lot.*

 Go also, tell them who and what they be,
That now do go on Pilgrimage with thee:
Say, Here's my neighbour Mercy, *she is one,*
That has long time with me a Pilgrim gone:
Come, see her in her Virgin face, and learn
'Twixt idle ones, and Pilgrims, *to discern.*
Yea, let young Damsels learn of her to prize
The World which is come, in any wise:
When little tripping maidens follow God,
And leave all doting Sinners to his Rod;
'Tis like those days wherein the young ones cry'd
Hosanna, *to whom old ones did deride.*

 Next tell them of old Honest, *who you found*
With his white hairs treading the Pilgrim's ground

Yea, tell them how plain-hearted this man was,
How after his good Lord he bare his Cross:
Perhaps with some gray head this may prevail
With Christ to fall in Love, and Sin bewail.

Tell them also, how Master Fearing *went*
On Pilgrimage, and how the time he spent
In solitariness, with fears and cries;
And how, at last, he won the Joyful Prize.
He was a good man, tho' much down in spirit:
He is a good man, and doth Life inherit.

Tell them of Master Feeble-mind *also,*
Who, not before, but still behind would go;
Shew them also how he had like been slain,
And how one Great-Heart *did his life regain:*
This man was true of Heart, tho' weak in Grace,
One might true Godliness read in his face.

Then tell them of Master Ready-to-halt,
A man with Crutches, but much without fault:
Tell them how Master Feeble-mind *and he*
Did love, and in Opinions much agree.
And let all know, tho' Weakness was their chance,
Yet sometimes one would Sing, the other Dance.

Forget not Master Valiant-for-the-Truth,
That man of courage, tho' a very Youth:
Tell every one his spirit was so stout,
No man could ever make him face about;
And how Great-Heart *and he could not forbear,*
But put down Doubting-Castle, *slay* Despair.

Overlook not Master Despondency,
Nor Much-afraid *his daughter, tho' they lie*
Under such mantles, as may make them look
(With some) as if their God had them forsook.
They softly went, but sure, and at the End
Found that the Lord of Pilgrims *was their Friend.*
When thou hast told the World of all these things,
Then turn about, my Book, and touch these strings;

Which, if but touched, will such musick make,
They'll make a Cripple dance, a Giant quake.
Those Riddles that lie couch'd within thy breast,
Freely propound, expound: And for the rest
Of thy mysterious lines, let them remain
For those whose nimble Fancies shall them gain.
Now may this little Book a blessing be
To those that love this little Book, and me:
And may its Buyer have no cause to say,
His money is but lost, or thrown away;
Yea, may this Second Pilgrim *yield that Fruit*
As may with each good Pilgrim's *fancy suit;*
And may it persuade some that go astray,
To turn their Foot and Heart to the right Way,

Is the Hearty Prayer of

The AUTHOR,

JOHN BUNYAN.

THE

PILGRIMS PROGRESS:

IN THE SIMILITUDE OF A DREAM.

The Second Part.

COURTEOUS COMPANIONS, some time since, to tell you my Dream that I had of *Christian* the *Pilgrim*, and of his dangerous Journey towards the Cœlestial Country, was pleasant to me, and profitable to you. I told you then also what I saw concerning his *Wife* and *Children*, and how unwilling they were to go with him on Pilgrimage; insomuch that he was forced to go on his Progress without them; for he durst not run the danger of that destruction, which he feared would come, by staying with them in the City of *Destruction*: Wherefore, as I then shewed you, he left them and departed.

Now, it hath so happened, through the multiplicity of business, that I have been much hindred and kept back from my wonted Travels into those parts whence he went, and so could not, till now, obtain an opportunity to make further enquiry after whom he left behind, that I might give you an account of them. But having had some concerns that way of late, I went down again thitherward. Now having taken up my lodgings in a Wood, about a mile off the place, as I slept, I dreamed again.

And as I was in my dream, behold an aged gentleman came by where I lay; and because he was to go some part of the Way that I was travelling, methought I got up and went with him. So as we walked, and as Travellers usually do, I was as if we fell into discourse, and our talk happened to be about *Christian*, and his Travels: For thus I began with the old man.

Sir, said I, what Town is that, there below, that lieth on the Left Hand of our Way?

Then said Mr. *Sagacity*, for that was his name, it is the City of *Destruction*, a populous place, but possess'd with a very ill-condition'd and idle sort of people.

I thought that was that City, *quoth I:* I went once myself thro' that Town; and therefore I know that this report you give of it is true.

Sag. Too true; I wish I could speak truth in speaking better of them that dwell therein.

Well Sir, quoth I, then I perceive you to be a well-meaning man, and so one that takes pleasure to hear and tell of that which is Good: Pray, did you never hear what happen'd to a man some time ago in this Town, (whose name was *Christian*) that went on Pilgrimage up towards the higher Regions?

Sag. Hear of him! Ay; and I also heard of the molestations, troubles, wars, captivities, cries, groans, frights, and fears that he met with and had in his Journey; besides, I must tell you, all our Country rings of him; there are but few houses that have heard of him and his doings, but have sought after, and got the Records of his Pilgrimage; yea, I think I may say, that his hazardous Journey has got many well-wishers to his ways: For tho' when he was *Christians are well spoken of when gone, tho' called Fools while they are here.* here, he was *Fool* in every man's mouth, yet now he is gone, he is highly commended of all; for, 'tis said, he lives bravely where he is: Yea, many of them that are resolved never to run his hazards, yet have their mouths water at his gains.

They may, *quoth I*, well think, if they think any thing that is true, that he liveth well where he is; for he now lives at, and in the Fountain of Life, and has what he has without labour and sorrow, for there is no grief mixed therewith. ['But pray, [Edit. 1728.] what talk have the people about him?']

Sag. Talk! The people talk strangely about him: Some say, that he now walks in white! that he has *Rev. 3. 4. Chap. 6. 11.* a chain of Gold about his neck, that he has a crown of Gold, beset with Pearls, upon his head: Others say, that the shining Ones that sometimes shewed themselves to him in his Journey, are become his companions, and that he is as familiar with them in the place where he is, as here one neighbour is with another. Besides, 'tis confidently affirmed concerning him, that the King of the place where he is, has bestowed upon him already, a very rich *Zech. 3. 7. Luke 14. 15.* and pleasant dwelling at Court, and that he every day eateth and drinketh, and walketh and talketh with him, and receiveth of the smiles and favours of him that is Judge of all there. Moreover, it is expected of some, that his Prince, the Lord of that country, will shortly come into these parts, and will know the reason, if they can give any, why his Jude 14, 15. neighbours set so little by him, and had him so much in derision, when they perceived that he would be a Pilgrim.

Christian's King will take Christian's part.

For they say, that now he is so in the affections of his Prince, and that his Sovereign is so much concern'd with the indignities that were cast upon *Christian*, when he became a Pilgrim, that he will *Luke 10. 16.* look upon all as if done unto himself; and no marvel, for 'twas for the Love that he had to his Prince, that he ventured as he did.

I dare say, *quoth I*, I am glad on't; I am glad *Rev. 14. 13.* for the poor man's sake, for that now he has Rest *Psal. 126. 5,* from his labour, and for that he now reapeth the *6.* benefit of his tears with Joy; and for that he has got beyond the gun-shot of his enemies, and is out of the reach of them that hate him. I also am glad, for that a rumour of these things is noised abroad in this country; who can tell but that it may work some good effect on some that are left behind? But, pray, Sir, while it is fresh in my mind, do you hear any thing of his Wife and Children? Poor hearts, I wonder in my mind what they do!

Good tidings of Christian's Wife and Children.

Sag. Who! *Christiana* and her Sons! They are like to do as well as did *Christian* himself; for though they all play'd the fool at the first, and would by no means be persuaded by either the tears or entreaties of *Christian*, yet second thoughts have wrought wonderfully with them, so they have pack'd up, and are also gone after him.

Better and better, *quoth I:* But, what! Wife and Children and all?

Sag. 'Tis true, I can give you an account of the matter, for I was upon the spot at the instant, and was throughly acquainted with the whole affair.

Then, *said I,* a man it seems may report it for a Truth?

Sag. You need not fear to affirm it; I mean, that they are all gone on Pilgrimage, both the good woman and her four boys. And being we are, as I perceive, going some considerable way together, I will give you an account of the whole matter.

This *Christiana* (for that was her name from the day that she with her children betook themselves to a Pilgrim's life,) after her husband was gone *over* the *River*, and she could hear of him no more, her thoughts began to work in her mind. First, for that she had lost her husband, and for that the loving bond of that relation was utterly broken betwixt them. For you know, said he to me, Nature can do no less but entertain the living with many a heavy cogitation in the remembrance of the loss of loving relations. This therefore of her husband did cost her many a tear. But this was not all, for *Christiana* did also begin to consider with herself, Whether her unbecoming behaviour towards her husband was not one Cause that she saw him no more; and that in such sort he was taken away from her. And upon this, came into her mind by *swarms*, all her unkind, unnatural, and ungodly carriage to her dear friend;

Part I. *page* 183.

Mark this, you that are churls to your godly relations.

which also clogg'd her conscience, and did load her with Guilt. She was moreover much broken with calling to remembrance the restless groans, the brinish tears, and self-bemoanings of her husband, and how she did harden her heart against all his entreaties, and loving persuasions (of her and her Sons) to go with him; yea, there was not any thing that *Christian* either said to her, or did before her, all the while that his Burden did hang on his back, but it returned upon her like a Flash of Lightning, and rent the caul of her heart in sunder; especially that

Part I. *pages* 1, 2.

bitter out cry of his, *What shall I do to be saved?* did ring in her ears most dolefully.

Then said she to her children, Sons, we are all undone. I have sinned away your father, and he is gone; he would have had us with him, but I would not go myself; I also hindred you of Life. With that the boys fell all into tears, and cried out to go after their father. Oh! said *Christiana*, that it had been but our lot to go with him, then had it fared well with us, beyond what 'tis like to do now. For tho' I formerly foolishly imagin'd concerning the Troubles of your father, that they proceeded of a foolish fancy

James i. 23, 24, 25.

that he had, or for that he was over-run with melancholy humours; yet now 'twill not out of my mind, but that they sprang from another cause, to wit, for

[1st Edit. ' *Light of Light.*']

that the Light of Life was given him; by the help of which, as I perceive, he has escaped the Snares of Death. Then they all wept again, and cry'd out, *Oh, Wo worth the day!*

Christiana's dream.

The next night, *Christiana* had a dream; and behold, she saw as if a broad Parchment was opened before her, in which were recorded the Sum of her ways, and the crimes, as she thought, look'd *very black upon her.* Then she cry'd out aloud in her sleep, *Lord have Mercy upon me, a Sinner;* and the little children heard her. Luke 18. 13.

After this, she thought she saw two very ill-favour'd Ones standing by her bed-side and saying, *What shall we do with this Woman? For she cries out for Mercy waking and sleeping: If she be suffer'd to go on as she begins, we shall lose her as we have lost her Husband.* Wherefore we must, by one way or other, seek to take her off from the thoughts of what shall be hereafter, else all the world cannot help it but she will become a Pilgrim. Mark this, this is the Quintessence of Hell.

Now she awoke in a great sweat, also a trembling was upon her; but after a while she fell to sleeping again. And then she thought she saw *Christian* her husband in a place of Bliss among many *Immortals*, with a *Harp* in his hand, standing and playing upon it before one that sat on a Throne, with a Rainbow about his head. She saw also as if he bowed his head with his face to the paved-work that was under the Prince's feet, saying, *I heartily thank my Lord and King for bringing me into this Place.* Then shouted a Company of them that stood round about and harped with their harps: But no man living could tell what they said, but *Christian* and his Companions. Help against Discouragement.

Next morning, when she was up, had pray'd to God, and talked with her children a while, one knocked hard at the door; to whom she spake out, saying, *If thou comest in God's name, come in.* So he said, *Amen;* and open'd the door and saluted her with *Peace be to this House.* The which, when

Convictions seconded with fresh tidings of God's Readiness to pardon.

he had done, he said, *Christiana*, knowest thou wherefore I am come? Then she blushed and trembled, also her heart began to wax warm with desires to know whence he came, and what his errand was to her. So he said unto her, My name is *Secret*, I dwell with those that are high. It is talked of where I dwell, as if thou hadst a desire to go thither; also there is a report that thou art aware of the Evil thou hast formerly done to thy husband, in hardning of thy heart against his Way, and in keeping of these thy babes in their Ignorance. *Christiana*, the Merciful One has sent me to tell thee, That he is a God ready to forgive, and

[1st edit. ' *To multiply to pardon offences.*' See Isa. 55. 7, margin.]

that he taketh Delight to multiply the pardon of offences. He also would have thee know, that he inviteth thee to come into his Presence, to his Table, and that he will feed thee with the fat of his house, and with the heritage of *Jacob* thy father.

There is *Christian* thy husband, *that was*, with Legions more, his companions, ever beholding that Face that doth minister Life to beholders: And they will all be glad when they shall hear the sound of thy feet step over thy Father's threshold.

Christiana at this was greatly abashed in herself, and bowed her head to the ground, this *Visiter* proceeded, and said, *Christiana*, here is also a Letter for thee, which I have brought from thy husband's

Song 1. 11, 12.

King; so she took it and opened it, but it smelt after the manner of the best perfume. Also it was written in letters of Gold. The contents of the letter was; *That the King would have her do as did* Christian *her husband, for that was the way to*

come to his City, and to dwell in his Presence with Christiana
Joy for ever. At this the good woman was quite
overcome : So she cried out to her Visiter, *Sir, will* *quite over-*
come.
you carry me and my Children with you, that we
also may go and worship this King?

Then said the Visiter, *Christiana! the Bitter is* *Further in-*
before the Sweet. Thou must through Troubles, as *structions to*
Christiana.
did he that went before thee, enter this Cœlestial
City. Wherefore I advise thee to do as did *Chris-*
tian thy husband : Go to the *Wicket-Gate* yonder
over the Plain, for that stands in the head of the
Way up which thou must go, and I wish thee all
good speed. Also I advise, that thou put this
Letter in thy bosom : That thou read therein to
thyself, and to thy Children, until you have got it
by root-of-heart : For it is one of the songs that Psal. 119. 54.
thou must sing while thou art in this House of thy
Pilgrimage : Also this thou must deliver in at the
further Gate.

Now I saw in my dream, that this old gentleman, as he told me this story, did himself seem to
be greatly affected therewith. He moreover proceeded, and said : So *Christiana* called her Sons together, and began thus to address herself unto them :
My Sons, I have, as you may perceive, been of late Christiana
under much exercise in my Soul, about the death *prays well for*
her Journey.
of your father; not for that I doubt at all of his
happiness; for I am satisfied now that he is well.
I have also been much affected with the thoughts
of mine own State and yours, which I verily believe is by Nature miserable. My carriage also to
your father in his distress, is a great load to my
conscience : For I harden'd both my own heart and

yours against him, and refused to go with him on Pilgrimage.

The thoughts of these things would now kill me outright, but that for a dream which I had last night, and but that for the Encouragement that this Stranger has given me this morning. Come, my children, let us pack up, and be gone to the Gate that leads to the Cœlestial Country, that we may see your father, and be with him and his companions in Peace, according to the laws of that land.

Then did her Children burst out into tears, for joy that the heart of their mother was so inclined: So their Visiter bid them farewell; and they began to prepare to set out for their Journey.

But while they were thus about to be gone, two of the women that were *Christiana's* neighbours, came up to her house, and knocked at the door: To whom she said as before, *If you come in God's name, come in.* At this the women were stunn'd; for this kind of language they used not to hear, or to perceive to drop from the lips of *Christiana.* Yet they came in: But behold, they found the good woman a preparing to be gone from her house.

Christiana's
*new language
stuns her old
neighbours.*

So they began, and said, Neighbour, pray what is your meaning by this?

Christiana answered, and said to the eldest of them, whose name was Mrs. *Timorous*, I am preparing for a Journey. (This *Timorous* was daughter to him that met *Christian* upon the Hill of *Difficulty*, and would ha' had him gone back for fear of the Lions.)

Part I. *page*
42.

Tim. For what Journey, I pray you?

Christ. Even to go after my good Husband; and with that she fell a weeping.

Tim. I hope not so, good neighbour; pray, for your poor children's sake, do not so unwomanly cast away yourself.

Christ. Nay, my children shall go with me, not one of them is willing to stay behind.

Tim. I wonder in my very heart, what or who has brought you into this mind.

Christ. Oh, neighbour, knew you but as much as I do, I doubt not but that you would go with me.

Tim. Prithee, what new Knowledge hast thou got, that so worketh off thy mind from thy Friends, and that tempteth thee to go no body knows where?

Christ. Then *Christiana* reply'd, I have been sorely afflicted since my husband's departure from me; but especially since he went *over the River.* But that which troubleth me most, is my churlish carriage to him, when he was under his distress. Besides I am *now*, as he was *then;* nothing will serve me, but going on Pilgrimage. I was a dreaming last night, that I saw him. O that my Soul was with him! He dwelleth in the Presence of the King of the Country; he sits and eats with him at his table; he is become a companion of *Immortals*, and has a House now given him to dwell in, to which the best palaces on Earth, if compared, seem to me to be but as a dunghill. The Prince of the Place has also sent for me, with promise of entertainment, if I shall come to him; his Messenger was here even now, and has brought me a Letter, which invites me to come. And with that she pluck'd out her

Timorous comes to visit Christiana with Mercy, one of her neighbours.

Death.

2 Cor. 5. 1, 2, 3, 4.

Letter, and read it, and said to them, what now will you say to this?

Tim. Oh! the Madness that has possessed thee and thy husband! to run yourselves upon such Difficulties! You have heard, I am sure, what your husband did meet with, even in a manner at the first step that he took on his Way, as our

Part I. pages 5 to 9. neighbour *Obstinate* can yet testify, for he went along with him; yea, and *Pliable* too, until they, like wise men, were afraid to go any further. We also heard over and above, how he met with the Lions, *Apollyon*, the Shadow of Death, and many

The reasonings of the Flesh. other things. Nor is the Danger that he met with at *Vanity-Fair* to be forgotten by thee. For if he, tho' a man, was so hard put to it, what canst thou, being but a poor woman, do? Consider also, that these four sweet babes are thy children, thy flesh, and thy bones. Wherefore, though thou shouldest be so rash as to cast away thyself; yet for the sake of the fruit of thy body, keep thou at home.

But *Christiana* said unto her, tempt me not, my neighbour: I have now a price put into my hand to get gain, and I should be a Fool of the greatest size, if I should have no heart to strike in with the opportunity. And for that you tell me of all these Troubles that I am like to meet with in the Way, they are so far off from being to me a Discouragement, that they shew I am in the right. *The Bitter*

A pertinent Reply to fleshly Reasonings. *must come before the Sweet*, and that also will make the Sweet the sweeter. Wherefore since you came not to my house *in God's name*, as I said; I pray you to be gone, and not to disquiet me farther.

Then *Timorous* also reviled her, and said to her

fellow, Come, neighbour *Mercy*, let's leave her in her own hands, since she scorns our counsel and company. But *Mercy* was at a stand, and could not so readily comply with her neighbour, and that for a twofold reason, 1st, Her bowels yearned over *Christiana :* So she said within herself, if my neigh-bour will be gone, I will go a little way with her, and help her. 2dly, Her bowels yearned over her own Soul, (for what *Christiana* had said, had taken some hold upon her mind :) Wherefore she said within herself again, I will yet have more talk with this *Christiana*, and if I find Truth and Life in what she shall say, myself with my heart shall also go with her. Wherefore *Mercy* began thus to reply to her neighbour *Timorous*.

Mercy. Neighbour, I did indeed come with you to see *Christiana* this morning ; and since she is, as you see, a taking of her last farewell of her Country, I think to walk this sun-shine morning, a little way with her, to help her on the Way. But she told her not of her second reason, but kept that to herself.

Tim. Well, I see you have a mind to go a fooling too ; but take heed in time and be wise ; while we are out of danger, we are out ; but when we are in, we are in. So Mrs. *Timorous* returned to her house, and *Christiana* betook herself to her journey. But when *Timorous* was got home to her house, she sends for some of her neighbours, to wit, Mrs. *Bat's-eyes*, Mrs. *Inconsiderate*, Mrs. *Light-mind*, and Mrs. *Know-nothing*. So when they were come to her house, she falls to telling of the story of *Christiana*, and of her intended Journey. And thus she began her tale.

Mercy's bow-els yearn over Christiana.

Timorous for-sakes her, but Mercy cleaves to her.

Timorous acquaints her friends, what the good Christiana in-tends to do.

Tim. Neighbours, having had little to do this morning, I went to give *Christiana* a visit; and when I came at the door, I knocked, as you know 'tis our custom; and she answered, *If you come in God's name, come in.* So in I went, thinking all was well: But when I came in, I found her preparing herself to depart the town, she and also her children. So I asked her, what was her meaning by that? and she told me in short, that she was now of a mind to go on Pilgrimage, as did her Husband. She told me also a dream that she had, and how the King of the Country where her Husband was, had sent her an inviting Letter to come thither

Mrs. Know-nothing.

Then said Mrs. *Know-nothing*, And what do you think she will go?

Tim. Ay, go she will, whatever comes on't; and methinks I know it by this; for that which was my great argument to persuade her to stay at home, (to wit, the Troubles she was like to meet with in the Way) is one great argument with her, to put her forward on her Journey. For she told me in so many words, *The Bitter goes before the Sweet:* Yea, and forasmuch as it so doth, it makes the sweet the sweeter.

Mrs. Bat's-eyes.

Mrs. *Bat's-eyes.* Oh, this blind and foolish woman, said she; will she not take warning by her Husband's afflictions? For my part, I see, if he was here again, he would rest him content in a whole skin, and never run so many hazards for nothing.

Mrs. Incon-siderate.

Mrs. *Inconsiderate* also replied, saying, Away with such fantastical fools from the town; a good riddance, for my part, I say, of her; should she stay where she dwells, and retain this her mind, who could live quietly by her; for she will either be dumpish or unneighbourly, or talk of such matters as no wise body can abide: Wherefore, for my part, I shall never be sorry for her departure; let her go, and let better come in her room; 'twas never a good world since these whimsical fools dwelt in it.

Then Mrs. *Lightmind* added as followeth; Come, put this kind of talk away. I was yesterday at Madam *Wanton's*, where we were as merry as the maids. For who do you think should be there, but I and Mrs. *Love-the-Flesh*, and three or four more, with Mr. *Lechery*, Mrs. *Filth*, and some others: So there we had musick, and dancing, and what else was meet to fill up the Pleasure. And I dare say, my Lady herself is an admirable well-bred gentlewoman, and Mr. *Lechery* is as pretty a fellow. By this time *Christiana* was got on her Way, and *Mercy* went along with her: So as they went, her Children being there also, *Christiana* began to discourse. And *Mercy*, said *Christiana*, I take this as an unexpected favour, that thou shouldest set foot out of doors with me, to accompany me a little in my Way.

Mercy. Then said young *Mercy*, (for she was but young) If I thought it would be to purpose to go with you, I would never go near the town any more.

Christ. Well, *Mercy*, said *Christiana*, cast in thy lot with me, I well know what will be the end of our Pilgrimage; my Husband is where he would not but be for all the Gold in the *Spanish* Mines. Nor shalt thou be rejected, tho' thou goest but upon *my Invitation*. The King who hath sent for me and my Children, is one that delighteth in *Mercy*. Besides, if thou wilt, I will hire thee, and thou shalt

Mrs. Light-mind. *Madam* Wanton, *she that had like to have been too hard for* Faithful *in time past,* Part I. *page* 74.

Discourse between Mercy *and good* Christiana.

Mercy *inclines to go.*

Christiana *would have her Neighbour with her.*

go along with me as my servant. Yet we will have all things in common betwixt thee and me, only go along with me.

Mercy doubts of Acceptance.

Mercy. But how shall I be ascertained that I also shall be entertained? Had I this Hope but from one that can tell, I would make no stick at all, but would go, being helped by him that can help, tho' the Way was never so tedious.

Christiana allures her to the Gate, which is Christ, and promiseth there to enquire for her.

Christ. Well, loving *Mercy*, I will tell thee what thou shalt do; go with me to the *Wicket-Gate*, and there I will further enquire for thee; and if there thou shalt not meet with encouragement, I will be content that thou shalt return to thy place; I also will pay thee for thy kindness which thou shewest to me and my Children, in thy accompanying of us in our Way as thou doest.

Mercy prays.

Mercy. Then will I go thither, and will take what shall follow; and the Lord grant that my lot may there fall, even as the King of Heaven shall have his heart upon me.

Christiana glad of Mercy's company.

Christiana then was glad at her heart, not only that she had a companion, but also for that she had prevailed with this poor maid to fall in love with her own Salvation. So they went on together, and *Mercy* began to weep. Then said *Christiana*, Wherefore weepeth my Sister so?

Mercy grieves for her carnal Relations.

Mercy. Alas! said she, who can but lament, that shall but rightly consider what a state and condition my poor relations are in, that yet remain in our sinful town: And that which makes my grief the more heavy, is because they have no instructor, nor any to tell them what is to come.

Christ. Bowels become Pilgrims; and thou dost

for thy friends, as my good *Christian* did for me Christian's
when he left me; he mourned for that I would not *Prayers were*
heed nor regard him, but his Lord and ours did *his Relations,*
gather up his tears, and put them into his bottle, *dead.*
and now both I and thou, and these my sweet Babes,
are reaping the fruit and benefit of them. I hope,
Mercy, these tears of thine will not be lost; for the Psal. 126. 5,
Truth hath said, *that they that sow in Tears, shall* 6.
*reap in Joy and singing. And he that goeth forth
and weepeth, bearing precious seed, shall doubtless
come again with rejoycing, bringing his Sheaves with
him.*

Then said Mercy,

> *Let the most Blessed be my Guide,*
> *If't be his blessed Will,*
> Unto *his Gate,* into *his Fold,*
> Up to *his Holy Hill :*

> *And let him never suffer me*
> *To swerve or turn aside*
> *From his Free Grace, and Holy Ways,*
> *Whate'er shall me betide.*

> *And let him gather them of mine,*
> *That I have left behind;*
> *Lord, make them pray they may be thine,*
> *With all their Heart and Mind.*

Now my old Friend proceeded, and said,—But *Part* I. *page*
when *Christiana* came to the Slough of *Despond,* *8, 9.*
she began to be at a stand; for, said she, This is *Their own Carnal Con-*
the place in which my dear Husband had like to *clusions in-*
have been smothered with mud. She perceived *Word of Life.*

also, that notwithstanding the command of the King to make this place for Pilgrims good, yet it was rather worse than formerly : So I asked if that was true ? Yes, said the old Gentleman, too true : For that many there be, that pretend to be the King's Labourers, and that say, they are for mending the King's Highway, that bring *dirt* and *dung* instead of stones, and so mar instead of mending. Here *Christiana* therefore, with her boys, did make a stand : But said *Mercy*, Come let us venture, only let us be wary. Then they looked well to the Steps, and made a shift to get staggeringly over.

Mercy the boldest at the Slough of Despond.

Yet *Christiana* had like to have been in, and that not once nor twice. Now they had no sooner got over, but they thought they heard words, that said unto them, *Blessed is she that believeth, for there shall be a Performance of the things that have been told her from the Lord.*

Luke I. 45.

Then they went on again, and said *Mercy* to *Christiana*, had I as good ground to hope for a loving reception at the Wicket-Gate, as you, I think no Slough of *Despond* would discourage me.

Well, said the other, you know *your* sore, and I know *mine ;* and, good friend, we shall all have enough evil before we come at our Journey's end.

For can it be imagined, that the people that design to attain such excellent Glories *as we do,* and that are so envied that happiness *as we are ;* but that we shall meet with what Fears and Scares, with what troubles and afflictions they can possibly assault us with, that hate us.

Prayer should be made with

And now Mr. *Sagacity* left me to dream out my dream by myself. Wherefore, methought I saw

Christiana and *Mercy*, and the Boys, go all of them up to the Gate : To which, when they were come, they betook themselves to a short debate, about *how* they must manage their calling at the Gate ; and what should be said to him that did open to them. So it was concluded, since *Christiana* was the eldest, that she should knock for entrance, and that she should speak to him that did open, for the rest. So *Christiana* began to knock, and as her poor Husband did, she *knocked*, and *knocked* again. But instead of any that answered, they all thought that they heard as if a Dog came barking upon them ; a Dog, and a great one too, and this made the Women and Children afraid, nor durst they for a while to knock any more, for fear the Mastiff should fly upon them. Now therefore they were greatly tumbled up and down in their minds, and knew not what to do ; Knock they durst not, for fear of the Dog ; Go back they durst not, for fear that the Keeper of that Gate should espy them as they so went, and should be offended with them : At last they thought of knocking again, and knocking more vehemently than they did at the first. Then said the Keeper of the Gate, Who is there ? So the Dog left off to bark, and he opened unto them.

Then *Christiana* made low obeisance, and said, Let not our Lord be offended with his hand-maidens, for that we have knocked at his Princely Gate. Then said the Keeper, Whence come ye ? And what is that you would have ?

Christiana answered, We are come from whence *Christian* did come, and upon the same errand as

Marginal notes:

Consideration and Fear, as well as in Faith and Hope.

Part I. page 20.

The Dog, the Devil, an enemy to Prayer.

Christiana and her Companions perplexed about Prayer.

he; to wit, to be, if it shall please you, graciously
admitted, by this Gate, into the Way that leads to
the Cœlestial City : And I answer, my Lord, in the
next place, that I am *Christiana*, once the Wife of
Christian, that now is gotten above.

With that the Keeper of the Gate did marvel,
saying, What is she become now a Pilgrim, that but
a while ago abhorred that Life ?   Then she bowed
her head, and said, Yes, and so are these my sweet
Babes also.

Then he took her by the hand and let her in, and
said also, *Suffer the little Children to come unto me,*
and with that he shut up the Gate.   This done, he
called to a Trumpeter that was above, over the
Gate, to entertain *Christiana* with Shouting, and
Sound of Trumpet, for Joy.   So he obeyed and
sounded, and filled the air with his melodious
notes.

*How Christi-
tiana is enter-
tained at the
Gate.*

Luke 15. 7.

Now all this while poor *Mercy* did stand without, trembling and crying, for fear that she was
rejected.   But when *Christiana* had gotten admittance for herself and her Boys, then she began to
make intercession for *Mercy*.

*Christiana's
Prayer for
her friend
Mercy.*

Christ. And she said, My Lord, I have a companion of mine that stands yet without, that is
come hither upon the same account as myself :
One that is much dejected in her mind, for that
she comes, as she thinks, without sending for;
whereas I was sent to by my husband's King to
come.

*The Delays
make the hun-
gering Soul
the ferventer.*

Now *Mercy* began to be very impatient, for
each minute was as long to her as an hour; wherefore she prevented *Christiana* from a fuller inter-

ceding for her, by knocking at the Gate herself. And she knocked then so loud, that she made *Christiana* to start. Then said the Keeper of the Gate, Who is there? And *Christiana* said, It is my friend.

So he opened the Gate and looked out, but *Mercy* was fallen down without in a swoon, for she fainted, and was afraid that no Gate would be opened to her. *Mercy faints.*

Then he took her by the hand, and said, *Damsel,* I bid thee arise.

O, Sir, said she, I am faint; there is scarce life left in me. But he answered, that one once said, *When my soul fainted within me, I remembred the* *Jonah 2. 7.* *Lord, and my Prayer came in unto thee, into thy Holy Temple.* Fear not, but stand upon thy feet, and tell me wherefore thou art come.

Mercy. I am come for *that* unto which I was never invited, as my friend *Christiana* was. Hers was from the King, and mine was but from her: Wherefore I fear I presume. *The Cause of her fainting.*

Did she desire thee to come with her to this place?

Mercy. Yes; and as my Lord sees, I am come. And if there is any Grace and Forgiveness of Sins to spare, I beseech that I thy poor hand-maid may be partaker thereof.

Then he took her again by the hand, and led her gently in, and said, I pray for all them that believe on me, by what Means soever they come unto me. Then said he to those that stood by, fetch something and give it *Mercy* to smell on, thereby to stay her fainting: So they fetch'd her *Mark this.*

a bundle of myrrh; and a while after, she **was** revived.

And now was *Christiana* and her Boys, and *Mercy*, received of the Lord at the head of the Way, and spoke kindly unto by him. Then said they yet further unto him, we are sorry for our Sins, and beg of our Lord his Pardon and further information what we must do.

I grant Pardon, said he, by word and deed; by word, in the Promise of Forgiveness; by deed, in the Way I obtained it. Take the first from my lips with a kiss, and the other as it shall be revealed.

Song 1. 2.
John 20. 20.

Now I saw in my dream, that he spake many good words unto them, whereby they were greatly gladded. He also had them up to the top of the Gate, and shewed them by what *Deed* they were saved; and told them withal, that that sight they would have again as they went along in the Way, to their comfort.

*Christ Cruci-
fied seen afar
off.*

So he left them awhile in a summer parlour below, where they entred into talk by themselves; and thus *Christiana* began: O Lord! how glad am I, that we are got in hither!

*Talk between
the Chris-
tians.*

Mercy. So you well may; but I of all have cause to leap for Joy.

Christ. I thought one time as I stood at the Gate, (because I had knocked and none did answer) that all our labour had been lost, 'specially when that ugly cur made such a heavy barking against us.

Mercy. But my worst fears was, after I saw that you was taken into his favour, and that I was left behind: Now, thought I, 'tis fulfilled which is

written; *Two Women shall be grinding together, the* Mat. 24. 41.
one shall be taken, and the other left. I had much
ado to forbear crying out, *Undone! Undone!*

And afraid I was to knock any more; but when
I looked up to what was written over the Gate, I
took courage. I also thought that I must either
knock again, or die: So I knocked, but I cannot Part I. p. 20.
tell how; for my spirit now struggled betwixt Life
and Death.

Christ. Can you not tell how you knocked? I
am sure your knocks were so earnest, that the very
sound of them made me start; I thought I never Christiana
heard such knocking in all my life; I thought you *thinks her
Companion*
would ha' come in by violent hands, or ha' took the *prays better
than she.*
Kingdom by storm. Mat. 11. 12.

Mercy. Alas! to be in my case, who that so
was, could but ha' done so? You saw that the
Door was shut upon me, and that there was a most
cruel *Dog* thereabout. Who, I say, that was so
faint-hearted as I, that would not ha' knocked with
all their might? But pray, what said my Lord unto
my rudeness? was he not angry with me?

Christ. When he heard your lumbring noise, he *Christ pleased*
gave a wonderful innocent smile: I believe what *with loud and
restless*
you did, pleased him well enough, for he shewed *Prayer.*
no sign to the contrary. But I marvel in my heart *If the soul at
first did know*
why he keeps such a Dog; had I known that afore, *all it should
meet with in*
I fear I should not have had heart enough to ha' *its journey to
Heaven, it*
ventured myself in this manner. But now we are *would hardly
ever set out.*
in, we are in, and I am glad with all my heart.

Mercy. I will ask, if you please, next time he
comes down, why he keeps such a filthy cur in his
yard; I hope he will not take it amiss.

The Children are afraid of the Dog. Ay do, said the Children, and persuade him to hang him, for we are afraid he will bite us when we go hence.

So at last he came down to them again, and *Mercy* fell to the ground on her face, before him, and worshipped, and said, Let my Lord accept the Sacrifice of Praise which I now offer unto him with the calves of my lips.

Jer. 12. 1, 2. So he said unto her, *Peace be to thee, stand up.*
Mercy expostulates about the Dog. But she continued upon her face, and said, *Righteous art thou, O Lord, when I plead with thee, yet let me talk with thee of thy Judgments:* Wherefore dost thou keep so cruel a Dog in thy yard, at the sight of which, such women and children, as we, are ready to fly from thy Gate for fear?

He answered and said, That Dog has another *Devil.* *Owner;* he also is kept close in another man's ground, only my Pilgrims hear his barking: He be*Part* I. *p.* 21.longs to the Castle which you see there at a distance, but can come up to the walls of this place. He has frighted many an honest Pilgrim from *worse* to *better*, by the great Voice of his Roaring. Indeed, he that owneth him, doth not keep him of any good-will to me or mine, but with intent to keep the Pilgrims from coming to me, and that they may be afraid to knock at this Gate for entrance. Sometimes also he has broken out, and has *worried* some that I love; but I take all at present patiently. I also give my *A Check to the carnal fear of the Pilgrims.* Pilgrims timely help, so they are not delivered up to his power, to do them what his doggish nature would prompt him to. But what! my purchased one, I tro, hadst thou known never so much before-hand, thou wouldest not have been afraid of a dog.

Mercy Swoons before the Gate

The Beggars that go from door to door, will, rather than they will lose a supposed alms, run the hazard of the bawling, barking, and biting too of a Dog : and shall a *dog*, a dog in another man's yard, a dog, whose barking I turn to the Profit of Pilgrims, keep any from coming to me ?   I deliver them from the Lions, and my darling from the power of the Dog.

Mercy. Then said *Mercy*, I confess my Ignorance: Christians I spake what I understood not; I acknowledge that *when wise enough, ac-* thou doest all things well.   *quiesce in the Wisdom of*

Christ. Then *Christiana* began to talk of their *their Lord.* Journey, and to enquire after the Way.   So he fed them, and washed their feet, and set them in the Way of his steps, according as he had dealt with her *Part* I. p. 23. Husband before.   So I saw in my dream, that they walked on in their Way, and had the weather very comfortable to them.

Then *Christiana* began to sing, saying,

> *Blest be the Day that I began*
>   *A Pilgrim for to be ;*
> *And blessed also be that man*
>   *That thereto mov-ed me.*
>
> *'Tis true, 'twas long ere I began*
>   *To seek to live* for ever :
> *But now I run fast as I can ;*
>   *'Tis better* late, *than* never.
>
> *Our* Tears *to* Joy, *our* Fears *to* Faith,
>   *Are turned as we see ;*
> *Thus our Beginning* (*as one saith*)
>   *Shews what our End will be.*

Now there was on the other side of the Wall, that

fenced in the Way up which *Christiana* and her companions was to go, a garden, and that garden belonged to him whose was that *barking Dog*, of whom mention was made before. And some of the fruit-trees that grew in that garden, shot their branches over the Wall; and being mellow, they that found them did gather them up and oft eat of them to their hurt. So *Christiana's* boys, as boys are apt to do, being pleased with the trees, and with

The Children eat of the Enemy's Fruit. the fruit that did hang thereon, did plash them and began to eat. Their mother did also chide them for so doing, but still the boys went on.

Well, said she, my Sons, you transgress, for that fruit is none of ours; but she did not know that they did belong to the Enemy: I'll warrant you, if she had, she would have been ready to die for fear. But that passed, and they went on their Way. Now, by that they were gone about two bows-shot from the place that let them into the Way, they espied

Two Ill-favoured Ones. two very ill-favoured Ones coming down apace to meet them. With that *Christiana*, and *Mercy* her friend, covered themselves with their veils, and kept also on their Journey: The Children also went on before; so that at last they met together. Then they that came down to meet them, came just up to the Women, as if they would embrace them; but *Christiana* said, Stand back, or go peaceably by as

They assault Christiana. you should. Yet these two, as men that are deaf, regarded not *Christiana's* words, but began to lay

The Pilgrims struggle with them. hands upon them; at that *Christiana* waxing very wroth, spurned at them with her feet. *Mercy* also, as well as she could, did what she could to shift them.

Christiana again said to them, Stand back, and be gone, for we have no money to lose, being Pilgrims as ye see, and such too as live upon the Charity of our friends.

Ill-Fav. Then said one of the two men, we make no assault upon you for money, but are come out to tell you, that if you will but grant one small request which we shall ask, we will make Women of you for ever.

Christ. Now *Christiana* imagining what they should mean, made answer again, *We will neither hear, nor regard, nor yield to what you shall ask. We are in haste, and cannot stay, our business is a business of Life and Death:* So again, she and her companions made a fresh essay to go past them: But they letted them in their Way.

Ill-Fav. And they said, We intend no hurt to your lives, 'tis another thing we would have.

Christ. Ay, quoth *Christiana*, you would have *She cries out.* us Body and Soul, for I know 'tis for that you are come; but we will die rather upon the spot, than suffer ourselves to be brought into such snares as shall hazard our well-being hereafter.   And with that they both shrieked out, and cried, *Murder,* Deut. 22. 23, *Murder:* And so put themselves under those laws 26, 27. that are provided for the protection of Women. But the men still made their approach upon them, with design to prevail against them.   They therefore cried out again.

Now, they being, as I said, not far from the Gate, *'Tis good to* in at which they came, their Voice was heard from *cry out when* *we are assault-* where they was, thither: Wherefore some of the *ed.* house came out, and knowing that it was *Christiana's* tongue, they made haste to her relief.   But by that they was got within sight of them, the women were in a very great scuffle, the children also stood crying by. Then did he that came in for their relief call out to the Ruffians, saying, What is that thing you do? Would you make my Lord's people to transgress? He also attempted to take them, but they did make their escape over the Wall into the garden of the man to whom the great Dog belonged; so the Dog became their protector. This *Reliever* then came up to the women, and asked them how they did. So they answered, we thank thy Prince, pretty well, only we have been somewhat affrighted; we thank thee also, for that thou camest in to our help, for otherwise we had been overcome.

Reliever. So after a few more words, this *Reliever* said, as followeth: I marvelled much when you was entertained at the Gate above, being ye knew that ye were but weak women, that you petitioned not the Lord there for a Conductor: then might you have avoided these troubles and dangers; for he would have granted you one.

Christ. Alas! said *Christiana*, We were so taken with our present blessing, that dangers to come were forgotten by us; besides, who could have thought, that so near the King's Palace, there should have lurked such naughty ones? Indeed, it had been well for us, had we asked our Lord for one; but since our Lord knew 'twould be for our profit, I wonder he sent not one along with us.

Rel. It is not always necessary to grant things not asked for, lest by so doing, they become of little esteem; but when the Want of a thing is felt, it then comes under, in the eyes of him that feels it, that estimate, that properly is its due, and so consequently will be hereafter used. Had my Lord granted you a Conductor, you would not neither so have bewailed that oversight of yours, in not asking for one, as now you have occasion to do. So all things work for good, and tend to make you more wary.

Christ. Shall we go back again to my Lord, and confess our folly, and ask one?

Rel. Your confession of your folly I will present him with: To go back again, you need not; for in all places where you shall come, you will find no want at all; for in every of my Lord's lodgings, which he has prepared for the reception of his Pilgrims, there is sufficient to furnish them against all attempts whatsoever: But as I said, he will be enquired of by them to do it for them; and it is Ezek. 36. 37. a poor thing that is not worth asking for. When he had thus said, he went back to his place, and the Pilgrims went on their Way.

Mercy. Then said *Mercy*, What a sudden blank *The mistake* is here? I made account we had been past all *of* Mercy. danger, and that we should never sorrow more.

Christ. Thy *innocency*, my Sister, said *Christiana* to *Mercy*, may excuse thee much; but as for me, my fault is so much the greater, for that I saw Christiana's this danger before I came out of the doors, and yet *Guilt.* did not provide for it where provision might ha' been had. I am much therefore to be blamed.

Mercy. Then said *Mercy*, How knew you this before you came from home? Pray open to me this riddle?

Christ. Why, I will tell you: Before I set foot

out of doors, one night, as I lay in my bed, I had
a dream about this; for methought I saw two
men, as like these as ever the world they could
look, stand at my bed's feet, plotting how they
might prevent my Salvation. I will tell you their
very words: They said, ('twas when I was in my
Troubles) What shall we do with this woman?
For she cries out waking and sleeping for Forgiveness; if she be suffered to go on as she begins, we
shall lose her as we have lost her Husband. This
you know might ha' made me take heed, and have
provided when Provision might ha' been had.

Christiana's dream repeated.

Mercy. Well, said *Mercy*, As by this neglect we
have an occasion ministred unto us, to behold
our own imperfections: So our Lord has taken
occasion thereby to make manifest the Riches of
his Grace; for he, as we see, has followed us with
unasked kindness, and has delivered us from their
hands that were stronger than we, of his mere
good Pleasure.

Mercy makes good use of their neglect of duty.

Thus now when they had talked away a little
more time, they drew nigh to a house which stood
in the Way, which house was built for the relief
of Pilgrims, as you will find more fully related in
the First Part of these Records of the *Pilgrims
Progress:* So they drew on towards the House,
(the house of the *Interpreter*) and when they came
to the door, they heard a great talk in the house,
they then gave ear, and heard, as they thought,
Christiana mentioned by name; for you must
know, that there went along even before her, a
talk of her and her Children's going on Pilgrimage. And this thing was the more pleasing to

Part I. p. 24, *&c.*

Talk in the Interpreter's house about Christiana's going on Pilgrimage.

THE MAN WITH THE MUCKRAKE

them, because they had heard that she was *Christian's* wife; that woman who was some time ago so unwilling to hear of going on Pilgrimage. Thus, therefore, they stood still, and heard the good people within commending her, who they little thought stood at the door. At last, *Christiana* knocked, as she had done at the Gate before. Now when she had knocked, there came to the door a young damsel, and opened the door, and looked, and behold, two women were there.

She knocks at the Door.

The Door is opened to them by Innocent.

Damsel. Then said the damsel to them, With whom would you speak in this place?

Christ. *Christiana* answered, We understand that this is a privileged place for those that are become Pilgrims, and we now at this door are such: Wherefore we pray that we may be partakers of that for which we at this time are come; for the day, as thou seest, is very far spent, and we are loth, to night, to go any further.

Damsel. Pray what may I call your name, that I may tell it to my Lord within?

Christ. My name is *Christiana;* I was the wife of that Pilgrim that some years ago did travel this Way, and these be his four children. This maiden also is my companion, and is going on Pilgrimage too.

Innocent. Then ran *Innocent* in (for that was her name) and said to those within, Can you think who is at the Door? There is *Christiana* and her Children, and her Companion, all waiting for entertainment here. Then they leaped for joy, and went and told their Master. So he came to the door, and looking upon her, he said, Art thou that *Christiana*

Joy in the house of the Interpreter, that Christiana is turned Pilgrim.

whom *Christian* the good man left behind him, when he betook himself to a Pilgrim's life?

Christ. I am that woman that was so hard-hearted as to slight my Husband's troubles, and that left him to go on in his Journey alone, and these are his four children; but now I also am come, for I am convinced that no Way is right but this.

Mat. 21. 29.   *Interp.* Then is fulfilled that which is written of the Man that said to his son, Go work to day in my vineyard; and he said to his Father, I will not; but afterwards repented and went.

Christ. Then said *Christiana*, So be it, *Amen*. God make it a true saying upon me, and grant that I may be found at the last of him in peace, without spot, and blameless.

Interp. But why standest thou thus at the door? Come in, thou daughter of *Abraham*; we was talking of thee but now, for tidings have come to us before, how thou art become a Pilgrim. Come, children, come in; come, maiden, come in; so he had them all into the house.

So when they were within, they were bidden sit down and rest them; the which, when they had done, those that attended upon the Pilgrims in the *Old Saints* house, came into the room to see them. And one *glad to see* *the young ones* smiled, and another smiled, and they all smiled, for *walk in God's* joy that *Christiana* was become a Pilgrim: They *ways.* also looked upon the boys; they stroked them over the faces with the hand, in token of their kind reception of them: They also carried it lovingly to *Mercy*, and bid them all welcome into their Master's house.

After a while, because supper was not ready, the

Interpreter took them into his *Significant Rooms,* and shewed them what *Christian, Christiana's* Husband, had seen some time before. Here therefore they saw the Man in the Cage, the Man and his Dream, the Man that cut his Way through his Enemies, and the Picture of the biggest of them all, together with the rest of those things that were then so profitable to *Christian.*

This done, and after these things had been somewhat digested by *Christiana* and her company, the *Interpreter* takes them apart again, and has them first into a room, where was a Man that could look no way but downwards, with a muckrake in his hand: There stood also one over his head, with a Cœlestial Crown in his hand, and proffered to give him that Crown for his muckrake; but the man did neither look up, nor regard, but raked to himself the straws, the small sticks, and dust of the floor.

Then said Christiana, I persuade myself, that I know somewhat the meaning of this: For this is a Figure of a man of this World: Is it not, good Sir?

Interp. Thou hast said the right, said he, and his muckrake doth shew his Carnal mind. And whereas thou seest him rather give heed to rake up straws and sticks, and the dust of the floor, than to what he says that calls to him from above, with the Cœlestial Crown in his hand; it is to shew, that Heaven is but as a Fable to some, and that things here are counted the only things substantial. Now, whereas, it was also shewed thee, that the man could look no way but downwards: It is to let thee know, that earthly things, when they are with power upon men's minds, quite carry their hearts away from God.

Christiana's Prayer against the muckrake. Prov. 30. 8.

Christ. Then said *Christiana*, Oh! deliver me from this muckrake.

Interp. That Prayer, said the *Interpreter*, has lain by 'till it is almost rusty; *Give me not Riches*, is scarce the prayer of one of ten thousand. Straws and sticks, and dust, with most, are the great things now looked after.

With that *Mercy* and *Christiana* wept, and said, It is, alas! too true.

When the *Interpreter* had shewed them this, he has them into the very best room in the house; (a very brave room it was) so he bid them look round about, and see if they could find any thing profitable there. Then they looked round and round; for there

Of the Spider.

was nothing to be seen but a very great Spider on the wall; and that they over-looked.

Mercy. Then said *Mercy*, Sir, I see nothing: But *Christiana* held her peace.

Interp. But said the *Interpreter*, look again; she therefore looked again, and said, Here is not any thing but an ugly spider, who hangs by her hands upon the wall. Then said he, is there but one spider in all this spacious room? Then the water stood in *Christiana's* eyes, for she was a woman

Talk about the Spider.

quick of apprehension: and she said, Yes Lord, there is here more than one. Yea, and Spiders, whose venom is far more destructive than that which is in her. The *Interpreter* then looked pleasantly upon her, and said, Thou hast said the Truth. This made *Mercy* blush, and the boys to cover their faces; for they all began now to understand the riddle.

Then said the *Interpreter* again, *The Spider tak-eth hold with her hands,* as you see, *and is in King's Palaces.* And wherefore is this recorded, but to shew you, that how full of the venom of Sin soever you be, yet you may, by the hand of Faith, lay hold of and dwell in the best room that belongs to the King's House above. *The Inter-pretation.* Prov. 30. 28.

Christ. I thought, said *Christiana,* of something of this; but I could not imagine it all. I thought, that we were like *spiders,* and that we looked like ugly creatures, in what fine room soever we were: But that by this *spider,* this venomous and ill-fa-voured creature, we were to learn *how to act Faith,* came not into my mind; and yet she has taken hold with her hands, as I see, and dwells in the best room in the house: God has made nothing in vain.

Then they seemed all to be glad; but the water stood in their eyes: Yet they looked one upon another, and also bowed before the *Interpreter.*

He had them then into another room, where was a Hen and chickens, and bid them observe a while. So one of the chickens went to the trough to drink, and every time she drank, she lifted up her head, and her eyes towards Heaven. See, said he, what this little chick doth, and learn of her to acknowledge whence your mercies come, by receiving them with looking up. Yet again, said he, observe and look; so they gave heed, and perceived that the Hen did walk in a four-fold method towards her chickens. *Of the Hen and chickens.*

1. She had a *common call,* and that she hath all day long. 2. She had a *special call,* and that she had but sometimes. 3. She had a *brooding note.* And, 4. She had an *out-cry.* Mat. 23. 37.

Now, said he, compare this Hen to your King, and these chickens to his obedient ones. For answerable to her, himself has his methods, which he walketh in towards his People; by his common Call, he gives nothing; by his special Call, he always has something to give; he has also a brooding Voice, for them that are under his Wing; and he has an Out-cry, to give the alarm when he seeth the enemy come. I chose, my darlings, to lead you into the room where such things are, because you are women, and they are easy for you.

Christ. And, Sir, said *Christiana*, pray let us see some more: So he had them into the slaughterhouse, where was a butcher killing a sheep: And behold the sheep was quiet, and took her death patiently. Then said the *Interpreter*, You must learn of this sheep to suffer, and to put up wrongs without murmurings and complaints. Behold how quietly she takes her death, and without objecting, she suffereth her skin to be pulled over her ears. Your King doth call you his Sheep.

Of the Butcher and the Sheep.

After this, he led them into his Garden, where was great variety of flowers: And he said, Do you see all these? So *Christiana* said, Yes. Then said he again, Behold the flowers are divers in *stature*, in *quality*, and *colour*, and *smell*, and *virtue;* and some are better than some: Also where the gardener has set them, there they stand, and quarrel not one with another.

Of the Garden.

Again, he had them into his Field, which he had sowed with wheat and corn: But when they beheld the tops of all was cut off, only the straw remained, he said again, This ground was dunged, and ploughed,

Of the Field.

and sowed, but what shall we do with the crop? Then said *Christiana*, burn some and make muck of the rest. Then said the *Interpreter* again, Fruit, you see, is that thing you look for, and for want of that you condemn it to the Fire, and to be trodden under foot of men: Beware that in this you condemn not yourselves.

Then as they were coming in from abroad, they *Of the* Robin espied a little *Robin* with a great *spider* in his mouth: *and the* Spider. So the *Interpreter* said, look here: So they looked, and *Mercy* wondered; but *Christiana* said, What a disparagement is it to such a little pretty bird as the *Robin-red-breast* is, he being also a bird above many, that loveth to maintain a kind of sociableness with man; I had thought they had lived upon crums of bread, or upon other such harmless matter; I like him worse than I did.

The *Interpreter* then replyed, This *Robin* is an emblem, very apt to set forth some professors by; for to sight they are, as this *Robin*, pretty of note, colour and carriage: They seem also to have a very great love for professors that are sincere; and above all other to desire to sociate with them, and to be in their company, as if they could live upon the good man's crums: They pretend also, that therefore it is, that they frequent the house of the godly, and the appointments of the Lord: But when they are by themselves, as the *Robin*, they can catch and gobble up *spiders*, they can change their diet, drink iniquity, and swallow down Sin like water.

So when they were come again into the house, *Pray, and you will get at* because supper as yet was not ready, *Christiana that which* again desired that the *Interpreter* would either *yet lies unrevealed.*

shew or tell of some other things that are profitable.

Then the *Interpreter* began and said : *The fatter the Sow is, the more she desires the mire; the fatter the Ox is, the more gamesomely he goes to the slaughter; and the more healthy the lusty man is, the more prone he is unto Evil.*

There is a desire in Women to go neat and fine, and it is a comely thing to be adorned with that, that in God's sight is of great Price.

'Tis easier watching a night or two, than to sit up a whole Year together: So 'tis easier for one to begin to profess well, than to hold out as he should to the End.

Every Ship-master, when in a Storm, will willingly cast that over-board that is of the smallest value in the vessel; but who will throw the Best out first? None but he that feareth not God.

One Leak will sink a Ship, and one Sin will destroy a Sinner.

He that forgets his friend, is ungrateful unto him; but he that forgets his Saviour, is unmerciful to himself.

He that lives in Sin, and looks for happiness hereafter, is like him that soweth cockle, and thinks to fill his barn with wheat or barley.

If a man would live well, let him fetch his last day to him, and make it always his Company-keeper.

Whispering and change of thoughts, proves that Sin is in the World.

If the World, which God sets light by, is counted a thing of that worth with men, what is Heaven that God commendeth?

If the Life that is attended with so many Troubles, is so loth to be let go by us, what is the Life above?

Every body will cry up the Goodness of men; but who is there, that is, as he should, affected with the Goodness of God?

We seldom sit down to meat, but we eat, and leave: So there is in Jesus Christ, more Merit and Right-eousness, than the whole World has need of.

When the *Interpreter* had done, he takes them out into his Garden again, and had them to a Tree, *Of the Tree* whose inside was all rotten and gone, and yet it *that is rotten at heart.* grew and had leaves. Then said *Mercy*, What means this? This tree, said he, whose outside is fair, and whose inside is rotten, it is, to which many may be compared that are in the Garden of God: Who with their mouths speak high in behalf of God, but indeed will do nothing for him; whose leaves are fair, but their Heart good for nothing but to be tinder for the Devil's tinder-box.

Now supper was ready, the table spread, and all *They are at* things set on the board; so they sat down and did *supper.* eat, when one had given thanks. And the *Inter-preter* did usually entertain those that lodged with him with musick at meals; so the minstrels played. There was also one that did sing, and a very fine voice he had. His Song was this:

> *The Lord is only my support,*
> *And he that doth me feed;*
> *How can I then want any thing*
> *Whereof I stand in Need?*

When the song and musick was ended, the *Inter-* *Talk at sup-* preter asked *Christiana*, What it was that at first *per. A Re-*

did move her thus to betake herself to a Pilgrim's life ? *Christiana* answered, *First*, the loss of my Husband came into my mind, at which I was heartily grieved ; but all that was natural affection. Then, after that came the troubles and Pilgrimage of my Husband into my mind, and also how like a churl I had carried it to him as to that. So Guilt took hold of my mind, and would have drawn me into the pond ; but that opportunely I had a dream of the well-being of my Husband, and a Letter sent me by the King of that country where my Husband dwells to come to him. The dream and the Letter together so wrought upon my mind, that they forced me to this Way.

Interp. But met you with no Opposition before you set out of doors ?

Christ. Yes, a neighbour of mine, one Mrs. *Timorous*, (she was akin to him that would have persuaded my Husband to go back, for fear of the Lions.) She also befooled me, for, as she called it, my intended desperate adventure ; she also urged what she could to dishearten me to it, the hardship and troubles that my Husband met with in the Way ; but all this I got over pretty well. But a dream that I had of two ill-look'd Ones, that I thought did plot how to make me miscarry in my Journey, that hath troubled me much : Yea, it still runs in my mind, and makes me afraid of every one that I meet, lest they should meet me to do me a mischief, and to turn me out of the Way. Yea, I may tell my Lord, tho' I would not every body know it, that between this and the Gate by which we got into the Way, we were both so sorely assaulted, that we

THE BUTCHER AND THE SHEEP

were made to cry out *Murder;* and the two that made this assault upon us, were like the two that I saw in my dream.

Then said the *Interpreter*, Thy beginning is Good, thy latter end shall greatly increase. So he addressed himself to *Mercy*, and said unto her, And what moved thee to come hither, Sweet-heart? *A Question put to Mercy.*

Mercy. Then *Mercy* blushed and trembled, and for a while continued silent.

Interp. Then said he, Be not afraid, only believe, and speak thy mind.

Mercy. So she began, and said, Truly, Sir, my want of experience is that, that makes me covet to be in silence, and that also that fills me with Fears of coming short at last. I cannot tell of Visions and Dreams, as my friend *Christiana* can : Nor know I what it is to mourn for my refusing of the counsel of those that were good relations. *Mercy's Answer.*

Interp. What was it then, dear heart, that hath prevailed with thee to do as thou hast done?

Mercy. Why, when our friend here was packing up to be gone from our Town; I and another went accidentally to see her. So we knocked at the Door, and went in. When we were within, and seeing what she was doing, we asked what was her meaning? She said, she was sent for to go to her Husband; and then she up and told us how she had seen him in a dream, dwelling in a curious Place, among *Immortals*, wearing a Crown, playing upon a Harp, eating and drinking at his Prince's Table, and singing Praises to him for bringing him thither, *&c.* Now methought while she was telling these things unto us, my heart burned within me. And I said in my heart, If this be true, I will leave my Father and my Mother, and the land of my nativity, and will, if I may, go along with *Christiana.*

So I asked her further of the Truth of these things, and if she would let me go with her; for I saw now, that there was no dwelling, but with the danger of Ruin, any longer in our town. But yet I came away with a heavy heart, not for that I was unwilling to come away, but for that so many of my relations were left behind. And I am come with all the desire of my heart, and will go if I may, with *Christiana,* unto her Husband and his King.

Interp. Thy setting out is Good, for thou hast given credit to the Truth; thou art a *Ruth*, who did for the love that she bore to *Naomi*, and to the Lord her God, leave Father and Mother, and the land of her nativity, to come out and go with a People that she knew not heretofore, *Ruth* 2. 11, 12. *The* Lord *recompence thy work, and a full reward be given thee of the* Lord God *of Israel, under whose Wings thou art come to trust.*

They address themselves for bed.
Mercy's good night's rest.

Now supper was ended, and preparations was made for bed, the women were laid singly alone, and the boys by themselves. Now when *Mercy* was in bed, she could not sleep for joy, for that now her doubts, of missing at last, were removed further from her than ever they were before; so she lay blessing and praising God, who had such favour for her.

In the morning they arose with the sun, and prepared themselves for their departure; but the

Interpreter would have them tarry a while, for said he, you must orderly go from hence. Then said he to the damsel that at first opened unto them, Take them and have them into the Garden to the *Bath*, and there wash them, and make them clean *The Bath of* from the Soil, which they have gathered by tra- *Sanctification.* velling. Then *Innocent* the damsel took them, and had them into the Garden, and brought them to the *Bath;* so she told them, that there they must wash and be clean, for so her Master would have the women to do, that called at his house as they were going on Pilgrimage. They then went in and washed, yea, they and the boys and all; *They wash in* and they came out of that *Bath*, not only sweet *it.* and clean, but also much enlivened and strength- ened in their joints. So when they came in, they looked fairer a deal, than when they went out to the washing.

When they were returned out of the Garden from the *Bath*, the *Interpreter* took them, and looked upon them, and said unto them, *Fair as the Moon.* Then he called for the *Seal*, wherewith they used to be *sealed* that were washed in his *Bath*. So the *Seal* was brought, and he set his Mark upon them, *They are* that they might be known in the places whither *sealed.* they were yet to go: Now the Seal was the con- tents and sum of the Passover which the children of *Exod.* 13. 8, *Israel* did eat, when they came out from the land of 9, 10. *Egypt;* and the Mark was set between their eyes. This *Seal* greatly added to their beauty, for it was an ornament to their faces. It also added to their gravity, and made their countenance more like them of Angels.

Then said the *Interpreter* again to the damsel that waited upon these Women, Go into the vestry, and fetch out Garments for these people: So she went and fetched out White Raiment, and laid it down before him; so he commanded them to put *They are* it on. *It was fine Linen white and clean.* When *clothed.* the women were thus adorned, they seemed to be a terror one to the other; for that they could not see that Glory each one on herself, which they could see in each other. Now therefore they began to *True Hu-* esteem each other better than themselves. For you *mility.* are fairer than I am, said one; and you are more comely than I am, said another. The children also stood amazed, to see into what fashion they were brought.

The *Interpreter* then called for a man-servant of his, one *Great-heart,* and bid him take *Sword,* and *Helmet,* and *Shield,* and take these my daughters, said he, and conduct them to the house called *Beautiful,* at which place they will rest next. So he took his weapons and went before them; and the *Interpreter* said, God speed. Those also that belonged to the family, sent them away with many a good wish. So they went on their Way, and sang;

> *This place has been our second stage,*
> *Here we have heard, and seen*
> *Those good things, that from Age to Age*
> *To others hid have been.*
>
> *The Dunghill-raker, Spider, Hen,*
> *The Chicken too, to me,*
> *Hath taught a lesson, let me then*
> *Conformed to it be.*

The Butcher, Garden. and the Field,
The Robin, and his bait,
Also the rotten Tree doth yield
Me argument of weight;

To move me for to Watch and Pray,
To strive to be sincere;
To take my Cross up day by day,
And serve the Lord with fear.

Now I saw in my dream, that they went on, and *Part* I. *page*
Great-heart went before them; so they went and 35.
came to the place where *Christian's* Burden fell off
his back, and tumbled into a Sepulchre. Here then
they made a pause; and here also they blessed
God. Now, said *Christiana*, it comes to my mind,
what was said to us at the Gate, to wit, that we
should have Pardon by *Word* and *Deed;* by word,
that is, by the Promise; by *Deed*, to wit, in the
Way it was obtained. What the Promise is, of that
I know something: But what is it to have Pardon
by deed, or in the Way that it was obtained? Mr.
Great-heart, I suppose you know; therefore, if you
please, let us hear your discourse thereof.

Great-heart. Pardon by the Deed done, is pardon *A Comment*
obtained by some one for another that hath need *upon what*
was said at
thereof: Not by the person pardoned, but in the *the Gate, or*
a Discourse of
Way, *saith another*, in which I have obtained it. *our being jus-*
So then to speak to the question more at large, the *tified by*
Christ.
pardon that you and *Mercy*, and these boys have
attained, was *obtained* by another; to wit, by him
that let you in at the Gate: and he hath obtained
it in this double way; he has performed Righteousness to cover you, and spilt Blood to wash you in.

Christ. But if he parts with his Righteousness to us, what will he have for himself?

Great-heart. He has more Righteousness than you have Need of, or than he needeth himself.

Christ. Pray make that appear.

Great-heart. With all my heart; but first I must premise, that he of whom we are now about to speak, is One that has not his fellow: He has two Natures in one Person, plain to be *distinguish'd*, *impossible* to be *divided*. Unto each of these natures a righteousness belongeth, and each righteousness is essential to that nature. So that one may as easily cause the nature to be extinct, as to separate its Justice or Righteousness from it. Of *these* righteousnesses therefore we are not made partakers, so as that they, or any of them, should be put upon us, that we might be made Just, and lively thereby. Besides these, there is a righteousness which this Person has, as these two natures are joined in one. And this is not the righteousness of the *God-head*, as distinguished from the *Manhood*; nor the righteousness of the *Manhood*, as distinguished from the *God-head*, but a righteousness which standeth in the Union of both natures; and may properly be called the righteousness that is essential to his being prepared of God to the capacity of the Mediatory Office, which he was to be entrusted with. If he parts with his first righteousness, he parts with his *God-head*: If he parts with his second righteousness, he parts with the Purity of his *Manhood*: If he parts with his third, he parts with that Perfection that capacitates him to the office of Mediation. He has therefore another righteousness, which standeth in *Performance*, or obedience to a revealed Will: And that is it that he puts upon Sinners, and that by which their Sins are covered. Wherefore he saith, *As by one man's Disobedience, many were made Sinners: So by* Rom. 5. 19. *the Obedience of one, shall many be made Righteous.*

Christ. But are the other righteousnesses of no Use to us?

Great-heart. Yes; for though they are essential to his Natures and Office, and so cannot be communicated unto another, yet it is by virtue of them, that the righteousness that justifies, is for that purpose efficacious. The *righteousness* of his *God-head* gives Virtue to his obedience; the *righteousness* of his *Manhood* giveth Capability to his obedience to justify, and the righteousness that standeth in the union of these two Natures to his Office, giveth Authority to that righteousness to do the work for which it was ordained.

So then here is a righteousness that Christ, as God, has no need of; for he is God without it: Here is a righteousness, that Christ, as Man, has no need of, to make him so, for he is perfect Man without it. Again, here is a righteousness, that Christ, as God-man, has no need of; for he is perfectly so without it. Here then is a righteousness, that Christ, as God, as man and as God-man, has no need of, with reference to himself, and therefore he can spare it a justifying righteousness, that he for himself wanteth not, and therefore he giveth it away: Hence it is called *the Gift of Righteousness*. This righteousness, since Christ Jesus the Lord has made himself under the Law, *must* be given away; for the Law doth not only bind him that is under it, *to do justly*, but to use Charity. Wherefore he must, he ought by the Law, if he hath two Coats, to give one to him that hath none. Now our Lord indeed hath two Coats, one for himself, and one to spare: Wherefore he freely bestows one upon those that have none; and thus, *Christiana* and *Mercy*, and the rest of you that are here, doth your Pardon come by *Deed*, or by the work of another man. Your Lord Christ is he that has worked, and has given away what he wrought for, to the next poor beggar he meets.

But again, in order to pardon by *Deed*, there must something be paid to God as a Price, as well as something prepared to cover us withal. Sin has delivered us up to the just Curse of a righteous Law: Now from this curse we must be justified by way of Redemption, a Price being paid for the harms we have done; and this is by the Blood of your Lord, who came and stood in your place and stead, and died your Death for your Transgressions: Thus has he ransomed you from your transgressions, by Blood, and covered your polluted and deformed Souls with Righteousness: For the sake of which, God passeth by you, and will not hurt you, when he comes to judge the world.

Christ. This is brave: Now I see that there was something to be learned by our being pardoned by *Word* and *Deed*. Good *Mercy*, let us labour to keep this in mind; and, my children, do you remember it also. But, Sir, was not this it that made my good *Christian's* Burden fall from off his shoulder, and that made him give three leaps for Joy?

Rom. 5. 17.

Rom. 4. 24.

Gal. 3. 13.

Christiana
*affected with
this Way of
Redemption.*

Great-heart. Yes, 'twas the Belief of this that cut *How the* out those strings, that could not be cut by other *Strings that bound* Chris- means; and 'twas to give him a proof of the virtue *tian's Burden to him were* of this, that he was suffer'd to carry his Burden to *cut.* the Cross.

Christ. I thought so; for tho' my heart was light- ful and joyous before, yet it is ten times more light- some and joyous now. And I am persuaded by what I have felt, tho' I have felt but little as yet, that if the most burdened man in the world was here, and did see and believe as I now do, 'twould make his heart the more merry and blithe.

Great-heart. There is not only Comfort, and the *How Affection* Ease of a Burden brought to us, by the sight and *to Christ is begot in the* consideration of these, but an endeared Affection *Soul.* begot in us by it: For who can (if he doth but once think that Pardon comes not only by Promise, but thus) but be affected with the way and means of Redemption, and so with the Man that hath wrought it for him?

Christ. True; methinks it makes my heart bleed to think that he should bleed for me. Oh! thou loving One: Oh! thou blessed One. Thou de- servest to have me; thou hast bought me: Thou deservest to have me all; thou hast paid for me ten *Part* I. *page* thousand times more than I am worth. No marvel *36.* *Cause of Ad-* that this made the water stand in my Husband's *miration.* eyes, and that it made him trudge so nimbly on: I am persuaded he wished me with him; but vile wretch that I was, I let him come all alone. O *Mercy,* that thy Father and Mother were here; yea, and Mrs. *Timorous* also: Nay, I wish now with all my heart, that here was Madam *Wanton* too. Surely,

surely, their hearts would be affected; nor could the
Fear of the one, nor the powerful Lusts of the other,
prevail with them to go home again, and to refuse
to become good Pilgrims.

Great-heart. You speak now in the warmth of
your affections: Will it, think you, be always thus
with you? Besides, this is not communicated to
To be affected every one, nor to every one that did see your JESUS
with Christ, bleed. There was that stood by, and that saw the
and with
what he has Blood run from the Heart to the ground, and yet
done, is a
thing Special. were so far off this, that instead of lamenting, they
laugh'd at him; and instead of becoming his Dis-
ciples, did harden their hearts against him: So
that all that you have, my daughters, you have by
a peculiar impression made by a divine contem-
plating upon what I have spoken to you. Remember that 'twas told you, that the *Hen*, by her
common call, gives no meat to her Chickens.
This you have therefore by a special Grace.

Now I saw still in my dream, That they went
on until they were come to the place, that *Simple*,
Simple, Sloth, and *Sloth*, and *Presumption*, lay and slept in, when
and Presump-
tion *hanged,* *Christian* went by on Pilgrimage: And behold
and why. they were hanged up in irons a little way off on
the other side.

Mercy. Then said *Mercy* to him that was their
Guide and conductor, What are those three men?
And for what are they hanged there?

Their *Great-heart.* These three men were men of
Crimes.
very bad qualities; they had no mind to be Pilgrims themselves, and whosoever they could, they
hinder'd; they were for *sloth* and *folly* themselves,
and whosoever they could persuade with, they

made so too ; and withal taught them to presume that they should do well at last. They were asleep when *Christian* went by, and now you go by, they are hanged.

Mercy. But could they persuade any one to be of their opinion ?

Great-heart. Yes, they turned several out of the Way. There was *Slow-pace* that they persuaded to do as they ; they also prevailed with one *Short-wind*, with one *No-heart*, with one *Linger-after-Lust*, and with one *Sleepy-head*, and with a young woman, her name was *Dull*, to turn out of the Way and become as they. Besides, they brought up an ill report of your Lord, persuading others that he was a task-Master. They also brought up an Evil report of the good Land, saying, it was not half so good as some pretended it was. They also began to villify his Servants, and to count the very best of them meddlesome, troublesome busy-bodies : Further, they would call the Bread of God *Husks ;* the *Comforts* of his Children *Fancies ;* the travel and labour of Pilgrims, *Things to no Purpose.*

Christ. Nay, said *Christiana*, if they were such, they shall never be bewailed by me ; they have but what they deserve ; and I think it is well that they hang so near the highway, that others may see and take Warning. But had it not been well if their

Whom they prevailed upon to turn out of the Way.

Behold here, how the Slothful are a sign
Hung up, 'cause Holy Ways they did decline :
See here too, how the Child doth play the Man,
And weak *grows* strong, *when* Great-heart *leads the van.*

crimes had been engraven in some plate of Iron or Brass, and left here, even where they did their mischiefs, for a caution to other bad men?

Great-heart. So it is, as you may well perceive, if you will go a little to the Wall.

Mercy. No, no; let them hang, and their names rot, and their Crimes live for ever against them: I think it a high favour that they were hanged afore we came hither; Who knows else what they might ha' done to such poor women as we are? Then she turned it into a Song, saying,

Now then you three hang there, and be a Sign
To all that shall against the Truth combine.
And let him that comes after, fear this End,
If unto Pilgrims he is not a Friend.
And thou, my Soul, of all such men beware,
That unto Holiness opposers are.

Part I. *page* 40.

Thus they went on, till they came at the foot of the Hill *Difficulty*, where again their good Friend, Mr. *Great-heart,* took an occasion to tell them of what happened there when *Christian* himself went by. So he had them first to the Spring; *Lo,* saith he, *this is the Spring that* Christian *drank of* before

Ezek. 34. 18.
'*Tis difficult getting of good Doctrine in erroneous Times.*

he went up this Hill, and then 'twas clear and good, but now 'tis dirty with the feet of some that are not desirous that Pilgrims here should quench their thirst: Thereat *Mercy* said, *And why so envious trow?* But, said the Guide, it will do, if taken up and put into a Vessel that is sweet and good; for then the dirt will sink to the bottom, and the water come out by itself more clear. Thus therefore

Christiana and her companions were compelled to do. They took it up and put it into an earthen pot, and so let it stand till the dirt was gone to the bottom, and then they drank thereof.

Next he shewed them the two *by-ways* that were at the foot of the Hill, where *Formality* and *Hypocrisy* lost themselves. And, said he, these are dangerous paths: Two were here cast away when *Christian* came by; and although as you see these *By-paths, tho' barred up, will not keep all from going in them.* ways are since stopped up with *Chains*, *Posts*, and a *Ditch*, yet there are that will choose to adventure here, rather than take the pains to go up this Hill.

Christ. The Way of transgressors is hard. 'Tis Prov. 13. 15. a wonder that they can get into those ways without danger of breaking their necks.

Great-heart. They will venture, yea, if at any time any of the King's servants doth happen to see them, and doth call upon them, and tell them, that they are in the wrong ways, and do bid them beware the danger; then they will railingly return them answer, and say, *As for the Word that thou hast* Jer. 44. 16, *spoken unto us in the Name of the King, we will not* 17. *hearken unto thee; but we will certainly do whatsoever thing goeth out of our own mouths*, &c. Nay, if you look a little farther, you shall see that these ways are made cautionary enough, not only by these *Posts*, and *Ditch*, and *Chain*, but also by being hedged up: Yet they will choose to go there.

Christ. They are Idle; they love not to take pains; up-hill Way is unpleasant to them: So it is fulfilled unto them as it is Written, *The way of the* *The reason why some do* *Slothful Man is a Hedge of Thorns.* Yea, they *choose to go in By-ways.* will rather choose to walk upon a Snare, than to Prov. 15. 19.

go up this Hill, and the rest of this Way to the City.

The Hill puts the Pilgrims to it.
Then they set forward, and began to go up the Hill, and up the Hill they went; but before they got to the top, *Christiana* began to *pant*, and said, I dare say; this is a breathing Hill; no marvel if they that love their Ease more than their Souls, choose to themselves a smoother way. Then said *Mercy*, I must sit down; also the least of the children began to cry. Come, come, said *Great-heart*, sit not down here, for a little above is the Prince's *Arbour*. Then took he the little boy by the hand, and led him up thereto.

They sit in the Arbour *Part I. p. 41.* Mat. 11. 28.
When they were come to the *Arbour*, they were very willing to sit down, for they were all in a pelting heat. Then said *Mercy, How sweet is Rest to them that labour?* And how good is the Prince of Pilgrims to provide such resting places for them? Of *this Arbour* I have heard much; but I never saw it before: But here let us beware of Sleeping; for as I have heard, for that it cost poor *Christian* dear.

Then said Mr. *Great-heart* to the little ones, Come, my pretty boys, how do you do? What
The little boy's answer to the Guide, and also to Mercy.
think you now of going on Pilgrimage? Sir, said the least, I was almost beat out of heart; but I thank you for lending me a hand at my need; and I remember now what my mother has told me, namely, that the Way to Heaven is as a ladder, and the Way to Hell is as down a hill. But I had rather go up the ladder to Life, than down the hill to Death.

Then said *Mercy*, But the proverb is, *To go down*

the hill is easy: But *James* said, (for that was his name) The Day is coming, when in my opinion, going down the Hill will be the hardest of all. 'Tis a good boy, said his Master, thou hast given her a right answer. Then *Mercy* smiled, but the little boy did blush. *Which is hardest, up hill or down hill.*

Christ. Come, said *Christiana*, will you eat a bit; a little to sweeten your mouths while you sit here to rest your legs? For I have here a piece of pome- granate, which Mr. *Interpreter* put into my hand just when I came out of his doors; he gave me also a piece of an honey-comb, and a little bottle of spirits; I thought he gave you something, said *Mercy*, be- cause he called you aside. Yes, so he did, said the other; but, *Mercy*, it shall be still as I said it should, when at first we came from home; thou shalt be a sharer in all the good that I have, because thou so willingly didst become my companion. Then she gave to them, and they did eat, both *Mercy* and the boys. And said *Christiana* to Mr. *Great-heart*, Sir, will you do as we? But he answered, You are going on Pilgrimage, and presently I shall return; much good may what you have do to you; at home I eat the same every day. Now, when they had eaten and drank, and had chatted a little longer, their Guide said to them, The day wears away, if you think good, let us prepare to be going. So they got up to go, and the little boys went before · But *Christiana* forgat to take her bottle of spirits with her; so she sent her little boy back to fetch it. Then said *Mercy*, I think this is a *losing* place. Here *Christian* lost his *Roll;* and here *Christiana* left her bottle behind her; Sir, what is the Cause of *They refresh themselves.* *Christiana forgets her bottle of Spi- rits.*

this? So their Guide made answer, and said, the cause is *Sleep*, or *Forgetfulness;* some *sleep* when they should keep *awake*, and some *forget* when they should *remember;* and this is the very cause, why often at the resting places, some Pilgrims, in *Mark this.* some things, come off losers. Pilgrims should watch, and remember what they have already received under their greatest enjoyments; but for want of doing so, ofttimes their rejoicing ends in *Part* I. *p.* 43, tears, and their sun-shine in a Cloud; witness the 44. story of *Christian* at this place.

When they were come to the place where *Mistrust* and *Timorous* met *Christian* to persuade him to go back for fear of the Lions, they perceived as it were a Stage, and before it, towards the road, a broad plate, with a copy of verses written thereon, and underneath, the reason of raising up of that Stage in that place, rendered. The Verses were these:

> *Let him that sees this Stage, take heed*
> *Unto his Heart and Tongue:*
> *Lest if he do not, here he speed*
> *As some have long agone.*

The words underneath the verses were, *This Stage was built to punish such upon, who, through* Timorousness *or* Mistrust, *shall be afraid to go further on Pilgrimage: Also on this Stage, both* Mistrust *and* Timorous *were burnt through the tongue with a hot Iron, for endeavouring to hinder* Christian *on his Journey.*

Then said *Mercy*, This is much like to the *Psal.* 120, 3, saying of the Beloved, *What shall be given unto* 4. *thee? Or what shall be done unto thee, thou false tongue? sharp arrows of the Mighty, with coals of juniper.*

So they went on, till they came within sight of the *Part* I. *p.* 45. Lions. Now Mr. *Great-heart* was a strong man, so he was not afraid of a Lion : But yet, when they were come up to the place where the Lions, were the boys that went before, were glad to cringe be- *An Emblem of* hind, for they were afraid of the Lions, so they stept *those that go on bravely* back, and went behind. At this, their Guide smiled, *when there is no danger, but* and said; How now, my boys, do you love to go *shrink when* before when no danger doth approach; and love to *Troubles come.* come behind so soon as the Lions appear?

Now, as they went up, Mr. *Great-heart* drew his Sword, with intent to make a Way for the Pilgrims in spite of the Lions. Then there appeared one *Of* Grim *the* that, it seems, had taken upon him to back the *Giant, and of his backing* Lions; and he said to the Pilgrims Guide, What is *the Lions.* the cause of your coming hither? Now the name of that man was *Grim,* (or *Bloody-Man,*) because of his slaying of Pilgrims, and he was of the race of the *Giants.*

Great-heart. Then said the Pilgrims Guide, These women and children are going on Pilgrimage, and this is the Way they must go, and go it they shall, in spite of thee and the Lions.

Grim. This is not their way, neither shall they go therein. I am come forth to withstand them, and to that end will back the Lions.

Now, to say the truth, by reason of the fierceness of the Lions, and of the *grim* carriage of him that did back them, this Way had of late lain much unoccupied, and was almost all grown over with grass.

Christ. Then said *Christiana*, though the High-ways have been unoccupied heretofore, and tho' the Travellers have been made in times past to walk through By-paths, it must not be so now I am risen, *Now I am risen a Mother in Israel.*

Judges 5. 6, 7.

Grim. Then he swore *by the Lions*, but it should, and therefore bid them turn aside, for they should not have passage there.

Great-heart. But their Guide made first his approach unto *Grim*, and laid so heavily at him with his Sword, that he forced him to a retreat.

A Fight betwixt Grim *and* Great-Heart.

Grim. Then said he, (that attempted to back the Lions) Will you slay me upon mine own ground ?

Great-heart. 'Tis the King's high-way that we are in, and in this Way it is that thou hast placed thy Lions; but these women, and these children, tho' weak, shall hold on their Way in spite of thy Lions. And with that he gave him again a down-right blow, and brought him upon his knees. With this blow he also broke his helmet, and with the next he cut off an arm. Then did the Giant roar so hideously, that his voice frighted the women, and yet they were glad to see him lie

The Victory. sprawling upon the ground. Now the Lions were chained, and so of themselves could do nothing. Wherefore, when old *Grim*, that intended to back them, was dead, Mr. *Great-heart* said to the Pilgrims, Come now, and follow me, and no hurt shall happen to you from the Lions. They there-fore went on, but the women trembled as they

They pass by the Lions. passed by them ; the boys also looked as if they would die, but they all got by without further hurt.

Now, then, they were within sight of the *Porter's* Lodge, and they soon came up unto it; but they made the more haste after this to go thither, because 'tis dangerous travelling there in the night. So when they were come to the Gate, the Guide *They come to* knocked, and the Porter cry'd, *Who is there?* but *the Porter's Lodge.* as soon as the Guide had said, *It is I,* he knew his voice, and came down; (for the Guide had oft before that come thither as a *Conductor of Pilgrims*) when he was come down, he opened the Gate, and seeing the Guide standing just before it, (for he saw not the women, for they were behind him) he said unto him, How now, Mr. *Great-heart,* what is your business here so late to-night? I have brought, said he, some Pilgrims hither, where, by my Lord's commandment, they must lodge: I had been here some time ago, had I not been opposed by the Giant that did use to back the Lions; but I, after a long and tedious combat with him, have cut him off, and have brought the Pilgrims hither in safety.

Porter. Will you not go in, and stay till morning?

Great-heart. No, I will return to my Lord to- *Great-heart attempts to go back.* night.

Christ. Oh, Sir, I know not how to be willing *The Pilgrims implore his company still.* you should leave us in our Pilgrimage, you have been so faithful and so loving to us, you have fought so stoutly for us, you have been so hearty in counselling of us, that I shall never forget your favour towards us.

Mercy. Then said *Mercy,* O that we might have thy company to our Journey's end! How can such poor women as we, hold out in a Way so full of troubles as this Way is, without a Friend and Defender?

James. Then said *James*, the youngest of the boys, Pray, Sir, be persuaded to go with us, and help us, because we are so weak, and the Way so dangerous as it is.

Great-heart. I am at my Lord's commandment: If he shall allot me to be your Guide quite through, I will willingly wait upon you; but here you failed at first; for when he bid me come thus far with you, then you should have begged me of him to have gone quite through with you, and he would have granted your request. However at present I must withdraw, and so, good *Christiana, Mercy,* and my brave children, Adieu.

Help lost for want of asking for.

Then the Porter, Mr. *Watchful,* asked *Christiana* of her country, and of her kindred, and she said, *I came from the City of* Destruction; *I am a widow woman, and my Husband is dead, his name was* Christian *the Pilgrim.* How, said the Porter, was he your husband? Yes, said she, and these are his Children; and this, pointing to *Mercy,* is one of my town's-women. Then the Porter rang his bell, as at such times he is wont, and there came to the door one of the damsels, whose name was *Humble-mind.* And to her the Porter said, Go tell it within, that *Christiana,* the Wife of *Christian,* and her Children are come hither on Pilgrimage. She went in therefore, and told it. But, oh, what a noise for Gladness was there, when the damsel did but drop that word out of her mouth!

Part I. *p.* 45. Christiana makes herself known to the Porter; he tells it to a damsel.

Joy at the noise of the Pilgrims coming.

So they came with haste to the Porter, for *Chris-*

tiana stood still at the door. Then some of the most grave said unto her, *Come in,* Christiana, *come in, thou Wife of that good Man ; come in, thou blessed woman, come in, with all that are with thee.* So she went in, and they followed her that were her children and her companions. Now, when they were gone in, they were had into a very large room, where they were bidden to sit down : So they sat down, and the Chief of the House was called to see and welcome the guests. Then they came in, and understanding who they were, did salute each other with a kiss, and said, Welcome, ye vessels of the Grace of God; Welcome to us your faithful Friends. *Christians' Love is kindled at the sight of one another.*

Now, because it was somewhat late, and because the Pilgrims were weary with their Journey, and also made faint with the sight of the fight, and of the terrible Lions, therefore they desired, as soon as might be, to prepare to go to Rest. Nay, said those of the Family, refresh yourselves with a morsel of meat : For they had prepared for them a Lamb, with the accustomed Sauce belonging thereto. For the Porter had heard before of their coming, and had told it to them within. So when they had supped, and ended their Prayer with a Psalm, they desired they might go to rest. But let us, said *Christiana*, if we may be so bold as to choose, be in that chamber that was my Husband's, when he was here; so they had them up thither, and they lay all in a room. When they were at rest, *Christiana* and *Mercy* entered into discourse about things that were convenient. *Exod.* 12. 3-8. *John* 1. 29. *Part* I. p. 54.

Christ. Little did I think once, that when my *Christ's Bo-*

som is for all Pilgrims. Husband went on Pilgrimage, that I should ever ha' followed him.

Mercy. And you as little thought of lying in his bed, and in his chamber to rest, as you do now.

Christ. And much less did I ever think of seeing his face with comfort, and of worshipping the Lord the King with him, and yet now I believe I shall.

Mercy. Hark! Don't you hear a noise?

Christ. Yes, 'tis, as I believe, a noise of musick, for Joy that we are here.

Musick. *Mercy.* Wonderful! musick in the house, musick in the Heart, and musick also in Heaven, for Joy that we are here.

Thus they talked awhile, and then betook themselves to sleep. So in the morning, when they were awake, *Christiana* said to *Mercy*,

Mercy *did laugh in her sleep.* *Christ.* What was the matter that you did laugh in your sleep to-night? I suppose you was in a dream.

Mercy. So I was, and a sweet dream it was; but are you sure I laughed?

Christ. Yes; you laughed heartily; but prithee, *Mercy*, tell me thy dream.

Mercy's dream. *Mercy.* I was a dreamed that I sat all alone in a solitary place, and was bemoaning of the hardness of my heart.

Now I had not sat there long, but methought many were gathered about me to see me, and to hear what it was that I said. So they hearkened, and I went on bemoaning the hardness of my heart. At this some of them laughed at me, some called me fool, and some began to thrust me about. With What her dream was. that, methought I looked up, and saw one coming with Wings towards me. So he came directly to me, and said, *Mercy*, What aileth thee? Now when he had heard me make my complaint, he said, *Peace be to thee:* He also wiped mine eyes with his handkerchief, and *clad* me in *Silver and Gold.* He put a Chain about my neck, and Ear-Rings in mine ears, Ezek. 16. 10, and a beautiful Crown upon my head. Then he ^{11, 12.} took me by the hand, and said, *Mercy*, Come after me. So he went up, and I followed, till we came at a Golden Gate. Then he knocked, and when they within had opened, the Man went in, and I followed him up to a Throne, upon which one sat; and he said to me, *Welcome, Daughter.* The place looked bright and twinkling, like the Stars, or rather like the Sun, and I thought that I saw your Husband there; so I awoke from my dream. But did I laugh?

Christ. Laugh! ay, and well you might, to see yourself so well. For you must give me leave to tell you, that it was a good dream; and that as you have begun to find the First Part true, so you shall find the Second at last. *God speaks once, yea twice,* Job 33. 14, *yet Man perceiveth it not, in a Dream, in a Vision of* 15. *the night, when deep Sleep falleth upon men, in slumbering upon the bed.* We need not, when abed, to lie awake to talk with God, he can visit us while we sleep, and cause us then to hear his Voice. Our heart oft-times wakes when we sleep, and God can speak to that, either by words, by proverbs, by signs and similitudes, as well as if one was awake.

Mercy. Well, I am glad of my dream, for I hope, Mercy *glad of* e're long, to see it fulfilled, to the making me laugh *her Dream.* again.

Christ. I think it is now high time to rise, and to know what we must do.

Mercy. Pray, if they invite us to stay a while, let us willingly accept of the proffer. I am the willinger to stay a while here, to grow better acquainted with these maids; methinks *Prudence, Piety* and *Charity*, have very comely and sober countenances.

Christ. We shall see what they will do. So when they were up and ready, they came down, and they asked one another of their rest, and if it was comfortable or not?

Mercy. Very good, said *Mercy*, it was one of the best night's lodgings that ever I had in my life.

Then said *Prudence* and *Piety*, if you will be persuaded to stay here a while, you shall have what the house will afford.

They stay here some time.

Char. Ay, and that with a very good will, said *Charity*. So they consented and staid there about a month or above, and became very profitable one to another. And because *Prudence* would see how *Christiana* had brought up her children, she asked leave of her to Catechise them: So she gave her free consent. Then she began at the youngest, whose name was *James*.

Prudence desires to Catechise Christiana's children.

James catechised.

Prudence. And she said, Come, *James*, canst thou tell me who made thee?

James. God the Father, God the Son, and God the Holy Ghost.

Prud. Good boy. And canst thou tell who saves thee?

Jam. God the Father, God the Son, and God the Holy Ghost.

Prud. Good boy still. But how doth God the Father save thee?

Jam. By his Grace.

Prud. How doth God the Son save thee?

Jam. By his Righteousness, Death, and Blood, and Life.

Prud. And how doth God the Holy Ghost save thee?

Jam. By his *Illumination*, by his *Renovation*, and by his *Preservation*.

Then said *Prudence* to *Christiana*, You are to be commended for thus bringing up your children. I suppose I need not ask the rest these Questions, since the youngest of them can answer them so well. I will therefore now apply myself to the youngest next.

Prud. Then she said, Come, *Joseph*, (for his name was *Joseph*) will you let me catechise you? *Joseph catechised.*

Joseph. With all my heart.

Prud. What is Man?

Jos. A reasonable Creature, made so by God, as my brother said.

Prud. What is supposed by this word *Saved?*

Jos. That Man, by Sin, has brought himself into a state of Captivity and Misery.

Prud. What is supposed by his being saved by the Trinity?

Jos. That Sin is so great and mighty a Tyrant, that none can pull us out of its clutches, but God; and that God is so good and loving to Man, as to pull him indeed out of this miserable state.

Prud. What is God's design in saving of poor men?

Jos. The glorifying of his Name, of his Grace, and Justice, *&c.* and the everlasting Happiness of his Creature.

Prud. Who are they that must be saved?

Jos. Those that accept of his Salvation.

Prud. Good boy, *Joseph,* thy mother has taught thee well, and thou hast hearkened to what she has said unto thee.

Then said *Prudence* to *Samuel,* who was the eldest but one:

Prud. Come, *Samuel,* are you willing that I should catechise you also?

Samuel *catechised.*

Samuel. Yes, forsooth, if you please.

Prud. What is Heaven?

Sam. A Place and State most blessed, because God dwelleth there.

Prud. What is Hell?

Sam. A Place and State most woful, because it is the dwelling-place of Sin, the Devil, and Death.

Prud. Why wouldst thou go to Heaven?

Sam. That I may see God, and serve him without weariness; that I may see Christ, and love him everlastingly; that I may have that fulness of the Holy Spirit in me, that I can by no means here enjoy.

Prud. A very good boy also, and one that has learned well.

Matthew *catechised.*

Then she addressed herself to the eldest, whose name was *Matthew;* and she said to him, Come, *Matthew,* shall I also catechise you?

Matthew. With a very good will.

Prud. I ask then, if there was ever any thing that had a Being antecedent to, or before God?

Matt. No, for God is Eternal ; nor is there any thing, excepting Himself, that had a being, until the beginning of the first day. *For in six days the Lord made Heaven and Earth, the Sea, and all that in them is.*

Prud. What do you think of the Bible ?

Matt. It is the Holy Word of God.

Prud. Is there nothing written therein, but what you understand ?

Matt. Yes, a great deal.

Prud. What do you do when you meet with places therein that you do not understand ?

Matt. I think God is wiser than I. I pray also that he will please to let me know all therein that he knows will be for my good.

Prud. How believe you as touching the Resurrection of the Dead ?

Matt. I believe they shall rise, the same that was buried ; the same in *Nature*, tho' not in Corruption. And I believe this upon a double account. *First*, Because God has promised it. *Secondly*, because he is able to perform it.

Then said *Prudence* to the boys, You must still hearken to your Mother, for she can learn you more. You must also diligently give ear to what good talk you shall hear from others ; for your *Prudence's conclusion upon the catechising of the boys.* sakes do they speak good things. Observe also, and that with carefulness, what the Heavens and the Earth do teach you ; but especially be much in the meditation of that Book that was the cause of your Father's becoming a Pilgrim. I, for my part, my children, will teach you what I can while you are here, and shall be glad if you

will ask me questions that tend to Godly edi-
fying.

Now, by that these Pilgrims had been at this
place a week, *Mercy* had a visiter that pretended
some good will unto her, and his name was Mr.
Brisk, a man of some breeding, and that pretended
to Religion, but a man that stuck very close to the
World. So he came once or twice, or more, to
Mercy, and offered love unto her. Now *Mercy*
was of a fair countenance, and therefore the more
alluring.

Her Mind also was, to be always busying of
herself in doing, for when she had nothing to do
for herself, she would be making of hose and garments for others, and would bestow them upon
them that had need. And Mr. *Brisk* not knowing where, or how she disposed of what she made,
seemed to be greatly taken, for that he found her
never idle. I will warrant her a good housewife,
quoth he to himself.

Mercy then revealed the business to the maidens
that were of the house, and enquired of them
concerning him, for they did know him better
than she. So they told her, that he was a very

busy young man, and one that pretended to religion ; but was, as they feared, a stranger to the
Power of that which is Good.

Nay then, said *Mercy*, I will look no more on him ;
for I purpose never to have a Clog to my Soul.

Prudence then replied, That there needed no
great matter of discouragement to be given to him,
her continuing so as she had begun to do for the
Poor, would quickly cool his courage.

So the next time he comes, he finds her at her old work, a making of things for the Poor. Then said he, What, always at it? Yes, said she, either *Talk betwixt* for myself or for others: And what canst thou *Mercy and Mr. Brisk.* *earn* a day, quoth he? I do these things, said she, *That I may be rich in good works, laying up in store a good foundation against the time to come, that I may lay hold on Eternal Life.* Why, Prithee, what 1 Tim. 6. 17, dost thou with them? said he. Cloathe the naked, 18, 19. said she. With that his countenance fell. So he forbore to come at her again. And when he was *He forsakes* asked the reason why, he said, that Mercy *was a* *her, and why* *pretty lass, but troubled with ill conditions.*

When he had left her, *Prudence* said, Did I not Mercy *in the* tell thee, that Mr. *Brisk* would soon forsake thee? *practice of Mercy reject-* yea, he will raise up an ill report of thee: For *ed, while Mercy in the* notwithstanding his pretence to Religion, and his name *of Mer-* seeming love to *Mercy*, yet *Mercy* and he are of *cy is liked.* tempers so different, that I believe they will never come together.

Mercy. I might have had husbands before now, tho' I spoke not of it to any; but they were such as did not like my conditions, tho' never did any of them find fault with my person. So they and I could not agree.

Prud. Mercy in our days is little set by, any further than as to its name: The practice, which is set forth by the conditions, there are but few that can abide.

Mercy. Well, said *Mercy*, if nobody will have Mercy's *Re-* me, I will die a maid, or my conditions shall be *solution.* to me as a Husband. For I cannot change my Nature; and to have one that lies cross to me in this, that I purpose never to admit of as long as I live. I had a sister named *Bountiful*, married to one of these churls ; but he and she could never agree ; but because my sister was resolved to do as she had begun, that is, to shew kindness to the Poor, therefore her husband first cried her down at the Cross, and then turned her out of his doors.

Prud. And yet he was a Professor, I warrant you.

Mercy. Yes, such a one as he was, and of such as he the world is now full ; but I am for none of them all.

Now *Matthew*, the eldest son of *Christiana*, fell sick, and his sickness was sore upon him, for he was much pained in his bowels, so that he was with it, at times, pulled as t'were both ends together. There dwelt also, not far from thence, one Mr. *Skill*, an ancient and well-approved Physician. So *Christiana* desired it, and they sent for him, and he came : When he was entred the room, and had a little observed the boy, he concluded that he was sick of the gripes. Then he said to his mother, What *diet* has *Matthew* of late fed upon ? Diet, said *Christiana*, nothing but what is wholsome. The Physician answered, This boy has been tampering with something that lies in his maw undigested, and that will not away without Means. And I tell you he must be purged, or else he will die.

Sam. Then said *Samuel*, Mother, mother, what was that which my brother did gather up and eat, so soon as we were come from the Gate that is at the head of this Way ? You know that there was an orchard on the left-hand, on the other side of the

How Mercy's *sister was served by her husband.*

Matthew *falls sick.*

Gripes of Conscience.

The Physician's Judgment.

Samuel *puts his mother in mind of the Fruit his brother did eat.*

Wall, and some of the trees hung over the Wall, and my brother did plash and did eat.

Christ. True, my child, said *Christiana,* he did take thereof and did eat; naughty boy as he was, I did chide him, and yet he would eat thereof.

Skill. I knew he had eaten something that was not wholsome food, and that food, to wit, that fruit, is even the most hurtful of all. It is the fruit of *Beelzebub's* orchard. I do marvel that none did warn you of it; many have died thereof.

Christ. Then *Christiana* began to cry, and she said, O naughty boy, and O careless mother, what shall I do for my Son?

Skill. Come, do not be too much dejected; the boy may do well again, but he must purge and vomit.

Christ. Pray, Sir, try the utmost of your skill with him, whatever it costs.

Skill. Nay, I hope I shall be reasonable. So he made him a purge, but it was too weak; 'twas said, it was made of the Blood of a Goat, the Ashes of a Heifer, and with some of the Juice of Hysop, *&c.* When Mr. *Skill* had seen that that purge was too weak, he made him one to the purpose: 'Twas made *Ex Carne, & Sanguine Christi,* (you know Physicians give strange medicines to their patients) and it was made up into pills, with a Promise or two, and a proportionable quantity of Salt. Now he was to take them three at a time fasting, in half a quarter of a pint of the tears of Repentance. When this potion was prepared, and brought to the boy, he was loth to take it, tho' torn with the gripes, as if he should be pull'd in pieces, Come, come, said the Physician, you must take it. It goes against my

[marginal notes:] Heb. 10, 1, 2, 3, 4. *Potion prepared.* Joh. 6. 54, 55, 56, 57. Mark 9. 49. *The Latin I borrow.* Heb. 9. 14. *The boy loth to take the Physick.*

Zech. 12. 10. stomach, said the boy. *I must have you take it*, said his mother. I shall vomit it up again, said the boy. Pray, Sir, said *Christiana* to Mr. *Skill*, how does it taste? It has no ill taste, said the doctor; and with that she touched one of the pills with the tip of her tongue. Oh, *Matthew*, said she, this potion is sweeter than honey. If thou lovest thy Mother, if thou lovest thy Brothers, if thou lovest *Mercy*, if thou lovest thy Life, take it. So with much ado, after a short prayer for the blessing of God upon it, he took it, and it wrought kindly with him. It caused him to purge, it caused him to sleep, and rest quietly; it put him into a fine heat, and breathing sweat, and did quite rid him of his gripes.

The Mother tastes it, and persuades him.

So in a little time he got up, and walked about with a Staff, and would go from room to room, and talk with *Prudence*, *Piety* and *Charity*, of his distemper, and how he was healed.

A Word of God in the hand of his Faith.

So when the boy was healed, *Christiana* asked Mr. *Skill*, saying, Sir, what will content you for your pains and care to and of my child? And he said, You must pay the *Master of the College of Physicians*, according to Rules made in that case and provided.

Heb. 13. 11, 12, 13, 14, 15.

Christ. But, Sir, said she, what is this pill good for else?

Skill. It is an universal pill; 'tis good against all the diseases that *Pilgrims* are incident to; and when it is well prepared, it will keep good, time out of mind.

This pill an Universal Remedy.

Christ. Pray, Sir, make me up twelve boxes of them: For if I can get these, I will never take other physick.

W.S.

MERCY AT HER WORK

Skill. These *pills* are good to prevent diseases, as well as to *cure* when one is sick. Yea, I dare say it, and stand to it, that if a man will but use this physick as he should, *it will make him live for ever.* But good *Christiana*, thou must give these John 6. 50. pills *no other way*, but as I have prescribed : For *In a glass of* if you do, they will do no good. So he gave unto *the tears of Repentance.* *Christiana* physick for herself, and her boys, and for *Mercy*, and bid *Matthew* take heed how he eat any more *green plums*, and kissed them, and went his way.

It was told you before, that *Prudence* bid the boys, that if at any time they would, they should ask her some Questions that might be profitable, and she would say something to them.

Matt. Then *Matthew* who had been sick, asked her, Why for the most part Physick should be *Of Physick.* bitter to our palates ?

Prud. To shew how unwelcome the word of God, and the effects thereof, are to a Carnal Heart.

Matt. Why does Physick, if it does good, purge, *Of the Effects of Physick.* and cause that we vomit ?

Prud. To shew that the Word, when it works effectually, cleanseth the Heart and Mind. For look what the one doth to the body, the other doth to the soul.

Matt. What should we learn by seeing the flame *Of Fire, and of the Sun.* of our fire go upwards ? And by seeing the beams and sweet influences of the Sun strike downwards ?

Prud. By the going up of the fire, we are taught to ascend to Heaven, by fervent and hot desires. And by the Sun his sending his heat, beams, and sweet influences downwards, we are taught, that the Saviour of the World, tho' high, reaches down with his Grace and Love to us below.

Of the Clouds.

Matt. Where have the Clouds their water?

Prud. Out of the Sea.

Matt. What may we learn from that?

Prud. That Ministers should fetch their doctrine from God.

Matt. Why do they empty themselves upon the Earth?

Prud. To shew that Ministers should give out what they know of God to the world.

Of the Rain-Bow.

Matt. Why is the Rain-Bow caused by the Sun?

Prud. To shew that the covenant of God's Grace is confirmed to us in Christ.

Of the Springs.

Matt. Why do the springs come from the Sea to us, through the Earth?

Prud. To shew, that the Grace of God comes to us through the Body of Christ.

Matt. Why do some of the springs rise out of the top of high Hills?

Prud. To shew, that the Spirit of Grace shall spring up in *some* that are great and mighty, as well as in *many* that are poor and low.

Of the Candle.

Matt. Why doth the fire fasten upon the candle-wick?

Prud. To shew that unless Grace doth kindle upon the heart, there will be no true Light of Life in us.

Matt. Why is the wick, and tallow, and all spent, to maintain the light of the candle?

Prud. To shew that Body and Soul, and all should be at the service of, and spend themselves to maintain in good condition, that Grace of God that is in us.

Matt. Why doth the *Pelican* pierce her own breast with her bill? *Of the Pelican.*

Prud. To nourish her young ones with her blood, and thereby to shew that Christ the Blessed so loveth his young, his People, as to save them from Death by his Blood.

Matt. What may one learn by hearing the cock to crow? *Of the Cock.*

Prud. Learn to remember *Peter's* Sin, and *Peter's* Repentance. The cock's crowing shews also, that Day is coming on; let then the crowing of the cock put thee in mind of that last and terrible Day of Judgment.

Now about this time their month was out; wherefore they signified to those of the House, that 'twas convenient for them to up and be going. Then said *Joseph* to his mother, it is con- *The Weak may sometimes call the Strong to Prayers.* venient that you forget not to send to the house of Mr. *Interpreter*, to pray him to grant that Mr. *Great-heart* should be sent unto us, that he may be our conductor the rest of our Way. Good boy, said she, I had almost forgot. So she drew up a petition, and prayed Mr. *Watchful* the Porter, to send it by some fit man, to her good friend Mr. *Interpreter*; who when it was come, and he had seen the contents of the petition, said to the messenger, Go tell them that I will send him.

When the Family where *Christiana* was, saw *They provide to be gone on their way.* that they had a purpose to go forward, they called the whole house together, to give thanks to their King for sending of them such profitable guests as these; which done, they said to *Christiana*, And shall we not shew thee something, according as our custom is to do to Pilgrims, on which thou may'st meditate, when thou art upon the Way? So they took *Christiana*, her children, and *Mercy* *Eve's Apple.* into the closet, and shew'd them one of the *Apples* that *Eve* did eat of, and that she also did give to her husband; and that for the eating of which, they were both turned out of Paradise, and asked her what she thought that was? Then *Christiana* *A sight of Sin* said, '*Tis Food or Poison*, I know not which. So *is amazing.* *Gen.* 3. 6. they opened the matter to her, and she held up *Rom.* 7. 24. her hands and wondered.

Then they had her to a place, and shewed her *Jacob's Lad-* *Jacob's Ladder*. Now at that time there were *der.* some Angels ascending upon it. So *Christiana* look'd and look'd to see the Angels go up, and so did the rest of the company. Then they were going into another place, to shew them something *A sight of* else; but *James* said to his mother, Pray bid them *Christ is tak-* stay here a little longer, for this is a curious sight. *ing.* So they turned again, and stood feeding their eyes *Gen.* 28. 12. with this *so pleasant a prospect*. After this they *Golden An-* had them into a place where did hang up a *Golden* *chor.* *Anchor*, so they bid *Christiana* take it down; for, said they, you shall have it with you, for it is of *John* 1. 51. absolute necessity that you should, that you may *Heb.* 6. 10. lay hold of that within the veil, and stand stedfast in case you should meet with turbulent weather: So they were glad thereof. Then they took them, *Of* Abraham and had them to the Mount upon which *Abraham* *offering up* our Father had offered up *Isaac* his Son, and *Isaac.* *Gen.* 22. 9. shewed them the *Altar*, the *Wood*, the *Fire*, and the *Knife*, for they remain to be seen to this very Day. When they had seen it, they held up their hands, and blest themselves, and said, Oh! What a man for Love to his Master, and for denial to himself was *Abraham!* After they had shewed them all these things, *Prudence* took them into the dining-room, where stood a pair of excellent virginals, so she played upon them, and turned what she had shewed them into this excellent Song, saying, *Prudence's Virginals.*

> Eve's *Apple we have shew'd you ;*
> *Of that be you aware :*
> *You have seen* Jacob's *Ladder too,*
> *Upon which Angels are.*
>
> *An* Anchor *you received have,*
> *But let not these suffice,*
> *Until with* Abra'm *you have gave*
> *Your Best, a Sacrifice.*

Now about this time one knocked at the door: So the Porter opened, and behold Mr. *Great-heart* was there; but when he was come in, what Joy was there! For it came now fresh again into their minds, how but a while ago he had slain Old *Grim* (*Bloody-man,*) the Giant, and had delivered them from the Lions. *Mr. Great-heart come again.*

Then said Mr. *Great-heart* to *Christiana*, and to *Mercy*, My Lord has sent each of you a bottle of wine, and also some parched corn, together with a couple of pomegranates: He has also sent the boys some figs and raisins, to refresh you in your Way. *He brings a token from his Lord with him.*

Then they addressed themselves to their Journey; and *Prudence* and *Piety* went along with them. When they came at the Gate, *Christiana* asked the Porter, if any of late went by. He said, No, only one some time since, who also told me, *Robbery.* that of late there had been a great robbery committed on the King's highway as you go: But, he saith, the thieves are taken, and will shortly be tried for their lives. Then *Christiana* and *Mercy* were afraid; but *Matthew* said, mother, fear nothing, as long as Mr. *Great-heart* is to go with us, and to be our conductor.

Christiana takes her leave of the Porter. Then said *Christiana* to the Porter, Sir, I am much obliged to you for all the kindnesses that you have shewed me since I came hither; and also for that you have been so loving and kind to my children; I know not how to gratify your kindness: Wherefore, pray, as a token of my respects to you, accept of this small mite: So she put a gold angel in his hand, and he made her a low obeysance, and *The Porter's blessing.* said, Let thy Garments be always white, and let thy head want no ointment. Let *Mercy* live and not die, and let not her Works be few. And to the boys he said, Do you fly youthful lusts, and follow after Godliness with them that are grave and wise; so shall you put gladness into your mother's heart, and obtain praise of all that are sober-minded: So they thanked the Porter, and departed.

Now I saw in my dream, that they went forward until they were come to the brow of the Hill, where· *Piety* bethinking herself, cried out, Alas! I have forgot what I intended to bestow upon *Christiana* and her companions· I will go back and fetch it;

so she ran and fetched it. While she was gone,
Christiana thought she heard in a grove a little
way off on the right hand, a most curious melodious
note, with words much like these :

> *Thro' all my Life thy Favour is*
> *So frankly shew'd to me,*
> *That in thy House for evermore*
> *My dwelling-place shall be.*

And listening still, she thought she heard another
answer it, saying,

> *For why? The Lord our God is good;*
> *His Mercy is for ever sure:*
> *His Truth at all times firmly stood,*
> *And shall from Age to Age endure.*

So *Christiana* asked *Prudence* what 'twas that
made those curious notes. They are, said she, *Song* 2. 11,
our Country birds; they sing these notes but sel   12.
dom, except it be at the Spring, when the flowers
appear, and the Sun shines warm, and then you
may hear them all day long. I often, said she, go
out to hear them ; we also oft-times keep them tame
in our House. They are very fine company for us
when we are melancholy ; also they make the woods
and groves and solitary places, places desirous to
be in.

By this time *Piety* was come again; so she said Piety *bestow-*
to *Christiana*, Look here, I have brought thee a *eth something*
on them at
Scheme of all those things that thou hast seen at our *parting.*
House, upon which thou may'st look when thou

findest thyself forgetful, and call those things again to remembrance for thy edification and comfort.

Part I. p. 58. Now they began to go down the Hill into the Valley of *Humiliation.* It was a steep hill, and the Way was slippery; but they were very careful, so they got down pretty well. When they were down in the Valley, *Piety* said to *Christiana,* this is the place where *Christian* your Husband met with the foul fiend *Apollyon,* and where they had that great Fight that they had: I know you cannot but have heard thereof; but be of good courage, as long as you have here Mr. *Great-heart* to be your Guide and conductor, we hope you will fare the better. So when these two had committed the Pilgrims unto the conduct of their Guide, he went forward and they went after.

Mr. Great-heart *at the Valley of* Humiliation.

Great-heart. Then said Mr. *Great-heart,* We need not be so afraid of this Valley, for here is nothing to hurt us, unless we procure it to ourselves. 'Tis true, *Christian* did here meet with *Apollyon,* with whom he had also a sore Combat; but that *fray* was the fruit of those slips that he got in his going down the Hill: For they that get *Slips there,* must look for *Combats here;* and hence it is, that this Valley has got so hard a name. For the common People, when they hear that some frightful thing has befallen such an one in such a place, are of an opinion that that place is haunted with some foul fiend, or evil spirit; when, alas! it is for the fruit of their doing, that such things do befal them there.

The Reason why Christian

This Valley of *Humiliation* is of itself as fruitful a place, as any the crow flies over; and I am per-

suaded, if we could hit upon it, we might find *was so beset here.*
somewhere hereabout something that might give
us an account why *Christian* was so hardly beset in
this place.

Then *James* said to his mother, Lo, yonder
stands a Pillar, and it looks as if something was
written thereon; let us go and see what it is. So
they went and found there written, *Let* Christian's *A Pillar with an Inscription on it.*
Slips, before he came hither, and the Battles that he
met with in this place, be a warning to those that
come after. Lo, said their Guide, Did I not tell
you that there was something hereabouts that
would give intimation of the reason why *Christian*
was so hard beset in this place : Then turning to
Christiana, he said, No disparagement to *Christian*
more than to many others whose hap and lot it was.
For 'tis easier going *up* than *down* this Hill, and
that can be said but of few hills in all these parts of
the World. But we will leave the good man, he
is at rest, he also had a brave Victory over his
enemy : Let Him grant that dwelleth above, that
we fare no worse when we come to be tryed than
he.

But we will come again to this Valley of *Hu-* *This Valley a brave place.*
miliation. It is the best and most fruitful piece of
ground in all those parts. It is a fat ground, and,
as you see, consisteth much in meadows ; and if a
man was to come here in the summer time, as we
do now, if he knew not any thing before thereof,
and if he also delighted himself in the sight of his
eyes, he might see that, that would be delightful
to him. Behold how green this Valley is, also
how beautified with *Lillies.* I have also known *Song* 2. 1.

Jam. 4. 6.
I Pet. 5. 5.

many labouring men that have got good estates in this Valley of *Humiliation.* (For God resisteth the Proud, but gives *more, more* Grace to the humble;)

Men thrive in the Valley of Humiliation.

for indeed it is a very fruitful soil, and doth bring forth by handfuls. Some also have wished, that the next way to their Father's House were here, that they might be troubled no more with either hills or mountains to go over; but the Way is the Way, and there's an end.

Now as they were going along, and talking, they espied a boy feeding his father's sheep. The boy was in very mean cloaths, but of a very fresh and well-favoured countenance; and as he sat by himself, he sung. Hark, said Mr. *Great-heart,* to what the Shepherd's boy saith; so they hearkened, and he said,

Phil. 4. 12,
13.

> *He that is down, needs fear no Fall;*
> *He that is low, no Pride:*
> *He that is humble, ever shall*
> *Have God to be his Guide.*
>
> *I am content with what I have,*
> *Little be it or much:*
> *And, Lord, Contentment still I crave,*
> *Because thou savest such.*

Heb. 13. 5.

> *Fulness to such, a Burden is,*
> *That go on Pilgrimage:*
> *Here little, and hereafter Bliss,*
> *Is best from Age to Age.*

Then said their Guide, Do you hear him? I will dare to say, that this boy lives a merrier life, and wears more of that herb call'd *Heart's-Ease* in his bosom, than he that is clad in silk and velvet; but we will proceed in our discourse.

In this Valley our Lord formerly had his country house, he loved much to be here: He loved also to walk in these meadows, for he found the Air was pleasant: Besides, here a man shall be free from the noise, and from the hurryings of this life: all states are full of noise and confusion, only the Valley of *Humiliation* is that empty and solitary place. Here a man shall not be so let and hindered in his contemplation, as in other places he is apt to be. This is a Valley that no body walks in, but those that love a Pilgrim's life; and tho' *Christian* had the hard hap to meet here with *Apollyon*, and to enter with him a brisk encounter, yet I must tell you, that in former times men have met with Angels here, have found Pearls here, and have in this place found the Words of Life. *Christ, when in the Flesh, had his country house in the Valley of Humiliation.* *Hos. 12. 4, 5.*

Did I say our Lord had here in former days his country-house, and that he loved here to walk? I will add, in this place, and to the People that live and trace these grounds, he has left a yearly revenue to be faithfully paid them at certain seasons for their maintenance by the way, and for their farther encouragement to go on their Pilgrimage. *Mat. 11. 29.*

Samuel. Now as they went on, *Samuel* said to Mr. *Great-heart:* Sir, I perceive that in this Valley, my father and *Apollyon* had their Battle; but whereabout was the Fight, for I perceive this Valley is large?

Great-heart. Your father had that Battle with

Apollyon, at a place yonder before us, in a narrow passage, just beyond *Forgetful Green:* And indeed that place is the most dangerous place in all these parts. For if at any time the Pilgrims meet with any brunt, it is when they forget what Favours they have received, and how unworthy they are of them: This is the place also where others have been hard put to it; but more of the place when we are come to it; for I persuade myself, that to this day there remains either some sign of the Battle, or some monument to testify that such a battle there was fought.

Forgetful Green.

Mercy. Then said *Mercy,* I think I am as well in this Valley as I have been any where else in all our Journey: The place, methinks, suits with my spirit. I love to be in such places where there is no rattling with coaches, nor rumbling with wheels: Methinks here one may, without much molestation, be thinking what he is, whence he came, what he has done, and to what the King has called him: Here one may think and break at heart, and melt in one's spirit, until one's eyes become like the *Fish-Pools of Hesh-bon.* They that go rightly through this Valley of *Bacha,* make it a Well, the rain that God sends down from Heaven upon them that are here also, *filleth the Pools.* This Valley is that from whence also the King will give to their vineyards, and they that go through it, shall sing, (as *Christian* did, for all he met with *Apollyon.*)

Humility a sweet Grace.

Song 7. 4.
Psal. 84. 5, 6, 7.
Hos. 2. 15.

Great-heart. 'Tis true, said their Guide, I have gone through this Valley many a time, and never was better than when here.

An Experiment of it.

I have also been a conduct to several Pilgrims,

and they have confessed the same: *To this man will I look, saith the King, even to him that is Poor, and of a contrite Spirit, and that trembles at my Word.*

Now they were come to the place where the afore-mentioned Battle was fought: Then said the Guide to *Christiana*, her children and *Mercy*, This is the place, on this ground *Christian* stood, and up there came *Apollyon* against him; and look, did not I tell you, here is some of your husband's blood *The Place* upon these stones to this day: Behold, also, how *where* Chris-here and there are yet to be seen upon the place, *Fiend did* some of the shivers of *Apollyon's* broken darts: See *signs of the* also how they did beat the ground with their feet *Battle re-* as they fought, to make good their places against *main.* each other; how also with their by-blows, they did split the very stones in pieces, verily *Christian* did here play the man, and shewed himself as stout as could, had he been there, even *Hercules* himself. When *Apollyon* was beat, he made his retreat to the next valley, that is called, *The Valley of the Shadow of Death*, unto which we shall come anon.

Lo, yonder also stands a monument, on which is *A Monument* engraven this Battle, and *Christian's* Victory, to his *of the Battle.* Fame, throughout all Ages: So, because it stood just on the Way-side before them, they stept to it, and read the writing, which word for word was this:

> *Hard-by here was a Battle fought,* *A Monument*
>   *Most strange, and yet most true;* *of* Christian's
> Christian *and* Apollyon *fought* *Victory.*
>   *Each other to subdue.*

The Man so bravely play'd the Man,
He made the Fiend *to fly :*
Of which a Monument I stand,
The same to testify.

Part I. p. 64.   When they had passed by this place, they came
upon the borders of the Shadow of Death, and this
Valley was longer than the other, a place also most
strangely haunted with evil things, as many are able
to testify : But these women and children went the
better through it, because they had Day-light, and
because Mr. *Great-heart* was their conductor.

Groanings
heard.
When they were entered upon this Valley, they
thought that they heard a groaning, as of dead
men ; a very great groaning. They thought also
they did hear words of Lamentation, spoken as of
some in extreme torment. These things made the
boys to quake, the women also looked pale and
wan ; but their Guide bid them be of good comfort.

The Ground
shakes.
So they went on a little further, and they
thought that they felt the ground begin to shake
under them, as if some hollow place was there ;
they heard also a kind of hissing, as of serpents,
but nothing as yet appeared. Then said the boys,
Are we not yet at the end of this doleful place ?
But the Guide also bid them be of good courage,
and look well to their feet, lest haply, said he, you
be taken in some snare.

James *sick*
with Fear.
Now *James* began to be sick, but I think the
cause thereof was fear ; so his Mother gave him
some of that Glass of Spirits that she had given
her at the *Interpreter's* house, and three of the

Pills that Mr. *Skill* had prepared, and the boy began to revive. Thus they went on, till they came
to about the middle of the Valley; and then *Chris-*
tiana said, Methinks I see something yonder upon *A* Fiend ap-
the road before us, a thing of such a shape, such *pears.*
as I have not seen. Then said *Joseph*, Mother,
what is it? An ugly thing, child; an ugly thing,
said she. But mother, what is it like? said he.
'Tis like I cannot tell what, said she. And now *The Pilgrims*
it was but a little way off: Then said she, It is *are afraid.*
nigh.

Well, said Mr. *Great-heart*, let them that are
most afraid, keep close to me: So the *Fiend* came
on, and the conductor met it; but when it was
just come to him, it vanished to all their sights:
Then remembered they what had been said some
time ago; *Resist the Devil, and he will fly from*
you.

They went therefore on, as being a little re- Great-Heart
freshed; but they had not gone far, before *Mercy*, *encourages*
looking behind her, saw, as she thought, something *them.*
'most like a Lion, and it came a great padding pace *A Lion.*
after; and it had a hollow voice of roaring; and at
every roar that it gave, it made all the Valley echo,
and their hearts to ake, save the heart of him that
was their Guide. So it came up, and Mr. *Great-*
heart went behind, and put the Pilgrims all before
him. The Lion also came on apace, and Mr.
Great-heart addressed himself to give him battle. 1 Pet. 5. 8, 9.
But when he saw that it was determined, that resistance should be made, he also drew back, and
came no further.

Then they went on again, and their conductor

did go before them, till they came at a place
where was cast up a Pit, the whole breadth of the
Way, and before they could be prepared to go over
that, a great mist and a darkness fell upon them, so
that they could not see.   Then said the Pilgrims,
Alas! Now what shall we do? But their Guide
made answer, Fear not, stand still, and see what
an end will be put to this also; so they staid there,
because their path was marr'd.   They then also
thought that they did hear more apparently the
noise and rushing of the Enemies; the fire also,
and the smoke of the Pit, was much easier to be
discerned.   Then said *Christiana* to *Mercy,* Now I
see what my poor Husband went through; I have
heard much of this place, but I never was here
afore now; poor man, he went here all alone in
the night; he had night almost quite through the
Way; also these Fiends were busy about him, as
if they would have torn him in pieces.   Many
have spoke of it, but none can tell what the Valley
of *the shadow of Death* should mean, untill they
come in it themselves.   *The heart knows its own
bitterness, and a stranger intermeddleth not with its
joy.*   To be here, is a fearful thing.

Great-heart. This is like doing business in great
waters, or like going down into the deep; this
is like being in the heart of the Sea, and like
going down to the bottoms of the mountains: Now
it seems as if the Earth, with its bars, were about
us for ever. *But let them that walk in darkness,
and have no light, trust in the name of the* LORD,
and stay upon their God.   For my part, as I have
told you already, I have gone often through this

A Pit and darkness.

Christiana *now knows what her Husband felt.*

Great-Heart's *reply.*

Valley, and have been much harder put to it than now I am; and yet you see I am alive. I would not boast, for that I am not mine own Saviour. But I trust we shall have a good deliverance. Come, let us pray for Light to him that can lighten our darkness, and that can rebuke, not only these, but all the Satans in Hell.

So they cried and prayed, and God sent light *They pray.* and deliverance, for there was now no let in their Way; no not there, where but now they were stopt with a Pit. Yet they were not got through the Valley; so they went on still, and behold great stinks and loathsome smells, to the great annoyance of them. Then said *Mercy* to *Christiana*, There is not such pleasant being here as at the Gate, or at the *Interpreter's*, or at the house where we lay last.

O but, said one of the boys, it is not so bad to *One of the* go through here, as it is to *abide* here always; and *boys reply.* for ought I know, one reason why we must go this way to the House prepared for us, is, that our home might be made the sweeter to us.

Well said, *Samuel,* quoth the Guide, thou hast now spoke like a man. Why, if ever I get out here again, said the boy, I think I shall prize light and good way, better than ever I did in all my life. Then said the Guide, We shall be out by and by.

So on they went, and *Joseph* said, Cannot we see to the end of this Valley as yet? Then said the Guide, Look to your feet, for you shall presently be among snares: So they looked to their feet, and went on; but they were troubled much with the snares. Now when they were come among the snares, they espied a man cast into the Ditch on the left hand, with his flesh all rent Heedless *is slain, and* Takeheed *preserved.* and torn. Then said the Guide, That is one *Heedless*, that was a going this Way; he has lain there a great while: There was one *Takeheed* with him, when he was taken and slain; but *he* escaped their hands. You cannot imagine how many are killed hereabouts, and yet men are so foolishly venturous, as to set out lightly on Pilgrimage, and to come without a Guide. Poor *Christian!* it was a wonder that he here escaped; but he was beloved of his God: Also he had a good heart of his own, or else he could never ha' done it. Now they drew towards the end of the Way, and just there where *Christian* had *Part* I. *p.* 70. seen the Cave when he went by, out thence Maul *a Giant.* came forth *Maul* a giant. This *Maul* did use to spoil young Pilgrims with Sophistry, and he called *Great-heart* by his name, and said unto him, How many times have you been forbidden to do these things? Then said Mr. *Great-heart*, *He quarrels with* Great-heart. What things? What things? quoth the Giant; you know what things; but I will put an end to your trade. But, pray, said Mr. *Great-heart*, before we fall to it, let us understand wherefore we must fight. (Now the women and children stood trembling, and knew not what to do.) Quoth the Giant, You rob the country, and rob it with the worst of thefts. These are but generals, said Mr. *Great-heart;* come to particulars, man.

Then said the Giant, Thou practisest the craft *God's Ministers counted* of a *Kidnapper*, thou gatherest up women and

children, and carriest them into a strange country, *as* Kidnap-
to the weakning of my Master's kingdom.   But now *pers.*
Great-heart replyed, I am a servant of the *God
of Heaven;* my business is to persuade Sinners to
Repentance: I am commanded to do my endeavour *The* Giant
to turn men, women, and children, from Darkness *and Mr.*
to Light, and from the Power of Satan to God; and *must fight.*
if this be indeed the ground of thy quarrel, let us
fall to it as soon as thou wilt.

Then the Giant came up, and Mr. *Great-heart*
went to meet him; and as he went, he drew his
Sword, but the Giant had a club.   So without
more ado they fell to it, and at the first blow the
Giant struck Mr. *Great-heart* down upon one of
his knees; with that the women and children
cried out: So Mr. *Great-heart* recovering himself
laid about him in full lusty manner, and gave the *Weak folks*
Giant a wound in his arm; thus he fought for the *Prayers do
sometimes help*
space of an hour, to that height of heat, that the *Strong folks
Cries.*
breath came out of the Giant's nostrils, as the heat
doth out of a boiling cauldron.

Then they sat down to rest them, but Mr.
Great-heart betook him to prayer; also the women
and children did nothing but sigh and cry all the
time that the battle did last.

When they had rested them, and taken breath,
they both fell to it again, and Mr. *Great-heart* with
a full blow fetch'd the Giant down to the ground: *The Giant*
Nay, hold, and let me recover, quoth he.   So Mr. *struck down.*
Great-heart fairly let him get up: So to it they
went again, and the Giant missed but little of
all-to-breaking Mr. *Great-heart's* skull with his
club.

Mr. *Great-heart* seeing that, runs to him in the full heat of his spirit, and pierced him under the fifth rib; with that the Giant began to faint, and could hold up his club no longer. Then Mr. *Great-heart* seconded his blow, and smit the head of the Giant from his shoulders. Then the women and children rejoiced, and Mr. *Great-heart* also praised God, for the deliverance he had wrought.

He is slain, and his head disposed of.

When this was done, they amongst them erected a *Pillar*, and fastened the Giant's head thereon, and wrote underneath in letters that passengers might read:

> *He that did wear this Head, was one*
>   *That Pilgrims did misuse;*
> *He stopt their Way, he spared none,*
>   *But did them all abuse:*
> *Until that I,* Great-heart *arose,*
>   *The Pilgrims Guide to be;*
> *Until that I, did him oppose,*
>   *That was their Enemy.*

Now I saw that they went to the ascent that was a little way off cast up to be a prospect for *Pilgrims*, (that was the place from whence *Christian* had the first sight of *Faithful* his brother.) Wherefore here they sat down, and rested, they also here did eat and drink, and make merry; for that they had gotten deliverance from this so dangerous an enemy. As they sat thus and did eat, *Christiana* ask'd the Guide, *If he had caught no hurt in the Battle?* Then said Mr. *Great-heart*,

Part I. p. 71.

No, save a little on my flesh; yet that also shall be so far from being to my detriment, that it is at present a proof of my love to my Master and you, and shall be a means, by Grace, to increase my reward at last.

But was you not afraid, good Sir, when you see him come out with his Club?

It is my duty, said he, to distrust mine own ability, that I may have reliance on Him that is stronger than all. But what did you think, when he fetch'd you down to the ground at the first blow? Why, I thought, quoth he, that so my Master himself was served, and yet he it was that conquered at the last.

*2 Cor. 4.
Discourse of
the Fights.*

Matt. When you all have thought what you please, I think God has been wonderful good unto us, both in bringing us out of this Valley, and in delivering us out of the hand of this Enemy; for my part, I see no reason why we should distrust our God any more, since he has *now*, and in *such* a place as this, given us such testimony of his love as this.

*Matt. here ad-
mires God's
Goodness.*

Then they got up, and went forward: Now a little before them stood an oak, and under it when they came to it, they found an old Pilgrim fast asleep; they knew that he was a Pilgrim by his *Clothes*, and his *Staff*, and his *Girdle*.

Old Honest
*asleep under
the Oak.*

So the *Guide*, Mr. *Great-heart*, awaked him, and the old gentleman, as he lift up his eyes, cried out, What's the matter? Who are you? And what is your business here?

Great-heart. Come, man, be not so hot, here is none but Friends: Yet the old man gets up, and

*One Saint
sometimes*

takes another for his Enemy. stands upon his guard, and will know of them what they were. Then said the *Guide*, my name is *Great-heart*, I am the guide of these Pilgrims, which are going to the Cœlestial Country.

Honest. Then said Mr. *Honest*, I cry you mercy; I fear'd that you had been of the company of those that some time ago did rob *Little-Faith* of his money; but now I look better about me, I perceive you are honester people.

Talk between Great-heart and he.

Great-heart. Why what would, or could you ha' done, to ha' help'd yourself, if we indeed had been of that company?

Hon. Done! Why, I would have fought as long as breath had been in me; and had I so done, I am sure you could never have given me the worst on't; for a *Christian* can never be overcome, unless he shall yield of himself.

Great-heart. Well said, father *Honest*, quoth the Guide; for by this I know thou art a cock of the right kind, for thou hast said the truth.

Hon. And by this also I know that thou knowest what true Pilgrimage is; for all others do think, that we are the soonest overcome of any.

Great-heart. Well, now we are so happily met, pray let me crave your name, and the name of the place you came from?

Whence Mr. Honest came.

Hon. My name I cannot, but I came from the town of *Stupidity;* it lieth about four degrees beyond the City of *Destruction.*

Great-heart. Oh! Are you that country-man then? I deem I have half a guess of you, your name is old *Honesty*, is it not? So the old Gentleman blush'd, and said, Not *Honesty* in the *abstract,* but *Honest* is my name, and I wish that my *nature* shall agree to what I am called.

Hon. But, Sir, said the old gentleman, how could you guess that I am such a man, since I came from such a place?

Great-heart. I had heard of you before, by my Master; for he knows all things that are done on the Earth: But I have often wondered that any should come from your place, for your town is worse than is the City of *Destruction* itself. *Stupified Ones are worse than those merely Carnal.*

Hon. Yes, we lie more off from the Sun, and so are more cold and sensless; but was a man in a mountain of Ice, yet if the Sun of Righteousness will arise upon him, his frozen heart shall feel a thaw; and thus it hath been with me.

Great-heart. I believe it, Father *Honest*, I believe it; for I know the thing is true.

Then the old gentleman saluted all the *Pilgrims* with a holy kiss of Charity, and asked them of their names, and how they had fared since they set out on their Pilgrimage.

Christ. Then said *Christiana*, My name I suppose you have heard of; good *Christian* was my husband, and these four were his children. But can you think how the old gentleman was taken, when she told him who she was! He skipped, he smiled, and blessed them with a thousand good wishes, saying: *Old Honest and Christiana talk.*

Hon. I have heard much of your husband, and of his travels and wars, which he underwent in his days. Be it spoken to your comfort, the name of your husband rings all over these parts of the world; his Faith, his Courage, his Enduring, and his Sincerity under all, has made his name famous.

Then he turned him to the boys, and asked them of their names, which they told him: And then said he unto them, *Matthew*, be thou like *Matthew* the publican, not in Vice but in Virtue. *Samuel*, said he, be thou like *Samuel* the prophet, a man of Faith and Prayer. *Joseph*, said he, be thou like *Joseph* in *Potiphar's* house, Chaste, and one that flies from temptation. And *James*, be thou like *James the Just*, and like *James* the brother of our Lord. Then they told him of *Mercy*, and how she had left her town and her kindred to come along with *Christiana*, and with her sons. At that

the old honest man said, *Mercy* is thy name: By *Mercy* shalt thou be sustain'd, and carried through all those difficulties that shall assault thee in thy Way, till thou shalt come thither, where thou shalt look the *Fountain of Mercy in the face with comfort.*

All this while the Guide, Mr. *Great-heart*, was very much pleased, and smiled upon his companion.

Now, as they walked along together, the Guide asked the old gentleman, If he did not know one Mr. *Fearing*, that came on Pilgrimage out of his parts?

Hon. Yes, very well, said he? He was a man that had the Root of the matter in him, but he was one of the most troublesome Pilgrims that I ever met with in all my days.

Great-heart. I perceive you knew him, for you have given a very right character of him.

Hon. Knew him! I was a great companion of

his; I was with him most an end; when he first
began to think of what would come upon us hereafter, I was with him.

Great-heart. I was his Guide from my Master's
house to the gate of the Cœlestial City.

Hon. Then you knew him to be a troublesome
one.

Great-heart. I did so; but I could very well
bear it; for men of my calling are oftentimes in-
trusted with the conduct of such as he was.

Hon. Well then, pray let us hear a little of
him, and how he managed himself under your
conduct.

Great-heart. Why, he was always afraid that *Mr.* Fearing's
he should come short of whither he had a desire *troublesome*
Pilgrimage.
to go. Every thing frightned him that he heard
any body speak of, that had but the least appearance of opposition in it. I hear that he lay roar-
ing at the *Slough* of *Despond*, for above a month *His behaviour*
together; nor durst he, for all he saw several go *at the Slough*
of Despond.
over before him, venture, tho' they many of them
offered to lend him their hand. *He would not*
go back again neither. The Cœlestial City, he
said he should die if he came not to it, and yet
was dejected at every difficulty, and stumbled
at every straw that any body cast in his Way.
Well, after he had lain at the *Slough* of *Despond*
a great while, as I have told you, one Sun-shine
morning, I do not know how, he ventured, and
so got over: But when he was over, he would
scarce believe it. He had, I think, a *Slough* of
Despond in his mind, a *Slough* that he carry'd
every where with him, or else he could never

have been as he was. So he came up to the
Gate, you know what I mean, that stands at the
head of this Way, and there also he stood a good
while before he would adventure to knock. When
His behaviour the Gate was opened, he would give back and
at the Gate. give place to others, and say, that he was not
worthy : For all he got before some to the Gate,
yet many of them went in before him. There
the poor man would stand shaking and shrink-
ing ; I dare say it would have pitied one's heart
to have seen him : *Nor would he go back again.*
At last he took the hammer that hang'd on the
Gate in his hand, and gave a small rap or two ;
then one opened to him, but he shrunk back as
before. He that open'd, stept out after him, and
said, Thou trembling one, what wantest thou ?
With that he fell to the ground. He that spoke
to him wonder'd to see him so faint. So he said
to him, Peace to thee, up, for I have set open
the Door to thee, come in, for thou art blest.
With that he gat up, and went in trembling ; and
when that he was in, he was ashamed to shew his
face. Well, after he had been entertained there
a while, as you know how the manner is, he was
bid go on his Way, and also told the Way he
His behaviour should take. So he came till he came to our
at the Inter- house, but as he behaved himself at the Gate, so
preter's door. he did at my master the *Interpreter's* door. He
lay thereabout in the cold a good while, before he
would adventure to call. *Yet he would not go back.*
And the nights were long and cold then. Nay,
he had a Note of *Necessity* in his bosom to my
Master to receive him, and grant him the comfort

of his House, and also to allow him a stout and
valiant conduct, because he was himself so *chicken-
hearted* a man; and yet for all that, he was afraid
to call at the door. So he lay up and down thereabouts, till, poor man, he was almost starv'd; yea,
so great was his dejection, that tho' he saw several
others for knocking got in, yet he was afraid to
venture. At last I think, I looked out of the
window, and perceiving a man to be up and down
about the door, I went out to him, and asked
what he was; but poor man the water stood in his
eyes: So I perceived what he wanted. I went
therefore in, and told it in the House, and we
shewed the thing to our Lord: So he sent me out
again, to entreat him to come in; but I dare say,
I had hard work to do it. At last he came in,
and I will say that for my Lord, he carry'd it wonderfully lovingly to him. There were but a few *How he was*
good bits at the table, but some of it was laid upon *entertained*
his trencher. Then he presented the *Note*, and my *there.*
Lord looked thereon, and said, his desire should
be granted. So when he had been there a good
while, he seemed to get some heart, and to be *He is a little*
a little more comfortable. For my Master, you *encouraged at*
must know, is one of very tender bowels, especi- *the Interpre-*
ally to them that are afraid; wherefore he carried *ter's house.*
it so towards him, as might tend most to his encouragement. Well, when he had had a sight
of the things of the place, and was ready to
take his Journey to go to the City, my Lord, as
he did to *Christian* before, gave him a bottle
of Spirits, and some comfortable things to eat.
Thus we set forward, and I went before him,

but the man was but of few words, only he would sigh aloud.

He was greatly afraid when he saw the Gibbet, cheary when he saw the Cross.

When we were come to where the three fellows were hanged, he said, that he doubted that that would be his end also: Only he seemed glad when he saw the *Cross* and the *Sepulchre*. There I confess he desired to stay a little to look; and he seemed for a while after to be a little cheary. When we came at the Hill *Difficulty* he made no stick at that, nor did he much fear the Lions: For you must know, that his trouble *was not about such things as those*, his fear was about his acceptance at last.

I got him in at the House *Beautiful*, I think before he was willing; also when he was in, I brought him acquainted with the damsels that were of the

Dumpish at the House Beautiful.

place, but he was ashamed to make himself much for company; he desired much to be alone, yet he always loved good talk, and often would get behind the *Screen* to hear it: He also loved much to see *ancient* things, and to be *pondering* them in his mind. He told me afterward, that he loved to be in those two houses from which he came last, to wit, at the Gate, and that of the *Interpreter*, but that he durst not be so bold to ask.

He went down into, and was very pleasant in the Valley of Humilia-tion.

When we went also from the House *Beautiful*, down the Hill, into the Valley of *Humiliation*, he went down as well as ever I saw a man in my life, for he cared not how mean he was, so he might be happy at last. Yea, I think there was a kind of Sympathy betwixt that Valley and him: For I never saw him better in all his Pilgrimage than when he was in that Valley.

Here he would lie down, embrace the ground, and kiss the very flowers that grew in this Valley. He would now be up every morning by break of day, tracing and walking to and fro in this Valley. Lam. 3. 27, 28, 29.

But when he was come to the entrance of the Valley of the *Shadow of Death*, I thought I should have lost my man; not for that he had any incli- nation *to go back*, that he always abhorred, but he was ready to die for Fear. O, the *Hobgoblins* will have me, the *Hobgoblins* will have me, cried he; and I could not beat him out on't. He made such a noise, and such an out-cry here, that had they but heard him, 'twas enough to encourage them to come and fall upon us. *Much per- plexed in the Valley of the* Shadow of Death.

But this I took very great notice of, that this Valley was as quiet while he went through it, as ever I knew it before or since. I suppose those Enemies here had now a special check from our Lord, and a command not to meddle until Mr. *Fearing* was passed over it.

It would be too tedious to tell you of all; we will therefore only mention a passage or two more. When he was come at *Vanity-Fair*, I thought he would have fought with all the men in the fair; I feared there we should both have been knock'd o' the head, so hot was he against their Fooleries; upon the inchanted ground he was also very wakeful. But when he was come at the *River*, where was no bridge, there again he was in a heavy case: Now, now, he said, he should be drowned for ever, and so never see that Face with comfort, that he had come so many miles to behold. *His behaviour at* Vanity- Fair.

And here also I took notice of what was very remarkable; The water of that river was lower at this time, than ever I saw it in all my life; so he went over at last, not much above wet-shod. When he was going up to the Gate, Mr. *Great-heart* began to take his leave of him, and to wish him a good reception above, so he said, *I shall, I shall:* Then parted we asunder, and I saw him no more.

His Boldness at last.

Hon. Then it seems he was well at last.

Great-heart. Yes, yes, I never had doubt about him, he was a man of a choice spirit, only he was always kept very low, and that made his life so burdensome to himself, and so troublesome to others. He was above many, tender of Sin; he was so afraid of doing injuries to others, that he often would deny himself of that which was lawful, because he would not offend.

Psal. 88.
Rom. 14. 21.
1 Cor. 8. 13.

Hon. But what should be the reason that such a good man should be all his days so much in the dark?

Reasons why good men are so in the Dark.
Matt. 11. 16, 17, 18.

Great-heart. There are two sorts of reasons for it; one is, The wise God will have it so, some must *pipe*, and some must *weep*: Now Mr. *Fearing* was one that played upon *this bass*. He and his fellows sound the *sackbut*, whose notes are more doleful than the notes of other musick are; though indeed some say, the bass is the ground of musick: And for my part, I care not at all for that profession, that begins not in heaviness of mind. The first string that the musician usually touches, is the *bass*, when he intends to put all in tune; God also plays upon this string first, when he sets the soul in tune for himself. Only here was the imperfection of Mr. *Fearing*, he could play upon no other musick but this, till towards his latter end.

I make bold to talk thus Metaphorically, for the ripening of the wits of young readers, and because in the book of the Revelations, the Saved are compared to a company of musicians that play upon their *Trumpets and Harps*, and sing their songs before the Throne. Rev. 8. 14. 2, 3.

Hon. He was a very zealous man, as one may see by what relation you have given of him; difficulties, Lions, or Vanity-Fair, he feared not at all; 'twas only Sin, Death, and Hell, that was to him a terror; because he had some doubts about his interest in that Cœlestial Country.

Great-heart. You say right: *Those* were the things that were his troublers, and they, as you have well observed, arose from the weakness of his mind thereabout, not from weakness of spirit as to the practical part of a Pilgrim's Life. I dare believe, that as the proverb is, *He could have bit a Fire-brand, had it stood in his Way:* But the things with which he was oppressed, no man ever yet could shake off with ease. *A Close about him.*

Christ. Then said *Christiana*, This relation of Mr. *Fearing* has done me good: I thought nobody had been like me; but I see there was some semblance 'twixt this good man and I, only we differ in two things. His troubles were so great, they brake out, but mine I kept within. His also lay so hard upon him, they made him that he could not knock at the houses provided for entertain- *Christiana's Sentence.*

ment ; but my trouble was always such, as made me knock the louder.

Mercy. If I might also speak my mind, I must say, that something of him has also dwelt in me. For I have ever been more afraid of the *Lake*, and the loss of a place in *Paradise*, than I have been of the loss of other things. O, thought I, may I have the happiness to have a habitation *there*, 'tis enough, though I part with all the World to win it.

Matt. Then said *Matthew*, *Fear* was one thing that made me think that I was far from having that within me that accompanies Salvation ; but if it was so with such a good man as he, why may it not also go well with me ?

James. No fears, no Grace, said *James ;* though there is not always Grace where there is the fear of Hell, yet to be sure there is no Grace where there is no fear of God.

Great-heart. Well said, *James*, thou hast hit the mark ; for the fear of God is the beginning of Wisdom ; and to be sure they that want the *beginning*, have neither *middle* nor *end*. But we will here conclude our discourse of Mr. *Fearing*, after we have sent after him this farewel.

Well, Master Fearing, *thou didst fear*
Thy God, and wast afraid
Of doing any thing, while here,
That would have thee betray'd.
And didst thou fear the Lake and Pit ?
Would others did so too !
For, as for them that want thy wit,
They do themselves undo.

Now I saw, that they still went on in their talk. For after Mr. *Great-heart* had made an end with Mr. *Fearing*, Mr. *Honest* began to tell them of another, but his name was Mr. *Self-will*. He pre- *Of Mr.* Self-tended himself to be a *Pilgrim*, said Mr. *Honest;* will. but I persuade myself, he never came in at the Gate that stands at the head of the Way.

Great-heart. Had you ever any talk with him about it?

Hon. Yes, more than once or twice; but he would *Old* Honest always be like himself, *self-willed*. He neither cared *had talked* *with him*. for man, nor Argument, nor yet Example; what his mind prompted him to, that he would do, and nothing else could he be got to.

Great-heart. Pray what principles did he hold? for I suppose you can tell.

Hon. He held, that a man might follow the Self-will's Vices as well as the Virtues of the Pilgrims; *Opinion*. and that if he did both, he should be certainly saved.

Great-heart. How? If he had said, 'tis possible for the best to be guilty of the vices, as well as to partake of the vertues of Pilgrims, he could not much have been blamed; for indeed we are exempted from no Vice absolutely, but on condition that we Watch and Strive: But this I perceive is not the thing; but if I understand you right, your meaning is, that he was of that opinion, that it was allowable so to be?

Hon. Ai, ai, so I mean, and so he believed and practised?

Great-heart. But what grounds had he for his so saying?

Hon. Why, he said he had the Scripture for his warrant.

Great-heart. Prithee, Mr. *Honest*, present us with a few particulars.

Hon. So I will. He said: To have to do with other mens wives, had been practised by *David*, God's beloved, and therefore he could do it. He said: To have more women than one, was a thing that *Solomon* practised, and therefore he could do it. He said, that *Sarah* and the godly midwives of *Egypt* lied, and so did save *Rahab*, and therefore he could do it. He said, that the disciples went at the bidding of their Master, and took away the owner's *Ass*, and therefore he could do so too. He said, that *Jacob* got the inheritance of his father, in a way of Guile and dissimulation, and therefore he could do so too.

Great-heart. High base! indeed. And are you sure he was of this opinion?

Hon. I have heard him plead for it, bring Scripture for it, bring arguments for it, *&c.*

Great-heart. An opinion that is not fit to be with any allowance in the World.

Hon. You must understand me rightly: He did not say that *any* man might do this; but, that those that had the Virtues of those that did such things, might also do the same.

Great-heart. But what more false than such a conclusion? For this is as much as to say, that because good men heretofore have sinned of Infirmity, therefore he had allowance to do it of a presumptuous mind: Or if because a child, by the blast of the wind, or for that it stumbled at a stone, fell down and so defiled itself in mire, therefore he might wilfully lie down and wallow like a boar therein. Who could ha' thought that any one could so far ha' been blinded by the power of Lust? But what is written must be true : They *stumble at the Word, being disobedient, whereunto also they were* 1 Peter 2. 8. *appointed.*

His supposing that such may have the godly man's Virtues, who addict themselves to their Vices, is also a delusion as strong as the other. ('Tis just as if the *dog* should say, I have, or may have the *qualities* of the *child*, because I lick up its stinking excrements.) To eat up the Sin of God's People, is no sign of one that is possessed Hos. 4. 8. with their Virtues. Nor can I believe, that one that is of this opinion, can at present have Faith or Love in him. But I know you have made strong objections against him, prithee what can he say for himself?

Hon. Why, he says, to do this by way of Opinion, seems abundance more honest than to do it, and yet hold contrary to it in opinion.

Great-heart. A very wicked answer; for though to let loose the bridle to lusts, while our opinions are against such things, is bad; yet, to sin, and plead a Toleration so to do, is worse; the one stumbles beholders accidentally, the other pleads them into the snare.

Hon. There are many of this man's mind, that have not this man's mouth, and *that* makes going on Pilgrimage of so little esteem as it is.

Great-heart. You have said the truth, and it is to

be lamented : But he that feareth the King of Paradise, shall come out of them all.

Christ. There are strange opinions in the world. I know one that said, 'twas time enough to repent when they came to die.

Great-heart. Such are not over wise : That man would ha' been loth, might he have had a week to run twenty mile in his life, to have deferred that Journey to the last hour of that week.

Hon. You say right, and yet the generality of them that count themselves Pilgrims, do indeed do thus. I am, as you see, an old man, and have been a traveller in this Road many a day ; and I have taken notice of many things.

I have seen some that have set out as if they would drive all the world afore them, who yet have in few days died as they in the Wilderness, and so never gat sight of the Promised Land.

I have seen some that have promised nothing at first setting out to be Pilgrims, and that one would ha' thought could not have lived a day, that have yet proved very good Pilgrims.

I have seen some that have run hastily forward, that again have, after a little time, run as fast just back again.

I have seen some that have spoke very well of a Pilgrim's Life at first, that after a while have spoken as much against it.

I have heard some, when they first set out for Paradise, say positively, there is such a place, who when they have been almost there, have come back again, and said there is none.

I have heard some vaunt what they would do in

case they should be opposed that have even at a false alarm fled Faith, the Pilgrim's Way, and all.

Now as they were thus in their Way, there came one running to meet them, and said, Gentlemen, and you of the weaker sort, if you love life, shift for yourselves, for the Robbers are before you. *Fresh News of trouble.*

Great-heart. Then said Mr. *Great-heart*, they be the three that set upon *Little-Faith* heretofore. Well, said he, we are ready for them; so they went on their Way: Now they looked at every turning when they should ha' met with the villains: But whether they heard of Mr. *Great-heart*, or whether they had some other game, they came not up to the Pilgrims. *Part* I. p. 143. Great-heart's *Resolution.*

Christ. Christiana then wished for an Inn for herself and her children, because they were weary. Then said Mr. *Honest*, There is one a little before us, where a very honourable disciple, one *Gaius*, dwells. So they all concluded to turn in thither, and the rather, because the old gentleman gave him so good a report. So when they came to the door, they went in, not knocking, for folks use not to knock at the door of an Inn. Then they called for the Master of the House, and he came to them: So they asked if they might lie there that night? Christiana *wisheth for an Inn.* Rom. xvi. 23. Gaius. *They enter in to his House.*

Gaius. Yes, Gentlemen, if you be true men, for my house is for none but Pilgrims. Then was *Christiana, Mercy*, and the *boys*, the more glad, for that the Innkeeper was a lover of Pilgrims. So they called for rooms, and he shewed them one for *Christiana* and her children, and *Mercy*, and another for Mr. *Great-heart* and the old gentleman. Gaius *entertains them, and how.*

Great-heart. Then said Mr. *Great-heart*, good *Gaius*, What hast thou for supper? for these Pilgrims have come far to-day, and are weary.

Gaius. It is late, said *Gaius*, so we cannot conveniently go out to seek food; but such as we have you shall be welcome to, if that will content.

Great-heart. We will be content with what thou hast in the house, forasmuch as I have proved thee; thou art never destitute of that which is convenient.

Gaius *his* Cook.

Then he went down and spake to the cook, whose name was, *Taste-that-which-is-Good*, to get ready Supper for so many Pilgrims. This done, he comes up again, saying, Come, my good friends, you are welcome to me, and I am glad that I have a house to entertain you; and while supper is making ready, if you please, let us entertain one another with some good Discourse: So they all said, content.

Talk between Gaius *and his* Guests.

Gaius. Then said *Gaius*, Whose wife is this aged matron? and whose daughter is this young damsel?

Great-heart. The woman is the wife of one *Christian*, a Pilgrim of former times; and these are his four children. The maid is one of her acquaintance; one that she hath persuaded to come with her on Pilgrimage. The boys take all after their

Mark this.

father, and covet to tread in his steps: Yea, if they do but see any place where the old Pilgrim hath lain, or any print of his foot, it ministereth joy to their hearts, and they covet to lie or tread in the same.

Gaius. Then said *Gaius*, Is this *Christian's* wife,

MARRIAGE OF *MERCY* AND *MATTHEW*

and are these *Christian's* children? I knew your husband's father, yea, also his father's Father. Many have been good of this stock, their ancestors dwelt first at *Antioch*. *Christian's* progenitors (I Acts 11. 26. suppose you have heard your husband talk of *Of* Christian's *Ancestors.* them) were very worthy men. They have, above any that I know, shewed themselves men of great virtue and courage, for the Lord of the Pilgrims, his ways, and them that loved him. I have heard of many of your husband's relations that have stood all trials for the sake of the Truth. Acts 7. 59, 60. *Stephen*, that was one of the first of the Family from whence your husband sprang, was knocked o' th' head with stones. *James*, another of this chap. 12. 8. generation, was slain with the edge of the sword. To say nothing of *Paul* and *Peter*, men anciently of the family from whence your husband came: There was *Ignatius*, who was cast to the Lions: *Romanus*, whose flesh was cut by pieces from his bones; and *Polycarp*, that played the man in the fire. There was he that was hanged up in a basket in the Sun, for the wasps to eat; and he who they put into a sack, and cast him into the Sea to be drowned. 'Twould be impossible, utterly to count up all of that family that have suffered injuries and death, for the love of a Pilgrim's life. Nor can I but be glad, to see that thy husband has left behind him four such boys as these. I hope they will bear up their Father's name, and tread in their Father's steps, and come to their Father's end.

Great-heart. Indeed, Sir, they are likely lads; they seem to choose heartily their father's ways.

Advice to Christiana about her Boys.

Gaius. That is it that I said, wherefore *Christian's* family is like still to spread abroad upon the face of the ground, and yet to be numerous upon the face of the earth : Wherefore, let *Christiana* look out some damsels for her sons, to whom they may be betrothed, *&c.* that the name of their father, and the house of his progenitors may never be forgotten in the world.

Hon. 'Tis pity this family should fall and be extinct.

Gaius. Fall it cannot, but be diminished it may ; but let *Christiana* take my advice, and that's the way to uphold it.

And *Christiana*, said this Inn-keeper, I am glad to see thee and thy friend *Mercy* together here, a lovely couple. And may I advise, take *Mercy* into a nearer relation to thee : If she will, let her be given to *Matthew* thy eldest son ; 'tis the way to preserve you a posterity in the earth. So this match was concluded, and in process of time they were married : But more of that hereafter.

Gaius also proceeded, and said, I will now speak on the behalf of Women, to take away their re-

Gen. 3.

proach. For as Death and the Curse came into the world by a woman, so also did Life and Health :

Gal. 4.

God sent forth his Son, made of a woman. Yea,

Why women of old so much desired children.

to shew how much those that came after, did abhor the act of their Mother, this sex in the old Testament coveted children, if happily this or that woman might be the Mother of the Saviour of the World. I will say again, that when the Saviour was come, women rejoyced in him, before

Luke 2.

either man or angel. I read not, that ever any

man did give unto Christ so much as one groat,
but the women followed him, and ministered to chap. 8. 2, 3.
him of their substance. 'Twas a woman that chap. 7. 37,
washed his feet with tears, and a woman that John 11. 2.
anointed his body to the burial. They were chap. 12. 3.
women that wept when he was going to the Cross ; Mat. 27. 55,
and women that followed him from the cross, and 56, 61.
that sat by his sepulchre when he was buried :
They were women that were first with him at his Luke 24. 22,
Resurrection-morn ; and women that brought tid- 23.
ings first to his disciples, that he was risen from
the dead : Women therefore are highly favoured,
and shew by these things, that they are sharers
with us in the Grace of Life.

Now the cook sent up to signify that Supper *Supper ready.*
was almost ready, and sent one to lay the cloth,
the trenchers, and to set the salt and bread in
order.

Then said *Matthew*, The sight of this cloth, and
of this fore-runner of a supper, begetteth in me a
greater appetite to my food than I had before.

Gaius. So let all ministring doctrines *to* thee in *What to be*
this life, beget *in* thee a greater desire to sit at the *gathered from laying of the*
Supper of the great King in his Kingdom ; for all *Board with*
preaching, books and ordinances here, are but as *the Cloth and Trenchers.*
the laying of the trenchers, and as setting of salt
upon the board, when compared with the Feast
that our Lord will make for us when we come to
his House.

So Supper came up, and first a *heave-shoulder*, Levit. 7. 32,
and a *wave-breast* were set on the table before 33, 34. ch.
them ; to shew that they must begin their meal Psalm 25, 1.
with Prayer and Praise to God. The *heave-shoulder* Deut. 32. 14.

Judg. 9. 13.
John 15. 1.

David lifted his Heart up to God with, and with the *wave-breast, where his Heart lay*, with that he used to lean upon his harp, when he played. These two dishes were very fresh and good, and they all eat heartily-well thereof.

Deut. 32. 14.
Judg. 9. 13.
John 15. 1.

The next they brought up, was a bottle of wine, red as blood.   So *Gaius* said to them, Drink freely, this is the juice of the true Vine, that makes glad the heart of God and man.   So they drank and were merry.

1 Pet. 2. 1, 2.
A Dish of
Milk.

The next was a dish of milk well crumbed: But *Gaius* said, *Let the boys have that, that they may grow thereby.*

Of Honey
and Butter.

Then they brought up in course a dish of *butter* and *honey*.   Then said *Gaius*, Eat freely of *this*, for this is good to chear up, and strengthen your judgments and understandings ; this was our Lord's

Isa. 7. 15.

dish when he was a child : *Butter and honey shall he eat, that he may know to refuse the Evil, and choose the Good.*

A Dish of
Apples.

Then they brought them up a dish of apples, and they were very good tasted fruit.   Then said *Matthew*, may we eat apples, since they were such, by and with which, the Serpent beguiled our first Mother ?

Then said *Gaius*,

Apples were they with which we were beguiled,
Yet Sin, *not Apples, hath our Souls defiled ;*
Apples forbid, if eat, corrupt the blood :
To eat such, when commanded, does us good ;
Drink of his Flagons then, thou Church, his Dove,
And eat his Apples, who are sick of Love.

Then said Matthew, *I made the Scruple, because I a while since was sick with eating of fruit.*

Gaius. Forbidden fruit will make you sick, but not what our Lord has tolerated.

While they were thus talking, they were presented with another dish, and 'twas a dish of *Nuts.* Then said some at the table, *Nuts* spoil tender teeth, 'specially the teeth of the children: Which when *Gaius* heard, he said:

Song 6. 61. A Dish of Nuts.

> *Hard* Texts *are* Nuts, (*I will not call them* Cheaters)
> *Whose* Shells *do keep their* Kernels *from the* Eaters.
> *Ope then the shells, and you shall have the Meat,*
> *They here are brought, for you to crack and eat.*

Then were they very merry, and sat at the table a long time, talking of many things. Then said the old gentleman, My good landlord, while ye are here cracking your *Nuts*, if you please, do you open this Riddle.

> *A man there was, tho' some did count him mad,*
> *The more he cast away, the more he had.*

A Riddle put forth by Old Honest.

Then they all gave good heed, wondering what good *Gaius* would say; so he sat still a while, and then thus replyed:

> *He that bestows his Goods upon the Poor,*
> *Shall have as much again, and ten times more.*

Gaius *opens it.*

Then said *Joseph*, I dare say, Sir, I did not think you could ha' found it out.

Oh! said *Gaius*, I have been trained up in this way a great while: Nothing teaches like experience; I have learned of my Lord to be kind, and have found by experience, that I have gained

thereby. *There is that scattereth, yet increaseth; and there is that with-holdeth more than is meet, but it tendeth to Poverty: There is that maketh himself Rich, yet hath nothing; there is that maketh himself poor, yet hath great Riches.*

Then *Samuel* whispered to *Christiana* his mother, and said, Mother, this is a very good man's house, let us stay here a good while, and let my brother *Matthew* be married here to *Mercy*, before we go any further.

The which *Gaius* the host over-hearing, said, *With a very good will, my child.*

So they stayed there more than a month, and *Mercy* was given to *Matthew* to wife.

While they stayed here, *Mercy*, as her custom was, would be making coats and garments to give to the poor, by which she brought a very good report upon the Pilgrims.

But to return again to our Story: After supper, the lads desired a bed, for that they were weary with travelling: Then *Gaius* called to shew them their chamber; but said *Mercy*, I will have them to bed. So she had them to bed, and they slept well, but the rest sat up all night: For *Gaius* and they were such suitable company, that they could not tell how to part. Then after much talk of their Lord, themselves, and their Journey, old Mr.

Honest, he that put forth the riddle to *Gaius*, began to nod. Then said *Great-heart*, What, Sir, you begin to be drowsy; come, rub up, now here is a *Riddle* for you. Then said Mr. *Honest*, Let's hear it. *Old* Honest *nods.*

Then said Mr. *Great-heart*,

> *He that will kill, must first be overcome:* *A Riddle.*
> *Who live abroad would, first must die at home.*

Ha! said Mr. *Honest*, it is a hard one, hard to expound, and harder to practise. But, come, landlord, said he, I will, if you please, leave my part to you, do you expound it, and I will hear what you say.

No, said *Gaius*, 'twas put to you, and it is expected you should answer it.

Then said the old Gentleman,

> *He first by Grace must conquer'd be,* *The Riddle opened.*
> *That Sin would mortify:*
> *And who, that lives, would convince me,*
> *Unto himself must die.*

It is right, said *Gaius*, good Doctrine and Experience teaches this. For first, untill Grace displays itself, and overcomes the soul with its glory, it is altogether without heart to oppose Sin; besides, if Sin is Satan's cords, by which the soul lies bound, how should it make resistance, before it is loosed from that Infirmity?

Secondly, Nor will any, that knows either reason or Grace, believe that such a man can be a living monument of Grace, that is a slave to his own Corruptions.

A Question worth the minding.

And now it comes in my mind, I will tell you a story worth the hearing. There were two men that went on Pilgrimage, the one began when he was young, the other when he was old: The young man had strong corruptions to grapple with, the old man's were decayed with the decays of nature: The young man trod his steps as even as did the old one, and was every way as light as he: Who now, or which of them had their Graces shining clearest, since both seemed to be alike?

A Comparison.

Hon. The young man's, doubtless. For that which heads it against the greatest opposition, gives best demonstration that it is strongest; specially when it also holdeth pace with that that meets not with half so much; as to be sure old age does not.

A Mistake.

Besides, I have observed, that old men have blessed themselves with this mistake; namely, taking the decays of nature for a gracious conquest over corruptions, and so have been apt to beguile themselves. Indeed old men that are gracious, are best able to give Advice to them that are young, because they have seen most of the emptiness of things: But yet, for an old and a young to set out both together, the young one has the advantage of the fairest discovery of a work of Grace within him, though the old man's corruptions are naturally the weakest.

Thus they sat talking till break of day. Now when the family was up, *Christiana* bid her son *James* that he should read a chapter; so he read

53d of *Isaiah:* When he had done, Mr. *Honest* asked why it was said, *that the Saviour is said to come out of a dry ground, and also that he had no Form nor Comeliness in him.* *Another question.*

Great-heart. Then said Mr. *Great-heart;* To the first I answer; Because the Church of the *Jews,* of which Christ came, had then lost almost all the sap, and Spirit of religion. To the second I say, the words are spoken in the person of the Unbelievers, who because they want that Eye that can see into our Prince's heart, therefore they judge of him by the meanness of his outside.

Just like those, that know not that precious stones are covered over with a homely crust; who when they have found one, because they know not what they have found, cast it again away, as men do a common stone.

Well, said *Gaius,* now you are here, and since, as I know, Mr. *Great-heart* is good at his Weapons, if you please, after we have refreshed ourselves, we will walk into the fields, to see if we can do any good. About a mile from hence, there is one *Slay-good,* a giant, that doth much annoy the King's High-way in these parts: And I know whereabout his haunt is, he is master of a number of thieves; 'Twould be well if we could clear these parts of him. *Giant* Slay-good *assaulted and slain.*

So they consented and went, Mr. *Great-heart* with his *Sword, Helmet,* and *Shield;* and the rest with Spears and Staves.

When they came to the place where he was, they found him with one *Feeble-mind* in his hands, whom his servants had brought unto him, *He is found with one* Feeble-mind *in his hand.*

having taken him in the Way; now the *Giant* was rifling him, with a purpose, after that, to pick his bones; for he was of the nature of *Flesh-eaters.*

Well, so soon as he saw Mr. *Great-heart* and his friends at the mouth of his Cave, with their Weapons, he demanded what they wanted.

Great-heart. We want thee; for we are come to revenge the Quarrel of the many that thou hast slain of the Pilgrims, when thou hast dragged them out of the King's High-way; wherefore come out of thy Cave. So he armed himself and came out, and to a battle they went, and fought for above an hour, and then stood still to take wind.

Slay. Then said the Giant, Why are you here on my ground?

Great-heart. To revenge the blood of Pilgrims, as I also told thee before; so they went to it again, and the giant made Mr. *Great-heart* give back; but he came up again, and in the greatness of his mind he let fly with such stoutness at the giant's head and sides, that he made him let his weapon fall out of his hand; so he smote him, and slew him, and cut off his Head, and brought it away to the *Inn.* He also took *Feeble-mind* the Pilgrim, and brought him with him to his lodgings. When they were come home, they shewed his head to the Family, and set it up as they had done others before, for a terror to those that shall attempt to do as he, hereafter.

Feeble-mind rescued from the Giant.

Then they asked Mr. *Feeble-mind,* how he fell into his hands?

Feeble-mind. Then said the poor man, I am a *How* Feeble- sickly man, as you see, and because *Death* did mind *came to be a Pilgrim.* usually once a day *knock at my door,* I thought I should never be well at home: So I betook my-self to a Pilgrim's life; and have travelled hither from the town of *Uncertain,* where I and my fa-ther were born. I am a man of no strength at all of body, nor yet of mind, but would, if I could, though I can but *crawl,* spend my life in the Pilgrim's Way. When I came at the Gate that is at the head of the Way, the Lord of that place did entertain me freely; neither objected he against my weakly looks, nor against my *feeble mind;* but gave me such things that were neces-sary for my Journey, and bid me hope to the end. When I came to the House of the *Interpreter,* I received much kindness there; and because the Hill of *Difficulty* was judged too hard for me, I was carried up that by one of his Servants. Indeed I have found much relief from Pilgrims, though none was willing to go so softly as I am forced to do: Yet still as they came on, they bid me be of good cheer, and said, that it was the will of their Lord, that comfort should be given to the *feeble-* 1 Thes. 5. 4. *minded,* and so went on their *own* pace. When I was come to *Assault-Lane,* then this Giant met with me, and bid me prepare for an *Encounter:* But alas! feeble one that I was, I had more need of a *Cordial:* So he came up and took me: I con-ceited he should not kill me; also when he had got me into his Den, since I went not with him *willingly,* I believed I should come out alive again: For I have heard, that not any Pilgrim that is taken *Mark this.*

captive by violent hands, if he keeps heart-whole towards his Master, is, by the Laws of Providence, to die by the hand of the Enemy. *Robbed* I look'd to be, and robbed to be sure I am ; but I am as you see escaped with life, for the which I thank my King as Author, and you as the means. Other brunts I also look for, but this I have resolved on, to wit, to *run* when I can, to *go* when I cannot run, and to *creep* when I cannot go. As to

Mark this. the main, I thank him that loves me, I am fixed ; my Way is before me, my mind is beyond the River that has no bridge, tho' I am, as you see, but of a *feeble mind.*

Hon. Then said old Mr. *Honest*, Have not you some time ago, been acquainted with one Mr. *Fearing* a Pilgrim.

Mr. Fearing *Mr.* Feeble-mind's *Uncle.*

Feeble. Acquainted with him, Yes ; he came from the town of *Stupidity*, which lieth four degrees *Northward* of the City of *Destruction*, and as many off, of where I was born ; yet we were well acquainted, for indeed he **was** mine uncle, my father's brother ; he and I have been much of a temper, he was a little shorter than I, but yet we were much of a complexion.

Feeble-mind *has some of* Mr. Fearing's *features.*

Hon. I perceive you know him, and I am apt to believe also, that you were related one to another ; for you have his whitely look, a cast like his with your eye, and your speech is much alike.

Feeble. Most have said so, that have known us both ; and besides, what I have read in him, I have for the most part found in myself.

Gaius *comforts him.*

Gaius. Come, Sir, said good *Gaius*, be of good cheer, you are welcome to me, and to my house, and what thou hast a mind to, call for freely ; and what thou would'st have my servants do for thee, they will do it with a ready mind.

Then said Mr. *Feeble-mind*, This is an unex- *Notice to be taken of Pro-vidence.* pected favour, and as the Sun shining out of a very dark cloud : Did Giant *Slay-good* intend me this Favour when he stopped me, and resolved to let me go no further ? Did he intend, that after he had rifled my pocket, I should go to *Gaius* mine host ! Yet so it is.

Now, just as Mr. *Feeble-mind* and *Gaius* were *Tidings how one Not-right was slain by a thunder-bolt, and Mr.* Fee-ble-mind's *comment upon it.* thus in talk, there comes one running, and called at the door, and told, that about a mile and a half off, there was one Mr. *Not-right* a Pilgrim struck dead upon the place where he was, with a *Thunder-bolt.*

Feeble. Alas! said Mr. *Feeble-mind*, is he slain ? He overtook me some days before I came so far as hither, and would be my company-keeper : He also was with me when *Slay-good* the Giant took me, but he was nimble of his heels, and escaped : But it seems, he escaped to Die, and I was took to Live.

What, one would think, doth seek to slay outright,
Oft-times delivers from the saddest plight.
That very Providence, *whose Face is Death,*
Doth oft-times to the lowly, Life bequeath :
I was taken, he did escape and flee ;
Hands crost, give Death to him, and Life to me.

Now about this time, *Matthew* and *Mercy* were married ; also *Gaius* gave his daughter *Phebe* to

James, Matthew's brother, to wife; after which time, they yet staid above ten days at *Gaius's* house; spending their time, and the Seasons, like as Pilgrims use to do.

The Pilgrims prepare to go forward. When they were to depart, *Gaius* made them a feast, and they did eat and drink, and were merry. Now the hour was come that they must be gone; wherefore Mr. *Great-heart* called for a reckoning. But *Gaius* told him, that at his house it was not the custom for Pilgrims to pay for their entertainment. He boarded them by the year, but

Luke 10. 33, 34, 35. *How they greet one another at parting.* looked for his pay from the good *Samaritan*, who had promised him, at his return, whatsoever charge he was at with them, faithfully to repay him. Then said Mr. *Great-heart* to him,

3 John 5. 6. *Great-heart.* Beloved, thou dost faithfully, whatsoever thou dost, to the Brethren and to Strangers, which have borne witness of thy Charity before the Church, whom if thou (yet) bring forward on their Journey, after a Godly sort, thou shalt do well.

Gaius's last kindness to Feeble-mind. Then *Gaius* took his leave of them all, and of his children, and particularly of Mr. *Feeble-mind.* He also gave him something to drink by the Way.

Now Mr. *Feeble-mind*, when they were going out of the door, made as if he intended to linger. The which when Mr. *Great-heart* espied, he said, Come, Mr. *Feeble-mind*, pray do you go along with us, I will be your conductor, and you shall fare as the rest.

Feeble-mind *for going behind.* *Feeble.* Alas! I want a suitable companion; you are all lusty and strong, but I, as you see, am weak; I choose therefore rather to come behind, lest by reason of my many Infirmities, I should be both a burden to myself and to you. I am, as I said, a man of a weak and a feeble mind, and shall be offended and made weak at that which others can bear. I shall like no Laughing : I shall like no gay Attire : I shall like no unprofitable Questions. Nay, I am so weak a man, as to *His Excuse* be offended with that which others have a liberty *for it.* to do. I do not know all the truth : I am a very ignorant *Christian man :* Sometimes, if I hear some rejoice in the Lord, it troubles me, because I cannot do so too. It is with me, as it is with a weak man among the strong, or as with a sick man among the Job 12. 5. healthy, or as a lamp despised, (he that is ready to slip with his feet, is as a lamp despised in the thought of him that is at ease :) so that I know not what to do.

Great-heart. But brother, said Mr. *Great-heart*, Great-heart's I have it in Commission to comfort the *feeble-* commission. *minded,* and to support the weak. You must needs Rom. 14. go along with us ; we will wait for you, we will chap. 9. 22. lend you our help ; we will deny ourselves of some things both *Opinionative* and *Practical,* for your *A Christian* sake : We will not enter into doubtful disputations *spirit.* before you ; we will be made all things to you, rather than you shall be left behind.

I Thes. 5. 15.
I Cor. 8.

Now all this while they were at *Gaius's* door ; and behold, as they were thus in the heat of their discourse, Mr. *Ready-to-halt* came by, with his Psalm 38. 17. *Crutches* in his hand, and he also was going on *Promises.* Pilgrimage.

Feeble. Then said Mr. *Feeble-mind* to him, Man ! How camest thou hither ? I was but just now complaining that I had not a suitable companion, but thou art according to my wish. Welcome, welcome, good Mr. *Ready-to-halt*, I hope thee and I may be some help.

Feeble-mind
glad to see
Ready-to-
halt *come by.*

Ready-to-halt. I shall be glad of thy company, said the other ; and good Mr. *Feeble-mind*, rather than we will part, since we are thus happily met, I will lend thee one of my crutches.

Feeble. Nay, said he, though I thank thee for thy good-will, I am not inclined to halt afore I am lame. Howbeit, I think, when occasion is, it may help me against a dog.

Ready-to-halt. If either myself, or my crutches can do thee a pleasure, we are both at thy command, good Mr. *Feeble-mind.*

Thus therefore they went on ; Mr. *Great-heart* and Mr. *Honest* went before, *Christiana* and her children went next, and Mr. *Feeble-mind* and Mr. *Ready-to-halt* came behind with his crutches. Then said Mr. *Honest*,

New talk.

Hon. Pray, Sir, now we are upon the Road, tell us some profitable things of some that have gone on Pilgrimage before us.

Part I. *pp.*
58, 64, 74-
80.

Great-heart. With a good will : I suppose you have heard how *Christian* of old did meet with *Apollyon* in the Valley of *Humiliation*, and also what hard work he had to go through the Valley of the *Shadow of Death.* Also I think you cannot but have heard how *Faithful* was put to it with Madam *Wanton*, with *Adam* the First, with one *Discontent* and *Shame;* four as deceitful villains, as a man can meet with upon the Road.

Hon. Yes, I have heard of all this ; but indeed

good *Faithful* was hardest put to it with *Shame*, he was an unwearied one.

Great-heart. Ay, for as the Pilgrim well said, he of all men had the wrong name.

Hon. But pray, Sir, where was it that *Christian* and *Faithful* met *Talkative?* That same was also a notable one.

Great-heart. He was a confident Fool, yet many follow his ways.

Hon. He had like to ha' beguiled *Faithful.*

Great-heart. Ay, but *Christian* put him into a way quickly to find him out. Thus they went on till they came at the place where *Evangelist* met with *Christian* and *Faithful*, and prophesied to them what should befall them at *Vanity-Fair.* *Part* I. *p.* 95.

Great-heart. Then said their guide, Hereabouts did *Christian* and *Faithful* meet with *Evangelist*, who prophesied to them of what troubles they should meet with at *Vanity-Fair.*

Hon. Say you so! I dare say it was a hard chapter that then he did read unto them.

Great-heart. 'Twas so, but he gave them en- couragement withal. But what do we talk of them, they were a couple of lion-like men; they had set their faces like flints. Don't you remember how undaunted they were when they stood before the Judge? *Part* I. *p.* 103.

Hon. Well, *Faithful* bravely suffered.

Great-heart. So he did, and as brave things came on't; for *Hopeful* and some others, as the story relates it, were converted by his death.

Hon. Well, but pray go on; for you are well acquainted with things.

Great-heart. Above all that *Christian* met with after he had passed through *Vanity-Fair,* one *By-Ends* was the arch one.

Part I. *p.* 110.

Hon. By-Ends, what was he?

Great-heart. A very arch fellow, a down-right Hypocrite; one that would be religious which way ever the world went; but so cunning, that he would be sure neither to lose nor suffer for it.

He had his *mode* of religion for every fresh occasion, and his wife was as good at it as he. He would turn and change from opinion to opinion; yea, and plead for so doing too. But so far as I could learn, he came to an ill end with his *By-Ends;* nor did I ever hear that any of his children were ever of any esteem with any that truly feared God.

They come within sight of Vanity-Fair. [Ps. 21. 16.? 1st edit.]

Now by this time they were come within sight of the town of *Vanity,* where *Vanity-Fair* is kept. So when they saw that they were so near the town, they consulted with one another how they should pass through the town, and some said one thing, and some another. At last Mr. *Great-heart* said, I have, as you may understand, often been a Conductor of Pilgrims through this town; now I am acquainted with one Mr. *Mnason* a *Cyprusian* by nation, an old disciple, at whose house we may lodge. If you think good, said he, we will turn in there?

They enter into one Mr. Mnason's *to lodge.*

Content, said Old *Honest;* content, said *Christiana;* content, said Mr. *Feeble-mind;* and so they said all. Now, you must think, it was even-tide by that they got to the outside of the town; but Mr. *Great-heart* knew the way to the old man's

house. So thither they came; and he called at
the door, and the old man within knew his tongue
so soon as ever he heard it; so he opened, and they
all came in. Then said *Mnason*, their host, How
far have ye come to-day? So they said, from the
house of *Gaius* our friend. I promise you, said he,
you have gone a good stitch, you may well be a
weary; sit down. So they sat down.

Great-heart. Then said their Guide, Come,
what cheer, Sirs, I dare say you are welcome to
my friend.

Mnason. I also, said Mr. *Mnason*, do bid you
welcome; and whatever you want, do but say, and *They are glad of entertainment.*
we will do what we can to get it for you.

Honest. Our great want, a while since, was
Harbour and good Company, and now I hope we
have both.

Mnason. For harbour, you see what it is; but
for good company, that will appear in the trial.

Great-heart. Well, said Mr. *Great-heart*, will you
have the Pilgrims up into their lodging?

Mnason. I will, said Mr. *Mnason*. So he had
them to their respective places; and also shewed
them a very fair dining-room, where they might
be, and sup together until time was come to go to
rest.

Now when they were set in their places, and
were a little cheary after their Journey, Mr. *Honest*
asked his landlord, if there were any store of good
people in the town?

Mnason. We have a few, for indeed they are
but a few when compared with them on the other
side.

Honest. But how shall we do to see some of them? For the sight of good men to them that are going on Pilgrimage, is like to the appearing of the Moon and Stars to them that are sailing upon the Seas.

Mnason. Then Mr. *Mnason* stamped with his foot, and his daughter *Grace* came up: So he said unto her, *Grace*, go you, tell my friends, Mr. *Contrite*, Mr. *Holy-man*, Mr. *Love-saint*, Mr. *Dare-not-lie*, and Mr. *Penitent*, that I have a friend or two at my house that have a mind this evening to see them.

So *Grace* went to call them, and they came; and after salutation made, they sat down together at the table.

Then said Mr. *Mnason*, their landlord, My neighbours, I have, as you see, a company of *Strangers* come to my house; they are *Pilgrims:* They come from afar, and are going to Mount *Sion.* But who, quoth he, do you think this is? pointing with his finger to *Christiana:* It is *Christiana*, the wife of *Christian*, that famous Pilgrim, who with *Faithful* his brother, were so shamefully handled in our town. At that they stood amazed, saying, We little thought to see *Christiana*, when *Grace* came to call us, wherefore this is a very comfortable surprize. Then they asked her of her welfare, and if these young men were her husband's sons. And when she had told them they were; they said, the King whom you love and serve, make you as your father, and bring you where he is in peace.

Hon. Then Mr. *Honest* (when they were all sat

down) asked Mr. *Contrite* and the rest, in what *Some talk be-* posture their town was at present. *twixt Mr. Honest and*

Contrite. You may be sure we are full of hurry *Mr. Contrite.* in Fair-time. 'Tis hard keeping our hearts and *The fruit of* spirits in any good order, when we are in a cum- *Watchful- ness.* bered condition. He that lives in such a place as this is, and that has to do with such as we have, has need of an *Item* to caution him to take heed every moment of the day.

Honest. But how are your neighbours now for quietness ?

Contrite. They are much more moderate now *Persecution* than formerly. You know how *Christian* and *not so hot at Vanity-Fair* *Faithful* were used at our town : But of late, I say, *as formerly.* they have been far more moderate. I think the blood of *Faithful* lieth with load upon them till now ; for since they burned him, they have been ashamed to burn any more ; in those days we were afraid to walk the streets, but now we can shew our heads. *Then* the name of a professor was odious; *now*, specially in some parts of our town, (for you know our town is large) Religion is counted honourable.

Then said Mr. *Contrite* to them, Pray how fareth it with you in your Pilgrimage ? How stands the country affected towards you ?

Hon. It happens to us, as it happeneth to way-faring men ; sometimes our Way is clean, some-times foul ; sometimes up hill, sometimes down hill ; we are seldom at a certainty : The wind is not always on our backs, nor is every one a Friend that we meet with in the Way. We have met with some notable rubs already ; and what are yet behind we know not; but for the most part we find it true, that has been talked of of old : *A good man must suffer trouble.*

Contrite. You talk of rubs, what rubs have you met withal?

Hon. Nay, ask Mr. *Great-heart*, our Guide, for he can give the best account of that.

Great-heart. We have been beset three or four times already: First, *Christiana* and her children were beset with two ruffians, that they feared would take away their lives. We were beset with giant *Bloody-man*, giant *Maul*, and giant *Slay-good:* Indeed we did rather beset the last, than were beset of him ; and thus it was : After we had been some time at the house of *Gaius, mine host, and of the whole Church*, we were minded upon a time to take our weapons with us, and so go see if we could light upon any of those that were Enemies to *Pilgrims;* (for we heard that there was a notable one thereabouts.) Now *Gaius* knew his *haunt* better than I, because he dwelt thereabout ; so we looked and looked, till at last we discerned the mouth of his Cave ; then were we glad, and pluck-ed up our spirits. So we approached up to his den, and lo, when we came there, he had dragged, by mere force, into his net, this poor man, Mr. *Feeble-mind*, and was about to bring him to his end. But when he saw us, supposing, as we thought, he had had another prey ; he left the poor man in his hole, and came out. So we fell to it full sore, and he lustily laid about him ; but, in conclusion, he was brought down to the ground, and his head cut off, and set up by the Way-side, for a Terror to such as should after practise such Ungodliness. That I tell you the truth, here is the man himself to affirm it, who was as a lamb taken out of the mouth of the lion.

Feeble-mind. Then said Mr. *Feeble-mind,* I found this true, to my cost and comfort; to my cost, when he threaten'd to pick my bones every moment; and to my comfort, when I saw Mr. *Great-heart* and his friends, with their weapons, approach so near for my deliverance.

Holy-man. Then said Mr. *Holy-man,* there are two things that they have need to be possessed with that go on Pilgrimage, *Courage,* and an *Unspotted Life.* If they have not courage, they can never hold on their Way; and if their lives be loose, they will make the very name of a *Pilgrim* stink. *Mr. Holyman's speech.*

Love-saint. Then said Mr. *Love-saint;* I hope this caution is not needful amongst you. But truly there are many that go upon the road, that rather declare themselves Strangers to Pilgrimage, than *Strangers and Pilgrims in the Earth.* *Mr. Lovesaint's speech.*

Dare-not-lie. Then said Mr. *Dare-not-lie,* It is true, they neither have the Pilgrim's *weed,* nor the Pilgrim's *Courage;* they go not uprightly, but all *awry* with their feet; one shoe goeth *inward,* another *outward,* and their hosen out behind; here a rag, and there a rent, to the disparagement of their Lord. *Mr. Darenot-lie his speech.*

Penitent. These things, said Mr. *Penitent,* they ought to be troubled for; nor are the Pilgrims like to have that Grace upon them and their *Pilgrims Progress,* as they desire, untill the Way is clear'd of such spots and blemishes. *Mr. Penitent his speech.*

Thus they sat talking and spending the time, untill supper was set upon the table. Unto which they went, and refreshed their weary bodies; so they went to rest. Now they staid in the Fair a great while, at the house of Mr. *Mnason*, who, in process of time, gave his daughter *Grace* unto *Samuel*, *Christian's* son, to wife, and his daughter *Martha* to *Joseph*.

The time, as I said, that they lay here, was long, (for it was not now as in former times.) Wherefore the Pilgrims grew acquainted with many of the good People of the town, and did them what service they could. *Mercy*, as she was wont, laboured much for the Poor, (wherefore their bellies and backs blessed her,) and she was there an ornament to her profession. And, to say the truth for *Grace*, *Phebe*, and *Martha*, they were all of a very good nature, and did much good in their places. They were also all of them very fruitful, so that *Christian's* name, as was said before, was like to live in the world.

A Monster.

While they lay here, there came a *Monster* out of the *woods*, and slew many of the people of the town. It would also carry away their children, and teach them to suck its whelps. Now no man in the town durst so much as face this *Monster;* but all men fled when they heard of the noise of his coming.

Rev. 17. 3.
His Shape.
His Nature.

The *Monster* was like unto no one beast upon the earth: Its body was like a Dragon, and it had seven heads and ten horns. *It made great havock of children, and yet it was governed by a woman.* This *Monster* propounded conditions to men; and

such men as loved their Lives more than their
Souls, accepted of those conditions. So they came
under.

Now this Mr. *Great-heart*, together with these
that came to visit the Pilgrims at Mr. *Mnason's*
house, enter'd into a covenant to go and engage
this beast, if perhaps they might deliver the people
of this town from the paw and mouths of this so
devouring a Serpent.

Then did Mr. *Great-heart*, Mr. *Contrite*, Mr.
Holy-man, Mr. *Dare-not-lie*, and Mr. *Penitent*,
with their weapons, go forth to meet him. Now *How he is en-*
the *Monster* at first was very rampant, and looked *gaged.*
upon these enemies with great disdain; but they
so belabour'd him, being sturdy men at arms, that
they made him make a retreat: So they came
home to Mr. *Mnason's* house again.

The *Monster*, you must know, had his certain
Seasons to come out in, and to make his attempts
upon the children of the people of the town: Also
these seasons did these valiant Worthies watch him
in, and did continually assault him; insomuch, that
in process of time he became not only wounded,
but lame; also he had not made the havock of the
townsmen's children, as formerly he has done.
And it is verily believed by some, that this beast
will certainly die of his wounds.

This therefore made Mr. *Great-heart* and his
fellows of great Fame in this town; so that many
of the people that wanted their taste of things, yet
had a reverend esteem and respect for them. Upon
this account therefore it was, that these Pilgrims
got not much hurt here. True, there were some

of the baser sort, that could see no more than a
mole, nor understand more than a beast; these
had no reverence for these men, nor took they
notice of their valour and adventures.

Well, the time grew on that the Pilgrims must
go on their Way, wherefore they prepared for
their Journey.   They sent for their friends, they
conferred with them, they had some time set
apart therein to commit each other to the Protection of their Prince.   There were again, that
brought them of such things as they had, that
were fit for the weak and the strong, for the
Acts 28. 10.   women and the men, and so laded them with such
things as were necessary.

Then they set forwards on their Way, and their
friends accompanying them so far as was convenient, they again committed each other to the
protection of their King, and departed.

They therefore that were of the Pilgrims company, went on, and Mr. *Great-heart* went before
them ; now the women and children being weakly,
they were forced to go as they could bear; by this
means Mr. *Ready-to-halt* and Mr. *Feeble-mind* had
more to sympathize with their condition.

When they were gone from the townsmen, and
when their friends had bid them farewel, they
quickly came to the place where *Faithful* was
put to death : Therefore they made a stand, and
thanked him that had enabled him to bear his
Cross so well; and the rather, because they now
found that they had a benefit by such a manly
Suffering as his was.

They went on therefore after this, a good way

further, talking of *Christian* and *Faithful*, and how *Hopeful* joined himself to *Christian*, after that *Faithful* was dead.

Now, they were come up with the hill *Lucre*, *Part* I. *p.* 120. where the *Silver-Mine* was, which took *Demas* off from his Pilgrimage, and into which, as some think, *By-ends* fell and perished; wherefore they considered that. But when they were come to the old Monument that stood over-against the hill *Lucre*, to wit, to the Pillar of Salt, that stood also within view of *Sodom*, and its stinking lake; they marvelled, as did *Christian* before, that men of that knowledge and ripeness of wit as they were, should be so blinded as to turn aside here. Only they considered again, that nature is not affected with the harms that others have met with, specially if that thing, upon which they look, has an attracting virtue upon the foolish eye.

I saw now that they went on till they came at the River that was on this side of the Delectable *Part* I. *page* 124. Mountains.

To the River where the fine Trees grow on both sides; and whose leaves, if taken inwardly, are good against surfeits, where the meadows are green Psalm 23. all the year long, and where they might lie down safely.

By this River side, in the meadow, there were cotes and folds for sheep, a house built for the nourishing and bringing up of those lambs, the babes of those women that go on ·Pilgrimage. Also Heb. 5. 2. Isa. 40. 11. there was here One that was entrusted with them, who could have compassion, and that could gather these lambs with his arm, and carry them in his bosom, and that could gently lead those that were with young. Now to the care of *this Man, Christiana* admonished her four Daughters to commit their little ones, that by these waters they might be housed, harboured, succoured, and nourished, and that none of them might *be lacking in time to come.* This man, if any of them go astray, or be lost, he will bring them again; he will also bind up that which was broken, and will strengthen them that are sick. Here they will never want meat and drink and cloathing; here they will be kept from thieves and robbers; for this man will die before one of those committed to his Trust shall be lost. Besides, here they shall be sure to have good *nurture* and *admonition*, and shall be taught to walk in right Paths, and that you know is a Favour of no small account. Also here, as you see, are delicate *waters*, pleasant *meadows*, dainty *flowers*, variety of *trees*, and such as bear wholsome *fruit;* fruit not like that that *Matthew* eat of, that fell over the wall, out of *Beelzebub's* garden; but fruit that procureth Health where there is none, and that continueth and increaseth where it is.

So they were content to commit their little ones to him; and that which was also an encouragement to them so to do, was, for that all this was to be at the charge of the King, and so was an Hospital to young children and *orphans*.

Now they went on; and when they were come to *By-Path* meadow, to the stile over which *Christian* went with his fellow *Hopeful*, when they were taken by Giant *Despair*, and put into *Doubting*

Jer. 23. 4.
Ex. 34. 11,
12, 13, 14,
15, 16.

John 10. 16.

*They being
come to By-
Path stile,
have a mind
to have a
pluck with*

Castle; they sat down, and consulted what was *Giant* Despair. *Part* I. *p.* 125-135.
best to be done; to wit, now they were so strong,
and had got such a man as Mr. *Great-heart* for
their conductor, whether they had not best to
make an attempt upon the Giant, demolish his
Castle, and if there were any Pilgrims in it, to set
them at liberty, before they went any further. So
one said one thing, and another said the contrary.
One questioned, if it was lawful to go upon *un-
consecrated* ground; another said they might, provided their end was good; but Mr. *Great-heart*
said, though that assertion offered last, cannot be
universally true, yet I have a commandment to resist Sin, to overcome Evil, to fight the good fight
of Faith: And I pray, with whom should I fight
this good fight, if not with Giant *Despair?* I will
therefore attempt the taking away of his life, and
the demolishing of *Doubting Castle.* Then, said
he, who will go with me? Then said old *Honest*,
I will; and so will we too, said *Christian's* four
sons, *Matthew, Samuel, James,* and *Joseph,* for they 1 John 2. 13, 14.
were young men and strong.

So they left the women in the Road, and with
them Mr. *Feeble-mind* and Mr. *Ready-to-halt,* with
his crutches, to be their guard, until they came
back; for in that place the Giant *Despair* dwelt
so near, they keeping in the Road, *a little child* Isa. 11. 6.
might lead them.

So Mr. *Great-heart,* old *Honest,* and the four
young men, went to go up to *Doubting-Castle,* to
look for Giant *Despair.* When they came at the
Castle-Gate, they knocked for entrance with an
unusual noise. At that the old Giant comes to

the gate, and *Diffidence* his wife follows: Then
said he, Who and what is he, that is so hardy, as
after this manner to molest the Giant *Despair?*
Mr. *Great-heart* replyed, It is I, *Great-heart*, one
of the King of the Cœlestial Country's conductors
of Pilgrims to their place: And I demand of thee,
that thou open thy gates for my entrance; prepare
thyself also to fight, for I am come to take away
thy head, and to demolish *Doubting-Castle.*

Now Giant *Despair*, because he was a Giant,
thought no man could overcome him; and again,

Despair *has*
overcome
Angels.

thought he, since heretofore I have made a conquest of Angels, shall *Great-heart* make me afraid?
So he harnessed himself, and went out: He had
a cap of steel upon his head, a breast-plate of fire
girded to him, and he came out in iron shoes, with
a great club in his hand. Then these six men made
up to him, and beset him behind and before: Also
when *Diffidence* the Giantess came up to help him,
old Mr. *Honest* cut her down at one blow. Then
they fought for their lives, and Giant *Despair* was

Despair *is*
loth to die.

brought down to the ground, *but was very loth to*
die: He struggled hard, and had, as they say, as
many lives as a cat; but *Great-heart* was his death,
for he left him not till he had severed his head
from his shoulders.

Doubting-
Castle *demo-*
lished.

Then they fell to demolishing *Doubting-Castle*,
and that you know might with ease be done, since
Giant *Despair* was dead. They were seven days
in destroying of that, and in it of Pilgrims they
found one Mr. *Despondency*, almost starved to
death, and one *Much-afraid* his daughter; these two
they saved alive. But it would ha' made you ha'

wondered, to have seen the dead bodies that lay here and there in the castle-yard, and how full of dead men's bones the dungeon was.

When Mr. *Great-heart* and his companions had performed this exploit, they took Mr. *Despondency*, and his daughter *Much-afraid* into their protection, for they were honest people, though they were prisoners in *Doubting-Castle* to that tyrant Giant *Despair*. They therefore, I say, took with them the head of the Giant, (for his body they had buried under a heap of stones) and down to the road, and to their companions they came, and shewed them what they had done. Now when *Feeble-mind* and *Ready-to-halt* saw that it was the head of Giant *Despair* indeed, they were very jocund and merry. Now *Christiana*, if need was, could play upon the *viol*, and her daughter *Mercy* upon the *lute:* So since they were so merry disposed, she played them a lesson, and *Ready-to-halt* would dance. So he *They have* took *Despondency's* daughter *Much-afraid* by the *musick and dancing for* hand, and to dancing they went in the road. True, *joy.* he could not dance without one crutch in his hand; but I promise you, he footed it well; also the girl was to be commended, for she answered the musick handsomely.

As for Mr. *Despondency*, the musick was not much to him, he was for feeding rather than dancing, for that he was almost starved. So *Christiana* gave him some of her bottle of Spirits, for present relief, and then prepared him something to eat, and in little time the old gentleman came to himself, and began to be finely revived.

Now I saw in my dream, when all these things

were finished, Mr. *Great-heart* took the head of Giant *Despair*, and set it upon a pole by the Highway-side, right over against the Pillar that *Christian* erected for a *caution* to Pilgrims that came after, to take heed of entring into his grounds.

Then he writ under it upon a marble-stone, these verses following :

> *This is the* Head *of him, whose* Name *only*
> *In former times did Pilgrims terrify.*
> *His Castle's down, and* Diffidence *his wife*
> *Brave Master* Great-heart *has bereft of life.*
> Despondency, *his daughter* Much-afraid,
> Great-heart, *for them also the Man has play'd.*
> *Who hereof doubts, if he'll but cast his eye,*
> *Up hither, may his scruples satisfy.*
> *This head also, when doubting cripples dance,*
> *Doth shew from Fears they have Deliverance.*

When these men had thus bravely shewed themselves against *Doubting Castle*, and had slain Giant *Despair*, they went forward, and went on till they came to the *Delectable* mountains, where *Christian* and *Hopeful* refreshed themselves with the varieties of the place. They also acquainted themselves with the Shepherds there, who welcomed them, as they had done *Christian* before, unto the *Delectable* mountains.

> *Though* Doubting-Castle *be demolished,*
> *And the Giant* Despair *hath lost his head,*
> Sin *can rebuild the Castle, make't remain,*
> *And make* Despair *the Giant live again.*

Now the Shepherds seeing so great a train follow Mr. *Great-heart*, (for with him they were well acquainted ;) they said unto him, Good sir, you have got a goodly company here ; pray where did you find all these ? Then Mr. *Great-heart* replyed,

The Guide's Speech to the Shepherds.

First, here's Christiana *and her train,*
Her Sons, and her Sons wives, who, like the wain,
Keep by the Pole, and do by Compass steer,
From Sin to Grace, else they had not been here :
Next here's old Honest *come on Pilgrimage,*
Ready-to-halt *too, who I dare engage,*
True hearted is, and so is Feeble-mind,
Who willing was, not to be left behind.
Despondency, *good man, is coming after,*
And so also is Much-afraid *his daughter,*
May we have entertainment here, or must
We further go ? Let's know whereon to trust ?

Then said the Shepherds ; This is a comfortable Company ; you are welcome to us, for we have for the *feeble*, as for the *strong;* our Prince has an eye to what is done to the least of these. Therefore Infirmity must not be a block to our entertainment. So they had them to the Palace door, and then said unto them, Come in Mr. *Feeble-mind,* come in Mr. *Ready-to-halt,* come in Mr. *Despondency*, and Mrs. *Much-afraid,* his daughter. These, Mr. *Great-heart,* said the Shepherds to the Guide, we call in by name, for that they are most subject to draw back ; but as for you, and the rest that are *strong,* we leave you to your wonted liberty. Then said Mr. *Great-heart,* This day I see that Grace

Their entertainment.

Mat. 25. 40.

doth shine in your faces, and that you are my Lord's Shepherds indeed; for that you have not *pushed* these diseased neither with side nor shoulder, but have rather strewed their way into the Palace with flowers, as you should.

A description of false Shepherds.
Ezek. 34. 21.

So the feeble and weak went in, and Mr. *Great-heart* and the rest did follow. When they were also set down, the Shepherds said to those of the weakest sort, What is it that you would have? For, said they, all things must be managed here to the supporting of the weak, as well as the warning of the unruly.

So they made them a feast of things easy of digestion, and that were pleasant to the palate, and nourishing: The which when they had received, they went to their rest, each one respectively unto his proper place. When morning was come, because the mountains were high, and the day clear; and because it was the custom of the Shepherds to shew to the Pilgrims, before their departure, some rarities; therefore, after they were ready, and had refreshed themselves, the Shepherds took them out into the fields, and shewed them first what they had shewed to *Christian* before.

Then they had them to some new places. The first was *Mount-Marvel*, where they looked, and behold a man at a distance, *that tumbled the hills about with words.* Then they asked the Shepherds what that should mean? So they told them, that that man was the son of one Mr. *Great-grace,* of whom you read in the First Part of the records of the *Pilgrim's Progress.* And he is set there to teach Pilgrims how to believe down, or to tumble

Mount Marvel.

Part I. *p.* 135.

Mark 11. 23, 24.

out of their ways, what difficulties they should meet with; by Faith. Then said Mr. *Great-heart*, I know him, he is a man above many.

Then they had them to another place, called *Mount Innocent;* and there they saw a man *Mount Inno-* cloathed all in white; and two men, *Prejudice* and *cent.* *Ill-will*, continually casting dirt upon him. Now behold the dirt, whatsoever they cast at him, would in little time fall off again, and his garment would look as clear as if no dirt had been cast thereat.

Then said the Pilgrims, What means this? The Shepherds answered; this man is named *Godly-man*, and the garment is to shew the innocency of his life. Now those that throw dirt at him, are such as hate his *well-doing;* but, as you see, the dirt will not stick upon his cloaths, so it shall be with him that liveth truly innocently in the world. Whoever they be that would make such men dirty, they labour all in vain; for God, by that a little time is spent, will cause that their *Innocence* shall break forth as the light, and their *righteousness* as the noon-day.

Then they took them, and had them to *Mount* *Mount Cha-* *Charity*, where they shewed them a man that had *rity.* a bundle of cloth lying before him, out of which he cut coats and garments for the poor that stood about him; yet his bundle, or roll of cloth, was never the less.

Then said they, What should this be? This is, said the Shepherds, to shew you, that he that has a heart to give of his labour to the poor, shall never want where-withal. He that watereth, shall be watered himself. And the cake that the widow gave to the prophet, did not cause that she had ever the less in her barrel.

The Work of one Fool, *and one* Want-wit. They had them also to a place, where they saw one *Fool*, and one *Want-wit*, washing of an *Ethiopian*, with intention to make him white; but the more they washed him, the blacker he was. They then asked the Shepherds, what that should mean? So they told them, saying, thus shall it be with the vile person; all means used to get such an one a good name, shall in conclusion tend but to make him more abominable. Thus it was with the *Pharisees*, and so shall it be with all *Hypocrites*.

Part I. *p.* 139. *Mercy has a mind to see the hole in the Hill.* Then said *Mercy*, the wife of *Matthew*, to *Christiana* her mother, I would, if it might be, see the hole in the Hill; or that commonly called the *By-way* to Hell. So her mother brake her mind to the Shepherds. Then they went to the door; it was in the side of an hill, and they opened it, and bid *Mercy* hearken awhile. So she hearkened, and heard one saying, *Cursed be my father for holding of my feet back from the way of Peace and Life;* and another said, *O that I had been torn in pieces, before I had, to save my life, lost my soul;* and another said, *If I were to live again, how would I deny myself, rather than come to this place.* Then there was, as if the very Earth had groaned and quaked under the feet of this young woman for fear; so she looked white, and came trembling away, saying, Blessed be he and she, that is delivered from this place.

Now when the Shepherds had shewed them all these things, then they had them back to the palace, and entertained them with what the house

would afford : But *Mercy* being a young and breed- *Mercy long- eth, and for what.*
ing woman, longed for something that she saw
there, but was ashamed to ask. Her mother-in-
law then asked her what she ailed, for she looked
as one not well. Then said *Mercy, There is a
Looking-Glass hangs up in the dining-room*, off of
which I cannot take my mind; if therefore I have
it not, I think I shall miscarry. Then said her
mother, I will mention thy wants to the Shepherds,
and they will not deny it thee. But she said, I am
ashamed that these men should know that I longed.
Nay, my daughter, said she, it is no shame, but a
vertue, to long for such a thing as that; so *Mercy*
said, Then mother, if you please, ask the Shepherds, if they are willing to sell it.

Now the Glass was one of a thousand. It would *It was the Word of God.* James I. 23.
present a man, one way with his own feature ex-
actly ; and turn it but another way, and it would
shew one the very face and similitude of the Prince
of Pilgrims himself. Yea, I have talked with them
that can tell, and they have said, that they have
seen the very Crown of Thorns upon his head, by
looking in that Glass; they have therein also seen
the holes in his hands, in his feet, and his side. I Cor. 13. 12. 2 Cor. 3. 18.
Yea, such an excellency is there in that Glass, that
it will shew him to one, where they have a mind
to see him; whether living or dead, whether in
Earth or Heaven; whether in a state of Humiliation, or in his Exaltation; whether coming to
Suffer, or coming to Reign.

Christiana therefore went to the Shepherds
apart, (Now the names of the Shepherds are
Knowledge, Experience, Watchful, and *Sincere*) and *Part* I. *p.* 137.

said unto them, there is one of my daughters a
breeding woman; that, I think doth long for something that she hath seen in this house, and she
thinks she shall miscarry, if she should by you be
denied.

She doth not lose her longing.

Experience. Call her, call her, she shall assuredly
have what we can help her to. So they called her,
and said to her, *Mercy*, what is that thing thou
wouldst have? Then she blushed and said, The
great Glass that hangs up in the dining-room: So
Sincere ran and fetched it, and with a joyful consent it was given her. Then she bowed her head,
and gave thanks, and said, By this, I know that I
have obtained favour in your eyes.

They also gave to the other young women such
things as they desired, and to their husbands great
commendations, for that they joined with Mr.
Great-heart, to the slaying of Giant *Despair*, and
the demolishing of *Doubting-Castle*.

How the Shep-herds adorn the Pilgrims.

About *Christiana's* neck the Shepherds put a
bracelet, and so they did about the necks of her
four daughters; also they put ear-rings in their
ears, and jewels on their foreheads.

When they were minded to go hence, they let
them go in peace, but gave not to them those certain Cautions which before were given to *Christian*

Part I. *p.* 140.

and his companion. The reason was, for that these
had *Great-heart* to be their Guide, who was one
that was well acquainted with things, and so could
give them their cautions more seasonably; to
wit, even then when the danger was nigh the
approaching.

What cautions *Christian* and his companion had

received of the Shepherds, they had also lost by *Part* I. *p.*
that the time was come that they had need to put *152.*
them in practice. Wherefore, here was the advantage that this company had over the other.

From hence they went on singing, and they
said,

> *Behold, how* fitly *are the Stages set !*
> *For their Relief that Pilgrims are become,*
> *And how they* us *receive without* one *let,*
> *That make the* other *Life the* mark *and Home.*
> *What Novelties they have, to us they give,*
> *That we, tho' Pilgrims, joyful lives may live.*
> *They do upon us too, such Things bestow,*
> *That shew we Pilgrims are, where-e'er we go.*

When they were gone from the Shepherds, they
quickly came to the place where *Christian* met with *Part* I. *p.*
one *Turn-away,* that dwelt in the town of *Apostacy.* *142.*
Wherefore of him Mr. *Great-heart,* their Guide,
did now put them in mind, saying, This is the
place where *Christian* met with one *Turn-away,*
who carried with him the character of his rebellion
at his back. And this I have to say concerning *How one*
this man, he would hearken to no counsel, but once *Turn-away*
managed his
afalling, persuasion could not stop him. *apostacy.*
Heb. 10. 26,
When he came to the place where the Cross 27, 28, 29.
and Sepulchre was, he did meet with one that did
bid him *look there,* but he gnashed with his teeth,
and stamped, and said, he was resolved to go back
to his own town. Before he came to the Gate,
he met with *Evangelist,* who offered to lay hands
on him, to turn him into the way again. But this

Turn-away resisted him, and having done much *despite* unto him, he got away over the Wall, and so escaped his hand.

Then they went on, and just at the place where *Little-faith* formerly was robbed, there stood a man with his sword drawn, and his face all bloody. Then said Mr. *Great-heart,* What art thou? The man made answer, saying, I am one whose name is *Valiant-for-truth.* I am a Pilgrim, and am going to the Cœlestial City. Now, as I was in my Way, there were three men did beset me, and propounded unto me these three things: 1. Whether I would become one of them? 2. Or go back from whence I came? 3. Or die upon the Place? To the first I answered, I had been a true man a long season, and therefore it could not be expected that I now should cast in my lot with thieves. Then they demanded what I would say to the second. So I told them that the place from whence I came, had I not found incommodity there, I had not forsaken it at all; but finding it altogether unsuitable to me, and very unprofitable for me, I forsook it for this Way. Then they asked me what I said to the third. And I told them, my Life cost more dear far than that I should lightly give it away. Besides, you have nothing to do thus to put things to my choice; wherefore at your peril be it, if you meddle. Then these three, to wit, *Wild-head, Inconsiderate,* and *Pragmatick,* drew upon me, and I also drew upon them.

So we fell to it, one against three, for the space of above three hours. They have left upon me, as you see, some of the marks of their valour, and

One Valiant-for-truth *beset with Thieves.*

Prov. 1. 10, 11, 13, 14.

How he behaved himself, and put them to flight.

have also carried away with them some of mine. They are but just now gone : I suppose they might, as the saying is, hear your horse dash, and so they betook them to flight.

Great-heart. But here was great odds, three against one.

Great-heart *wonders at his valour.*

Valiant. 'Tis true ; but *little* and *more* are nothing to him that has the Truth on his side : *Though an Host should encamp against me*, said one, *my heart shall not fear : Though War should rise against me, in this will I be confident*, &c. Besides, said he, I have read in some records, that one man has fought an army : And how many did *Sampson* slay with the jaw-bone of an ass ?

Ps. 27. 3.

Great-heart. Then said the Guide, Why did you not cry out, that some might ha' came in for your succour ?

Valiant. So I did to my King, who I knew could hear, and afford invisible Help, and that was sufficient for me.

Great-heart. Then said *Great-heart* to Mr. *Valiant-for-truth*, Thou hast worthily behaved thyself ; let me see thy Sword ; so he shewed it him.

When he had taken it in his hand, and looked thereon a while, he said, Ha ! It is a right *Jeru-salem* blade.

Is. 2. 3.

Valiant. It is so. Let a man have one of *these blades*, with a hand to wield it, and skill to use it, and he may venture upon an Angel with it. He need not fear its holding, if he can but tell how to lay on. Its edges will never blunt. It will cut *flesh*, and *bones*, and *soul*, and *spirit* and all.

Ephes. 6. 12, 13, 14, 15, 16, 17.
Heb. 4. 12.

Great-heart. But you fought a great while, I wonder you was not weary.

2 Sam. 23. 10.
The Word.

Valiant. I fought till my Sword did cleave to my hand, and when they were joined together, as

The Faith.
Blood.

if a sword grew out of my arm; and when the blood ran through my fingers, then I fought with most courage.

Great-heart. Thou hast done well, thou hast resisted unto blood, striving against Sin; thou shalt abide by us, come in, and go out with us, for we are thy companions.

Then they took him and washed his wounds, and gave him of what they had to refresh him; and so they went together. Now as they went on, because Mr. *Great-heart* was delighted in him (for he loved one greatly, that he found to be a man of his hands) and because there was with his company them that were feeble and weak: Therefore he questioned with him about many things; as first, what Country-man he was?

Valiant. I am of *Dark-Land,* for there I was born, and there my father and mother are still.

Great-heart. Dark-Land, said the Guide, doth not that lie upon the same coast with the City of *Destruction?*

How Mr. Va-
liant *came to
go on Pilgrim-
age.*

Valiant. Yes, it doth. Now that which caused me to come on Pilgrimage, was this; we had one Mr. *Tell-true* came into our parts, and he told it about what *Christian* had done, that went from the City of *Destruction:* Namely, how he had forsaken his wife and children, and had betaken himself to a Pilgrim's life. It was also confidently reported, how he had killed a *Serpent,* that did come out to resist him in his Journey; and how he got through to whither he intended. It was also told, what welcome he had at all his Lord's lodgings, specially when he came to the Gates of the Cœlestial City: For there, said the man, he was received with sound of Trumpet, by a company of shining ones. He told it also, how all the bells in the city did ring for joy at his reception, and what golden garments he was cloathed with; with many other things that now I shall forbear to relate. In a word, that man so told the story of *Christian* and his Travels, that my heart fell into a burning haste, to be gone after him; nor could father or mother stay me; so I got from them, and am come thus far on my Way.

Great-heart. You came in at the Gate, did you not?

Valiant. Yes, yes; for the same man also told us, that all would be nothing, if we did not begin to enter this Way at the Gate. *He begins right.*

Great-heart. Look you, said the Guide to *Christiana*, the *Pilgrimage* of your husband, and what he has gotten thereby, is spread abroad far and near. *Christian's name famous.*

Valiant. Why, is this *Christian's* wife?

Great-heart. Yes, that it is; and these are also her four sons.

Valiant. What! and going on Pilgrimage too?

Great-heart. Yes verily, they are following after.

Valiant. It glads me at heart! good man! How joyful will he be, when he shall see them that would not go with him, yet to enter after him, in at the Gates into the City? *He is much rejoiced to see Christian's wife.*

Great-heart. Without doubt it will be a comfort to him ; for next to the joy of seeing himself there, it will be a joy to meet there his wife and his children.

Valiant. But now you are upon that, pray let me hear your opinion about it. Some make a Question, whether we shall know one another when we are there ?

Great-heart. Do they think they shall know themselves then ? or that they shall rejoice to see themselves in that Bliss, and if they think they shall know and do these, why not know others, and rejoice in their welfare also ?

Again, since relations are our second self, though that state will be dissolved there, yet why may it not be rationally concluded, that we shall be more glad to see them there, than to see they are wanting ?

Valiant. Well, I perceive whereabouts you are as to this. Have you any more things to ask me about my beginning to come on Pilgrimage ?

Great-heart. Yes ; Was your father and mother willing that you should become a Pilgrim ?

Valiant. Oh no. They used all means imaginable to persuade me to stay at home.

Great-heart. Why what could they say against it ?

The great stumbling-blocks that by his friends were laid in his way.

Valiant. They said, it was an idle life ; and if I myself were not inclined to sloth and laziness, I would never countenance a Pilgrim's condition.

Great-heart. And what did they say else ?

Valiant. Why, they told me that it was a dangerous Way, yea, the most dangerous Way in the world, said they, is that which the Pilgrims go.

Great-heart. Did they shew wherein this Way is so dangerous?

Valiant. Yes; and that in many particulars.

Great-heart. Name some of them.

Valiant. They told me of the *Slough of Despond,* ^{The first} where *Christian* was well-nigh smothered. They *stumbling-block.* told me, that there were archers standing ready in *Belzebub-Castle,* to shoot them that should knock at the *Wicket* gate for entrance. They told me also of the Wood, and dark Mountains, of the Hill *Difficulty;* of the Lions, and also of the three Giants, *Bloody-man, Maul,* and *Slay-good:* They said moreover, that there was a foul *Fiend* haunted the Valley of *Humiliation;* and that *Christian* was by them almost bereft of life. Besides, said they, you must go over the *Valley of the Shadow of Death,* where the *Hobgoblins* are, where the Light is Darkness, where the Way is full of snares, pits, traps, and gins. They told me also of Giant *Despair,* of *Doubting-Castle,* and of the *ruin* that the Pilgrims met with there. Further, they said, I must go over the Enchanted ground, which was dangerous: And that, after all this, I should find a River, over which I should find no bridge; and that that River did lie betwixt me and the Cœlestial Country.

Great-heart. And was this all?

Valiant. No; they also told me, that this Way *The second.* was full of *deceivers,* and of persons that laid await there to turn good men out of the path.

Great-heart. But how did they make that out?

Valiant. They told me, that Mr. *Worldly-wise-* *The third.* *man* did lie there in wait to deceive.

They also said, that there was *Formality* and

Hypocrisy continually on the road. They said also, that *By-ends*, *Talkative*, or *Demas*, would go near to gather me up : that the *Flatterer* would catch me in his net ; or that, with green-headed *Ignorance*, I would presume to go on to the Gate, from whence he always was sent back to the hole that was in the side of the Hill, and made to go the by-way to Hell.

Great-heart. I promise you, this was enough to discourage ; but did they make an end here ?

The fourth.　*Valiant.* No, stay. They told me also of many that had tried that Way of old, and that had gone a great way therein, to see if they could find something of the Glory there, that so many had so much talked of from time to time ; and how they came back again, and befooled themselves for setting a foot out of doors in that path, to the satisfaction of all the Country. And they named several that did so, as *Obstinate* and *Pliable*, *Mistrust* and *Timorous*, *Turn-away* and old *Atheist*, with several more ; who, they said, had some of them gone far to see if they could find, but not one of them found so much advantage by going, as amounted *to the weight of a feather.*

Great-heart. Said they any thing more to discourage you ?

Valiant. Yes, they told me of one Mr. *Fearing*, who was a Pilgrim ; and how he found this Way so *solitary*, that he never had a comfortable hour therein : Also that Mr. *Despondency* had like to have been starved therein : Yea, and also which I had almost forgot *Christian* himself, about whom there has been such a noise, after all his ventures for a Cœlestial Crown, was certainly drowned in the black *River*, and never went a foot further; however, it was smothered up.

Great-heart. And did none of these things discourage you?

Valiant. No, they seemed but as so many Nothings to me.

Great-heart. How came that about?

Valiant. Why, I still believed what Mr. *Tell-true* had said, and that carried me beyond them all. *How he got over these stumbling-blocks.*

Great-heart. Then this was your Victory, even your Faith.

Valiant. It was so, I believed, and therefore came out, got into the Way, fought all that set themselves against me, and by believing, am come to this place:

> *Who would true Valour see,*
>   *Let him come hither;*
> *One here will constant be,*
>   *Come wind, come weather:*
>
> *There's no Discouragement*
> *Shall make him once relent,*
> *His first avow'd intent*
>   To be a Pilgrim.
>
> *Whoso beset him round*
>   *With dismal stories,*
> *Do but themselves confound,*
>   *His Strength the more is.*
>
> *No Lion can him fright;*
> *He'll with a Giant fight,*

But he will have a right
To be a Pilgrim.

Hobgoblin, nor foul Fiend
Can daunt his spirit;
He knows, he at the End
Shall Life inherit.

Then Fancies fly away,
He'll fear not what men say,
He'll labour Night and Day
To be a Pilgrim.

By this time they were got to the *enchanted Ground,* where the air naturally tended to make one *drowsy:* And that place was all grown over with briars and thorns, excepting here and there, where was an *enchanted Arbour,* upon which if a man sits, or in which if a man sleeps, 'tis a question, say some, whether ever they shall rise or wake again in this world. Over this Forest therefore they went, both one and another, and Mr. *Great-heart* went before, for that he was the Guide, and Mr. *Valiant-for-truth,* he came behind, being there a Guard, for fear, lest peradventure some *Fiend,* or *Dragon,* or *Giant,* or *Thief,* should fall upon their rear, and so do mischief. They went on here, each man with his Sword drawn in his hand, for they knew it was a dangerous place. Also they cheered up one another, as well as they could; *Feeble-mind,* Mr. *Great-heart* commanded should come up after him, and Mr. *Despondency* was under the eye of Mr. *Valiant.*

Now they had not gone far, but a great Mist

Part I. *p.*
156.

and Darkness fell upon them all; so that they could scarce, for a great while, see the one the other: Wherefore they were forced, for some time, to feel for one another, by words; for they walked not by Sight.

But any one must think, that here was but sorry going for the best of them all; but how much worse for the women and children, who both of *feet* and *heart* were but tender. Yet so it was, that through the encouraging words of he that led in the front, and of him that brought them up behind, they made a pretty good shift to wag along.

The Way also was here very wearisome, through dirt and slabbiness. Nor was there on all this Ground, so much as one *Inn,* or *Victualling-house,* therein to refresh the feebler sort. Here therefore was *grunting,* and *puffing,* and *sighing:* While one tumbleth over a bush, another sticks fast in the dirt; and the children, some of them, lost their shoes in the mire: While one cries out, I am down; and another, Ho, where are you? And a third, The bushes have got such fast hold on me, I think I cannot get away from them.

Then they came at an *Arbour,* warm, and pro- *An Arbour on* mising much refreshing to the Pilgrims: For it *the Enchant-* *ed ground.* was finely wrought above-head, beautified with *greens,* furnished with *benches* and *settles.* It also had in it a soft couch, whereon the weary might lean. This, you must think, all things considered, was tempting; for the Pilgrims already began to be foiled with the badness of the Way; but there was not one of them that made so much as a motion to stop there. Yea, for ought I could perceive, they

continually gave so good heed to the advice of their
Guide, and he did so faithfully tell them of *dangers*,
and of the *nature* of dangers when they were at
them, that usually when they were nearest to them,
they did most pluck up their Spirits, and hearten
one another to deny the Flesh.   This *Arbour* was

The name of the Arbour. call'd, *The Slothful's friend*, on purpose to allure,
if it might be, some of the Pilgrims there, to take
up their Rest, when weary.

I saw then in my dream, that they went on in
this their *solitary* ground, till they came to a place
at which a man is apt to lose his Way.   Now,

The Way is difficult to find. though when it was light, their Guide could well
enough tell how to miss those ways that led wrong,

The Guide has a Map of all ways leading to or from the City. yet in the dark he was put to a stand : But he had
in his pocket a map of all ways leading to or from
the Cœlestial City ; wherefore he struck a light,
(for he never goes also without his tinder-box) and
takes a view of his Book or map, which bids him
be careful in that place, to turn to the Right-hand-
way.   And had he not here been careful to look in
his map, they had all in probability been smothered
in the mud ; for just a little before them, and that
at the end of the cleanest Way too, was a Pit, none
knows how deep, full of nothing but mud ; there
made on purpose to destroy the Pilgrims in.

God's Book.   Then thought I with myself, who, that goeth
on *Pilgrimage*, but would have one of these maps
about him, that he may look when he is at a *stand*,
which is the Way he must take.

They went on then in this *enchanted Ground*,

An arbour, and two asleep therein. till they came to where there was another *Arbour*,
and it was built by the High-way-side.   And in

that *Arbour* there lay two men, whose names were *Heedless* and *Too-bold*. These two went thus far on Pilgrimage; but here, being wearied with their Journey, they sat down to rest themselves, and so fell fast asleep. When the Pilgrims saw them, they stood still, and shook their heads; for they knew that the Sleepers were in a pitiful case. Then they consulted what to do, whether to go on, and leave them in their sleep, or step to them, and try to awake them. So they concluded to go to them, and wake them; that is, if they could; but with this caution, namely to take heed that themselves did not sit down nor embrace the offered benefit of that *Arbour*.

So they went in, and spake to the men, and called each by his name, (for the Guide it seems *The Pilgrims try to wake them.* did know them) but there was no voice, nor answer. Then the Guide did shake them, and do what he could to disturb them. Then said one of them, *I will pay you when I take my Money.* At which the Guide shook his head. *I will fight so long as I can hold my Sword in my hand,* said the other. At that, one of the children laughed.

Then said *Christiana,* What is the meaning of this? The Guide said, *They talk in their sleep;* *Their endeavour is fruitless.* if you strike them, beat them, or whatever else you do to them, they will answer you after this fashion; or as one of them said in old time, when the waves of the Sea did beat upon him, and he *Prov. 23. 34, 35.* slept as one upon the mast of a ship; *When I awake, I will seek it again.* You know, when men talk in their sleep, they say any thing, but their words are not governed either by Faith or Reason.

There is an incoherency in their words now, as there was before betwixt their going on Pilgrimage, and sitting down here. This then is the mischief on't, when *heedless* ones go on Pilgrimage, 'tis twenty to one but they are served thus. For this *Enchanted Ground* is one of the last refuges that the Enemy to Pilgrims has; wherefore it is, as you see, placed almost at the end of the Way, and so it standeth against us with the more advantage. For when, thinks the Enemy, will these Fools be so desirous to sit down, as when they are weary? and when so like to be weary, as when almost at their Journey's end? Therefore it is, I say, that the *Enchanted Ground* is placed so nigh to the Land *Beulah*, and so near the end of their race. Wherefore, let Pilgrims look to themselves, lest it happen to them, as it has done to these, that, as you see, are fallen asleep, and none can wake them.

Then the Pilgrims desired with trembling to go forward, only they prayed their Guide to strike a light, that they might go the rest of their Way

The Light of the Word. 2 Pet. I. 19.

by the help of the light of a Lantern. So he strook a light, and they went by the help of that through the rest of this Way, though the darkness was very great.

The Children cry for weariness.

But the children began to be sorely weary, and they cried out unto him that loveth Pilgrims, to make their Way more comfortable. So by that they had gone a little further, a wind arose, that drove away the fog, so the air became more clear.

Yet they were not off (by much) of the *Enchanted Ground*, only now they could see one another better, and the Way wherein they should walk.

Now, when they were almost at the end of this ground, they perceived that a little before them was a *solemn* noise, of one that was much concerned. So they went on, and looked before them, and behold they saw, as they thought, a man upon his knees, with hands and eyes lift up, and speaking, as they thought, earnestly to one that was above; they drew nigh, but could not tell what he said; so they went softly till he had done. When he had done, he got up, and began to run towards the Cœlestial City. Then Mr. *Greatheart* called after him, saying, soho, friend, let us have your company, if you go, as I suppose you do, to the Cœlestial City. So the man stopped, and they came up to him. But so soon as Mr. *Honest* saw him, he said I know this man. Then said Mr. *Valiant-for-Truth*, Prithee, who is it? 'Tis one, said he, that comes from whereabouts I dwelt, his name is *Standfast;* he is certainly a right good Pilgrim.

So they came up one to another, and presently *Standfast* said to old *Honest*, Ho, Father *Honest*, are you there? Ay, said he, that I am, as sure as you are there. Right glad I am, said Mr. *Standfast*, that I have found you on this Road. And as glad am I, said the other, that I espied you upon your knees. Then Mr. *Standfast* blushed, and said; But why, did you see me? Yes, that I did, quoth the other, and with my heart was glad at the sight. Why, what did you think, said *Standfast?* Think, said old *Honest*, what should I

Standfast upon his knees in the Enchanted Ground.

The story of Standfast.

Talk betwixt him and Mr. Honest.

think? I thought we had an honest man upon the road, and therefore should have his company by and by. If you thought not amiss, how happy am I? But if I be not as I should, I alone must bear it. That is true, said the other; but your fear doth further confirm me, that things are right betwixt the Prince of Pilgrims and your soul: For he saith, *Blessed is the man that feareth always.*

They found him at Prayer.

Valiant. Well, but brother, I pray thee tell us what was it that was the cause of thy being upon thy knees even now? Was it for that some special Mercy laid obligations upon thee, or how?

What it was that fetch'd him upon his knees.

Standfast. Why, we are, as you see, upon the *Enchanted Ground;* and as I was coming along, I was musing with myself of what a dangerous Road the Road in this place was, and how many that had come even thus far on Pilgrimage, had here been stopt, and been destroyed. I thought also of the manner of the death, with which this place destroyeth men. Those that die here, die of no violent distemper; the death which such die, is not grievous to them. For he that goeth away in a *Sleep* begins that Journey with desire and pleasure. Yea, such acquiesce in the Will of that disease.

Hon. Then Mr. *Honest* interrupting of him, said, Did you see the two men asleep in the arbour?

Standfast. Ay, ay, I saw *Heedless* and *Too-bold* there; and for ought I know, there they will lie

Prov. 10. 7. till they rot. But let me go on with my tale: As I was thus musing, as I said, there was one in very pleasant attire, but old, that presented herself unto me, and offered me three things, to wit, her body, her purse, and her bed. Now the truth is, I was both weary and sleepy: I am also as poor as a howlet, and that perhaps the witch knew. Well, I repulsed her once and twice, but she put by my repulses, and smiled. Then I began to be angry, but she mattered that nothing at all. Then she made offers again, and said, if I would be ruled by her, she would make me great and happy. *Madam* Bubble: *Or this* ble: *Or this vain World.* For, said she, I am the mistress of the World, and men are made happy by me. Then I asked her name, and she told me it was Madam *Bubble.* This set me further from her; but she still followed me with enticements. Then I betook me, as you see, to my knees, and with hands lift up, and cries, I prayed to him that had said he would help. So just as you came up, the gentlewoman went her way. Then I continued to give thanks for this my great deliverance; for I verily believe she intended no good, but rather sought to make stop of me in my Journey.

Hon. Without doubt her designs were bad. But stay, now you talk of her, methinks I either have seen her, or have read some story of her.

Standfast. Perhaps you have done both.

Hon. Madam *Bubble!* is she not a tall, comely dame, something of a swarthy complexion?

Standfast. Right, you hit it, she is just such an one.

Hon. Doth she not speak very smoothly, and give you a smile at the end of a sentence?

Standfast. You fall right upon it again, for these are her very actions.

Hon. Doth she not wear a great purse by her side, and is not her hand often in it, fingering her money, as if that was her heart's delight?

Standfast. 'Tis just so; had she stood by all this while, you could not more amply have set her forth before me, nor have better described her features.

Hon. Then he that drew her picture was a good limner, and he that wrote of her said true.

Great-heart. This woman is a *Witch*, and it is *The World.* by virtue of her sorceries, that this ground is *enchanted*: Whoever doth lay their head down in her lap, had as good lay it down upon that block over which the axe doth hang; and whoever lays their eyes upon her beauty, are counted the Enemies of God. This is she that maintaineth in their splendor, all those that are the enemies of Pilgrims. Yea, this is she that has bought off many a man from a Pilgrim's life. She is a great gossipper; she is always, both she and her daughters, at one Pilgrim's heels or other, now commending, and then preferring the excellencies of this life. She is a bold and impudent slut; she will talk with any man. She always laugheth poor Pilgrims to scorn, but highly commends the rich. If there be one cunning to get Money in a place, she will speak well of him from house to house; she loveth banqueting and feasting mainly well; she is always at one full table or another. She has given it out in some places, that she is a Goddess, and therefore some do Worship her. She has her times, and open places of cheating; and she will say, and avow it, that none can shew a Good comparable to hers. She promiseth to dwell with children's children, if they will but love and make much of her. She will cast out of her purse gold, like dust, in some places, and to some

Jam. 4. 4.
1 John 2. 15.

persons. She loves to be sought after, spoken well of, and to lie in the bosoms of men. She is never weary of commending her commodities, and she loves them most that think best of her. She will promise to some crowns and kingdoms, if they will but take her advice; yet many has she brought to the halter, and ten thousand times more to Hell.

Standfast. Oh! said *Standfast,* what a Mercy is it that I did resist her; for whither might she hav' drawn me?

Great-heart. Whither! nay, none but God knows whither. But in general, to be sure she would hav' drawn thee *into many foolish and hurt-* 1 Tim. 6. 9. *ful Lusts, which drown men in Destruction and Perdition.*

'Twas she that set *Absalom* against his Father, and *Jeroboam* against his Master. 'Twas she that persuaded *Judas* to sell his Lord; and that prevailed with *Demas* to forsake the Godly Pilgrim's life; none can tell of the mischief that she doth. She makes variance betwixt rulers and subjects, betwixt parents and children, 'twixt neighbour and neighbour, 'twixt a man and his wife, 'twixt a man and himself, 'twixt flesh and the heart.

Wherefore, good Master *Standfast,* be as your name is, and when you have done all, *stand.*

At this discourse there was among the Pilgrims, a mixture of joy and trembling, but at length they brake out and sang:

> *What danger is the Pilgrim in?*
> *How many are his Foes?*

How many ways there are to Sin,
  No living mortal knows.
Some in the ditch shy are, yet can
  Lie tumbling on the mire.
Some, though they shun the frying-pan,
  Do leap into the fire.

Part I. *page*
178.
After this, I beheld until they were come unto the land of *Beulah*, where the Sun shineth night and day. Here, because they were weary, they betook themselves a while to rest. And because this country was common for Pilgrims, and because the orchards and vineyards that were here, belonged to the King of the Cœlestial Country, therefore they were licensed to make bold with any of his things. But a little while soon refreshed them here ; for the bells did so ring, and the trumpets continually sound so melodiously, that they could not sleep, and yet they received as much refreshing, as if they had slept their sleep never so soundly. Here also all the noise of them that walked the streets, was, *More Pilgrims are come to town.* And another would answer, saying, And so many, went over the Water, and were let in at the Golden Gates to day. They would cry again, There is now a Legion of shining ones just come to town ; by which, we know, that there are more Pilgrims upon the road ; for here they come to wait for them, and to comfort them after all their sorrow. Then the Pilgrims got up, and walked to and fro : But how were their ears now filled with heavenly noises and their eyes delighted with Cœlestial Visions ? In this land they *heard* nothing, *saw* nothing, *felt* nothing, *smelt* nothing,

tasted nothing, that was offensive to their stomach
or mind ; only when they tasted of the water of the
River, over which they were to go, they thought *Death bitter*
that tasted a little *bitterish* to the palate, but it *to the Flesh,*
but sweet to
proved sweeter when 'twas down. *the Soul.*

In this place there was a Record kept of the
names of them that had been Pilgrims of old, and
a history of all the famous Acts that they had done.
It was here also much discoursed, how the River to *Death hath*
some had had its *flowings*, and what *ebbings* it has *its ebbings*
and flowings
had while others have gone over. It has been in a *like the Tide.*
manner *dry* for some, while it has overflowed its
banks for others.

In this place, the Children of the town would
go into the King's Gardens, and gather nosegays
for the Pilgrims, and bring them to them with much
affection. Here also grew *camphire*, with *spikenard*,
and *saffron*, *calamus*, and *cinnamon*, with all its trees
of *frankincense*, *myrrh*, and *aloes*, with all *chief*
spices. With these the Pilgrims' chambers were
perfumed while they staid here ; and with these
were their bodies anointed, to prepare them to go
over the River, when the time appointed was come.

Now while they lay here, and waited for the *A messenger*
good hour, there was a noise in the town, that *of Death sent*
to Christiana.
there was a post come from the Cœlestial City,
with matter of great importance to one *Christiana*,
the wife of *Christian* the Pilgrim. So enquiry was
made for her, and the house was found out where
she was, so the post presented her with a letter :
The contents whereof were, *Hail good woman !* *His message.*
I bring thee tidings, that the Master calleth for
thee, and expecteth that thou shouldest stand in his

Presence, in clothes of Immortality, within this ten days.

When he had read this letter to her, he gave her therewith a true token that he was a true messenger, and was come to bid her make haste to be gone, The token was, *an Arrow with a point sharpened with Love, let easily into her heart, which by degrees wrought so effectually with her, that at the time appointed she must be gone.*

How welcome is Death to them that are willing to die.

When *Christiana* saw that her time was come, and that she was the first of this company that was to go over, she called for Mr. *Great-heart* her Guide, and told him how matters were. So he told her, he was heartily glad of the news, and could have been glad, had the post come for him. Then she bid that he should give advice how all things should be prepared for her Journey.

Her speech to her Guide.

So he told her, saying, thus and thus it must be, and we that survive, will accompany you to the River-side.

Then she called for her children, and gave them *her Blessing,* and told them, that she yet read with comfort, the Mark that was set in their foreheads, and was glad to see them with her there, and that they had kept their garments so white. Lastly, she bequeathed to the Poor that little she had, and commanded her sons and her daughters to be ready against the messenger should come for them.

To her Children.

When she had spoken these words to her Guide, and to her children, she called for Mr. *Valiant-for-Truth,* and said unto him, Sir, you have in all places shewed yourself true-hearted, be *faithful unto Death,* and my King will give a *Crown of Life.* I would also intreat you to have an eye

To Mr. Valiant.

to my children; and if at any time you see them
faint, speak comfortably to them. For my daughters, my Sons' wives, they have been faithful, and
a fulfilling of the Promise upon them will be their
end. But she gave Mr. *Standfast* a ring.

To Mr. Stand-*fast.*

Then she called for old Mr. *Honest*, and said
of him, *Behold an Israelite indeed, in whom is no
Guile.* Then said he, I wish you a fair day, when
you set out for Mount *Sion*, and shall be glad to
see that you go over the River dry-shod. But she
answered, come *wet*, come *dry*, I long to be gone;
for however the weather is in my Journey, I shall
have time enough when I come there, to sit down
and rest me, and dry me.

To Old Ho-nest.

Then came in that good man Mr. *Ready-to-halt*,
to see her. So she said to him, thy travel hither
has been with difficulty; but that will make thy
Rest the sweeter. But watch and be ready; for
at an hour when you think not, the messenger may
come.

To Mr. Rea-dy-to-halt.

After him came in Mr. *Despondency*, and his
daughter *Much-afraid;* to whom she said, you
ought, with Thankfulness, for ever, to remember
your deliverance from the hand of Giant *Despair*,
and out of *Doubting-Castle.* The effect of that
mercy, is that you are brought with safety hither.
Be ye watchful, and cast away Fear; be sober, and
hope to the end.

To Despon-dency, *and his Daughter.*

Then she said to Mr. *Feeble-mind*, Thou wast
delivered from the mouth of Giant *Slay-good*, that
thou mightest live in the Light of the Living for
ever, and see the King with comfort: Only I advise thee to repent thee of thy aptness to fear and

To Feeble-mind.

doubt of his Goodness, before he sends for thee; lest thou shouldest, when he comes, be forced to stand before him for that fault, with blushing.

Her last day, and manner of departure. Now the day drew on, that *Christiana* must be gone. So the Road was full of people, to see her take her Journey. But behold all the banks beyond the River were full of horses and chariots, which were come down from above, to accompany her to the City Gate. So she came forth, and entred the *River*, with a *beckon* of farewell, to those that followed her to the River-side. The last word she was heard to say, here, was *I come, Lord, to be with thee, and bless thee.*

So her children and friends returned to their place, for that those that waited for *Christiana* had carried her out of their sight. So she went and called, and entred in at the Gate with all the ceremonies of Joy, that her husband *Christian* had done before her.

At her departure her children wept, but Mr. *Great-heart* and Mr. *Valiant* play'd upon the welltuned cymbal and harp for Joy. So all departed to their respective places.

Mr. Ready-to-halt *summoned.* In process of time, there came a post to the town again, and his business was with Mr. *Ready-to-halt.* So he enquired him out, and said to him, I am come to thee in the name of him whom thou hast Loved and followed, tho' upon *Crutches:* And my message is to tell thee, that he expects thee at his table to sup with him in his Kingdom, the next day after *Easter;* wherefore prepare thyself for thy Journey.

Then he also gave him a token that he was a Eccles. 12. 6. true messenger, saying, *I have broken thy golden bowl, and loosed thy silver cord.*

After this, Mr. *Ready-to-halt* called for his fellow Pilgrims, and told them, saying, I am sent for, and God shall surely visit you also. So he desired Mr. *Valiant* to make his *Will.* And because he had nothing to bequeath to them that should survive him, but his *crutches*, and his *good* Promises His will. *wishes*, therefore thus he said : *These crutches I bequeath to my son, that shall tread in my steps, with an hundred warm wishes, that he may prove better than I have done.*

Then he thanked Mr. *Great-heart* for his conduct and kindness, and so addressed himself to his Journey. When he came at the brink of the River, he said, Now I shall have no more need of these *crutches*, since yonder are Chariots and Horses for me to ride on : The last words he was His last Words. heard to say, was, *Welcome Life.* So he went his Way.

After this, Mr. *Feeble-mind* had tidings brought Feeble-mind summoned. him, that the post sounded his horn at his chamber-door. Then he came in, and told him, saying, I am come to tell thee that thy Master has need of thee ; and that in very little time thou must behold his Face in Brightness : And take this as a token of the truth of my message : *Those that look out at the windows, shall be darkned.*

Then Mr. *Feeble-mind* called for his friends, and told them what errand had been brought unto him, and what token he had received of the truth of the

message.   Then he said, Since I have nothing to
He makes no will.
bequeath to any, to what purpose should I make
a will ?   As for my *feeble Mind,* that I will leave
behind me, for that I have no need of that in the
place whither I go ; nor is it worth bestowing upon
the poorest Pilgrims : Wherefore, when I am gone,
I desire, that you, Mr. *Valiant,* would bury it in
a dunghill.   This done, and the day being come
in which he was to depart, he entered the River as
His last Words.
the rest : His last words were, *Hold out, Faith and
Patience.*   So he went over to the other side.

When days had many of them passed away, Mr.
Despondency was sent for ; for a post was come,
Mr. Despondency's *summons.*
and brought this message to him : *Trembling man,
these are to summon thee to be ready with thy King
by the next Lord's Day, to shout for Joy, for thy
deliverance from all thy doubtings.*

And, said the messenger, that my message is
true, take this for a proof.   So he gave him the
Eccles. 12. 5.
grasshopper to be a *burden* unto him.   Now Mr.
His Daughter goes too.
Despondency's daughter, whose name was *Much-
afraid,* said, when she heard what was done, that
she would go with her father.   Then Mr. *Despondency* said to his friends ; myself and my daughter,
you know what we have been, and how trouble-
somely we have behaved ourselves in every com-
His Will.
pany.   My will, and my daughter's is, that our
Desponds and slavish fears be by no man ever
received, from the day of our departure, for ever :
For I know, that after my death, they will offer
themselves to others.   For, to be plain with you,
they are *ghosts,* the which we entertained when we
first began to be Pilgrims, and could never shake

them off after: And they will walk about, and seek entertainment of the Pilgrims; but for our sakes, shut ye the doors upon them.

When the time was come for them to depart, they went to the brink of the River. The last words of Mr. *Despondency*, were, *Farewel night*, *Welcome day.* His daughter went through the River singing, but none could understand what she said. *His last Words.*

Then it came to pass a while after, that there was a post in the town, that enquired for Mr. *Honest.* So he came to his house, where he was, and delivered to his hands these lines: *Thou art* *Mr. Honest summoned.* *commanded to be ready against this day seven-night, to present thyself before thy Lord, at his Father's house.* And for a token that my message is true, *All thy daughters of Musick shall be brought low.* *Eccles. 12. 4.* Then Mr. *Honest* called for his friends, and said unto them, I die, but shall make no will. As for *He makes no Will.* my Honesty, it shall go with me; let him that comes after, be told of this. When the day that he was to be gone was come, he addressed himself to go over the River. Now the River at that time over-flow'd the banks in some places; but Mr. *Honest* in his life-time had spoken to one *Good-Conscience* to meet him there, the which he *Good-Conscience helps Mr. Honest over the River.* also did, and lent him his hand, and so helped him over. The last words of Mr. *Honest* were, *Grace Reigns:* So he left the World.

After this, it was noised abroad, that Mr. *Va-* *Mr. Valiant summoned.* *liant-for-Truth* was taken with a summons by the same post as the other; and had this for a token Eccles. 12. 6. that the summons was true, *That his pitcher was broken at the fountain.* When he understood it, he called for his friends, and told them of it. Then, said he, I am going to my Father's, and tho' with great difficulty I am got hither, yet now I do not repent me of all the trouble I have *His Will.* been at to arrive where I am. *My Sword* I give to him that shall succeed me in my Pilgrimage, and my *Courage* and *Skill* to him that can get it. My *marks* and *scars* I carry with me, to be a witness for me, that I have fought His battles, who now will be my Rewarder. When the day that he must go hence was come, many accompany'd him to the River-side, into which as he went, he *His last* said, *Death, where is thy Sting?* And as he went *words.* down deeper, he said, *Grave, where is thy Victory?* So he passed over, and all the Trumpets sounded for him on the other side.

Mr. Stand-
fast *is sum-*
moned.

Then there came forth a summons for Mr. *Standfast;* (this Mr. *Standfast* was he that the rest of the Pilgrims found upon his knees in the *Enchanted ground;*) for the post brought it him open in his hands. The contents whereof were, *That he must prepare for a change of life, for his Master was not willing that he should be so far from him any longer.* At this Mr. *Standfast* was put into a muse: Nay, saith the Messenger, you need not doubt of the truth of my message; for here is a *Eccl. 12. 6.* token of the truth thereof: *Thy wheel is broken at* *He calls for* *the cistern.* Then he called to him Mr. *Great-* *Mr.* Great-
heart. *heart,* who was their Guide, and said unto him, Sir,

although it was not my hap to be much in your *His speech to* good company in the days of my Pilgrimage, yet, *him.* since the time I knew you, you have been profitable to me. When I came from home, I left behind me a wife, and five small children; let me intreat you, at your return, (for I know that you will go and return to your Master's house, in hopes that you may yet be a conductor to more of the Holy Pilgrims) that you send to my family, and let them be acquainted with all that hath, and shall happen unto me. Tell them moreover of my happy arrival to this place, and of the present late blessed condition that I am in. Tell them also of *His errand to Christian* and *Christiana* his wife, and how *she* and *his family.* her children came after her husband. Tell them also, of what a happy end she made, and whither she is gone. I have little or nothing to send to my family, except it be Prayers and Tears for them; of which it will suffice if you acquaint them, if peradventure they may prevail.

When Mr. *Standfast* had thus set things in order, and the time being come for him to haste him away, he also went down to the River. Now there was a great calm at that time in the River; wherefore Mr. *Standfast*, when he was about halfway in, stood a while, and talked to his companions that had waited upon him thither: And he said,

This River has been a terror to many, yea, the *His last* thoughts of it also have often frighted me; but now *Words.* methinks I stand easy, my foot is fixed upon that *Jos. 3. 17.* upon which the feet of the Priests that bare the

Ark of the Covenant stood, while *Israel* went over this *Jordan.* The waters indeed are to the palate bitter, and to the stomach cold; yet the thoughts of what I am going to, and of the conduct that waits for me on the other side, doth lie as a glowing coal at my heart.

I see myself now at the end of my Journey; my *toilsome* days are ended. I am going now to see *that* Head that was crowned with thorns, and *that* Face that was spit upon for me.

I have formerly lived by hear-say and Faith; but now I go where I shall live by Sight, and shall be with him in whose company I delight myself.

I have loved to hear my Lord spoken of; and where-ever I have seen the print of his shoe in the earth, there I have coveted to set my foot too.

His Name has been to me as a *civet-box;* yea, sweeter than all perfumes. His Voice to me has been most sweet; and his Countenance I have more desired than they that have most desired the light of the Sun. His Word I did use to gather for my food, and for antidotes against my faintings. He has held me, and I have kept me from mine iniquities; yea, my steps hath he strengthened in his Way.

Now, while he was thus in discourse, his countenance changed, his *strong man* bowed under him; and after he had said, *Take me, for I come unto Thee*, he ceased to be seen of them.

But Glorious it was to see, how the open Region was filled with Horses and Chariots, with Trumpeters and Pipers, with Singers and Players on stringed instruments, to welcome the PILGRIMS as they went up, and followed one another in at the Beautiful Gate of the City.

As for *Christian's* children, the four boys that *Christiana* brought with her, with their wives and children, I did not stay where I was till they were gone over. Also since I came away, I heard one say, that they were yet alive, and so would be for the increase of the Church in that place where they were, for a time.

Shall it be my lot to go that way again, I may give those that desire it, an account of what I here am silent about; mean time, I bid my Reader *Adieu.*

THE END.

Christian setting out.   Evangelist.   Slough of Despond.

ission & Patience.   The Fire.   Palace   The Man of Despair   Christian at the Cross.

Christian passing the Lions.   The Study.   The Armoury.

Faithful at the Stake.   Chariot waiting for Faithful.   Demas at the Hill Lucre.

The Delectable Mountains   Mount Clear.   Pilgrims in the Net.